Studies in Historical Archaeoethnology

Volume 2

THE ANGLO-SAXONS
FROM THE MIGRATION PERIOD TO THE EIGHTH CENTURY

AN ETHNOGRAPHIC PERSPECTIVE

Studies in Historical Archaeoethnology

SERIES EDITOR: GIORGIO AUSENDA

Already published:

After Empire: Towards an Ethnology of Europe's Barbarians
edited by Giorgio Ausenda

Franks and Alamanni in the Merovingian Period: An Ethnographic Perspective
edited by Ian Wood

The Visigoths from the Migration Period to the Seventh Century: An Ethnographic Perspective
edited by Peter Heather

The Scandinavians from the Vendel Period to the Tenth Century: An Ethnographic Perspective
edited by Judith Jesch

The Continental Saxons from the Migration Period to the Tenth Century: An Ethnographic Perspective
edited by Dennis H. Green and Frank Siegmund

Forthcoming:

The Ostrogoths from the Migration Period to the Sixth Century: An Ethnographic Perspective
edited by Sam Barnish and Federico Marazzi

The Langobards from the Migration Period to the Eighth Century: An Ethnographic Perspective
edited by Paolo Delogu and Chris Wickham

Vandals and Suebi from the Migration Period to the Sixth Century: An Ethnographic Perspective

Forthcoming conferences:

The Burgundians from the Migration Period to the Sixth Century

The Bavarians from the Migration Period to the Eighth Century

THE ANGLO-SAXONS

FROM THE MIGRATION PERIOD TO THE EIGHTH CENTURY

AN ETHNOGRAPHIC PERSPECTIVE

Edited by

JOHN HINES

THE BOYDELL PRESS

Center for Interdisciplinary Research on Social Stress
San Marino (R.S.M.)

First published 1997
The Boydell Press, Woodbridge
Reprinted in paperback 2003

ISBN 978 085115 479 4 hardback
ISBN 978 1 84383 034 4 paperback

Transferred to digital printing

The Boydell Press is an imprint of Boydell & Brewer Ltd
PO Box 9, Woodbridge, Suffolk IP12 3DF, UK
and of Boydell & Brewer Inc.
668 Mt. Hope Avenue, Rochester NY 14620, USA
website: www.boydellandbrewer.com

This volume contains the papers presented
at the second conference on "Studies on in Historical Archaeoethnology"
organized by the Center for Interdisciplinary Research on Social Stress,
which was held in San Marino from 26th to 31st August 1994.

A CIP catalogue record for this title is available
from the British Library

Library of Congress Catalog Card Number 97-11117

This book is printed on acid-free paper

CONTENTS

LIST OF MAPS

FOREWORD

JOHN HINES

School of English Studies, Communication and Philosophy, University of Wales Cardiff, PO Box 94, Cardiff GB-CF1 3XB

The symposium on the Anglo-Saxons, the proceedings of which are published in this volume, was the second in the series devoted to Historical Archaeoethnology held under the auspices of the Center for Interdisciplinary Research on Social Stress in San Marino (R.S.M.).

The principles of this series were extensively discussed at the inaugural meeting in the summer of 1993 (Ausenda 1995:1-13, 281-304). The aim of the symposia is to encourage and make progress towards the holistic study and understanding of the changes that European societies underwent in what is generally regarded as the great historical transition from the Roman period—the ancient world—to the medieval one. Such an undertaking necessitates an interdisciplinary and collaborative approach to both the acts and the ideology of the people of this era. When considered in the light of various other schools of anthropological-ethnological history and archaeology that have appeared on the scholarly scene during the last half-century this is nothing startingly innovative. Nevertheless it is still a sufficiently undeveloped approach that collaborative work of this kind must at present largely take the form of exploratory and evaluative discussion—towards 'an ethnographic perspective' as our subtitle puts it.

From one viewpoint, the point of the whole enterprise is both self-evident and self-validating. If an integrated analysis of history of this kind is possible, it is virtually implicit that the identification and description of the essential and unifying character of the historical era will be of fundamental importance to historical understanding. Even if such interdependency in the whole range of past culture can still be in doubt, it is so strongly established as a principle of historical interpretation that a case study which empirically tests its validity must be of value. It is, however, instructive that when an attempt was made at the initial symposium to discuss the purpose(s) of such an approach (Ausenda 1995:282-91) the fundamental theoretical question of the very nature of culture did not emerge as a major topic for investigation. Rather—and perhaps paradoxically—the value of the unified approach could best be appreciated as a way of improving understanding of specific historical issues such as urbanization, trade, migration, and political relations, which themselves can each be classified as the province of a single branch of history — economic, social, political etc. This does not denote a fundamental inconsistency nor mere lip-service to the idea of a holistic understanding on the participants' part. In a favourable light, it can be seen as emblematic of the complete interdependency of the parts and the whole in current historical and cultural studies. It is, however, recognized that these symposia test the underlying theory empirically rather than analysing it in its own theoretical terms.

The Anglo-Saxons were an appropriate topic for the first specially focussed symposium in the series. This is a historical field in which the research traditions of several disciplines—archaeology, history and philology—are both deep-rooted and reasonably vigorous. Of central importance is the fact that the historical, archaeological and linguistic sources for early England are relatively substantial and well-balanced between themselves—despite the fact that specialists will always run into and lament the limitations and lacunae within their own particular material! Purely pragmatically, it was helpful that this field is ideally suited to discussion and publication in the current scholarly lingua franca of English. It was thus possible to convene a symposium with a team of research-active scholars with wide knowledge and experience over a broad range of issues, disciplines and methods.

There is an all-too-easily perceived discrepancy between the stated aim of a holistic understanding of social and cultural change in post-Roman Europe and the organization of the symposia around particular groups such as the Anglo-Saxons. Actually this discrepancy is largely superficial. Certainly one cannot in practice take in the whole of Europe in one draught, and pragmatic limits had to be fixed. But a much more positive point can be made, concerned with the nature of the groups themselves. Anglo-Saxon culture and identity—as many other cultures and identities—are especially worthy of study in this period because they are both composite and changing entities. As the following papers and discussions show, it is impossible to study the Anglo-Saxons in isolation from, on the one hand, the Celtic-speaking communities and British and Irish cultures in the British Isles, and the Germanic powers on the Continent and the Church of Rome on the other. Specialists whose primary experience lies in other areas of European history and anthropology were invited to participate in the discussions. The risk of convening symposia that actually reinforce field-of-study boundaries which are essentially incompatible with the comparative and integrative goals of this series is recognized; we have done our best to deal with this problem.

No historical field of this kind can be free of problems, however. In the case of the earlier Anglo-Saxons the coverage provided by the sources is, of course, incomplete. It is very easy for interdisciplinary studies in such a context never to get beyond the use of comparative analysis in the inferential reconstruction of the past to the whole—ethnographical— study of that past, observable and reconstructed. It is broadly true that the archaeological sources become sparser in the seventh century as the documentary/textual sources become more substantial. Meanwhile the finite range of Anglo-Saxon sources and specialists available could not match a 'shopping list' drawn up from a purely ethnological perspective. This mismatch was particularly felt in the level of detail it is possible to go into in terms of social relations. In consequence, the theme and programme of this symposium had to be constructed with a view to doing as good a job of meeting the ideal objectives of the series as could be done.

Hence the focal date-range: 'from the Migration Period to the eighth century'. Even this range is, properly, transgressed in several discussions. The results can be claimed to vindicate this pragmatic decision. The net was cast wide enough to catch an appropriate diversity of forms of evidence, and certainly wide enough to encompass quite sufficient social and cultural change—one of the primary interests of the institute organizing the symposium—and the comparative ethnological study of Anglo-Saxon, native Romano-British and Continental Romanized and Germanic groups or cultures. At the same time it was not too diffuse for the intrinsic unity of the group and culture, the earlier Anglo-Saxons, at the centre of attention to appear a worthlessly artificial or illusory construct. Another conscious reason for this chosen date-range was the perception that the weight of available archaeological and historical evidence has tended to polarize Anglo-Saxon studies into early (fifth to seventh century) and late (ninth to eleventh century) branches respectively. A deliberate effort to pay more attention to the intermediary period seemed timely.

This foreword is not an apologia seeking to persuade you, the reader, that the motives, planning, organization and results of this symposium were clinically logical and academically flawless. It seeks to advertise those principles that were consciously followed in arranging the meeting, and so to explain both the wider context and the intrinsic character of these proceedings. This having been done, the contributors will speak for themselves.

References:

Ausenda, G. (ed.)
   1995   Concluding discussion. In *After Empire: Towards an Ethnology of Europe's Barbarians*. G. Ausenda (ed.), pp.281-304. Woodbridge: The Boydell Press.

Roman name		Modern name
Calleva	=	Silchester
Camulodunum	=	Colchester
Corinium	=	Cirencester
Deva	=	Chester
Durnovaria	=	Dorchester
Durovernum	=	Canterbury
Eburacum	=	York
Glevum	=	Gloucester
Isca	=	Exeter
Isurium	=	Aldborough
Lindum	=	Lincoln
Londinium	=	London
Luguvalium	=	Carlisle
Moridunum	=	Carmarthen
Noviomagus	=	Chichester
Petuaria	=	Brough-on-Humber
Ratae	=	Leicester
Venta Belgarum	=	Winchester
Venta Icenorum	=	Caistor
Venta Silurum	=	Caerwent
Verulanium	=	St. Albans
Viroconium	=	Wroxeter

Map of Roman Britain

Notes: The names in capitals are those of British *civitates*. • The name *Picti* occurs in sources from the late 3rd century onwards, apparently referring to a new confederation of previously distinct northern tribes.

Map of Anglo-Saxon territories in the 7th/8th centuries

ETHNIC NAMES AND IDENTITIES IN THE BRITISH ISLES: A COMPARATIVE PERSPECTIVE

WALTER POHL

Institut für Österreichische Geschichtsforschung, Universität Wien, Dr. Karl Lueger-Ring, A-1010 Wien

> The Sibyl does not invariably mention events in their order, much less construct a well-arranged narrative, but after uttering some verse or other concerning the troubles in Lybia she leaps straightaway to the land of Persia, thence proceeds to mention the Romans, and then transfers the narrative to the Assyrians. And again, while uttering prophecies about the Romans, she foretells the misfortunes of the Britons (Procopius, *Wars* V.xxiv.35).

I have to apologize that my paper cannot offer much more. Much less equipped to present a well-arranged narrative about Anglo-Saxon ethnogenesis than the other contributors in this volume, I shall jump between Britain and the Continent, presenting more questions than answers. But at least this European perspective may be excused by the Sybil of Cumae, for Britain was, in the middle of the sixth century, still part of her world, as it was for Procopius, the Byzantine intellectual from Palestine. That it was the misfortunes of the Britons that came to his mind was, after all, not so different from the view held by his British contemporary, Gildas.

General observations: ethnic processes in the early middle ages

I would like to start with a brief list of criteria for the study of early medieval ethnicity as they have been developed by the 'Vienna School' and in my own work.[1] Some of my propositions represent generally accepted opinions in the field (although nationalist ideologies have not completely retreated from academic studies of ethnicity, and have regained some ground recently, especially in Eastern Europe). Some of my suggestions respond to comparatively new challenges, especially to semiotic and textual theories. In the light of recent discussions, we cannot simply go on assuming that texts and artefacts reflect a reality of the past that can be adequately represented in modern historical language. The relationship between texts and realities, texts and texts, and texts as realities seems to be far more complex. I do not, however, argue for a purely textual understanding of ethnicity; I retain the concept that the testing-ground for ethnicity lies in the field of social practice, a practice that is of course shaped by language and communication. As I will try to show, such a point of view, tested against the

---

[1] See the works by Herwig Wolfram and the author in the References.

evidence, sometimes seems to raise more questions than it answers. But it is a model that allows for the ambiguity, the multiplicity and the contradictions that are characteristic for ethnic processes. Let me formulate a few basic assumptions:

* Ethnicity is not a biological, but a historical phenomenon; peoples and tribes develop, change and may also disappear in the course of time. At a given moment, their members are, as a rule, of diverse origin ('polyethnic'), even if they have ceased to be aware of this diversity.

* The process of ethnogenesis, therefore, is not determined by any ethnic essence, linguistic heritage, common natural feature or territorial prefiguration. Not even islands (like the British Isles) necessarily determine the evolution of an ethnically homogeneous population.

* The decisive criterium of ethnicity is the subjective consciousness of belonging to an ethnic group, which is often also expressed in outward signs and is therefore obvious to the others concerned (Ernest Renan's famous 'plebiscite de tous les jours').[2] None of the objective criteria by which ethnicity has been defined since antiquity (language, dress and customs, territory etc.) offer more than a statistical clue, and all of them can be shown to be inapplicable in some cases.

* Nevertheless, ethnicity is not purely subjective or even arbitrary. Ethnic identity only matters when it is practised, when it motivates decisions and efforts (which can go as far as being ready to die for an ethnic group). This opens up a wide field of ethnic practice(s). The success of ethnic communities, up to a certain point, depends on the efforts of their members to give shape to them.[3]

* Not all ethnic practices, however, necessarily include the conscious purpose of strengthening the ethnic group itself. They are 'ethnic' in so far as they help to preserve the group's identity or establish its political success. In our early medieval sources, most of the ethnic activities recorded are political or military and are intended to stabilize power on the basis of ethnic groups; economic activities and ecological factors are far more difficult to assess.

* An important field of ethnic practices that can be reconstructed is that of symbolic strategies and the preservation and propagation of ethnic traditions. As in the field of politics, their implicit goal is to construct stability and meaning beyond the span of individual lives. This includes a wide range of religious creeds and rituals, of burial practices, of myths and symbols, of norms and modes of behaviour, but also of information about recent events.

* Wenskus and Wolfram have stressed the close connection between myths and norms, between *origo* and *religio/lex* within ethnic traditions, and have seen the

---

[2] In early medieval studies this has been demostrated at length in Wenskus 1977.

[3] I understand 'practice' (with, for instance, Pierre Bourdieu) in a general sense, not as the opposite of theory, but as including the production of texts and meanings. But I would not see ethnicity, as does Wenskus 1977, as exclusively a question of 'Geistgeschichte', a 'Denkform', or, to put it in a more up-to-date way, a 'literary construct' (see below).

preservation and adaptation of tradition as an achievement of a core group, a 'kernel of tradition' (*Traditionskern*), not necessarily identical to but as a rule close to the political élite (Wolfram 1994; cf. Pohl 1994). Traditional norm systems (like the *leges*) may be seen as traces of ethnic practices; it is open to discussion whether they directly constitute and define an ethnic group.

* The term 'tradition' has provoked many misunderstandings, mostly between German-speaking and other scholars, and is hard to define.[4] Certainly, it should neither be used to argue for the archaic character of texts transmitted only much later, nor as a concept that presupposes 'Germanic' authenticity or continuity. The flexibility of myths, genealogies, rituals, and norms that formed a body of ethnic tradition in changing circumstances has already been underlined by Wenskus and Wolfram. The decisive factor for the success of ethnic '*Traditionen*' (like the *Origo gentis Langobardorum*) is that for their audience, they were credible in their claims to ancient origins, which does not mean that they are factual accounts of actual origins.[5]

* Myths, norms and other information had to be communicated to become influential. Communication could be symbolic, oral or written, and was not limited to members of a group. Our evidence comes from traces of this communication process in which ethnically relevant information was diffused. Archaeologists have to deal with objects that were symbolically significant, while historians and philologists are confronted with texts and, frequently, just with names. Ethnic interpretation of these data involves considerable methodological problems; more often than not, ethnic labels have too easily been used in modern historical research.

* The most common form of ethnically significant texts are narratives (especially '*origines gentium*'). Recent research on the 'fiction of fact' can lead to a better understanding of the way in which narratives shaped the self-perception and perception of ethnic groups; it should not lead to a purely aesthetic or literary interpretation of these texts (Goffart 1988; Smith 1986). This type of fiction responded to realities and helped change them by motivating action. Although its function for ethnic groups can only be reconstructed from fragmentary evidence, it should not be forgotten that the impact of these narratives varied widely; its success and diffusion must be studied specifically in each case.

* In these narratives, there is no clear distinction between myth and history, between ancient and contemporary matters. Important figures or events were stylized in legendary form almost immediately, as can be shown, for instance, in the case of Alboin. Ethnic tradition had to establish a direct link between legitimating origins and present times. The same constructed continuity becomes obvious in the rudimentary but highly structured narratives of genealogies.

---

4 Cf. Dumville 1990:192: "We cannot accept a text, or an item in a text, simply on the ground that it appears to derive from 'tradition.'"

5 The comparative analysis of origin legends could still offer interesting perspectives (see for instance Carey 1994, Howe 1989, Sims-Williams 1983:22-3, Wolfram 1994).

* Greek and Roman tradition had developed a rich and varied discourse of ethnicity that helped to shape communication about ethnic processes and locate them within a Roman cultural sphere (Geary 1988). Our surviving texts have to be seen within this intertextual matrix, although certain elements in them transcend the horizons of ancient ethnography. But ancient ethnography, in spite of all the stereotypes it had accumulated, was well equipped to allow for a multiplicity of ethnic traditions, just as, politically, the Empire had always been open to integrate a multiplicity of ethnic groups within the *res publica*.

* Latin-barbarian ethnic discourse could therefore accompany and often justify the integration of the *gens* into the Roman world; Roman rhetoric could be used to affirm the existence of a people as a distinct ethnic and political group. Without this type of communication that led to some sort of ethnic definition neither a stable identity nor integration was possible; even conflicts could not be managed in a regular manner. The means of organizing the barbarians into large and politically structured ethnic groups were limited; but these attempts were successful in most parts of the Western Empire. The ethnic factor was not the only cohesive force in this process; but, in the long run, none of the barbarian successor states could do without it. However, ethnicity was much less important in the East, where the early Slavs only slowly and gradually formed regional ethnic units, the core areas of the Byzantine empire upheld the imperial tradition, and in the Islamic world even political fragmentation did not presuppose or create ethnic diversity.

* Nevertheless, one of the fundamental changes within the Roman world at the end of antiquity was that, contrary to the Roman model, ethnicity began to become a basis for power. Successful groups of warriors manipulated and sometimes even monopolized ethnic discourses and traditions. Theoderic's Gothic kingdom in Italy was maybe the most ambitious of a series of attempts to achieve that. An extreme case of monopolized ethnic identity is constituted by the Avar Khaganate, outside of which Avars soon lost their identity. On the other hand, ethnic groups could be constituted of several power centres, which is obviously the case of the Angles and Saxons. In this case, identities tended to be less clear-cut and more flexible.

How was ethnic identity achieved? The texts that have come down to us have the advantage of being part of a communication process in which identities were formed. The way in which they contributed to this, if at all, obviously varies. But I think it is methodologically advisable not to exclude any texts from our analysis because they are thought to lack any basis in 'hard fact'. It seems especially important to me not to start by drawing a line between self-perceptions and perceptions from the outside, between 'authentic' traditions and prejudices. Quite probably, ethnic identities in the British Isles were not formed by their inhabitants alone. Was the identity of the *Angli* based only on genealogies going back to Woden and on the Offa myth, or did Gregory the Great have a part in it? This is the kind of question that I had in mind when testing my hypotheses against texts about the Anglo-Saxons. Those who are more familiar than I am with the material will be able to judge if there is anything to gain from the questions I have tried to ask.

Names and ambiguities

In Anglo-Saxon studies, there seems to be fundamental agreement between historians, philologists and archaeologists about the common subject, the Anglo-Saxons. There may be some debates about numbers, and the archaeological evidence hardly allows a clear delimitation, but that is due more to the difficulty of finding the Britons than to that of defining the Anglo-Saxons. Philology can offer clear linguistic criteria, so convincing to modern minds who are used to differentiate peoples by their language. The name for this people, the Anglo-Saxons, can also, be found in early medieval sources. Thus, a scholarly tradition that projects a notion of clear-cut ethnic identities into a distant past prevails. In many countries, scholars still expect to find an early medieval population with an unmistakable name, sharing a common political organization, language and culture. If such an ideal object of interdisciplinary research proves too elusive, they tend to explain this as an anomaly—or assume flaws in the reconstruction (or in the sources).

But, somehow, the historical evidence seems to trouble that clear-cut notion of ethnic identity. Ethnic names tell a story that is much more opaque and contradictory. The history of ethnonyms in the British Isles is, as elsewhere, full of paradox. Their inhabitants may nowadays be called 'British' or 'Britons', although they have little to do with those who bore that name in late antiquity and then gradually disappeared from history. Those Britons who retained their identity came to be called 'Welsh', which is the Germanic term for Romance-speaking populations, although they had ceased to speak Latin long ago; only on the Continent, is there still a 'British' country called Brittany. *Scotti*, in the early Middle Ages, was the name for the Irish but moved to Scotland; the term for the Celtic language preserved in modern Ireland is related to the name of ancient Gaul. The name 'English' goes back to one of the conquering groups of the fifth century, whereas that of the Saxons continues as the root of the Welsh and Gaelic words for 'English'. The last successful invaders, who established the modern kingdom, called Normans (although they came from the South), did not manage to establish their name in the country as they had in Normandy where they came from. National terminology in Europe is full of that kind of paradox. The Germans are called Germans by the British, *Allemands* by the French, *Tedeschi* by the Italians and *Niemeci* (or similar) by their Slavonic neighbours. They are not called French, although the first German state developed from the East Frankish kingdom where the language of the Franks was preserved, unlike in France where even the Romance language came to be called French.

All this is too well known to make one wonder as one should, for it does not tell stories of clear-cut identities or of the correspondence of ethnicity, language, political institutions and culture but of conflicting allegiances, shifting perceptions, competition for successful political terms and concepts, and complex identities. This does not mean that we have to accept this confusion in our own terminology and that all these generic names, like French, German, English or Anglo-Saxons, have to disappear from the covers of scholarly books. It should just warn us not to take them too much for granted. Ethnic names are abstractions; they do not simply reflect natural facts but represent the construction of a historical model—by Bede just as much as by ourselves. Likewise, the ethnic communities they indicate are not the subjects of history, they are only one type of community that may have given a meaning to peoples' actions. Here, the difference between modern nations and early medieval peoples becomes relevant. Most Anglo-Saxons may have acted in the name of their kin or their kingdom, of their social group or their religious confession, but not in the name of a people called 'the Anglo-Saxons'. Of course, there were, by Bede's time, more or less recognizable groups of Angles and Saxons in Britain. But was their—shared or separate—sense of identity strong enough to leave a clear stamp on contemporary ethnic terminology? I would like to consider ethnic names in this respect: do they lend themselves to the kind of classification that we try to establish? In what way do they contribute to the construction of ethnic identities or reflect it? What is the relationship between perceptions from outside and ethnic traditions? I cannot offer a systematic study of the matter, as scholars from German-speaking countries have recently done for ethnic terminologies in early and high medieval France and Germany (Brühl 1990; Ehlers 1994; Schneidmüller 1987; Thomas 1990; Wolfram 1995). But I hope to raise some questions, at least.

Multiplicity of ethnic terminology is certainly not the exception but the rule in early medieval Europe, especially where no power centre was able to monopolize names and traditions. Some names coexist with a wealth of alternative designations, as that of the Goths who are also called Scythians, Getae or Gog (apart from the names differentiating between Gothic groups, like the *Tervingi, Vesi,* Visigoths, Ostrogoths, *Tetraxitae,* etc.) (Pohl 1993; Wolfram 1990a:30-46). The same is true for the Franks, whom Greek authors call Celts and later Germans, whereas in the West they are often styled as *Sygambri* and sometimes specified by the obscure term 'Salians'. A fundamental ambiguity that led early medieval authors to many misunderstandings lies in the names *Alamanni* and *Suevi;* by Carolingian scholars in and around St Gall, this was further confused by a retrospective identification of *Alamanni, Vindelici* and *Vandali,* which was based on Isidore and on Bede's account of the Vandal invasion of Gaul (Pohl 1988:284). The Slavs were called both *Sclavi* and *Vinedi* (a self-designation and one by outsiders, respectively). The Avars appear in some of the early Greek sources as *Varchonitai,* and Theophylactus Simocatta tells us that these 'Pseudo-Avars' wrongly adopted the name Avars to frighten their neighbours (Pohl 1988). And of course, things get even more complicated with the Byzantine 'Romans' who were Greeks and did not want to be called Hellenes because that had turned into a synonym for pagans.

Another common feature in early medieval sources is the importance of local and regional designations that are usually ignored by modern terminology. Isidore's *Etymologiae* (IX.2) are a good example. In an attempt to give a systematic catalogue of peoples that can be traced back genealogically to the sons of Noah in the Bible, he not only includes what we would regard as peoples of his day, like the Goths or the Langobards, but also regional communities like the Tuscans and Umbrians, the Asturians or Cantabrians. In Anglo-Saxon England, the co-existence of local, regional and larger communities is admirably exemplified by the Tribal Hidage, enumerating thirty-four units ranging from Wessex with 100,000 hides, East Anglia and Mercia with 30,000, down to a number of units with only three to six hundred hides, without any distinction of principle (Dumville 1989:225-31). Most of the smaller units never made it to the pages of narrative history, but we may ask ourselves at which level group affiliations and ethnic identities were really felt. Early medieval ethnicity never is a clear-cut system as we would expect to find it in a historical atlas but usually includes several layers of territorial and ethnic units that may overlap or even put parts and the whole on the same list.

Especially problematic are general names like Germans or Scythians. Their application is purely situational. Even in the fifteenth century, the humanist Enea Silvio Piccolomini, later Pope Pius II, found it hard to decide whether the English were Germans or not. The Byzantines, in the sixth century, got used to using the general name Germans for the Franks; on the other hand, the idea that *Germania* was east of the Rhine lingered on. Bede is our witness for a third use of the name when he writes that the neighbouring Britons called the Anglo-Saxons *Garmani*. Early medieval Britain is certainly a good example of the ambiguity of ethnic names and the difficulty of finding appropriate terms for 'ethnic' or territorial units that stretched far beyond the horizons of most of their members.

In Bede, there is a strong notion of ethnic plurality in Britain. Right at the beginning of his *Ecclesiastical History*, he states that at present the truth is studied in *quinque gentium linguis...Anglorum videlicet, Brettonum, Scottorum, Pictorum et Latinorum* (*HE* I.1).[6] Each of these peoples, Bede says, has its own language, but they are united in the study of the fifth, Latin, which they get from the Scriptures. He is far from regarding this linguistic diversity as a disadvantage; he even compares the number of languages to the five books of the Divine Law. Latin, in this list, is not so much the language of the Romans but the language of the Scriptures.[7] In the subsequent narrative, Bede unfolds his ethno-historical model, as each of the peoples of Britain is shown to land successively on its shores: Britons from Armorica/Brittany, Picts from 'Scythia', and *Scotti* from Hibernia. The last of the four peoples to arrive, the *Angli*, are in fact a group of peoples; and this takes us to Bede's second, and most famous, list of peoples. But unlike the straightforward linguistic division presented in the first chapter, we are confronted with a rather opaque piece of ethnic rhetoric here.

---

[6] Geoffrey of Monmouth (1.2) gives an only slightly modified list for the twelfth century, consisting of Normans, Britons, Saxons, Picts and *Scotti*.

[7] This view leaves no room for any differentiation between the Latin of the Scriptures and native Romance dialects that might or might not have survived (but that did not matter to Bede).

First, Vortigern invites the *gens Saxonum* (*HE* I.14), then the *gens Saxonum sive Anglorum* comes in three ships (*HE* I.15), and immediately afterwards the newly-arrived are said to have come *de tribus Germaniae populibus*, from the Saxons, the Angles and the Jutes. It is worth mentioning that Bede does not explicitly say here that these three groups came to England and settled there as distinct peoples. Ethnic divisions among the newcomers, according to him, were territorial and on the whole corresponded to political entities. In Bede's version, these fall into loose groups according to their ethnic origin before the invasion: from the Jutes, he writes, are descended the people of Kent and the Isle of Wight, from the Saxons, the East, South and West Saxons, and from the Angles, the East and Middle Angles, the Mercians, and the Northumbrians—the Humber, as Bede states elsewhere, divides the *meridiani et septentrionales Anglorum populi* (*HE* I.25), and the plural makes it clear enough that Bede perceived of the Angles as of a plurality of peoples. Although the boundaries between the kingdoms shifted quite frequently and sometimes radically, these kingdoms were certainly the foci of politically meaningful ethnic identities. Bede himself allows for an exception to this ethno-political equation between wandering tribes and contemporary ethno-political geography: opposite the Isle of Wight, there is that *gens* in the 'kingdom (*provincia*) of the West Saxons which is still today called the nation of the Jutes'—this passage, interestingly enough, is omitted in the Anglo-Saxon (or rather Anglian) translation of the *Ecclesiastical History*.[8]

There is a third list in the *Ecclesiastical History* (*HE* V.9): Bishop Ecgberht, we are told, knew that there were many pagan *nationes* in *Germania, a quibus Angli vel Saxones, qui nunc Britanniam incolunt, genus et originem duxisse noscuntur.* Therefore, Angles and Saxons were *corrupte* called *Garmani* by the *vicina gens Brittonum*. But in spite of his reservations about the name '*Garmani*' for the Angles and Saxons, Bede goes on to name the pagan peoples in *Germania* from whom Angles and Saxons derived their origins: the *Fresones, Rugini, Danai, Hunni, Antiqui Saxones, Boructuarii*. From what we know about early medieval ethnogenesis, there is no problem in accepting most of these groups as parts of the polyethnic force that came to Britain and settled there under Anglian and Saxon leadership. One may debate which of them were more or less likely to have taken part, using literary and archaeological evidence from the Continent (see Myers 1970; Wood, this volume, pp. 41-2). The list of the inhabitants of Britain given by Procopius, however legendary the context, also includes the Frisians: he has "*Angíloi, Fríssones kaì Bríttanes*" (*Wars* VIII.xx). I would just like to make a remark about the 'intertextual' connections of the list. This type of list of ethnic names, combining classical stereotypes with contemporary information, is frequent enough in late antiquity; to give just a few examples: Claudian (*Paneg. de IV cons. Hon.* 446-52) has the *Bructerus* as inhabitant of the Hercynian Forest together with *Sygambri, Franci, Alamanni, Bastarni, Cimber, Cherusci* along the Rhine as

---

[8] For the anomaly of the Jutes in Bede's list that was otherwise "influenced, if not determined, by the political geography and the nomenclature of his own day" (see Myres 1970:149-51).

peoples pacified by Stilicho. Sidonius Apollinaris, writing about Attila's invasion in 451 (*carm.* VII 321-325), lists *Rugus, Gelonus, Gepida, Scirus, Burgundio, Chunus, Bellonotus, Neurus, Bastarna, Toringus, Bructerus* and *Francus*. Venantius Fortunatus, in the second half of the sixth century, is especially fond of this kind of display of learning; in a poem to celebrate Chilperic's victories (*carm.* IX.i.73), he lists *Geta, Vasco (...), Danus, Euthio, Saxo, Britannus* together with the *Fresones* and the *Suebi*.

Whatever their context, the function of these lists was usually similar: they either amplified the multitude of barbarians that threatened the Roman state or the Christian faith, or the victories of a ruler who had stood up to these dangers or even subdued them (or, later, a churchman who had spread the word of God among them). Therefore, their aim was not ethnographic but atmospheric, we might say. They usually contained names that were more emotionally charged than others—eastern peoples like the Huns could often fulfill that purpose, evoking a universe of stereotypes about Scythian barbarians. They also often incorporated allusions to barbarians from classical literature which may have stimulated a sense of the fundamental continuity of these barbarians and tapped another reservoir of rich lore about barbarian habits—this might also be the function of the traditional name *Boructuarii* in Bede's list. And there had to be names from the headlines of the day, names that were in everybody's mind at the moment, like Bede's *Fresones*: Frisian mission is what his story is basically about, although the Boructuari and the Old Saxons also figure in the following account (*HE* V.11). Basic and factual as they may seem, lists of peoples were a highly stylized form of literature. They relied a lot on what Umberto Eco has called the *lector in fabula*, the reader whose knowledge, prejudice and emotions any text would try to mobilize (Eco 1979).

Of course, it is hard to tell how Bede's contemporary 'model reader'—the reader that he had, in Umberto Eco's terminology, in his mind when writing— would have reacted to the passage. Bede opened up a world of pagan peoples right across the Channel as a goal for English missions; at the same time he made it clear enough that the origins of the Angles and Saxons lay in that barbarian world. A double phrase, *genus et origo*, underlines this point. The grammar, on the other hand, is imprecise enough to leave it to the reader to judge whether all those barbarians, Huns (which the contemporaries would identify with the Avars) included, were actually the forefathers of the Angles and Saxons; but, suggestively enough, the Huns even figure right before the *Antiqui Saxones* whose direct relation to the inhabitants of Britain is unmistakable. On the other hand, Bede explicitly refuses to call the Angles and Saxons Germans like their Continental relatives. We can assume that this is a passage highly charged with conflicting attitudes and deliberate ambiguity. Obviously, Bede's intention was to underline how many pagans there still were east of the Rhine, and that missions among them could continue the conversion of the Anglo-Saxons they were related to. On the other hand, a dream soon persuaded Ecgberht that it was still more important to deal with problems in Britain itself. And, in a sense, the number of pagan relatives on the Continent made the achievement of the Anglian Church look more extraordinary.

Do the ethnic names in Bede's lists reflect contemporary self-perceptions and identities, or are they influenced by classical traditions? Bede is a good example of how difficult it is to distinguish between these elements in our early medieval sources. For a long time, scholars have tried to arrive at a neat reconstruction of authentic Germanic traditions. But in most cases, we must acknowledge that written records owe a lot to classical perceptions. As the *gentes* adapted to post-Roman statehood in a Christian universe, their myths and identities changed shape according to categories of classical ethnography. Ethnic names have to be understood in this context. Neither traditional self-denominations nor the terminology of Greek and Latin ethnography could adequately describe ethnogenetic processes; when they overlapped, they created even greater contradictions and ambiguities. For a modern scholar, it may be hard to deal with names that were not just descriptive but charged with overtones and implicit evaluations.

Names told stories, like that of the Langobards which is explained by an elaborate origin myth about women with long beards. Ethnonyms fell into groups and patterns that were believed to explain genetic and geographical relationships. The most widespread model was, of course, biblical and traced back all known peoples to the sons of Noah. A classical statement of this model is found in Isidore's *Etymologies* (IX.II). The *Historia Brittonum* (c.16-7) also goes back to Japhet; in the seventeenth generation, Hessitio becomes the forefather of the Franks, the Romans, the Britons and the *Albani* (cf. Dumville 1994:409).[9] This is a slightly changed version of the so-called 'Frankish table of nations', probably compiled in Theoderic's Italy (Goffart 1983). The name Hessitio ultimately goes back to one of the three sons of *Mannus* in Tacitus from which the *Istaevones*, *Ingaevones* and *Herminones* sprung. In the second century AD, this had been a genealogy of Germanic peoples. The 'table of nations' does not distinguish between *Germani* and non-*Germani* any more and instead presents Romans, Franks and Britons as related, more or less in the context of the Roman origin myth from Troy. The list is found in many variants, for instance in a southern Italian manuscript of Langobardic law written around the year 1000; instead of the *Albani*, the other versions have the *Alamanni*.[10] The *Historia Brittonum* list is the only one that connects the table of nations with a genealogy going back to Japhet, thus combining three strains of origin legends in one list: biblical-Isidorian, Roman-Frankish and classical-Germanic ethnography.

Names also held semantic and etymological connotations which Isidore of Seville developed into an all-inclusive semantic system. Many names were

---

[9] For the symbolic significance of the seventeenth generation, or seventeenth ruler (Romulus, Athalaric, Rothari) see Wolfram 1990a:26.

[10] The Codex Cavensis, Cava de Tirreni n. 4, has the form: *Hostius genuit Romanos, Brittones, Francos et Alamannos.*

connected to those of other peoples purely because they sounded alike, like the Goths with the Getae or even the Scythians (Isidore explains that by dropping the 'S' you could show that this was in fact the same name). In Britain, the Jutes were later linked with the Goths for similar reasons, as Asser (I.2) clearly does at the end of the ninth century. Furthermore, a Latin speaker had no difficulty in deciphering many contemporary ethnic names. He could easily link the name of the Avars with avarice, the Bulgars with vulgarity, whereas the name of the Slavs later replaced the classical term *servus* as slave. Less negatively than these eastern barbarians, the Langobards were easily to be identified as *Longibarbae*, the Burgundians could be traced to the *burgi* or *castra* in which the Romans had stationed them, and the name of the Franks came to be understood almost as the exact opposite of that of the Slavs.

British ethnonyms were just as telling. The *Picti* stimulated ethnographic phantasies of painted bodies, even in Isidore (*Etym.* XIX.xxiii.7; cf. Jordanes, *Getica* 14) who then applied the same etymology to the *Scotti*, which he explained as the word for 'painted body' in their own language (*Etym.* IX.ii.103). The Britons, according to Isidore, have their name *eo quod bruti sint* (*Etym.* IX.ii.102).[11] The Saxons are much better off, with their association with *saxum* that comes so naturally that Isidore does not even mention it when he calls them a *durum et validissimum genus hominum* (*Etym.* IX.ii.100); the Spanish ninth-century list *De proprietatibus gentium* (see below) attributes *duritia* to the Saxons. Isidore does not refer to the sax, the Germanic knife, as for instance Widukind did in the tenth century (*Res gestae saxonicae* I.6-7), which of course reinforces the military note in the name of the Saxons. The famous equation of *Angli* and *Angeli* even has Papal authority to support it; Bede's anecdote (*HE* II.1) reflects how easily names were seen as omens. If there were no easy parallels, one could use one's imagination as when Pope Gregory interprets the inhabitants of Deira as 'from the wrath' (of God), *de ira eruti*. There was, however, an alternative explanation for the name *Angli*, which is already implicit in Bede's name for their country of origin, *angulus*; Widukind even understood it as a mere geographical qualification of the Saxons who had come to Britain, to an island in an angle of the sea: *quia illa insula in angulo quodam maris sita est, Anglisaxones usque hodie vocitantur*.

It is surprising to see that in a way these etymologies corresponded to the image these peoples had among contemporary writers. Greed and avarice is a stock characteristic in texts about the Avars, and authors have speculated about the Bulgars as the 'bastards' of the steppes (even as late as our own century). Of course, attitudes could vary, as, for instance, the diffused lists about the characteristics of the people (*De proprietatibus gentium*) show (Mommsen 1894:389-90; cf. Meyvaert 1991:749-59 n.14). Apart from two Cambridge manuscripts, it is also contained in the British Library manuscript Harley 3271,

---

11 The *Historia Brittonum*, the version of the 'Frankish table of nations' that is copied in one of its manuscripts, and Geoffrey of Monmouth (1.3) have Brutus or Bruto/Britto as *heros eponymos* instead (Dumville 1990; Dumville 1994:407-10; Goffart 1983).

immediately following the 'Tribal Hidage' (Fol. 6v; see facsimile in Dumville 1989:226). It lists, among others, the *crudelitas Pictorum*, the *superbia uel ferocitas Francorum, ira Bryttanorum, stultitia Saxonum uel Anglorum, libido Iberniorum*. The Angles are an addition in this manuscript; the Britons are always connected with anger, whereas the Saxons, in a late ninth century Spanish version, are credited with *duritia* (in other manuscripts attributed to the Picts). Later lists give both positive and negative attributes; here, the Saxons may boast their *instantia*, the *Scotti fidelitas*, the Picts *magnanimitas* and the Britons *hospitalitas*.

But generally, since late antiquity, the names of the Britons and of Britain often appear in negative contexts—although they were also regarded as related to Romans and Franks, as in the so-called 'Frankish table of nations' (Goffart 1983:111). The Church fathers, in their polemic against Pelagius, often dwelt on his British (or Irish) origin (Bury 1904/5). In one instance, Jerome (*Hieronymus, In Hieremiam prophetam libri sex*) compares him to Cerberus, alluding to ancient mythologies that place the entrance to the underworld in the North West. This idea reappears in an eerie anecdote Procopius tells in his *Wars* (VIII.xx.47-58), stressing that he does not believe it but cannot omit it lest he should "gain a lasting reputation for ignorance of what takes place there". At night, he writes, the fishermen from the opposite side of the Channel have to row the souls of the dead over to Britain, because that is the place where they all have to go; in reward, these fishermen are exempt from Frankish taxes. Procopius had some more strange stories about Britain to tell. The island, according to him, is cut in two by a wall beyond which the weather gets very bad, and wild animals abound; indeed, the difference in climate is so drastic that people who go to the other side of the wall are supposed to die immediately (VIII.xx. 42-46). Jordanes had a similar idea (prejudice or not) about bad weather in Britain; he cites Strabo as a witness for the permanent fogs there (*Getica* XII). But admittedly, the most striking feature in the Gothic historian's chapter on Britain is that, writing in Constantinople around 550, he relied exclusively on books that were hundreds of years old; his only non-classical reminiscence is a strange hint about Gothic captivity in Britain. Ecclesiastical writers writing about the British often dwelt on moral values; when Pope Gregory III sent Boniface to Bavaria, he warned the Bavarians to be on guard against "pagan rites and doctrines, arriving Britons, false and heretic priests and adulterers" (Boniface, *Epistulae* n. 44).[12] In England, writers from Gildas and Bede onwards complain about the sinful lives of the Britons, but also their cowardice as reasons for their defeats; this view culminates in Wulfstan's *Sermo Lupi ad Anglos*, where it reaches apocalyptic dimesions and serves as a warning for the Anglo-Saxons of his day. Defeat, for Christian writers, had to have a moral reason. In Byzantium, the "misfortunes of the Britons" (as in Procopius, *Wars* V.xxiv.35) seem to have been proverbial. *Optimi Saxones, miseri*

---

[12] Boniface, who came from Britain too, rather stressed his origin from the *gens Anglorum* (n. 46, n. 80, n. 111) although he does not spare the *Angli* severe criticism, for instance about their heavy drinking, the *malum speciale paganorum et nostrae gentis*, or about the *meretrices gentis Anglorum* in Continental towns (n.78).

Bretti, is the catchy phrase in which Widukind (c.8) renders his quintessence of Bede's narrative. Nevertheless, as a name for the island, *Britannia* could hardly be replaced—like *Italia* and *Hispania*, and unlike Gaul, which became *Francia*, or *Pannonia*, which turned into Hungary.

The perceptions of Angles and Saxons, we might even say the 'Angels' and the 'Rocks', developed quite differently.[13] In Bede, Saxons usually turn up for military victories, whereas the Angles are often mentioned in matters of religion. The Saxons rather than the Angles are connected with the migration to Britain (as in the anonymous Cosmography of Ravenna 5.31, compiled in different stages between the sixth and the eighth century). The Church is the *ecclesia Anglorum* (*HE* IV.2) or the *ecclesiae Anglorum* (*HE* III.28), even though in the epilogue, Bede seems less clear where he calls the work *historia ecclesiastica Brittaniarum, et maxime gentis Anglorum* (the Saxons are not mentioned). Again in the spiritual field, the *Angli* have to confront the *Scotti* in the Easter controversy. It is, I suppose, generally accepted that in this respect, the choice was Gregory the Great's (Wormald 1994:12). His letter to Æthelberht of Kent (*HE* I.32; *Greg. Reg.* XI.37) calls him *rex Anglorum*, and successive popes generally stuck to that title in their letters to Anglo-Saxon kings (Scharer 1988:40). But Gregory only used Byzantine terminology. Procopius knows *Angíloi*, but no Saxons in Britain; and he mentions that the king of the Franks had recently sent an embassy to Justinian bringing a few Angles that had emigrated to the Frankish kingdom "to establish his claim that this island was ruled by him" (*Wars* VIII.xx.10; see also Wood 1984:25). One may debate how far Byzantine usage influenced ethnic identities in Britain, given the relative scarceness of direct political contact. Within the political sphere of the Empire, diplomatic relationships, military conflicts and treaties closely followed the pattern established by ethnographic perceptions. The Byzantines did not negotiate with groups they could not name and identify, which, for these groups, meant a considerable disadvantage against barbarian rivals. This lack of communication about ethnic and political identities seems to have constituted a major obstacle to the integration of the early Slavs in the late Roman world, with far-reaching consequences. In the case of the Angles and Saxons, the Church, more than the Roman state, seems to have contributed a lot towards the stabilization of ethnic identities.

Missionary terminology gave the name of the *Angli* a general meaning which that of the Saxons had only in some contexts, for instance in Celtic languages (Kuhn 1973:305). But even with the term *Angli*, no clear-cut name system evolved. We read both of the *gens* and of the *gentes Anglorum*—the plural seems to be more frequent in a political sense, where *gens* means the population of a single kingdom, whereas a single, inclusive *gens Anglorum* often evokes the idea of a religious community, as in the title of Bede's *History*.[14] This was paralleled by

---

[13] See also Patrick Wormald's observations on the "implications of Englishness" (1994:14 ff.)

[14] For some observations on the terminology of the *gens Anglorum* see Fanning 1991:20-2; Hines 1990:32, with n.43; Wormald 1983:122-3. Alcuin, in his letters, also used both the singular and the plural, e.g. *gens Anglorum* (*ep.* 3, 82), *populi Anglorum* (*ep.* 61).

the Anglo-Saxon term *Engle* (Kuhn 1973:285, 304). In both senses it is not always clear whether Saxons and others are included, this usually depended on explicit or implicit semantic oppositions. The term *populi Anglorum* usually carries a strong overtone of orthodoxy and Church organization. But, as far as I can see it, there was no strong territorial equivalent; there was Bede's *Angulus* for the Continental homeland of the Angles (*HE* I.15), and there were specific regions like *Anglia Orientalis*, but no overwhelming use of *Anglia* for the whole of Britain or its Anglo-Saxon parts.[15] Instead, we hear of *terra* or *provinciae Anglorum*, which seems to be the Latin eqivalent of *Engla land* (Ælfric, *Life of King Oswald*; Sweet 1967: n. 15.77).[16] In Old English, the composite *Angel-cynn* could acquire a territorial meaning, for instance in King Alfred's letter prefixed to his version of the *Cura pastoralis* (Sweet 1967: n. 2).[17] In some cases, *Saxonia* could be used instead as a term covering also Anglian territory, as in a letter by the abbot of Jarrow in *Saxonia* to the Pope cited by Bede (*Vita sanctorum abbatum* c.19) or in a letter by Boniface to Pope Zachary in which he locates London *in transmarina Saxonia* (*Epistulae*, n. 50). An interesting form is used by Alcuin in 786 in the subscription of a report about two British Synods to Pope Hadrian I (*ep.* 3), "*Synodus, quae facta est in Anglorum Saxonia*". This formula already points towards the collective Anglo-Saxons, and obviously serves to distinguish the insular Saxons from those on the Continent.

With the name of the Saxons, as we can see in the last two examples, the problem was to distinguish the English Saxons from those on the Continent whom Bede and Boniface (*Epistulae,* n. 73) sometimes call *antiqui Saxones* (cf. *Cosmographus ravennatis* 5.31), and a letter by Pope Gregory II even *Altsaxones* (*Epistulae,* n. 21). The same applies to the problems of distinguishing between the Insular and the Continental *Britannia*; Carolingian annals normally use *Britannia* for Brittany and have to qualify Britain as *Britannia insula*. Only the *Angli* have no Continental counterpart, although even here qualifications like *gens Anglorum advena Britannia* appear.[18]

Royal titles, as they are preserved in seventh- and eighth-century charters, mostly refer to specific kingdoms: *rex Cantiae/rex Cantuariorum, rex Marciae/rex Merciorum* etc. But there were also attempts to adopt more general terms, chiefly

---

[15] On the Continent, *Anglia* was used more naturally, for instance in a late eighth century addition to the *Annales Xantenses* where it is repeatedly used as a synonym with *Britannia* (e.g. a. 730: *Obiit domnus Beda presbiter et monachus in Anglia*).

[16] For the shifting terminoloogy of *provinciae* and *regiones* see Bassett 1989:18; cf. Wormald 1994:11 ff.

[17] The excerpt referred to in Sweet is *ciricean giond all Angelcynn*; of course it could, like *Angel-theod*, also mean the Angles or the Anglo-Saxon people (cf. Ealdorman Alfred's ninth century will [Sweet 1967: n. 34, n. 48] and the *Anglo-Saxon Chronicle* [Parker-Chronicle, a. 896]). Again, the closeness to *engelcynn*, the 'order of angels' (Sweet 1967: n. 22.1) is remarkable. These composites with *Angel-* seem to be more frequent than the corresponding *Seax-theod*; see, for instance, the Old English Bede I. 15, where *Anglorum sive Saxonum gens* is translated *Angeltheod and Seaxna*.

[18] Letter by Archbishop Cuthbert of Canterbury about the death of Boniface (*Epistulae*, n. 11).

when a king had extended his dominion, as with Æthelbald or Offa. Æthelbald occasionally styled himself *rex Suutanglorum*, or, more elaborately, *rex non solum Marcersium sed et omnium provinciarum quae generale nomine Sutangli dicuntur*, or similar (Sawyer 1968: S 89; Scharer 1988:57). Confronted with this not very elegant attempt to be precise, the famous subscription *Ego Aetdilbalt rex Britanniae* becomes comprehensible (Sawyer 1968: S 89).[19] Offa generally used the title *rex Merciorum*; none of the charters calling him *rex Anglorum* seems to be genuine, *rex Mercensium simulque in circuitu nationum* is doubtful, although similar to Aethelbald's (Sawyer 1968: S 96), and the absolute title (*rex dei dono* or similar), rather than any geographical term, reflected the dominating position Offa achieved towards the end of his reign (Scharer 1988:63-70; cf. Wormald 83:109).

All this suggests that there was no clear notion of, or terminology for an ethnic collective of Anglo-Saxons up to at least 800, although a number of conceptual efforts were made to describe larger units that exceeded the single kingdoms. In narrative sources, the most common inclusive term to cover both the Angles and the Saxons is the formula *Angli vel Saxones*, or similar.[20] Only in Carolingian times do Continental writers seem to have started using the composite *Anglisaxones*, which is found in Paul the Deacon's *Historia Langobardorum,* written between 788 and 796 (*HL* IV.22; VI.15)[21], along with the specific terms *Angli* and *Saxones*—as in Bede, we get *Angli* in ecclesiastic contexts (*HL* III.25; V.30; VI.37) and *Saxones* in the political sense (*HL* V.33; VI.28). The *Angli Saxones* also appear in the *Annales Bertiniani* (*s.a.* 844 and 855). But here it becomes apparent that it is used because the author cannot differentiate between Angles and Saxons. A person as conspicuous as Prudentius of Troyes, chaplain at the court of Charles the Bald, calls King Alfred's father, Æthelwulf of Wessex, indiscriminately *rex Anglorum Saxonum* (*s.a.* 855), *rex Occidentalium Anglorum* (*s.a.* 856) and *rex Occidentalium Saxonum* (*s.a.* 858)—he only gets the correct title after he has died.[22]

Lives of Anglo-Saxon saints in the ninth century also occasionally use the new composite form, for instance the *Vita Bertuini* (*Vita Bertuini episcopi et sancti maloniensis, Mer.* 7, 177), who *ex provincia Anglisaxonis oriundus fuit*. Another early occurence is in the *Vita Alcuini* (c.18) written under Louis the Pious, probably in the 820s. The priest Aigulfus, *Engelsaxo et ipse*, comes to Tours where

---

[19] For a thorough discussion of Bede's use of the term '*Britannia*' see Scharer 1988:58-60.

[20] Translating the Latin *vel* by a simple 'and' removes much of its ambiguity that still carries the notion of 'or'; you do not really use *vel* when you have a clear distinction in your mind. However, Anglo-Saxon translations, for instance of Bede, put 'and'.

[21] For the date see Pohl 1994b; for the earliest use of the term see Levison 1946; see also Scharer 1993:124.

[22] The same equation appears already in Paul's *Historia Langobardorum*, where the list of contents of Book 6 contains a chapter *de duobus Anglorum regibus*, whereas the chapter heading (6, 28) talks of *duo reges Saxonum*, as does the *Liber pontificalis* 90 (Constantine) from where Paul took the information. A ninth-century Anglo-Saxon scribe at Fulda, possibly not by sheer chance, wrote *Angelorum regibus* instead.

Alcuin stays. Not all of the monks welcome his visit; Alcuin overhears some of them saying: *Venit iste Britto vel Scoto ad illum alterum Brittonem, qui intus iacet. O Deus, libera istud monasterium de istis Brittonibus; nam, sicut apes undique ad matrem revertuntur, ita hi omnes ad istum veniunt.*

This anecdote is not only a good example of xenophobic tendencies in Carolingian monasteries, but it also shows that prejudiced monks simply confused Anglo-Saxons, British and Irish and used old stereotypes about the Britons for Anglo-Saxon clerics. It seems that Carolingian writers often did not bother to distinguish between Angles, Saxon and British anymore. Ruodolf's *Translatio S. Alexandri*, written around 850, has the Continental Saxons come directly *ab Anglis Britanniae*. Thus, it might be that our scholarly term for the Anglo-Saxons was coined by Continental clerics who had ceased to perceive a difference between Angles and Saxons, and probably did not even care.

In the second half of the ninth century, however, political changes in Britain itself led to a change in terminology, for the fall of the eastern kingdoms in the Viking raids and the rise of Alfred's Wessex destroyed the old plurality of ethno-political units (cf. Scharer 1993). Bede's world of Anglian and Saxon kingdoms had collapsed. Asser's *Life of King Alfred*, most likely written in 893, is among the first Insular sources to use the collective term 'Anglo-Saxons'. As early as the first chapter, it styles Alfred as *angul saxonum rex*. That usage still varied is shown in the preceding dedication to *omnium Britanniae insulae christiano rectori Aelfred Anglorum Saxonum regi* (Keynes-Lapidge 1983:66, with the 1722 facsimile from the lost *ca* 1000 manuscript).[23] In charters of the period, the forms *rex Anglorum et Saxonum* (Sawyer 1968: S 346), *Anglorum Saxonum rex* (Sawyer 1968: S 347), *Angol Saxonum rex* (Sawyer 1968: S 348) and *Angulsaxonum rex* (Sawyer 1968: S 354) all appear, suggesting that the Anglo-Saxons did not burst on the scene as a revolutionary change in concept but in a gradual, though ideologically significant transition. Tenth century royal titles show a renewed variety: *rex Angligenarum omnium gentium, rex totius Britanniae, rex Angulosaxonum, rex Angulseaxna, basileus* (or *rex*) *(totius) Albionis, Angligenae et diversarum nationum rex* and many other forms, besides the most successful form *rex Anglorum* (only in the Norman period did *rex Angliae* become common) (Kleinschmidt 1988:115 n.148).

Strategies of ethnic definition

In most of the cases I have cited here (without claiming that I have got anywhere near being systematic), it may be debated whether they have any bearing on actual identities in Britain. One thing, however, should have become clear. Studies of ethnogenesis in medieval Europe cannot simply resort to ethnological models that

---

[23] The commentary (Keynes-Lapidge 1983:227-8) assumes that "Asser here uses a regnal style (*Angul-Saxonum rex*) that appears to have become current during the 880s, probably in connection with the submission to Alfred in 886 of 'all the English people that were not under subjection to the Danes (*ASC s.a.* 886)'".

have been developed in case studies in Polynesia (one of the favourite areas to study migrations and their consequences) or the Amazon jungle. I do not say this to minimize the many ways in which modern ethnology has inspired historical studies. But ethnic processes in early medieval Europe did not happen within a small, ethnocentric world where a tribe could simply perceive of itself as the focus of the world, but in a wide universe full of *gentes*, stretching as far as the biblical Middle East and the Russian steppe. This wide horizon is not just the construction of a few Christian intellectuals. It corresponds, especially between the fourth and sixth centuries but also later, to the collective experience of secular élite groups, mainly of warriors, with far-reaching connections. These were the people who formed the 'kernels of tradition', as Wenskus has put it, around which new ethnic groups developed; but, at the same time, they seem to have looked far beyond the small world of their regional kingdoms. The prestige goods that surrounded them demonstrate this, from Tournai and Sutton Hoo to Pietroasa and Malaja Pereščepina.

Anglo-Saxon epic has a similar bias. Historians have, quite correctly, studied every little piece of evidence related to Hengist and Horsa and the *adventus Saxonum*—but this fragmentary *origo gentis* comes from Bede, and not from Anglo-Saxon poetry. This is not unusual; our main witness for the origin of the Goths is a Roman senator, Cassiodorus, and for the Langobards a monk from Montecassino (whereas the one major text we have in Gothic is Ulfila's bible). Among Anglo-Saxon texts, *Widsith* in particular offers a world-view that is anything but insular—his list of ethnonyms surpasses any late Roman panegyrist by far.[24] He emphatically presents all of Europe from the Emperor of the Greeks to Scandinavia, from Ermanaric to Alboin's Italy, and from Attila to Picts and Scots as a stage for personal exploits and a common quest for honour. *Widsith*'s topography of honour relies mainly on a body of what moderns have called *Germanische Heldensagen*. This term may be linguistically correct; but the point of view in *Widsith* as in many of the Germanic legends is certainly not Germanic. Huns and Greeks, Persians and Wends, Picts and Welsh figure in it without any distinction. Neither is there any geographical order that treats British matters separately.

Apart from *Widsith*, it is surprising to find that many other Anglo-Saxon texts—even *Beowulf*—treat travel and adventures in foreign countries, while ethnic identities do not seem to matter much. "The Beowulf poet does his best to attach his pagan champion to as many peoples as possible—Danes, Geats, Swedes, Wulfings, and Waegmundings", Roberta Frank concluded (1982:64). Only with the accounts of battles against Vikings from the ninth century onwards does a note of 'we-consciousness' become apparent. We do, of course, come rather close to an *argumentum ex silentio* in this case; and as vernacular literature is only preserved (on the Continent) in writing from rather late dates, the comparison becomes difficult. Still, interest in writing down *origines gentium*, as far as our evidence goes, is a matter for Latin texts. This need not mean that it was a concern of small minorities; it

---

[24] This observation remains valid even if one accepts a rather late date for the composition of *Widsith*, as proposed by Hill (1984:305-15).

might be that there was a continuous tradition of argument about the *adventus Saxonum*, as Nicholas Howe (1989) has recently tried to prove. It is impressive to see how the Anglo-Saxon *Exodus* poem makes an emblematic event of the people of Israel crossing the Red Sea; one of a number of instances in which metaphors for migration narratives have been taken from the *Exodus* (Schneider 1993:11-58).

Paul the Deacon, for instance, makes Alboin climb a mountain to look into Italy before entering it, just as Moses looked into the Promised Land. But still, this type of allegory is rather different from actual migration myths; it is not a controlled discourse that defines space and time, actors and identities, as Bede's chapter about the *adventus Saxonum* is, but an open text that allows widely different inter-pretations. After all, the peoples in Britain were all thought to have come by sea. Retrospectively, their migration myths could also be turned around; Bede has the Britons come from Brittany and the Saxons from the Continent, whereas according to a redaction of the Carolingian Court Annals the Bretons of Brittany came from Britain, and both Ruodolf's ninth-century *Translatio S. Alexandri* (Pertz 1829:674) and Widukind's *Res gestae saxonicae* tell us that it was the Continental Saxons who migrated from their British homeland. Early medieval scholars often argued about conflicting origin stories, or tried to harmonize them without completely resolving their contradictions (cf. Carey 1994).

Our Latin texts, in Britain as on the Continent, presuppose a certain form of organized memory, oral or written, and an audience that could fill in the gaps between the rather scrappy information given by authors like Jordanes, Gregory of Tours, Bede or Paul the Deacon. Herwig Wolfram's studies on *origines gentium* have certainly established that there is information in these texts that cannot be explained otherwise (Wolfram 1994). Thus, I would not go as far as Walter Goffart who, at the 1994 Kalamazoo conference, has argued for the total disappearance of heroic literature and oral tradition between 550 and 800. But, on the other hand, ethnic discourse did not have to rely on archaic material alone. Heroic poetry was not necessarily the most important medium for the construction of ethnic identities. The conflicts described in it hardly ever develop along ethnic lines, and they do not as a rule give models for ethnic identity, although they presuppose it as a kind of personal quality. Thus, Angles and Saxons—like *Widsith*—could regard myths about Ermanaric, Theoderic or Alboin as parts of their own heritage. Paul the Deacon remarks that Alboin legends were also popular among Bavarians, Saxons and others. Semiotically speaking, the code of heroic poetry was rather restricted in a social sense, but quite open as far as ethnic identities were concerned.

Paradoxically as it seems, churchmen were more interested than heroic poetry in defining ethnic groups in writing.[25] One might even go so far as to say, as J. N. L. Myres did a quarter of a century ago, that "Bede invented the Angles, the Saxons, and the Jutes" (1970:146).[26] This meant, firstly, relating ethnic groups to certain territories.

---

[25] For some general observations on Old English poetry and Christian writing see Lerer (1991:4 ff.); for the development of Christian discourse see Cameron (1991:1 ff.).

[26] Myres goes on to say: "What Bede did for the Angles, the Saxons, and the Jutes was to put them firmly on the map: or rather on two maps, the map of Germany and the map of Britain".

Widsith hardly ever does that, and only in very vague form; more often, his lists follow the logic of assonance than that of topography. Bede's lists, on the other hand, are systematic and exclusive. Secondly, ethnic groups could be defined by identifying them with one or several political entities, even if that was as problematic as in the case of the Anglo-Saxon kingdoms. And thirdly, constructing ethnic identities could mean codifying the *origo gentis*. It is remarkable that both the Gothic and the Langobardic histories, in the form preserved for us, were written down by witnesses of the final defeat of the Ostrogothic and the Langobardic kingdoms respectively—Jordanes and Paul the Deacon—when perhaps a final redaction was thought appropriate. This is obviously different in Bede's case. But still, the written text must have contributed to codify memories that had been more flexible up to that point.[27] In Bede's ethnic model, there is no room for what we would call ethnogenetic processes—people can come and go, or even be destroyed, but they do not mix or change. Thus, after almost 400 years of Roman rule, the Romans can simply leave or be killed, and leave the Britons they have once conquered to themselves. Bede also disregards—or rather denies—the possibility that many Britons might have become Angles or Saxons (Dumville 1993). This is a point of view common to the whole discourse of ethnicity in late antiquity and the early Middle Ages. Such a view could in the long run lead to contradictions between the actual situation and a text as influential as Bede's *Ecclesiastical History*. But it could also contribute to stabilizing ethnic identities as a basis for political legitimacy. We have some reason to assume that ethnic constructions like Bede's, or Cassiodorus's and Jordanes's, were embedded in a much broader ethnic discourse that was at the same time more flexible in its combination of certain basic elements. But we can also suppose that authoritative writers like these had a tremendous influence on such discourse. We can show that, for instance, in the case of the Ostrogothic kingdom or of the Langobardic principalities of southern Italy. Ian Wood (1990:64) has arrived at a similar conclusion in a study of Burgundian ethnicity: "the Burgundians—he writes—were not defined by blood but by those who wrote about them". The influence of ethnic discourse on the consciousness of the people is, of course, largely a matter of speculation. For us, it is hard to tell whether Bede's contemporaries regarded themselves as Northumbrians, as Angles, as *Angli vel Saxones*, as *Garmani*, as inhabitants of Britain or of their local environs, or as something different altogether. In any case, we should remember that there is a point to all of these possibilities. Calling them Anglo-Saxons may give us a sense of their ethnic identity that they did not necessarily share. We need not conclude that ethnic identities did not matter to them at all—Bede would not talk about the matter repeatedly if that were the case. But ethnic processes were open to political and personal shaping and re-shaping, to constructions and re-constructions of ethnic identities.

---

[27] It would be interesting to take Anglo-Saxon regnal lists, with their oscillation between codified memory and ideological manipulation, into account here (Dumville 1990c:72 ff.).

Acknowledgements—I would like to thank the participants in the discussion at San Marino, especially David Dumville, John Hines and Ian Wood, for their advice and guidance on my venture into the little-known universe of Anglo-Saxon studies.

References

Textual sources:

[Abbreviations: *ASC* = *Anglo-Saxon Chronicle*; *HE* = *Historia ecclesiastica gentis Anglorum*; *Mer.* = *MGH, Script. rerum merovingicarum*; *S* = Document number in Sawyer 1968; *SS* = *Scriptores*]

Ælfric
              Life of King Oswald: see Skeat 1871-1887.
Alfred the Great
              Cura pastoralis: see Kerr 1956.
Anglo-Saxon Chronicle: see Whitelock 1961.

Annales Bertiniani: see Rau 1958.

Annales Xantenses: see Rau 1958.

Asser
              Life of King Alfred: see Keynes & Lapidge 1983.
Bede
              Historia ecclesiastica gentis Anglorum: see Colgrave & Mynors 1969.
              Vita sanctorum abbatum: see King 1930.
Boniface
              Epistulae: see Rau 1968.
Claudian
              Paneg. de IV cons. Hon. 446-452: see Hall 1985.
Codex Cavensis: ms. n.4, Badia di Cava.

Cosmographus ravennatis: see Schnetz 1940.
Cuthbert of Canterbury
              Letter about the death of Boniface: see Rau 1968: n. 111.
De proprietatibus gentium: see Mommsen 1894.
Geoffrey of Monmouth
              Historia regum Britanniae: see Wright 1985.
Gregory the Great
              Registrum epistolarum: see Ewald & Hartmann 1891/1899.
Gregory II
              Letters: see Rau 1968.
Historia Brittonum: see Mommsen 1898.
Isidore of Seville
              Etymologiae: see Lindsay 1911.
Jerome
              In Hieremiam prophetam libri sex: see Reiter 1913.
Jordanes
              Getica: see Mommsen 1882.
Liber pontificalis: see Duchesne 1955.
Paul the Deacon
              Historia Langobardorum: see Waitz 1878.

Procopius
> *Wars*: see Dewing 1919.

Ruodolf
> *Translatio Sancti Alexandri*: see Pertz 1829.

Sidonius Apollinaris
> *Carmina*: see Luetjohann 1887.

Tribal Hidage: see Dumville 1989.

Venantius Fortunatus
> *Carmina*: see Leo 1881.

Vita Alcuini: see Arndt 1887.

Vita Bertuini episcopi et sancti maloniensis: see Levison 1920.

Widsith: see Chambers 1912.

Widukind
> *Res gestae saxonicae*: see Hirsch & Lohmann 1935.

Wulfstan
> *Sermo Lupi ad Anglos*: see Bethurum 1957.

Bibliography:

Arndt, W. (ed.)
> 1887   *Monumenta Germaniae historica, Scriptores*, 15, pp 182-197. Hannover: Hahn.

Bassett, S. (ed.)
> 1989   *The Origins of Anglo-Saxon Kingdoms*. London: Leicester University Press.

Beumann, H., & W. Schröder (eds.)
> 1978   *Aspekte der Nationenbildung im Mittelalter*. (*Nationes* 1). Sigmaringen: Thorbecke.

Bethurum, D. (ed.)
> 1957   *The Homilies of Wulfstan*. Oxford: Clarendon Press.

Bourdieu, P.
> 1977   *Outline of a Theory of Practice*. Cambridge: Cambridge University Press.

Brühl, C.
> 1990   *Deutschland-Frankreich*. Die Geburt zweier Völker. Köln: Böhlau Verlag.

Bury, J. B.
> 1904/5   The Origin of Pelagius. *Hermathena* 13: 26-35.

Cameron, A.
> 1991   *Christianity and the Rhetoric of Empire. The Development of the Christian Discourse*. Berkeley: University of California Press.

Campbell, J.
> 1979   Bede's *Reges and Principes*. The Jarrow Lecture.
> 1986   *Essays in Anglo-Saxon History*. London: Hambledon.

Carey, J.
> 1994   *The Irish National Origin-Legend: Synthetic Pseudo-History*. Cambridge: Dept. of Anglo-Saxon.

Colgrave, B., & R. A. B. Mynors (eds. & trans.)
> 1969   *Bede's Ecclesiastical History of the English People*. Oxford: Clarendon Press.

Chambers, R. W. (ed.)
> 1912   *Widsith*. Cambridge: Cambridge University Press.

Dewing, H. B. (ed.)
1919   *Procopius, Wars*, vol. 3 (1919), vol. 4 (1924), vol. 5 (1928). London: Heinemann/Cambridge, MA: Harvard University Press.
Duchesne, L. (ed.)
1955   *Liber pontificalis*, vol. 1-2. Paris: Bibliothèque des écoles françaises d'Athènes et de Rome.
Dumville, D.
1984   The Chronology of *De excidio Britanniae*, Book 1. In *Gildas: New Approaches*. Lapidge & Dumville (eds.), pp. 61-84. Woodbridge: The Boydell Press.
1989   The tribal hidage: An introduction to its texts and their history. In *The Origins of Anglo-Saxon Kingdoms*. S. Bassett (ed.), pp. 225-230. London: Leicester University Press.
1990a   *Histories and Pseudo-Histories of the Insular Middle Ages*. Aldershot: Variorum.
1990b   *The Historical Value of the Historia Brittonum*. Dumville 1990, VII, 1-26. Aldershot: Variorum.
1990c   *Kingship, Genealogy and Regnal Lists*. Dumville 1990, XV, 72-104, 1-5. Aldershot: Variorum.
1993a   *Bretons and Anglo-Saxons in the Early Middle Ages*. Aldershot: Variorum.
1993b   *Essex, Middle-Anglia, and the Expansion of Mercia in the South-East Midlands*. Dumville 1993, IX, 11-3. Aldershot: Variorum.
1994   *Historia Brittonum: an Insular History from the Carolingian Age*. In *Historiographie im frühen Mittelalter*. A. Scharer & G. Scheibelreiter (eds.), pp. 406-434. Wien/München: Oldenbourg.
Eco, U.
1979   *Lector in fabula. La cooperazione interpretativa nei testi narrativi*. Milano: Bompiani.
Ewald, P., & L. Hartmann (eds.)
1891/1899 *Monumenta Germaniae historica, Epistolae*, vol. 1 & 2. Berlin: Weidmann.
Ehlers, J.
1994   *Die Entstehung des deutschen Reiches*. München: Oldenbourg.
Fanning, S.
1991   Bede, *Imperium* and the Bretwaldas. *Speculum* 66: 1-26.
Frank, R.
1982   The Beowulf Poet's Sense of History. In *The Wisdom of Poetry*. L. Benson & S. Wenzel (eds.), pp. 53-65. Kalamazoo: Western Michigan University Press.
Geary, P.
1983   Ethnic Identity as a Situational Construct in the Early Middle Ages. *Mitteilungen der anthropologischen Gesellschaft in Wien* 113: 15-26.
1988   *Before France and Germany*. Oxford: Oxford University Press.
Goffart, W.
1983   The Supposedly 'Frankish' Table of Nations. *Frühmittelalterliche Studien* 17: 98-130.
1988   *The Narrators of Barbarian History: Jordanes, Gregory of Tours, Bede, and Paul the Deacon*. Princeton: Princeton University Press.
Hall, J. B. (ed.)
1985   *Claudian: Carmina*. Leipzig: Täubner.
Higham, N.
1992   *Rome, Britain and the Anglo-Saxons*. London: Seaby.

Hill, J.
1984   Widsith and the Tenth Century. *Neuphilologische Mitteilungen* 85: 305-315.
Hines, J.
1990   Philology, Archaeology and the *adventus Saxonum vel Anglorum*. In *Britain 400-600: Language and History*. A. Bammesberger & A. Wollmann (eds.), pp. 17-36. Heidelberg: Carl Winter Verlag.
Hirsch, P., & H. Lohmann (eds.)
1935   *Monumenta Germaniae historica, Scriptores rerum germanicarum*, 60. Hannover: Hahn.
Howe, N.
1989   *Migration and Mythmaking in Anglo-Saxon England*. New Haven-London: Yale University Press.
Kerr, N. R. (ed.)
1956   *Alfred the Great: The Pastoral Care*. Copenhagen: Rosenkilde & Bagger.
Keynes, S., & M. Lapidge
1983   *Alfred the Great. Asser's 'Life of King Alfred' and Other Contemporary Sources*. Harmondsworth: Penguin.
King, J. E. (ed.)
1930   Bede, *Historical Works*. Cambridge, MA: Harvard University Press.
Kleinschmidt, H.
1988   Die Titulaturen englischer Könige im 10. und 11. Jahrhundert. *Intitulatio III*. H. Wolfram & A. Scharer (eds.), pp. 75-130. Wien: Böhlau Verlag.
Krusch, B., & W. Levison (eds.)
1951   *Monumenta Germaniae historica. Scriptores rerum merovingicarum* 2. Hannover: Hahn.
Kuhn, H.
1973   Angeln. Angelsachsen. *Reallexikon der Germanischen Altertumskunde RGA*, 2nd ed., vol.1, pp. 285-286 & 303-306. Berlin: de Gruyter.
Lapidge, M., & D. Dumville (eds.)
1984   *Gildas: New Approaches*. Woodbridge: The Boydell Press.
Leo, F. (ed.)
1881   *Monumenta Germaniae historica, Auctores antiquissimi* 4.1. Berlin: Weidmann.
Lerer, S.
1991   *Literacy and Power in Anglo-Saxon Literature*. Lincoln/London: University of Nebraska Press.
Levison, W. (ed.)
1920   *Monumenta Germaniae historica, Scriptores rerum merovingicarum* 7, pp. 175-182. Hannover: Hahn.
Levison, W.
1946   *England and the Continent in the Eighth Century*. Oxford: Clarendon.
Lindsay, W. M. (ed.)
1911   *Isidore of Seville, Etymologiae*. Oxford: Clarendon.
Luetjohann, C. (ed.)
1887   *Monumenta Germaniae historica, Auctores antiquissimi* 8. Berlin: Weidmann.
Mayvaert, P.
1991   'Rainaldus *est malus scriptor Francigenus*': Voicing National Antipathy in the Middle Ages. *Speculum* 66: 743-763.

Mommsen, T. (ed.)
   1882   *Monumenta Germaniae historica, Auctores antiquissimi 5.1.* Berlin:
               Weidmann.
   1894   *Monumenta Germaniae historica, Auctores antiquissimi 11.* Berlin:
               Weidmann.
   1898   *Monumenta Germaniae historica. Auctores antiquissimi 13*, pp. 111-222.
               Berlin: Weidmann.
Müller-Wille, M. (ed.)
   1993   *Ausgewählte Probleme europäischer Landnahmen des Früh- und
               Hochmittelalters*, vol.1. Sigmaringen: Thorbecke.
Myres, J. N. L.
   1970   The Angles, the Saxons, and the Jutes. *Proceedings of the British Academy*
               56: 145-174.
Pertz, G. (ed.)
   1829   *Monumenta Germaniae historica, Scriptores* 2, pp. 673-681. Hannover: Hahn.
Pohl, W.
   1988   *Die Awaren. Ein Steppenvolk in Mitteleuropa, 567-822 n.Chr.* München:
               C. H. Beck Verlag.
   1990   Verlaufsformen der Ethnogenese. Awaren und Bulgaren. In *Typen der
               Ethnogenese*, vol. 1, pp. 113-124. Wien: Verlag der Oesterreichischen
               Akademie der Wissenschaften.
   1991   Conceptions of Ethnicity in Early Medieval Studies. *Archaeologia Polona*
               29: 39-49.
   1993   I Goti d'Italia e le tradizioni delle steppe. In *Teoderico il Grande e i Goti
               d'Italia*. Atti del XIII Congresso internazionale di studi sull'Alto Medioevo
               1992, pp. 227-251. Spoleto: CISAM.
   1994a   Tradition, Ethnogenese und literarische Gestaltung: eine Zwischenbilanz. In
               *Ethnogenese und Überlieferung. Angewandte Methoden der
               Frühmittelalterforschung.* K. Brunner & B. Merta (eds.), pp. 9-26.
               Wien/München: Oldenbourg.
   1994b   Paulus Diaconus und die 'Historia Langobardorum'. In *Historiographie im
               frühen Mittelalter*. A. Scharer & G. Scheibelreiter (eds.), pp. 375-405.
               Wien/München: Oldenbourg.
Rau, R.
   1958   *Quellen zur karolingischen Reichsgeschichte*, vol. 2.   Berlin:
               Wissenschaftliche Buchgesellschaft.
   1968   *Ausgewählte Quellen zur deutschen Geschichte des Mittelalters*, vol 4b.
               Frankfurt: Wissenschaftliche Buchgesellschaft.
Reiter, S.
   1961   *Corpus scriptorum ecclesiasticorum latinorum 59*. Wien: Tempsky.
Renan, E.
   1947   *Oeuvres complètes 1*. Paris: Paschari.
Sawyer, P.
   1968   *Anglo-Saxon Charters*. London: Royal Historical Society.
Scharer, A.
   1988   Die *Intitulationes* der angelsächsischen Könige im 7. und 8. Jahrhundert.
               Intitulatio III. H. Wolfram & A. Scharer (eds.), pp. 9-74. Wien: Böhlau
               Verlag.
   1993   Von der Vielfalt zur Einheit? Die Geschichte der Angelsachsen bis zum Ende
               des 9. Jahrhunderts. *Bericht über den 19. österreichischen Historikertag*, pp.
               124-130. Graz: Verband österreichischer Historiker und Geschichtsvereine.

Schneider, R.
   1993   Zur Problematik eines undifferenzierten Landnahmesbegriffes. In *Ausgewählte Probleme europäischer Landnahmen des Früh- und Hochmittelalters*, vol.1. M. Müller-Wille (ed.), pp. 11-58. Sigmaringen: Thorbecke.

Schneidmüller, B.
   1987   Nomen patriae: *Die Entstehung Frankreichs in der politisch-geographischen Terminologie (10.-13.Jh.). (Nationes* 7). Sigmaringen: Thorbecke Verlag.

Schnetz, J. (ed.)
   1940   *Itineraria romana*, vol. 2. Leipzig: Teubner.

Simson, B.
   1909   *Monumenta Germaniae historica, Scriptores rerum germanicarum 12*. Hannover: Hahn.

Sims-Williams, P.
   1983   Gildas and the Anglo-Saxons. *Cambridge Medieval Celtic Studies* 6: 1-31.

Skeat, W. W. (ed.)
   1871-1887   *Ælfric's Lives of Saints*. Oxford: Oxford University Press [repr. 1966].

Smith, A.
   1986   *The Ethnic Origins of Nations*. Oxford: Blackwell

Sweet, H.
   1967   see Whitelock 1967.

Thomas, H.
   1990   Zur Geschichte von *theodiscus* und *teutonicus* im Frankenreich des 9. Jahrhunderts. In *Beiträge zur Geschichte des Regnum Francorum*. R. Schieffer (ed.), pp. 67-95. Sigmaringen: Thorbecke Verlag.

Timpe, D.
   1986   Ethnologische Begriffsbildung in der Antike. In *Germanenprobleme in heutiger Sicht*. H. Beck (ed.), pp. 22-40. Berlin: de Gruyter Verlag.

Waitz, G. (ed.)
   1878   *Monumenta Germaniae historica, Scriptores rerum langobardicarum*. Hannover: Hahn.

Wenskus, R.
   1977   *Stammesbildung und Verfassung. Das Werden der frühmittelalterlichen Gentes*. [2nd ed] Köln-Graz: Böhlau Verlag.

Whitelock, D. (ed.)
   1961   *The Anglo-Saxon Chronicle*. London: Eyre & Spottiswoode.

   1967   *Sweet's Anglo-Saxon Reader*, 15th edition. Oxford: Clarendon Press.

Wolfram, H.
   1990a   *Die Goten. Von den Anfängen bis zur Mitte des 6. Jahrhunderts*. 3rd ed. München: C. H. Beck Verlag. [(Engl.) *The Goths* (1989). Berkeley: University of California Press].

   1990b   *Das Reich und die Germanen. Zwischen Antike und Mittelalter*. Berlin: Siedler Verlag.

   1994   *Origo et Religio*. Ethnic Traditions and Literature in Early Medieval Texts. *Early Medieval Europe* 3: 19-38.

   1995   *Grenzen und Räume*. Österreichische Geschichte (AD 375-907). Wien: Ueberreuter Verlag.

Wolfram, H., & W. Pohl
   1990   *Typen der Ethnogenese*, vol. 1. Symposion Zwettl 1986. H. Wolfram & W. Pohl (eds.), Denkschriften der Österreichischen Akademie der Wissenschaften 201. Wien: Verlag der Oesterreichischen Akademie der Wissenschaften.

Wood, I.
  1984   The End of Roman Britain: Continental Evidence and Parallels. In *Gildas:*
            New Approaches. M. Lapidge & D. Dumville (eds.), pp. 1-26. Woodbridge:
            The Boydell Press.
  1990   Ethnicity and the Ethnogenesis of the Burgundians. In *Typen der*
            Ethnogenese, vol. 1. H. Wolfram & W. Pohl (eds.), pp. 53-70.
            Denkschriften der Österreichischen Akademie der Wissenschaften 201.
            Wien: Verlag der Oesterreichischen Akademie der Wissenschaften.
  1994   *The Merovingian Kingdoms.* London: Longman.
Wormald, P.
  1983   Bede, the *Bretwaldas* and the Origins of the *Gens Anglorum*. In *Ideal and*
            Reality in Frankish and Anglo-Saxon Society. P. Wormald & D. Bullough
            (eds.), pp. 99-129. Oxford: Basil Blackwell.
  1994   Engla Lond: The Making of an Allegiance. *The Journal of Historical*
            Sociology 7 (1): 1-24.
Wright, N. (ed.)
  1985   Geoffrey of Monmouth, *Historia regum Britanniae*. Cambridge: Brewer.

Discussion

HÄRKE: I have a general question. That is, is ethnicity infinitely malleable? If one carries your argument to the logical conclusion then that would be the end point. Peter Heather has argued that there are perhaps some hard cores to ethnic identity which are not so malleable, at least not over a short period of time (Heather n.d.). And he points to a number of ethnic groups and names that disappeared into larger political units and then reappeared after these larger political units had disintegrated. Another question I have is perhaps much more mundane, arising from a R.A.I. seminar in Oxford about two years ago where somebody gave a paper on cooking habits in the Pyrenees. It turns out there is actually a very sharp division between the types of cooking the Spaniards and the French do even if they live in the same community in the same small valley in the Pyrenees. Now, if there is no ethnic conflict, if there is no need to stress one's ethnicity, how come that such things are continued? Is there some kind of mundane hard core in some ethnic perceptions or life styles?

POHL: Well, that is a question that's easy to answer. I don't think that ethnicity is infinitely malleable. I have heard Peter Heather's paper. I think it is an important example of ethnic continuity that the Rugians survived as a distinct group within the Ostrogothic kingdom, strong enough to be able to name their own king after a certain time. Now you could argue that when they reappear in the sources a couple of decades later and name a king again this was not a king of the Rugians but a king of the Ostrogoths. The point is that we also hear from Procopius that these Rugians had made a conscious effort to keep their identity by specific ethnic practices like obligatory intermarriage and clinging to their traditions—so the preservation of their identity is not just a natural process. I have actually argued so strongly for the flexibility of ethnicity because I think we are still confronted with a deep-rooted scholarly tradition that regards ethnicity as biological, not historical. I don't know about Britain but it is certainly deeply rooted in my Central European environment, especially in Eastern Europe where these concepts are threatening to become a basis for renewed nationalism and are used as arguments in national struggles. At the Slavistic conference in Bratislava last year somebody argued that the Great Moravians had already come into being in the second century AD and that there was direct continuity between them and the Slovak nation of today. Now, of course, that is a bit bizarre even for somebody like me living fifty kilometres from Bratislava. But, in a way, in a lot of research that is being done the habit still is to look, for instance in archaeology, for an ethnic label, and once you have found one to regard it as an answer.

What I want to propose is that these ethnic labels are not the answer we are looking for. It would be more interesting to go on asking what it means to call these people Anglo-Saxons, Jutes or whatever, and what kind of entity this is. The example of the Rugians shows that ethnic identity mattered more to some than to others, and the point up to which they tried to manipulate ethnic traditions differed. I sometimes get the impression that in the early Middle Ages many ethnic traditions could be more easily manipulated than at other times. I certainly agree that people living in the Pyrenees may have a stronger sense of ethnic identity. The Basques are a famous example of a really stubborn claim to ethnic identity even if it means bombing the Guardia Civil and so on. Mountain inhabitants tend to be more stubborn than city people.

SCULL: You began by characterizing the ethnic group as self-defined, but I wonder in fact whether the need for opposition to some other group is something which is equally important in the definition of ethnicity. The second point I want to make is that when we are talking of the Anglo-Saxons we should distinguish between the identities perceived in the seventh and eighth centuries as a result of Christian sources and the identities which may have preceded those—and from which they presumably derived or evolved—for which we don't have contemporary textual sources and which create rather greater problems.

You asked how ethnic identities are constructed. In order to answer this for Anglo-Saxon identities in the seventh and eighth centuries we have to go back into the Migration period. I just want to make an obvious point here: a case can be made for Anglo-Saxon identities of the fifth and sixth centuries being derived from incoming groups, apex groups or apex families bearing with them a kernel of tradition; and if we see such groups as important, relatively powerful, and perhaps in direct competition with each other, you have a situation in which strong expressions of identity might be expected.

POHL: The first point is very important, of course: the need for opposition and to have another group to define yourself against. This holds true in a psychological sense: you understand what you are yourself or you understand your own identity versus another group, and it also holds true in a kind of semantic sense. Looking for instance at Angles and Saxons there is a problem with the name *Angles*. Does it mean Angles in opposition to Saxons and Jutes, or are these regarded as part of the

Angles versus the Britons, or does it mean the population of the Island versus someone else from the Continent? Ethnic names often appear in opposed pairs.

As to the question about Anglo-Saxon identity, I completely agree that these identities really start to form in the Migration period and that kernels of tradition and apex groups coming from the Continent started a process that shaped identity. But this does not necessarily mean that a strong sense of identity was widely diffused. The problem that turns up with ethnogenesis on the Continent is the social content of ethnic designations. In the case of Avars, for instance, the name Avars sometimes is used for a core group within that population, for an élite group, while everybody else in the Avar army, can be split up into units of Slavs, Gepids, Bulgarians and so on. Interestingly enough this usually happens when the Byzantines take prisoners and these prisoners prefer not to be Avars but claim to belong to other groups. In other instances the name Avar is used for everybody living within the Avar Khaganate. A similar thing might be true for the early Saxons, that there is a strong concept of Anglian or Saxon or Anglo-Saxon identity within élite groups or core groups—and those are the people who do turn up in our sources regularly—whereas with something like 80 or 90 per cent of the population, we don't really know. These are people who often have very regional or local identities. We may ask whether they would regard themselves as part of their local unit like in the Tribal Hidage, or of a sub-kingdom, but certainly a basic unit of identity was a kingdom like Northumbria or Wessex. It is hard to tell whether the identity people had was really Saxon or Anglian, or on several levels at once, or only in kin groups.

CHARLES-EDWARDS: What you say reminds me of Ine's laws. Ine is the king of the West Saxons, but in the text of the laws (e.g. Ine 46.1), when he is contrasting people of different status according to their ethnic identity, he contrasts *wilisc* with *englisc* (British with English). Now this really matters for people, because of status. If you get killed, your wergild varies depending on what you are. So it does actually matter within the local group because there is a possibility of Welsh and English living side-by-side, even within what we call Wessex. Now this is a clear and specific example to show that what we think of as the biggest contrast, Britons vs English, does matter locally.

POHL: That is interesting. In Continental, for instance Langobardic sources, you sometimes get curious absences of Romans, although you know they must have been there; only in very specific circumstances are they mentioned. From the charter-evidence of the Langobardic kingdom you cannot argue for a very clear-cut distinction between Langobards and Romans. In some cases, people who are obviously Roman behave like Langobards in the charters; some people with Roman names put *genere Langobardus* to say they want to be treated according to Langobardic law. This is, as you said, a question of status. It is probable, of course, that some overall concept of Anglian versus British identity was there, again in a binary opposition. I just wonder if that was an inclusive concept of the kind that it is usually supposed to be. In other situations different loyalties would matter. It might be that in a context where King Ine and his army were marching upon some other kingdom, solidarity in relation to another regional group would have been much more important than the difference in legal status.

DUMVILLE: Heinrich very politely tried a *reductio ad absurdum* of your central point; I would like to try it in another direction. I don't suppose anybody would quarrel with the proposition that ethnicity is fundamentally a historical phenomenon, nor with Wenskus's proposition that it is a subjective phenomenon. But the corollary of this seems to be that a biological element is to be rejected altogether and I wonder whether here there is not too much of a reaction to the role which ideological perceptions of nationalism have played in this century, and perhaps threaten to play again so in the scholarship, one reacts to contemporary concerns, or to the concerns of the twentieth century. Carried to extremes, the proposition would essentially mean for Anglo-Saxons that the people one is looking at in the seventh and eighth centuries are not the biological heirs of those who arrived in the fifth and sixth centuries (if they did). This of course would suit some current ideas about how England developed. In other words I worry about the direction of this perception of ethnicity; about where it is going, whether there is not a danger that it will go off the rails in the way that earlier, (strongly biologically based) perceptions of ethnicity, did and become absurd or, even dangerous.

Tied up with that in your exposition is a series of problems associated with terminology. You started on the problem of what the word 'tradition' means and how it has been used, but within the English-speaking tradition of scholarship it has also come to be used as a formula to validate information when there is no other way of validating it. You eventually got down to the word 'tribe' in your paper, and used it a lot. There is one term which cries out for definition. And *gens* too: one has got into the habit, after Wenskus, of using the word *gens* for a 'people'.

POHL: That would give me a lot to talk about, if I were to answer it properly. Firstly the general point about the Anglo-Saxons not being the biological heirs of the migrants who came from the Continent. I certainly do not mean to deny that there is a steady biological process of procreation [laughter]. But what that means for the organization of any given society is shaped by language and concepts, by laws and perceptions. Societies may be matrilinear or patrilinear, agnatic or cognatic, tribal or national, they may regard class distinctions or ethnic distinctions as fundamental. All these mechanisms are quite stable, so they can be confused with biological facts; but what we are looking for is not the biological determination but the social mechanism, the concept. Wolfram once said, quite off the record, that 'ethnicity is not shaped in the wombs of women but in the heads of men'.

DUMVILLE: That is a *reductio ad absurdum*.

POHL: What I am trying to do is to argue against a biological reading of our sources. They talk a lot about biological relationships, for instance in genealogies, but these are social constructions, not biological facts. You also hinted at a possible ideological use of these excluding the biological element, which I find very important. Now the question of terminology: for me this is difficult in a double sense. For, as you said, German ethnic terminology is terribly dangerous because almost all of it has been used in an ideological complex that makes it very hard to use it any more. I am always rather surprised to see how easy it is in Italian or in English to use the term 'race' in relation to a group of people, and it always sends a chill down my spine whenever I read it. Even now in German-speaking scholarship you cannot easily use the term 'race' any longer.

CHARLES-EDWARDS: Supposing a man, in a marriage, crossed national boundaries; the children will presumably adopt one nationality or the other, and yet this is, in a sense, racial inheritance. The biological inheritance permits a political choice.

POHL: Well, I guess so, yes. But I wonder if it is necessary to call this 'objective' component race. I just used this as an example of how difficult these terms are, especially in German, at the moment; and the same goes for 'Volk' and all the other terms.

HÄRKE: I think part of the problem really is terminology. I noticed that in Germany nobody uses the term 'Rasse'. Everybody in Germany would jump on you if you used 'Rasse' as against 'Ethnizität'. You wouldn't even be able to finish your sentence.

SCULL: I think that Thomas has already made the crucial point here: you may inherit culturally-constructed identities from your parents, but these should not be confused with biological—genetic—inheritance.

POHL: Basically this goes back to the sociological discussion which was à la mode in the 60s and 70s: what, in people in general, is social and what is biological. There is the usual example of twins growing up under very different circumstances, will they be similar? Do people who move as babies from one culture to another really adapt to that culture or not? I guess I would lean more to the social than to the biological side in this case although in some cases this argument has been taken *ad absurdum*.

Let me just go back for a moment to the question of terms that has come up because that is essential. I just mentioned one problem I have which is the ideological minefield in the German language in everything which is connected with ethnicity. That's the reason why Wenskus chose the term *gens* in the first place. Of course, it is ambiguous itself. There can be a *gens Agilolfingorum*—a dynasty—and a *gens Baivariorum*, a people. My second problem is that of translation, and I recently realized that this is much more difficult than I used to think. There are terms which seem to be very easy, *Tradition*, 'tradition', yet I am always surprised to discover new connotations and overtones to all these familiar sounding terms which actually go back to the Latin tradition, in most cases, or even the Greek tradition. You can only define these terms in connection with concepts and as you try to re-define them these concepts get more and more complex and difficult. What I actually set out to do was to put the concept into very short hypotheses without getting lost in any long-drawn-out discourse, and to set these terms into the context of a formulated model. I can see that I have left out many presuppositions or bases, and I did not talk about what I think is clear anyway, but it is not very clear to others, obviously. It is really hard to define the terms. In the case of 'tribe', for instance, again it is largely a question of overtones. There is that old ethnocentric ring, at least in the German term 'Stamm'. I do not know if it is the same in Britain, but in Austria in the nineteenth century, two museums were set up: a Naturgeschichtliches Museum, Natural History, and Kunstgeschichtliches Museum, for Cultural History and the History of Art. What was supposed to be high culture went to the Kunsthistorisches Museum and prehistoric finds went to the Naturhistorisches, because tribes were seen as a part of nature. Absurdly, the treasure of Nagyszentmiklós, a famous Avar, as we now believe, or maybe Hungarian gold hoard is at the Kunsthistorisches Museum because it was considered a work of high art, but the Avar finds from normal graves are in the other museum. The term 'tribe' or 'Stamm' clearly belonged to the realm of nature and to the Natural History Museum, and so trying to avoid any connotation that 'these are primitive peoples' I avoid the term 'tribe', although sometimes it probably would be appropriate.

HOOKE: Many of the names are actually given by outsiders. They can make decisions on merely visual, if incorrect, biological grounds. In this period this probably was quite relevant. We need to look very carefully whether ethnicity has been allotted to people or whether they are actually claiming it themselves.

POHL: Of course this distinction is basic, and in some cases, as with the Slavs, it seems to be clear that Slavs originally was the name the Slavs had for themselves, whereas '*Venedi*' would be the name given them by outsiders. However these terms appear very soon in the Latin or in the Greek sources where almost from the start we find them called Slavs as well. In the West, the distinction between internal and external perceptions soon wears off: would Bede be an inside or an outside witness, writing in Latin, which is an outside language, and using a lot of tradition which goes back to Isidore and others? He is firmly rooted in a Latin-speaking world and intellectual tradition and he also uses that, to a certain degree, to describe ethnicity in Britain itself. But he is not only somebody watching from outside; he has a lot of obviously Anglo-Saxon material to rely on as well. Is that material genuine, or is Bede just somebody locked in his monastery who does not really know what people really think they are? This is the sort of problem that I think should be discussed. How do we handle the overwhelmingly Roman cultural tradition which is so prominent in our sources: do we just dismiss it as being outside information, and how far can we really rely on it?

One further remark that came to my mind when you talked about biological features and being categorized because you looked different. There are a lot of instances in history of people being killed because they looked different. There are also a lot of instances in history of people killed although they did not look different. In Bosnia, I really doubt that by looking at the people anybody would be able to tell a Serb from a Croat or from a Muslim Bosnian. Again, this is a case where concepts shift and do not make clear what 'Bosnian' is. Can a Serb be a Bosnian? The Serbs say that Bosnians are in reality Serbs, the Bosnian government says that all Bosnian Serbs are Bosnians, and outsiders try to distinguish between Serbs, Croats and 'Muslims' and/or Bosnians within Bosnia. This is the sort of thing I am talking about—when seemingly simple facts of biology turn into a mess by concepts (and finally obliterate concepts), and it turns out that these seemingly simple biological facts are much more ambiguous and leave more options open—

although still a limited range—than most people assume. The German Jews are another example of people who were not killed by the Nazis for their appearance but on the basis of documents: that is, of a social construct which was only one of several possible definitions of Jewish identity.

AUSENDA: Concerning 'race', apart from the fact that since 1945 it is a bad word in anthropology, there does not seem to be any objective way of clearly identifying 'races'. Scientists are still floundering. One of the differences concerns blood groups, but these have a very, very wide distribution. They are toying now with immunity factors. Size and dimensions of bones have been shown not to have anything to do with 'race'. Bringing it in sharp scientific focus is very difficult. I would stay away from an attempt at a biological definition of 'race'.

I would also like to talk about *origines*. Amongst Beni Amer, origins are entrusted mostly to genealogies. Table 1-1 from a Beni Amer ethnography (Ausenda n.d.) gives a synopsis of Beni Amer origins for both dominant and client clans.

One notes that preferred descent is from a *sherìf* (Ar.), a nobleman related to the Prophet, the only descent befitting dominant clans. This parallels the Woden ancestor of dominant Anglo-Saxon dynasties. Client clans favour someone belonging to the Quraish, the Prophet's clan. Nowadays, after 'freedom' was granted by the British in 1948, even client clans may aspire to a *sherìf* in their genealogies: it is not difficult to obtain one from a compliant holy man.

Dominant clans, the Nabtab among Beni Amer and Beit Asgadé among Habab, possess a legend of origin. The Nabtab consider themselves linked to the Ja'alìn, a Sudanese tribe whose territory is at the confluence of the Nile and the Atbara rivers, which had considerable trading and religious influence over the Nabtab. The latters' descent is made to go through the Ja'alìn, who in turn claim descent from the Prophet's uncle.

The Beit Asgadé's (the Habab dominant clan) legend of origin has them coming from Abyssinia. Again, Abyssinia was the hegemonic power over their territory from which they obtained their war drums (Beni Amer got them from the Funj, riverine neighbours and overlords of the Ja'alìn). Even the Beit Asgadé, who were Christian until the 1830s, claim descent from the same uncle of the Prophet. Thus their paradoxical genealogy has the last six or seven generations with Moslem names, the preceding ten or fifteen generations with Christian names, and earlier still it returns to Moslem names, going back to the Prophet's uncle. This clashes with Moslem orthodoxy, but is readily acceptable to present Beit Asgadé and their followers.

One also notes that genealogies are divided into two parts, one corresponding to 'demonstrated descent' listing the ancestors up to some three or four ascending generations. The preceding portion of the genealogy represents 'stipulated descent' (Fried 1967:124-5) and may be divided in turn into a more recent portion, just beyond 'demonstrated descent', listing the ancestors up to the kinship group's founder and providing the 'political map' connecting the various sections of the group, while the most ancient portion lists ancestors backwards in time from the legendary founder and supplies the 'legitimating background' to justify the group's privileges, be they dominance or related claims.

Table 1-1

Summary of genealogical characteristics of Beni Amer and related clans.

Clan and section		Origin claimed	Depth of origin: n. of generations	Depth of founder: n. of generations	Number of fractions
	Dagga			12	6
	Ad Ibrahìm			9	5
	Ad Naseh	Sherìf	64	9	7
	Ad Omar			8	16
Nabtab	Ad Okud	and		8	11
	Ad Gultana			8	4
	Ad Al Bakhìt			7	6
	Ad Hasri	Ja'ali	32	6	14
	Tauliàb			6	5
	Ad Saleh			5	2
Belaw		Autochtonous	?	?	8
Ejeilab		Quraishi	38	9	12
Faidab		?		?	5
Beit Ma'la		Sherìf	19	18	12
Ab Hashela		"	19	11	15
Ad Fadl "		19	13	10	
Hamasèn		"	14	12	8
Ma'la Qattàn		"	16	15	7
Ad Dyrk'ey		Sherìf	?	10	7
Ad Muallem		NA	NA	NA	NA
Ad Sheikh Hamed		Sherìf	18	10	11
Ad Sheikh Soliman		Sherìf	45	6	11
Aflanda		Melhitkinab			10
Aglemba		were w. Regbat		8	
Aitama		Sherìf	14		11
Almadà		Quraish (mother from Dob'at)	30	13	13
Asfadà		Arabian	15	14	12
Bahadùr		Ja'ali	7	7	?
Beit Awad		Sherìf	24	10	10
Dagdaghé		Almadà			6 or 11
Dagher		Abyssinian		14	4
Dob'at			17	16	12
Harabsò		NA	NA	NA	31
Hassa-Tokar		Beit Ma'la	19	10	1
Kabbé				10	
Labad		Hadendowa	?	?	21
Maghallab		Sherìf	14	11	3
Meekàl		Da. of Almadà	13	12	30
Regbàt		Quraish	14	13	17
Welednoho		Funj		>15	33
Sab l'alìth (Asawurta)		Sherìf	45		6
Saiho		Asawurta		9	2
Ad Heptès		Sherìf	34	16	22
Ad Taklès		"	34	10	7
Ad Temariàm		"	34	11	2
Bahailài		"	34	16	10
Ad Hamdòi		Abyssinian	?	8	2

I wonder whether the human predilection for 'origins', not only in pedigrees, but also in science, in addition to a desire to add status to one's pedigree, may be dictated by a trait inherent in mankind, the fact that humans are loath to account for continuity and infinity so that they have to mask negative infinity with origins and positive infinity with paradise or hell.

POWLESLAND: I do not know why ethnicity is important. Who is it important for? Is it important to us as we try to understand these peoples in the past giving them labels, or is it a matter of how important it was to them? I think it would be very easy to go a long way down the road of believing that what is important to us was important to them. In terms of trying to understand the past, the level of importance which we apply to some interpretation like ethnicity has to be stated, and the importance to whom, because otherwise I think we can move away from understanding the past to the very opposite.

POHL: I absolutely agree. It is important to ask when and to whom ethnicity did matter. But we cannot say that it is not in the sources. There are frequent lists of peoples, ethnic titles (like *rex Francorum*), legal categories with an ethnic basis, *origines gentium* and all the rest. What I do not want to do is to represent this as the tip of the iceberg, or as an all-inclusive phenomenon that comprises everything else. I certainly think that a lot of other aspects of identity, such as social status, were more important for most people most of the time.

References in the discussion

Textual sources:

Laws of Ine: see Lierbermann 1903:89-123.

Bibliography:

Ausenda, G.
    n.d.   Beni Amer and Habab: A Diachronic Ethnography.
Fried, M. H.
    1967   *The Evolution of Political Society: An Essay in Political Anthropology.*
                New York: Random House
Heather, P.
    n.d.   Disappearing and reappearing tribes. In *Strategies of Distinction - The
                Construction of Ethnic Communities, 300-800.* W. Pohl (ed). Leiden: Brill.
Liebermann, F.
    1903   *Die Gesetze der Angelsachsen.* Bd. 1. Halle: Niemeyer.
Wenskus, R.
    1961   See References at end of paper.

BEFORE AND AFTER THE MIGRATION TO BRITAIN

IAN WOOD

School of History, University of Leeds, Leeds, GB-LS2 9JT

The historiography of the migration of Germanic peoples to the British Isles begins famously with Bede's comment in Book I, chapter 15 of the *Ecclesiastical History*: *Advenerunt autem de tribus Germaniae populis fortioribus, id est Saxonibus, Anglis, Iutis* ("They came from the strongest peoples of *Germania*, that is from the Saxons, the Angles and the Jutes"). The problems of this epigrammatic account and its relationship to Gildas' description of the arrival of the Saxons in three ships have long been recognized (Campbell 1992:23-7, 28-9). Nevertheless even a book as recent as Torsten Capelle's *Archäologie der Angelsachsen* provides a map of the 'Wanderungswege der Sachsen, Angeln und Jüten' (Capelle 1990:8).

Despite this continuing attachment to the Angles, Saxons and Jutes, it may be, as James Campbell has pointed out (Campbell 1982:31), that Bede himself contradicts his own account of the migration of the Angles, Saxons and Jutes in chapter 9 of Book 5 of the *Ecclesiastical History*: *Quarum in Germania plurimas noverat esse nationes, a quibus Angli vel Saxones, qui nunc Brittaniam incolunt, genus et originem duxisse noscuntur; unde hactenus a vicina gente Brettonum corrupte Garmani nuncupantur. Sunt autem Fresones, Rugini, Danai, Hunni, Antiqui Saxones, Boructuari.* ("He knew that there were many of these nations in *Germania*, from whom the Angles and Saxons, who now live in Britain, are known to have derived their tribal origin; as a result they are wrongly called *Garmani* by the neighbouring people of the Britons. They are the Frisians, the *Rugini*, the Danes, the Huns, the Old Saxons and the *Boructuarii*.") This list differs in interesting ways from that of Bede's first account: there are no Angles and no Jutes. Instead there are Frisians and Danes, *Rugini* (i.e. *Rugi*, who came from southern Denmark) and *Boructuarii* (i.e. *Bricteri*, a group sometimes described as Frankish and sometimes as Saxons; see Wenskus 1991:522-3), and Huns. This last group certainly raises problems, if by Huns we understand the Asiatic tribe whose most famous ruler was Attila. If, however, we understand the phrase more generally to refer to groups ultimately of Asiatic origin, an Alan contingent among the migrants to Britain is not impossible. The Alans were, after all, active in northern Gaul where a substantial group of them were settled in the first half of the fifth century (Constantius, *Vita Germani* 28; Bachrach 1973:59-71, 77-99).

Bede's second account of the origins of the peoples who migrated to Britain cannot be said to be unproblematic. For a start it is not quite clear that it is really meant to be an accurate list of the ancestors of the Anglo-Saxons—it is introduced as a list of the peoples whom the monk Ecgberht wanted to evangelize. Nevertheless, what can be said is that its basic tenor is closer to the evidence of the archaeology of the early Anglo-Saxon inhumation cemeteries than is that of the simple story of three boatloads of Angles, Saxons and Jutes.

THE ANGLO-SAXONS FROM THE MIGRATION PERIOD TO THE EIGHTH CENTURY:
AN ETHNOGRAPHIC PERSPECTIVE

The majority of the earliest inhumation evidence is to be found south of the Thames, most particularly in Kent. A notable aspect of the material from these cemeteries is its variety. Rather than being exclusively 'Anglian', 'Saxon' or 'Jutish'—whatever those terms may mean in this context—there are also objects whose best parallels are to be found in Frankish, Alamannic and Thuringian regions (Evison 1965; Hawkes 1982:72; Eagles 1994:13-5). To take a single example, Bifrons has Frankish, Jutish, Scandinavian and Thuringian material (Hawkes 1982:72). The archaeology, in other words, does not suggest that the migrants of the fifth and sixth centuries who settled south of the Thames were necessarily culturally, let alone biologically, pure groups, such as might be implied by the labels Angle, Saxon and Jute.

The great cremation cemeteries of East Anglia and East Yorkshire may, however, tell a different story—one of greater cultural uniformity. The differences suggest that no single model for the history of the Anglo-Saxon migration will work, and that there are profound geographical variations. Nor does there seem to be much of a time-lag between the two cemetery-types. Chronology, therefore, does not appear to be a factor in this instance. Elsewhere, however, precise chronology is important, for the closer one comes to the seventh century, the further one moves from evidence for the Migration period, and the more one is likely to be looking at evidence for a new society created in the aftermath of settlement—a society which will have had its own methods of social and political expression.

But, to return to the evidence of the inhumation cemeteries, here the findings of such scholars as Sonia Chadwick Hawkes can be set alongside the interpretation of tribal formation set out by a school of Continental scholars whose work essentially derives from that of Reinhard Wenskus (1961). Wenskus' concern was to examine the creation of the tribal groups before, during and after the Migration period. While recognizing some factors, he emphasized the fluidity of tribal groups, which tended to form around successful military leaders, but which could dissolve with equal facility. More recently scholars influenced by Wenskus have explored the question of the creation of a tribal past, that is the question of ethnogenesis, with regard to the most successful of the barbarian tribes (e.g. Pohl 1994; Wolfram 1979; Wolfram 1994). Although these approaches have not been completely ignored in recent Anglo-Saxon historiography, as yet their full potential has not been recognized by a number of scholars.

Three questions, derived from the work of Wenskus and his Continental followers, may be asked in the context of the migration of Germanic peoples to Britain. First, what is known of the structure of the tribes from whom the migrants were drawn at the time of migration? Second, what can be said about the development of tribal structures within Britain in the fifth and sixth centuries? And third, what ethnogeneses came to be developed to explain the origins of the Anglo-Saxon tribes in the course of the seventh and eighth centuries?

The peoples of Frisia, the North German plain and Denmark are covered direct by Wenskus, although the relation of these peoples to the question of the formation of the English is certainly not fully explored. Here, in fact, a start had been made long before in H. M. Chadwick's remarkable, if much criticized, work, *The Origin of the English Nation* (1907). Perhaps the most important general point to emerge from studies of the northern Germanic tribes is the comparatively recent origins of most of the major tribal units to be found in the region of the east of the lower Rhine in the fourth and fifth centuries. Certainly these peoples incorporated tribes which had long been known to the Romans. Indeed, sometimes they are referred to, even in the sixth century, by the names of groups whom they had swallowed up: thus Gregory of Tours uses the archaic term *Sicamber* to describe the Frankish king Clovis (*Libri historiarum decem* II.21). What is important is the fact that the political geography of northern *Germania* in the fourth and fifth centuries was a relatively new one.

If, on the one hand, the political structures of northern *Germania* were fluid in the fourth and fifth centuries, that is not to say that the structures of the different tribal groups were all interchangeable. Here it is worth pausing to look at what is known, or what can be inferred, about the social and political structures of the major groups from which the migrants who crossed to the British Isles are likely to have been drawn.

It is reasonable to start with Bede's Angles, Saxons and Jutes. The Saxons are a people who cannot easily be distinguished from the Franks in sources of the fourth and even fifth centuries, so much so that the same activities are ascribed to each of them in different sources (Wood 1990). On the other hand, by the eighth century at the latest, the Continental Saxons and the Franks had very different political systems. The Franks, for instance, are already known to have had kings in the fourth century (Ammianus Marcellinus XXX.3.7; XXXI.10.6). No Saxon king is known at this period, and in the eighth century Bede and others specifically tell us that the Continental Saxons did not have kings (*Historia ecclesiastica* V.10). This situation may, of course, have developed in the intervening centuries, but it is equally possible that, despite their close association with the Franks, the Saxons had a markedly different political structure throughout the late and post-Roman periods.

The Continental Angles are almost impossible to investigate since in literature they appear rarely if at all outside lists of tribes, while the archaeology associated with them is scarcely adequate to underpin a reconstruction of their political and social structures. Their Jutish neighbours may be equally obscure. More, however, can be said about neighbouring, perhaps even related, Danish groups. Archaeologically at least one central place of great importance is coming to light at Gudme (Thrane 1988). A king of the Danes, Chlochilaicus (Hygelac) is known from Gregory of Tours (*Libri historiarum decem* III.3). A stratified society, with some sort of kingship, is therefore apparent. It may have been from such a society that Hengest came. There is little, if anything, that can be said with certainty about Hengest (Brooks 1989:58-64; Sims-Williams 1983). Bede provides our earliest evidence: he calls Hengest and Horsa the first leaders of the Angles, and identifies them as the sons of Wictgils, son of Uitta, son of Uecta, son of Woden (*Historia ecclesiastica* I.15). He places Horsa's death in Kent. His account is elaborated by the Welsh *Historia Brittonum* of *ca* 829, which strengthens the association of

Hengest and Horsa with Kent (*Historia Brittonum* XXXI.44). Hengest also appears is *Beowulf* (ll. 1083, 1091, 1095, 1127), and in the *Finnsburgh Fragment* (l. 17), where he is associated with heroes who fell in Chlochilaicus/Hygelac's raid. If Hengest, the legendary foil of Vortigern, really can be seen as a companion of Chlochilaicus, the literary evidence for this Danish king and the archaeological evidence for contemporary Denmark may provide some sort of entrée into understanding the Continental Jutes—but it must be said that none of the literary sources has any claim to reliability (for an uncritical reading of the evidence relating to Hygelac, see Storms 1970).

If we turn to the additional names on Bede's second list of ancestors of the Anglo-Saxons we may find some further information on the social and political structures to which they were accustomed. The Frisians, like the Saxons, are not always easy to distinguish from the Franks. Detailed evidence for Frisia itself only begins in the late seventh century, long after the Migration period. There is, however, nothing to suggest that the Frisians had a well-developed pattern of kingship before that date: Aldgisl and Radbod, in the late seventh and early eighth centuries, appear to have been the first and the last powerful Frisian kings (Wood 1994a:160-1, 297-8). The next name in Bede's list is that of the *Rugini*: assuming them to be related, as Plummer claimed, to the *Rugi* of Tacitus, who subsequently followed Attila, and later still fell in first with Odovacer and then with Theoderic the Great (Plummer 1896:286; Procopius *Wars* VI.xiv.24; VII.ii.1-4; Wolfram 1988:266, 278-82), we return to a Continental group ruled by kings—at least in the case of those Rugians who had moved south to the region of modern Austria (Eugippius, *Vita Severini*: V.1; VIII.1; etc.). As for the *Boructuarii*, they bring us back to the Franks, since they are in all probability to be equated with the *Bricteri* of Gregory of Tours (*Libri historiarum decem* II.9).

Although Bede does not actually refer to *Franci*, as opposed to *Boructuarii*, by name, Frankish involvement in the earliest phases of Germanic settlement in Britain seems to be attested archaeologically (Evison 1965; Eagles 1994:13-5). There can be no doubt that the Franks were a highly stratified society by the late fourth century, and having long been neighbours of the Roman Empire they were also deeply romanized (Geary 1988:73-5; Wood 1994a:35-8). The Thuringians were another group whose involvement in the Germanic settlement of Britain may be attested archaeologically. In political and dynastic terms they were closely associated with the Franks (Wood 1994a:37-8). Like them they were also highly stratified, with a royal dynasty of considerable importance (Gregory of Tours, *Libri historiarum decem* III.1.7; Cassiodorus, *Variae* III.3; IV.1), even though they were based as far from the Roman *limes* as the valley of the Unstrut (Wenskus 1961:551-60).

Such a tour of the peoples from whom the Germanic settlers of Britain came cannot be said to produce any detailed model for understanding the earliest social and political history of the Anglo-Saxons. What it does provide, on the other hand, is a very clear indication of the amount of social and political diversity within these peoples. They were distinguished not only by types of pottery or metalwork.

Although the tribes of the fourth, fifth and sixth centuries were fluid and cannot always be distinguished one from the other, some were subject to royal government, and others were apparently used to an oligarchy. Some as long-term neighbours of Rome were deeply influenced by the Empire, others were not.

There are other factors to be considered as well. The Franks, Frisians, Saxons and Danes were maritime peoples (Wood 1990). Indeed to a very large extent they can be seen as nations of pirates (Heywood 1991:54-62). No one studying the migration of the Anglo-Saxons should ignore the evidence in the writings of Sidonius Apollinaris for their simultaneous attacks in the mid-fifth century on the coasts of Aquitaine (*carm.* VII 369-70; *ep.* VIII 6, 3, 13), or Gregory of Tours' account of the activities of Adovacrius and his Saxons on the Loire, which apparently took place in the 460s (*Libri historiarum decem* II.18-19). Yet rising sea-levels are more likely than any search for a new piratical base to have been the cause of substantial migration. In either context possession of a seaworthy boat will have been an important consideration, and will have privileged the powerful, even in a supposedly egalitarian society like that of the Continental Saxons. Power structures will have affected the ability to migrate, just as the problems of transfretation will have affected the scale of migration (Jones 1987).

Yet the migrants were not all sea-going peoples. The presence of Thuringian objects in Anglo-Saxon graves may reflect the actual presence of Thuringians, even though they were a people whose traditional homeland had no coastline—they are, however, known to have had close links with the coastal Angles and the *Varni* (Wenskus 1961:556-7). Moreover, naval power may not have been an issue for the very first group of settlers. If we are able to believe Gildas, they were mercenaries, called in by the government of Britain to provide protection against the Picts and Scots of the North and West {*De excidio Britanniae* 23; compare Procopius (*Wars* VIII.xx.1) relating to *ca* 550, where the Angles are described as soldiers living in *Brittia*}. All these factors made the migrants a very heterogeneous body of people, although within this overall diversity there will have been some very close-knit groups. It might perhaps be possible to identify and map features which could help to distinguish relatively homogeneous groups, who might have migrated because of marine transgression, from pirate groups and from mercenaries.

At this point it is also worth remembering that among the Anglo-Saxon tribes settled in Britain there may also have been individuals who were British by blood, even if they chose to identify themselves, in time, as English. Such people will have included slaves (Laws of Ine 23.3; 24.2; 32; 33; 46.1; 54.2; 74), but also aristocrats, to judge by the names of such kings as Cerdic and Cædwalla (perhaps half-British, through marriage) (Eagles 1994:27-8). The survival of certain British patterns of building also suggests significant local influence on the migrants (Dixon 1991:67). The ultimate profile of the Anglo-Saxons could in no way have been predicted from the Continental world from which they were drawn.

When we turn from our first subject, the societies from which the migrants came, to our second, the societies which they developed, a new set of issues comes to the fore. Assuming Gildas to be right, rebellious mercenaries were responsible for the first breach between the Saxons and the British. One would like to know more about this initial period. It could either have been one of very considerable dislocation, or one in which a rapid military takeover, in certain areas at least, allowed for a relatively steady transformation from Roman to barbarian state (cf. Dark 1993 for a reading of possible developments on the British side). It is more than likely that some places saw rapid takeover with minimum disruption, others saw instances of carnage, and yet others saw a slow, destructive infiltration. These patterns of expansion will each have instigated different processes of state-formation.

Gildas provides some insight into the original mid-fifth-century rebellion of the Saxons against the sub-Roman British government. He also allows us to see a continuing military force active until some point in the first half of the sixth century, when he completed the *De excidio Britanniae*. Unfortunately he does not provide any evidence to elucidate the evolution from rebellion to tribal- or state-formation among the Anglo-Saxons. If we are to discuss this question in the light of contemporary evidence, as we should at least initially, we are forced back to a consideration of archaeology, which for this period poses considerable problems of chronology and of interpretation, and to a consideration of the equally contentious written evidence from the Continent.

The archaeological evidence may be simply divided between that of settlement sites and that of cemeteries. Settlement archaeology has revealed a remarkable amount about the clusters of fifth-, sixth-, and seventh-century farms at such sites as Mucking (Hamerow 1992), Charlton, Cowdery's Down and West Stow (West 1985). These sites, however, have not always provided an indication of absolute, as opposed to relative, dates. Moreover, for an understanding of the development of the broader social and political structures of the English kingdoms they are of limited use, since their status as settlement sites within the early kingdoms is unclear. For an excavated site of unquestionably central importance to the development of a kingdom one has to wait for the seventh-century royal vill at Yeavering—a site, one should add, which has markedly British features (Hope-Taylor 1977).

The cemeteries are more complex. First, there are marked differences between inhumation cemeteries, such as those south of the Thames, whose grave goods display a wide 'ethnic' variety, and the great 'Anglian' cremation cemeteries, like Sancton and Spong Hill—though even Spong has its inhumation area (Welch 1992:87). Of course this distinction may be related in part to the destruction of certain goods in the cremation process. Nevertheless, the urns from these cremation cemeteries may suggest more cultural uniformity among the local inhabitants, even by the beginning of the sixth century, than do the southern inhumation fields. Parallels to the cremation rite in Saxony (Welch 1992:66-9) may also suggest that something more like tribal migration was at stake in the areas of cremation burial than elsewhere. But it is the inhumation cemeteries with high-status burials that are perhaps most valuable for an understanding of developing Anglo-Saxon political structures (Welch 1992:88-96), not least because some can be linked with likely early royal centres, as can the cemetery of

Finglesham with the royal vill at Eastry in Kent (Campbell 1982:24). Once again, however, the best evidence comes from a seventh-century site, that of Sutton Hoo (Bruce-Mitford 1975-83).

A chronologically more precise framework against which to interpret this archaeological material can perhaps be gained from consideration of the sixth-century literary evidence from the Continent. Curiously, the earliest piece of evidence is probably to be found in a law code, the Frankish *Pactus legis salicae*, issued probably between 481 and 507 (Wood 1994a:108-12). The clause in question (39, 2) runs as follows:

> If someone entices away another man's slave and takes him overseas and there he is found by his lord, [the slave's lord] away from his homeland, and he [the lord] should have three witnesses there [in court]. When the slave has been recalled from overseas, [his lord] should name [the enticer] before a second court, and he should have there three witnesses who are suitable men; and the same should be done before a third court so that there will be nine witnesses in all who can attest that they heard the slave speaking at three courts, and afterward he who enticed him away shall be liable to pay fourteen hundred *denarii* in addition to the return of the slave plus a payment for the time his labor was lost. If the confession of the slave is admitted [and indicates] that there were up to three enticers, he [the slave's lord] should always name the names of the men and their villages in the same way (trans. Drew 1991).

Although this is a clause from Frankish legislation, drawing perhaps on earlier imperial legislation (Novel of Valentinian III.33), it is difficult to see what is meant by 'overseas' other than the British Isles. The clause thus suggests a reciprocal legal system on either side of the English Channel. This in its turn suggests that the political structure of some southern English kingdoms could accommodate a complex pattern of courts even as early as the first decade of the sixth century.

The other information for this period is not so illuminating. The vast majority of it reflects Frankish claims to hegemony over their neighbours—claims that related not just to the Anglo-Saxon settlements in England, but also to other neighbours of the Franks east of the Rhine (Wood 1983; Wood 1992; Wood 1994a:176-80). Most of the evidence for these claims throws little or no light on the developing structure of the Anglo-Saxon kingdoms. There are, however, exceptions.

Most important is the evidence for an embassy sent by a king of the Franks to the imperial court in Constantinople in around 548. The king claimed that he had jurisdiction in *Brittia*, apparently to be identified with Britain, since the island was said to be inhabited by Angles, Frisians and Britons, a group of peoples which is more easily associated with Britain than anywhere else (Procopius, *Wars* VIII.xx.7). The claim was based on the settlement within the Frankish kingdom of Angles who had left the island (Procopius, *Wars* VIII.xx.8-10). The inclusion of Angles within the Frankish legation may not reflect much of the state of any English kingdom, since the Angles in question are likely to have been drawn from those settled in *Francia*. Nevertheless the Continental settlement of the Angles from Britain can be linked with archaeological evidence from the region round Bayeux, and at Herpes on the Garonne (James 1988:101-4, 114), and the activities of the settlers can be traced in the pages of Gregory of Tours (*Libri historiarum decem* V.26, X.9; Heywood 1991:59).

For the Byzantines the evidence of Anglo-Saxon settlement in *Britannia* may have come as something of a surprise. Supposedly in 547 the Byzantine general Belisarius had offered Britain (*Brettania*) to the Goths (Procopius, *Wars* VI.vi.28), though it is important to note that this offer may have been no more than a comic response to the Goths' offer of Sicily to the Byzantines. On the other hand, according to Procopius, Justinian had sent subsidies to the barbarians in Britain (*Bretannia Secret History* XIX.13). The island of Britain, and its new Anglo-Saxon settlers, was therefore drawn into a web of international diplomacy, Frankish and Byzantine, however little the state of the island was understood.

Two further indications of this diplomatic world may be considered. First, Anglo-Saxon kings were already connected to Continental houses by marriage alliances in the first half of the sixth century. The earliest of these marriages is only known from a strange, rather folkloric account, contained within Procopius' *History of the Wars* (VIII.xx.1-41), concerning the relations between Radigis, son of King Hermegisclus of the *Varni*, and the sister of a king of the Angles living in the island of *Brittia*. Radigis had been betrothed to the princess, but when his father died he married his step-mother, who was the sister of the Merovingian king Theudebert (533-48). The Anglian princess took this badly, raised an army, attacked the *Varni* and forced Radigis to accept her as wife. Whatever the reality behind the story, it is fairly clear that ties between the migrants to Britain, and the peoples of north *Germania* had not been broken by the migration.

The most famous and best attested diplomatic marriage involving the Anglo-Saxons in the sixth century is that of Bertha, daughter of king Charibert of Neustria, to Æthelberht, son of King Irminric of Kent (Wood 1983:15-6). At the time of the marriage, which must have taken place sometime between 562 and 573/5, Bertha may well have been an orphan (her father died in 567). Æthelberht was still no more than a prince. It was, in other words, not an alliance of great importance at the time, although it was to have considerable religious repercussions through Æthelberht's conversion to Christianity. Moreover it was probably not the only marriage between Anglo-Saxon and Frankish royalty to take place in the sixth century. The East Anglian prince Sigbert, son of the wife of King Rædwald, had a name common in the Merovingian dynasty of the Franks. Further, he fled to Gaul from his father or step-father (Bede, *Historia ecclesiastica* III.18). Given his name, it would not be unreasonable to see his flight as a return to his maternal kin.

It is not surprising that the Continental evidence only allows us to see the Anglo-Saxons in their dealings with the Continent. That is, after all, what concerned Frankish and Byzantine writers. Nevertheless there is enough in the Continental evidence to show that the development of, at least, the southernmost Anglo-Saxon kingdoms had a Continental context. The migrants did not break off contacts with the Continent once they had reached the shores of Britain. Some Angles migrated from Britain to the Frankish kingdom. At a level of royalty at least one Anglo-Saxon prince married a Frankish princess, and at least one Anglian princess married a Continental prince in the sixth century. Moreover the Merovingians exploited their new transmarine neighbours in order to boost their prestige at home (Wood 1992) and in Constantinople. It is inconceivable that such Frankish interest did not in turn have an impact on the Anglo-Saxon kingdoms of Britain. The Merovingian court is likely to have provided a model for such kingdoms as Kent and East Anglia. Frankish law may even have influenced Anglo-Saxon law at this time (Wallace-Hadrill 1971:37-9). In the light of all this it is not surprising that Æthelberht appears to have turned to the Merovingians in the first instance, when he decided to convert his kingdom to Christianity (Wood 1994b:8-9).

While the Continental sources reveal the development of the Anglo-Saxon kingdoms exclusively within the context of relations between Britain and the Continent, seventh- and eighth-century Anglo-Saxon sources present a rather different picture of dynastic history against a background of war. To a large extent the resulting pictures are ethnogeneses deliberately constructed for political and cultural reasons. As a result they are not necessarily reliable reconstructions, although they may well contain a kernel of truth. They do, however, bring us to the third of our questions: that concerned with the ethnogenesis of the Anglo-Saxons, as constructed by the people themselves.

In strictly narrative terms the history of the Anglo-Saxons in the period of migration and settlement only came to be written down long after the event. In *ca* 731 Bede knew a little about Hengest and Horsa, but misplaced the story badly (*Historia ecclesiastica* I.15). Just over a century later the *Historia Brittonum* (24-7) was able to elaborate on the dealings of Hengest and Vortigern. Then in the early 890s the *Anglo-Saxon Chronicle* arranged a series of military origin stories into a coherent whole. That whole however has no evidential standing: traditions seem to have been juxtaposed to make points about the status of individual kingdoms. Nor do individual traditions necessarily have any value, even though it is possible that some may have been taken from earlier sources which have been lost (cf. Davies 1977). Some of the stories, like that relating to Port, are no more than historicized etymologies (*Anglo-Saxon Chronicle, s.a.* 501). Even the early dynasty history of the West Saxon kings, about which the *Chronicle*, written in Wessex, might have been expected to be authoritative, is clearly a construct (Yorke 1989).

Perhaps more important than the narratives are the genealogies that the Anglo-Saxons came to construct in the late seventh and eighth centuries (Dumville 1976; Dumville 1977). These genealogies tend to trace the descent of royal dynasties from Woden (see most recently John 1992). The genealogies appear to be reasonably accurate once they record kings who existed after a particular historical horizon. This horizon essentially falls in the third quarter of the sixth century, that is in the generation before the arrival of Augustine's mission in Kent, and the subsequent development of a tradition of written Christian record in England (Dumville 1977:91). On the whole it is to this same period, the third and last quarters of the sixth century that historians seem to be attributing the general creation of Anglo-Saxon kingdoms (Bassett 1989).

In the earlier parts of the Anglian genealogies there are figures who were clearly thought of as the founders of their dynasties: for example Oisc of the Oiscingas, and Wuffa of the Wuffingas (Dumville 1977:91). There may be a case for accepting these figures as having played some significant role either in the Migration period or in the subsequent establishment of a dynasty of kings, but there is no way that this can be proved. There is one piece of possible corroborative evidence, an entry in the eighth-century *Ravenna Cosmographer* (V 31): *In oceano vero occidentale est insula quae dicitur Britania, ubi olim gens Saxonum veniens ab antiqua Saxonia cum principe suo nomine Ansehis modo habitare videtur* ("There is an island in the western ocean which is called Britain, where once the people of the Saxons, coming from old Saxony, with their leader called Ansehis, are seen to live"). Unfortunately, however, although the Cosmographer did draw on Ostrogothic sources of the early sixth century (Straab 1976), it cannot be shown that his information relating to the British Isles was so early, nor is it certain whether he was referring to Hengest or to Oisc (Wallace-Hadrill 1988:215; Sims-Williams 1983:21-5)—indeed one might wonder whether the name Ansehis is not a corruption of one or other of these names intended to conjure up a parallel with Anchises, father of Aeneas. It is better to take the early generations of the genealogies together with the narratives of invasion and see both of them as constructs developed during the seventh and eighth centuries in order to reveal each Anglo-Saxon kingdom as being the creation of an identifiable group of invaders. Thus the complexity of the early migration process was forgotten.

The seventh and eighth centuries indeed saw a pseudo-historical reconstruction of the origins of the English kingdoms. This process of reconstruction culminated in Bede's *Ecclesiastical History*, but it began before that. It can be seen in the changing nomenclature of the Anglo-Saxons. At its most influential level it can be seen in the growing significance of the term *Angli* over *Saxones*, occasioned apparently by Gregory the Great's support of the former term (Wormald 1983). Arguably more instructive is the evidence supplied by Bede for the renaming of the group known as the *Gewisse* as West Saxons (*Historia ecclesiastica* IV.15). It is unfortunate that the etymology of *Gewisse* is unclear, but it is at least possible that the origins of the word are British (e.g. Jenkins 1964), in which case King Ine, successor to Cædwalla, an Anglo-Saxon king with a British name, may deliberately have been rejecting any hint of British tradition among his people (Laws of Ine, pref.). What is clear, whatever the origin of the name *Gewisse*, is that the followers of Ine were now ostentatiously being identified as Saxon—a point which is of a piece with the evidence for a streamlining of Anglo-Saxon history and, therefore, of Anglo-Saxon identity in the seventh century.

For all their Englishness, the Anglo-Saxons did not lose their Continental contacts. Even in the first half of the seventh century Anglo-Saxon politics were influenced by the Continent (Wood 1991; Wood 1992; Wood 1994a). And by the end of the same century potential Anglo-Saxon missionaries were remembering their Continental cousins (Bede, *Historia ecclesiastica* V.9; for the early eighth century, Boniface, ep. 46). Indeed it is in the context of Ecgberht's missionary idea that Bede provides his second origin list of the Anglo-Saxons. By the late seventh and early eighth centuries, however, the Anglo-Saxons had recreated the past, seeing the origins of their insular kingdoms in terms of a simplified pattern of migration and conquest—one which, by 731, emphasized Angles, Saxons and Jutes, and which would come later to settle on the single name of 'English'. Like all rewritings of history it was a rewriting which ignored the true complexity of the formation of a people—neglecting the diversity of Continental origins, the influence of indigenous peoples and the continuing influence of the outside world.

References

Textual sources:

Ammianus Marcellinus
    Res gestae: see Rolfe 1935-9.
Anglo-Saxon Chronicle: see Whitelock 1979.
Bede
    Historia ecclesiastica: see Plummer 1896.
Beowulf: see Swanton 1978.
Boniface
    Epistles: see Tangl 1916.
Cassiodorus
    Variae: see Mommsen 1894.
Constantius of Auxerre
    Vita Germani: see Borius 1965.
Eugippius
    Vita Severini: see Régérat 1991.
Finnsburgh Fragment: see Hill 1983.
Gildas
    De excidio Britanniae: see Winterbottom 1978.
Gregory of Tours
    Libri historiarum decem: see Krusch & Levison 1951.
Historia Brittonum: see Dumville 1985.
Laws of Ine: see Whitelock 1979.
Novels of Valentinian III: see Pharr 1952.
Pactus legis salicae: see Drew 1991.
Procopius
    The Secret History: see Dewing 1935.
    Wars: see Dewing 1914-28.
Ravenna Cosmographer: see Schentz 1940.

Bibliography:

Bachrach, B.
    1973   *A History of the Alans in the West*. Minneapolis, Minnesota Monographs.
              Minneapolis: University of Minnesota Press.
Bassett, S. (ed.)
    1989   *The Origins of Anglo-Saxon Kingdoms*. London: Leicester University Press.
Borius, A. (ed.)
    1965   Constantius of Auxerre, *Vita Germani. Sources chrétiennes* 112. Paris:
              Éditions du Cerf.
Brooks, N. P.
    1989   The creation and early structure of the kingdom of Kent. In *The Origins of
              Anglo-Saxon Kingdoms*. S. Bassett (ed.), pp. 55-74. London: Leicester
              University Press.
Bruce-Mitford, R. (ed.)
    1975-83   *The Sutton Hoo Ship Burial*. London: British Museum Publications.
Campbell, J. (ed.)
    1982   *The Anglo-Saxons*. Oxford: Phaidon.
Capelle, T.
    1990   *Archäologie der Angelsachsen*. Darmstadt: Wissenschaftliche Buch-
              gesellschaft.
Chadwick, H. M.
    1907   *The Origin of the English Nation*. Cambridge: Cambridge University Press.
Dark, K.
    1993   *From Civitas to Kingdom*. London: Leicester University Press.
Davies, W.
    1977   Annals and the Origin of Mercia. In *Mercian Studies*. A. Dornier (ed.),
              pp. 17-30. London: Leicester University Press.
Dewing, H. B. (ed.)
    1914/28   Procopius, *The Wars*. London: Heinemann.
Dewing, H. B. (ed.)
    1935   Procopius, *The Secret History*. London: Heinemann.
Dixon, P.
    1991   Secular Architecture. In *The Making of England*. L. Webster &
              J. Backhouse (eds.), pp. 67-70. London: British Museum Publications.
Drew, K. F. (trans.)
    1991   *The Laws of the Salian Franks*. Philadelphia: Pennsylvania University Press.
Dumville, D. N.
    1976   The Anglian Collection of Royal Genealogies and Regnal Lists. *Anglo-Saxon
              England* 5: 23-50.
    1977   Kingship, Genealogies and Regnal Lists. In *Early Medieval Kingship*. P. H.
              Sawyer & I. N. Wood (eds.,), pp. 72-104. Leeds: Leeds University Printing Service.
    1985   *Historia Brittonum: The Vatican Recension*. Woodbridge: The Boydell Press.
Eagles, B.
    1994   The Archaeological Evidence for Settlement in the Fifth to Seventh
              Centuries AD. In *The Medieval Landscape of Wessex*. M. Aston &
              C. Lewis (eds.), pp. 13-32. Oxford: Oxbow.
Evison, V.
    1965   *The Fifth-Century Invasions south of the Thames*. London: Athlone Press.

Geary, P. J.
  1988   *Before France and Germany*. Oxford: Oxford University Press.
Hamerow, H.
  1992   *Excavations at Mucking*, vol. 2. London: English Heritage.
Hawkes, S. C.
  1982   Anglo-Saxon Kent c. 425-725. In *Archaeology in Kent*. P. Leach (ed.),
           pp. 64-78. (CBA Research Report 48). London: CBA.
Heywood, J.
  1991   *Dark Age Naval Power*. London: Routledge.
Hill, J. M. (ed.)
  1983   *Old English Minor Heroic Poems*. Durham: Department of English
           Language and Medieval Literature, University of Durham.
Hope-Taylor, B.
  1977   *Yeavering: an Anglo-British centre of early Northumbria*. London: HMSO.
James, E.
  1988   *The Franks*. Oxford: Blackwell.
Jones, M. E.
  1987   The logistics of the Anglo-Saxon invasions. In *Papers in the Sixth Naval
           History Symposium held at the U.S. Naval Academy on 29-30 September
           1983*. M. Daniel (ed.), pp. 62-69. Wilmington: Scholarly Resources, Inc.
Krusch, B., & W. Levison (eds.)
  1951   Gregory of Tours, *Libri historiarum decem. Monumenta Germaniae
           historica. Scriptores rerum merovingicarum* 1. Hannover: Hahn.
Mommsen, T.
  1894   Cassiodorus, *Variae. Monumenta Germaniae historica, Auctores antiquissimi* 12.
           Berlin: Weidmann.
Pharr, C., (trans.)
  1952   *The Theodosian Code*. Princeton: Princeton University Press.
Plummer, C.
  1896   *Baedae Venerabilis Opera Historica*. Oxford: Oxford University Press.
Pohl, W.
  1994   Tradition, Ethnogenese und literarische Gestaltung: eine Zwischenbilanz. In
           Ethnogenese und Überlieferung. K. Brunner & B. Merta (eds.), pp. 9-26.
           Wien: Oldenbourg.
Régérat, P. (ed.)
  1991   Eugippius, *Vita Severini, Sources Chrétiennes* 374. Paris: Éditions du Cerf.
Rolfe, J. C. (ed.)
  1935/9   *Ammianus Marcellinus*. London: Heinemann.
Schnetz, J. (ed.)
  1940   *Ravenna Cosmographer, Itineraria romana* II. Stuttgart: Teubner.
Sims-Williams, P.
  1983   The Settlement of England in Bede and the Chronicle. *Anglo-Saxon
           England* 12: 1-41.
Storms, G.
  1970   The significance of Hygelac's raid. *Nottingham Medieval Studies* 14: 3-26.
Straab, F.
  1976   Ostrogothic geographers at the court of Theoderic the Great: a study in some
           sources of the Anonymous Cosmographer of Ravenna. *Viator* 7: 27-64.
Swanton, M. (ed.)
  1978   *Beowulf*. Manchester: Manchester University Press.

Tangl, M. (ed.)
    1916   Boniface, *Epistolae. Monumenta Germaniae historica. Epistolae selectae* 1.
                Berlin: Weidmann.
Thrane, H.
    1988   Import, Affluence and Cult – Interdependent Aspects. In *Trade and
                Exchange in Prehistory.* B. Hårdh (ed.), pp. 187-196. Stockholm:
                Almqvist & Wiksell.
Wallace-Hadrill, J. M.
    1971   *Early Germanic Kingship in England and on the Continent.* Oxford:
                Clarendon.
    1988   *Bede's Ecclesiastical History of the English People: A historical
                commentary.* Oxford: Oxford University Press.
Welch, M.
    1992   *Anglo-Saxon England.* London: English Heritage.
Wenskus, R.
    1961   *Stammesbildung und Verfassung.* Köln: Böhlau Verlag.
West, S.
    1985   *West Stow: The Anglo-Saxon Village.* Ipswitch: Suffolk Planning Department.
Whitelock, D. (trans.)
    1979   *English Historical Documents* I, 2nd ed. London: Methuen.
Winterbottom, M. (ed.)
    1978   Gildas, *De excidio Britanniae.* Chichester: Phillimore.
Wolfram, H.
    1988   *History of the Goths.* Berkeley: University of California Press.
    1994   *Origo et religio.* Ethnic traditions and literature in early medieval texts.
                Early Medieval Europe 3 (1): 19-38.
Wood, I. N.
    1983   *The Merovingian North Sea.* Alingsås: Viktoriabokförlag.
    1990   The Channel from the 4th to the 7th centuries AD. In *Maritime Celts,
                Frisians and Saxons.* (CBA Research Report 71). S. McGrail (ed.), pp. 93-97.
                London: CBA.
    1991   The Franks and Sutton Hoo. In *People and Places in Northern Europe 500-
                1600.* I. N. Wood & N. Lund (eds.), pp. 1-14. Woodbridge: The Boydell Press.
    1992   Frankish Hegemony in England. In *The Age of Sutton Hoo.* M. Carver (ed.),
                pp. 235-241. Woodbridge: The Boydell Press.
    1994a   *The Merovingian Kingdoms 450-751.* London: Longman.
    1994b   The Mission of St Augustine of Canterbury to the English. *Speculum* 69: 1-17.
Wormald, P.
    1983   Bede, the *Bretwaldas* and the Origins of the Gens Anglorum. In *Ideal and
                Reality in Frankish and Anglo-Saxon Society.* P. Wormald (ed.), pp. 99-129.
                Oxford: Blackwell.
Yorke, B.
    1989   The Jutes of Hampshire and Wight and the Origins of Wessex. In *The
                Origins of Anglo-Saxon Kingdoms.* S. Bassett (ed.), pp. 84-96. London:
                Leicester University Press.

Discussion

HINES: I am in agreement with you on many basic points though there are details that one can argue about, and opinions which can differ, particularly in respect of the use of archaeological material. To start with, I would like to clarify what, ultimately, you yourself believe and were trying to encourage us to believe about that second list in Bede's *Ecclesiastical History*, Book V, Chapter 9—where he may or may not be trying to list more people from whom the Angles and Saxons drew their origins.

WOOD: I agree with you that James Campbell (1976:123-4) pushes it far too far. I do not think that the passage means what James Campbell seems to say it means.

CHARLES-EDWARDS: Why not?

WOOD: Well, what Bede says in that passage is that these are peoples of the Continent from whom the peoples who have migrated to England were drawn. He does not say that these peoples on the Continent each provided groups which migrated to England.

CHARLES-EDWARDS: What's the difference?

WOOD: That here is a list of people on the Continent who are going to be worth evangelizing and some of them provided people who migrated to England.

CHARLES-EDWARDS: The phrase *genus et originem duxisse noscuntur* suggests descent from the people who are then listed, *Fresones, Rugini*, etc.

HINES: There are some critical words. What about "from amongst whom" for *a quibus*, and what is the sense of *sunt autem*?

WOOD: It also depends on the emphasis put on *sunt*. Is the *sunt* the peoples from whom the Angles and Saxons are drawn, or does the *sunt* refer to *plurimas nationes*?

CHARLES-EDWARDS: There is no difficulty about *sunt*: the contrast is between "*Sunt autem Fresones...*" and "*sunt alii perplures...*". The second clause refers to the larger group for which the *Fresones*, etc. are distinguished by kinship with *Angli vel Saxones*.

WOOD: No, I think that *sunt* is a problem as well. It depends whether it refers to all the *nationes* or just the *Angli* and *Saxones*.

CHARLES-EDWARDS: What is quite clear in the first sentence is that he is talking about the *Angli* and *Saxones* who derive from a very large number of *nationes*. That is useful in your point of view. It shows us a change in ethnic identity: they are transformed from many different peoples to *Angli* and *Saxones*. I can well see that as far as the *Saxones, Rugini, Dani*, etc. are concerned it is not necessarily intended to be the list which includes all those who are *plurimae gentes* or *nationes*: that's fine.

WOOD: Yes, but the issue is whether all those produce the Anglo-Saxons, or whether that list is just a list of the *plurimas nationes* in *Germania*.

CHARLES-EDWARDS: I think *sunt autem* suggests that this is illustrative.

WOOD: Of which part of the sentence?

CHARLES-EDWARDS: Oh, it has to be the *plurimas nationes*.

WOOD: Not the *Angli vel Saxones*?

CHARLES-EDWARDS: That's the same.

WOOD: No, it's not.

POHL: One question is how Bede intended it; another question is what the bits and pieces were from which Bede put this list together. To me it does not look like a homogeneous piece of evidence. Bede says "Germany on the whole is the place where these Angles and Saxons originated" and he obviously has some information about who are the most important *gentes* in that *Germania*. I tried in my paper to link it up with the whole tradition of lists of peoples, in other contexts, like Venantius Fortunatus and Sidonius Apollinaris. I think it is going too far to argue that each of them must, according to Bede, have been a group from which people living in his day in the British Isles actually originated. But it is interesting that Bede certainly does not want to exclude that. You are right that *genus et originem* is really a very strong statement. It is not just implying that they might have come from there, it is putting it very emphatically.

HINES: Can we move from that to the archaeological points? I shall try to sum up a few of the points which are involved here. Let me take an example of the Anglo-Saxon cemetery (Bifrons) which has Frankish, Jutish, Scandinavian and Thuringian material. I would query Jutish *and* Scandinavian, because Jutish comes within the Scandinavian category and, although there are cases where one can distinguish Jutlandic material from other Scandinavian material, they are very few. You also refer to Thuringian material. But just how much identifiable Thuringian material has been found in England?

HÄRKE: And even if it is there, what exactly does it mean for the presence of people there? Was it just the artefacts that moved?

WOOD: No, I think you can put it into the context of what I said before about the Saxons and Franks. Saxons and Franks certainly become distinguishable within the fifth century. To find material in Saxon graves which would normally be identified as Frankish merely highlights the point that these people were not very easily distinguished.

SCULL: There is, of course, the question of who is doing the distinguishing. Is it possible that you are perpetuating a Late Classical view of an undifferentiated mass of barbarians—a sort of `red peril'—whereas in reality there were a multitude of individual groups or tribal identities? You are heavily dependent on a 'Roman' rather than a 'barbarian' viewpoint.

WOOD: Yes, except I think that you are making an assumption about the state of those peoples on the Continent. Where do you think the Franks are in the year 400?

CHARLES-EDWARDS: But surely, you can actually, as your story has it, reconstruct a Frankish identity in the late fourth century, and as a part of this construction you might include practices of this populace.

WOOD: By the time you have got this created identity, you are in the late seventh century, by which time you do not actually find a lot of grave goods or cremation urns.

CHARLES-EDWARDS: But the Franks were surely creating some kind of identity for themselves in the Lower Rhine in the very late Roman period.

WOOD: They are not calling themselves *Franci*.

CHARLES-EDWARDS: You mean they are calling themselves *Bructeri*...

WOOD: ...or *Salii*, or *Sigambri*, or....

CHARLES-EDWARDS: Couldn't they be both?

WOOD: Yes, but there isn't that much coherence. Let me come to it another way around. At this date it is perfectly possible that the term Frank has both general and specific meanings. There is no reason to think that Thuringians were Franks before they became defined as Thuringians. I think these categories slithered around for political reasons.

HINES: It seems to me to be an important point that eventually, retrospectively, the historical sources tell us where to look for these peoples. As you say, from the late third century onwards, the notion that there was a people around called the Franks is attested. Gradually we get information that tells us where to look for Franks. Likewise we gradually get information that tells us where to look for Saxons and one can examine the evidence to see how far back in history this distinction would fit. Now the question of the material cultural reflection of that sort of group identity is something that I have been looking into, and my conclusion is that by the second half of the fourth century you can certainly distinguish the material culture of the area of the Frankish Rhineland from that of the Saxon homeland in Niedersachsen very clearly. And, quite interestingly, it is originally somewhere in that area of Niedersachsen that one first gets the deliberate manipulation of material culture to define a distinct province which fits seductively well the Saxon provinces we are told about by history.

One then can see neighbouring groups gradually doing the same thing. If the Saxons start this about 350, by 400 their neighbours to the North-West, the Angles, have started doing it, and the practice moves into Scandinavia from there. The Franks are really quite interesting. In the Frankish area of the Rhineland, the women are dressed predominantly in Roman-derived types of costume and dress accessories. It is, therefore, extremely difficult in that area to say there is anything distinctively Frankish in material culture. This situation seems to continue all the way down into the second half of the fifth century when the garnet styles that do look distinctively Frankish are developed. So it looks as if we do have more in terms of material culture marking off the groups than you suggest.

WOOD: You are making a distinction between Saxons and Franks in 350, which suggests that Romans were really the actors.

HINES: I do not suggest that this interpretation discredits the historical sources; rather that the evidence is harmonious. Perhaps we can push the Saxons more to the fore. At least we can allow for them earlier than 420.

WOOD: You get an absolutely steady development of the language describing these people, from Franks, to Franks and Saxons, and to Saxons, and Franks to Saxons. The use of the phrase 'Franks and Saxons' as opposed to just 'Franks' comes in about the 340s or 350s.

DUMVILLE: I took it that you saw a progression of activity which was changing from one group to another, rather than a progression in terminology.

Now what you have stressed here and in discussing this is simply the terminological questions.

WOOD: I think I was doing both. I do stress the question of terminology but then claiming that the terminology gets sorted out between peoples active largely on the north side of the Channel and people active in the Rhineland. In other words, I don't think the two points can be separated out.

HÄRKE: Several times you stress the point about the homogeneity of groups that may have come across to England because they were forced out by marine transgression. If you look at the extent of that transgression, certainly along the North German coast or the Dutch coast, the groups that would have been forced out cannot have been very large, and their movement would have spanned quite an extensive period. Michael Gebühr (1986) has drawn up what I find a more convincing model, at least for parts of the Anglian migration, which is that you basically have economic collapse on the northern fringes as a consequence of Roman economic disintegration, because the northern tribes had been drawn very much into the orbit of the Roman economy and had orientated themselves in that direction, and so were badly affected by any downturn in the Roman economy. What you would then have as a first reaction up there is male groups turning to piracy, and that is, as we know from other cases, often the first stage of a migration because it also provides the explorers. In the end you may have homogeneous groups going out, but in the first stages they look rather different. I am rather worried about this question of homogeneity anyway, because it may be the result of the way we look at the rather uniform evidence from the cremation cemeteries on the Continent and in eastern England. Inhumation cemeteries appear to provide more diversity at first sight, but a) what do we know about what was going on by way of ritual when they practised cremation; and b) cremation is a rather destructive rite, and therefore does not leave much in the way of diversity in the archeological record.

WOOD: This is why I used the verb 'may' throughout my paper [laughter].

HÄRKE: Perhaps the other archaeologists here might want to comment on the question of how we can actually distinguish these homogeneous groups, if they existed, from the others? If I may be allowed one other point which relates to what you say about people of northern *Germania* not having been broken by the emigration. This hardly ever happens in any kind of migration because it is very rare for complete, homogeneous groups to move in one block and to leave a wasteland behind. There is a very enlightening story about the Vandals who stayed in their homelands and actually sent a delegation to the Vandals in North Africa to settle the property rights the emigrants still had over fields in their original homelands. We have to imagine such contacts going on all the time; I believe we also see it reflected in the migration of art styles and the way they travel back to Scandinavia.

WOOD: I agree with you.

DUMVILLE: Could I ask about the two lists, Bede's two lists? Can I put in a plug for J. N. L. Myers, who does not get many plugs these days. He did give some consideration to this question, lecturing in 1970, and I suspect that is one of the things that set James Campbell thinking. From time to time I have hoped people would produce arguments that the list in I.15 arises at the end of Bede's process of consideration of these questions and that therefore what is in V.9 is in some way a more preliminary, or less well-digested, set of thoughts on Bede's part. I have heard Eric John argue with great enthusiasm about there being an antecedent document behind I.15 which Bede obtained late and incorporated. A lot of these speculations one has heard people put forward over the years have not found their way into print. How do you see the relations between these two chunks?

WOOD: I think the two lists have functions in their precise contexts in the text. Chapter I.15 is a response to Gildas's three boats, and the V.9 one is the response to a comment on Willibrord's conversion. I think that the lists have functions quite different from the ones that historians want to place upon them.

DUMVILLE: So there is no need, then, to set them up against one another as providing different phases of Bede's thought or as contradicting one another?

WOOD: No, these are ways of responding to certain bits of information that Bede has in front of him or is writing about at a certain moment.

CHARLES-EDWARDS: I don't agree at all [laughter]. I admit that there is the 'three' element behind the three keels and the three peoples, but isn't there a more plausible explanation? We are told that the *Anglorum siue Saxonum gens* derive from the peoples who came over—Saxons, Angles, Jutes. Bede then defines the *origo* of various population groups, Kentishmen, *Uictuarii*, etc.; and, finally, he says that the leaders of the migration, the *duces*, were Hengest and Horsa. They are given a genealogy going back to Woden which links with Æthelberht's pedigree in *HE* II.5 (note the phrase in II.5, *ut supra retulimus*). In other words, the legendary ancestors of the Kentish kings were the *duces*, not just of a Jutish migration, but of Angles and Saxons as well. The story asserts the original leadership of the Kentish line and thus supports Kentish claims to hegemony. There are similar things in Irish origin-stories: "...we led the first migration and settlement and therefore we should rule here and now".

WOOD: I don't see how that contradicts what we were just saying.

CHARLES-EDWARDS: It is simply a response to the 'three', namely that it has a political message, and it is not Bede's political message. That this is Kentish, is absolutely right.

DUMVILLE: Yes, and now we are back to this wretched question which we will have to come back to again, about Kentish input into Bede's views of English politics. Again an awful lot of extraordinary stuff has crept marginally into the scholarship, which has never actually been explored and discussed in print. You say that Bede's account is elaborated by the *Historia Brittonum*, which strengthens the association of Hengest and Horsa with Kent. This is very ambiguous writing. What are you actually driving at; what is strengthening what? It seemed to me that you were looking for a history of Hengest.

WOOD: No, most certainly not. I thought it wrong to ignore Hengest and Horsa altogether, but it doesn't seem to me that you can make anything out of them.

DUMVILLE: The strengthening then is that Bede's account is given detail and pressed harder.

WOOD: Yes.

DUMVILLE: Well, OK. About the Procopius story, I even see a way of deconstructing that easily. In fact I was much more worried about the fact that as your paper progressed, you seemed to be happy, happier and happier, to use this as a statement of relations between Angles and Franks exactly as they were in the sixth century. That seems to me to go far too far until you found a way of deconstructing the story.

WOOD: Oh, I agree with you there. I think there is a real problem with that story.

DUMVILLE: But if that story appeared in a seventh- or eighth-century English source, your language about it, I suspect, would be very different from the language you used here for Procopius. In other words you allow yourself to be better disposed towards this because of the relative antiquity and Mediterranean nature of the source from which it is drawn.

WOOD: I just do not know how to treat that story. It seems to be an important story if only one could see how one could get a methodological hold on it. I do not believe that anybody has managed to.

DUMVILLE: I agree.

HINES: I would like to go back again to the question of archaeological evidence. This relates primarily to your comments on the evidence for relations between Britain and the Continent. The archaeological evidence for early Anglo-Saxon activity and influence on the Continent is, I think, seriously neglected; the amount of it is not as widely recognized as it should be. In fact, this brings Thuringians back in, because there are some Anglo-Saxon objects in Continental Thuringian contexts. In the wider context those finds in Normandy are rather minor. The Herpes cemetery does stand out because there is so much material of Kentish character concentrated there. But all the way down the Rhineland you have good evidence for consistent and regular Anglo-Saxon influence. This is not just about objects moving around but influence whereby Anglo-Saxon motifs penetrate the art styles and the artefact range and are then locally produced.

CHARLES-EDWARDS: At what date?

HINES: The sixth century, but from the very beginning of the century.

POWLESLAND: Archaeologists excel themselves in trying not to identify the re-export of material culture to the Continent, particularly with the pots. Until we actually do have very detailed comparisons of huge assemblages we will not be able to tell whether the pottery is local products and local designs, or imported products and imported designs; whether the stuff we find in eastern England is actually stuff which comes from the Continent or of Continental design.

HINES: The biggest problem area in this respect is in fact Frisia. A thesis published last year on the archaeology of the coastal regions of the northern Netherlands (Knol 1993) provided, in quantity, illustrations of extraordinarily close parallels between material in England and in Frisia. However, the direction of the relationship is obscure.

CHARLES-EDWARDS: Transport of that kind of material is easy by sea. It can go in both directions so producing a cultural province.

HINES: Absolutely.

POWLESLAND: By the late ninth century the Frisians are controlling the seaways in respect of trade and it is particularly interesting that parallels are turning up in Frisia at a much earlier date.

SCULL: I am a little uneasy about this. It may be slightly anachronistic to talk about trade in these items across the North Sea. I can see contact which leads to similarities in cultural traditions, but I am not convinced there was any large-scale trade in hand-made pottery in the Migration period. You could argue more convincingly that there were cultural similarities, cultural contacts.

POWLESLAND: There is probably a substantial percentage of it that we are quite happy get carried around incidentally but there is also a percentage which was definitely moved as high status-products.

SCULL: May I develop this? There is a crucial distinction to be drawn between everyday material which can be produced domestically or acquired by local exchange and scarce material which must be acquired over long distances. Anglo-Saxon pottery could be produced on a bonfire in your back garden and there is no reason to trade it over long distances. We have to bear in mind the context of production and the availability of resources, and the organization of exchange and the desirability and scarcity of commodities. I do not believe that there is trade in low-value everyday items across the North Sea: we have to explain similarities in material culture between Britain and the Continent in other ways (cf. Scull 1995).

HINES: Trade is something that goes on within a network, but you cannot use trade as a catch-all term to cover all contacts.

POWLESLAND: I think we have tended to take a view of these people as hopping out of their ships from the Continent and not sending letters back home as though their level of communication was very low. I believe we have said that their level of communication was quite high. There was a lot of to-ing and fro-ing and with that there is an amount of to-ing and fro-ing of items, some of which will be very high-status items but also things like designs, things like ideas, things like ways of doing things. And architectural or ceramic or clothing styles are invisible in the political, and documentary record. But if we try and reconstruct a living world, this must have gone on.

WOOD: But the written evidence all points to very considerable activity across the Channel. Even the Procopius stories, however you take them, are stories about things happening on both sides of the Channel. The legal evidence suggests the same. The fact that you can actually register a claim in an Anglo-Saxon law court from *Francia* seems to me absolutely amazing. My view actually, is that we understate the evidence. One of the reasons for underestimating the contact is the inaccessibility of some of the archaeological evidence.

AUSENDA: I have two ecological enquiries: firstly, did the overseas migration happen in a condensed period or did it go on during the fifth, sixth and seventh centuries? And was there a preferred season for migration? Or did they come at any time of the year?

WOOD: That is one of the problems which has not been fully integrated in the discussion. People tend to talk about migration as if it was a brief phenomenon. It may well be something which continued right up to the mid-seventh century, in which case, there may be considerable consequences on one's reading of numbers. A small migration is more likely if one is talking about fifth-century migration. If one is talking in fact about three centuries it is a very different picture. And, it must be seasonal, because one thing you would not do is cross the North Sea before March.

POWLESLAND: Did they cross the North Sea? It's a major question, because there is massive evidence in the Middle Saxon period of people following the coast of Europe to cross the Channel.

WOOD: It must be seasonal because of the wind.

HÄRKE: Yes, but you would not even want to row along the Danish and the German North Sea coast during winter. It is a very dangerous coast to row along in bad weather. Read the medieval and early modern stories of what has actually gone down along that coast.

DUMVILLE. What do you do if you are starving in Frisia in January? Do you wait calmly or do you set out to sea, and try to do something else than die and die out at sea?

AUSENDA: I am interested in the question of the time of the year. Would they have come over in the spring or in the fall? Professor Fowler might be able to tell us, because it is a question of whether they came when they were sure of their supplies, or they preferred to come and sow before the agricultural season started. It should be possible to reconstruct the conditions fairly easily. There must be some logic to that.

LENDINARA: "Spring is the worst month", according to the poem *Maxims* II (line 5); spring is the worst month to travel because ice forms bridges across the rivers (see also *Maxims* I, 71-4a). If you look at the descriptions of nature in Old English poetry you will gather that spring was the worst season to travel.

HÄRKE: Well, it is not so much the worst time because of ice, but because by then you would have exhausted all your provisions for the winter. What you need for travelling and for migration is well-stocked granaries and, before that, the time to convert your immovable wealth into movable wealth. That is described in some detail in Caesar's passage on the preparation of the Helvetian migration, because they systematically prepared for migration over a long period. Giorgio, I am sure, is right in that it was less haphazard than we think. I am also sure that agrarian societies, like the ones we are talking about, are very much bound to the agrarian cycle. You can migrate in considerable numbers only after you have brought in the harvest, or possibly then prepared the fields for next year before the next group leaves.

POHL: We also know in the case of Theoderic and the Goths that in two consecutive years, 488 and 489, they departed in August, and waited for the harvest to come in. And that was not even a group of peasants moving, that was an army consisting largely of specialized warriors. It does not really make much difference if you have to harvest yourself or you have to use other people to harvest. With the Langobards we have Paul the Deacon's information that their migration started after Easter. But, of course, that is open to discussion because there might be a hagiographic model with this just supposed to be a good date. It would be a strange thing for the largely pagan Langobards. In the course of the narrative he has King Alboin climb a mountain to look at the promised land, like Moses, before entering Italy.

AUSENDA: Professor Fowler, if you were a barbarian, when would you start? [Laughter].

FOWLER: I don't really like your question because it begs so many other questions. It depends on what you want to do. What nobody has mentioned is the question of the reconnaissance and preparation which you do a year before. That, for example, is a technique which was often used in colonization of North America: for instance, people in the east of North America moving out into the Plains. Very often a member of the family or some males in a group went out in advance. When you have done your preparation you have the time to get ploughed and to look forward to getting the first harvest. They learnt from some of the disastrous early episodes in American history. I think what happened in America in the sixteenth century is very germane to what we are talking about here. One of the things we have learnt from there is that it was disastrous just to move out. Most people died if they just moved into an alien territory.

I do not see the Angles being a large, highly organized group of people. I think there were a lot of individuals taking individual decisions. But some of them (particularly raiders), I would see coming out at the low point of the year, which is April/May. You take the risk of bad weather, because you have got very little left at home; you are looking for the profit of raiding. Or, if you are basically in the temperate zone, you do exactly what we are doing now: after the results of exams have been gathered in, we all migrate because it is all in the bag at home, and if it does not work in San Marino we can all go back. The equivalent is after you have got your harvest in late September. Especially if you face battles, because if you lose you can go back.

If you are in an area where transhumance is built in as an integral part of your annual cycle, there is, theoretically, an argument for doing it in June/July, after you have got your grain in and sent the children and the women up to the pastures. The menfolk who are underemployed in that period can go off and do some raiding and possibly stake out some areas to go back to after the harvest or in the following year.

HOOKE: This is in the tradition of Welsh raiding.

FOWLER: Exactly.

HINES: Can I make one further point on this question of the organization of migration and the relations between natives and settlers? It doesn't have to be an entirely speculative discussion. We have one rather nice block of evidence, which is the location of early Anglo-Saxon settlements just south of London, where three of our earliest Anglo-Saxon cemeteries, Mitcham, Croydon and Orpington, are placed on main roads at regular distances out of London. These were probably Roman collection points related to the city of London. So here we have got our earliest Anglo-Saxon communities, occupying important roads of the old Romano-British supply system. I do not assume that this is typical of the rest of the country, but at least in this case one does seem to have communities, perhaps with a military role, moving into a well-organized system.

References in the discussion

Textual sources:

Maxims I and *Maxims II*: see Krapp & Dobbie 1936; Dobbie 1942.

Bibliography:

Campbell, J.
    1976   *Essays in Anglo-Saxon History*. London: Hambledon Press.
Dobbie, E. van K.
    1942   *The Anglo-Saxon Minor Poems*. New York/London: Columbia University
                Press/Routledge & Kegan Paul.
Gebühr, M.
    1986   Ursachen für den "Siedlungsabbruch" auf Fünen im 5. Jahrhundert n.Chr.
                Unpublished Habilitationsschrift. Christian-Albrechts-Universität, Kiel.
Knol, E.
    1993   *De Noordnederlandse Kustlanden in de vroege Middeleeuwen*. Academisch
                Proefschrift. Amsterdam: Vrije Universiteit.
Krapp, G. P., & E. van K. Dobbie
    1936   *The Exeter Book*. New York/London: Columbia University Press/Routledge
                & Kegan Paul.
Scull, C.
    1995   Approaches to the material culture and social dynamics of the Migration
                Period in eastern England. In *From Roman to Medieval in Europe: Current
                Perspectives*. H. Hamerow & J. Bintliffe (eds), pp. 71-83. Oxford: BAR.

THE ANGLO-SAXONS IN ENGLAND IN THE SEVENTH AND EIGHTH CENTURIES: ASPECTS OF LOCATION IN SPACE

DELLA HOOKE

Department of Geography and Geology, Cheltenham and Gloucester College of Higher Education, Francis Close Hall, Swindon Road, Cheltenham, Gloucestershire, GB-GL50 4AZ

The background

> In just punishment for the crimes that had gone before, a fire heaped up and nurtured by the hand of the impious easterners spread from sea to sea. It devastated town and country round about, and, once it was alight, it did not die down until it had burned almost the whole surface of the island and was licking the western ocean with its fierce red tongue (Gildas, *De excidio, ca* 540, XXIV.1).

Gildas's words have been viewed as exaggerated rhetoric, giving an account of the Anglo-Saxon invasions which viewed them as divine retribution for lax morality in a supposedly Christian world. He also claimed that "the wretched survivors" were either forced to flee, some of them "trusting their lives with constant foreboding to the high hills, steep, menacing and fortified, to the densest forests, and to the cliffs of the sea coast" or "were fated to be slaves for ever" (XXV.1). Gildas was writing in the middle of the sixth century, some hundred years after the events he describes and the veracity of his words has been, with some foundation, questioned. But who are we to know better? Certainly the Anglo-Saxon invasions were one of the most traumatic episodes of post-Roman Britain and hardly less devastating than the attacks of the Vikings so similarly bemoaned by the Anglo-Saxons in their turn.

I start by mentioning this earlier period because I think we are in danger of belittling the Anglo-Saxon take-over which we must acknowledge if we are to understand the situation in the seventh and eighth centuries, the period under discussion in the present paper. As the *Gallic Chronicle* also claims, under the year AD 441: "The provinces of Britain...are brought under the control of the Saxons" (Jones & Casey 1988).

The Anglo-Saxon Chronicle itself tells a different side of the story. Composed in the late ninth century, it belongs to a time when social hierarchies amongst the invaders had become well established, when kingdoms had been recognized across England; interested in bolstering the power of particular dynasties, it gives a distorted image acceptable to the dominant royal house of Wessex. Here we find "Hengest and Horsa" succeeding to the kingdom of Kent in the middle of the fifth century and the British fleeing "as one flies from fire" from continued attacks, but much of the conquest is described as the achievement of small groups of intrepid invaders coming in as few as two, three or five ships at a time to conquer whole

THE ANGLO-SAXONS FROM THE MIGRATION PERIOD TO THE EIGHTH CENTURY:
AN ETHNOGRAPHIC PERSPECTIVE

regions around the turn of the century: a sort of 'Wild West' scenario which seems to have played as major a role in Anglo-Saxon tradition as its short-lived counterpart in the American West. The remainder of the sixth century is seen as one of consolidating kingdoms and continued efforts to maintain and extend supremacy over the British. Thus we find the warlike king of the new kingdom of Wessex, Ceawlin, defeating the Britons at Old Sarum in 552, at Barbury hillfort, Wiltshire, in 556, Cutha defeating them at *Bedcanford* (Bedford) in 571, and Ceawlin and Cuthwine slaying the three British kings of Gloucester, Cirencester and Bath at Dyrham in 577, thus obtaining control over one of the richest and longest surviving enclaves of Roman culture in the Cotswolds and Severn valley (cf. Sims-Williams 1983:31).

I believe that much recent work has tended to 'sanitize' our attitude to the effects of the Anglo-Saxon takeover. We are told that the economic situation in late Roman Britain was already so bad that any decay in town life, for instance, can be explained away by the economic climate prevailing by the end of the fourth century. The trappings of Roman culture as expressed in formal urban buildings had indeed, for the most part, fallen into decay long before the events of the fifth century. Agriculture, however, had still to maintain some form of urban life, commerce and trade, and more especially, the army until the latter's withdrawal. Subsequently, however, we have to envisage a rural economy more heavily biased towards subsistence farming. Pottery sherds on the Celtic fields of the upper downlands of southern England seem to suggest that these native type fields continued to be farmed until the late fourth century. Given that pottery then became much less widely available, the date may perhaps be extended somewhat, but the pressure on marginal regions seems to have been lessened as the necessity to meet the demands of the townspeople and the army was withdrawn.

Invading armies lived off the land, and we have only to look at recent events in Europe, the Middle East or Africa today, and more particularly in Bosnia or Rwanda, two very different types of society, to see how any farming community can be devastated by attack. Given the ruthlessness of an opposing army with little to lose and everything to gain, the resistance of poor farmers, living little above subsistence level, must have been minimal. Two sections of society are likely to have suffered most: the landless labourer and the richer landowner; the latter was almost invariably dispossessed, the former driven to slavery or, at worst, forced to 'live off his wits' as a thief or brigand. As Costen argues:

> With little or no land of his own and no prospect of finding work in towns, poverty and vagabondage would be the lot of those labourers no longer needed.... Men do not simply turn to farm for themselves when their services are no longer required; they starve if they have no land (Costen 1992:56).

Given our present knowledge of population numbers, the effects upon population levels can only be pure speculation. Many Romanists argue that the population of Roman Britain varied from somewhere between two and three million (Esmonde Cleary 1989:174), although some would argue that it reached as much as five million (Taylor 1983:106); yet after apparent growth during the Anglo-Saxon period it is estimated that levels only reached two million again at the time of the compilation of Domesday Book. Clearly a drastic population loss has to be accounted for if these figures have any basis in reality.

As yet, it is impossible to judge the numbers of Anglo-Saxons involved in either the early migrations or in subsequent waves. It seems that extensive areas of the North Sea littoral were deserted in this period, never to be reoccupied, and many of these migrants must have added to the numbers hoping to carve out a new life in Britain. The Anglo-Saxon burial evidence has been taken by some to indicate that the numbers have, in the past, been grossly exaggerated. But it is hardly likely that more than a minority of burials have been discovered (Welch 1992:11-3), and many of the recorded sites are chance discoveries made in the nineteenth century and only haphazardly recorded. Neither is it known what proportion of the settlers were buried in cemeteries or how representative those that were buried in this way were of the general population. Of the British population, burial tells us very little and this section of the population, undeniably a substantial portion in some midland and western regions, if not elsewhere, remains largely absent from the archaeological record.

In a very short time, genetic evidence will help to answer this question. Already enclaves of Viking settlement have been identified in the central parts of the Lake District from an examination of the genetic make-up of the present-day inhabitants and a Norman enclave similarly identified in Pembrokeshire, long known as 'Little England beyond Wales' (Mackie 1993)—once again, revealing the truth in a number of long-held folk traditions. Such discoveries may encourage us to give greater weight to the early traditions concerning the impact of the Anglo-Saxons upon the British population.

It was, however, through the role of minor landlord that the Anglo-Saxon finally dominated the country: in particular, through creating or altering ways of holding land. The evidence for this is manifold: in language and in territorial organization.

Language and place-names

Margaret Gelling has long argued that the numbers of Anglo-Saxons entering the country must have been huge to explain the almost total language change that occurred by the sixth and seventh centuries: "...the renaming of the vast majority of settlements is inconceivable without the influx of a mass of peasant settlers" (Gelling 1993:51). Others have proposed a different situation and have shown how language could change over a period of time without the replacement of the native population: the late Professor Jackson (1953) argued that such a change could occur over merely a few generations.

We have later historical situations for comparative changes, particularly in the role played by English in Wales. Language is an instrument of power. In Wales it was the language adopted by the landlord and the administrative élite; later, the speaking of Welsh in schools was both forbidden and punished. Yet, Welsh survived amongst the working class, the smaller farmers and those employed in industry and, above all, it survived for the majority of ordinary minor place-names throughout the country. In medieval Fifeshire, English gradually supplanted Gaelic amidst the middle classes in a similar but less pressured way because it was the language of merchants and tradespeople (Taylor 1994).

What does this tell us about the numbers of 'newcomers' involved? Let us look for a moment at the far south-west of England. Although most of Devon was to fall under the sway of the English by the seventh century, Cornwall was not fully assimilated until the tenth century; the British population was not supplanted by large numbers of immigrants and the Cornish language was spoken until recent times; Cornish place-names survive throughout the country. This would seem to confirm Gelling's arguments for large numbers of people being necessary to precipitate language change. Similarly, the British exodus to Brittany in the post-Roman period established "a little Britain beyond the sea, with a Cornwall and a Dumnonia of its own (Cornouaille and Domnonee), and a distinct and still enduring identity and language" (Campbell 1982:22). In general, local place-names, as witnessed in Wales, Cornwall or Brittany, are likely to reflect the speech of the majority of the local people. If an established population was to change its language it had to be deeply penetrated by newcomers at many levels of the social hierarchy. The Norman domination of England after 1066, involving relatively small numbers of Norman-French forming a social élite, had singularly little effect upon either everyday speech or place-names. We are certainly forced to consider more Anglo-Saxon incomers than the few boat-loads referred to in *The Anglo-Saxon Chronicle*!

Admittedly, Old English, as we should term the language of the Anglo-Saxons, had other factors contributing to its ultimate success. Firstly, it was the language of what was to become a dominant race. As Greenblatt (1993) has noted, when colonists and explorers moved to the New World the first thing they did was to rechristen the places at which they landed. These places already had native names, but Columbus renamed one island in the West Indies, the native name of which was *Samoet*, 'Isabella' in honour of his queen; other places acquired the names of Roman Catholic saints. His diary entry for Monday, October 15th, 1492, for instance, notes how he landed on an island not far distant from San Salvador: "To this island I gave the name *Santa Maria de la Concepcion....* It was...my wish not to pass any island without taking possession of it" (Columbus 1960 [edn]:29). The island was already inhabited and presumably already had a name but the very act of naming by Columbus in itself was a mark of possession. By doing this, a linguistic authority was established and the place was appropriated for the new ruling race.

Second, the new language both maintained group identity and power. Just as the Norman kings and officials held themselves apart from the populace by speaking French after the Norman Conquest of England, so the Anglo-Saxon leaders must have enjoyed the common bond of language in their mead halls and through the works of their poets. The power of language is again expressed today in the resurgence of national feeling displayed in Wales and by such groups as the Welsh Language Society. In Anglo-Saxon England the dominant race must inevitably have stood apart in its linguistic seclusion—at first. When, inevitably, the suppressed people had to communicate with their new overlords the latter were hardly likely to take a course in Neo-Brittonic!

Third, and an equally powerful factor, was the fact that the Anglo-Saxons, at least in the royal courts and in the Church, were literate and had frequent recourse to the written document. Admittedly Latin was the language used of official documentation, but the newly recorded place-names which were written down for the first time were Old English and, once written down, were less likely to change.

The fact that many new settlements and newly recognized minor estates or 'proto-manors' were coming into being in this period was undoubtedly another very important reason for the coining of new Old English place-names. Here, however, we need to pause and consider, for the place-name evidence has been subject to close scrutiny. It may be noted how charters, mostly from the eighth century onwards, strongly suggest that Old English had by then become the language of the people in many regions. After the beginning of the ninth century, boundary clauses, relating landmarks along the boundaries of estates, well known to the local people, are invariably in Old English outside Cornwall, and charters also frequently refer to a place-name as the one commonly used by the inhabitants.

The earliest reference in charters to a place-name being that known to the local inhabitants has yet to be established but a Kentish charter of AD 686 (Birch 1885/99: B 67; Sawyer 1968: S 9) notes that a boundary landmark of Stodmarsh *...appellatur fordstreta publica indirectum...*, which may imply that 'Ford street', possibly the road to Fordwich, was so-called locally (*stræt* was initially a loan-word from Latin *strata*). I am not qualified to comment upon the linguistic date of Old English charter material but a charter of Shottery in Warwickshire (Birch 1885/99: B 123; Sawyer 1968: S 64) of AD 699 x 709 includes a relatively simple boundary clause in which the landmarks are given in Old English:

> *balgandun. billes læh. westgraf. heofentill. baddan dun...wudan bergas. ruggan broc.*
> *bromhlinces dene...sture...afene.*

This may be an indication of the names known locally. Although it appears that this charter, long regarded as authentic, may now prove to be a forgery based upon a genuine early Mercian charter (Susan Kelly, pers. comm.) it still apparently emanates from the eighth century. However, boundary places named in another authentic mid eighth-century charter of Ismere in Worcestershire (Birch 1885/99: B 154; Sawyer 1968: S 89), a location much closer to the Welsh Borderland, are names of British type: *Cynibre*, for instance, later Kinver, for which Ekwall suggests a Welsh *Cynfre*, containing the mutated form of Welsh *bre* 'hill'; and *Moerheb*, later Morfe, for which Ekwall suggests a reduction from OW *mor-dref* 'big village' (Ekwall 1960:278, 331). By the ninth century landmarks are commonly given in Old English.

One has to remember that several hundred years had elapsed since the Anglo-Saxon migrations, a period which allows ample time for any community to adopt the language of what it sees as the superior order if it so wishes, especially in a climate of new aspirations and opportunities. One might make comparisons with the way in which earlier peoples of Britain had apparently accepted Roman styles of dress and of building, a change perhaps made most willingly by the more ambitious members of the native community.

There can be little doubt that the survival of British names increased westwards and that such names were markedly few in number in eastern England. In spite of additional names of British origin or containing British elements now being recognized, the picture has not changed significantly since Kenneth Jackson produced his map in 1953. Some Romano-British settlement names survived without change and a narrow area along the Kentish coast is of interest, where *Duroverno* remained, for instance, the name of Canterbury (Hogg 1964; Gelling 1978) and the Roman sites of Pevensey, Lympne, Dover, Reculver, Richborough, Rochester and London retained their early names. The speed with which this region traditionally passed into Anglo-Saxon control may have been a factor in such name survival.

Place-name scholars have, however, had cause to lose faith in the long accepted chronology of place-names. In particular, the *-ingas, -inga-* names, once thought to indicate groups settling "at the time of the Anglo-Saxon and perhaps for some time afterwards" (Ekwall 1923:113) are now recognized as names of secondary colonization. I use the term colonization deliberately, for there is still evidence to suggest that these terms may be connected with actual group settlement. The studies of John Dodgson and Martin Welch have shown that throughout eastern and south-eastern England the terms occur in place-names which appear to be in sites secondary to the main thrust of pagan burials (Dodgson 1966; Welch 1983; the nature of such groups is also discussed by Charles-Edwards 1972). In Sussex, for instance, although the Hastings names are mainly concentrated within the Rape of that name, this area to the west of the River Rother is devoid of early burials, the latter concentrated along the coastal lowlands to the west between Pevensey and Chichester.

If the *-ingas, -inga-* names have been placed in a secondary period of Anglo-Saxon settlement, the same is not true for topographical type names. The naming of regions and settlements after obvious, mainly, physical features in the landscape was characteristic in Roman Britain, and although subsequent names were of Old English origin—or of mixed origin—the trend continued. The work of Barrie Cox (1976) has shown how topographical type names formed one of the main groups of names recorded in the period between AD 400 and AD 730. Such terms as *burna* 'bourne', *dūn* 'hill', *eg* 'land partly surrounded by water, island', *feld* 'open country', *ford* 'ford', *lēah* usually 'wood', and perhaps *hamm* 'land in a river bend, river meadow, etc', appear most frequently in the early records. To these must be added, in addition to the *-ingas, -inga-* names, the district-forming name *gē* and a number of habitative terms which include *burh, ceaster, hām, hām-stēde* and *wic*, the significance of which has been discussed elsewhere (cf. Gelling 1978).

One local example must suffice. In that part of the later county of Warwickshire which lay within the Anglo-Saxon kingdom of the Hwicce, charter evidence refers to a group known as the *Stoppingas* (Birch 1885/99: B 157; Sawyer 1968: S 94). A minster was established within their territory in the mid eighth century after a substantial grant of land there had been made to Æthelric, son of the late King Oshere of the Hwicce, by Æthelbald, king of the Mercians, specifically for this purpose. The land was said to lie *in regione quae antiquitus nominatur Stoppingas*, "in the territory which in former times is called the *Stoppingas*", and was granted *intra terminos ab antiquis possessoribus constitutos*, "within (the) boundaries established by (the) ancient (former) owners", the grant extending to 20 *cassati*.[1]

When the *parochia* of the later Wootton Wawen monastery is plotted from post-Conquest sources it is found to encompass an area lying across the headwaters of the River Alne, probably representing the region of the *Stoppingas*, an area shown by the evidence of Domesday Book (Plaister 1976) to have been only just short of 50 hides (49 hides and an estate of 12 acres) (Fig. 3-1).

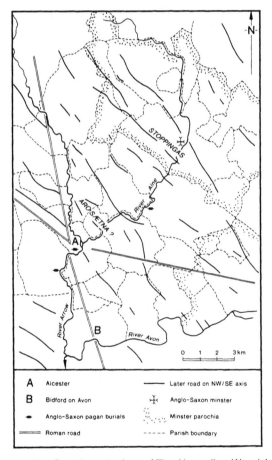

Fig. 3-1: The *Stoppingas* territory of The Alne valley, Warwickshire.

---

[1] A *cassatus* is defined in the Revised Medieval Latin Word-List of the British Academy (1965) as a "measure of land appurtenant to a household: a hide".

The River Alne, like the River Arrow, was a tributary of the River Avon and both the Alne and Arrow drained southwards from an upland wooded region known as the Arden (British *ardu* 'high land'). The Arden was a relatively sparsely settled region which provided wood-pasture and timber for the long settled estates in the south of the county. Evidence of Roman settlement in this northern region is sparse and it is quite likely that this was a relatively marginal zone upon the fringe of less developed land. However, the very fact that a minster was to be established there implies that Wootton Wawen was already a focus of settlement in the region. The place-name *Wudu tūn* may indicate a settlement near a wood or perhaps one associated with the extraction of timber, but the *tūn* element itself is one which comes into common usage only after the beginning of the eighth century (Cox 1976:510) and is often related to newly emerging village clusters (Hooke 1985b).

When this settlement region is viewed against the known incidence of pagan burials and estate hierarchies, it is clear that the land associated with the later *parochia* was secondary to a focal region of settlement in the lower Arrow valley, itself possibly the region of a folk-group known as the *Arosǣtna* (Davies & Vierck 1974). Situated at the confluence of the rivers Alne and Arrow, the urban centre of *Alauna*, Alcester (named after the River Alne), had dominated this region in Roman times. This may have been "the celebrated place called Alne" at which an ecclesiastical council was held in AD 709 (Haddan & Stubbs 1871:281, 283), suggesting the presence of an undocumented minster there, while a nearby **ecles* name suggests the presence of a surviving British Christian community after the Anglo-Saxon takeover. However, archaeological investigation has yet to find substantial evidence of Anglo-Saxon occupation on the site of the Roman town and the focus of settlement appears to have moved southwards.

Several pagan burials are known from sites along the Arrow, with one further up the valley of the Alne itself (Meaney 1964:257-63), but the most extensive cemetery evidence comes from Bidford, located where the Roman Ryknield Street from Alcester crosses the River Avon. Both inhumation and cremation burials come from a cemetery which had a long life, apparently in use from *ca* AD 500 into the seventh century. Domesday Book (see Plaister 1976, 1.3) records that Bidford, like the unrecorded Alcester, was part of a royal estate and rich items, such as brooches, have been found there from time to time. We appear to be looking, in the *Stoppingas* territory, at a substantial grant of land to incoming Anglo-Saxons soon after their domination of this part of central England; by the mid-eighth century it was felt that they had indeed held this land "from ancient times".

Names and estate structure

If examples such as the *-ingas* settlements suggest deliberate Anglo-Saxon colonization, the general pattern in most densely settled areas away from east coast regions must have been one largely influenced by lordship. By the eighth century, large multiple estates were well-established features across England. These operated through a system of federated holdings in which the peasantry was almost certainly in the lower echelons of serfdom, probably not dissimilar in role to that of the bond communities of medieval Wales. There, the most tied peasants were those of the *maerdrefi,* responsible for maintaining the royal vill, and bond communities can be recognized around the focal centres of most Welsh commotes in North Wales, with many others in regions which served as the summer *hafodydd* of the king (noted, for instance in the *Record of Caernarvon*). There is little evidence about the status of serfs in Anglo-Saxon England but multiple estates centred upon royal vills are not uncommon in England in this period and these clearly had a dependent peasantry to maintain them.

The recognition of such multiple estates in recent years has been one of the greatest steps forward in understanding Anglo-Saxon territorial organization in the period in question. Some, notably Glanville Jones (e.g. 1978:51), have argued strongly that such estates were firmly based on older territorial groupings of British origin. Essentially, the multiple estate was of unified ownership and organized on a large scale but comprised many integral units which "involved economic, jurisdictional and political relationships" (Costen 1992:87) and numerous settlements in which some degree of specialization is often suggested (Jones 1976). In Somerset, Costen argues that "It would be absurd to suggest that the English failed to utilize the pre-existing structure which they found" (Costen 1992:86) and discusses Somerton as a probable estate centre. This was a royal vill administering a 50-hide estate and was close to the site of Roman Ilchester; there is even a fortification in the vicinity at Cadbury Castle that saw renewed activity in the post-Roman period. The Anglo-Saxon name means 'the summer *tūn*', perhaps a place visited in summer (Ekwall 1960:431).

Others are more hesitant in accepting British origins for such an arrangement (e.g. Gregson 1985) and it may be that such an arrangement was common in both societies at this time, with new multiple estates forming as Anglo-Saxons adapted the situation they met, some no doubt based upon donations of land like that suggested for the *Stoppingas* in Warwickshire. Continuity of focus probably persisted, in any case, in those regions already regarded as important either economically or administratively. Very often, early estate centres were chosen as the sites of minsters and, as parochial boundaries became more firmly drawn, their territories fossilized those of the early estates. Whether one should envisage firm boundaries at first or merely frontiers of weaker control is arguable. Certainly it was the margins/frontier regions of the *parochiae* which were the first to be lost as minster control waned (Hooke 1994a:86-99; 1994b:84-6). Even the multiple estates themselves probably represent only parts of once larger territories which initially comprised both the heavily cultivated regions and the more distant seasonal pastures (Hooke 1985a).[2]

---

[2] For evidence of linkage of this type, see the eighth-century charter of Shottery in Warwickshire, already referred to, in which two parcels of woodland in Arden and in north Worcestershire are granted with a riverine estate situated in the valley of the River Avon.

Several place-names may be discussed at this point. The regions recognized as belonging to particular groups of peoples often referred to these as the *sǣte* and there is ample evidence for the use of this term at a relatively early date. The *Magonsǣte*, for instance, were the people whose kingdom extended across much of modern Herefordshire and south Shropshire. The name may be derived from the same British root as the district-name Maund, and *Magnis* was the Roman settlement later called Kenchester. If this name is indeed derived from British **magno,* 'stone, rock' (Rivet & Smith 1979:407), it may apply to the hilly ground to the north of Kenchester and must have become known to English speakers before AD 550. The kingdom itself is not recorded until the later seventh century when it was recognized by the Anglo-Saxons under its first king Merewalh.

Further to the north, the *Wreocensǣte* were recorded in the seventh-century document known as the Tribal Hidage and occupied the area around the Wrekin in Shropshire. In Mercia, two folk groups who occupied valley regions in what was to become Staffordshire were termed the *Pencersǣte* and the *Tomsǣte*. Such names were not uncommon for those occupying such valley territories—the *Wilsǣte* of the Wylye valley of Wiltshire, for instance—while others, like the *Meonware* of the Meon area of Hampshire, noted by Bede, were described as *ware*, 'dwellers', in a particular region. Klingelhöfer has argued that valley territories were the earliest recognizable form of territorial organization in Anglo-Saxon Hampshire, clearly linked to the period of pagan burial, with such territories offering a "community-wide" rural economy of the Early Anglo-Saxon period which lasted into the eighth century (Klingelhöfer 1992:24).

There is one aspect in which Klingelhöfer's work disagrees with many other interpretations of multiple estate organization: in Hampshire he finds no evidence of links with distant woodlands, hill grazings and marshes such as those which frequently served as summer pastures in such places as the Weald, the Warwickshire Arden, County Durham or North Wales. Certainly such links may be found in the charter evidence of Late Anglo-Saxon Hampshire (Hooke 1986) but the problem awaits further investigation.

A number of habitative place-name terms appear to indicate possession by named individuals who bore Anglo-Saxon names. The earliest of these is *hām*, recorded on a number of occasions in the seventh century. In Kent, for instance, *Botdeshām*, Bodsham, is referred to in an authentic charter of *ca* AD 690 (Sawyer 1968:S 110) and may be either 'Boda's *hām*' or contain a topographical element related to OE *bodig* 'body, main part' (Wallenberg 1931:9-10) but *Chebeham*, Chobham in Surrey, is certainly 'Ceabba's *hām*', recorded in AD 672 x 674 (Sawyer 1968: S 1165).[3] The element *hām*, meaning 'village, estate', has been shown by Cox (1976) to have been in use at a relatively early period.

In general, the element *tūn* comes into frequent usage only after the middle of the eighth century when it appears to be related to newly emerging nucleated settlements (Hooke 1985b:134). It does occur before this time and appears to be first recorded in AD 675-92 as *Tomtūn*, probably an early name for the royal vill of Tamworth in Staffordshire (Cox 1976:37; Sawyer 1968: S 1804).

---

[3]   This charter is thought to be based on a genuine seventh-century text (S. Kelly pers. comm.).

A clear case of possession including a personal name with *tūn* also occurs in a Kentish charter of AD 697 or 712 in which 4 *aratra* at *Wieghelmes* or *Pleghelmes tūn*, possibly Wilmington near Berwick on Romney Marsh, is granted to St Mary's church, Lyminge. Such grants indicate settlements or estates associated with named individuals in existence by the end of the seventh century in Kent which were to become individual holdings. Apart from a lost *Humantūn* on the island of Thanet in Kent, these remain the only seventh-century recordings. In the eighth century the term occurs on four occasions, recorded for instance in a charter of AD 714 (for ?717; Sawyer 1968: S 42) in which Nunna, king of Sussex, grants land at *Herotunum* in Sussex to the brethren of Selsey and in a grant of AD 718 (for ?727) in which Æthelbald, king of Mercia, grants land at Acton Beauchamp in Herefordshire (here compounded with OE *ac,* 'oak-tree') (Sawyer 1968: S 85). But after *ca* AD 730 the element *tūn* became widely used as a habitative place-name and may be telling us something about the nature of settlement related to estate subdivision.

In view of its frequent usage throughout southern England after the middle of the eighth century it is somewhat surprising to find the term *tūn* used with such frequency for the multiple estate centres of Somerset. Elsewhere one would normally expect such foci to bear a topographical type name, continuing a naming tradition already familiar in Roman Britain. Costen, however, finds that seven out of the seventeen estate centres he has been able to recognize in this county carry the *tūn* suffix, among them Taunton and Somerton itself. This may be a reflection of the relatively late date of Anglo-Saxon penetration into the area, for the British estate structure was only penetrated and exploited here in the mid-seventh century and one might expect any British names of estate centres to be changed at this time, given the change in leadership.[4] We can also see, in Somerset, the renaming process taking place, for an estate at Biddisham was apparently earlier known as *Ternuc/Tornoc*, while other British names merely acquired an OE suffix: thus Cannington may be derived from a British *cantaco*, 'a district divided off', but had become *Cantuctūn* by the ninth century (Costen 1992:61-3). Taunton and Bruton similarly have *tūn* added to British river-names. The *tūn* element in these cases appears to apply to a newly designated or newly recognized manorial focus. It is of interest that *Tomtūn*, in Mercia, noted earlier, if this is indeed an early name for the royal centre of Tamworth, also refers to a new nucleation of the Anglo-Saxon period.

One might expect a similar high incidence of such names for the estate centres of Devon, also an area of late conquest. A complete assessment of such names has yet to be carried out but in Devon the names of several centres were based upon earlier British river-names, among them Exeter, a pre-existing Roman walled town. Crediton, a name compounding a British river-name with *tūn*, was the site of a minster re-established by the Anglo-Saxons in 739, probably renamed at this date. Here an element of replanning was probably involved. Conversely, in Kent, an area which seems to have been taken over rapidly in the early stages of the

---

[4] Apparently supporting this hypothesis is the loss of such a notable British name as *(æt) Peonnum* (Br. 'head, end'), the site of a battle between Cenwalh and the Welsh in AD 658.

conquest, *tūn* is very rarely found in the names of estate centres. Of 49 estate centres recognized by Everitt (1986:76-7), eight were based upon the British names of rivers (Crayford, Dartford, Darenth, Lympne, Lyminge, Dover, ? Sarre, Sturry) and a further five (Reculver, Eynsford, Chevening, Rochester, Canterbury) contained other British elements, although these were matched by a medley of names containing OE elements known to be early, such as *gē, ing, hām, -ing-*, and the *wīchām* of Latin derivation.

This brings me to my third place-name element: OE *w(e)alh* 'Welshman, foreigner'. Faull's (1975) work has shown that although the term later carried with it the derogatory interpretation of 'slave', this meaning was not pre-eminent at first, when the term merely alluded to a 'Celt, Briton', and Cameron has little doubt that the term "was used originally in personal names to denote people of British stock or mixed parentage" (1980:6). Strangely, the term does not generally occur before the end of the seventh century. What is relevant here is the relationship of many *w(e)alh* place-names to multiple estates. The term is compounded with *cot, worth* or *tūn*, obviously referring to a hamlet or settlement cluster, and sometimes these occur in pairs within one such estate. For instance, two Waltons lie alongside the River Dene to the south of the Wellesbourne estate centre in Warwickshire; another lies closer to the Staffordshire estate centre of Eccleshall, itself bearing a name of hybrid Celtic-English origin; a fair proportion of these lie in the West Midlands and in the Anglo-Saxon/Welsh Borderland extending from Devon to Cheshire. As Cameron comments, "This is such a marked feature that it cannot be purely coincidence" (1980:30). I should like to ask whether these settlements had any special role to play within the estate structure, for they are often as indicative of the presence of nearby estate centres as the Charltons discussed by Finberg (1964:157-8).

A second British term, **ecles,* is now known to clearly allude to the presence of a surviving British Christian community and this is also highly relevant to the recognition of estate centres in some parts of the country. At Eccleshall, in Staffordshire, the term was attached to the estate centre itself, but on some occasions it remained attached to a subordinate village or hamlet, like the two Exhalls in Warwickshire near the later minster centres of Alcester and Coventry. Might such hamlet/estates have had a special role to play in the support of a British Christian church prior to the foundation of the Anglo-Saxon minster? Do either of these terms imply anything about the antiquity of estate composition?

It may be concluded that, although faith has been lost in the simplistic chronological interpretation of place-names, this source of evidence still has much to tell us about the Anglo-Saxon takeover and the establishment of Anglo-Saxon territorial organization during the ensuing centuries.

The subdivision of estates

Probably the most significant change that was to take place during the period in question, however, was the subdivision of these early regions and multiple estates between petty landlords or thegns who were, or now saw themselves, as 'Anglo-Saxon'. But how early did this occur? Some, mostly archaeologists, have argued for the systematic subdivision of valley territories as early as the pagan period, basing their arguments largely upon the location of pagan barrows upon estate and parish boundaries. I believe that the demarcation of individual estates must be set firmly within the Anglo-Saxon period. The sixth and seventh centuries were largely a period of consolidation, witnessing the growing prosperity of those 'Anglo-Saxons' who were to aspire to thegnly status. Until the seventh century, it is doubtful whether Anglo-Saxon England had a middle tier of society sufficiently widely and well established to fill the role of landed thegn. This prosperity may have been based upon a status in society established when their ancestors had arrived with the later self-styled aristocratic war leaders, or upon the opportunist acquisition of land and stock. Some may even have been descended from 'turn-coat' Britons clever enough to adopt the Anglo-Saxon way of life as readily as their forefathers had adopted the Roman toga. It is interesting to note how in India, in the days of the British Raj, minor administrative positions were often held by those of mixed descent; these were not only better educated than the general populace but probably had looser ties with native tradition. Certainly, by the middle of the Anglo-Saxon period most of the minor thegns, whatever their racial origins, saw themselves as Anglo-Saxon and sported such names as Wiglaf or Wulfhere, badges of a Germanic outlook.

The first question that must be addressed is whether subdivision occurred as a planned feature, with valley estates, for instance, being subdivided at a particular period in time, or were pieces of land gradually shorn off from a larger territory as they were allotted to minor thegns or bodies acting in this capacity? This remains one of the unanswered questions of this period.

There are several approaches to the problem. First, may personal names be expected to indicate the possession of small estates? Personal names associated with particular locations are not uncommon in the earliest English records: *Batrices ēge*, present-day Battersea, is for instance 'Beaduric's island', noted in a grant of AD 693, and *æt Baeccesōre*, Batsford, recorded in a grant of AD 727 x 736 is 'at Bæcci's slope'. Such names have been listed by Cox (1976:52). Obviously estates themselves were often to take the names of well-known topographical features which were associated with named individuals, but when do such names cease to denote local ownership or holding of land and refer to the ownership of whole estates? In some cases a personal name occurs with an early habitative element such as *hām* or *tūn*, as previously discussed, but in itself this does not offer conclusive proof of estate subdivision as such a settlement could well have operated within the context of a larger multiple estate.

Taking one of Klingelhöfer's valley regions, that based upon Micheldever (Fig. 3-2), the estate centre bore a British river-name while all those of the subdivisions were entirely of Old English derivation but only one, Wonston, 'Wynsige's *tūn*' was of the type discussed here while a further three incorporated cardinal points of the compass referring to their position relative to the river or the estate centre. Looking

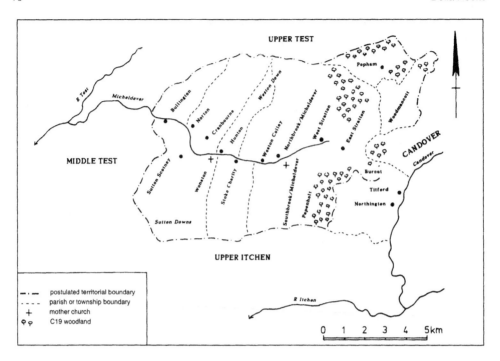

Fig. 3-2: The Micheldever valley, Hampshire (based upon Klingelhöfer 1992).

at the Wylye valley of Wiltshire, the area of the *Wilsæte*, we find the focus at Wilton itself, a royal estate again incorporating the pre-English river-name with *tūn* (recorded 838; Ekwall 1928:457-60), but with an estate of Wylye in a central location within the valley itself. Only four of the 15 valley estates bore *tūn* names compounded with the name of an individual. An interesting case here of three separate estates bearing the same topographical name Langford, 'the long ford', poses the question whether subdivision may not have been a more gradual process than has sometimes been suggested.

It has been suggested that the numerous estate grants concerning the Vale of the White Horse in Oxfordshire reveal the renaming of larger land holdings when granted in the later Anglo-Saxon period. Gelling (1976:675) draws attention to the region apparently known as Ashbury, after *Æscesbyrig*, the hillfort later known as Uffington Castle, where linear estates granted in AD 856 and 958 acquired the name Woolstone, Wulfric's *tūn*, from their tenth-century owner, once he had obtained them both. A further part of the original Ashbury became known as Uffington after AD 953. These occurrences may imply relatively late subdivision but the place-name evidence seems to be of limited usefulness in resolving this problem.

Second, the subdivision of territories can also be examined through the medium of charter grants. The earliest authentic Kentish charter concerns a grant of only 3 *aratra* in the marsh called Stodmarsh near Fordwich, granted to St Peter's minster in Canterbury (Sawyer 1968: S 7). Although a substantial grant of 44 *manentes* was made to Eafe for her minster in Thanet in AD 689 (Sawyer 1968: S 10), other relatively small pieces of land in Thanet and in north-east Kent were also granted to her and also to Canterbury minster.

The West Midland charter evidence, on the other hand, shows only substantial grants, involving large areas of land, to minster foundations in the seventh century, the majority of these of spurious antiquity, with smaller individual estates appearing as the eighth century progresses. Nevertheless, the authentic grants relating to the later county of Worcestershire are also at first only related to large holdings, such as the large estate of *Wican* which lay to the west of the Severn on the margins of the woodland known as *Weorgorenaleah*, granted in AD 757 to the Church of Worcester (Sawyer1968: S 142). Such estates encompassed a number of integral parts which are individually named but did not necessarily enjoy any individual status as estate centres. It is a remarkable fact that all the grants relating to individual parish estates in Worcestershire in the eighth century are of questionable authenticity. However, the Warwickshire charters do include some individual parish estates: the bishop of Worcester's estates of Hampton Lucy and Stratford were separately administered by AD 781 (Sawyer 1968: S 1257) and Hampton Lucy was allegedly leased to Abbess Eanburh in the same year (S 120). Here, some small grants merely referred to blocks of woodland such as Nuthurst in Arden (Sawyer 1968: S 64).

None of these estate-names were associated with named landowners but if a charter of Tredington recording a grant by the underkings of the Hwicce to the Church of Worcester is based upon authentic mid-eighth-century documentation (Sawyer 1968: S 55) (and its boundary clause is certainly later), then Tyrdda appears to have been the name of its former holder. Here we see the equivalent of the Kentish Wilmington established in the West Midlands by the middle of the eighth century. This may, of course, merely reveal the chance recording of such places in charter grants, and a study of the whole country has yet to be carried out, but it offers a possible line of enquiry that has not yet been fully investigated.

If one moves to the south-western part of England, Devon was part of the British kingdom of Dumnonia but was taken over by the Anglo-Saxons by the end of the seventh century. Further to the south-west, Cornwall continued to be ruled by its own king until at least AD 870. It is interesting to note that estate subdivision was well attested in Cornwall by the tenth century, largely due to the establishment of lesser churches in the areas around the British monasteries, so that this was not a feature confined to the Anglo-Saxon regions of England (Olson & Padel 1986). There are no early charters for Cornwall, the one true surviving British charter dating only from the tenth century (Padel 1978), and, as elsewhere, early grants were mostly to the Church. In Devon, a substantial grant was made to the minster of Crediton in AD 739 but small parcels of land were also being granted to individuals by the eighth century. In this county they formed little part of the geometrical division of land that has lured some archaeologists and geographers to suggest large-scale planning.

Can we then, thirdly, turn to the evidence of settlement and fields—the basis of the estate-subdivision that was occurring in the seventh and eighth, and subsequent centuries? There is ample evidence now available to show that the pattern of settlement which characterized Roman Britain continued through the early centuries of the Anglo-Saxon period. Settlement sites might change, but overall a dispersed pattern remains evident in those areas where it can be identified. The changes begin to occur only towards the end of the mid-Anglo-Saxon period, involving the nucleation of settlement. Although this did not necessarily presuppose regular settlement planning, vestiges of this can be identified at two sites in eastern England, North Elmham in Norfolk and Wickham Bonhunt in Essex, by the late sixth or early seventh century (Wade 1980; Wade-Martins 1980). The latter may have been a royal vill and it seems likely that major reorganization may have begun on the estates of royal or major landholders (such as the Church).

The reasons for change are less clearly understood. Some have argued that economic factors were predominant: as subdivision occurred, each tiny manor had to improve its efficiency in order to sustain a relatively self-sufficient economy with, moreover, adequate surplus revenue to maintain its lord and his retainers. That nucleation was strongest in the main crop-growing areas has been seen by Higham (1990) as the result of a rationalization of plough-teams: if outlying farms could be dispensed with, so could their teams, with the organization of shared teams easier within a single clustered community. Others (Pesez 1992) have pointed out that settlement clustering might offer a lord greater opportunities to both organize and control his tenants. There has been some disagreement as to whether the motive for change arose within the peasant community or was initiated by its overlords. Personally, I would hardly expect change to be initiated by any peasant community in itself; these are notoriously opposed to change and unlikely to have had the power to implement it; in all regions where the farming community enjoyed any measure of freedom, such change is less apparent.

It is likely that settlement nucleation spread rather more slowly across England than has frequently been thought. West Midland charters clearly show the presence of minor settlements near estate boundaries in the Late Anglo-Saxon period which had entirely disappeared by medieval times (Hooke 1985b). There seem little doubt that it was carried out most efficiently within arable regions and may have begun on royal or Church estates. These were the very estates that had the power to initiate change and had probably held their peasants in the strictest degrees of bondage. Certainly the necessity appears to have been felt most in areas most dependent upon crop cultivation and had less to offer in pastoral regions, but even in the latter the manorial centre appears to have had attached to it a small dependent settlement focus, often with a patch of mainly arable land farmed under an open field system. These settlement clusters with their associated arable strips were often dissipated soon after the Norman Conquest on manors on which a degree of individual freedom was allowed (Roberts 1968). In the Warwickshire Arden the Earls of Warwick encouraged their tenants to establish new farms on the margins of the uncultivated waste and the relatively small area of open field that was tied to the manorial centre was short-lived. In the parish of

Tanworth-in-Arden there is an indication that the open field itself may have been laid out over land previously worked as an Anglo-Saxon farm (Hooke n.d.).

The strongest evidence of open field farming (Hooke 1988b) comes from regions that were already under the plough in Roman time. Little is known about Roman field systems but, increasingly, a pattern of large squarish fields is being identified in areas farmed under a villa system in the south of England. These seem to have been more systematically laid out than the small rectangular fields often termed 'Celtic fields' which seem to have been associated with native farming methods from the Iron Age through into the Roman period. Indeed, subdivision of such large square fields would produce a pattern of strip holdings closely akin to those actually recorded on post-medieval estate maps: the interlocking furlongs of the so-called 'Midland system'. Some drastic change in the way that land was owned as well as managed may be indicated, taking place in the period under discussion. Even the change from a slave-dominated economy to one of common ownership within a system of serfdom might be sufficient to produce the subdivided furlongs and intermingled strips which seem to have replaced the suggested pattern of regular fields. Certainly the field system seems to have been adapted to the underlying patterns in parts of the Midland region. That the area under open field arable was, subsequently, remarkably constant from Anglo-Saxon into medieval times is clear from the evidence from several valley regions of Wiltshire and Berkshire but the system appears to have spread far beyond the main regions of villa estates (Hooke 1988a).

But discussion of the spread of the open field system carries us beyond the period of our debate and has only been mentioned because of the hints of the beginnings of settlement nucleation may already be detected in a limited number of areas before the end of the eighth century and because settlement nucleation seems to have gone hand in hand with the reorganization of the fields, the latter documented by the late ninth century. Both occurred on the new manorial subdivisions that were clearly coming into being within our period.

Few changes occurred rapidly. Although the consequences of war may have been drastic in their effect upon populations and cultures, these were seldom catastrophic. It is unlikely that many within England felt themselves to be anything other than 'Anglo-Saxon' at the end of the eighth century: indeed, the groups distinguished by *walh* place-names were obviously distinguished in this way because they were unusual. To judge from the charter evidence, the rural population shared a common tongue and language had become the unifying element it was intended to be.

Other cultural developments in the organization of land and attitudes to land ownership were taking place, reflected in administrative and territorial arrangements which were to form the basis for organization throughout the ensuing centuries. Thus, over these two centuries under discussion, the basis was laid for the growth of a nation.

References

Textual sources:

[B = Document number in Birch 1885/99; S = Document number in Sawyer 1968]

The Anglo-Saxon Chronicle: see Garmonsway 1953.
Domesday Book: see Record Commission 1783; Plaister 1976.
Gallic Chronicle: see Jones & Casey 1988.
Gildas
　　　　　De excidio Britanniae: see Winterbottom 1978.
The Journal of Christopher Columbus: see Jane 1960.
Record of Caernarvon: see Ellis 1838.

Bibliography:

Birch, W. de Gray
1885/99　　*Cartularium Saxonicum*, 3 vols. London: Whiting & Co (Ltd). [Rep. 1964 by Johnson reprint Co, New York/London].
Cameron, K.
　1980　　The meaning and significance of Old English walh in English place-names. *Journal of the English Place-Name Society* 12 (1979-80): 1-53.
Campbell, J.
　1982　　The lost centuries: 400-600. In *The Anglo-Saxons*. J. Campbell (ed.), pp. 20-44. Oxford: Phaidon.
Charles-Edwards, T. M.
　1972　　Kinship, status and the origins of the hide. *Past and Present* 56: 3-33.
Costen, M.
　1992　　*The Origins of Somerset*. Manchester: Manchester University Press.
Cox, B.
　1976　　The place-names of the earliest English records. *Journal of the English Place-Name* Society 8 (1975-76): 12-66.
Davies, W., & H. Vierck
　1974　　The contents of the Tribal Hidage: social aggregates and settlement patterns. *Frühmittelalterliche Studien* 8: 224-236.
Dodgson, J. McN.
　1966　　The significance of the distribution of the English place-name in *ingas, -inga-* in south-east England. *Medieval Archaeology* 10: 1-29.
Ekwall, E.
　1923　　*English Place-Names in -ing*. Lund: Gleerup.
　1928　　*English River Names*. Oxford: Oxford University Press.
　1936　　*The Concise Oxford Dictionary of English Place-Names*. [1960 ed.] Oxford: Clarendon Press.
Ellis, H. (ed.)
　1838　　*Record of Caernarvon*. London: Eyre & Spottiswoode.
Everitt, A.
　1986　　*Continuity and Colonization: The Evolution of Kentish Settlement*. Leicester: Leicester University Press.

Faull, M.
    1975   The semantic development of Old English *wealh*. *Leeds Studies in English*
           18: 20-44.
Finberg, H. P. R.
    1964   *Lucerna: Studies of some Problems in the Early History of England.*
           London: Macmillan.
Gelling, M.
    1976   *The Place-Names of Berkshire, Part 3.* (English Place-Name Society 51).
           Cambridge: Cambridge University Press.
    1978   *Signposts to the Past.* London: Dent.
Greenblatt, S.
    1993.   *New World Encounters.* Berkeley, CA: University of California Press.
Gregson, N.
    1985   The multiple estate model: some critical questions. *Journal of Historical*
           Geography 11: 339-351.
Haddan, A. W., & W. Stubbs
    1871   *Councils and Ecclesiastical Documents relating to Great Britain and*
           Ireland, 3. Oxford: Clarendon.
Higham, N.
    1990   Settlement, land use and Domesday ploughlands. *Landscape History* 12:
           33-44.
Hogg, A. H. A.
    1952   The survival of Romano-British place-names in southern England. *Antiquity*
           38: 296-299.
Hooke, D.
    1985a   *The Anglo-Saxon Landscape, the Kingdom of the Hwicce.* Manchester:
           Manchester University Press.
    1985b   Village development in the West Midlands. In *Medieval Villages, a Review*
           of Current Work. D. Hooke (ed.), pp. 125-154. (University of Oxford
           Committee for Archaeology Monograph No. 5). Oxford: Oxford Committee
           for Archaeology.
    1986   Territorial organisation in the Anglo-Saxon West Midlands. In *Central*
           Places, Archaeology and History. E. Grant (ed.), pp. 79-93. Sheffield:
           Department of Archaeology, University of Sheffield.
    1988a   Regional variation in southern and central England in the Anglo-Saxon
           period and its relationship to land units and settlement. In *Anglo-Saxon*
           Settlements. D. Hooke (ed.) pp. 123-151. Oxford: Blackwell.
    1988b   Early forms of open-field agriculture in England. *Geografiska Annaler* 70B
           8 (1): 123-131.
    1994a   *Pre-Conquest Charter-Bounds of Devon and Cornwall.* Woodbridge: The
           Boydell Press.
    1994b   The administrative and settlement framework of early medieval Wessex. In *The*
           Medieval Landscape of Wessex. M. Aston & C. Lewis (eds.), pp. 83-95. (Oxbow
           Monograph No. 46). Oxford: Oxford University Committee for Archaeology.
    n.d.   Place-names and settlement patterns in west Warwickshire. In *Names, Time*
           and Place. Festschrift for R. A. McKinley. Leicester: Leopard's Head Press.
Jackson, K.
    1953   *Language and History in Early Britain.* Edinburgh: Edinburgh Univ. Press.
Jane, C. (ed. & trans.)
    1960   *The Journal of Christopher Columbus*, [1960 ed.]. London: Hakluyt Society.

Jones, G. R. J.
    1976   Multiple estates and early settlement. In *Medieval Settlement*. P. H. Sawyer (ed.), pp. 15-40. London: Edward Arnold.
    1978   Celts, Saxons and Scandinavians. In *An Historical Geography of England and Wales*. [2nd ed.]. R. A. Dodgson & R. A. Butlin (eds.), pp. 45-68. London: Academic Press.

Jones, M. E., & J. Casey
    1988   The Gallic Chronicle restored: a chronology for the Anglo-Saxon invasions and the end of Roman Britain. *Britannia* 19: 367-398.

Klingelhöfer, E.
    1992   *Manor, Vill, and Hundred*. Toronto: Pontifical Institute.

McKie, R.
    1993   Genetic patchwork of an island nation. *Geographical Magazine*. (June): 25-28.

Meaney, A.
    1964   *A Gazetteer of Early Anglo-Saxon Burial Sites*. London: Allen & Unwin.

Oldon, B. L., & O. J. Padel
    1986   A tenth-century list of Cornish parochial saints. *Cambridge Medieval Celtic Studies* 121: 33-71.

Padel, O. J.
    1978   Two new pre-Conquest charters for Cornwall. *Cornish Studies* 6: 20-27.

Pesez, J-M.
    1992   The emergence of the village in France and in the west. *Landscape History* 14: 31-50.

Plaister, J.
    1976   *Domesday Book, 23, Warwickshire*. Chichester: Phillimore.

Record Commission
    1783   *Domesday Book*. London: Record Commission

Rivet, P. L. F., & C. Smith
    1979   *The Place-Names of Roman Britain*. London: Batsford.

Roberts, B. K.
    1968   A study of medieval colonization in the Forest of Arden, Warwickshire. *Agricultural History Review* 16: 101-113.

Sawyer, P. H.
    1968   *Anglo-Saxon Charters, an Annotated List and Bibliography*. London: Royal Historical Society.

Sims-Williams, P.
    1983   The settlement of England in Bede and the *Chronicle*. *Anglo-Saxon England* 12: 1-41.

Smith, A. H.
    1964   *The Place-Names of Gloucestershire, Part II*. (English Place-Name Society 39). Cambridge: Cambridge University Press.

Smith, R.
    1988   Human resources. In *The Countryside of Medieval England*. G. Astill & A. Grant (eds.), pp. 188-212. Oxford: Blackwell.

Taylor, C.
    1983   *Village and Farmstead*. London: G. Philip.

Wade, K.
    1980   A settlement site at Bonhunt Farm. In *Archaeology in Essex to A.D. 1500*. D. Buckley (ed.), pp. 96-103. (CBA. Research Report 34). London: CBA.

Wade-Martins, P. (ed.)
    1980   *Excavation in North Elmham Park 1967-72.* (East Anglian Archaeology 9).
             Gressenhall: Norfolk Archaeological Unit.
Wallenberg, J. K.
    1931   Kentish Place-Names. *Uppsala Universitets Årsskrift.* Uppsala: University
             of Uppsala Press.
Welch, M. G.
    1983   *Early Anglo-Saxon Sussex.* (British Archaeological Reports, British Series
             191). Oxford: BAR.
    1992   *Anglo-Saxon England.* London: English Heritage.
Winterbottom, M. (ed. & trans.)
    1978   *Gildas, The Ruin of Britain and other Works.* Chichester: Phillimore.

Discussion

AUSENDA: I have a few questions on Dr. Hooke's paper. Language change does not require large numbers. I do not believe that dominance produces language change. In fact in *Francia* and in *Langobardia* the dominant groups were Germanic and yet the language remained Romance. I believe that trade and the language spoken in the market are more influential in bringing about language change.

HOOKE: I suggested that that was the reason in Fife. I do not think it was sufficient to explain the other changes.

AUSENDA: In fact you suggested that "in medieval Fifeshire, English gradually supplanted Gaelic amidst the middle classes in a similar but less pressured way because it was the language of merchants and tradespeople". The lower pressure was not due to weaker dominance but to slower trade.

HOOKE: So why didn't the Welsh change over to English and why did the Cornish retain their language?

AUSENDA: Probably because their economy was mainly a subsistence economy and there was very little trade getting into Cornwall.

HOOKE: No, I do not think that it was that. Language change did not happen in Wales and there trade was important and relied very much on the use of the English language, especially in Tudor times. Yet trade did not change the language. The people continued to speak Welsh.

AUSENDA: This is what I am saying: English landlords were dominant but they did not change the language. People went on speaking Welsh.

HOOKE: But in Fife they did change the language.

AUSENDA: We are talking about two different things. I say that language is not necessarily changed by the 'dominance' of another population speaking another language, but more often by the predominance of a given language in trade.

CHARLES-EDWARDS: Curiously, in the case of the Franks you rightly say that the language in western *Francia* did not change, but they do change their personal names: there is an intermediate situation with some linguistic expression of the domination but not a wholesale linguistic change. The Welsh case is rather special because there are other factors involved, such as religion. So the trade might well be important on the one hand, but there might be other ways of explaining the Cornish and Welsh survival.

AUSENDA: I entirely agree with you. At the same time dominance is not the only explanation, it is part of an explanation. You also mentioned 'serfdom'. I believe that 'serfdom' is an ill-defined term. It was even used by early ethnographers to describe the relation between certain agro-pastoral groups and groups which were 'foreign' to their territories. For these cases the term 'client' is preferred.

HOOKE: I am not sure what you are arguing here.

AUSENDA: That 'serfdom' is an ill-defined term.

HOOKE: It is defined in Welsh law codes where it is very precise.

DUMVILLE: Not in the tenth century.

HOOKE: Agreed, but some have attempted to extrapolate backward from these documents.

CHARLES-EDWARDS: Welsh law texts are late twelfth-century at the earliest, or thirteenth- to fourteenth-century. I think there is clear evidence of change occurring at that period in terms of which groups are regarded as free or unfree. So, there is a possibility that one shouldn't read back. We have terminological problems here of a quite serious kind. I suppose there is the slave who can be bought and sold personally; the operative medievalist who could not leave the land, the estate; the lord; and a number of possible indications of lack of freedom as expressed by Maitland. Clientship can be a useful concept, but within the client class, the umbrella term which one might use is the term *bound* for the unfree who are somewhere near the bottom of the hierarchy.

LENDINARA: They were liable to be fined, so they had property.

CHARLES-EDWARDS: They were unfree.

LENDINARA: They were unfree but they had property at the same time. 'Serfdom' is too general a term. What is the Celtic term?

CHARLES-EDWARDS: There is no Celtic term. There is the term *caeth* which means 'the one who is personally subjected to constraint'; then there are other terms. There is a range of terms from the most unfree up to the most free.

HOOKE: Well there is someone in charge and then there are those tilling the land with very little choice regarding their position.

AUSENDA: The term *tūn*, presumably 'town', is rare until after AD 730 (Cox 1977). This coincides with Chris Scull's analysis concluding that town life had all but disappeared.

HOOKE: The *tūn* is not a town in the sense of an urban centre. *Tūn* is an Old English word; originally it meant an enclosure but became adapted to an enclosed settlement; in geographical usage it appears to have been applied to some type of nucleated settlement. It came down in Middle English as 'town', in fact, but without any urban connotation.

LENDINARA: It came to mean 'town' in the *Menologium*: 'when March comes in town'. That is one of the first occurrences of *tūn* in the meaning of 'town', in Old English and post-966. It is some sort of syntagm, 'to come in town', like 'downtown': it is hard to construe it as 'to come in an enclosure'.

HOOKE: It may imply a nucleated settlement, but not necessarily an urban one.

LENDINARA: What is relevant is the kind of syntagms in which *tūn* occurs: *tō tūne* (line 34), *on tūn* (line 138). It is hard to conceive of months coming to an enclosure.

HOOKE: These little things were not towns—mere clusters of farmsteads.

FOWLER: 'Church-town' is still a common descriptive name in western Britain, describing exactly what is meant by *tūn* except that it is the *tūn* which has a church in it, the centre of an ecclesiastical estate. This is how I try to convey this idea of what a *tūn* was.

I found this a most stimulating paper. There are many, many points here. I would like to take them up in the order in which you presented them. As far as population is concerned, you said that you wished that archaeologists could make up their minds, since guesses about population figures range between 2 and 5 million. In fact, they range between 2 and 7 million, but there may have been other guesses. I suppose it was about ten or fifteen years ago now that it occurred to a number of people more or less simultaneously that whatever the figure was, it was certainly bigger than the 2 million which was the conventional wisdom—which has just been re-enshrined in print in the latest edition of the Frere's *Britannia* (Frere 1987:301-2), where despite the long discussions I had with him, he has completely ignored my advice and all the evidence. By the 70s the large size of the rural population had become clear. I opted for about 4 or 5 million in total, which upset some but others thought it still too low. This was, almost entirely (about 99 per cent), on the basis of the new evidence from rural settlement. It was not the discovery of large numbers of new Roman towns or re-estimates of the Roman urban populations, it was the sheer density of settlement that had become visible in the Romano-British countryside, certainly by, say, AD 300. And the other major implication it seemed to us arose from that, that again, whatever the figure was, it was larger than the conventional wisdom about the population of Domesday England. This led to a lot of discussions with historians (such as Peter Sawyer) as to whether that 2 million was correct or not. Assuming that that 2 million was of the right order, there had to be some form of population collapse, as you just said, in between. You have to postulate an extraordinary set of circumstances to go from 5 million to 2 million over 600 years. Then you get into arguments about the size of collapse and the speed of collapse, and its nature and causes. That is the historiography of this particular idea. The interesting thing is that the revolutionary idea of, say, 4 million of a dozen or fifteen years ago, is now accepted wisdom. I am not aware of any major criticism of it. I think people have pulled back a bit from some of the wilder excesses, like 7 million. I think everybody, archaeologists, would feel comfortable with 4 to 5 million in say 300 to 350 AD.

DUMVILLE: Could I ask one thing about your exposition on that? You said that a group of people decided that the previous figure was too small, because of re-estimation of the size and density of rural settlement. And I can see how one could go up. But what was the reliability of the previous figure?

POWLESLAND: It was off the shelf.

FOWLER: It was largely a discussion in the pages of *Antiquity* between Wheeler and Myres in the 1950s. Wheeler at that stage was trying to get the figure up from 1 to 2 million, which was, after all, a 100 per cent increase. There was a great deal of debate on that largely on the basis of the excavations at Verulamium and that involved urban excavations, reconsideration of the Silchester evidence, and an argument over whether all those empty spaces, which apparently there were in Roman towns like Verulamium and Silchester, were really gardens, or, as one or two daring souls were beginning to say, were there where bad excavations had missed the timber buildings. But the main thing, in one sentence, which led to the revised guesstimate going up was the visual revolution brought about by the wide availability of air photography evidence from 1965 onwards and, of course, the impact of motorways and all sorts of programmes in the countryside which churned up Roman settlements all over the place. And whatever the number of the population, this has led to this idea, deeply embedded in my paper, that in the fourth century the countryside was very densely used. That is not quite the same as lots of people living everywhere, but it was like a chess-board and there was no spare space, as it were. And, incidentally, Della's *Stoppingas* example exactly fits the model in my paper of finding an empty square in an already laid out and densely used landscape into which you can put all your odd groups.

HOOKE: I don't think it was empty because it was already a functioning estate. Its very location is also of interest, at the junction of two very different kinds of countryside. To be fair, we have also got to question Domesday figures because those are equally dubious.

CHARLES-EDWARDS: If Ferdinand Lot was right on population density in West *Francia* in the ninth century (as against Georges Duby; Lot 1921), Domesday Book may suggest a contrast between dense population south of the Channel and relatively low population levels north of the Channel.

SCULL: I think one point Peter has made which is extremely important is the distinction which should be drawn on the one hand between the landscape being full from the point of view of subsistence agriculture and on the other fully exploited from the point of view of some sort of more commercial agriculture as might be expected on a Roman estate. There is archaeological evidence from the upper Thames valley for a switch to a less intensive system of agriculture during the course of the fifth century. Thus the countryside may have been able to accommodate a number of incomers without actually causing any form of subsistence stress.

HOOKE: It might have been overfarmed in some areas; if you look at the arguments for the chalk downs there is some evidence for the tops of the chalk downs having been worked out, with soil pests rife—a situation ripe for abandonment.

SCULL: Some regions or soil types may have been overexploited. But on the contrary it has been argued that in the fifth and sixth centuries climatic change may have made eastern England potentially more fertile than it had been in the fourth century. East Anglia is an area of soil moisture deficit: climatic change in the fifth and sixth centuries to a slightly cooler and wetter climate would have enhanced the agricultural potential of previously marginal soils.

HINES: I must say that listening to the discussion convinces me that really I am not all that interested in this sort of long-term history and long-term processes of change in the landscape. These questions are just circulating around again and again; figures are plucked out of the air—they may be doubled, and may be halved, and so on. It seems to me that in the midst of this we are missing a big topic for potential research which is perhaps the most seriously neglected area of Anglo-Saxon studies. This is the question of how we might relate the evidence we have now for landholding and estate structures to the increasingly well-documented and well-studied evidence for the nature of settlement sites and then to such evidence as we have for social structures. What would we expect a given social arrangement to look like on the ground in terms of estate structures? What sort of housing would we expect it to be accommodated in? Is there anything that can actually be done to relate given changes of settlement pattern to changes that are postulated in social organization and in landholding?

Finally, just one specific question on your *Stoppingas* group: is there actually a good reason for regarding the *Stoppingas* group as a substantial, newly-introduced, colonizing group in an area rather than just a renamed, or re-defined, group where the one new arrival might have been a man called *Stoppa*?

HOOKE: *Stoppa* is not thought to be a personal name.

HINES: Well, few roots of *-inga-* names are obviously personal names. But the identification of these as personal names is actually a substantial factor in the argument that these are actually colonizing groups; they are meant to be followers of *N*.

HOOKE: I would argue that there were a lot of people already there whom the newcomers were moving in to dominate. I firmly believe in a British underlay. As you know, most people are arguing more on the side of an Anglo-Saxon colonization than I would be.

HINES: I may have misunderstood, but it sounded as if here was an empty, marginal area that you could put people in. It sounded as if the *Stoppingas* were meant to be that group.

HOOKE: No, I argue that there was probably an existing estate (as the charter claims), even if it was in a relatively lightly settled area—a functioning estate which someone was able to take over. It may be accepting conventional thought that the *-ingas* people involved a group leader with followers; I do not think we can actually come to any more conclusions about that any more than about what these settlements might have looked like. We have been running around in circles because we have not yet got the archaeological evidence to argue more precisely—we are working with documents, imagination, if you like, and really all you are saying is that we might as well go away for the next twenty years and wait until we have got something to argue with.

HINES: I am not saying that at all. What I was trying to do was to clear out what seemed to me to be an assumption about the nature of these groups, which I wrongly supposed to be couched in conventional and traditional terms when actually it was not. If we are all in agreement, that's fine.

HOOKE: I do not think we are moving hundreds of people and saying, 'this is an empty area of countryside—go and live there'. But I do think you are probably allotting an area within a functioning landscape to somebody with perhaps a small group of followers, but with people already there. I think there is a recognizable new person or persons going into that patch.

HÄRKE: I think that kind of model, with an immigrant group of limited size and a new lord or controller coming in, and taking over the native population as well, is something that can be seen in the German 'East Colonization', for example in East Prussia where this happened in the thirteenth and fourteenth centuries.

HOOKE: The only evidence you've got here is a small group of pagan burials.

POWLESLAND: I have been considering a similar question concerning place-names. I find the idea that place-names show that there were millions of Anglo-Saxons completely unacceptable. Numbers and place-names are two entirely different questions and this idea of invoking place-names whenever it's convenient is the most irritating thing that people have been doing in the last ten years. Look at the place-name evidence and look at what we actually have archaeologically: we have place-name evidence for a lot of places that exist, those places are *not* early Anglo-Saxon settlements. There is no early Anglo-Saxon settlement for which we have a place-name, and it would be nice if people who play with place-names and people who play with history could actually accept that the places that have an early Anglo-Saxon population, i.e. Anglo-Saxon settlements and their cemeteries, we do not have a single place-name for.

HOOKE: That's because of a gap of 200 or 300 years in the evidence.

POWLESLAND: It is two problems together, one of which comes back to John's point and one to your point: to deal with what we do with the landscape and what's going on in terms of movement. For a long time we have recognized the mid Anglo-Saxon shuffle and I believe it is in association with this that all these places get these place-names, which is a way of politically imposing the Anglo-Saxon language on the population and on the landscape by establishing new towns which are a brave new world—or they might be new hamlets or new villages. What also appears to occur is an early Anglo-Saxon shuffle. There is evidence for early Anglo-Saxon activity on a number of late Roman sites, but what is very clear is that it does not continue. Something happens at the end of Roman Britain, or within the later part of Roman Britain, that creates an environment in which people *can* move. I have spent a lot of time looking at this particular problem, and trying to work out why the settlement gets to be where it is. I wonder whether during, say, the last century of Roman control, the entire landscape belongs to someone and is controlled and we see late Roman settlements and environments which are decidedly antisocial—it has become a lot wetter at the end of the Roman period and there are lots and lots of people living in environments which are extremely wet; nobody in their right mind would wish to build houses in these increasingly fenland environments by choice. The reason they do it is not because they choose to do so but because they can't go anywhere else. And they cannot go anywhere else because somebody owns and controls the land. Once that system breaks down, people move, not because of some desire to move in the first instance, but because they can do. So we have two shuffles: one in the early period in response to the freeing-up of the landscape; then one in the middle period which may be a consequence of establishing a new landscape under a Christian-controlled population. Whether Christianity is involved I am not really sure but it is not a necessary component; I have a feeling that it is, because I have a feeling that the building of churches is a crucial part in the establishment of these new shifted settlements.

HOOKE: Is the expression of lordship not a primary factor?

POWLESLAND: Yes, it is all combined, because it all comes back to the elements of control. Within this sort of environment I can quite happily deal with these moving settlements and moving populations. But we do not actually understand or know anything about the estate structure of late Roman Britain. There seems to be no way that we can find out. One thing that we do know is that very often things like estate boundaries follow consistent boundaries that go back in time. We have a number of demonstrable examples—not necessarily for minor boundaries, but major boundaries seem to last a very long time. I throw these ideas out to the floor because I think it is very important that we scotch this business about place-names pronto because you cannot say because you have a place-name at *x* attached to a settlement that is a mile away from an early Anglo-Saxon settlement that the two things are in any way related. I'm delighted that you brought that up.

HOOKE: I personally regard place-names often as estate names. I cannot agree with those place-name scholars who necessarily equate a name with a specific village and do not envisage that the name could have referred to any different kind of settlement or any different location. Even once names have been allotted to a settlement, that settlement can change either its position or its form. Alternatively, even a static settlement may change its name. I would, however, strongly agree that we usually have *no* names for the earliest settlements and most place-names post-date the eigth-century. Barry Cox's study was an attempt to consider which were the earliest types of names being coined before the mid eighth century. A recent study that has been published in *Landscape History* is a paper by Christopher Balkwill (1993) on early *wic* names.

POHL: I want to say something quickly because it supports what has just been said about place-names. I want to introduce a Continental comparison from Langobardic Friuli. There has been a lot of argument based on the distribution of Langobardic, Germanic, or Roman place-names in Italy and there is a particularly impressive example along the Isonzo river of two names of neighbouring villages, one is called Romans d'Isonzo, and the other one is called Farra d'Isonzo. Now, as we know from Marius of Avenches, the Langobards moved into Italy 'in *fara*', a notion probably similar to the one implied in the discussion about the Stoppingas, that there is a kind of kin group moving in and taking over a bit of land and establishing a new settlement pattern there. So the *fara* place-names all around Italy have been interpreted in that way. There were new groups which came in and founded these *fara* settlements and there were isolated groups of Romans nearby who were so isolated that 'Roman' could be used as a place-name. Now over the last few years there have been two excavations, one at Romans and one at Farra d'Isonzo. Strangely enough, at Romans, a beautiful Langobardic cemetery with rich weapon graves was found and at Farra you have a Roman population, so it diametrically contradicts the evidence of the place-names.

LENDINARA: There are so many *fara* place-names in Italy that if they were all founded and inhabited by Germanic populations one would have to imagine a large number of Langobards, etc. invading Italy and arriving far south.

POHL: I would not really argue that all these theories completely break down because of one archaeological excavation, but still it calls for some caution in semantic interpretation.

HOOKE: Do you have a change of overlord in that type of situation?

POHL: The point about the Langobards, of course, is that the archaeological evidence shows that within three generations after the migration the Langobards were more or less Christianized and romanized, and the grave goods disappear. Thus, we can date the Langobardic evidence to the first three generations from 568 to the seventh-century Langobardic population, and we do not know what happens after this. Our chronological evidence is even more restricted to a certain period than it is in the case of the Anglo-Saxons.

SCULL: Thomas's point about Mucking is important. At Mucking there is an archaeological site, and a settlement or a land unit to which at some point that name has been attached. One problem with place-name studies is the spurious attempt to date place-name strata by archaeological association. Just because a parish has an Anglo-Saxon name and a sixth-century cemetery does not mean that the name was given in the sixth century nor that the cemetery (or its associated settlement) was ever known by that name. I absolutely agree with Dominic on this: you simply cannot couple sites and place-names in this way.

CHARLES-EDWARDS: An interesting example is Bede's *In getlingum* (Gilling West), which describes a place as being 'among the Getlingas' (*HE* III.14 & 24); in this instance it is quite clear that in its early period the name did not apply to a place but to a group of people.

HOOKE: As you say, many place-names are not *place*-names at all, they may be 'folk' names.

WOOD: Can I just ask about the minster at Wootton Wawen. What's the Latin word used for this? Is it *monasterium?* If you found an equivalent of this in *Francia* you would be looking at an Ardennes-style monastery.

HOOKE: The estate is given *in ius monastica(e)* 'into tenure of monastic type'.

WOOD: Why can't it be a monastery deliberately founded somewhere out of the way?

HOOKE: It says it is in the territory anciently called that of the *Stoppingas*, a territory estimated from that of the medieval *parochia*.

WOOD: I wonder whether in origin this isn't a passive monastery with somebody going with a group of people or founding something deliberately deep in a forest.

HOOKE: Well, it is not an empty forest.

WOOD: Neither is the Ardennes. The sort of model that is constructed for a minster in Anglo-Saxon England is completely different from the sort of model that is constructed for a *monasterium* on the Continent and I just wonder whether there is any real reason for constructing two different models from the evidence that we have.

HOOKE: You find in this area, incidentally, that, in addition to the one at Wootton Wawen, there was another minster at Upper Stratford and possibly a lost *monasterium* at Alcester. The latter was described as 'the celebrated place called Alne' when an ecclesiastical council was held there. But there is no documented minster and much of the area was taken into the estates of Evesham Abbey. There is a suggested pattern, however, of three different minster *parochiae*, one primary one around Alcester, although it cannot be proved, and subsidiary ones at Stratford and Wootton Wawen—a rather neat pattern as if the minsters were established to serve recognized territories.

DUMVILLE: Returning to place-names, may I ask something about your *walh* place-names? It is unclear as to your chronology on this because I suspect that might affect the nature of the argument.

HOOKE: They are either a feature of the eighth century onwards or were too minor to find their way into earlier documents or else it is a late nomenclature for some group that is standing out as different from the rest at that date. I refer to Kenneth Cameron's study on this term in place-names (1988:42-3).

DUMVILLE: The mere fact that there is opposition within the argument means that nothing can be based on their distribution.

HOOKE: The term *walh* is, however, found linked to other place-name elements which appear to be late in date (Cox 1976). There is also a distinct relationship to estate centres. Sometimes they occur in couples near an estate centre, like the two Waltons near Wellesbourne in Warwickshire. These do seem to represent something more than 'a dirty little village' of people the general population did not wish to claim as their own.

DUMVILLE: Yes, but the implication of what you were saying earlier and in your paper seemed to be that one could be reasonably certain that the *walh* names were brought into existence in the eighth century plus, sufficiently so to start building further hypotheses upon this. Whereas that is not in fact demonstrable, is it? I have never been entirely persuaded that any conclusions could be drawn from that particular paper of Cox's: it is all very interesting in terms of delivery of information but any argument from it depends essentially upon negative reasoning.

HINES: Yes, you do have to assume the sources are a reliable guide, which is not consistently a satisfactory argument. It is especially difficult when you have a rare place-name element which haphazardly might or might not be recorded before 730. When you get something like *-hām* or *-tūn* which is very common indeed, the situation is different. One such element is *stōw*—a very common element now in the English place-name set, and yet completely unrecorded in Cox's list. It is wrong to take a single view of the whole list in respect of setting up a chronology of different types.

HOOKE: But few settlements stay in the same place or have stayed in the same place through to the eighth century.

HINES: I nonetheless see a possibility for the place-names; the situation is not totally hopeless.

POWLESLAND: It's very interesting that two examples of *stōw* and *tūn* are both represented by significant early Anglo-Saxon settlements (West Stow, Suffolk, and Heslerton, Yorkshire) that are not actually at the location of those place-names.

DUMVILLE: We presumably have to be careful about assuming that when the shuffle takes place, the place-name either does or does not go with the shuffle.

POWLESLAND: These might support the idea than when they shuffle, they re-name.

CHARLES-EDWARDS: The Mucking shuffle is a slow shuffle.

POWLESLAND: Some people would argue that, others would disagree.

CHARLES-EDWARDS: Basically it's a slow shuffle. It gradually shifts along that ridge. Then you wouldn't expect any great moment at which you can say a new name should appear.

POWLESLAND: But Mucking does not shuffle in the eighth or ninth century, does it?

SCULL: Mucking is an early- to middle-Saxon settlement which is abandoned in the eighth century. We do not know whether there is a successor settlement adjacent or nearby.

CHARLES-EDWARDS: Are you saying that the middle-Saxon shuffle is always a very sharp shift?

SCULL: No, I am saying that the middle-Saxon shuffle model postulates a relocation of a settlement on a new site. This is not the case at Mucking where you have in effect a static settlement in the broadest sense: that within a settlement zone there is shift over time. That does not seem to me to accord with the model of the middle-Saxon shuffle as I understand it.

POWLESLAND: The middle-Saxon shuffle would be what happens at the end of Mucking. So in the concept Mucking fits quite nicely. Again, you have an early Anglo-Saxon settlement deserted.

SCULL: This is my point: we have so few settlement sequences spanning the Anglo-Saxon period that we cannot model settlement development in detail. The 'middle-Saxon shuffle' is a very poorly defined idea.

FOWLER: Don't lets get too excited about the 'shuffle'. The demonstration of the shuffle at Mucking and other places is a great achievement logistically but intellectually all it really has done is show that, far from being specifically of this period, and far from it being specifically Anglo-Saxon, what we are looking at there is something which has been happening all over western Europe, and indeed further afield, ever since people were there. The outstanding characteristic of the first settlements we have, the earliest Neolithic settlements in south-eastern Europe, and in the north European plain, is that they shuffle. And exactly the same thing has happened in this interpretation of the early prehistoric period as is happening in Anglo-Saxon studies: the shift from 'my word, how tremendous it is that we've found some settlements' to 'my word, aren't these settlements big?' to 'oh well, they're actually little ones all the time that they have been going along the sand ridge'. It's exactly the same thing.

CHARLES-EDWARDS: There may be a difference between the 'shifting settlement' and the situation which would produce a change in name; let me suppose we have got two competing principal settlements in a multiple estate. In this multiple estate type you have got at least two settlements; one declining the other growing in size. As one is going down the other is coming up. If the name for the multiple estate derives from the principal settlement within that estate, a change from one principal settlement to another should produce a different name for the multiple estate.

FOWLER: Could I make just a short general point about this and really go back to John's remarks. Obviously I find it distressing, not because he upsets me, but because he is missing so much intellectually in saying he does not see the importance of long-term change. The answer to this, surely, is that we must look at things in a relatively long time span—and we are looking at about four or five hundred years in the landscape—as it is only by doing that, that we can begin to get a grip on the sort of problem you've just raised, which is subsumed within one word, which is 'dynamics'. And unless we can understand the dynamics of social change and the working of the landscape, then we are in no position to start understanding the dynamics of, for example, minor subjects like religion. [Laughter]

HINES: Obviously my comments were meant to be provocative. But I think this is actually a classic case of the theoretical clash that arose fifteen or twenty years ago between the functionalists and the historians. The point I really wanted to make was that it seemed to me that attempts to explain through history had become over-dominant in relation to this question, and in fact we could probably now help ourselves to understand that history by paying more attention to the synchronic function of these elements in the landscape in the Middle-Saxon period.

DUMVILLE: I would like to make a point about literacy. You seem to say both in your paper and in your remarks, Della, that you are contrasting Old English as a literate, a literary, language with British as a non-literary language. This got me rather confused and wondering about what time frame you were talking about.

HOOKE: There appears to be rather more documentation in Old English and not very much in British.

DUMVILLE: Well, that begs many questions. Most British documents are in Latin. Take your text: "a third and equally powerful factor was the fact that the Anglo-Saxons, at least in the royal courts and the Church, were literate".

There is no way of contrasting that with the British situation where in a comparable context we are dealing with literate groups.

CHARLES-EDWARDS: I looked at this in a different way. I thought you were supposing that if there were surviving lower-status British groups they would not have been literate; or are we making a contrast between the Britons when they were powerful in western Britain, when they had courts and kings and so forth, and the Anglo-Saxons?

HOOKE: I implied that the Anglo-Saxons were more ready to record minor and major items in writing than the British were—in the vernacular—as in charter boundary clauses, for instance.

CHARLES-EDWARDS: It depends on the dating of the Anglo-Saxon evidence.

LENDINARA: Do you mean in the early seventh century?

HOOKE: I was trying to concentrate in this paper only on the period *from* the seventh century, rather than the period before that.

LENDINARA: I could not accept the idea of Old English vernacular written down in the early seventh century.

HOOKE: Yes. I was not referring to the early period.

CHARLES-EDWARDS: My feeling is that as far as western Britain is concerned, what does not come out strongly enough is that a Romance language survived in western Britain alongside British until probably around AD 600 at least. Now that means we have two competing vernaculars which means a complicated situation if people are going to write documents. The British have two vernaculars: this is quite different from the situation of the English who speak just English, with no Romance counterpart in competition. When people were engaged in things like pastoral work, they were bound to be concerned with the language in which they could do pastoral work, just as Bede was anxious to translate Saint John's gospel.

Could I also ask about your concept of the large multiple estate as proposed by Glanville Jones (1976) and Geoffrey Barrow (1973)? As I understand it, there are usually two elements. First, there is usually a principal centre, very often royal, and that is the centre at which the king might occasionally turn up to consume food renders; so it is tied to the political power of itinerant kings. Then there is the other element which, in your account, is a distinction of function between different satellites within this multiple estate. So, I assume, you might have transhumance, for example, or your barton/*beretūn* settlements.

HOOKE: Those might be some of the functions within a multiple estate.

CHARLES-EDWARDS: So they are complementary functions.

HOOKE: In other words, a feature of the multiple estate is lesser units which are themselves only part of a larger whole.

CHARLES-EDWARDS: But is this because they are trading within the group.

HOOKE: They don't need to be self-sufficient, but later—once these multiple estates have been broken up—the smaller units must be self-contained and must maintain their lordly contributions from within their own boundaries. If, for instance, they lack sufficient land for hay meadow, then they are sometimes granted additional land beyond their boundaries for that purpose. As I see it, in the multiple estate the individual settlement units do not have to be self-sufficient, they are merely part of the whole.

SCULL: So there is a redistribution between the component parts of the multiple estate?

HOOKE: Yes.

CHARLES-EDWARDS: Is the trade vertical not horizontal?

HOOKE: It is vertical if goods are sent to a central vill for the maintenance of the lord in person.

CHARLES-EDWARDS: So it is largely an expression of lordship.

HOOKE: I think so.

HINES: If you do have continuity of considerable antiquity, and a redistributive structure like that, surely you would expect to recognize that situation archaeologically? One should be able to find that pattern of redistribution from certain types of surviving artefacts and the sites of storage places. One would expect a hierarchy of settlement if you do have vertical redistribution.

HOOKE: They haven't excavated enough to say you haven't.

CHARLES-EDWARDS: Cheddar is a very grand example of just that.

HINES: Yes, that might be an appropriate example, but we are in the early to mid-seventh century before we actually do get the examples of this sort of thing. My point was not a rhetorical question saying, "Your assumptions are wrong because you haven't found the archaeological evidence"; it is rather suggesting again that the question of function hasn't been sufficiently consistently asked of the evidence.

HOOKE: Nobody is necessarily claiming antiquity for that particular type of estate management. I am not.

POWLESLAND: It's a Middle-Saxon characteristic.

LENDINARA [to Scull]: You provide evidence about that in your paper.

SCULL: Glanville Jones's model envisages considerable antiquity for multiple estates, but the archaeological evidence for Anglo-Saxon England in the seventh century is not consistent with this. If there is a settlement hierarchy with special dependent settlements looking to an estate centre, then it should be archaeologically recognizable; and Middle-Saxon sites such as Flixborough would appear to be higher-status centres which exploit an agrarian rural hinterland. John is saying that if there is such a settlement hierarchy in estate structure, with functionally dependent settlements, then it ought to be recognizable.

There are one or two rural settlements which you might argue are dependent settlements and they do appear to have had specialized functions: it has been suggested that the Ramsbury site in Wiltshire is one of them (Haslam 1980). Theoretically John is right.

CHARLES-EDWARDS: Suppose we had such an estate, and suppose there is a standard shopping list in your food render of what the king or lord wanted to consume; this is evident in charters. Is it going to be recognizable in the archaeological record unless he makes a distinction between one settlement and another: unless he says, "I want this and that from this or that settlement"? If everything is being redistributed you may not recognize dependent settlements.

SCULL: I'm talking about the model as I understand it, not necessarily arguing for it. My understanding of the model is that there would be different shopping lists for different constituents of the estate.

FOWLER: Can I come in with an example from the other end of that period which you may say is not relevant. In the North, we have to use the Bolden Book instead of

Domesday Book. Now, it can be argued that when you look at the estates there—and I'm thinking of the bishop of Durham's in particular—that you are looking at a late version of a multiple estate. There are two concepts here to answer the questions that have been raised. One is that it looks as if the bishop of Durham's estate was not put together in the way that has just been envisaged. That is that the estate is made up of components which are scattered across the landscape, each one of which has to produce the needs of the king. It's actually the other way around. The king, or in this case the bishop, requires a range of resources and looks around the landscape to find the places which produce the resources which in total, one by one plus one plus one, support the bishop. To take an extreme example. One of the things that the bishop required was to have recreation, i.e. hunt, and some of the best examples of the basis of what looks like a multiple estate are on the bishop's land in the Durham Dales. There, are certain holdings which make absolutely no sense unless they are seen in terms of the whole of the bishop's properties. In one there is one man living in a building which is mentioned, and his duty is to supply a dog and to make sure that everything is ready when the bishop chooses to come. Now that's a 'service', not a food render but a very specific purpose for a clearly defined area of land.

The other question that was asked was "Can we recognize such a part of a multiple estate?" Well in this case I say quite definitely, "No". As part of the project up there in Weardale and in the north Tyne area, we did try to locate on the ground these specific bits of this multiple estate, not for the reasons pertaining here, but because the theory was that if we could find these places then we might find well-preserved bits of landscape in which there would be good archaeological preservation because there would only have been hunting over the years, no ploughing. We totally failed; although we had a place-name like Muddleswick, there was nothing distinctive about those landscapes in archaeological terms, like a bank or ditch around, them or a particular form. We looked and did not find, yet the documentary evidence is absolutely wonderful. There was just nothing.

SCULL: There is an interesting dichotomy here between the two views of the multiple estate. On the one hand the idea that things were very tightly controlled, and on the other the view that there is free enterprise and that the nature of the control was in the right to extraction rather than the right to control everything. Maybe we should be looking at that second model.

FOWLER: I wish I could feel confident in that sort of thing. Bolden Book is locationally very extensive over Northumbria; the bishop's and other estates are dotted around all over the area. I just wish that we had confidence that we could project the pattern retrogressively back to 900 never mind to 600.

HOOKE: What you're implying is that archaeology will never supply us with the answers.

POWLESLAND: If archaeology supplies some of the answers, historians will never have the courage to believe them. [Laughter].

FOWLER: You'll never answer questions of tenure. That's the important thing.

References in the discussion

Textual sources:

Menologium: see Dobbie 1942

Bibliography:

Balkwill, C.
    1993   Old English *wīc* and the origins of the Hundred. *Landscape History* 15: 5-12.
Barrow, G. W. S.
    1973   *The Kingdom of the Scots*. London: Edwin Arnold.
Cameron, K.
    1988   *English Place-Names*. [Rev. ed.]. London: Batsford.
Cox, B.
    1976   See References at end of paper.
Dobbie, E. van K.
    1942   *The Anglo-Saxon Minor Poems*. New York/London: Columbia University Press/Routledge & Kegan Paul.
Frere, S.
    1987   *Britannia*. [3rd ed.]. London: Routledge & Kegan Paul.
Haslam, J.
    1980   A middle Saxon iron smelting site at Ramsbury, Wiltshire. *Medieval Archaeology* 24: 1-68.
Jones, G. R. J.
    1976   See References at end of paper.
Lot, F.
    1921   Conjectures démographiques sur la France au IXe siècle. *Le Moyen Age* 32: 109-137.

EARLY ANGLO-SAXON SETTLEMENTS, STRUCTURES, FORM AND LAYOUT

DOMINIC POWLESLAND

Heslerton Parish Project, The Old Abbey, Yeddingham, Yorkshire, GB-YO17 8SW

Although some hundreds of early Anglo-Saxon cemeteries have been identified in southern and eastern England over the last one hundred and fifty years, the same cannot be said for the contemporary settlements. Even though the number of well-documented and fully excavated cemeteries is small, the situation in respect of settlements is far worse. The record of over three hundred years of post-Roman occupation, the formative years of English society, is so biased towards funerary evidence that it can to some extent be summed up as merely a pile of pots and old brooches and their associated typologies.

Historians have attempted to create a romantic 'Dark Ages' populated with Hengest, Horsa, Arthur and others derived from late, essentially speculative and politically biased documents designed more to demonstrate the supremacy of Wessex than to chronicle precisely the formation of English society. The late documents and cemetery evidence have been drawn upon to provide the basis for elaborative invasion theories according to the fashion of the day. At various times, place-name evidence has been invoked to play a supporting role for either invasion or mass migration theories, and yet these very place-names which so perfectly demonstrate either the acceptance or imposition of Anglo-Saxon language are again mostly documented very late in the Anglo-Saxon period.

It is unfortunate that our understanding of late-Roman Britain is likewise so poor, so that an understanding of the transition from Roman to Saxon remains the least understood part of the sequence, providing little of the context for what appears to be a massive social and economic change.

The lack of contemporary documentary evidence means that only archaeology can provide a sound basis for a social and economic reconstruction of the period. Only when a balanced archaeological record has been generated will we have the raw materials for a detailed analysis of early Anglo-Saxon society, trade and economy. If the historical models that we construct are not to be mere toys, then the models require detailed testing based on the use of the archaeological sources. If we cannot correlate the archaeological and historical sources then we need to exercise considerable caution if we are to avoid generating insupportable and dogmatic views of the Early Anglo-Saxon period. The archaeology of early Anglo-Saxon England offers exciting research challenges on account of the paucity of the evidence that has accrued as well as opportunities for fundamental discoveries pertaining to the transition from Roman to Saxon.

The present position is however, less bleak than it may at first appear. Excavations at Mucking, West Heslerton and a handful of other sites have provided an insight into early Anglo-Saxon settlement and economy that offers the

THE ANGLO-SAXONS FROM THE MIGRATION PERIOD TO THE EIGHTH CENTURY:
AN ETHNOGRAPHIC PERSPECTIVE

© C.I.R.O.S.S.
San Marino (R.S.M.)

potential to redress the current imbalance in the record (Jones 1973; 1979). Leaving aside the issues of invasion/colonization, recent scholarship, in attempting to redress an essentially isolated English view, has looked more to the Continent to provide a contextual framework for the interpretation of early Anglo-Saxon settlement. However, we must be careful in attempting to identify the Continental model in the English context; the continuity of the Continental Iron Age within the Anglo-Saxon homelands contrasts with the picture in Britain, where the period of Roman occupation and subsequent romanization radically changed the political, social and economic landscape. There has been much discussion of continuity/discontinuity between Roman and Saxon in the urban context; however the broader questions concerning the late Roman to early Anglo-Saxon transition have remained unanswered.

Roman to Saxon: a cultural transition?

Material culture, settlement structure and morphology, patterns of trade and exchange, and rituals associated with death and burial would appear to be quite different in the Early Anglo-Saxon from those in the Roman period. What is less clear are the differences between, for instance, the situation at AD 350 and that at AD 450. Recent work in towns has produced a wealth of evidence concerning the decline of the urban centres during the fourth century AD. Evidence from the countryside, however, has been less forthcoming, simply as a function of work undertaken rather than a lack of available known sites. A tendency for fieldwork to be concentrated upon the examination of Roman towns, villas and military sites has given us little insight into rural life for large tracts of the country in that period. There is considerable evidence for a shift in settlement in the post-Roman period, a shift which can be demonstrated over wide areas of lowland Britain. The mechanics and reasons behind this 'Early Saxon shuffle', as we may call it, are not well understood. The evidence indicates that there is a major shift in settlement by a majority of early Anglo-Saxon settlements, not over their Roman predecessors, but to apparently deserted or *de-novo* sites. What is clear is that this shift in settlement appears not to be localized; rather that it occurs widely over the area of early Anglo-Saxon settlement.

The roots of this shift however, need not be an early Anglo-Saxon phenomenon. Work at West Heslerton indicates that this shift may have been initiated during the late Roman period. Elsewhere in the Vale of Pickering, sample excavations on an Iron-age and Roman linear settlement on the southern margins of the valley, but about a kilometre north of the geomorphological zone occupied by the West Heslerton settlement, indicate that during the latter stages of occupation at the site, which, importantly, does include a number of early Grubenhäuser, there were severe ground water problems. Despite a rising water table, occupation continued under increasingly adverse conditions; it is surprising that the settlement was not deserted in favour of a better drained location. That the settlement remained static in a declining environment may indicate that other factors restricted settlement mobility, perhaps the pattern of landholding. We seem to be without any clear model which covers the transition from Roman to Saxon at the overall population level; the concept of a largely depopulated post-Roman landscape taken over by an overwhelming immigrant population seems insupportable.

The evidence now emerging through human bone studies from a number of cemeteries indicates that, in some cases at least, distinctive features make it possible to discriminate to some degree between native and non-native individuals, or perhaps more precisely between physically distinctive groups which may or may not represent Anglian and native. Whilst it has been possible to identify physical differences amongst some of the male burials this has been less feasible with the females; in addition, generally poor bone preservation means that ratios between the groups cannot be securely quantified (Powlesland & Haughton n.d.). That there is a social and economic relationship between these two groups is indicated at West Heslerton by the presence of weapons accompanying the burials of a group of distinctive taller and more slender individuals; these are presumed to represent the 'Anglian' members of the community.

If we are to argue for an initial Germanic population of clients to late-Roman masters, then at what point and through what mechanism does this role reverse, as the distinctive material culture of the early Anglo-Saxon cemeteries indicates it has done? If on the other hand we are to argue for a mass migration, then where is the archaeological evidence? If the evidence is the widespread acceptance of Anglo-Saxon material culture, then we must also attempt to identify the level of migration at the beginning of the Roman period when a radically different material culture was introduced and evidently immediately accepted. Whatever the case, by the end of the fifth century the material culture of a large part of former Roman Britain had effectively been completely displaced by the distinctive mix that is early Anglo-Saxon in character.

Disregarding the questions of urban continuity and looking only at the countryside, the differences are perhaps less than we tend to suppose. The most striking changes in the archaeological record are in the ceramics and evidence of long-distance trade on the one hand, and a change in the preferred structural types and building technology on the other, although, even here, the antecedents for the early Anglo-Saxon post-built structures are as likely to be native and British as Continental. If we disregard changes in ceramic technology and the question of trade patterns we are left with a very much smaller comparative assemblage, in which the dominant early Anglo-Saxon metalwork may be viewed not as totally different but as a development from what went on before. Other material such as worked bone items show a continued sequence of development extending back into the Iron Age. From this we may argue that the principal differences between the romanized British and early Anglo-Saxon material cultures is a radical change in trade networks following the complete collapse of the economy of the later Roman Empire in the West.

If we are to argue that the early Anglo-Saxon material culture is imported and imposed from the Continental homelands then this should be reflected in all aspects of the material culture not simply in the pots and brooches, and this is not necessarily the case. The evidence from the settlements is crucial in determining the cultural relationship between the Anglo-Saxons and the Angles, Saxons, Frisians and Jutes on the Continent, and the presence of brooch-types and other items of adornment found in the cemeteries need not indicate more than a change in fashion or a change in the trade network, a trade network that is as likely to have included the export of hybrid Anglo-Saxon material and ideas as well as imports from the Continent.

The collapse of the urban economy of late Roman Britain is now well documented through excavations at a number of sites. That this collapse occurs effectively entirely within a late Roman rather than an early Anglo-Saxon context is of great importance if we are to try to identify the differences between the immediately post-Roman and early Anglo-Saxon settings, and it is particularly unfortunate that the archaeological record for the immediately post-Roman period is currently so limited.

With the collapse of the urban economy and with it of a substantial portion of the trade network and industrial base, as exemplified by the ceramics industry, a reversion to an 'Iron Age' type of rural economy has to be envisaged. The late occupancy argued for some of the Roman villas need not preclude a rural reversion since even where occupation occurs late in the sequence, the role of the villas may have radically changed as their economic base must certainly have done. The emergence of the early Anglo-Saxon settlements need not be seen, in the light of a rural reversion, as anything more than a natural development within a newly established trade and economic base focused on northern Europe rather than on the Roman world.

Early Anglo-Saxon settlements: distinctive features

Although there are only a handful of extensively and well-documented excavations of early Anglo-Saxon settlements, isolated features and fragments of settlements have been examined throughout the area of early Anglo-Saxon occupation.

The preference for building in timber and a limited range of building plans and styles has left a remarkably limited but uniform range of archaeological features. The distinctive nature of the principal components of these settlements are such that when encountered they can be readily assigned to the Early Anglo-Saxon period.

There are three classes of feature that can easily be identified and which form the principal physical components of these settlements. These are briefly summarized below:

a) **Grubenhäuser**
The Grubenhaus is the most distinctive structure from sites of this period. They are found widely in Britain in early Anglo-Saxon settlements and are paralleled by

a wealth of broadly similar examples on the Continent from which the structural form is derived.[1]

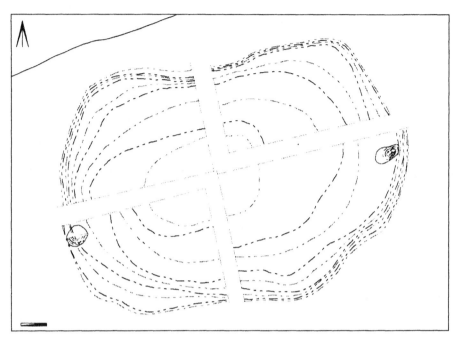

Fig. 4-1: Plan of a Grubenhaus from West Heslerton, North Yorkshire.

The Grubenhaus was the first structural feature of Anglo-Saxon settlements to be identified in this country, and, following their identification at Sutton Courtney in 1922, they were initially thought to represent the housing of the period (Leeds 1936). They are distinctive not only on account of their form, a subrectangular steep-sided pit with post-holes against the sides at either end, but also on account of their fills which generally contain high volumes of rubbish in an organically enriched but relatively uniform fill sequence. Where animal bone survives it is usually the dominant inclusion. These ubiquitous features have been interpreted in a wealth of different ways but have remained remarkably little understood; recent work, however, indicates that we have tended in the past to make too close a connection between the contents of the features and their supposed function (Jones 1979:53-9).

Even the exact mode of construction has been the subject of debate since their initial discovery. There is considerable variation in the scale of these features, which can be as small as two metres square and as large as eight metres by five. The suggestion that these structures were crudely built tent-like constructions is

---

[1] The term SFB meaning 'Sunken Featured Building' is not used here since the letters SFB may be mistaken to mean 'Sunken Floored Building', a term now considered to be inappropriate (Rahtz 1971).

not supported by the evidence of carefully squared timbers utilized in one of the West Heslerton examples. The discovery of carbonized timbers at West Stow, demonstrating that at least some of these structures were cavity floor buildings, is of great significance. At West Heslerton only in one of 115 such structures was there even a hint of wear in the base of the pit, which hardly indicates the use of the base of the pit as a floor.

An obvious use for these structures substantiated by plant macro-fossil evidence from West Heslerton is as grain storage buildings, in which the dry air space beneath the cavity floor is an essential component. Their function as weaving-sheds, suggested in the past on account of the distribution of loom-weights in their fills, seems insupportable in the light of other material derived from these features: these items, almost always unfired and made from locally available clay, must surely simply be discards. The remainder of the assemblages from these features tend to be dominated by animal bone, occasionally whole carcasses and often articulated sections. The accumulations of rotting animal bones, dog faeces etc. which make up the larger part of the material derived from these features are important on account of their single period, or even single event, nature and also for what they reveal about discard policy on these sites. The lack of evidence for latrines and the general lack of discarded material in the 'housing areas' indicates that this part of settlement was well maintained and generally kept clean. Given

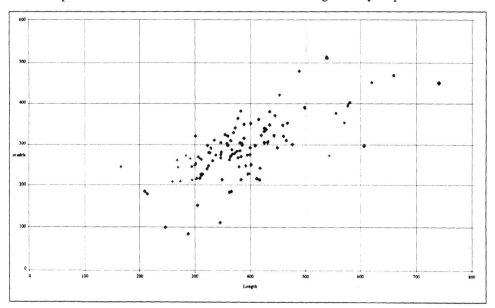

Fig. 4-2: Scatter diagram showing the length to breadth ratio of Grubenhäuser at West Heslerton, North Yorkshire.

the lack of latrines and or cess pits, night soiling was presumably practised if so, it is likely that a considerable body of other material evidence may have been discarded beyond the confines of the settlement itself. It remains to be seen from the analysis of the ceramics what the average vessel percentage recovered was, as this may help in determining a rough guide to the level of off-site disposal.

The considerable variation in scale and the high frequency of these features as well as their distribution suggests that we should take a flexible view of their function: some were almost certainly grain storage buildings, while others seem to have served as more generalized storage buildings which may have been associated with crafts such as spinning and weaving. One thing we can be reasonably certain of is that these structures did not provide housing.

b) **Rectangular post-hole structures**

Rectangular post-hole structures were first identified on sites of this period in the 1960s and since then the excavations at West Heslerton, Cowdery's Down, West Stow, Charlton, Mucking and other sites have provided data which indicate that these were built using a limited series of uniform designs at a small variety of scales (Addyman *et al.* 1973; Millett 1983; West 1985). In the Middle Saxon period true post-hole structures appear in some cases to be superseded by post-in-trench structures which follow the same general plan but utilize a different constructional technique at ground level.

The structural forms utilized in England are remarkable on account of the widespread use of almost identical ground plans and also by the complete lack of any Continental-style aisled longhouses. The lack of Continental-style longhouses may perhaps be attributed to a difference in the agricultural regime in which there was less need for winter stabling or byres as part of the structure. There is as yet no evidence for the use of any of the English examples as byres, whilst the lack of the Continental-style buildings which combine housing for both people and animals indicates a radically different agrarian economy.

Although a small number of Continental sites include small post-hole structures, their plans and constructional techniques are somewhat different from those found in England, one major difference being the lack of hearths in all but one example in England. In this case, West Stow, Hall 2, the inclusion of the hearth is a feature only identified in the final report where discussion is minimal. Dixon has observed that while the roots of the early Anglo-Saxon building tradition can be identified within structures on some of the Continental sites, the Anglo-Saxon type should perhaps best be seen as a localized hybrid combining local with Continental influences (Dixon 1988). It is not implausible that the presence of similar post-built structures in the Continental context could reflect influences from Britain rather than the reverse; the exceptional difficulties in dating material from this period makes the tracking of influences in any direction speculative in any case.

The construction methods employed indicate sophisticated carpentry skills and, although there is considerable debate as to the nature of the superstructures of these buildings, they frequently incorporate evidence of the innovative use of multiple plank uprights to create strong yet flexible structures (James *et al.* 1984). The subject of early Anglo-Saxon building design has been much discussed recently with a number of sophisticated reconstructions being offered. Whilst appealing, the elaborate reconstructions put forward by James, Marshall and

Millett are not the only solutions. A detailed re-assessment of building plans undertaken by Heather Clemence as part of an undergraduate thesis has revealed that although there is considerable variation in building length, the breadth of the structures rarely exceeds 4.5m (Clemence 1993). This evidence strongly supports the use of tie-beam construction, the limiting factor being the size of timbers available for tie-beams. A distinctive feature of many of the larger buildings is the use of an internal cross-wall not much more than a metre from one of the end walls, perhaps indicating that these structures incorporated an upper storey accessed via a stair well between the end-wall and adjacent cross-wall. Another aspect which has considerable bearing upon the potential for interpretation of structural function is the preference for supported timber floors. There is not a single structure known from early Anglo-Saxon England where the presence of an earth or mortar floor can be demonstrated; not even where the old ground surface remains relatively intact in one part of West Heslerton was there any evidence that floor joists were situated at ground level. The potential for examining the use of space within these structures is, therefore, currently zero; only when a burnt down or waterlogged example has been identified will we be able to investigate the use of interior space in these structures.

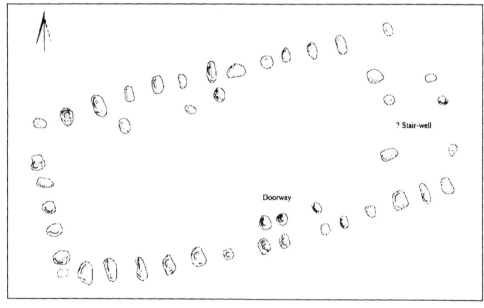

Fig. 4-3: Posthole structure from West Heslerton, North Yorkshire.

c) Cooking or fire pits

The third type of feature which seems to be distinctive of the Anglian areas at least, is small subrectangular fire pits which occur in external locations with no clear association with any particular structure, and which are found extensively on the Continent, at West Heslerton, West Stow (where they are assigned to the prehistoric period), Catterick and a number of other sites (West 1990). These pits, which are generally small, measuring little more than a metre long by 50 centimetres wide and deep, contain large quantities of charcoal and fire-cracked stone and appear to represent cooking pits ideal for barbecuing sides of meat. Their occurrence in relatively small numbers and their distribution with no very obvious structural association raises questions regarding their broader function: are they a product of special feasts or ritual meals? At West Heslerton fewer than ten examples have been identified; at West Stow there were only five, which thus cannot have provided for daily cooking. The question of food preparation and diet is rarely raised beyond the broadest terms in archaeological reports and yet tremendous resources are put into the detailed examination of the faunal remains looking for butchery marks and so on. The presence of nearly a million animal bones from the excavation at West Heslerton tends to lead us towards assumptions about the importance of meat in the diet merely on account of the tremendous visibility of the faunal material. If we view the livestock as mobile wealth more important for its wool, milk and traction power, as it so often is in agrarian economies, then we should be careful in our assessment of the faunal material. It must be of interest that the last meals of so many of the late Iron-age bog bodies reflect a diet of porridge rather than of pork.

Farmstead, village or town in early Anglo-Saxon England

Whilst the standard components that comprise the bulk of the features found in early Anglo-Saxon settlement sites are distinctive enough not to go unrecognized, the lack of totally excavated sites means that our comprehension of settlement layout is minimal. The difficulty in dating early Anglo-Saxon deposits in particular, and the limited number of well-documented examples, make interpretation of settlement planning, development, and economy unusually challenging. The choice of *de-novo* or abandoned sites and the open nature of the settlements which seem generally to have been deserted by the end of the Middle Saxon period have not facilitated the development of deep stratigraphic sequences. This, coupled with the generally short duration of occupation, has exacerbated the problems of reconstructing the sequence of development of these sites particularly. The choice of situations, generally located on sands and gravels and on the margins of the heavier soils, has meant that many of the sites have been discovered during mineral extraction with the archaeological deposits having been truncated either by ploughing or by topsoil removal, making spatial analysis and the interpretation of the use of space difficult on most sites and impossible on others.

Attempts to define social hierarchies in the excavated cemeteries have led some to identify highly stratified societies, something which has not left an obvious record in the settlements. In one recent work, Higham has even suggested that the Anglo-Saxon settlements only represent the élite portion of the population, the remainder as yet unidentified in the archaeological record, an insupportable and unlikely view from an otherwise good scholar (Higham 1993).

A variety of different models of settlement development have been proposed, ranging from simple farmsteads comprising a small group of structures which move around in the landscape as each phase is replaced as at West Stow, to what appears to be a planned settlement at West Heslerton where the settlement is divided into a number of distinctive functional zones. Clearly much of the debate which relates to settlement morphology is fuelled by the lack of well-documented and well-dated excavation sites: only at Mucking and West Heslerton can we argue that at least most of the settlement area has been examined, and in the latter case this currently excludes what is seen as the high-status core of the site.

Air photography has revealed a complex of post-hole structures at Sutton Courtney, Oxon, which is situated at some distance from the areas examined by E.T. Leeds in the 1930s and may form an integral part of a site of similar layout to West Heslerton. At West Stow it is not clearly demonstrated that the full extent of the settlement was examined. The evidence from both Mucking and West Heslerton reveals that these sites can be very large indeed and that the density of features is often relatively low; it is important that at both these sites very large areas were stripped and that the relative distribution of Grubenhäuser and post-hole structures shows remarkable variation.

It is unfortunate that Hamerow devoted so little space to the discussion of the post-hole structures in the Mucking report since the evidence from West Heslerton and, indeed, from the Mucking plans does not fully support the hypothesis that substantial numbers of post-hole buildings were simply not observed during the excavation (Hamerow 1993). This view seems to derive from a feeling that a lack of post-hole structures in some parts of the site was a function of poor observation rather than a true picture. Since any model of settlement morphology must take on board a social and economic dimension, it is clear that the difference between settlements merely represented by the occasional farmstead and sites such as West Heslerton indicates a radically different social pattern behind the 'planned', or at least deliberately laid out, settlements. The evidence from West Heslerton raises a wealth of new questions that indicate a need for a radical reappraisal of early Anglo-Saxon settlement patterns.

If we can see a remarkable uniformity in the structural styles employed in these settlements, as indeed we can, then it would be unsurprising if we were also to identify a similar and equally sophisticated overall structure within the settlements of which these structures form a part. If we are to argue for planned or organized development, then is this displayed by the components which combine to form the settlement, and what status can we reliably assign to these sites? The example from West Heslerton is particularly important because it appears to be just one of a number; there is no evidence that the site possessed special status such as that of Yeavering—rather it seems somehow to lack any particular status and yet the overall picture emerging is that here we have what may be described as a proto-type village or even proto-type town (Hope-Taylor 1977). Do we see in the settlement examples of co-operative behaviour or social domination by an élite, and if so does this incorporate a physical presence in the form of structural layout?

The settlement covered an area of some 20 ha and was occupied, possibly continuously, from the late fourth century until the late eighth or early ninth centuries. What is less clear at present is to what extent there was true continuity and to what extent this is reflected in the continued occupancy of an appreciable population. It appears at present that there may have been a considerable fluctuation of population, with few in the late Roman period and again few in the Middle Saxon period. Whatever the case, by the end of the sixth century the settlement reached its fullest extent. The layout of the settlement includes a number of distinctive zones with a stream running from the heart of the settlement through the centre of the site; a similar example may be suggested for the site at Sykeham a few kilometres away on the northern side of the Vale of Pickering (Moore 1966). Preliminary analysis of the plan and associated material culture indicates that the site can be broken into five basic components.

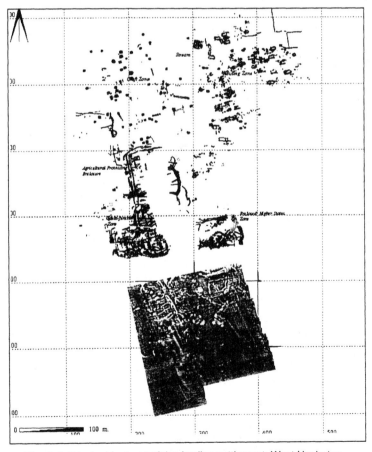

Fig. 4-4: Principal features of the Anglian settlement, West Heslerton.

- A housing area to the east of the stream channel.
- A craft/industrial zone covering much of the north-western area.
- A crop and livestock processing area on the western bank of the stream, re-using part of the late-Roman enclosure sequence.
- A multi-function zone adjacent to the west of the spring that provided the source of the stream.
- A regularly enclosed area, which appears to have had a higher status, to the east and above the spring,

Housing zone

More than 75 post-hole structures have been examined, all but three being of post-hole rather than post-in-trench construction, and the majority being located in the area to the east of the stream channel. For the most part, there were no indications of any physical property boundaries in the form of fence lines and gullies; had these existed, evidence would have survived in the parts of the site where the old ground surface had effectively been protected from erosion by aeolian sands and hill-wash deposits. Associated with these post-hole structures were a small number of Grubenhäuser, fire-pits and a few other pits, mostly a by-product of small-scale quarrying activity to recover iron-enriched chalk which was preferred as a matrix for furnace construction.

Although a natural hollow ran through the area there was only limited evidence of paths and tracks. The majority of the structures respected each other and rebuilding on the same site appears to be limited to two phases. A number of the Grubenhäuser were evidently replaced by post-hole structures, which probably served the same function. Carbonized grain recovered from the area appears on an initial scan to have incorporated more wheat than the grains from other parts of the site, which gives some support to the suggestion that the Grubenhäuser in the area served primarily as grain storage buildings. By comparison with other parts of the site this zone produced very little material, the evidence indicating that all the structures had had supported floors and that the whole area was kept clean and well maintained. Small pits located just inside the wall lines at one end of a number of structures may represent foundation deposits.

Craft/industry zone

This area, which comprised more than 50 Grubenhäuser contained not a single post-hole structure. The scale of the Grubenhäuser varied from a single tiny example less than 2 metres square to the large example examined measuring 7.5 by 4.5 metres, bigger in floor area than some of the post-hole structures. Also located in this area were a number of metal-working furnaces, a malt kiln, and tremendous quantities of rubbish, particularly animal bone. These rubbish deposits had survived to a remarkable degree sealed beneath the headland of a later field system, thus amplifying the apparent differences between this and the 'housing zone'.

Agricultural processing zone

This area, defined by a sub-rectangular enclosure of Roman origin, contained only a few cut features including a Middle-Saxon post-in-trench structure in the north-

west corner and post holes indicating a single structure in the interior and a third in
the south-west corner. The interpretation that this served mainly as an agricultural
processing area has been given some support from the assessment of the plant
macro-fossil evidence.

Multi-function zone

In the southern part of the settlement the picture is more mixed, with a combination of
post-hole structures, Grubenhäuser and extensive evidence of industrial activity. The
complex of enclosures established in this area during the late Roman period continued
to be redefined during the Early Anglo-Saxon period, but were ultimately replaced by a
series of fenced enclosures during the Middle Saxon period which show remarkable
similarity to those established at Catholme, Staffs. (Losco-Bradley 1974). This area,
located to the west of the spring and stream, was somewhat less regular than that to the
east, perhaps indicating a lesser degree of control over the development.

Enclosed higher status zone

To the east of the spring at the most elevated position, a series of radiating
enclosures, with their focus in an unexcavated area to the south, showed a regular
sequence of development. Just to the north of this area an area of clay was without
any features and may perhaps have supported woodland providing an effective
barrier demarcating this area from the rest of the site. The cultural material derived
from this area spans the complete life of the settlement and includes a higher than
usual frequency of glass and metalwork and a different faunal assemblage.

To the south the enclosures, identified through a gradiometer survey, are arranged
around a central core which may form the political centre of the settlement. Once
again the features displayed in the geophysical survey indicated that the western
half of the area is less organized and more cluttered than that to the east.

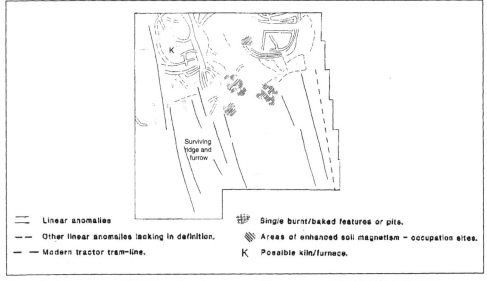

Fig. 4-5: Interpretation of the Magnetometer Survey of the southern part of the West Heslerton
settlement. English Heritage, Ancient Monuments Laboratory, Geophysical Survey.

Conclusion

The detailed recording procedures that were employed at West Heslerton offer us opportunities for spatial analysis not possible with other data sets from sites of this period but this work has yet to take place. If we are to build any models for the development and functioning of these settlements then it is to the spaces between the structures that we should look rather than simply looking at the structures themselves.

It would be stretching the point to describe any of these settlements as 'urban' in character, although many of the features used later to define urban centres can be applied to these sites. Clearly, settlements like Mucking, Essex, West Heslerton, North Yorkshire, and Sutton Courtney, Oxon, are of such a scale that they acted as central places, maintaining, one assumes, extensive agricultural land-holdings. Although the population of these centres was probably no more than between one and two hundred at most, this is a great deal more significant that if we are dealing only with large farmsteads. Agriculture was important, not only for day to day food supplies but also for supporting the wool-producing livestock that offered the potential for surplus production of trade items.

That trade was significant is shown by the quantity of material from further afield, whether it be cowrie shells from the Red Sea, hone-stones from northern Scandinavia, or even ivory purse rings, that is found in both the settlements and cemeteries in numbers suggesting that these are not merely survivals from the Roman period. The role of wool and textile production as a generator of surplus is probably overstated simply because of the famous letters between Offa and Charlemagne which document the 'cloth for stones' trade in which textiles were traded, almost certainly for Mayen lava quern stones.

The quantities of spinning and weaving debris are significant enough to register, but they are not overwhelming and should perhaps be seen as substantially concerned with production for local needs rather than for trade. So much of the interpretation of textile production has depended on the relative weight given to this part of the assemblage and a tendency by finds specialists in the past to view their materials in isolation from the assemblages as a whole. Whether the population travelled to beach-markets on the coast for trading purposes or whether travelling salesmen, as we would know them today, travelled from village to village we have no idea, but large settlements do provide a context for both long distance and short-distance trade.

The lack of documentary evidence for the early period makes assessment of the legal status of these sites impossible, although the later practice of strengthening urban control through legal restrictions to trading and legal processes which could only be undertaken within the *burhs* may represent a formalized process of population and land control. Unless the area interpreted as an agricultural processing area at West Heslerton also served as a 'village green' there is no obvious open public place within these settlements, nor is there evidence of any 'ritual space', streets or defences.

The separation between housing and craft/storage/industry over the northern half of the settlement could perhaps be a function not of deliberate planning but of intelligent development in which the population chose to live upwind of the stench of rotting carcasses, burning furnaces etc. on the opposite side of the stream. One could perhaps identify planning in the way that the structures are laid out, almost all being aligned east-west with plentiful space around them; this incidentally being a feature of other sites as well. There seems to be some correlation between the distribution of the Grubenhäuser related to the post-hole structures in the housing area; here, groups of Grubenhäuser extend away from the main post-hole structures, perhaps indicating a land-holding unit that extended from the stream channel to the more elevated post-hole structures beyond; the picture is, however, far too incoherent and may of course change radically once detailed examination of the cultural material has been completed. The lack of physical boundaries and streets which are fundamental in the definition of the later '*burh*' is significant and could be used to argue that while the settlement is organized it was not planned in a formal fashion.

Whether we see sites like West Heslerton and Mucking as proto-villages or not, what is clear is that the early Anglo-Saxon settlements were well organized, well maintained and formed part of a sophisticated network of trade and exchange. From a purely structural point of view they display a remarkable degree of uniformity, indicating an unanticipated degree of social equality. The symbols of wealth that dominate the assemblages from cemeteries appear so far to be absent from the settlement record, or at least our interpretation of it.

It is unfortunate that at West Heslerton the one area that offers the potential for examining the Roman-Saxon interface, a portion that appears to be of different status to the rest of the site and the one area where the relationship between Early and Middle Saxon can be examined in detail, remains unexcavated at the time of writing. The rise of the early settlements and the decline and shift in the middle Saxon period remains as enigmatic a question as that of the location of their latrines, and only further excavation and re-examination of older data sets can help us move forward. If, as I am convinced, the scale and layout of West Heslerton is the norm rather than the exception, we will have to re-evaluate the evidence from all the sites that have produced settlement evidence if we are not to do the early Anglo-Saxon population the same sort of injustice served out by E. T. Leeds in his description of a people living in "something that hardly deserves a better title than a hovel" (Leeds 1936:21).

References

Bibliography:

Addyman, P. V. A., D. Leigh & M. J. Hughes
  1973   The Anglo-Saxon houses at Chalton, Hampshire. *Medieval Archaeology* 17: 13-31.

Clemence, H.
    1993   The Timber-Framed Structures at West Heslerton Anglo-Saxon Settlement:
                Analysis and Comparison. Unpublished undergradute dissertation,
                Nottingham University, Dept. of Archaeology.

Dixon, P. W.
    1988   How Saxon is the Saxon house? In *Structural Reconstruction: Approaches
                to the Interpretation of Excavated Remains of Buildings.* P. Drury (ed.), pp.
                275-296. (British Archaelogical Series 100). Oxford: BAR.

Hamerow, H.
    1993   *Excavations at Mucking, Vol. 2: The Anglo-Saxon Settlement.* (English
                Heritage Research Report 21). London: English Heritage.

Higham, N. J.
    1992   *Rome, Britain and the Anglo-Saxons.* London: Seaby.

Hope-Taylor, B.
    1977   *Yeavering: an Anglo-Saxon Centre for early Northumbria.* London:
                H.M.S.O.

James, S. T., A. Marshall & M. Millett
    1984   An early medieval building tradition. *Archaeological Journal* 141: 182-215.

Jones, M. U.
    1973   An ancient landscape palimpsest at Mucking. *Essex Archaeology and
                History* 5: 6-12.
    1979   Saxon sunken huts: Problems of interpretation. *Archaeological Journal*
                136: 53-59

Leeds, E. T.
    1936   *Early Anglo-Saxon Art and Archaeology.* Oxford: Clarendon Press.

Losco-Bradley, S.
    1974   The Anglo-Saxon settlement at Catholme, Staffordshire. *Trent Valley
                Archaeological Committee Report,* 8.

Millett, M.
    1983   Excavations at Cowdery's Down, Basingstoke, Hants., 1978-1981.
                Archaeological Journal 140: 151-178.

Moore, J. W.
    1966   An Anglo-Saxon Settlement at Wykeham, North Yorkshire. *Yorkshire
                Archaeological Journal* 41: 403-444.

Powlesland, D. J.
    1989   West Heslerton 1989, The Anglian Settlement, an Interim Report.
                Unpublished mss.

Powlesland, D. J., & C. A. Haughton
    n.d.   *West Heslerton - The Anglian Cemetery.* (English Heritage Monograph).
                London: English Heritage.

Powlesland, D. J., C. A. Haughton & J. H. Hanson
    1986   Excavations at Heslerton, North Yorkshire, 1978-82. *Archaeological Journal*
                143: 53-173.

Pye, G. R.
    1976   Excavations at Crossgates, near Scarborough in 1957-65. *Transactions of
                the Scarborough Archaeological and History Society* 3/19: 1-22.

1983 Further Excavations at Crossgates near Scarborough 1966-1981. *Transactions of the Scarborough Archaeological and Historical Society.* 3/25: 3-12.

Rahtz, P. A.
1971 Buildings and rural settlement. In *The Archaeology of Anglo-Saxon England.* D. M. Wilson (ed.), pp. 49-98. London: Methuen.

Rutter, J. G., & G. Duke
1958 Excavations at Crossgates near Scarborough 1947-56. *Scarborough and District Archaeological Society, Res. Rep. 1.*

West, S. E.
1985 *The Anglo-Saxon village at West Stow*, vols. 1 & 2. (East Anglian Archaeology 24). Ipswich: Suffolk County Planning Department.

1990 *West Stow, Suffolk: the prehistoric and Romano-British occupation.* (East Anglian Archaeology 48). Burg St Edmunds: Suffolk County Planning Department.

Wilson, D. M. (ed.)
1976 *The Archaeology of Anglo-Saxon England.* London: Methuen.

Discussion

SCULL: You argued that other sites may be like Heslerton, but appear different because they have only been partially excavated. However, at West Stow, for instance, the structure appears to be different. I do not see on the plan of West Heslerton any area where you have the same ratio of Grubenhäuser to ground-level timber buildings as at West Stow. You have a housing zone which shows a different ratio from West Stow, and you have a craft zone which shows a different ratio. So I wonder if the settlement at West Stow is not genuinely different; both smaller and structured differently.

POWLESLAND: We have an area which is the same as West Stow which is just north of the housing zone. I think you will find the ratios are not much dissimilar.

SCULL: But I do not see on your plan any area the size of West Stow with sixty or seventy sunken-feature buildings and six or seven ground-level buildings. Both size and structural arrangement appear to be different here; and just as we should be careful not to pre-judge West Heslerton according to patterns evident at other sites, so we should be cautious about interpreting other sites in the light of West Heslerton. There may well be diversity; especially regional diversity.

POWLESLAND: I would like to see what we get in this summer's excavations. The bit which is most like West Stow is an area at the southern end of the site.

SCULL: I would like to make two other points: one is to clarify the chronology of the site. Are you saying that the high-status area to the south is Middle-Saxon, and the rest of the site is not?

POWLESLAND: There is the question of what status spans the life of the settlement. I would argue that it starts in the Roman period and goes right the way through. But in the Middle Saxon period the site has contracted to cover about the same area as the Roman.

SCULL: The other point concerns the cemetery. I see no real problem in the supposed dichotomy presented by evidence for ranking in the cemetery but not in the settlement. This is a fairly widespread phenomenon which can be explained by the hypothesis that these communities are composed of more-or-less equal households/families, which are themselves internally ranked (see Hamerow 1993; Scull 1995; Sherlock & Welch 1992). If you do have a high-status focus to the settlement all the way through, then one would look for evidence in the cemetery. And I wonder where your Middle-Saxon cemetery is.

POWLESLAND: I would hope that the Middle-Saxon cemetery would turn up. I am very interested in that, but as yet have no evidence.

FOWLER: On Chris's point about laying one settlement on the other, I understood Dominic to say that one could very specifically relate buildings, not settlement typology. This is a significant point that quite remarkably cuts across the supposed cultural, ethnic and political divisions that there are within this country at 500 AD, 600 or whatever, in terms of the most important thing in people's lives: this remarkable homogeneity in construction.

CHARLES-EDWARDS: I would ask Dominic what he makes of West Stow. What seems striking about organized settlements is that different bits have different functions. Are they all organized but in slightly different ways? You are saying, I think, that West Stow is organized, but organized somewhat differently.

SCULL: What you find at West Stow, in a much smaller area than at Heslerton, is a different ratio of one type of structure to another and a different spatial organization. So my argument is that this may indicate that we are dealing with a different form of settlement, and that it may not simply be a part of a larger Heslerton-like settlement.

POWLESLAND: But I would argue that it is part of a larger settlement. I don't think we have any evidence that suggests it is not.

SCULL: Only the topography, and the excavator's opinion. My point is that the structure at West Stow appears to be different from that at Heslerton, and that such differences between settlements may be worth investigating.

HINES: Your higher status area would seem a rather speculative entity for the moment, with relatively little of it having been excavated. You are very confident in arguing that it was occupied throughout the whole period. Are you as confident that it was of the same status relative to the rest of the site throughout that time?

POWLESLAND: It's late Roman status is implicit in the enclosures, and there is a higher percentage of good stuff turning up here than over the rest of the site: fine metalwork and glass are concentrated down here. There is still heavy metalwork and glass associated with features right out at the extremities, but there seems to be a higher concentration at the southern end.

I would argue that there may be signs here of some sort of manorial grain store. You have four Grubenhäuser contained by a nice little enclosure. The various enclosures there seem to be peripheral to whatever it is that's going on on the other side of the track across the site. We are hoping to excavate this last piece next year; if we can't it is going to be almost impossible to interpret the site in the report.

HINES: You refer, for instance, to the first 'metalworking evidence'. Have you evidence of both bronzeworking and ironworking on the site?

POWLESLAND: We have evidence of ironworking in the so-called crafts zone in three furnace bases and some associated bits of slag and other by-products. We have got one or two bits of mould frames. But we have not got good evidence of bronzeworking by any stretch of the imagination. We have a lot of slag turning up at the southern end of the site for which there is no obvious context.

HINES: So the slag is at the southern end?

POWLESLAND: We've got it in the craft zone and then we have other bits at the southern end which appear to have no particular context, so they may be derived. I would argue that there is a good chance we will find more, I suppose we may call them more important crafts, industrial stuff in the area to the south and west. There were a lot of tiny fragments of furnace-type material over the area to the west of the stream, quite different in nature from the ironwork to the north.

AUSENDA: You mentioned grain storage. Is there any indication for hay storage?

POWLESLAND: Yes, there are hayrick gulleys. It looks as if they had hayrick gulleys all around the outside of the settlement. Another aspect I forgot to mention is that we believe there was a mill. We have geophysics that indicate that they were managing water coming out of the spring. They ran it down first one alignment and then cut across it at almost 90° where the stream channel changes direction. We believe this was to maintain the mill pond.

HOOKE: This is quite early for a mill, isn't it?

POWLESLAND: It would be, yes.

HÄRKE: There are several seventh-century water mills from Ireland. What's the earliest in England? Early eighth-century (at Tamworth and Old Windsor)?

AUSENDA: You wrote of a radical change in trade networks following the complete collapse of the economy of the late Roman Empire in the West. I totally agree with you. As Chris Scull pointed out in his paper, this must have gone on throughout the British Isles during and after the fall of the Western Empire, when there was a major shift in trade. Roman trade was centripetal, probably based on the extraction of strategic raw materials and the slave trade, and it gradually declined to zero, when a new 'tangential' trade gradually developed along peripheral lines to the Continent with the establishment of the *emporia*. Then with your reversion to a more 'Iron-age' rural economy, a return to subsistence economy was probably a major factor in chasing away most romanized Britons who were used to better living conditions.

You also talk about 'night soiling'. If this means what I think it does, having spent a few weeks in a Beja encampment and several months in an east Sudanese village, one should call it 'early morning soiling' [laughter]. I remember my worst problem was keeping growling dogs at bay in the process. Latrines are late even in Western society. In a hamlet in the Alps latrines were unknown until the end of the last century.

Then you mention a "lack of Continental-style longhouses". Perhaps this is due to smaller extended families because of migration. You also mention "craft/industry". Could these be deposits of wood, which must be kept dry or it will rot?

POWLESLAND: What is going on in the Grubenhäuser, I'm really not sure. They do have a very distinctive nature, these deposits, and I think it is just because there is a very high organic component. But in a number of them we have whole carcasses of animals and they must have been absolutely disgusting. They are quickly created deposits containing very high levels of organic material and 90 per cent animal bone. And again coming back to the use of livestock, it is particularly interesting that we've got a number of whole animals represented, because if we see all this stuff as just conventional butchery waste from a large amount of meat eating, how can we get these huge carcasses and complete sheep and cows? The animal-bone specialists can't understand it. I think there are major questions we have to ask about the livestock because it is so crucial to understanding the wider aspect.

FOWLER: I just wondered if one or two generalities might emerge from all these new data which Dominic has put before us. I'm thinking about the relationship between British and Anglians in this case. In the middle of your plan, you've got a double ditch thing, your agricultural processing enclosure, which in morphological terms reminds me straightaway of the non-Anglian enclosures at Yeavering. I'm not sure whether the scale is right, but I did wonder if that was a possible pointer towards one sort of relationship that might be developing here, given your early start in the late fourth century. That may well be the right date for the early phase of Yeavering.

The other one is to take you up on a remark you made and to explore the relationship within another model. As you said, you could apply your interpretation here in other parts of the country, where we have a similar evidence. So I'd invite you to talk your way through this, in terms of the model of the relationship between Anglians and British that you see here.

POWLESLAND: I suppose I should clarify now why I said that. Many sites are excavated just as a fifty-metre square, with a few Grubenhäuser in it, so we can easily say 'right, this site is not dissimilar to that one'. The big question is, do we need to go and investigate these other sites to see if we haven't completely missed the housing zone? I did some experiments in which we randomly sampled the data from this area. You had to have about 25 per cent of the remains before you even found the site properly. So it would be so easy to miss the post-hole area completely unless you work on this scale. Had we started at the opposite corner of the site, we might possibly never have got there. My main worry is that the interpretations that we have across the country are generally based on very small parts of sites. I propose to assess all the other excavated sites, and to compare them, and to try and look forward to trial work on one or two of them. I think Sutton Courtney is the best example for this because the scale of the site is broadly similar.

HÄRKE: I wonder if we want to speculate on the social background to this zoning; it is striking, is it not? It is not exactly what you would expect from what we know so far of early Saxon settlements.

POWLESLAND: I know. I would argue here that Grubenhäuser are not part of the settlements to start with. But the worrying thing is that the settlement seems to indicate a highly homogenized, relatively high-status population in this area. They go to work in the morning to their appropriate sheds and do their thing. The thing that as an excavator I found most striking is that we had good deposits in which things like fences would have survived but there weren't any.

Another aspect which is of some interest is that we certainly have two major construction phases within the early Anglo-Saxon material and we can see a number of Grubenhäuser being replaced by post-hole buildings, while a number of the bigger Grubenhäuser, which can be very large, have exactly the same length-breadth proportions as some of the smaller post-hole buildings. There is some danger in seeing the types as completely separate because a number of the post-hole buildings were also storage sheds and similar things. These are double-storey anyway, the bigger ones. At the moment socially it looks slightly different from the cemetery, and that worries me because I would like to see a very high-status controlling property here which is not defended or well fortified in any way, but does have natural barrier covers; then a great sweep of open settlements on the one side, and this great sweep of general craft and industry and agricultural processing in another place.

HÄRKE: What I am struck by is these kin groups in the cemetery. Could it be that one of these groups is in control of the community, which is why we have the zoning in the settlement rather than individual properties with their ancillary buildings?

POWLESLAND: I agree.

CHARLES-EDWARDS: Could I come back to a question about kin groups that I wanted to raise anyway? Are you identifying them in the cemetery because there is a founder who is earlier, who is of very high status?

POWLESLAND: We have there rectangular groups that cover the whole period of the life of the settlement and all different wealth and property attributes. The groups don't just run continuously all over. There seem to be little clusters and it's easy to conclude we've got six big families and that's jolly good; just what we would like to see.

CHARLES-EDWARDS: I would agree that the servants are in the same place.

POWLESLAND: Servants? I did not mention servants.

CHARLES-EDWARDS: I took your point about tall people buried alongside people who were apparently not Anglian.

POWLESLAND: But I did not say they were necessarily servants. The thing that worries me is that I am not utterly convinced that they are a dominated population. I think that very rapidly you have an assimilated population and this is why I am particularly interested in it. I am trying to find out what happens at the end of the Iron Age, and I see no reason why we shouldn't have an assimilated society very quickly. And the Anglian character is something we see dominating everything because of the change of material culture from Roman, but it's not such a big change from the Iron Age.

HÄRKE: I would have brought up that point sooner or later. For this kind of cemetery pattern, it has been suggested that these are household groups rather than kin groups or family groups, and I believe there is at least one cemetery (Berinsfield) where you can actually demonstrate this on the basis of epigenetic traits.

WOOD: I want to go back to the question of animals. I think that Giorgio's model cannot actually be used for England, because of how temperature affects human needs. As I understand it, the further you move away from a hot zone the more humans actually need to eat meat or some nutritional equivalent. Therefore you can't actually use a model from the Sudan to speculate on what people would be eating in Northumbria. And there is not actually a huge problem with people using animals until they cease to be productive and then killing and eating them. You can keep your sheep. You've just got to be very wary about reducing the meat content too much.

POWLESLAND: I would not argue they were vegetarians. But the difficulty here is that when you find these things in overwhelming quantities it makes an immediate impression on people. You say 'we have a million animal bones'. It doesn't actually have to represent very many animals. Likewise when spinning and weaving is overemphasized because of the loom-weights found. It is a question of scale and what is visible in the data set that we recover.

FOWLER: You keep referring to the Iron Age. Can I just make two points about that. One is that the Iron Age is just a label, it is not a homogeneous period. In fact all the problems we have been talking about exist in the last centuries BC. You mustn't fall into the trap of thinking that the Iron Age was necessarily just a period of subsistence and basically tribal peoples. In fact, in terms of European culture, Britain was quite advanced in some respects by the time you get to the middle of the first century AD. That's one point.

Now, if I can just go back to the site plan and its analogies. Unless we forget the historical model in which inevitably we are having this discussion, we have a plan which in a sense hasn't taken us any further because we are still presented, in dramatically graphic form, with the basic dichotomy for interpretation. Look at that plan and you say that it is a perfect pattern: it represents organization, presumably an organized community. But because of that we still have to decide if it represents the land settlement of a people coming in, lock, stock and barrel, with fixed ideas of what a settlement should be. If so, a direct analogy for that would be Jamestown, where the burgers moved the idea of an English village over to Jamestown and built it. You could say that your plan is so organized that it was not produced by first-generation colonists coming in higgledy-piggledy from Europe; indeed that it represents a relatively late stage, perhaps when there is much intermingling of the indigenous population with the incoming population.

POWLESLAND: Do we have a single Continental site which has a great deal in common with this for a plan? I would argue that the earliest Anglian population in this particular area are located about on a site, just over 1.5 km to the north within a declining Roman settlement where we have a group of Grubenhäuser and, we believe, a post-hole building.

Until we've actually seen and quantified this much more carefully I must be very guarded about what I say. But, as far as I can see, the impetus for the move is late Roman, and this settlement starts as a complex site in the late Roman period. I wonder whether you had a collapse in the Roman rural land tenure which freed up the population so they can move, and once the members of the population start this they move like nations. We might be looking at a period of transition of fifty or seventy years in which the populations from the areas just to the north moved to a site like this. The northern settlement did die out.

AUSENDA: In talking about a rural model, I was not saying that they did not eat meat, rather that it is very unlikely that they grew livestock to eat meat. Now the reason for that is that you should not look at livestock only from the point of view of the climate in which the people who eat it live, but also from the point of view of the amount of work that goes into keeping livestock throughout the winter. You have to cut fodder for it, you've got to feed it fatty foods. And this I know not from the eastern Sudan, where they do not have such problems, but from the southern Alps. I have a very interesting informant who told me that they did not keep oxen: out of 52 families only 6 kept oxen. They were too expensive because they ate too much food so as to 'work' hard and they did not produce anything. So you have to bear in mind this energy balance every time you talk about livestock. I was going to ask Dominic whether he found also traces of manuring.

POWLESLAND: We have evidence of sheep and we believe they were kept in a compound to the east of the stream, and there is evidence that they were feeding them leaf mulch, leaves and things. It's argued that this is winter fodder and that they were herded in and fed vast amounts of leafy stuff.

AUSENDA: The only animals they raised for food in the southern Alps were pigs, because of the fat. Did they have any other fat to cook with? Did they use linseed oil?

POWLESLAND: There is no evidence for any linseed. There is butter.

HÄRKE: Late-Saxon documents record some very large pig herds. The advantage of pork is that it is 'fast food': pigs put on weight (i.e. meat) faster than other livestock. The Romans, for example, switched to providing pork in the early phases of their occupation of the Rhineland in order to cope with the increase in demand for food.

POWLESLAND: Pigs are supposed to be relatively high-status in the Middle Saxon period.

CHARLES-EDWARDS: I think it is usually said that peasants only ate pork, or pig products; they didn't eat any other form of meat.

References in the discussion

Hamerow, H.
    1993   *Excavations at Mucking, Vol. 2: The Anglo-Saxon Settlement.* London: English Heritage.

Scull, C.
    1993   Archaeology, Early Anglo-Saxon society and the origins of Anglo-Saxon kingdoms. *Anglo-Saxon Studies in Archaeology and History* 6: 65-82.

Sherlock, S. J., & M. Welch
    1992   *An Anglo-Saxon Cemetery at Norton, Cleveland.* London: CBA.

EARLY ANGLO-SAXON SOCIAL STRUCTURE

HEINRICH HÄRKE

Department of Archaeology, University of Reading, Whiteknights, PO Box 218, Reading, GB- RG6 6AA

This paper is intended to provide an overview of the main features of social structure in England during the fifth to seventh/eighth century AD. The term 'social structure' is applied loosely here, referring to all aspects of social organization and differentiation. The emphasis is squarely on archaeological data, and, given the state of research and the nature of the available evidence, burials and cemeteries figure prominently in this survey. Historical evidence will be brought to bear on the various questions where possible, but neither special expertise nor exhaustive treatment is claimed here for the evaluation of written sources. It hardly needs emphasizing that the two main types of evidence relate to different, but overlapping phases: the burial evidence dates mainly to the fifth to seventh centuries whereas written sources do not start before the seventh century.

Archaeological evidence, in particular cemetery evidence, has been used for social inferences since the nineteenth century. While most archaeologists accept the validity of such an approach, not everybody agrees. Wilson has clearly stated his view that Anglo-Saxon archaeology provides "practically no clues to political structure, to national boundaries, to marital practices or to the rights of the individual. Occasionally a very rich grave may give an idea of social structure and the wealth of a particular person, but such indications are rare" (Wilson 1976:3; for a radically different view, see Addyman 1976). Even if we accept the possibility of social interpretation of cemeteries, their analysis raises two basic questions. To what degree does archaeological evidence reflect social relations? And in particular: does funerary evidence reflect social relations as they were active in living society, or does it reflect them in a way which is specific to ritual and the realm of the dead? This is not the place to tackle these questions in detail (cf. Härke 1994a), but it would be wrong to ignore them entirely because they pose fundamental problems for the social interpretation of Anglo-Saxon funerary evidence. Some of these problems should become apparent below.

The structure of this paper is determined by archaeological methodology (i.e. possible approaches and available evidence) as much as by general considerations. It begins with a look at age and sex, both of them biological categories which assume cultural significance in a social context. They are followed by a discussion of social groups and aggregates up to the level of local communities. Social classes and hierarchies, categories which have often been central to archaeologists' perceptions of social structure, are considered next, supplemented by a glance at the role of ethnic divisions in early Anglo-Saxon society.

THE ANGLO-SAXONS FROM THE MIGRATION PERIOD TO THE EIGHTH CENTURY:
AN ETHNOGRAPHIC PERSPECTIVE

© C.I.R.O.S.S.
San Marino (R.S.M.)

Age groups

In social anthropology, age grades or sets have long been recognized as important subdivisions of tribal societies, the transition from one age group to the next often marked by rites of passage (Van Gennep 1960). In complex societies, the importance of such age grades is often obscured by the variety of other factors, but age distinctions persist into our own times and our own society, together with their attendant rites of passage. It seems that early medieval societies have rarely been analysed from this perspective, and most studies have tended to concentrate on children (e.g. K. Arnold 1986; Herlihy 1995: 215-43; Ottinger 1974; Schwab 1982).

Following Ariès' suggestion of the "discovery of childhood" after the Middle Ages (Ariès 1962), there has been some debate on the medieval recognition of childhood (K. Arnold 1986:57; Herlihy 1995:215-9), and on the differentiation of children from adults in the Anglo-Saxon period (Keufler 1991).[1] Herlihy has distinguished Classical, barbarian and medieval childhood, with the barbarian childhood of the Migration and post-Roman periods being characterized by "an atmosphere of affectionate neglect" (Herlihy 1995:225). However this essentially psychological question is answered, it seems sufficiently clear that several age distinctions can be recognized in the earliest Anglo-Saxon sources. The extant laws suggest that children were comparatively well protected (Keufler 1991:827). They also identify the age of 10 as an important legal threshold: it marks the age of inheritance {Hlothere and Eadric 6 (AD 673-685?} and criminal responsibility {Ine 7.2 (AD 688-694); later raised to 12 years, cf. II Athelstan 1 (*ca* AD 925-930)}.

The biographical information in saints' lives and heroic poetry suggests several age thresholds which do not coincide with the one in the laws: 7-8 years, 14-15 years and mid-20s. The first threshold signalled the end of childhood and the beginning of light work or education, for high-status children not infrequently in fosterage outside the family (Felix, *Life of St Guthlac*, I; Bede, *HE* V.24; *Beowulf*, ll. 2428-2430). This threshold appears to have been a widespread feature in northwest European societies, from Ireland to Scandinavia. For boys of noble background it meant the beginning of weapon training and hunting as a preparation for the life of a warrior (Davidson 1989:11-12, 20-1). The second threshold at 14-15 years of age marks the boy's entry into adult life (Eddius Stephanus, *Life of St Wilfred*, II.7; Bede, *HE* V.19; Felix, *Life of St Guthlac*, II and XVII-XVIII). In the case of noble warriors, this phase may last about 10 years after which the mature man retires to the monastery (Felix, *Life of St Guthlac*, XIX) or to his acquired or inherited estate. A *comitatus* would therefore have comprised warriors mostly between the ages of about 15 and 25, with various levels of experience (cf. *Beowulf*, ll. 2626-2628; *Finnesburh*; *Battle of Maldon*, ll. 152-154), but made up of what is essentially one age set.[2] Further distinctions

---

[1]   Anglo-Saxon children were the object of a recent doctoral thesis (Crawford 1991). Regrettably, permission was not given to quote from the thesis in this paper.

[2]   Is it coincidence that in our days the age set 15 to 25 is the most prominent group in traffic

are blurred; the sources refer to old warriors in halls as well as noble advisers and friends of the king (Bede, *HE* II.13; *Beowulf*, ll. 356-357), both presumably older than the ordinary *comitatus* warriors.

Archaeological evidence can supplement some of this textual information, and redress the social and gender bias in favour of noble males shown in the written sources. Most of the following observations are based on inhumation burials which offer better preservation of grave goods, and an easier and more reliable age determination from skeletal remains, than cremations. There are some continuous trends which run across all age groups: the frequency of burial in multiple graves decreases with age, and the average number of grave goods increases steadily. More specific evidence of age sets and thresholds can be found in several aspects of the burial ritual, and in types and sizes of objects deposited in graves.

A first observation which may provide an idea of the attitude to infants in early Anglo-Saxon society relates to the possible under-representation of the youngest age groups in the early furnished cemeteries. In a sample of 47 cemeteries with just under 3,000 aged individuals, only some 2.3 per cent fall into the neonate and young infant categories (up to about 18 months of age; Härke 1992a:184, tab. 28). A separate analysis of 12 cemeteries arrived at a compatible figure of 6 per cent under the age of three (Crawford 1993:84). This low proportion represents a problem because infant mortality should be considerably higher if data from pre-industrial, Third World communities are anything to go by. This problem is common to virtually all early medieval (and many prehistoric) cemeteries across western Europe. It was recognized by Continental scholars several decades ago, and has been discussed at some length in the archaeological and anthropological literature (for a summary, see Steuer 1982:513-5). The alternatives are that either the comparative figures from Third World contexts cannot be applied to pre-industrial Europe, or that young infants were disposed of in different ways. Actually, both may apply to some degree: the former is now advocated by a number of physical anthropologists (Herrmann *et al.* 1990); and there seems to be some evidence (albeit not much) to substantiate the latter. Also, it appears that most late Roman and late Saxon cemeteries have somewhat higher proportions of infants (cf. Watts 1989). The disposal outside formal burial grounds of individuals under the age of two to three years of age would imply a low esteem of this age group, and a low status in society. This is underlined by the fact that the majority of individuals of this age were buried in multiple graves, and that two-thirds of them were buried without grave goods.

A first threshold seems to have been reached around two to three years of age. Burial in individual graves and the deposition of grave goods are more common from this age, and a weapon (mostly a single spear, occasionally an arrow) may now be put into the grave, although this still remains a rarity (Härke 1992b:156, tab. 4). Girls reached another threshold in the age group 7 to 14 years: there is a

---

accident and crime statistics? For a recent confirmation of this well-established and recognized trend, cf. the US murder statistics for 1994 (Lacayo 1996:34).

steep increase in the number and variety of objects in their graves, resulting from the increasing frequency of burial in full dress kit (a pair of brooches, necklace, keys or chatelaine/girdle hanger). A closer look at the relevant cases suggests that this point was reached at an age of between 10 and 12 years. The age of 12 certainly marked a threshold for boys: shields and swords were deposited occasionally from the age of 12 onwards (Härke 1992a:186-8; 1992b:156; Dickinson & Härke 1992:68, tab. 19). From the age of 15, there is a further, slight increase in the number of objects deposited in female graves, suggesting an elaboration of the dress kit in the juvenile age group. In male burials, the deposition of the body on its side in a flexed position all but disappears after the age of 15.

The attainment of 'adult' age (in our modern definition), at around 18 to 20 years, is connected with further changes in the burial ritual. The orientation of bodies becomes more standardized, with the head pointing roughly west; coffins and other grave structures become much more frequent (about double their frequency in sub-adult graves), and the rare chamber graves make their appearance in this age group. But it is the grave goods that most clearly distinguish the adult group from children and juveniles: artefacts such as musical instruments, scales, gaming pieces, horse harness, axes and seaxes have been found only in adult burials (Härke 1992a:160, fig. 26). Differentiation within the group of adult males is difficult to identify on the basis of the archaeological and skeletal evidence, but horse gear, axes and seaxes appear to be deposited preferentially with older adults (aged 30 and over). A similar analysis is still lacking for female adult burials.[3]

Skeletal evidence can provide additional information. Mortality peaks provide indirect evidence of particular stress at certain ages, but interestingly enough the picture that emerges from mortality figures is too unclear for interpretation because of marked local variations. The study of Harris lines is of greater weight because it provides direct indicators of periods of arrested growth through stress, malnutrition and illness, but not many cemetery populations have been analysed for this feature. At the late Anglo-Saxon site of North Elmham, girls experienced most of their growth-arresting episodes after the age of seven, while boys underwent more such episodes, and most of them after the age of 12 (Wells & Cayton 1980:298). This suggests gender differences in upbringing and socialization, and it may even mean that from the age of 12, "boys were exposed to something like the full rigours and physical demands of adulthood" (Wells & Cayton 1980:298). Although this would tie in with threshold ages suggested by other types of evidence, it is difficult to extrapolate from this one sample, and to extend this conclusion back to the Early Anglo-Saxon period without further supporting studies of this kind.

Settlement evidence does not contribute anything to our understanding of age divisions and age-related status in Anglo-Saxon society, except perhaps in the

---

[3] A detailed analysis of Anglo-Saxon female inhumations has been carried out by N. Stoodley (Reading) in his doctoral research; it was completed in April 1997.

absence of any subdivisions or partitions in buildings and settlements which could be related to specific age groups. All that this absence of special residential or activity areas of children, adults or old people suggests is that all age groups lived and worked side by side in social groups which cross-cut age divisions.

The above outline provides us with three series of age thresholds from various types of evidence (Table 5-1). The age grades suggested, in particular, by the biographical data are strikingly similar to those encountered in societies with gerontocratic structures. For example, the Lokop of northern Kenya have a system in which the males proceed through three age grades (Larick 1990): boys (7-15 years), warriors (15-30 years), and elders (over 30 years). Age structures in other post-Roman societies appear to have been similar to the Anglo-Saxon pattern, but not identical. In the Visigothic laws, the ages of 1, 10, 15, 20, and 45/50 (females/males) mark changes in wergild levels, with the decline in its value after the age of 45/50 reflecting the low value of ageing members to society (Herlihy 1995:222-3).

Table 5-1
Threshold ages

biographical data	laws	burial evidence
7/8 14/15 mid-20s+	10 (later 12)	2/3 12 (10/12 for females) 18/20 30+ (males only)

However, the divergences between Anglo-Saxon literary perception, legal codes, and ritual expression of age grades are conspicuous. The biographical data appear to suggest four relatively clear-cut age groups which are at odds with the five groups which can be inferred from burial ritual. The only coincidence between written sources and archaeological evidence is provided by the age of criminal responsibility and the onset of burial with full female dress or sword and/or shield, respectively, somewhere between the ages of 10 and 12. There are, at least, two possible explanations for these discrepancies. We may be looking at two different chronological horizons, and Christianity may have had an impact on the later horizon represented by the biographical data (cf. Crawford 1993; Herlihy 1995:225-8; Watts 1989). Alternatively, we may have to consider the possibility of a systematic divergence between the cultural perception of biographical age, on the one hand, and the biological age inferred from skeletal evidence, on the other.

Finally, it is interesting to note a possible change in the attitude towards children in the seventh/eighth centuries. Children were included in the (largely symbolic) weapon burial rite which ended around AD 700 (Härke 1992b). But the deposition of weapons in sub-adult burials ceased earlier than in adult burials: weapons were phased out gradually over the seventh century, first from children's burials, then from juvenile burials, and finally from adult burials (Härke 1992a:184). Also, children are never found on their own, i.e. without an adult burial, under barrows of seventh- or eighth-century date. Shephard (1979:67) has interpreted this as evidence that adult status was part of the 'superordinate' social status represented in the barrows. If this reflects a change in attitude, it may be connected with the introduction and spread of Christianity (cf. above), or with the emergence of early state structures which might also have led to a change in the status of children through the formalization of inheritance rules and the decline in importance of kinship.

Sex and gender

Interest in aspects of sex and gender[4] in Anglo-Saxon society started well before the recent popularity of gender and feminist perspectives. For a number of reasons, the study of gender has usually been equated with the study of women's place in society. For Anglo-Saxon England, the starting point of the debate was Sir Frank Stenton's pioneering study of place-names which suggested that "women were associated with men on terms of rough equality in the common life of the countryside" (F. M. Stenton 1943:13). This was echoed by his wife, Doris Mary Stenton's book in which she concluded that "women were then more nearly the equal companions of their husbands and brothers than at any other period before the modern age" (D. M. Stenton 1957:348). Later writers on this subject tended to concur (e.g. Dietrich 1980:43-4; Fell 1984a), but there has also been some disagreement. Klinck, in particular, has argued on the basis of the laws that women's rights increased during the Anglo-Saxon period, but even so Anglo-Saxon women had never been the equals of men (1982:115, 118). There appears to be evidence to support both sides of the debate, although to varying degrees. One aspect that all commentators have agreed on, though, is the clear assumption in virtually all extant sources that marriage was monogamous.

In *Beowulf*, wives and daughters of men of high rank appear mostly as peaceweavers and cupbearers, and other women do not appear at all (Fell 1984a:67). The *Anglo-Saxon Chronicle* and Bede present a very similar picture of a male scheme of social and political power relations. Where females are mentioned in the laws, from Æthelberht's (between AD 597 and 616) to Alfred's (between AD 885 and 899), a woman's status is almost invariably determined by that of her father: marriage did not lead to a change of social class (Loyn

---

[4] In contrast to a current theoretical trend which views both sex and gender as culturally determined (so in several papers given at the Theoretical Archaeology Group conference, Reading, December 1995), 'sex' is taken here to be a biological category, 'gender' a cultural category. This distinction makes sense when dealing with skeletal as well as archaeological evidence: the latter would normally reflect gender as expressed in material culture and ritual, whereas skeletal evidence gives information on the biological sex of individuals (in terms of a probability statement rather than in absolute terms). It also follows that written sources would reflect either sex or gender, depending on the type of source and the context of the reference.

1974:206). Apart from her class, the most important status distinction of a free woman is her marital status (unmarried, married, widow); in the case of men, this is less often mentioned and clearly of much less importance (Fell 1984a:62). And the laws of Ine mention almost in passing, as a matter of course, that a woman must obey 'her lord' (Ine 57), i.e. her husband.

But there are also indications of less uneven economic and power relations between the sexes. Some female rulers are referred to in the *Anglo-Saxon Chronicle* (e.g. Queen Seaxburh of Wessex ruling after Cenwealh's death, *ASC s.a.* 672; and later Æthelflæd, 'Lady of the Mercians', ruling in AD 911-918 after her husband's death, *ASC s.a.* 910, 913, 916, 917, 918; cf. Wainwright 1959). Æthelburh, the wife of King Ine of Wessex, is even mentioned as having destroyed Taunton (*s.a.* 722) during the reign of her husband, suggesting the possibility of military leadership by a noblewoman. This would tie in with the brief hint in *Beowulf* (line 2060) that Freawaru, the daughter of Hrothgar, would take her own followers abroad to the wedding. The poem, unambiguously male-centred as it is, also refers to several queens, Wealhtheow, Hygd and Freawaru (*Beowulf*, ll. 612-661, 1926-1931, 2015-2069) who distribute gifts to warriors, giving them an important role in the male world of the hall, and possibly implying some control over property. Bede's *Ecclesiastical History* portrays several women from noble or royal families as instrumental during the Conversion and in leadership positions in the early Church, mainly as abbesses (e.g. *HE* IV.21). This would be surprising if they could not have held similar positions of authority in contemporary secular society.

Fell (1984a:59-61; 1984b) has argued that a law of Æthelberht (73) may mean that a woman could be in control of keys to treasure stores, and made a connection with the keys (chatelaines, girdle-hangers) found in the burials of many female adults and juveniles (from the age of about 12). Certainly, the much later laws of Cnut (76.1a; AD 1020-1023) stipulate that the wife must look after the keys to her storeroom, her chest and her coffer. Earlier laws also define, or imply, a degree of independence of the wife from her husband. In Kent, rules were drawn up about the division of the marriage goods in case the woman went away, with or without her children (Æthelberht 79 and 80). And in both Kent and Wessex, a woman's criminal responsibility was judged independently of that of her husband: she was not to be punished if she was not aware of his crime {Wihtred 12 (AD 695); Ine 7 and 57}.

Charters and wills (predominantly of middle and late Saxon date) provide a picture of male economic dominance punctuated by instances of female equality or independence. Some 93 per cent of all charters were granted to men (Meyer 1980). Charters granted to women did not differ in form or content, but they were predominantly given to women of royal families (Meyer 1980:59-60). And while many charters were granted to husband and wife together, giving the impression of economic partnership, the reason behind this may be that a woman was not guaranteed possession of her husband's land after his death unless this had been specified in the charter. However, of the 39 wills compiled by Whitelock (1930), ten are by female testators alone, and four more by wives together with their husbands (Lancaster 1958:362). In other words women are represented in more than a quarter of the extant wills (cf. Sheehan 1963:70-1), which is more than one would expect if Anglo-Saxon women had a uniformly low economic status.

A certain measure of economic control, albeit over one particular item, is suggested by the regulations concerning bride payment and morning gift (Æthelberht 81). Fell (1984a:56-7) has concluded from laws and later charters that women kept control of land received as morning gift. And if a woman died childless, the morning gift would go to her paternal kinsmen (Æthelberht 81), not to her husband, implying a separate economic identity at least in this respect. Middleton has pointed out that societies with a bridewealth system (involving the payment of bride price and/or morning gift to the wife and her family, as against the dowry system) are usually characterized by high female productivity (Middleton 1995:57-8). Therefore, the Anglo-Saxon marriage system may be an indicator of the economic significance of female agricultural or craft production (Middleton 1995:58-9). It is also worth mentioning that Cynethryth, the wife of King Offa, had coins struck in her name (D. M. Stenton 1957:2), but it is not clear if this can be taken to indicate a measure of economic independence.

It has often been suggested that Christianity brought about a change in women's status because ecclesiatical writings protraying women as inferior and impure are assumed to have affected social attitudes. However, Fell (1984a:13-4) has emphasized that these writings largely remained theoretical, and that—at least initially—little changed at the practical level. One may add that, if there was any change in the perception and status of women after about AD 600, this may have had as much to do with Christian theories as with the emergence of statehood in England. One concomitant of the development of state structures is the decline in importance of kinship and family links, and this is likely to have affected gender relations as it probably affected the status and treatment of children (cf. above).

Early Saxon burial ritual put a remarkably strong emphasis on gender display through artefacts which formed part of the dress or were deposited separately in inhumation graves. While there are gender-neutral burials without diagnostic objects or without any grave goods at all (these are the majority of infants and young children, and a proportion of up to 44 per cent of juveniles and adults), the majority of adult burials show a marked male/female dichotomy. This phenomenon is more pronounced in inhumation graves (Brush 1988) than in cremations (Richards 1987), but it is present in both. The male 'kit' consists of weapons and tools (excluding textile-working tools); the female 'kit' is made up of dress ornaments (two or three brooches, bead necklace, pins), keys and girdle hanger (chatelaine) suspended from the belt, and textile-working tools (spindle whorls, loom weights, weaving batten).

The mutually exclusive gender attribution of these artefacts has been supported, in the overwhelming number of cases (over 99 per cent), by skeletal sexing. There is a small number of exceptions where archaeological and skeletal sexing are in disagreement. It is not impossible that some of them are genuine cases of cross-dressing, but the very rarity of this phenomenon suggests that it may be the product of the error span inherent in skeletal sexing. This suspicion is confirmed by a current re-study of the archaeology and biology of key cases from this group.[5] Also, there is not a single unambiguous case of mixing of the gender-specific artefact kits in undisturbed graves. The rare instances of brooches in graves with weapons involve single brooches, reminiscent of Roman and Celtic male dress, but not of Anglo-Saxon female dress; and the few cases of weapons in graves with female kit show features which are best explained as secondary re-use of parts of weapons as tools (Härke 1992a:179-82). The only exception may be arrowheads found with female children, an observation matched elsewhere in post-Roman Europe (Härke 1992a:181).

Even supposedly gender-neutral artefacts may show some degree of gender differentiation. The humble iron knife, by far the most frequent object in burials of either sex and all age groups, is a good example (Härke 1989b). Adult women were never buried with knives the blades of which were longer than 126 mm (5 inches); such large knives were only found with adult men. A parallel for this may be found among the Lapps (Saami) of northern Scandinavia where knives are part of the display dress, with men carrying the longer knives. Among Anglo-Saxon children, there is no gender-related difference in sizes of knives, but children with a male kit (i.e. weapons) are twice as likely to be accompanied by a knife than are children with a female kit (63 and 31 per cent, respectively).

Other aspects of the inhumation ritual confirm the emphasis on gender display. While the standard deposition of the body was extended on the back, with the head pointing somewhere around west, females were more often deposited with the head to the south than males were (under 10 per cent of male adults); and they were more often in a flexed position on the side than males (only about 5 per cent of male adults; Härke 1992a:151-5). Both traits link the mortuary treatment of female adults with that of children (*ca* 20 per cent with head to south, and *ca* 20 per cent flexed; cf. above). In her analysis of the East Anglian cemetery of Holywell Row, Pader (1982:130) suggested that this could mean that women and children were assigned a similar status, different from (and by implication, inferior to) men. It should, however, be noted that the gender-specific differences in burial treatment vary from cemetery to cemetery. This need not weaken Pader's interpretation, but it does indicate local variations in gender-linked ritual symbolism. It is conceivable that this also implies local and regional variations in gender relations.

Gender differences in burial ritual, and in particular the marked gender dichotomy in grave goods, are likely to relate to Anglo-Saxon perceptions of

---

5 This re-study deals with the 'cross-gender' cases from the cemeteries of Dover, Kent (Evison 1987) and Norton, Cleveland (Sherlock & Welch 1992), and is being carried out by N. Stoodley (archaeology; Reading), T. Molleson (physical anthropology; London) and J. Bailey (DNA; Oxford). The results to date (early 1997) suggest that in some cases, the original skeletal sexing was faulty; and where it was not, it is mostly contradicted by the DNA analysis (pers. comm. J. Bailey & N. Stoodley). As a result, there are no certain cases of females with weapons, and only a tiny number of probable males with jewellery from Anglo-Saxon cemeteries.

gender roles and statuses in society. The frequency of weapons in male burials, just under 50 per cent of male adults (Härke 1989a), and the exclusive appearance of textile-working tools in female burials is echoed several centuries later in the Will of Alfred which refers to the 'spear side' and the 'distaff side' of his family (Whitelock 1979:537, fn. 1). This material-cultural symbolism should not, however, tempt anybody to draw seemingly straightforward interpretations: not all males buried with weapons had been warriors (Härke 1990); similarly, probably not all females buried with tools had been weavers or spinners.

Burial wealth, i.e. the number and quality of objects in a grave, can be understood and interpreted in either symbolic or economic terms. Christlein (1973) has seen the wealth of male burials as directly reflecting the economic power of individuals, and this is a widespread assumption underlying many quantitative analyses of post-Roman burials. Comparisons of male and female burial wealth in Anglo-Saxon cemeteries agree on one key point: female burials are 'richer' than male burials (Arnold 1980:110, tab. 4.6; Pader 1982; Shephard 1979). They are furnished, on average, with a larger number of objects, a larger variety of artefact types, and a higher proportion of objects made of, or decorated with, precious metals or other rare materials, amber, rock crystal, etc. (see Table 5-2). This wealth differential is absent among infants and young children, but starts abruptly among older children (aged 7-14 years), and continues through all age groups.

Table 5-2

Male and female burial wealth after Arnold (1980, tab. 4.6)

REGION cemetery	average wealth scores		average number of artefact types	
	males	females	males	females
KENT				
Lyminge II	26.8	25.3	2.0	1.4
Polhill*	22.5	33.6	1.7	2.0
UPPER THAMES				
Abingdon I	16.4	69.8	1.2	3.0
Berinsfield	30.4	54.1	2.5	3.0
Long Wittenham I	29.1	41.3	3.1	2.1
WESSEX				
Petersfinger	32.7	81.8	2.5	1.5
Pewsey (Blackpatch)	34.8	65.3	2.7	3.4
Worthy Park	39.7	43.8	2.8	4.0
Winnall II*	8.6	25.9	0.5	1.4

*   late cemetery (7th/8th-century)

There is broad agreement that this wealth differential is a consequence of the differences between male and female dress, but interpretations vary. Chris Arnold (1980:132) has suggested that the wealth of a woman reflects not just her own status, but that of her husband as well. Shephard (1979:58) has claimed that the difference between the sexes was also a difference between social status and economic power: male grave goods were determined by social status, female grave goods by wealth. Pader, however, has pointed out that costume styles are not a suitable starting point for wealth analysis because costume may be determined by many other factors (Pader 1982:132). On the Continent where the gender differential is similar, Jørgensen has come up with a different explanation: families expressed their status through the burial of the first deceased of the heads of families, and because of the lower life expectancy of women, the result was a preponderance of rich female burials (Jørgensen 1987; 1990:66 fig. 48, 88; 1991:30-1).

Skeletal evidence provides some information on gender differences in living conditions and economic status. In the Early Anglo-Saxon period, women had a shorter life expectancy: 33.1 years as against 34.7 years for men, calculated on adults only (Brothwell 1972:83, tab. 25). While life expectancy appears to have risen in the Middle and Late Anglo-Saxon periods, e.g. to 35.8 and 38.2 years respectively at North Elmham (Wells & Cayton 1980:252), the gender differential persisted. The lower female life expectancy is significant because it must have led (as it did in early and high medieval societies across Europe) to a higher proportion of male adults in the living population, a trend which was only reversed in the later Middle Ages (Herlihy 1995:59-60). Physical anthropologists have interpreted this mortality differential as a consequence of biological rather than economic conditions, resulting from childbearing, in general, and a high rate of death in childbirth, in particular.

Differential access to food cannot be excluded as a contributory factor, though. At the Early Saxon cemetery of Worthy Park, Wells has observed that 25 per cent of women had enamel hypoplasia, but only 10 per cent of men, suggesting that girls were more likely to suffer from stress and malnutrition than boys (Hawkes & Wells 1983). However, this seems to be contradicted by the fact that at this particular site, the mean age at death of male adults (36.2 years) is lower than that of female adults (37.0 years; unpubl. report by C. Wells, pers. comm. S. C. Hawkes). Gender differences in health patterns may provide further insights on differential living conditions, but skeletal data have not yet been analysed systematically from this perspective.

Theoretical and anthropological considerations suggest what to look for in future research. If Anglo-Saxon society was the product of large-scale migration from the Continent (a view no longer as widely accepted as it was a decade ago), colonial societies might provide some clues. Stoodley's survey of gender roles in modern frontier societies suggests that distinctions of gender roles become more blurred, and gender differentiation of work more flexible among settlers than they were in the societies of origin: women have to carry out heavy 'male' work whereas men have to care for children and do more household chores (Stoodley 1993). This finding is strikingly reminiscent of Doris Mary Stenton's pronouncement on the "rough and ready partnership" (D. M. Stenton 1957:348) between the sexes in Anglo-Saxon England, and of Dietrich's suggestion of "role flexibility...for Anglo-Saxon women" (Dietrich 1980:44). It is surprising in another respect: the theoretical expectation of blurred gender roles contrasts with the marked gender dichotomy in burial ritual. Is the 'frontier society' model wrong for post-Roman England? Or was ritual a way of coping with the erosion of traditional gender roles in real life? The clearly symbolic function of Anglo-Saxon burial ritual would lend considerable support to the latter interpretation, as do anthropological observations on the role of ritual in reconciling ideal and reality (Leach 1964).

Settlement sites may provide information on the gender aspect of social relations (cf. Hastorp 1991), but there is not much gender-specific evidence in either the buildings or the finds from early Anglo-Saxon habitation sites. The mostly undifferentiated interiors of the typical timber-built dwellings (sometimes called 'halls') do not allow to identify separate activity areas. However, about a quarter of all timber 'halls' on a variety of fifth- to seventh-century sites, from ordinary to royal, have a partition at one end (Marshall & Marshall 1993:399). This provides a screened-off area of about one fifth of the interior (usually less than 2 x 5 metres), without a hearth of its own. The purpose of these compartments is unknown (Rahtz 1976:88), but it is often presumed that they were "private quarters" (Addyman 1972:304; Addyman & Leigh 1972:23, n. 5) for the higher-ranking members of the household. Given the existence of such partitions in large halls on high-status sites such as Cowdery's Down (Millett & James 1983: fig. 31) and Yeavering (Hope-Taylor 1977:127 fig. 60, 130 fig. 61) where written sources suggest that the highest-ranking individuals may have had their sleeping quarters in separate buildings (*Beowulf*, l. 1236; Addyman 1972:304), it is conceivable that this feature provided a bower for the women. Other functions such as storage, byre or stairwell cannot be excluded, though (Marshall & Marshall 1993:399; Powlesland, this volume). Heroic poetry gives the impression of the rest of the hall being an almost exclusively male activity area, but this may well be a biased representation, and in any case, it relates to high-status halls.

There has been a good deal of speculation and discussion concerning the function of the numerous sunken-floor buildings (SFBs) in early Anglo-Saxon settlements. Only in exceptional cases are they still seen as dug-out dwellings, e.g. for the first phase of Mucking (Dixon 1993:129; but cf. Hamerow 1993:86). On most sites, they seem to have been used as ancillary buildings. Occasionally this may have been in connection with metalworking, e.g. in sixth-/seventh-century Mucking (Hamerow 1993:17); much more often, though, they contain evidence of textile working (Rahtz 1976:76, 77 fig. 2.12; Arnold 1988:25 fig. 2.3). The concentration of loom weights and spindle whorls in SFBs varies from site to site (Bell 1977:226; Hamerow 1993:15, 17-9, 64; Losco-Bradley 1977:362; West 1985:138-9), but overall there can be little doubt about the link between many buildings of this type and textile production. Significantly, the two largest SFBs found on Early Saxon sites (at Upton and Charlton, with sizes around 9 x 5.5 metres) have produced loom weights the association of which with the respective buildings is clear because both had been destroyed by fire (Addyman 1972:281; Champion 1977:365).

The exclusive association of textile tools with female burials is strongly suggestive of textile production having been (or been presented as being) in the hands of women. The even distribution of SFBs within settlement sites means that weaving sheds were not concentrated to create a female activity area for the entire settlement. Rather, each household or farmstead had its own female activity area defined by its own weaving shed (if it had one). Other gender-specific areas in settlements of this period have yet to be identified.

Social groups: family, household, community

The *raison d'être* of this seemingly diverse section is the nature of the archaeological evidence in which kinship units, economic units and settlement units cannot always be distinguished easily, neither in cemeteries nor in settlements, and therefore require discussion side by side. It stands to reason that in Anglo-Saxon society these categories overlapped substantially anyway.

Kinship was essential to the working of early Anglo-Saxon society: it determined personal status, provided genealogical links, and gave access to land; equally importantly, the kindred guaranteed individual safety by paying part of the wergild to avert feuds and by conducting feuds on behalf of its members (Loyn 1974). Further discussion of kinship structures can be kept brief here because a separate paper is devoted to it (Charles-Edwards, this volume). The Anglo-Saxon kinship system was most likely bilateral, with a weak patrilateral bias, and probably virilocal residence (Lancaster 1958). Such a system which characterized early medieval kinship before the twelfth century (Herlihy 1995:143-5) militates against the creation of large descent groups as they are typical of unilateral kinship systems (Lancaster 1958:232, 359; but cf. Charles-Edwards 1972). In keeping with this theoretical expectation, there is indeed an emphasis in Anglo-Saxon kinship terminology on the nuclear family, and an absence of evidence for territorial clans in the charters (Loyn 1974:198, 202). In spite of these limitations: it is conceivable that kinship was also the initial basis of larger political units, as in most pre-state societies. Scull (1993) has suggested that regional structures, and eventually kingdoms, were created by the rise to dominance of individual lineages. The rise of territorial lordship and Christian kingship from the seventh century, in turn, suppressed the further development of kin groups into strong, land-holding institutions (Loyn 1974:209).

Textual references to households and other residential units are not very frequent, and they provide only limited information on their composition, sizes and structures. The early laws imply the existence of dependants, or other persons of lower status, in the households of kings (Ine 33) and freemen (Æthelberht 16 and 25; Ine 22 and 63). In Kent and Wessex, the master of the house was responsible for the acts of free and unfree persons of his household (Hlothere and Eadric 1; Wihtred 14; Ine 50). Thus, the evidence of the laws suggests that individuals of different status lived under one roof, or in very close and constant proximity, and that such households were not just residential units, but also to a certain degree legal units.

Other types of sources are not very helpful in the elucidation of this aspect. Charters are generally later than the period under discussion, and their nature, and the kinds of details they provide, have not encouraged an analysis of the demographic and social structures of residential units. The gift of 87 hides at Selsey to St Wilfred included an unspecified number of free men as well as 250 slaves (John 1964:26). On the conventional assumption that one hide should supply one man for military service, these figures give us an idea of the proportion of slaves to free households of a certain status on this particular estate. But the absence of further information, here and in other cases, makes it impossible to draw more precise inferences of the kind facilitated by Carolingian records on the Continent (Herlihy 1985:62-77; Le Jan 1995).

Cemeteries provide more direct evidence for sizes of local communities and their structures. At the upper end of the scale, some cremation cemeteries (such as Sancton I or Spong Hill) may originally have contained several thousand urns, which has led to the suggestion that these were the cemeteries of several settlements or local communities (C. J. Arnold 1981; Hills & Penn 1981:22). Inhumation and mixed cemeteries appear to correlate much better with the sizes of excavated settlement sites (cf. below). Chris Arnold (1984a:125; 1988:166) has used the evidence from 13 cemeteries to calculate the sizes of living communities; he arrived at figures between 15 and 36 individuals. While the cemetery chronologies used for these calculations may need some adjustment, the figures nevertheless give a useful idea of the size of a community which buried their dead together.

Internal structuring of cemeteries suggests the existence of distinct sub-groups within local communities. This structuring does not take the form of tangible partitions of cemetery areas, but of burial clusters identified on the basis of similarities in grave goods or other aspects of ritual treatment (cf. Pader 1982), horizontal stratigraphy, spatial relationships between graves of men, women and children, or occasionally skeletal evidence. Cemeteries may be classified by the type of internal structuring observed (arranged in the order of their frequencies; cf. Härke 1992a:169-72):

(1) polycentric cemetery, with independent development of several contemporaneous sectors (plots) which coalesce over time (e.g. Alfriston, Andover, Holywell Row, Polhill, Sewerby and Spong Hill inhumations);

(2) monocentric cemetery, with several contemporaneous sectors radiating out from a common focus (e.g. Bergh Apton, Berinsfield and Collingbourne Ducis, possibly Petersfinger; Spong Hill cremations);

(3) cemetery with simple horizontal stratigraphy, expanding in one direction (e.g. Finglesham);

(4) irregular development (possibly Abingdon I).

All these types appear to occur all over England throughout the Early Anglo-Saxon period. While types 3 and 4 do not have any unambiguous social implications, types 1 and 2 clearly do. Their contemporaneous sectors, and other conspicuous clusters of apparently related burials, have often been intuitively interpreted as 'family groups' (Adams 1982:145-6; Aldsworth 1978:162; Cook & Dacre 1985:54; Evison 1987:145; Philp 1973:200-1; Welch 1980:266). But at

Sewerby, Hirst (1985:102) observed that burials within each plot showed remarkable differences in status (as indicated by burial wealth), and concluded that these clusters probably represent households rather than families. A similar situation may be given at Broughton Lodge (Willoughby-on-the-Wolds) where poor burials, perhaps the "slave element in the population" (Kinsley 1993:72), were found on the fringes of the main burial cluster, but the incomplete excavation makes it impossible to judge how many such clusters there were at this site. However, internal wealth differentials within distinct burial clusters need not invalidate the 'family' interpretation: Steuer (1982:518-25) has suggested that Merovingian society was an "offene Ranggesellschaft" (open ranked society) in which social differences within families were as important as status differences between families.

In the future, the combination of biological information (skeletal data or DNA) and archaeological data may provide new insights. In the cemetery of Berinsfield (Oxfordshire), three sectors radiate out from a common focal area in the centre. For one of the three sectors, the skeletal evidence is detailed enough to suggest that this was the burial plot of a social group consisting of between 10 and 15 individuals at any one time, and comprising two or three distinct sub-groups whose members did not intermarry (Härke 1992a:205-6 Abb. 41; 1995). This structure would imply that the plot represents a large household; and if this interpretation is extended to the other two plots (where there is not enough skeletal evidence), one may conclude that the cemetery was the burial ground of three households, perhaps farmsteads, representing the community of a hamlet or similar settlement.

Biological data may also help us to decide whether monocentric and polycentric origins of cemeteries imply further differences in the social development of the communities buried in type 1 and type 2 cemeteries, respectively. Is a type 2 cemetery the reflection of a primary settler group splitting up to form several households in subsequent generations, while type 1 reflects several separate households without initial ties (kinship or otherwise)?

Settlement evidence can supplement some of the above inferences. The main types of buildings found in Early Saxon settlements are sunken-floor buildings (SFBs), predominantly used as ancillary buildings (cf. above), and above-ground, timber-built 'halls' which are the normal dwelling of this period. In the fifth to eighth centuries, the majority of these 'halls' are between 6 and 12 metres long, and between 3.5 and 7 metres wide (Addyman 1972; James *et al.* 1984; Marshall & Marshall 1993; Rahtz 1976; Zimmermann 1988). Taking mean length and width (about 10 x 5 metres; Marshall & Marshall 1993:381, ill. 10), and assuming that there was no upper floor (firm evidence for which exists only from the Late Anglo-Saxon period; Rahtz 1976:90; but cf. Powlesland, this volume), we arrive at average floor areas around 50 sq.metres (cf. Hamerow 1993:10). Given that this space was contiguous, it could have accommodated up to about a dozen or so people, assuming that several of them would have been children. Buildings with larger floor areas seem to have been a feature of later, high-status sites (cf. below).

The internal partition found in many timber buildings may have provided a separate area, perhaps sleeping area (cf. Rahtz 1976:69, fig. 2.8), for one group within the household, defined by status, gender or age. Alternatively, such separate areas may, on some sites, have been provided by a smaller type of timber building with only one door which some authors have identified with the *būr* (bower) known from later sources (Addyman & Leigh 1972:23). A complete farmstead consisted of a main building, the 'hall', and a few (one to four) smaller, ancillary buildings which rarely appear to have been dwellings (Addyman & Leigh 1973:19; West 1985:168). Thus, if there were two or more groups of different status living and working in any given household or farmstead, in most cases they must have lived under one roof.

Rural settlements were usually made up of several farmsteads, arranged in a loose conglomeration without any regular lay-out. Sizes range from a single farmstead to about ten or more, but the incomplete nature of most settlement plans of the Early Anglo-Saxon period makes this aspect difficult to judge. The East Anglian 'village' of West Stow comprised three, or possibly four, farmsteads at any one time between the early fifth and mid-seventh century (West 1985:150 tab. 68, 168). Further south, the site of Mucking is estimated to have consisted of a minimum of eight to ten contemporary units (Hamerow 1993:90), and the plan of Chalton indicates a sixth-/seventh-century hamlet of similar size (Champion 1977:364). Catholme in the Trent valley shows a continuous development of five, or possibly seven, 'holdings', clearly demarcated by ditches, from the late fifth to the tenth century (Losco-Bradley 1977:359).

The settlement evidence, then, suggests local community sizes of between a dozen and well over fifty people, but rarely touching one hundred. This ties in well with the cemetery evidence, although there are few inhumation cemeteries which could represent communities at the upper end of this scale (cf. above). In the future, the analysis of settlements with adjacent cemeteries should provide more concrete figures. At Mucking, on the basis of the grave numbers, Hamerow has calculated a population of 94 (± 10 per cent) for the eight to ten farmsteads in the settlement (Hamerow 1993:90), suggesting a household size of nine to 12 persons each. Unfortunately, there are few such cases so far (for West Heslerton, cf. Powlesland, this volume), and all too often half of their evidence is incomplete, e.g. the West Stow cemetery (West 1985:64-9), and the Bishopstone settlement (Bell 1977).

Overall the evidence seems to point to small communities made up of a few farmsteads each. It is suggested here that households formed the basic residential and economic units in the fifth to mid-seventh centuries. They comprised individuals and groups of different status, most likely the family of the master of the household, and unfree or semi-free dependants. This suggestion, based primarily on the archaeological and skeletal evidence, agrees well with Lancaster's analysis of the Anglo-Saxon kinship system which led her to postulate that local groups are more likely to have consisted of households with dependants, rather than extended kin groups (Lancaster 1958:373-4). Moreover, simple calculations show that the low life expectancy (cf. above) would result in two rather than three generations under one roof, and an average number of, perhaps, three to four surviving children per family. The latter figure ties in closely with statistics produced by analyses of Carolingian sources which suggest an average family size of 5.79 persons (Herlihy 1985:69, 70 tab. 3.2), or 3.52 surviving children per family, respectively (Le Jan 1994:287). These figures belong to the ninth century by which time household structures had been transformed by social and religious change (Herlihy 1985:78). If we want to account for earlier social conditions, we may add the one or the other unmarried brother or sister and surviving parent, plus a few unfree individuals, and we begin to see for early Anglo-Saxon England quite a good correspondence between theoretical expectations, written sources, cemetery data and settlement evidence.

Social classes and legal status

The key issue in the historical debate over social status distinctions in early Anglo-Saxon society has been the status of freemen, the nature of their freedom, and (intimately linked with this issue) the nature of land tenure and the extent of military service (cf. Pelteret 1995:4-24). The disagreements have not been resolved, but the debate appears to have resulted among historians in a shift of opinion away from the assumption of an essentially free peasant society (as advocated, e.g., by F. M. Stenton 1971). Among archaeologists, the intellectual shifts in the discipline (see below) have resulted in a split: many of the younger archaeologists who have studied Anglo-Saxon social structures have eschewed the use of written sources, while many of their older colleagues who are more comfortable with the use of historical concepts and sources appear to be more familiar with the opinion of Stenton and his contemporaries than with more recent historical opinion.

Some of the most useful textual evidence for vertical social differentiation is contained in the wergild clauses of the early laws. The classic model of a three-tier social hierarchy has been inferred from their provisions for the various levels of compensation to be paid for murder or manslaughter (cf. F. M. Stenton 1971:277-318; Whitelock 1974:83-114):
- nobility (*eorl* in Kent, *gesith* in Wessex; the latter from the tenth century)
- freeman (*ceorl*)
- slave (*þēow, esne*).
In addition, the laws of Æthelberht of Kent (26) mention the *læt* who have widely been interpreted as semi-free persons, perhaps manumitted slaves (Loyn 1962:10; Whitelock 1979:392 n.7; Pelteret 1995:294-6), but neither is this certain, nor can it be assumed that such a distinction existed in all Anglo-Saxon kingdoms.

A number of other points emerge from the laws, the most important ones being the internal differentiation of these classes, and some mobility within and between them. In Kent, the unfree and semi-free classes were divided into three sub-classes each (Æthelberht 11 and 26), and noble widows into four (ibid. 75). In Wessex, free peasants of lower status are mentioned (*gafolgelda* and *gebūr*; Ine 6.3; cf. Whitelock 1979:399 n.4), suggesting subdivisions within the class of freemen. But status could change: a slave could be given freedom (Wihtred 8); freemen could go into slavery if convicted of theft (Wihtred 26; Ine 7.1) or found to work on a Sunday (Ine 3.2); and service for the king or in the royal household increased the wergild of unfree (Æthelberht 7; Ine 33) and free individuals (Ine 19). This conforms to expectations of a certain amount of upward mobility which is typical of stratified societies (Lancaster 1958:366-7), but also to theoretical expectations of increased social mobility during migration and new settlement. On the other hand, Wormald (1978:35, 91-2) has pointed out that the terms *gesithcund* and *eorlcund* demonstrate the existence of nobility by birth as early as the seventh century. Also from the seventh century onwards, the status of freemen changed as a consequence of the introduction of land charters, shifting the meaning of 'freedom' from the right to be granted the protection of the law to the power to leave an estate (Pelteret 1995:251).

Apart from the problem that the surviving law codes relate to Kent and Wessex only, it should be borne in mind that the wergild classes are a differentiation in law, and there is no guarantee that legal status and social status always coincided (James 1989:38). This distinction becomes even more critical when we begin to look for the reflection of such classes in the archaeological record, in particular burial evidence which is, after all, the result of ritual behaviour and may not faithfully reflect legal and social differentiations. In German archaeology, the evidence from post-Roman cemeteries has routinely been interpreted in social terms since the 1930s, using primarily male burials and their weaponry (for a survey, cf. Steuer 1982; for summaries in English, see James 1989; Samson 1987). The reason for the predominant use of men's graves for this kind of social analysis is the smaller range of objects in them compared with female burials, facilitating a subdivision by 'wealth' and resulting in a much clearer differentiation than can be achieved for female grave assemblages, both on the Continent and in England.

In Anglo-Saxon archaeology, there was no extensive debate on the social interpretation of burials before the 1970s, but in what would now be termed the 'traditionalist' (or 'cultural-historical') school, the equation of quality of grave goods with legally defined social classes has always been widespread. The often implicit premise of this approach has been spelt out by S. C. Hawkes (in Philp 1973:186-7): "There was nothing haphazard about the ownership of weapons: it was a matter of legal right and obligation". Accordingly, she postulated the equation of certain weapon-types in graves with social classes mentioned in the sources:

- sword   freemen of higher status
- seax   freemen of intermediate status
- spear   ordinary freemen and some half-free
- no weapons   majority of half-free, and all slaves.

She claimed that these equations should apply not just to Kent, but to all of England.

Alcock (1981) has suggested a more systematic scheme which was similar to S. C. Hawkes's in that he tried to identify the various quality levels of grave goods with equivalent social classes known from written sources. He concentrated on male burials, but also provided a tentative scheme for females. Below the royal level, indicated by graves with helmets and mail coats, he distinguished three social grades (Table 5-3). A very similar scheme has more recently been drawn up by Evison (1987:146-50) for the social interpretation of the cemetery of Dover-Buckland, but she added a fourth level of 'findless' graves identified as slaves, thus elevating the Dover-Buckland equivalents of Alcock's gamma grade to "poor relations in the free class" (Evison 1987:149). One of the implications is that no slaves were buried in this cemetery, and that these must have been buried elsewhere (Evison 1987:150).

Table 5-3

Burial grades and social classes after Alcock (1981)

grade	males	females	social class
alpha	sword	gilt brooches, gold/silver bracelets, amber or crystal beads, bronze bowl, glass vessel, weaving batten	*thegn*
beta	spear	brooches, necklace	*ceorl*
gamma	knife	knife or buckle, or 2-3 beads	unfree

The main drift of Alcock's argument, though, related to regional differences. He observed a marked difference between southern England, where the alpha/beta ratio of 1:3.6 suggests a broad stratum of free Saxon peasants, and Bernicia, where the much rarer alpha burials suggest a small Anglian élite over a large, indigenous population, continuing the Celtic social system of the sub-Roman period (Alcock 1981:177-9). This observation is important because it is an indicator of profound differences in social structure between the various polities of Anglo-Saxon England (but cf. Cramp 1983). However, Alcock's approach assumes a direct correspondence between ritual symbols (in this case, grave goods) and social classes, with both categories treated as broadly uniform across England and over the Early Anglo-Saxon period. Even if later sources appear to suggest a correlation between weapon-types and social status, this related to the status of the *living*; and Brooks (1978:83) has emphasized that, whatever the texts might suggest, in reality the differences between weapons of the nobility and of freemen were probably blurred.

By the time Alcock put forward his views on Anglo-Saxon social structure, quantitative approaches to the social analysis of burials had come into fashion in Anglo-Saxon archaeology, inspired by the neo-evolutionist 'New Archaeology' (processual archaeology). The basic processualist premise has been that of a more or less direct correlation between social complexity, and the complexity of the funerary ritual of any given society. In practice, virtually the only archaeological indicator used to infer complexity has been burial wealth, measured by a quantitative analysis of the grave goods. The observed levels of wealth have been interpreted as social strata, but no attempt has been made to compare them with the social classes in the written sources: the proponents of the processualist approach have tended to distrust the historical sources, stressing instead the information potential inherent in the archaeological evidence.

Quantitative social analysis became a regular feature of most Anglo-Saxon cemetery publications of the 1980s, but there are only two studies which analysed large samples and attempted to draw inferences on Anglo-Saxon social structure overall. Shephard (1979) analysed some 400 burials in order to elucidate the social background of the barrow burials of the late sixth to eighth centuries. As a result of statistical analyses, he identified five levels of wealth (Shephard 1979:62-3; Table 5-4). He observed that the proportion of category A burials is less than 10 per cent in flat inhumation cemeteries, but just under 30 per cent of barrow burials, and concluded that individuals in barrows belonged to a 'superordinate' class emerging from the late sixth century onwards. In spite of the fact that children have never been found under tumuli on their own, without adults, he suggested that the high rank displayed in barrows was ascribed, in contrast to the earlier phase when high social status could be achieved (Shephard 1979:70).

Table 5-4
Wealth categories after Shephard (1979)

category	males	females
A	broad range of rich finds, incl. ring sword, bronze bowl; *later:* seax, bronze bowl	gilt brooches, gold braiding, crystal ball, bracteates, bronze bowl; *later:* union sets, cabochon garnets, biconical gold beads
B	sword, shield, spear; *later:* seax + spear	(poorer versions of A objects)
C	shield, spear	(continuum; difficult to distinguish)
D	spear	
E	knife or unfurnished	knife and/or buckle or unfurnished

Chris Arnold (1980) analysed a sample of 27 cemeteries, of variable data quality, in order to identify the social factors in the development of the southern Anglo-Saxon kingdoms. He found an average of six levels of wealth across his study area, but noted that their number varied from four to eight in individual cemeteries (Arnold 1980:131). At the regional level, he found a difference in burial wealth between coastal and inland regions, which he attributed to differential trade opportunities and access to raw materials and imported goods: "The complexity of social structure, population densities, and levels of armament decrease with distance from commercial centres" on the coast (Arnold 1980:138; see Tab. 5-5).

Hodges (1989) has also applied the economic argument to the regional differences in social structures, but with a different conclusion. He pointed out that

Table 5-5

Regional differentiation of wealth and social structure after C. J. Arnold (1980)

socio-economic characteristics	coastal regions	inland regions
wealth levels	up to 7	up to 5
general wealth	rich	poor
external trade	much	little
weapon burial frequency	high	low

the early Kentish law codes appear to imply a much narrower gap between nobleman and freeman than in Wessex, and this may be explained with a more plentiful access to imported goods in Kent (Hodges 1989:39; for distribution maps of imports in early Anglo-Saxon contexts, see Huggett 1988).

Such quantitative analyses of grave goods have since been criticized by post-processualists for their functionalist and materialist outlook. But while post-processualist studies (e.g. Pader 1982; Richards 1987) have convincingly demonstrated the pervading symbolism in the early Anglo-Saxon burial ritual, they have shied away from attempting to present overall conclusions on Anglo-Saxon social structure. In that sense, Arnold's and Shephard's work still provides a useful starting point for any discussion of vertical social differentiation from a purely archaeological point of view.

One possible way forward is a multidimensional approach which combines the quantitative analysis of large samples with the consideration of symbolism in the various aspects of burial ritual. The analysis of male burials from 47 cemeteries of the fifth to seventh/eighth centuries, using archaeological and skeletal evidence (Härke 1989a; 1990; 1992a; 1992b), has demonstrated that weapon symbolism, burial treatment and living conditions do not coincide neatly. This underlines that the simple equation of burial wealth levels with social classes (let alone legal classes) may be misleading. Perhaps more importantly, the results also suggest that weapon symbolism changed over time, from a predominantly ethnic to a predominantly social meaning. This makes it necessary to distinguish clearly between early (fifth-/sixth-century) and late (seventh-century) graves. Within the group of males buried with weapons, a ranking by frequency of weapon-types and associated burial wealth reveals a top group characterized by the presence of sword, axe or seax (single-edged battle knife), followed at some distance by a group identified by shield and/or spear (see Table 5-6).

In spite of all the complications of the evidence, and many local and regional variations, it is sufficiently clear that the male members of the social élite are to be found among the men buried with sword, axe and/or seax: they were accompanied by the highest average number of grave goods; they had the highest proportion of drinking vessels (most likely symbolizing hospitality and the feast); their graves showed above-average labour investment in grave construction; their group includes an unusually high proportion of men with strong physique (suggesting regular exercise, perhaps weapon training and better nutrition); and their stature remained above average throughout the Early Anglo-Saxon period (unlike that of men with other weapons; cf. below, next section).

Table 5-6
Male grave equipment over time

weapons	proportion of male adults in:	
	5th/6th cent. %	7th cent. %
sword axe (5th/6th cent.) seax (6th/7th cent.)	6	6
shield spear	42	17
no weapons	52	77
	100	**100**

The changes over time are intriguing: while the proportion of male élite burials remained static throughout the Early Anglo-Saxon period, the proportion of intermediate burials dropped dramatically in the seventh century, and the proportion of graves without weapons rose accordingly (see Table 5-6). Religious and ritual change may well have played a role in this change, but given other archaeological indications of social change in the seventh century, such as the growing wealth differential between élite burials and others (C. J. Arnold 1982), social change is equally likely to have been a factor. This change appears to have involved a decline in status of many males of intermediate social standing, swelling the ranks of the lowest social orders. The historian Brooks has argued that in Anglo-Saxon society, as in other Germanic societies, the possession and bearing of arms was a symbol of legal freedom (Brooks 1978:83). If this argument has any relevance at all for the Anglo-Saxon weapon burial rite (which is by no means clear), we may be looking at a decline in the seventh century in numbers of ordinary freemen, with many of them descending to the status of semi-free or unfree.

The available settlement evidence provides some further clues as to the nature of vertical stratification in post-Roman England, and confirms the impression of social change in the seventh century. The mostly undifferentiated fifth-/sixth-century hamlets, with their haphazard lay-out, seem to be made up of groups of equal social standing. Where there are fences or ditches within these hamlets, as at Chalton, Catholme and West Stow, they separate farming units of comparable size (Champion 1977:367; Losco-Bradley 1977:359; West 1985:54, fig. 302); fenced enclosures on high-status sites are a different matter (cf. below). Accordingly, the timber-built 'halls' at Chalton have been seen as the "normal dwelling of the freeman, holder of one hide" (Addyman & Leigh 1972:24; 1973:19), and the entire settlement as a "village of ceorls" (Addyman & Leigh 1972:24).

Such interpretations have gained widespread, explicit or tacit acceptance, but they highlight the contrast to contemporary cemeteries which display distinctions of wealth and status. Attempts to identify farms of slightly higher status, on the basis of location within the settlement (West 1985:169) or number of ancillary buildings (Losco-Bradley 1977:363-4), have not produced very convincing results. Occasionally, small finds such as an enamelled mount from a hanging bowl and imported Frankish pottery at Chalton (Addyman and Leigh 1973:19-20; Champion 1977:369) or an iron tripod lamp at West Stow (West 1985:169), provide glimpses of possible differentials in material belongings and access to goods. But they are not enough to dispel the growing impression that the social differentiation seen in cemeteries may reflect status differences within rather than between families and/or households.

This picture changed from the late sixth century onwards, but most markedly during the seventh century. Parallel to signs of increasing social stratification in the burial evidence, we see in this phase the emergence of a settlement hierarchy and the appearance of larger buildings on high-status sites. The various elements of the settlement hierarchy develop from the early seventh century. By the end of the seventh century, at least three levels can be distinguished (C. J. Arnold 1984:278-9): rural settlements concerned with food production, trading sites engaged in craft production and commerce (Scull, this volume), and royal residences as centres of administration. Also from the seventh century onwards, ecclesiastical sites comprising churches, monasteries and episcopal palaces were forming their own settlement hierarchy.

The recent analysis of Anglo-Saxon buildings has shown that, from the end of the sixth century, some structures with a floor area above 80 sq.metres appear, sufficiently larger than average 'halls' (around 50 sq. metres; cf. above) to warrant an interpretation in terms of élite dwellings (Marshall & Marshall 1993:398). Annexes attached to timber buildings made their appearances at the same time, hinting at a connection with élite accommodation or the functions of élite farms.

The rise of an Anglo-Saxon élite is exemplified by two excavated high-status sites. The social status of Cowdery's Down (Hampshire) could only be inferred from the sizes of buildings on the site, from their superior building techniques, and the investment of timber and labour into their construction (Millett & James 1983:247). Over its occupation period in the sixth and seventh centuries, the settlement grew from three to six, and finally to ten, major buildings, with the size of the largest residential building in each phase increasing from 108 to 194 sq.metres. Two fenced enclosures attached to, and accessed through, buildings suggest the existence here of several social units. The size of the largest timber building (C12) at Cowdery's Down has led to its interpretation as the seasonal residence of a peripatetic élite (Millet & James 1983:249), or even the palace of a tribal leader (Marshall & Marshall 1993:400).

At Yeavering (Northumberland), a seventh-century royal estate of the kings of Bernicia has been identified from place-name evidence and the testimony of Bede (*HE* II.14; Hope-Taylor 1977). The 'township' was made up in each phase of a major timber-built hall, a few smaller buildings including a temple (later a church), a timber grandstand, and a large enclosure next to the residential complex (Hope-Taylor 1977: figs. 75-8). The successive timber halls, A2 and A4, (Hope-Taylor 1977:127 fig. 60, 130 fig. 61) of the early and mid-seventh century are the largest domestic structures uncovered so far on any early Saxon site. With their internal length of *ca* 25 m and their floor areas of 260 and 290 sq.metres respectively, each could have accommodated the 60 men who defended the Finnesburh hall (*Finnesburh Fragment*), or the 30 warriors killed by Grendel in King Hrothgar's hall (*Beowulf*, l. 123). Fenced enclosures were attached to the main hall in each phase, and like the partitions inside the halls (two in A2, one in A4), they hint at social and functional differentiations among the residents. The grandstand capacities of approximately 150 (later 320) people indicate the size of the group or groups assembled here, probably for council meetings, highlighting the function of this estate as an administrative centre (Hope-Taylor 1977:279).

It is interesting to note that social distinctions apparent in the seventh-century settlement evidence are mostly between sites, rarely within sites. This mirrors the appearance, in the seventh century, of isolated barrow burials in which the élite buried their members, away from 'ordinary' community cemeteries. Enclosures on high-status settlements which suggest some kind of internal differentiation are so far ill understood in terms of their exact functions and implications. Defended sites are virtually non-existent in early Anglo-Saxon England, with the exception of the strange, empty enclosure at Yeavering which was located next to the royal complex, not around it. It seems that social differentiation, as gender dichotomy, was expressed much more clearly in burial ritual than in domestic architecture or settlement lay-out. In this respect, Anglo-Saxon England differed from the Celtic areas of Britain where we find an earlier, and more pronounced, settlement hierarchy (Alcock 1987), but no social differentiation in the burial evidence.

Ethnicity and social structure

In many post-Roman societies, social structure and ethnic differentation were interrelated, usually as a result of immigrant groups achieving control over native populations. Nowhere is this interrelation clearer than in the early Anglo-Saxon laws where the Old English term *wealh* could mean either 'Welshman' or 'slave' (Pelteret 1995:43; Whitelock 1979:402 n.5). This illustrates at the same time the ambiguity and fluidity of the concept of ethnic identity in Migration-period Europe (cf. Pohl, this volume). The 'tribal' distinctions between Angles, Saxons, Jutes and others do not seem to have had any social significance and, while they provide interesting case studies in their own right, the discussion will be limited here to native Britons ('Welsh') and their relationship with the immigrant *Germani* and their descendants.

The narrative sources report the wholesale slaughter of the natives by the invaders, with the survivors going into "perpetual servitude" (Bede, *HE* I.15, following Gildas XXIV.3-XXV.1). The best evidence for the status of Britons in an Anglo-Saxon kingdom is provided by the late seventh-century laws of King Ine of Wessex (extant as an appendix to Alfred's laws). They list six different wergild levels for the Welsh, four of them below the wergild level of a freeman (Ine 23.3 and 32); but the king's Welsh horseman had the wergild of a freeman (Ine 33), and a Welshman with five hides had three times the wergild of a freeman, or half that of a nobleman (Ine 24.2). One clause implies that a Welsh slave could have free kindred (Ine 74.1). But it appears that in some respects, all Welsh were considered to have a lower status than the English: if accused of cattle theft by an Englishman, the accused had to deny it with double the oath than if the accusation came from a Welshman (Ine 46.1). Kentish laws do not mention the Welsh as such, but it has been suggested that the semi-free *læt* in the laws of Æthelberht (26) may have been Britons (cf. above).

The laws imply that, while some Britons could be wealthy freemen, the majority were of low legal status. On the other hand, not all slaves were of British extraction: Englishmen as well as Welshmen could become penally enslaved (Ine 24 and 54.2). At the same time, the laws also imply a close co-existence of both groups within the same kingdom and under the same jurisdiction. This co-existence is confirmed by Celtic river names and place-names in England, the analysis of which has suggested that bilingual Britons had transmitted Celtic names to Germanic-speaking immigrants (Jackson 1956:220-46). However, the small number of Celtic loan-words in the English language indicates a low level of intermarriage between the two groups (Loyn 1962:12-4), except possibly for Northumbria where personal names suggest a larger number of mixed marriages (Whitelock 1962:18). Thus, the assimilation of Britons into an English-speaking language community must, at least initially, have been the result of cultural rather than biological processes. This large-scale assimilation and its one-sided linguistic outcome would have been facilitated by the low social and political status of the Britons and their language (Charles-Edwards 1995:729-30).

Among archaeologists, the recent re-assessment of the Anglo-Saxon 'invasion' (C. J. Arnold 1984a; Garwood 1989; Higham 1992; Hodges 1989) has led to renewed interest in the question of British survival which is crucial to the revisionist argument of minimal immigration. However, the search for natives in the archaeological record has not been very successful so far. The identification of native, post-Roman settlements has been rare, tentative, and limited to the northern and western fringes of the Anglo-Saxon settlement areas (Higham 1992:106 fig. 4.11, 107). But even if the search for British farmsteads or villages were successful, their identification may not tell us much about their position within the social structures of post-Roman England. Any attempt to find in the Anglo-Saxon settlement sites the low-status Britons mentioned in the sources comes up against two problems: the ambiguity of internal subdivisions within houses and settlements, which may be economic, gender or status related (or a combination of these factors); and the absence of a distinctive, native material culture.

The latter problem also affects the interpretation of grave goods in terms of ethnic affiliation, but other aspects of the burial ritual as well as skeletal evidence may provide further clues. The native sub-Roman burial rite is known from sites such as Cannington, Somerset (Rahtz 1977): inhumation without grave goods, the body extended on its back, head approximately to the west. This is a useful contrast to Anglo-Saxon cremations, but it raises the question of how to distinguish Anglo-Saxon and native inhumations. The analysis of the archaeological and, where available, skeletal data of a sample of 1600 male and juvenile burials from early Anglo-Saxon cemeteries has suggested that in the fifth and sixth centuries, burial with weapons was used as an ethnic marker by the immigrants and their descendants (Härke 1990; 1992a). The main arguments leading to this conclusion are (Härke 1992a:195-200):

(1)   the origin of the weapon burial rite on the Continent, and the absence of weapon deposition in graves in Roman Britain and Celtic post-Roman Britain and Ireland;

(2)   the stature differential of 1 inches to 2 inches (2.5 to 5 cm) between men with and without weapons (compared separately for each cemetery).

While the latter may, in principle, be a purely social phenomenon created by preferential diet and living conditions of the élite, this is unlikely to be the case here. For a start, the two groups do not show any differential at all in indicators of stress and malnourishment. Secondly, the proportion of men buried with weapons (see Table 5-6) does not encourage an interpretation in terms of an 'élite'. Thirdly, the stature differential disappears in the 7th century, but social differences do not—quite the opposite in fact (cf. above). Finally, the differential in question is virtually the same as that between British Iron-age and Romano-British male stature on the one hand, and post-Roman male stature in northern Germany and England, on the other.

The key implication of the argument is that in the fifth/sixth centuries, up to half of the men (i.e. those without weapons) buried in 'Anglo-Saxon' inhumation cemeteries may have been native Britons. The weapon symbolism suggests that the Germanic population was expressing its dominance in ritual; and its higher average number of grave goods suggests that it had more disposable wealth. It is as yet impossible to say if the proportion of natives to immigrants was similar among the females. In her thesis, Brush (1993) was unable to unambiguously identify British females on the basis of dress items. It may be that a combination of archaeological and skeletal data, as used for males, will be more successful, but the wider spectrum of female grave goods and burial wealth may make it difficult.

In addition to the considerable proportion of natives in Anglo-Saxon cemeteries, further Britons must have lived in their own enclaves in southern and eastern England. Evidence for them is provided by river, hill and place-names (Jackson 1956:234-41); by the Upper Thames cemetery of Queenford Farm, post-Roman but without Anglo-Saxon artefacts (Chambers 1987); by an East Anglian cluster of enamelled dress ornaments (Scull 1985); by Anglo-Saxon pottery scatters on Romano-British settlement sites on Salisbury Plain (pers. comm. M. G. Fulford and R. Entwistle); and indirectly by a general drop in male stature in the seventh/eighth centuries which was most pronounced in Wessex. The latter is best explained as the consequence of the acculturation and assimilation of British populations which had previously been invisible in the archaeological record.

Two other developments suggest that the increasing assimilation of the native population and their integration into Anglo-Saxon society during the seventh and eighth centuries may have been connected with changes in the social structure. During that period, burial with weapons became less frequent, was more and more concentrated in rich burials, and was no longer used as an ethnic marker (Härke 1992b). The other development was the location of barrows and other, contemporaneous burial sites next to, in, or around, prehistoric barrows or Roman sites. A case in point is the mid-seventh-century barrow on Lowbury Hill, Oxfordshire (Härke 1994b). It is located next to a Roman temple site, and only a few miles from Wallingford, the name of which indicates the existence here of a British enclave. The rich male burial in the barrow contained two objects (a hanging bowl and a unique spearhead) with enamel decoration which is widely accepted as a Celtic marker. The seventh- and eighth-century evidence suggests that the social élite transformed the weapon burial rite into a mere status symbol, and attempted to establish a link to the indigenous, pre-Anglo-Saxon past, conceivably to legitimate their rule over an increasingly mixed population.

There can be little doubt that ethnic factors played an important role in early Anglo-Saxon social structure. Archaeological, historical and linguistic evidence are in agreement on this point. Parallels for this overlap of social and ethnic differentiations may be found in tribal and early state societies around the world where such situations have often been the consequence of immigration and conquest.

Conclusion

Even though this paper draws on a variety of data, it turned out to be easier to construct static descriptions of certain aspects of society in certain phases than to infer something about the actual workings of society. Also, the various types of evidence surveyed above give uneven and differential weight to the key factors of Anglo-Saxon social organization before the ninth century. The paramount importance of kinship is quite clear in the written sources: it provided the fabric of society, and determined to a large degree an Anglo-Saxon's status and, literally, his or her value. By contrast, the archaeological evidence, by its very nature, puts the emphasis on the material expression of status, relegating kinship to being one of the possible inferences.

Interestingly, though, archaeology highlights a number of aspects which are less prominent in the sources: household, gender and age. In fact, only a sophisticated analysis can achieve the distinction between household and family in the archaeological record, but the units we perceive in the organization of cemeteries are better explained in terms of residential units with internal social differentiation (i.e. households) than kinship units (i.e. families). The marked display of gender and age in early Saxon burial ritual poses problems. Not only are these factors less pronounced in the historical sources and virtually invisible in the settlement evidence: the emphasis on gender is in stark contrast to theoretical expectations concerning blurred gender roles in settler societies; and the evidence for age groups is inconsistent, with the written sources stressing different age thresholds from those apparent in burial ritual.

But both, written sources (the laws in particular) and the inferences possible from cemetery evidence agree on the key role played by ethnic affiliation in the Early Anglo-Saxon period. Britons seem to have made up a large proportion of the population buried in 'Anglo-Saxon' cemeteries, and most of them appear to have been of unfree, or otherwise low, status. Differences between the kingdoms in the proportions of Britons are likely to have played a role in creating regional differences in social structure. Increasing intermarriage with Britons in Anglo-Saxon settlements, and increasing assimilation of Britons in enclaves, may have been an important part of social change in England. The shift of emphasis in burial ritual from ethnic affiliation to social differentiation in the seventh century appears to mark a crucial transition: from ethnically divided conquest societies to the formation of early states.

Acknowledgements—I am grateful for the incentive that the CIROSS invitation gave me to clarify in my own mind a number of issues relating to early Anglo-Saxon society, and to bring into better focus those questions for which clarification could not be achieved. I benefitted immensely from the seminar discussions at San Marino even though this paper may not show it: points discussed or corrected during the meeting were not altered for this version as it would have rendered the publication of the discussion pointless. Helena Hamerow (Durham) kindly read and commented on the draft paper.

References

Textual sources:

[Abbreviations: *ASC = Anglo-Saxon Chronicle*; *HE* = Bede, *Historia ecclesiastica gentis Anglorum*] *Anglorum*]

The Anglo-Saxon Chronicle: see Earle & Plummer (eds.) 1892; Dumville & Keynes (eds.) 1983-.
Battle of Maldon: see Dobbie (ed.) 1958; Whitelock 1979 (trans.).
Bede
        Historia ecclesiastica gentis Anglorum: see Colgrave & Mynors 1969.
        Life of St Cuthbert: see Colgrave (ed.) 1940.
Beowulf: see Swanton 1978.
Eddius Stephanus
        Life of St Wilfred: see Colgrave (ed.) 1927.
Felix
        Life of St Guthlac: see Colgrave (ed.) 1956.

Finnesburh Fragment: see Dobbie (ed.) 1958.
Gildas
        De excidio Britanniae: see Winterbottom (ed.) 1978.
Laws of Æthelberht, Alfred, Athelstan, Cnut, Hlothere and Eadric, Ine, Wihtred:
      see Liebermann 1903 (ed.).

Bibliography:

Adams, B. D.
   1982   The Anglo-Saxon cemetery at Wakerley, Northamptonshire. M. Phil. thesis, Birkbeck College, London.
Addyman, P. V.
   1972   The Anglo-Saxon house: a new review. *Anglo-Saxon England* 1: 273-307.
   1976   Archaeology and Anglo-Saxon society. In *Problems in economic and social archaeology*. G. de G. Sieveking, I. H. Longworth & K. E. Wilson (eds.), pp. 309-322. London: Duckworth.
Addyman, P. V., & D. Leigh
   1972   Anglo-Saxon houses at Chalton, Hampshire. *Medieval Archaeology* 16: 13-31.
   1973   The Anglo-Saxon village at Chalton, Hampshire: second interim report. *Medieval Archaeology* 17: 1-25.
Alcock, L.
   1981   Quantity or quality: the Anglian graves of Bernicia. In *Angles, Saxons and Jutes: essays presented to J. N. L. Myres*. V. I. Evison (ed.), pp. 168-183. Oxford: Clarendon. (Reprinted in Alcock 1987:255-266).
   1987   *Economy, society and warfare among the Britons and Saxons.* Cardiff: University of Wales Press.
Aldsworth, F. R.
   1978   The Droxford Anglo-Saxon cemetery, Soberton, Hampshire. *Proceedings of the Hampshire Field Club Archaeological Society* 35: 93-182.
Ariès, P.
   1962   *Centuries of childhood. A social history of family life.* London: Jonathan Cape.
Arnold, C. J.
   1980   Wealth and social structure: a matter of life and death. In *Anglo-Saxon cemeteries 1979*. P. Rahtz, T. Dickinson & L. Watts (eds.), pp. 81-142. (British Archaeological Report 82). Oxford: BAR.
   1981   Early Anglo-Saxon pottery: production and distribution. In *Production and distribution: a ceramic viewpoint*. H. Howard & E. L. Morris (eds.), pp. 243-255. (British Archaeological Report, S 120). Oxford: BAR.
   1982   Stress as a stimulus to socio-economic change: England in the seventh century. In *Ranking, resource and exchange*. C. Renfrew & S. Shennan (eds.), pp. 124-131. (New Directions in Archaeology). Cambridge: Cambridge University Press.
   1984a   *Roman Britain to Saxon England.* (Croom Helm Studies in Archaeology). London: Croom Helm.
   1984b   Social evolution in post-Roman western Europe. In *European social evolution*. J. Bintliff (ed.), pp. 277-294. West Chiltington: Chanctonbury Press.
   1988   *An archaeology of the early Anglo-Saxon kingdoms.* London & New York: Routledge.

Arnold, K.
    1986   Die Einstellung zum Kind im Mittelalter. In *Mensch und Umwelt im Mittelalter*.
                B. Herrmann (ed.), pp. 53-64. Darmstadt: Deutsche Verlags-Anstalt.
Bell, M.
    1977   Excavations at Bishopstone, Lewes. *Sussex Archaeological Collections* 115.
Brooks, N. P.
    1978   Arms, status and warfare in Late-Saxon England. In *Æthelred the Unready*.
                D. Hill (ed.), pp. 81-103. (British Archaeological Report 59). Oxford: BAR.
Brothwell, D.
    1972   Palaeodemography and earlier British populations. *World Archaeology*
                4: 75-87.
Brush, K. A.
    1988   Gender and mortuary analysis in pagan Anglo-Saxon archaeology.
                Archaeological Review from Cambridge 7 (1): 76-89.
    1993   Adorning the Dead. Unpubl. Ph.D. thesis. Cambridge University.
Chambers, R. A.
    1987   The Late- and Sub-Roman cemetery at Queenford Farm, Dorchester-
                on-Thames, Oxon. *Oxoniensia* 52: 35-69.
Champion, T.
    1977   Chalton. *Current Archaeology* 59: 364-369.
Charles-Edwards, T.
    1972   Kinship, status and the origins of the hide. *Past and Present* 56: 3-33.
    1995   Language and society among the insular Celts AD 400-1000. In *The Celtic
                world*. M. J. Green (ed.), pp. 703-736. London & New York: Routledge.
Christlein, R.
    1973   Besitzabstufungen zur Merowingerzeit im Spiegel reicher Grabfunde aus
                West- und Süddeutschland. *Jahrbuch des Römisch-Germanischen
                Zentralmuseums* 20: 147-180.
Colgrave, B. (ed.)
    1927   *Life of Bishop Wilfred by Eddius Stephanus*. Cambridge: Cambridge
                University Press.
    1940   *Two Lives of Saint Cuthbert*. Cambridge: Cambridge University Press.
    1956   *Felix's Life of St Guthlac*. Cambridge: Cambridge University Press.
Colgrave, B., & R. A. B. Mynors (eds.)
    1969   *Bede's Ecclesiastical History of the English People*. Oxford: Clarendon Press.
Cook, A. M., & M. W. Dacre
    1985   *Excavations at Portway, Andover, 1974-5*. (Oxford University Committee for
                Archaeology, Monograph 4). Oxford: Oxford Committee for Archaeology.
Cramp, R.
    1983   Anglo-Saxon settlement. In *Settlement in North Britain 1000 BC - AD
                1000*. J. C. Chapman & H. C. Mytum (eds.), pp. 263-297. (British
                Archaeological Report 118). Oxford: BAR.
Crawford, S.
    1991   Age differentiation and related social status: A study of Early Anglo-Saxon
                childhood. Unpublished Ph. D. thesis, Oxford University.
    1993   Children, death and the afterlife in Anglo-Saxon England. *Anglo-Saxon
                Studies in Archaeology and History* 6: 83-91.
Dickinson, T. M., & H. Härke
    1992   *Early Anglo-Saxon Shields*. (Archaeologia 110). London: Society of
                Antiquaries.

Dietrich, S. C.
1980　　　An introduction to women in Anglo-Saxon society. In *The Women of England from Anglo-Saxon Times to the Present*. B. Kanner (ed.), pp. 32-56. London: Mansell.

Dixon, P. H.
1993　　　The Anglo-Saxon settlement at Mucking: an interpretation. *Anglo-Saxon Studies in Archaeology and History* 6: 125-147.

Dobbie, E. V. K. (ed.)
1958　　　*The Anglo-Saxon minor poems*. (The Anglo-Saxon poetic records, Vol. VI). New York: Columbia University Press.

Dumville, D. N., & S. Keynes (eds.)
1983-　　　*The Anglo-Saxon Chronicle. A Collaborative Edition*. (23 vols.). Cambridge: Brewer.

Earle, J., & C. Plummer
1892　　　*Two of the Saxon Chronicles Parallel*. (2 vols). Oxford: Clarendon Press.

Evison, V. I.
1987　　　*Dover: The Buckland Anglo-Saxon cemetery*. (Historic Buildings and Monuments Commission for England, Archaeological Report No. 3). London: English Heritage.

Fell, C.
1984a　　　*Women in Anglo-Saxon England*. London: British Museum.
1984b.　　　A *friwif locbore* revisited. *Anglo-Saxon England* 13: 157-165.

Garwood, P.
1989　　　Social transformation and relations of power in Britain in the late fourth to the sixth centuries A.D. *Scottish Archaeological Review* 6: 90-106.

Härke, H.
1989a　　　Early Saxon weapon burials: frequencies, distributions and weapon combinations. In *Anglo-Saxon weapons and warfare*. S. C. Hawkes (ed.), pp. 49-61. (Oxford University Committee for Archaeology, Monograph 21). Oxford: Oxford Committee for Archaeology.
1989b　　　Knives in Early Saxon burials: blade length and age at death. *Medieval Archaeology* 33: 144-148.
1990　　　'Warrior graves'? The background of the Anglo-Saxon weapon burial rite. *Past and Present* 126: 22-43.
1992a　　　*Angelsächsische Waffengräber des 5. bis 7. Jahrhunderts*. Zeitschrift für Archäologie des Mittelalters, Beiheft 6. Köln & Bonn: Rheinland-Verlag & Habelt.
1992b　　　Changing symbols in a changing society: the Anglo-Saxon weapon burial rite in the seventh century. In *The age of Sutton Hoo*. M. Carver (ed.), pp. 149-165. Woodbridge: The Boydell Press.
1994a　　　Data types in burial analysis. In *Prehistoric graves as a source of information*. B. Stjernquist (ed.), pp. 31-39. (Kungl. Vitterhets och Antikvitets Akademiens Konferenser 29). Stockholm: Almqvist & Wiksell.
1994b　　　Lowbury Hill, Oxon: A context for the Saxon barrow. *Archaeological Journal* 151: 202-206.
1995　　　Weapon burials and knives. In *Two Oxfordshire Anglo-Saxon cemeteries: Berinsfield and Didcot*. A. Boyle, A. Dodd, D. Miles & A. Mudd (eds.), pp. 67-75. (Thames Valley Landscapes Monograph 8: 67-75). Oxford: Oxfordshire Archaeological Unit.
n.d.　　　The nature of burial data. In *From burial to society*. K. H. Nielsen & K. Jensen (eds.). Århus: Århus Universitet.

Hamerow, H.
1993   *Excavations at Mucking. Vol. 2: The Anglo-Saxon settlement.*
          (Archaeological Report 21). London: English Heritage.

Hastorp, C.
1991   Gender, space and prehistory. In *Engendering archaeology.* J. M. Gero &
          M. W. Conkey (eds.), pp. 132-159. Oxford: Blackwell.

Hawkes, S. C., & C. Wells
1983   The inhumed skeletal material from an early Anglo-Saxon cemetery in
          Worthy Park, Kingsworthy, Hampshire, South England. *Palaeobios* 1: 1-36.

Herlihy, D.
1985   *Medieval households.* (Studies in Cultural History). Cambridge, MA:
          Harvard University Press.

1995   *Women, family and society in medieval Europe: historical essays,
          1978-1991.* Providence, RI: Berghahn.

Herrmann, B., G. Grupe, S. Hummel, H. Piepenbrink & H. Schutkowksi
1990   *Prähistorische Anthropologie: Leitfaden der Feld- und Labormethoden.*
          Berlin: Springer Verlag.

Higham, N.
1992   *Rome, Britain and the Anglo-Saxons.* (The Archaeology of Change series).
          London: Seaby.

Hills, C., & K. Penn
1981   *The Anglo-Saxon cemetery at Spong Hill, North Elmham. Part 2: Catalogue
          of cremations, Nos. 22, 41 and 1691-2285.* (East Anglian Archaeology 11).
          Gressenhall: Norfolk Archaeological Unit.

Hirst, S. M.
1985   *An Anglo-Saxon inhumation cemetery at Sewerby, East Yorkshire.* (York
          University Archaeological Publications 4). York: University of York Press.

Hodges, R.
1989   *The Anglo-Saxon Achievement: Archaeology and the Beginnings of English
          Society.* London: Duckworth.

Hope-Taylor, B.
1977   *Yeavering: an Anglo-British centre of early Northumbria.* (Department of
          Environment Archaeological Reports 7). London: H. M. S. O.

Huggett, J.
1988   Imported grave-goods and the early Anglo-Saxon economy. *Medieval
          Archaeology* 32: 63-96.

Jackson, K. H.
1956   *Language and history in early Britain.* (Edinburgh Univ. Publications,
          Language & Literature 4). Edinburgh: Edinburgh University Press.

James, E.
1989   Burial and status in the early medieval west. *Transactions of the Royal
          Historical Society* (5th series) 39: 23-40.

James, S., A. Marshall & M. Millett
1984   An early medieval building tradition. *Archaeological Journal* 141: 182-215.

Jørgensen, L.
1987   Family burial practices and inheritance systems: The development of an Iron
          Age society from 500 BC to AD 1000 on Bornholm, Denmark. *Acta
          Archaeologica* 58: 17-53.

1990   *Bäkkegård and Glasergård: Two cemeteries from the Late Iron Age on
          Bornholm.* (Arkæologiske Studier 8). Copenhagen: Akademisk Forlag.

1991   Castel Trosino and Nocera Umbra: A chronological and social analysis of family burial practices in Lombard Italy (6th - 8th cent. AD). *Acta Archaeologica* 62: 1-58.

John, E.
1964   *Land tenure in early England: a discussion of some problems.* (Studies in Early English History 1). Leicester: Leicester University Press.

Keufler, M. S.
1991   "A wryed existence": attitudes toward children in Anglo-Saxon England. *Journal of Social History* 24: 823-834.

Kinsley, A. G.
1993   *Broughton Lodge. Excavations on the Romano-British settlement and Anglo-Saxon cemetery at Broughton Lodge, Willoughby-on-the-Wolds, Nottinghamshire, 1964-8.* (Archaeological Monographs 4). Nottingham: University of Nottingham.

Klinck, A. L.
1982   Anglo-Saxon women and the law. *Journal of Medieval History* 8: 107-121.

Lacayo, R.
1996   Law and order. TIME 147 no. 5 (January 29, 1996): 30-35.

Lancaster, L.
1958   Kinship in Anglo-Saxon society. *British Journal of Sociology* 9: 230-250, 359-377.

Larick, R.
1990   'Gender, social age and personal adornment in Northern Kenia'. Unpublished paper given at a Theoretical Archaeology Group Conference (TAG 90). Lampeter.

Leach, E. R.
1964   *Political systems of Highland Burma.* London: Athlone Press.

Le Jan, R.
1995   Entre maîtres et dépendants: reflexions sur la famille paysanne en Lotharingie, aux IXe et Xe siècles. In *Campagnes médiévales: l'homme et son espace. Études offertes à Robert Fossier*, pp 277-296. Paris: Sorbonne.

Liebermann, F.
1903   *Die Gesetze der Angelsachsen.* Halle: Niemeyer.

Losco-Bradley, S.
1977   Catholme. *Current Archaeology* 59: 358-364.

Loyn, H. R.
1962   *Anglo-Saxon England and the Norman Conquest.* (Social and Economic History of England). London: Longman.
1974   Kinship in Anglo-Saxon England. *Anglo-Saxon England* 3: 197-209.

Marshall, A., & G. Marshall
1993   Differentiation, change and continuity in Anglo-Saxon buildings. *Archaeological Journal* 150: 366-402.

Meyer, M. A.
1980   Land charters and the legal position of Anglo-Saxon women. In *The women of England from Anglo-Saxon times to the present.* B. Kanner (ed.), pp. 57-82. London: Mansell.

Middleton, P.
1995   Weaving Destiny: changes in the significance of textile production to the economy of Anglo-Saxon England and its impact on female labour and status. Unpubl. M. A. thesis, University of Reading.

Millett, M., & S. James
    1983   Excavations at Cowdery's Down, Basingstoke, Hampshire, 1978-81.
                Archaeological Journal 140: 151-279.
Ottinger, I.
    1974   Waffenbeigabe in Kindergräbern. In *Studien zur vor- und früh-
                geschichtlichen Archäologie (Werner-Festschrift)*. Vol. 2. G. Kossack &
                G. Ulbert (eds.), pp. 387-410. (Münchener Beiträge zur Vor- und
                Frühgeschichte, Erganzungsband 1/II). München: Beck.
Pader, E. J.
    1982   *Symbolism, social relations and the interpretation of mortuary remains.*
                (British Archaeological Report, S 130). Oxford: BAR.
Pelteret, D.
    1995   *Slavery in early mediaeval England: from the reign of Alfred until the twelfth
                century.* (Studies in Anglo-Saxon History 7). Woodbridge: The Boydell Press.
Philp, B.
    1973   *Excavations in West Kent 1960-1970.* (Research Reports in the Kent Series 2).
                Dover: Kent Archaeological Rescue Unit.
Rahtz, P. A
    1976   Buildings and rural settlement. In *The archaeology of Anglo-Saxon England.*
                D. M. Wilson (ed.), pp. 49-98. Cambridge: Cambridge University Press.
    1977   Late Roman cemeteries and beyond. In *Burial in the Roman world.*
                R. Reece (ed.), pp. 53-64. (CBA Research Report 22). London: CBA.
Richards, J. D.
    1987   *The significance of form and decoration of Anglo-Saxon cremation urns.*
                (British Archaeological Report 166). Oxford: BAR.
Samson, R
    1987   Social structures from Reihengräber: mirror or mirage? *Scottish
                Archaeological Review* 4: 116-126.
Schwab, H.
    1982   Bemerkenswert ausgestattete Kindergräber der Merowingerzeit.
                Archäologisches Korrespondenzblatt 12: 251-262.
Scull, C.
    1985   Further evidence from East Anglia for enamelling on early Anglo-Saxon
                metalwork. *Anglo-Saxon Studies in Archaeology and History* 4: 117-124.
    1993   Archaeology, early Anglo-Saxon society and the origins of Anglo-Saxon
                kingdoms. *Anglo-Saxon Studies in Archaeology and History* 6: 65-82.
Sheehan, M.
    1963   *The will in medieval England.* (Studies and Texts 6). Toronto:Pontifical
                Institute of Mediaeval Studies.
Shephard, J.
    1979   The social identity of the individual in isolated barrows and barrow
                cemeteries in Anglo-Saxon England. In *Space, hierarchy and society.* B. C.
                Burnham & J. Kingsbury (eds.), pp. 47-79. (British Archaeological Report,
                S 59). Oxford: BAR.
Sherlock, S. J., & M. Welch
    1992   *An Anglo-Saxon cemetery at Norton, Cleveland.* (CBA Research Report 82).
                London: Council for British Archaeology.
Stenton, D. M.
    1957   *The English woman in history.* London & New York: Allen & Unwin.

Stenton, F. M.
1943   The historical bearing of place-name studies: the place of women in Anglo-Saxon society. *Transactions of the Royal Historical Society* (4th series) 25: 1-13.
1971   *Anglo-Saxon England*. 3rd ed. (Oxford History of England 2). Oxford: Clarendon Press.

Steuer, H.
1982   *Frühgeschichtliche Sozialstrukturen in Mitteleuropa*. (Abhandlungen der Akademie der Wissenschaften in Göttingen, Phil.-Hist. Klasse, 3. Folge, 128). Göttingen: Vandenhoeck & Ruprecht.

Stoodley, N.
1994   Gender relations within frontier societies. Unpubl. typescript, Reading University.

Swanton, M.
1978   *Beowulf*. (Manchester Medieval Classics). Manchester: Manchester University Press.

Turton, D.
1995   History, age and the anthropologists. In *After Empire: Towards an Ethnology of Europe's Barbarians*. G. Ausenda (ed.), pp. 95-108. Woodbridge: The Boydell Press.

Van Gennep, A.
1960   *The rites of passage*. London: Routledge & Kegan Paul.

Wainwright, F. T.
1959   Æthelflæd, Lady of the Mercians. In *The Anglo-Saxons: Studies presented to Bruce Dickins*. P. Clemoes (ed.), pp. 53-70. London: Bowes & Bowes.

Watts, D. J.
1989   Infant burials and Romano-British Christianity. *Archaeological Journal* 146: 372-383.

Welch, M. G.
1980   The Saxon cemeteries of Sussex. In *Anglo-Saxon cemeteries 1979*. P. Rahtz, T. Dickinson & L. Watts (eds.), pp. 255-283. (British Archaeological Report 82). Oxford: BAR.
1983   *Early Anglo-Saxon Sussex*. (British Archaeological Report 112) Oxford: BAR.

Wells, C., & H. Cayton
1980   The human bones. In *Excavations in North Elmham Park, 1967-1972*. P. Wade-Martins (ed.), pp. 247-314. (East Anglian Archaeology 9). Gressenhall: Norfolk Archaeological Unit.

West, S.
1985   *West Stow: The Anglo-Saxon village*. (2 vols). (East Anglian Archaeology 24). Ipswich: Suffolk County Planning Department.

Whitelock, D.
1930   *Anglo-Saxon Wills*. (Cambridge Studies in English Legal History). Cambridge: Cambridge University Press.
1962   *The beginnings of English society*. (Pelican History of England 2). Harmondsworth: Penguin.
1979   *English historical documents*. Vol. 1. London: Eyre Methuen.

Wilson, D. M.
1976   *The Archaeology of Anglo-Saxon England*. Cambridge: Cambridge University Press.

Winterbottom, M. (ed.)
  1978   *Gildas: The Ruin of Britain and Other Sources.* (Arthurian Period Sources).
            London & Chichester: Phillimore.
Wormald, P.
  1978   Bede, Beowulf and the conversion of the Anglo-Saxon aristocracy. In *Bede
            and Anglo-Saxon England.* R. T. Farrell (ed.), pp. 32-95. (British
            Archaeological Report 46). Oxford: BAR.
Zimmermann, W. H.
  1988   Regelhafte Innengliederung prähistorischer Langhäuser in den
            Nordseeanrainerstaaten: Ein Zeugnis enger, langandauernder kultureller
            Kontakte. *Germania* 66: 465-488.

Discussion

AUSENDA: You discuss the underrepresentation of the youngest age groups in
pagan cemeteries. Among Hadendowa and Beni Amer, no formal funeral and
burial ceremony is performed for infants who were not circumcized. The age for
circumcision varies between 1 and 5 for both males and females. This may have
been also the case for Anglo-Saxon infants who had not undergone the first
socializing transition.

You also discuss high infant mortality figures. These were not only true of Third
World societies but of European societies until World War I. Here is a tabulation of
infant mortality including infants up to 5 years of age in the crown lands of the
Austro-Hungarian Empire which had one of the most thorough statistical services
in Europe (Table 5-7)). It shows values gradually decreasing from peaks as high as
56 per cent in Galicia in 1873 to lows of about 25 per cent just before World War I.

On carrying swords: Hadendowa carry long (about one metre) straight swords
hanging from the left shoulder. Swords are carried by most adults living in the
bush as a token of prestige, usually when they go to market in the village. For
defence they carry a heavy curved throwing stick about a metre long. Those who
have settled in large villages no longer carry swords because they have other
tokens of prestige at their disposal, such as property, stores and pick-ups.

You quote Stenton who concluded that "...women were then more nearly the
equal of their husbands and brothers". There is a parallel among Beni Amer in that
women in the bush had considerable independence (Münzinger 1890:257-8) and
they still do nowadays. The reasons are manifold: first of all tents, made of mats of
palm leaves, are made and erected by women and, therefore, belong to them. If a
man should have an argument with his wife he would have to leave the tent and
sleep on the ground outside the encampment. In the second place, they are
independent as a consequence of the 'endogamic' marriage system: women in an
encampment are closely related among themselves and have their close agnatic kin
to defend them in case of prevarication by their husbands. Lastly livestock
obtained at marriage is shared in a *byrik* (Ti.), a partnership in which the wife owns
as many head as her bridegroom plus one. The picture changes when they become

Table 5-7
Infant Mortality as a % of Live Births in crown lands of Austria-Hungary

Year	Co.A.	Styria	Carin.	Carn.	Littoral	Tirol	Bohem.	Morav.	Siles.	Galic.	Buko.	Dalm.	Hung.	Cr.S.
1872	44.5	33.9	28.9	30.5	▲44.7	29.5	40.4	41.3	▲47.8	44.6	42.8	26.4		
3	44.2	33.4	31.6	▲40.6	40.6	33.5	▲42.0	▲47.9	39.6	▲56.8	44.4	29.2		
4														
5														
6	39.3	29.0	25.6	28.5	36.1	30.2	35.0	34.3	32.9	39.6	▲49.0	▲42.3		
7														
8														
9														
1880														
1	37.6	▲35.2	30.7	31.2	32.6	29.2	39.5	39.5	35.8	41.3	45.7	23.1	41.7	35.3
2	39.7		33.4		29.2	35.9	40.3	▲36.1						
				44.9	36.5									
3	36.9	33.5	▲31.9	31.4	34.5	31.3	36.7	35.6	36.5	40.3	40.2	31.8	37.1	37.5
4	36.8	30.4	28.4	28.1	36.3	30.5	39.0	35.9	33.0	38.6	37.4	29.4	36.0	36.0
5	39.9	32.1	31.6	29.6	34.8	31.7	37.1	36.7	36.2	38.6	45.2	26.3	38.9	32.5
6	37.4	30.8	30.9	29.4	39.1	28.7	38.8	38.4	38.6	38.4	38.7	26.7	38.9	31.2
7	35.9	31.9	28.6	32.3	34.2	28.4	37.1	35.2	35.7	40.4	37.4	26.1	42.2	35.1
8	35.9	29.7	29.4	33.1	34.8	29.8	39.7	35.2	26.1	38.4	41.6	31.8	38.2	34.6
9	33.8	30.8	32.2	34.4	30.3	28.5	35.3	36.4	34.1	36.0	36.3	31.3	35.5	34.2
90	36.8	33.1	33.9	34.2	38.2	29.4	39.2	41.8	38.4	40.5	41.3	28.9	41.4	40.2
1	36.2	32.4	28.0	29.6	36.2	30.7	36.6	33.2	30.9	37.4	42.2	28.9	41.3	39.4
2	35.8	33.3	29.6	38.0	35.3	30.0	38.0	38.4	35.8	39.9	45.3	31.6	▲45.5	▲50.1
3	32.4	31.3	35.1	33.1	33.1	28.1	35.0	35.0	35.8	33.0	32.3	25.6	37.8	39.3
4	32.4	29.6	30.4	33.5	35.0	27.0	36.6	39.8	37.3	39.5	37.6	28.6	38.7	38.4
5	32.9	31.0	28.2	32.8	28.0	30.8	33.1	33.8	35.9	39.5	42.6	31.7	36.6	35.7
6	29.8	33.6	30.7	37.4	37.8	27.0	31.7	32.2	30.9	35.8	39.4	35.6	35.1	38.9
7	29.9	31.5	30.9	33.3	30.1	28.0	32.5	33.5	34.0	34.5	36.2	28.1	34.0	39.2
8	29.6	28.7	28.9	27.2	33.4	25.5	32.3	31.7	30.8	33.8	31.8	29.2	36.0	34.7
9	29.2	27.9	29.9	29.0	29.4	25.1	32.4	30.0	34.3	36.1	33.0	27.7	32.4	30.2
1900	29.0	28.2	28.4	28.7	33.7	30.1	31.2	30.8	32.3	33.5	33.0	32.8	32.8	32.5
1	26.2	27.9	28.0	26.2	28.1	24.0	29.5	29.7	28.4	33.1	30.2	34.5	30.6	32.8
2	27.3	26.9	30.7	29.2	30.1	23.1	29.7	28.7	28.2	35.1	37.9	26.1	33.8	32.
3	27.4	26.4	29.0	26.8	30.7	26.2	29.7	28.3	29.3	33.0	35.0	29.5	33.3	32.6
4	26.4	25.2	24.9	25.8	27.3	25.6	29.4	29.7	34.1	31.5	27.4	32.0	29.4	30.3
5	28.5	30.0	29.9	28.9	27.3	25.6	31.8	31.0	31.0	34.9	35.0	32.3	35.2	36.0
6	25.4	23.8	24.2	25.4	25.8	26.8	26.0	27.7	27.4	31.7	33.8	25.1	31.4	31.8
7	25.1	25.3	25.4	27.9	29.7	23.8	26.8	28.0	32.0	30.5	35.5	26.8	31.5	29.6
8													29.7	31.6
9	26.5	27.6	27.1	27.3	28.5	27.3	27.4	28.3	28.2	33.0	37.6	28.0	31.4	30.8
10	24.4	Δ22.9	25.0	24.0	26.4	20.3	24.7	Δ23.4	28.4	30.7	30.7	Δ21.9	29.0	29.9
1	24.8	27.1	26.2	29.1	30.6	28.8	25.0	25.6	26.5	31.6	34.1	28.6	30.8	33.3
2	Δ21.6	23.6	Δ20.1	Δ21.8	Δ24.4	Δ18.8	24.7	23.8	Δ25.5	Δ27.2	Δ27.7	24.0	Δ26.6	Δ29.5
3	23.5	23.6	23.1	22.7	27.1	20.6	Δ23.3	24.1	26.2	29.8	34.7	26.3		
4	22.9													
5	31.9													
6	30.7													

▲ : Max. for the period.　　Δ: Min. for the period.

Source: *Statistisches Jahrbuch für das Jahr....* (relev. years); *Ungarisches Statistisches Jahrbuch, Neue Folge....* *
(relev. years).

Co.A. = Core Austria　　　　Cr.S. = Croatia/Slavonia

(After Ausenda 1992:179)

settled in villages because houses are built by men and are generally owned by men. The *shariah*, Islamic religious law, applies and it is more favourable to men. In general women are considered legally worth one half as much as men of the same status. It is true that women still wield considerable power in the privacy of their homes, but their segregation and fractionation gives them less short-term, visible political clout.

Something of the kind may have obtained among the Anglo-Saxons in that women were entrusted to their fathers' and husbands' *mund*. At marriage they were 'handed over' to their bridegroom and his agnatic kin. Still, there were women with considerable political power, but that was not necessarily attached to gender but to their genealogical ties.

You also discuss gender roles and I would like to bring up parallels from the groups I worked with. Gender roles are strictly respected both among Hadendowa and Beni Amer. Men milk and butcher animals, women are forbidden to do so because they would defile the milk and the animals. Women grind grain, cook and make pots and goatskins, they erect tents covered with dom palm mats they have made themselves. Tools and activities are completely separate. Women are seen as active in the dwelling and men in the wilderness. I do not see how such rigid separation could be overcome by a frontier situation. When America was colonized, gender activity had become much less rigidly segregated at the source, in Europe. Stoodley's survey can be applied only to contemporary society.

You mentioned the genesis of regional structures. That they were created by the rise to dominance of individual lineages can be verified also in contemporary pre-industrial society. In general, lineages most favourably located with respect to communications, represented in pre-industrial society mostly by trade, become dominant. This was the case of the Nabtab among Beni Amer, through whose territory passed most of the trade from the western lowlands, of what today is part of Eritrea, to the plateau and beyond to the coast, and of the Beit Asgadé among Habab who commanded the heights between the valleys of the Falkàt and Motsabét rivers, both important trade routes.

On the question of the status of the *læt*, I would like to draw a parallel again from the Beni Amer. The *læt* mentioned in Æthelberht's laws could be similar to 'clients' in agro-pastoral societies in the Middle East, North and East Africa. They were not slaves but were 'foreigners' in the dominant clan's territory, hence unable permanently to own land and sometimes even livestock. This was given them by members of dominant clans in exchange for services or part of the crop or both.

You also discuss the likelihood that among Anglo-Saxons the ownership of weapons was 'legally' fixed. Among Hadendowa and Beni Amer ownership of weapons is only a matter of wealth, it is not subject to legal rights or obligations. Swords are the most expensive weapons and antique swords are prized, most of all the so-called *Franji*, i.e. 'Frankish' for Western Europeans in general—some are said to go back several centuries—, spears come next, while throwing sticks are the most common. A parallel from Germanic groups may be drawn from late Langobardic legislation, namely Ahistulf 2 and 3 (AD 750). These laws detail armament for different statuses, mostly in connection with wealth, only to specify the 'minimum' with which an individual of given wealth should present himself to the mustering centre.

HÄRKE: Just two things. This survey of frontier societies that Nick Stoodley has done has persuaded me for one. He used examples from North America and Australia, and the gender role comparisons were with contemporaneous European societies. We are talking here about the actual settlers on the frontier; the situation was totally different where the incomers were in administrative positions, such as the English in India. As to the Beni Amer possession of weapons being simply a matter of wealth, I'm sure that varies from society to society. In post-Roman England we have what I believe is an ethnically divided society and the situation there is bound to be different from societies with a different make-up.

HAWKES: In the Old English poetry there seems to be a difference in the *comitatus* between the *witan*, *geoguð* and *duguð*: the younger and older warriors, who seem to be separate from those wise advisors whom you mention to us around the king. There is also a reference to what you call the problem of women. What comes most readily to mind is the character of Queen Wealhtheow who may well be a serf, a captured British slave. But she, in *Beowulf*, literally has the power of gift-giving and you see her trying to make an alliance. She tries to form an alliance with Beowulf to protect her two sons and their inheritance.

SCULL: May I make a point about inferring wealth from grave goods? If you look around this room, the women carry more portable wealth. If we were buried as we are, by the standards of the argument we are conducting here we would conclude that the women were wealthier. I am not sure that this is so: there are cultural factors affecting material expression here.

HÄRKE: So, basically what you are saying is that this whole discussion about wealth between men and women is irrelevant to social structure.

SCULL: We may be looking at a difference in expression rather than a genuine difference in personal wealth.

HAWKES: I have another point arising from the hagiographic literature. You ask about the age-difference in respect of the military context. In such literary contexts the 'ages of man' is a topos related to the 'ages of the world'—in turn related to notions of the end of the world/salvation, etc. I'm not sure of the extent to which this is relevant to 'real-life' in terms of 'coming of age' etc. in Anglo-Saxon society.

HÄRKE: We have, I believe, an age threshold of about 7 for fosterage right across north-west Europe, in Scandinavia, Iceland, in Anglo-Saxon England and in Celtic society. Does that mean that it is a shared perception rather than a shared reality?

HAWKES: It's represented in the literature, particularly the hagiographic literature and I would say it is a shared literary convention. Are there any distinctions in the cemeteries? When you get church cemeteries you sometimes have women buried on a different side of the church from the men, and the children of course have a different area. Is there some distinction in earlier cemeteries?

HÄRKE: In early Anglo-Saxon cemeteries, as a rule, no. There are some cemeteries where you find what could be called a degree of clustering by gender or by age groups. But in most cases I am sure if you would run a Nearest Neighbour analysis, the clustering would come out as statistically insignificant. When do we have it in Christian cemeteries?

HAWKES: The only one I know as a Christian cemetery is Raunds. In the Christian cemetery the women are on the (cold) north side of the church and the men and the young infants are on the sunny, south side, and very, very young children are put right up against the church wall, close to the churches.

POWLESLAND: Yes, infants. I was told by human-bone specialists that the reason we don't find any dead babies in our cemeteries is that there weren't any. But we find a lot in settlements. It looks as if the method of disposal was to place them in the nearest hole in the ground. We have them in the *Grubenhäuser*, quite a number of them.

HÄRKE: Could you quantify that off the top of your head?

POWLESLAND: I am sure that we've got more than fifteen instances.

SCULL: At the Watchfield cemetery in Oxfordshire, about 20 per cent of the individuals in the area we excavated were infants or young children. All the intact infant graves were found within or at the base of the ploughsoil. They were shallower, and would be destroyed by ploughing or machine stripping of the topsoil before archaeological excavation. I think that this is one reason why the burials of infants and children are under-represented.

HINES: One reason for believing that infant mortality may have been lower than one would expect if one took the nineteenth century as the norm and assumed that things were the same in the Anglo-Saxon period is, as I understand it, that the pathological study of skeletons has suggested that female fertility was very much lower. Unlike Victorian women having a dozen or so babies and carrying on having babies until they died, Anglo-Saxon women may have had three or four children as a maximum, so that for the maintenance of population one can believe that infant mortality should have been lower than one might otherwise have thought. Thus the idea is not entirely an assumption based on the apparent absence of skeletons.

HÄRKE: I believe that physical anthropologists are divided on that question.

SCULL: Evidence from the Spitalfields excavation shows that assessment of pregnancy, childbirth and the numbers of births from skeletal evidence is much more complex and difficult than used to be thought.

CHARLES-EDWARDS: Since it is crucial in terms of population, can you tell the age at which the women have their first child?

SCULL: At Spitalfields they were able to check a very large eighteenth-century biological sample against the records of the individual, and the correlation between skeletal pathology and the record of the number of children born by an individual is *very* complex (Molleson *et al.* 1993:135-6).

POHL: I want to go back to the grave goods in women's graves. It's a well-known feature in some Continental cultures like Langobardic Italy or in the Alemannic region that, when people get Christianized, for a while you find a lot of grave goods in women's graves while men cease to have any grave goods in their graves. I wonder if that might indicate that the symbolic function of grave goods is different according to gender?

HÄRKE: I wouldn't quarrel with that point. It is an interesting argument.

POHL: Sometimes people have tried to explain it as Christian men living with pagan women. But wherever we have written sources we learn of pagan men with Christian women. So this cannot be the whole explanation.

HINES: I would like to go back to the question of infant burials and your statement that 'the majority of individuals of this age [young infants] are buried in multiple graves'. Could I ask you to expand on that? In multiple graves with whom? Is there any consistent pattern?

HÄRKE: Multiple burial does not show any consistency whatsoever concerning age groups or gender, with one exception, and that is that a very high proportion of infants are buried in multiple burials.

HINES: You may have already answered the next question I was going to ask, which is on the topic of double burials, where one gets an adult man and an adult woman buried together. Looking at that phenomenon one is tempted to speculate on practices of suttee. Have you looked at the statistics for these burials?

HÄRKE: I have, although perhaps not quite as systematically as I would have wished. My sample suggests that there is a very close correlation with one factor, subsoil. The highest proportion of multiple burials is found in areas with chalk. Another factor is wealth: multiple burials are on average poorer, have fewer artefacts than others in the same cemetery. One cemetery where there are some epigenetic data from multiple burials is Finglesham, and there are several double burials where the same trait occurs with both individuals in the grave, so it is likely they are from the same family. So, the connections are with laziness, with absence of wealth, and with family links.

HINES: Absence of wealth in the grave?

HÄRKE: That's right. The argument that multiple burials reflect suttee (*Totenfolge*) has been expounded a few years ago by Oeftiger (1984) in respect of Iron-age burials. I'm not saying that it didn't exist in the Anglo-Saxon period; I just do not see it reflected in the archaeological evidence.

POWLESLAND: There are not actually many convincing double burials. At West Heslerton, we do have two examples which look pretty genuine although it is difficult to fit all the bones in together. Given the soils which these are cut into, it is very, very difficult to identify the cuts. The graves are frequently relatively shallow and all pretty much the same depth. We have an example where they clearly started to dig a grave, cut into another grave, stopped, and moved to a new location. So, when they disturb something, they are not going to pound straight through in true mediaeval style; maybe they just decided to utilize this hole even if there was somebody already in it.

HÄRKE: The general lack of intersections between graves in Anglo-Saxon cemeteries would indicate that they were clearly marked on the surface at least for a while. So, it shouldn't have been too difficult to actually re-open a grave and put a new body in after a slight widening.

LENDINARA: At Sutton Hoo there are burials with what you might call 'multiple burials', for example two heads in the same grave. These and other graves which have been called 'satellite burials' might be seen as sacrifices (Carver 1992a; 1992b). I do not know if it is correct to call them 'multiple burials': there is also a mound where a young man and a horse were laid.

HÄRKE: Decapitation, once you start looking for cases, is not that rare at all in the Anglo-Saxon record. But it need not have anything to do at all with criminal proceedings.

POWLESLAND: At West Heslerton, we have a body that was decapitated in the process of the grave being disturbed and the head was then moved and put on the chest. This is quite clear in the archaeological record. Had we not had goods and good visible evidence of disturbance, this would have been a burial of a young adult with his head upside-down on his chest, which we could have gone to town on. But there's a very simple explanation.

SCULL: One of the problems with the burials at Sutton Hoo is that there is little skeletal evidence, and it is impossible to investigate the pathology of body stains—the so-called 'sandmen'.

POWLESLAND: With a cemetery in sand you are free to invent as you go. One must be very cautious, and I'm very cagey about the suggestion that there is a huge amount of ritual going on with these burials which are supposed to be buried in strange positions. The burials from West Heslerton, a very large percentage of them, are either prone or the graves were not big enough and many bodies were in very strange and interesting and perverse positions. I don't think it suggests that they were ritually killed: the idea that forty per cent of the population of the settlement rushed out and had themselves ritually killed every now and then seems to me very, very bizarre. It looks more as if they just threw them away. There is a psychology about excavating in cemeteries that you assume there should be a nicely vertically cut, flat-bottomed grave. But particularly the early Anglo-Saxon cemeteries are usually dug in crappy soils, so you can't actually see the grave-cut well defined. And so you make a nice rectangular hole with nice vertical sides and flat bottom, but very careful examination of the stuff that we found shows that most of them are just scruffy little holes in the ground. And it is almost as if they just threw the body in. One or two of them are carefully laid out.

HÄRKE: Well, here as in all aspects of burial ritual you have quite a variation throughout Anglo-Saxon England. And whilst at first glance the ritual looks pretty standard, there are cemeteries where the layout is relatively regular and where graves were carefully dug; and then there are cemeteries where the graves intersect all the time, where they were too small so that the spears were broken to fit in, and so on.

LENDINARA: Analogous stories are met with in Anglo-Latin literature. One such story is told by Bede (*HE* IV.11) about the sarcophagus in which the corpse of Sebbi, King of Wessex, had to be laid.

CHARLES-EDWARDS: I was going to raise a problem about these age grades. I'm wondering whether there would be any complication about things like weapons. Perhaps someone of noble status is given a set of weapons which mark a certain age, but that might not be the same age at which that person starts to learn to use them, and you might then get complications about the age at which they were put in the ground also not necessarily being the age at which they learnt to use them. Similarly with women, the age at which you *can* be given in marriage is not the same as the age at which you *are* given in marriage. So there is a fair amount of possible leeway.

WOOD: With regard to gender I would like to ask a question I suspect the literary people can answer rather than the archaeologists. In Classical antiquity it was assumed that all the creative properties for the conception of the foetus came from the male, and that the female was simply a bed for the foetus to grow in. I suspect that if you have that sort of society, you can look on women in a very different way than if you actually need both male and female to create the foetus. Now, at some point between about the first century AD and the fourth century AD the Classical world seems to have forgotten that. I don't know when that happens. What I wanted to ask is, what do we know about Anglo-Saxon views of procreation: is it entirely a male activity or is it a male and female activity?

HAWKES: I don't know the actual answer. I just picked up a book on the subject, on the history of things gynaecological going through antiquity to the late mediaeval (McLaren 1990). It does seem that in the Anglo-Saxon period women did practise contraception and induce abortions. But the extent to which this notion that the man is the one who has the spirit of life and woman is the bed in which the foetus is developing came through from the Classical period into the Anglo-Saxon does make one suspect it was re-introduced in the Christian context.

WOOD: I cannot find this at all on the Continent in the Migration period. I wonder when the idea comes back.

LENDINARA: There are provisions against women who expose their babies on the roof of the house (*Canones Theodori* I.15). I cannot remember any clause against abortion, either in this or in other early penitentials. What needs to be stressed when dealing with Anglo-Saxon literary sources (both Latin and vernacular) is that they are likely to reflect the views of their authors. It is often said that women were portrayed quite fairly in the Early Anglo-Saxon period, that is at the time of our first Latin sources in the seventh century. Such 'positive' descriptions might be traced back to the existence of double monasteries, which gave the ecclesiastical writers a chance to know women. In the following centuries there were no double monasteries and several authors relied too much on their patristic sources, as is the case with Ælfric in the tenth century. Culture and its transmission were in the hands of men belonging to the clergy, who could interfere with the documents they were copying. Anglo-Saxon poetic documents do not give space to procreation, or the like. An exception is provided by the poem *The Fortunes of Men* which begins with a touching expression of child raising: "Full often it comes to pass...that man and woman bring forth a child into the world and clothe it with coloured garments, fondle and cheer it" (ll. 1-41). There is no description of miscarriages, but this omission is, once again, quite natural owing to the scribes through whose hands all the documents which have come down to us passed. There is one piece of evidence concerning women in literary sources, which could be of use to you. Anglo-Saxon medical literature often concerns itself with delayed birth. There is a charm against miscarriage (Storms 1948, no. 10), one for a woman big with child (no. 45) and one for a woman who cannot bear a child (no. 63). In the *Lācnunga* and the *Leechbook* there are remedies for women who cannot bear a child or cannot bring it forth. This means that such problems were widespread and were possibly the cause of much mortality.

FOWLER: Given that the title of this symposium is 'early Anglo-Saxon' it is fair enough that we spend an hour and a half talking about the Anglo-Saxons, but I wonder before the end if we can just say a word about the other 90 per cent of the population. I'm just being generous. Before 600 you're quite probably safe in saying that the British are almost invisible, certainly archaeologically. This is true in a very general sense. But it is worth just describing one of three ways in which they are visible. The very weakest argument is that unaccompanied burials, inhumations usually, are turning up all the time, literally daily as earth is disturbed. Some of them are probably from the period we are talking about. Because such inhumations are not accompanied, they usually do not get much archaeological attention. This is actually quite a serious point. We are talking about several thousand burials a year which turn up in Britain. But I do stress that's the weakest argument.

The second argument is that amongst various regional types of burial which exist archaeologically, which are very difficult to date, some belong to the period we are talking about, that is pre-seventh century. The most obvious sort, other than the obviously Anglo-Saxon cemeteries, are the long-cist cemeteries of southern Scotland, particularly south-eastern Scotland, which have got into the literature as late Iron age, which in Scottish terms they are, although in terms of absolute chronology they come in the first 500 years of the first millennium AD. So there are some British who are hovering around that area. And in this area, as I understand, some new cemeteries and settlements of Anglian type have recently turned up. Some of the Welsh cemeteries and burials, undatable because they are unaccompanied, are also probably of our period. The strongest argument is in that most productive area of western Wessex, Dorset and Somerset. I know this is a special case because I am talking about the fifth and sixth centuries and pre-Anglo-Saxon. But here are very specifically late-Roman and later cemeteries like Poundbury where you can look at the British in the fifth century and later. Equally convincing is the site at Cannington, overlooking the Bristol Channel, a large inhumation cemetery of around 500 AD which will soon be published. It lies close to an unexcavated hillfort, Cannington hillfort, which almost certainly is in general terms the same as South Cadbury, late-Roman/fifth-/sixth-century, and a re-occupied Iron-age hillfort. Probably this is the cemetery of the people living on the hill top. The other major thing about this cemetery is the length of time that it was in use. With about eight- or nine-hundred burials it may not be a very large community, because it runs from 500 to 800, probably into the ninth century, on the radiocarbon dates. There must be other Canningtons around and there are in Somerset—we've had glimpses of one or two of them. But, I think largely because they are unglamorous, because there are few grave goods, they don't show. But, 'invisible' though they may be, the British are there.

DUMVILLE: I would like to try inverting Peter's order of importance in these matters. I don't doubt that the British are there in all these places which we know were in British control at given times. But where are the Canningtons, in early Anglo-Saxon England?

SCULL: There is a late Roman cemetery by Dorchester-on-Thames (Queenford Farm) which is in use until the sixth century according to radiocarbon dates (Chambers 1987).

DUMVILLE: That is one. This is where the lists are needed to make this point.

HÄRKE: I think there may also be a conceptual problem for us. Once you start looking for these Britons with specific questions in mind, some preconceptions about what an Anglo-Saxon should look like might dissipate. I recently looked at the Anglo-Saxon cemetery at Wallingford; there are no weapons in that cemetery, and Leeds (1938) remarked on the strange brooches and slightly different dress in that cemetery. In view of the place-name, 'the ford of the people of the Welshman', I'm beginning to wonder whether that was one of these semi-Saxonized British enclaves we should expect in southern England in the Early Saxon period.

References in the discussion

Textual sources:

Edictus Langobardorum: see Bluhme 1868.
The Fortunes of Men: see Krapp and Dobbie 1936.
Lācnunga: see Cockayne 1864-66.
Leechbook: see Cockayne 1864-66.
Theodore of Canterbury
        Canones Theodori cantuariensis: see Finsterwalder 1929.

Bibliography:

Ausenda, G.
   1992   War and nationalities problem. The end of the Austro-Hungarian Empire. In *Effects of War on Society*. G. Ausenda (ed.), pp. 149-180. San Marino: AIEP Editore for CIROSS.
   n.d.   Beni Amer and Habab: a diachronic ethnography.
Bluhme, F.
   1868   Edictus Langobardorum. *In Monumenta Germaniae historica, Legum Tomus IIII*. G. H. Pertz (ed.), pp. 1-234. Hannover: Hahn.
Cameron, M. L.
   1993   *Anglo-Saxon Medicine*. (Cambridge Studies in Anglo-Saxon England, Vol. 7). Cambridge: Cambridge University Press.

Carver, M. O. H.
> 1992a   The Anglo-Saxon cemetery at Sutton Hoo: an interim report. In *The Age of Sutton Hoo*. M. O. H. Carver (ed.), pp. 343-371. Woodbridge: The Boydell Press.
>
> 1992b   Conclusion: the future of Sutton Hoo. In *Voyage to the Other World*. C. B. Kendall & P. Wells (eds.), pp. 183-200. (Medieval Studies at Minnesota 5). Minneapolis: University of Minnesota Press.

Chambers, R. A.
> 1987   The Late- and Sub-Roman cemetery at Queenford Fram, Dorchester-on-Thames, Oxon. *Oxoniensa* 52:36-69.

Cockayne, T. O.
> 1864-66   *Leechdoms, Wortcunning and Starcraft of Early England*, 3 vols. (Rolls Series 35). London: Longman. [repr. New York: Kraus 1965].

Finsterwalder, P. W.
> 1929   *Die Canones Theodori Cantuariensis und ihre Überlieferungsformen*. Weimar: Böhlau.

Krapp, G., & E. van K. Dobbie
> 1936   *The Exeter Book*. New York/London: Columbia University Press/Routledge & Kegan Paul.

Leeds, E. T.
> 1938   An Anglo-Saxon cemetery at Wallingford, Berkshire. *Berkshire Archaeological Journal* 42: 93-101.

Molleson, T., M. Cox, A. H. Waldron & D. K. Whittaker
> 1993   *The Spitalfields Project. Vol. 2: The Anthropology*. York: Council for British Archaeology.

Münzinger, W.
> 1890   *Studi sull'Africa Orientale*. Rome: Tipografia Voghera, Carlo.

Oeftiger, C.
> 1984   *Mehrfachbestattungen im Westhallstattkreis: zum Problem der Totenfolge*. Bonn: Antiquitas.

Storms, G.
> 1948   *Anglo-Saxon Magic*. The Hague: Nijhoff.

ANGLO-SAXON KINSHIP REVISITED

THOMAS CHARLES-EDWARDS

Jesus College, Oxford, GB-OX1 3DW

It is more than twenty years since Henry Loyn (1974) wrote his paper on Anglo-Saxon kinship. Since then important work has been done on particular topics, such as baptismal kinship, and Jack Goody (1983) has given us an anthropologist's view of the broad evolution of Western European kinship and marriage in the early medieval period. I shall address many of the same issues that have confronted earlier scholars, but I shall concentrate on two fundamental themes: the relationship between kinship and other forms of friendship and the way in which kinship varied according to the social rank of the person in question. I have chosen these themes, not just for their intrinsic importance, but because they reveal limitations in the view of the subject elegantly expressed by Loyn, but shared also by many scholars of his generation.

Two such limitations stand out. First, Loyn was preoccupied with the question whether there was a 'territorial clan'; the expectation lurking behind his discussion was that, for such a clan to exist, it ought, as a clan, to own land. Collective or communal property was the foundation of the territorial clan, as, perhaps of other 'tribal institutions' (Loyn 1974:206-7). 'Property' in this discussion was an undifferentiated concept, with no distinction being made between the right to cultivate land and the right to alienate it or the right to share in partible inheritance. Secondly—and this was the issue which, above all, preoccupied Loyn, as it had others—there was the claim that the growing strength of kingship and lordship entailed a corresponding weakening of the bonds of kinship. "Kingship in action trimmed the power of the kindred, and indicates the predominance of legal concepts quite different from those operating between kinsman and kinsman" (Loyn 1974:203). What was not asked was whether the power of the king or the power of the lord had the same effect on the king's kindred or the lord's kindred as on the kindreds of lesser men, nor, more generally, whether there might not be different forms of kinship depending on the status of those concerned. The analysis ran according to the assumptions of nineteenth-century anthropology, in spite of the dismissive reference to "these fringe anthropological matters" (Loyn 1974:207).

First, then, my first main theme: kinsmen and other friends. The best way to set the argument going may be to explain what I take to have been the crucial social values of the Anglo-Saxons. The views I shall present are sufficiently general in nature that they have a fair chance of being true—or, of course, false—both of the seventh and of the tenth century. The Anglo-Saxons tended to perceive other Anglo-Saxons as either friend or enemy, *frēond* or *fēond*.[1] Roughly, there is a

---

[1] E.g. the Ordinance of the Bishops and Reeves of the London District = VI Athelstan, c. 7: "we were all in one friendship and in one enmity".

THE ANGLO-SAXONS FROM THE MIGRATION PERIOD TO THE EIGHTH CENTURY:
AN ETHNOGRAPHIC PERSPECTIVE

strong tendency to give personal interaction a value, either positive or negative. Positive interaction creates friends and is required from friends; negative interaction creates and is expected from enemies. Gift-exchange is one form of positive interaction; feud is a serious case of negative interaction. So much may seem only to be expected, but the crucial point is that there is very little of what we would call impersonal interaction. By 'impersonal' is meant not interaction which somehow manages not to be between persons, but rather interaction which is not intended to carry any value in terms of expressed attitude towards another person. Impersonal interaction is indeed, therefore, between persons, but carries no implication of a positive or negative stance. Such impersonality is characteristic of bureaucratic government and modern market economies; and whatever may have been the wonders of late Anglo-Saxon government, it was quite as much a domination by the king's friends as an administration by the king's officers. Canute did not get rid of the ruling group of tenth-century England because they were found with their hands in the king's money-chest, but because they were the friends, not of him, but of the heirs of Alfred (Fleming 1991: ch. 2).[2]

This division of the social world into *frēond* and *fēond* was reinforced by a conception of personal honour which demanded consistent reciprocity: a person's duty was to be friendly to his friends and *fēondlīc* to his *fēond*. Thus, if, by the settlement of some enmity, *fēond* was converted into *frēond*, prospects for future friendship were much greater if the persons concerned had been consistent enemies in the past. If they had taken seriously the reciprocities of the feud, they might also take seriously the parallel reciprocities of friendship. The passage which best brings out the use of *frēond* is in Hrothgar's farewell speech to Beowulf before the latter sets out to return home.

> You have so brought it about that among these peoples,
> the men of the Geatas and the Spear Danes,
> peace shall be shared and strife cease,
> the hostile acts which they formerly carried out;
> that while I rule this broad kingdom
> treasures shall be shared; that many a man
> shall greet his fellow with good things over the gannet's bath; ·
> that a ring-prowed ship shall bring gift
> and token of affection across the sea. I know that people
> they take a consistent line both with foe and friend
> blamelessly with both according to the old custom.
> (*Beowulf*, ll. 1855-1865)

Hrothgar's words and assumptions are instructive. The Geats deal honourably with friend and foe alike, *gē wið fēond gē wið frēond*; and because they have been dependable enemies, so they will be dependable friends.

Kinship and marriage were sources of friends. To put it in context, I shall set out in a rough and ready way, what I take to have been the principal sources of

---

[2] The process by which the tenth-century élite was destroyed was begun in the later period of Æthelred II's reign under the pressure of defeat, but deliberately completed by Cnut.

friendship. The first division is between friendship which is given by a situation not of one's making, and friendship which is made by deliberate action. Yet, as we shall see, the Anglo-Saxons were good at overriding this distinction: much of the fun is producing 'given friendship' out of 'constructed friendship' and *vice versa*. So, for example, one may have a relationship between lord and man which arose indeed from a deliberate act, but which has been inherited for generations, and thus, for the current generation, is effectively given. Using the Scottish term 'the kindly tenant', I call this 'kindly lordship'. The attitude is immortalized by a couplet in a poem of about 1730 by the Irishman Aodhagán Ó Rathaille (Dinneen & Donoghue 1911), lamenting the fall of the native aristocracy of Munster:

I shall follow the beloved among heroes to the grave,
The lords my forefathers served before Christ was crucified.

Alongside such a given, though originally constructed, friendship, there is the opposite situation exemplified by baptismal kinship, a friendship which is itself constructed, yet modelled on one which was given. Moreover, baptismal kinship was only one example of a whole class of constructed kinships generated by other sacraments, such as confirmation, or by fosterage or by such rituals as hair-cutting and the giving of arms. Adoption, however, in the sense of an unrestricted right to make someone not only one's child—as baptismal sponsorship did—but a child with full rights of inheritance, seems not to have existed in Anglo-Saxon England. There may have been a more limited right enabling parents in old age or sickness whose children refused to support them, and who were then supported by another kinsman or a non-kinsman, to adopt that person as an heir (Goody 1983:74-5); but the evidence comes from a section of the *Leges Henrici primi* (c. 88.15, see Downer 1972:274-6) which is quite close to a rule in the *Collectio canonum hibernensis* (xxxii, 20-22; see Wasserschleben 1885:116-7), a text known to have circulated in tenth-century England (cf. Liebermann 1903-16: ii.1, Rechts- und Sachglossar, s.v. 'Adoption').

	primary forms	secondary forms
given friendship	(neighbourhood (kinship	'kindly lordship'
constructed friendship	(marriage (lordship (guilds	'constructed kinship'

The Anglo-Saxon feud is sometimes considered as if it were principally a matter of private vendettas between kindreds, an institution which kings struggled to bring under a modest degree of control. Nothing could be further from the truth. First, feud was not just a state of potentially active hostility between kindreds. Lords were involved in the feuds of their men; men in the feuds of their lords; godfathers in the feuds of their godsons. Any alliance between men, whether given or constructed, might draw one side into the feud of the other. Furthermore, feud was not so much a particular institution as a way of looking at the world. God himself and his faithful followers have enemies, led by the pre-eminent *feond*, Satan. Kings were themselves the greatest feuders, above all because there was no clear distinction between feud and war. Feud, then, deserves particular attention both because it has been taken to be the supreme example of the power of kinship set against the supposedly more progressive institutions of lordship and kingship and because the reality exemplifies some of the points I have been making.

An excellent corrective to oversimplified views of the feud is Bede's account of the Battle of the Trent between the Northumbrians and the Mercians in 679 and the story of Imma's capture after that battle and eventual release. A few years earlier, Wulfhere, king of the Mercians, had attempted to subject the Northumbrians to the payment of tribute, but he had been defeated and the Mercians had, in their turn, been compelled to pay tribute to the Northumbrian king Ecgfrith. When Wulfhere's brother, Æthelred, succeeded to the kingship of Mercia in 675 there was a period of peace between the two kingdoms. Æthelred was the husband of Ecgfrith's sister, Osthryth, and the marriage alliance between the two kings appeared for a time to keep the old hostility between the two kingdoms under control (*Vita S. Wilfridi*, 20, last sentence; Bede, *HE* IV.21/19).[3]

In 679, however, Æthelred defeated Ecgfrith at the Battle of the Trent. Ælfwine, Ecgfrith's brother and joint-king, was killed and the lands south of the Humber passed, for good, into Mercian hands. Bede comments on the death of Ælfwine as follows:

> Since it seemed that in this way there had been created the basis for fiercer warfare and more enduring enmity between fierce kings and peoples, bishop Theodore, beloved of God, availing himself of divine aid, completely extinguished by his wholesome persuasions this great and dangerous conflagration when it had only just begun. He had such success that the kings and peoples on both sides were restored to peace and no man's life was forfeit for the king's dead brother, but rather the appropriate compensation was paid to the avenger king (*HE* IV.21/19).

The prospect, then, was of vengeance: Ecgfrith was a *rex ultor*, an avenger king, who could be expected to respond with violence to his brother's death. Theodore, however, acted as a go-between (he performed the function of the later-attested *semend*) {*Wer*, 4 (Liebermann 1903-16, i.392)}. He was perhaps particularly effective as a complete outsider, having no inherited links to either party. As a result of his success, vengeance was averted by the payment of wergild. From Bede's words we can infer that for Ælfwine's death there was due an amount of *pecunia*, probably 'wealth' rather than 'money' at this period.[4] Although no legal text would so much as mention a king's wergild for over three hundred years, there must already have been a recognized compensation. One may compare the *Anglo-Saxon Chronicle*'s notice of a compensation paid by the Kentishmen after the killing of a member of the West Saxon royal family named Mul (*Anglo-Saxon*

---

[3] Ælfwine was *utrique prouinciae multum amabilis. Nam et sororem eius, quae dicebatur Osthryd, rex Aedilred habebat uxorem* (*HE* IV. 21/19).

[4] Bede's term is *debita multa pecuniae*.

Chronicle A, *s.a.* 694). The Alfredian *Chronicle* may have preserved the memory of this event because of its bearing upon the supremacy won by the West Saxons over Kent and because Alfred's ancestor Ingild was, like Mul, Ine's brother. Whatever the reason, the sum said to have been paid agrees well enough with the figure given in Archbishop Wulfstan's small tract on status probably written early in the eleventh century.[5]

Although these compensations were paid by one king and his people to another, they reveal the classic pattern of the feud: either vendetta or wergild. We may therefore feel fairly confident that Bede's *inimicitia* stands for Old English *fǣhþu*, 'hostility', 'feud'. In this war that was also a feud, kinship was indeed fundamental to the problem faced by Theodore: the *rex ultor* was the brother of the slain Ælfwine. Yet the participants were far from being confined to the royal kindreds on either side, as the story of Imma makes clear. Imma belonged to the *militia* of the dead king Ælfwine. As other examples of the word make clear, there is something aristocratic about a *militia*. Thus the *milites* of *HE* III.3 were the *iuuentus* of III.1, the young companions of Oswald when he was in exile; and the *iuuentus* is probably to be identified with the *geoguð* (as opposed to *duguð*) of *Beowulf*. It is not so much an army but rather a *comitatus*, an aristocratic war-band. Its loyalty to its lord is based upon a solemn oath whose violation stamps a man as a *trēowloga* 'troth-breaker'—as dishonoured and therefore deserving of disinheritance (S 362=*CS* 595=*EHD* i, n. 100; *Beowulf*, l. 2947). Imma's conduct in the battle was entirely honourable: although his lord, Ælfwine, was killed, he himself was left for dead upon the field. When he came to his senses he was picked up by some Mercians and taken before their lord, a *comes*. Imma was afraid to admit to being a *miles* and claimed that he was a *rusticus* and a *pauper*, and, furthermore, that he was married and had come on the hosting only for the purpose of transporting supplies for the *milites*. Imma, in other words, in spite of his wounds, did some very fast talking. Eventually, his captors noticed "from his appearance and dress and from his conversation that he was not of the poor people, as he had said, but of the nobility", whereupon the *comes* declared, "I had realized from each of your replies that you were not a *rusticus*, and now indeed you are worthy of death for all my brothers and kinsmen were killed in that battle" (*HE* IV.22, see Colgrave & Minors 1969:404).

Plummer's explanation of this passage, accepted by Wallace-Hadrill (1988:162), is as follows:

> From this it would appear that any member of an army, if captured, might be held liable by the relations of any man on the other side who had fallen in the battle (Plummer 1896:243).

This is a possible explanation, but it may well be too wide. According to Plummer, Imma was liable to the feud merely on the grounds that he had participated in the battle. Yet he was also *de nobilibus*, a *minister regis* and a *miles* from the *militia* of

---

5 *Norðleoda Laga*, cc. 1-2, allowing for difficulties over the nature of the monetary units involved (*þrymsas* in the legal text; the different versions of the *Chronicle* offer different readings).

the Northumbrian joint-king Ælfwine. In Bede's account there are two statements of the basis on which someone was judged either liable or not liable to the feud after such a battle as that of the Trent. The first is Imma's initial reply to the questions put by the *comes* of the Mercian king Æthelred; the second is in the words put into the mouth of the *comes* later on when he had just discovered that Imma's replies were false. Only in the first is there any reference to whether Imma had fought or not. In the second passage the fierce statement of the Mercian *comes* that Imma was now liable to the feud followed his discovery that Imma was not a peasant, a *rusticus*, "that he was not from the poor people, as he had said, but from the nobility" (*HE* IV.22/20). In this second passage the issue is solely one of status, and, what is more, a status implying a close relationship to the king (see also Alcock 1987:263; Brooks 1971:74 n.1; John 1966:136-7).

It is evidence of some weight that Alcuin, in his summary of Bede's story in the poem on the Church of York, concentrated on the issue of status and did not bother to mention that Imma claimed that he did not fight (Alcuin in Godman 1982:799-801, 819-22).[6] A Northumbrian reader of the eighth century was in a far better position to appreciate the implications of Bede's story than we can ever be. Following Alcuin, we can take Imma's assertion that he only brought up supplies and did not fight as an extra embellishment, not the essence of the matter. The crucial point for him was whether Imma was *de nobilibus*, because if he was a noble, not only did he fight but he did so as one so bound to his lord that he shared in his lord's feuds. We know, of course, that lords were involved in the feuds of their men—hence the *manbōt*, the compensation due to a lord for the loss of his man—and it is a natural corollary that noblemen bound by oath to their royal lord would be involved in his feuds also.

It becomes a great deal easier to account for Imma's liability to the feud once it is recognized that his noble status was the crucial issue. Imma was a member of Ælfwine's *militia*; as a young man he was still a king's thegn, a *minister regis*, rather than a *gesith*, a *comes*; this is perhaps why he claimed married status—a man of his age would probably not have been married if he were a noble (Bede, *Historia abbatum*, 1, and *Epistola ad Ecgberhtum*, 11). He had, no doubt, sworn the oath of loyalty taken by all those admitted to a king's *comitatus*. There is no doubt that the bond between lord and man entailed, for both sides, support in the feud; and we may infer that, as it entailed support, so it entailed liability to the feud. True, kinship was involved in the reaction of the Mercian *comes* to Imma's noble status: all his brothers and kinsmen were killed in the battle. Yet there was no implication that Imma was himself responsible for their deaths: he was not liable because of any particular action in the battle nor because of kinship between him and the killers. The attitude of the Mercian *comes* amounts to treating the *militia* of Ælfwine as a group capable of carrying on the feud; it was not a kindred but in this respect it behaved like a kindred. A constructed friendship was as relevant to Imma's chances of survival in the household of the Mercian *gesith* as was kinship.

---

6   The issue of whether he fought or not is the one aspect he leaves out.

Kinship itself might be, as we have seen, a constructed friendship. Baptismal kinship has been well covered in the work of Angenendt and Lynch and I do not therefore propose to spend much time on it (Angenendt 1984; Lynch 1986). One or two aspects, however, merit comment. The first is the role of baptismal kinship in the feud. The most interesting evidence here is given by a series of rules at the end of Ine's laws:

76. If anyone kills the godson or godfather of another, the compensation for the relationship is to be the same as that to the lord; the compensation is to increase in proportion to the wergild, the same as the compensation for his man does which has to be paid to the lord.

76.1. If, however, it is the king's godson, his wergild is to be paid to the king the same amount as to the kindred.

76.2. If, however, he was resisting him who slew him, then the compensation to the godfather is remitted, in the same way as the fine to the lord is.[7]

76.3. If it is a spiritual son at confirmation, the compensation is to be half as much (Trans. *EHD* i. 372 with modifications).

There are curious elements in these decrees. First, the spiritual kinship involved excludes the relationship between a man and his 'co-father', *cumpæder*.[8] The usual pattern of baptismal kinship bound together both godparent and godchild and also godparent and natural parent; thus the godfather was *cumpæder* to the natural father. This seems to be because spiritual kinship, at least so far as wergild payments are concerned, was modelled on lordship rather than natural kinship, with the one exception that it was two-way: whereas the *manbōt* was paid to the lord for the killing of his man, the compensation for spiritual kin was paid either to the godfather or to the godson. To that extent it was more like kinship. The next oddity is that killing the king's godson entails liability to two wergilds, one to the kindred as usual, but the other to the king. In terms of the size of the compensation, therefore, the king's sponsorship of a child at baptism is treated as creating full kinship; yet from another point of view, this relationship is even more like lordship than normal godparenthood. As we have seen, for the latter the equivalent of the *manbōt* was paid either to the godfather for the killing of a godson or to the godson for the killing of his godfather. When the king is the godfather, full wergild was paid; but no mention is made of a wergild paid to the godfather of the king when the latter was killed. Some spiritual kinship, it seems, is more lordship than kinship.

One of the crucial points about spiritual kinship was that, unlike natural kinship, it did not generate rights of inheritance. This did not have to be the case. When the

---

[7] *Leges Henrici primi*, c. 88, 19-20 (Downer 1972:276) provides a more intelligible variant of this rule, whereby, if someone was *coactus ad homicidium*, "forced to commit homicide"—and compulsion included the necessity to take revenge—no compensation was paid to the lord or to the godfather.

[8] E.g. *ASC* A *s.a.* 894, where Æðelred, ealdorman of the Mercians is *cumpæder* to Hæsten, the Viking leader, because he sponsored the latter's son at baptism; cf. *gefæðere*, 'godmother' S 1485 {Whitelock 1930: no. 9 (p. 22, l. 22)}.

Frankish king Guntram proposed to sponsor his nephew, Chlothar II, at baptism, his other nephew, Childebert II, declared himself outraged at the idea (Gregory of Tours, *Libri historiarum decem*, X.28). Guntram, who had no surviving son to succeed him, had previously adopted Childebert as his heir (Gregory of Tours, *Hist.* V.17, VII.33).[9] Childebert, therefore, maintained that Guntram was going back on the previous adoption; in other words, he claimed that baptismal sponsorship amounted to adoption, and that, because of the previous adoption of himself, Guntram was disqualified from sponsoring Chlothar. One English transaction, reported by Bede, looks a little similar. Wulfhere, king of the Mercians, sponsored the first Christian king of the South Saxons, Æthelwalh, at his baptism which took place in Mercia (*HE* IV.13). Bede says that Æthelwalh "was accepted as if he were a son", "*loco filii susceptus est*", and that as a "sign of adoption", "*signum adoptionis*", Wulfhere gave him two provinces, the Isle of Wight and the Meonware. At this stage, the Isle of Wight had its own dynasty, and the Meonware were said by Bede to belong to the people of the West Saxons. What Æthelwalh was being given was a pair of highly contentious assets which he could only keep by virtue of Wulfhere's power as overlord of the Southern English; after Wulfhere's death, Æthelwalh was to lose not only the two provinces but also his life at the hands of the West Saxons. However grim Æthelwalh's ultimate fate, however, at the time of the baptism, overlordship over the two provinces was Wulfhere's to give, and he gave them, even though they did not belong to the South Saxon kingdom, because he was adopting Æthelwalh as his son.

This ingenious manoeuvre by Wulfhere apart, however, spiritual kinship was valuable precisely because it did not generate rights of inheritance. As far as kings were concerned, it resembled the kinship created through marriage. Indeed, this can be seen in the background to Wulfhere's dealings with Æthelwalh. The latter had already been married to a princess of the Hwicce, in other words a kingdom much more firmly within the Mercian hegemony than any of those south of the Thames. Æthelwalh's links with the Mercian kingdom may therefore be represented as follows:

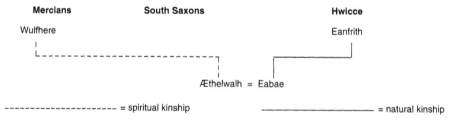

Just as his supposed adoption gave Æthelwalh no right to contend for a share of the Mercian kingdom, so also his marriage to Eabae gave him no rights of inheritance among the Hwicce nor were any transmitted to their children. For that very reason both spiritual kinship and kinship through marriage were ideal means

---

[9] He had done this twice.

to build an alliance. As we shall see when we come to royal kinship, princes of the one dynasty were natural rivals because they were entitled to compete for the kingship. Here we have an excellent illustration of the truth that there were different forms of kinship. For kings, agnatic kinsmen were natural rivals precisely because they shared rights of succession. For the very same reason, because baptismal kinsmen did not have rights of succession, they were natural allies. To put the same point in a sharper way, at the top of society natural agnatic kinsmen made unnatural allies while constructed kin made natural allies.

The other rites which created kinship in neighbouring countries, leaving aside fosterage for a moment, were the giving of arms to a boy, the first cutting of an infant's hair and the first cutting of an adolescent's beard. All three were widespread on the Continent (Cassiodorus, *Variae* IV.2; Gregory of Tours, *Hist.* X.16; Paul the Deacon, *Historia Langobardorum* IV.38, VI.53; *Pactus legis salicae*, LXVII; cf. Franz 1909:245-52, 253-7) and the hair-cutting rituals are also attested in the *Historia Brittonum* (c. 39). I know of no examples of any of these in Anglo-Saxon England. This is perhaps not surprising for the hair-cutting rites, since they appear to be Roman in origin and so are not attested in Ireland (Charles-Edwards 1993:180 n.45). It is more surprising for the giving of arms, exemplified among the Franks by the giving of arms to Charles the Bald (*Vita Hludovici*, 59; see Rau 1968:366). It may well be that by chance we have no evidence, or that the evidence exists but has escaped my notice. The usual pattern is that these rites are attached to points of transition in the life-cycle; it looks as though the taking of arms was such a point of transition in Anglo-Saxon England and this makes it more likely that it could generate constructed kinship (Asser, *Vita Ælfredi*, c. 75). The position with fosterage is only a little clearer: although it did generate kinship, it was of vastly less importance than in the Celtic countries, where it was the pre-eminent form of constructed kinship.[10]

Marriage also created kinship. For the generation of the married partners a formal marriage was an alliance made by a contract, but if the union produced children, the latter regarded their maternal kindred as part of their kin also. To judge by provisions about support in the feud, the maternal kindred was less important in general than the paternal {*Wer*, 3 (see Liebermann 1903-16: i.392); *Leges Henrici primi* 88, 11a (see Downer 1972:272)}, but the Anglo-Saxon laws were quite prepared to envisage a situation in which a person might not have any paternal kindred {Alfred, 30 (Attenborough, Whitelock) = 27 (Liebermann)}.

The legal texts relevant to marriage are predominantly early (Æthelberht and Ine) and late (*Be Wifmannes Beweddunge*). They appear to reveal two main changes: the disappearance of bridewealth (by which I mean a gift from the bridegroom to the wife's kinsmen in exchange for their gift of their kinswoman in marriage)—or, possibly, its transmutation into a *fosterlēan*, a reward for bringing her up—and the appearance of the notion that the marriage itself should be blessed

---

[10] The will of the ætheling Æthelstan, includes a bequest of an estate at Weston *"Ælfswyðe, mīnre fostermeder"* (Whitelock 1930: n. 20), but this is exceptional. On Irish and Welsh fosterage, see Charles-Edwards 1993:78-82.

by a priest. *Be Wīfmannes Beweddunge* gives a detailed account of the betrothal, called the *beweddung* (see Liebermann 1903-16:442-4). It goes according to a rhythm: the bridegroom makes a series of promises which he guarantees by a pledge (gage) while his friends guarantee them by surety; finally, the bride's kinsmen give a pledge to the bridegroom and the principal one among them (called the controller of the pledging) goes surety for her behaviour. The sequence, therefore, goes as follows (for convenience, I shall call the man the bridegroom and the woman the bride even when we have only got as far as the betrothal):

(1) (a) the bridegroom gives a pledge to the bride's advocate that he will conduct himself towards her so as to discharge his obligations entirely;
     (b) his friends provide a surety;
(2) (a) the bridegroom gives a pledge for the *fosterlēan*;
     (b) his friends provide a surety.

The bridegroom then announces what he will give to the bride because she has 'chosen his will' and what he will give to her if she should outlive him (the *weotuma*, 'dower' or *Wittum*).

(3) (a) the bridegroom gives a pledge to guarantee these two promises;
     (b) his friends give a surety;
(4) (a) her kinsmen give a pledge that they will marry their kinswoman to the bridegroom and that her manner of life will be all that it should be.

As can be seen 'friends' are prominent in these transactions; kinsmen appear only once, when the bride's *magas* pledge her *tō wīfe 7 tō rihtlīfe*. True, 'friends' may include kinsmen, both given and constructed, but they were not confined to kinsmen. The way in which the text speaks of the friends of the bridegroom but of the kinsmen of the bride may well be correct: the contract is between the bridegroom and the bride's kindred. Friends thus play a supporting role as providers of sureties to guarantee the numerous promises by the bridgroom which are one side of the betrothal, whereas kinsmen are at the centre of this making of a new friendship as parties to the contract.

Both in the late *Be Wīfmannes Beweddunge* and the early texts, the marriage itself is the *gyft*, the gift of the woman to the man {*Be Wīfmannes Beweddunge*, 8; Ine 31 (Liebermann 1903-16: i.442, 102)}. The *gyft* is one of the two things promised by her kinsmen at the betrothal (the other being that she will conduct herself as she should). In the early texts, however, the bridegroom is said to buy his wife (*gebycgan, ciepan*). It is both a gift by the bride's kinsmen and a purchase by the bridegroom. The two are not seen as different kinds of transaction, presumably because it all constitutes an exchange designed to promote an alliance between sets of friends and kinsmen by means of an alliance between man and wife. It is uncertain whether the *fosterlēan* of *Be Wīfmannes Beweddunge* is the old bridewealth under a new name: the person who fosters is not always the parent.[11] On the other hand, the same text makes no mention of any dowry (from the bride's family to the couple).

---

[11] II Cnut 74, (see Liebermann 1903-16: i. 360) may be hostile to bridewealth.

There is no good evidence that the disappearance or transformation of bridewealth had much to do with the Church. Ecclesiastical influence was, however, making itself felt, in three main directions: first, in prohibition of remarriage while a former partner was still alive;[12] secondly, in the definition and gradual extension of prohibited degrees {e.g. VI Æthelred 12 (see Liebermann 1903-16: i.250)}; and, finally, in the aspiration to bless the union. These developments were of very different importance; for example, the last was only an aspiration, since no one claimed that an ecclesiastical blessing was an essential part of a marriage. Similarly, there was no law declaring children born outside marriage to be ineligible to inherit. The notion was in the air, but it is found in a testator's preference rather than in a general law (S 1497; see Whitelock 1968:10-11). For this reason, it does not seem very likely that the reason why, in the will of Ealdorman Alfred (871 x 888), his son Æthelwold seems to be at a disadvantage is that he was illegitimate {S 1508 (see Harmer 1914, no. 10; *EHD*, i, no. 97)}.[13] What did make a child ineligible was a failure or refusal by the father to acknowledge paternity (Ine 27).[14]

Marriage demonstrates that 'given' kinship needs to be set in the context of 'constructed' kinship and, more broadly, of 'constructed' friendship. The standard starting-point of the process of marriage, the formal contract of betrothal, constructed a friendship; but it was a friendship which, so all hoped, would create, through the children of the union, a given kinship uniting both sides. A constructed friendship might thus turn into a given kinship. Marriage also illustrates, however, our second theme, the principle that kinship varied according to status. Before Ælfwine was killed in the Battle of the Trent, fighting against the Mercians, he was welcomed among those same Mercians as a kinsman and a friend (*HE* IV.21/19).[15] The reason given by Bede was that Ælfwine's sister, Osthryth, was married to Æthelred, king of the Mercians. Yet this was only one of three marriages between the Northumbrian and Mercian dynasties in a single generation (*HE* III.21).

	Mercia		**Northumbria**	
children	Peada	=	Ælhfled	children
of	Cyneburh	=	Alhfrith	of
Penda	Æthelred	=	Osthryth	Oswiu

The marriages of this generation, like the fated union of Ingeld and Freawaru in *Beowulf*, illustrate only too well the Zulu proverb, "They are our enemies: we marry them"; but Bede's observation about Ælfwine's welcome among the Mercians before 679 shows that, even in this unpromising case, marriage could, however temporarily, create friendship. Likewise Peada was said by Bede to have

---

[12] Separation of the wife from a living husband is mentioned by Æthelberht without disapproval {Æbt. 79 (see Liebermann 1903-16: i. 8)}.

[13] An alternative explanation is that Æthelwold had committed an offence which would render him ineligible to succeed.

[14] "Illegitimate child" in Whitelock's translation, *EHD:* i. 367, may give the wrong impression.

[15] Ælfwine was *"utrique prouinciae multum amabilis"*.

been persuaded to accept Christianity by Alhfrith, "who was his kinsman and his friend" (*HE* III.21). The marriages of Anglo-Saxon royals were, hardly surprisingly, conditioned by their rank. Those of lesser men and women were much less likely to be both born and destroyed in feud.

In Anglo-Saxon England social rank counted for a great deal. In Imma's case it nearly made all the difference between life and death. We should therefore expect kinship to differ according to the rank of the persons concerned. The tendency has been, I think, to admit that royal kinship may be different, but scholars have not grasped the general point of which royal kinship is only one example, namely that the character of kinship was always strongly influenced by status. One cannot dismiss royal kinship as untypical any more than noble kinship or the kinship of slaves. As, perhaps, with any inegalitarian society, there were Anglo-Saxon kinships rather than one Anglo-Saxon kinship.

We may begin with royal kinship, for which the evidence is relatively good. Bede, the *Chronicle* and the Anglian Collection of royal genealogies all appear to share the same general picture of royal kindreds. In Bede's chronological summary in chapter 24 of Book V, he states under the year 547 that "Ida began to reign, from whom the royal lineage of the Northumbrians derives its origin, and he continued to rule for twelve years". Bede was here using two types of source, closely related and both present in the Anglian Collection, the royal genealogy and the king-list (Dumville 1975). In the Anglian Collection there are four pedigrees pertaining to the Bernician royal kindred. They have the following general structure:

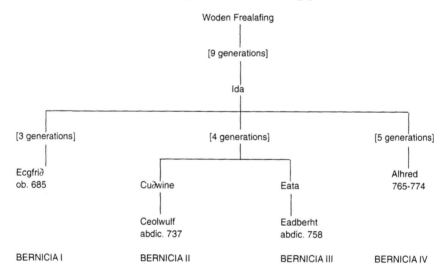

There are some oddities here. The order of the pedigrees is chronological going by the reign of the person at the bottom end of the pedigree. The earliest, however, ends before it should: one would have expected the last part to go as follows:

Oswiu

Aldfrið
ob. 705

Osred
ob. 716

The explanation may be that some refused to accept the legitimacy of Aldfrith's succession. Even during his reign, the *Anonymous Life of St Cuthbert* makes it plain that his half-sister, Ælffled, was astonished at the prospect of him succeeding Ecgfrith {*Vita S. Cuthberti anonyma*, III.6 (see Colgrave 1940:104)}. In Bede's *Prose Life*, probably written after the killing of Aldfrith's son, Osred, in 716, the expression of this surprise has been hardened: Aldfrith "was said to be the son of Ecgfrith's father" and was Ælffled's "bastard brother". The difficulties of Osred's reign may well have encouraged rivals to raise doubts about Aldfrith's right to succeed, as suggested by Bede's cautious phrase "who was said to be the son of Ecgfrith's father" (see Kirby 1974:19-21). Oswiu may never have formally acknowledged paternity to the Northumbrian nobility.

Apart from that puzzle, however, the general pattern is evident enough. We have an agnatic descent-group, whose common ancestor is the Ida from whom Bede says the Northumbrian royal lineage took its origin. Yet comparison between Bede's statement and the Anglian Collection throws up another puzzle. According to Bede, Ida was the *origo* of the *regalis Nordanhymbrorum prosapia*; yet the Anglian Collection also contains another pedigree—indeed it is the first in order—which gives the descent of the Deiran Edwin back, not to Ida, but to Yffi and Wuscfrea, and then on through many generations to Woden. All of them are ascribed in the collection to the Northumbrians. If we proceed by the chronological order of the last of any given line of descent, the text follows a consistent order: the first pedigree ends with Edwin and he died in 633, well before Ecgfrith, the subject of the next pedigree, who died in 685. We thus appear to have a flat contradiction between Bede, who says that Ida was the ancestor of the Northumbrian royal kindred, and the Anglian Collection, which gives as the first of its Northumbrian lines, a pedigree which has nothing to do with Ida. Of course we know what the explanation of this contradiction is: Bede is talking of the Northumbria after 651 when the last king of the Deiran dynasty was killed. Moreover, the Northumbrian people referred to in those terms by both Bede and the Anglian Collection was created by the destruction of the Deiran royal kindred, since there was an identification of royal lineage with the people and their land (*HE II*.1). We shall come in a moment to some ways in which Deiran identity was expressed even after the end of its dynasty, yet the fact remains that gradually Deirans were being subsumed into a new entity created by the kings of their hated northern neighbours, the Bernicians.

We are used to the notion that the larger Anglo-Saxon kingdoms were created out of smaller ones. There has been rather less emphasis on the way this was normally achieved: the destruction of royal kindreds. The most unnerving example of this brutal reality is the West Saxon conquest of the Isle of Wight—unnerving partly because of the alarmingly speedy tergiversation of Wilfrid, the friend successively of Æthelwalh, king of Sussex, and of his killer, Cædwalla, king of Wessex, partly also because of Bede's ability to see Christian triumph in political tragedy. The conquest of the Isle of Wight was sealed because all the members of its royal kindred were hunted down and executed. An abbot Cyneberht asked Cædwalla that, even if it were necessary that two royal brothers, who had fled to the province of the Jutes opposite the Isle of Wight and had been betrayed, should be executed, nevertheless he, Cyneberht, should be given permission to catechize and baptize them. For this Cædwalla gave Cyneberht permission, but there was no possibility of changing his decree that they should be executed. To have done so would have been to throw away the fruits of victory. Much of the history of Anglo-Saxon royal kindreds is a record of competition between different branches; yet in circumstances such as those faced by Deira and the Isle of Wight the royal kindred lived or died as one entity.

Before leaving the Northumbrians for the Mercians, we may note two things: how kings succeeded one another, and how the ghost of a destroyed royal lineage might live on by means of descent through women.

All Northumbrian kings of the Bernician line claimed, as Bede makes clear, descent from Ida. A pedigree connecting the claimant to the founder of the royal lineage was a prerequisite before one could make any bid for the kingship. That was only the first step. Some reached their goal by killing their predecessors, but there were other routes to power. Two are specified by Bede and by the Northumbrian annalist who continued his chronological summary. Bede says of the succession of Ceolwulf to Osric that the latter had decreed that Ceolwulf, brother to his predecessor, Coenred, should follow him as king (*HE* V.23). In this instance, the kingship passed from one branch of the kindred to another by designation.[16] Another succession later in the eighth century took place by a mixture of assassination and election:

> Oswulf was slain in criminal fashion by his own thegns; and the same year Æthelwald, having been elected by his people, succeeded to the kingship {*Baedae continuatio, s.a.* 768, perhaps for 769 (see Plummer 1896: i.363)}.

Whatever the route to power, however, Bede takes it for granted that only princes of the royal blood, *regii uiri*, are entitled to make a bid.

After the killing of Oswine in 651, the Deiran dynasty was at an end, apart from Trumhere, a monk who became abbot of the monastery of Gilling West, founded by Oswiu as an expiation of his deed (*HE* III.24; cf. III.14). Yet Oswiu, the killer, was married to Eanfled, daughter of Edwin and therefore cousin of the slain Oswine. Their sons were of the Bernician line; and yet, together with her daughter Ælffled, Eanfled was able to maintain some kind of focus for the sentiment of Deiran identity.

---

[16] More normal, of course, were kings who wished to designate their sons as heirs, as in *Baedae continuatio, s.a.* 768, Eadberht abdicated and "left his kingdom to his son Oswulf".

This is revealed by the Whitby *Life of Gregory the Great*, which shows how the monastery attempted to promote a cult of Edwin, how even in the early eighth century some Deirans could continue to regard Æthelfrith, father of Oswiu, as a tyrant who violently usurped power over their country, and how Eanfled was revered as the daughter of Edwin rather than as the wife of Oswiu—and all this in spite of the fact that Oswiu had made Whitby his burial church (Colgrave 1968:102). Some of this is explained by the special circumstance that Hild, first abbess of the monastery, was Edwin's niece (*HE* IV.23/21). Yet the pattern of succession to Whitby shows that it was more than the influence of one woman:

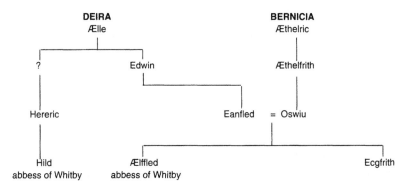

The connection between Hild and Ælffled through Eanfled and the Whitby writer's enthusiasm for the memory of Edwin show how loyalties to an old kingdom could survive its incorporation into a larger unit. They also show how flexible kinship could be. The royal agnatic lineage had been destroyed by the killing of Oswine. From Oswiu's point of view, as king of Bernicia, the killing of Oswine was just as necessary as Cædwalla judged the execution of the two royal youths from the Isle of Wight; yet he was married to one focus of Deiran identity, who demanded a form of wergild for Oswine, and along with Eanfled was buried in another, Whitby.

The kinship of Hild, Eanfled and Ælffled is comparable with that revealed by a pair of documents about the monastery of Withington dated to 736-37 and 774 (S 1429 and 1255 = *CS* 156 and 217 = *EHD* i, nos. 68 and 75):

Note: Δ = male person, 0 = female person

Dunne and Bucge had been the recipient of a grant of land by Æthelred, king of the Mercians (675-704), and Oshere, sub-king of the Hwicce. They left the monastery which they had built on the land to Hrothwaru on the understanding that she was to be abbess; but, because she was as yet only a child, her mother, a married woman, was put in charge and was given the charter to keep until her daughter came of age. When the time came, however, she claimed that the charter had been stolen. The dispute came before a synod which upheld Hrothwaru's claim, commanded that copies of the charters of the kings and of Dunne were to be made and that the thief of the original charter was to be condemned. The later document of 774 is a charter by Mildred, bishop of Worcester, in which it is recorded that Hrothwaru subsequently granted the monastery to the bishop, and he then, in 774, granted it to Abbess Æthelburh, daughter of Alfred, for her lifetime. There are many interesting aspects of this story, but one of them is the way in which, as at Whitby, a house ruled by women could generate its own special form of inheritance. These possibilities were created, of course, by bookland, to which I shall return later.

In the first half of the seventh century, the feud between the royal kindreds of Bernicia and Deira had the effect of successively exiling members of one royal kindred or the other. We know from Bede that Edwin was in exile during the period when Æthelfrith of Bernicia ruled over Deira, while during Edwin's reign Æthelfrith's sons, Eanfrith, Oswald and Oswiu fled to the Irish and the Picts. What is difficult to decide is how far this exiling went—whether it applied only to one branch of the royal kindred or more widely. Edwin's nephew, Hereric, the father of Hild, was in exile during Æthelfrith's reign; on the other hand, the long list of Bernician princes given in the E version of the *Anglo-Saxon Chronicle*, *s.a.* 617, may all have been sons of Æthelfrith.[17] The surviving descendants of Edwin all had to leave Deira during Oswald's reign (*HE* II.20), but it is unclear whether the same fate befell Oswine, the son of Osric, Edwin's first cousin, who had briefly been king of Deira, 633-4. It is quite likely that it did, since Oswine only began to rule Deira in 644, two years after Oswald's death (*HE* III.14).[18] There was no question of an automatic revival of the Deiran dynasty on Oswald's death; I suspect that Oswine may have revived Deiran independence with help from Penda. The most prominent victims of the feud were, however, the immediate lines of descent within the two royal kindreds that were currently monopolizing succession to the kingship; and, as David Kirby has made very clear for Bernicia, the descendants of Æthelfrith were not the only branch of the Idingas; others were to come to the fore in the eighth century, among them the recipient of Bede's *Historia ecclesiastica*, Ceolwulf (Kirby 1974:19-21). To the extent that the feud was between two branches of the two kindreds, Deiran and Bernician, one on either side, it resembled struggles within a single royal kindred. They too led to exiles, as the case of Guthlac, Æthelbald and the Iclingas of Mercia makes clear.

The table below represents the picture of the Mercian royal kindred given by the Anglian Collection, leaving out the ancestors of the dynastic founder, Icel, and also making some additions.

---

[17] *ASC* E *s.a.* 617 may be compared with the *Annals of Tigernach*, *s.a.* 626, which mention an Osric son of Albruit whom they call *rígdamnae*, i.e. someone fitted to be king. For his father's name Moisl (1983:105-6, 109 n.) maintains that Albruit represents Ælfred. For the Northumbrian material in ASC, see Hunter Blair 1948:105-12.

[18] *HE* says that Oswine reigned for seven years and was killed in 651, which suggests that his first regnal year was 644 (following Levison's proposal about Bede's use of regnal years).

The Iclingas (names in brackets are not included in the Anglian Genealogies):

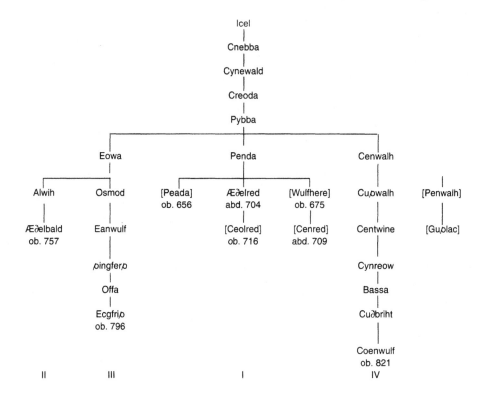

The archetype (David Dumville's α) was written during the reign of Coenwulf (796-821) and almost certainly in the first year of Coenwulf. The possibility is that the ordering of the pedigrees (I-IV) reflects the chronological layering of the text. No. I ends first but is the one to be taken back to Icel, and beyond Icel to Woden Frealafing. At the other end, Coenwulf's line is the last, even though he was the new king when the archetype was written. David Dumville argued that the *Historia Brittonum* provides evidence for an earlier state of the text composed between 787 and 796, after Ecgfriþ's unction but before his death (Dumville 1976:45). The relationship between III and IV is thus fairly clearly textual, IV having been added to an existing text without disturbing the sequence of the source. If we understand the text in this way, as a series of layers, each layer consisting of one pedigree, it becomes easier to understand. Pedigree I ends with Æthelred, omitting his son and nephew who both reigned after him. In other words, it does not trace the descent down to the last king of the line of Penda. Pedigree I may therefore be taken as much the earliest layer of the text, roughly a century before its compilation. What each pedigree does is to provide for the current ruler the *cynn* which makes him *cyning*; as the latter term shows, it is of the essence of a king's legitimacy that he be descended by a *rihtfæderencynn* (see e.g. *ASC* A *s.a.* 784), direct paternal descent, from the founder of the dynasty, in this instance Icel. *Cynn* in this context means a pedigree or line of descent, not the kindred as a whole. In their final form, the Mercian pedigrees in the Anglian Collection give us some indication of the branching of the dynasty: they approximate to what early Irish genealogists called 'a branch of kinship'. This, however, is largely fortuitous; it is produced by a simple process of additions to existing texts. We will come back to some problems associated with the *cynn* and the *cyning* when we get to the West Saxons. What I want to examine first is the position of Guthlac and Æthelbald as an illustration of the tensions, but also the possible alliances, within a ruling kindred.

The Life of Guthlac, written by Felix in the second quarter of the eighth century, records that the saint's father, Penwalh, was descended from Icel {*Vita S. Guthlaci*, 2 (see Colgrave 1956:74)}. His father is also said to have had his principal residence among the Middle Angles {*Vita S. Guthlaci* 1 (see Colgrave 1956:72)}. This may reflect a policy by which the currently dominant branch of the Iclingas, Penda and his descendants, killed two birds with one stone: they extended the power of the Mercian royal kindred among the Middle Angles and they ensured that a potentially threatening branch of the Iclingas was based outside the Mercian homeland. In the same way, perhaps, Offa's ancestors had land in the kingdom of the Hwicce where his grandfather, Eanwulf, built the monastery of Bredon, which Offa himself was later to enrich (S 116 = *CS* 236). Guthlac himself clearly made a bid for the kingship of the Mercians. The *Chronicle* gives his obit as 714 and the text of the Life itself shows that he died a year or two before the accession of Æthelbald to the Mercian throne. The bid for the kingship occupied about nine years—to judge by Felix's chronological indications *ca* 688-697—when he was aged about 15-24.[19] It involved recruiting a warband as well as enduring exile, including a period among the Britons (Felix, *Vita S. Guthlaci*, 16-18, 34). His renunciation of political ambitions was signalled by his entry into the monastery of Repton, closely associated with the Mercian royal house (*ASC s.a.* 755);[20] he would presumably not have been welcome unless he had made his new stance entirely clear. Later, however, Guthlac was said by Felix to have given crucial comfort to another Icling hopeful, Æthelbald, when he was suffering exile during the reign of Ceolred {Felix, *Vita S. Guthlaci,* 49 (Colgrave 1956:148-50); cf. 52 (Colgrave 1956:164-6)}. In other words, not only had he challenged the ascendancy of the descendants of Penda in his own youth but his authority as a royal saint was firmly attached by Felix to the cause of the Icling who finally put an end to that ascendancy. This case points to one reason why such ascendancies were not more enduring. On the whole, if a branch of an Irish ruling kindred had been out of power as long as were, for example, the ancestors of Cenwulf of Mercia or Cenred and Ceolwulf of Northumbria, no member of such a branch would have had much hope of ever succeeding (Charles-Edwards 1993:99-101; O Corráin 1971:28). In pre-Viking England, however, it was apparently not easy to exclude branches permanently; one reason may have been that those

---

[19] Felix, *Vita S. Guthlac*i, c. 18, mentions the nine years; c. 19 that he was 24 when he renounced a secular and military life; c. 24 says that he spent two years at Repton; c. 27 that he was about 26 when he began his eremitical life at Crowland; c. 50 that he spent 15 years as a hermit. He was therefore born *ca* 673.

[20] Æthelbald was to be buried at Repton.

branches currently out of the kingship may have combined to undermine the branch in possession, as Guthlac gave his blessing to Æthelbald; another reason may have been the policy of giving royal kinsmen bases in subject kingdoms and thereby a springboard from which to establish their power within Mercia itself. Both of these reasons, however, may have applied as strongly in Ireland as in England; what seems to have made the difference was the greater weight attached in Ireland to the number of kings a contender could count in his immediate pedigree (Charles-Edwards 1993:98-9).

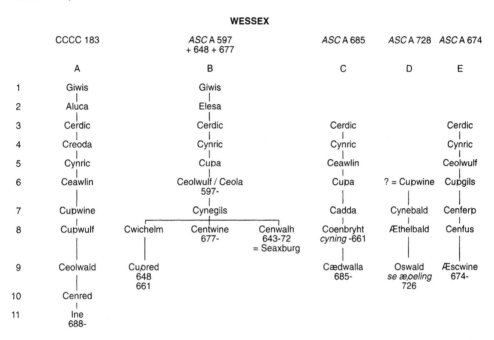

WESSEX

	CCCC 183	ASC A 597 + 648 + 677			ASC A 685	ASC A 728	ASC A 674
	A	B			C	D	E
1	Giwis	Giwis					
2	Aluca	Elesa					
3	Cerdic	Cerdic			Cerdic		Cerdic
4	Creoda	Cynric			Cynric		Cynric
5	Cynric	Cupa			Ceawlin		Ceolwulf
6	Ceawlin	Ceolwulf / Ceola 597-			Cupa	? = Cupwine	Cupgils
7	Cupwine	Cynegils			Cadda	Cynebald	Cenferp
8	Cupwulf	Cwichelm	Centwine 677-	Cenwalh 643-72 = Seaxburg	Coenbryht cyning -661	Æthelbald	Cenfus
9	Ceolwald	Cupred 648 661			Cædwalla 685-	Oswald se æpeling 726	Æscwine 674-
10	Cenred						
11	Ine 688-						

The Anglian Collection gives only a single pedigree for the West Saxon royal house; even that is absent from the earliest manuscript.[21] The *Chronicle* makes up for this scant attention; but it is important to note the context in which it makes its genealogical statements. The standard pattern is for a pedigree to be given at the beginning of a king's reign: its function, as we have already seen, is to legitimate accession, and the positioning of pedigrees in the *Chronicle* provides ample confirmation of the point. Thus when, in the table above, Æscwine is given the date 674-, that means that the pedigree occurs at his accession in 674. There are one or two interesting exceptions: the ætheling Oswald disputed the succession against Æthelhard after Ine's abdication; curiously, Æthelhard's descent is not given, although he was the victor.[22]

---

[21] Dumville (1976:40) suggested that the West Saxon genealogy, which comes last in MSS C and T, may have been omitted from V rather than added to the common exemplar of the other two; the position of the genealogy may be relevant, in that it is uncertain whether the collection in V, a fragment of three bifolia, is complete.

[22] From this point on there is a clear change of practice in the *Chronicle*: kings are not given pedigrees until we get to Æthelwulf, Alfred's father, and moreover his pedigree occurs at his death, not at his succession.

The most striking characteristic of early Wessex, however, is the number of *cyningas*. This was not confined to the years after Cenwalh's death in 672, when, according to Bede, the West Saxon kingdom was ruled by *subreguli*, such as the Baldred who appears in two charters of uncertain authenticity (*HE* IV.12; S 236 = *CS* 61; S 1170 = *CS* 71). Cædwalla's father, Coenbryht, is described at his obit in 661 (during Cenwalh's reign) as *cyning*, although there is no other evidence that he was king. In recounting Edwin's revenge expedition for the attempt by Cwichelm to assassinate him, the E version of the *Chronicle* says that the Northumbrian army slew five *cyningas* (*ASC* E *s.a.* 626 = *EHD* i. 149, *s.a.* 627). This entry can hardly be contemporary. It appears to perceive the situation very much from a Northumbrian standpoint—Edwin's vengeance is more than ample—and yet is not simply derived from Bede; nor is talk of five West Saxon *cyningas* likely to derive from Wessex at a later period. It may belong to the group of early Northumbrian annalistic entries preserved in *ASC*, D and E (Hunter Blair 1948:106-12). These seem to be contemporary from the late seventh century. If the entry for 626 belongs to that period, it may have been written close enough to the event to preserve genuine information of this kind, inconsistent with a picture, such as that presented by Bede, of a unitary kingship exercised by Cynegils over the West Saxons.

The likelihood is, therefore, that there were more kingdoms around in Wessex than the Alfredian *Chronicle*'s picture of the career of the House of Cerdic would allow (Kirby 1991:48-51). There are, however, problems about the very notion of a *cyning* which make a clear solution difficult to attain. Literally, *cyning* means something like 'kin-offspring'.[23] To explain how it could come to mean 'king', one has to assume that *cynn* had a central role in moulding the concept of kingship. *Cynn*, however, had two distinct senses, so far as kings were concerned: the collective *cynn*, the kindred as a whole, and *cynn* in the sense of 'pedigree'. These two senses may conveniently be distinguished as $cynn_1$ and $cynn_2$. As we have seen, $cynn_2$, 'pedigree' legitimated accession to the kingship, whereas a usurper was a *rex dubius uel externus* for Bede, and according to the *Chronicle* an *ungecynde cyning* (an 'unkindly' in the sense of 'unkinly' king) (*HE* IV.26/24; *ASC* 867). An 'outside king', *rex externus*, would be external to the entire royal kindred, $cynn_1$; but the dubiousness of the *rex dubius* was presumably his untrustworthy pedigree, $cynn_2$. The *ungecynde cyning* was thus an unkinly king both because he was outside the royal kindred and because he lacked an appropriate and accepted pedigree. The two went together, since a sound pedigree made one a member.

The problem remains, however, that the *cynn* relevant to the kinliness of kingship must be a very special kin. This is nicely illustrated by the way one could specify that a kindred was royal, namely by calling it a *cynecynn*, literally a 'kinly kin', *cyne-* being simply the compositional form of *cynn*. The use of this compositional form, however, extends even further the curious relationship

---

[23] Probably not just 'kin-member' because of the importance of providing a *cynn* '(royal) pedigree' to legitimate accession: the *cynn* 'pedigree' shows that a person is the offspring of a line of descent deriving from the founder of the dynasty.

between kinliness and kingliness: *cynelīc*, which one might have expected to mean 'kinly', in fact means 'kingly'; *cynedōm*, by derivation 'kin-dom', means 'kingdom'. It is almost as if the only kin or the only pedigree that mattered was a royal kindred or royal pedigree, and yet that cannot be the explanation: non-royals also had kindreds and pedigrees.

Part of the explanation for this association of kin and king has been seen already. When Cædwalla annexed the kingdom of the Isle of Wight, he destroyed the royal *cynn*: destruction of *cynn* led directly to annexation of *cynedōm*. There was, then, a very special *cynn*, a *cynecynn*, on which the survival of the *cynedōm* depended. A *cyning*, however, was more than simply a male offspring of this special *cynn*; such a person was not a *cyning*, but an *æþeling*, a prince, and, so far as pedigree, *cynn₂*, went, a potential *cyning* (Dumville 1979). The trio of *cynn*, *cyning* and *æþeling* exist in a curious misalignment of meaning and formation suggesting that there has been semantic change, especially since, in poetry, *æþeling* can have its natural meaning 'noble'. The misalignment can be represented as follows:

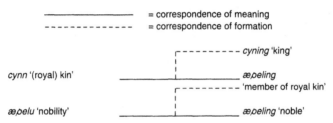

A possible explanation is suggested by a distant Irish parallel. Around the tenth century a new designation of Irish rulers was evolved. No longer was the king of Cenél Coirpri, 'the kindred of Coirpre', simply *rí Ceniúil Choirpri*. If he was king of that branch of the Kindred of Coirpre which ruled Northern Tethbae, he might now be called 'Ua Ciardai', 'The Descendant of Ciardae'. Of course, there were many who could trace their pedigrees from Ciardae, but the ruler was 'the Chief of his Name' and thus simply Ua Ciardai. Another man might be Colum ua Ciardai, but only the ruler of the kingdom, now itself often called Coirpre Uí Chiardai, 'Coirpre of Ua Ciardai', was the head of the royal kindred and so plain Ua Ciardai, 'The Descendant of Ciardae'. The analogy with the English situation is not exact: the Mercian royal kindred was called the Iclingas, but the king was not, so far as we know, 'The Icling'. Yet, to call him *cyning* was to associate kingliness with kinliness, the rule exercised by a *cyning* over a kingdom with headship of a royal *cynn*.

The title *cyning* may originally have been used, as *æþeling* was later, for royal princes, *regii uiri*, rather than just for kings. Frankish princes appear occasionally to have called themselves kings,[24] but cognates of *cyning* are found in all well-

---

[24] For example Chramn, Gregory of Tours, *Hist.* iv. 13. Was Ælfwine, brother of Ecgfrith of Northumbria, a case in point or just sub-king of Deira? In *HE* IV.21/19, he is *frater regis*, but in *HE* IV.22/20 he is *rex*, as he is in Stephen's *Vita S. Wilfridi*, 17. If a close kinsman of the king, such as Ælfwine were allowed to maintain his own *militia* that might, in effect, represent designation.

attested Germanic languages apart from Gothic and they mean 'king'. The change must, therefore, antedate the Anglo-Saxon settlement in Britain, so that the many *cyningas* of early Wessex should represent a plurality of kings rather than of princes. In the fifth and sixth centuries there may well have been several royal, or incipiently royal, dynasties in what was to become Wessex, but by the seventh century most of them were probably members of the kindred tracing its descent from Cerdic. Wessex may, therefore, have gone through a period as a group of sub-kingdoms, with their separate dynasties, one of which was beginning to gain an overlordship over the rest, and then another period still with sub-kingdoms but now ruled by a kinsman of the over-king.

One might imagine that, as someone's *cynn* in the sense of his pedigree was crucial to his status as *æpeling*, and then as king, some care would be taken to get them right. However, as several scholars have observed, the pedigrees in the *Chronicle* are an unholy mess especially in the generations numbered 5 and 6 in the table above. Part of the problem arises from short forms of names, such as Cupa for Cupwine (but then it could be for Cupwulf or even for Cupgils) or Ceola for Ceolwulf. More generally, however, it looks as though one could quite reliably take one's pedigree back two, three or even four generations, but then the intervening steps before one reached Cynric and then Cerdic were less well remembered because less important, or less well remembered because they had been edited inconsistently.[25] Founding a unified kingdom might necessitate creating or adapting an origin-legend of the kingdom as well as editing the pedigrees of the royal *cynn*, as is clear from what the *Chronicle* has to say about the Anglo-Saxon settlement of the Isle of Wight (Yorke 1989:84-6).

The problem of the ætheling leads conveniently to the topic of noble status. By the tenth century the title seems to have been more restricted in its use—to close agnatic kin of the ruling monarch rather than to any descendant of Cerdic (Dumville 1979:29-32; Stafford 1989:40-4). That has the consequence that, by then, an important element of the nobility, no longer marked off from the rest by the title ætheling, will have been composed of the descendants of kings, men like the chronicler Ealdorman Æthelweard, descended from Alfred's elder brother, Æthelred. One implication is that in late Anglo-Saxon England there may have been less of a distinction between royal and noble kinship than at an earlier period.

One thing that bound them together was the importance of bookland. This was not confined to the nobility, as the will of the reeve Abba shows (S 1428 = Harmer 1914: no.2), but possession of some bookland became characteristic of noble status {cf. *Rectitudines singularum personarum* 1 (Liebermann 1903-16, i.444)}. The implications for the law of inheritance of the introduction of charters as a result of the Conversion have been much discussed and no clear agreement has yet emerged

---

[25] E.g. D. N. Dumville (1985:21-66) argued that the date of the origin of the Cerdicing dynasty was put back into the fifth century, possibly in order to give the Cerdicings an antiquity equal to Bede's Kentish origin story. There might then have been inconsistent revision of the genealogies to fit the longer time-span.

(Campbell 1989; Chadwick 1905:367-77; Charles-Edwards 1976; John 1960:24-63, 1966; Jolliffe 1935; Stenton 1971:307-12; Vinogradoff 1893; Wormald 1984). It is accepted that one of the functions of charters was to confer a privileged possession of land: it might be held with 'the right of ecclesiastical freedom' (e.g. S 114 = *CS* 230), and so was 'bookland' because it was held under the terms of a charter, a 'book'. What I take to be the most likely view of bookland is as follows. It is relatively easy to say how bookland was created, relatively difficult to say what the consequences may have been—what rights were implied by possession of bookland. Bede's *Letter to Ecgberht*, bishop of York, shows that in his day land might be granted by the king by means of a royal edict orally promulgated in the presence of his council (11-13, 17 (Plummer 1896:415-17, 421)). A written charter, a book, was evidence of this oral transaction. It was evidence that one was foolish to do without, but it was not the effective act (S 1164=*CS* 107 and *EHD* i. no.55). The words 'I have consented' which follow the names of the witnesses to charters can be misinterpreted. What the affixing of a name—preceded by a cross—signified was that the person named was prepared to witness to the oral edict promulgated in his presence, to which he gave his consent: *consensi* refers to the oral consent, to which the written name is a witness, just as the charter witnesses to the oral edict as a whole. The effects of the transaction to which the charter witnessed are much more difficult to define. Bede's phrase for the rights which were granted by means of a charter, *ius haereditarium*, is echoed in the vernacular *ēce yrfe*, 'perpetual inheritance'.[26] Yet most early charters sought to confirm a *ius perpetuum*, 'a perpetual right' rather than specifically 'an hereditary right': they seem to have been more concerned to stress the *ēce* rather than the *yrfe* in the vernacular phrase {e.g. *in perpetuum* (S 8=*CS* 45, S 19=*CS* 97), *perpetualiter trado* (S 1171 in Hart 1966:127-8)}. There appear to be four strands in the rights granted. The first is perpetual or hereditary right; the second, apparently opposed to hereditary succession, is the right to grant the land to whomsoever one may wish;[27] thirdly, there is freedom from secular dues (e.g. S 186=*CS* 370=*EHD:* i, no. 83; see Brooks 1984:135-6, 195-6); and, finally, there is the notion that the rights are specifically ecclesiastical. These rights are referred to in a letter of Æthelbald to Wilfrid, bishop of Worcester, 727 x 736, *ut sit iuris ecclesiastici* (S 101=*CS* 163); and when an immunity is specified and can be described as 'ecclesiastical freedom' as it is in a letter from Offa, king of the Mercians, to the monastery of Bredon (Worcs.) (S116 =*CS* 236).

---

[26] The will of Badanoth Beotting, S 1510 (Robertson 1956: no.6), has a good range of terms: *mīn ærfe lond, mid fullum frīodōme on ēce ærfe, on ēce ærfe*; similarly, S 204 (Harmer 1914: no.3), a grant by Brihtwulf, king of the Mercians to his thegn Forthred, 844 x 845.

[27] The first two strands are combined in e.g. S 95=CS 153 (Æthelbald, king of Mercia, to Cyneburg, 723 x 737), *"ut fiat eius possessio in perpetuum et cuicumque voluerit tradere, vel in vita illius vel post obitum eius habeat [potestatem] tradendi"*; cf. S 1177=CS 122 (Æthelhard and Æthelweard to Cuthswith, 704 x 709, *"ut in tua potestate sit habendi et donandi cuicumque volueris"*.

The importance of each of these four strands varied both according to the period in which the grant was made and according to the particular purpose of the grant. To take an extreme case, the toll-charters of the reign of Æthelbald of Mercia conferred upon a church the privilege of bringing a ship into the port of London free of toll (Kelly 1992). In such cases the grant was not of land but of immunity from royal dues. The usual charter, however, witnessed a grant of land to a church; since the church was intended to endure indefinitely, the grant of land was likewise to be perpetual. Although, therefore, the precise effects of grants varied from case to case, there was at least a common theme, the giving, or the passing on to another person, of an enduring privilege (cf. Bede, *Epistola ad Ecgberhtum* 12).

For the purposes of kinship, charters are important in that they may govern the inheritance or alienation of land. Here too, however, there are different cases. First, the king may be granting his land, in which case he may need to guard against the rescinding of his grant by successors to his kingship or heirs to his land; thus a grant by Eadberht, king of Kent, of 738 (S 27=CS159), guards against both *propinqui mei* and *successores mei*. Secondly, the king might be granting land held, for his lifetime, by a *gesith*; if it were not for the grant, the land would be liable to revert to the king on the death of the *gesith*. What was crucial here was to confer an enduring right as opposed to a temporary one; the most likely person to seek to reverse such a grant would be the king's successor. Thirdly, the king's grant might be giving force to an arrangement within a kindred determining the succession to a church founded on hereditary land belonging to the kindred. In this case the danger would be likely to arise from later generations within the kindred. There is no reason to think, therefore, that bookland, land whose status was governed by an edict witnessed by a charter, was all of one and the same character. As late as Alfred's time we know that there could be crucial differences between one piece of bookland and another, in that one might be alienated to anyone while the other had to remain within the kindred (Alfred 41; see Liebermann 1903-16: i.74).

Apart from the general purpose of conferring a privilege, the main connection between the four strands appears, firstly, to be that a royal edict was required to enable subjects to grant land to churches in perpetuity. This led to the second strand, the right to give the land to whomsoever one wishes: one standard situation was that a king granted to a nobleman the right to alienate to a church either the nobleman's own land or land newly granted to him by the king. The third strand, freedom from secular dues, was also appropriate to the foundation of a church; and the effect of all this was the fourth, the creation of specifically ecclesiastical rights.

Perpetual right came to be identified with hereditary right, since the heads of churches were conceived as succeeding to one another in a way analogous to ordinary heirs (cf. Stephen, *Vita S. Wilfridi* 63; in Colgrave 1927:136-8). Furthermore, many churches were in fact hereditary in the sense that their heads came from a single family.[28] Bede's Letter to Ecgberht contains the claim that

---

[28] A good example of ecclesiastical land tied to a single family is S 1446 (in Harmer 1914): "so long as there was any man in their family who was willing to take holy orders, and qualified to do so,

since the death of Aldfrith in 705 Northumbrian noblemen had been active in obtaining grants of land to themselves by royal edict, attested by charter, but had not then gone on to found proper monasteries. It is of such monasteries, perhaps in a deliberately sarcastic tone, that Bede uses the term 'hereditary right', *ius haereditarium* (cf. Wormald 1984:22-3). Either they had set themselves up as lay abbots ruling over genuine monks or the entire community had been made up of married laymen purporting to be monks. In any event, the effect of this trend had been to deprive the king both of a sufficient supply of secular warriors, *copia militiae secularis*, and of enough land to endow new *milites* (Bede, *Epistola ad Ecgberhtum* 11).[29] The previous norm had apparently been for a nobleman to receive a grant of land for life from the king which would sustain his rank and enable him to marry.[30] The effect of a former *miles* purporting to become a monk and to establish a monastery which then passed down in his direct line of descent was twofold: that he and his kinsmen, in that they were supposedly monks, were no longer obliged to do military service and that his possession of the bookland was hereditary.

The next stage was for it to be accepted that noblemen could receive grants of land in hereditary right even when they might have no intention of founding a monastery.[31] They would then remain unambiguously liable to military service. It seems, therefore, that kings got out of the crisis created by noble desire for hereditary possession of land, not by the policy advocated by Bede, namely disendowing monasteries which did not live up to their name, but by cutting the link between book-right and grants of land to churches, between *ius haereditarium* and *ius ecclesiasticum*. Nobles then ceased to have the same incentive to found bogus monasteries and kings could grant land under conditions more appropriate to laymen.

There was also, however, a further element in the royal recovery of power over the transmission of land. When, in the seventh century, a *minister regis* such as Benedict Biscop received a royal grant of land, it went without saying that the

---

he should succeed to the estate at Sodbury". This corresponds closely to the Irish conception of the *damnae apad*, 'material of an abbot', that is, a person fit and qualified to be an abbot; in order to share in the succession to the headship of a church the kindred had to provide such a person.

[29] Bede writes *"neque illa [loca] milites siue comites secularium potestatum, qui gentem nostram a barbaris defendant, possident"; "rarescente copia militiae secularis"; "ut omnino desit locus, ubi filii nobilium aut emeritorum militum (= duguð?) possessionem accipere possint"*. The word *miles* almost certainly has the same sense as it had when used of Imma and the *militia* of King Ælfwine: Imma was, as a *minister regis*, a member of the *militia*. Bede is not referring to, still less denying, any obligation by non-nobles, whether on or off church lands, to fight (cf. Brooks 1971:73-4).

[30] Bede (*Historia abbatum*, c. 1) speaking of Benedict Biscop, *minister Oswiu regis*, says that when aged about twenty five he was due to receive a grant of land *suo gradui competentem*.

[31] The standard example is S 114=*CS* 230, a grant by Offa to his thegn, Dudda, of four hides *"in ius ecclesiasticae liberalitatis in perpetuum possid[endas]"*, by which Dudda was to have it during his lifetime and was specifically enabled to grant the land after his death to anyone *suae propinquitatis*. The grant also gave an exceptional privilege by which, if any of his heirs was liable to lose the land for committing a crime, he should be permitted to retain the land provided he paid an appropriate fine.

grant had to be earned: a period as a royal servant led to the royal grant. *Ius haereditarium* might appear to have weakened such notions: once the grant had been made it was, in theory, perpetual. But in the event nobles ended up having to earn their bookland,[32] just as they could easily lose it by wrongful behaviour {e.g. S 1447 (in Robertson 1956: no.44)}.[33] Moreover, Bede's phrase, when speaking of the grant of land to Benedict Biscop, that it was to be appropriate to his rank (*possessionem terrae suo gradui competentem*) is echoed by the frequent use of the term *ār*, 'honour, rank', for land.[34] Surviving histories of disputes over estates make it evident that royal support was crucial if even the noblest in the land were to retain possession of their lands.[35] Lack of such support meant loss of material possessions and therefore loss of *ār*, 'estate' in the sense of both rank and land. However much rhetoric charters might expend on the permanent and unalterable nature of grants, in practice they were often neither permanent nor unalterable; to keep them one needed good friends in large numbers, such as Archbishop Dunstan who could muster "a good thousand men who gave the oath" {S 1458 (Robertson 1956: no.41); S 1454 (Robertson 1956: no.66)}.

While one retained possession of bookland, there were valuable rights which were attached to it. Much the most important for the topic of kinship was testamentary freedom. This might enable someone to grant the land outside his kindred, provided that the original charter did not prohibit such an act (Alfred 41; Liebermann 1903-16: i.74). So, for example, Abbot Ceolfrith granted to Worcester land which earlier King Æthelbald had granted to Ceolfrith's father, Ealdorman Cyneberht, in order to found a monastery {S 1411=*CS* 220 (757 x 775); see Ismere charter, S 89=*CS* 154=*EHD* i. no.67}. Ceolfrith insists that he is granting the land 'by hereditary paternal right', *iure paterno ereditario*, and that what he is granting is the inheritance of his father Cyneberht. Since we have the original charter, we

---

[32] S 1283 (in Robertson 1956:no. 16): if Cyneswith does not have children, she is to "leave it to whichever of her kinsmen is willing to earn it from her". This may, however, refer to purchase of the land; but this is unlikely to be true of S 1503 (in Whitelock 1930: no. 20), where the Ætheling Æthelstan declares how he has disposed of his estates which he earned (*geearnode*) from his father King Æthelred II. There he is giving expression to the axiom that possession of bookland depends upon faithful service. In S 1211 (in Harmer 1914: no. 23) it is part of a reciprocity: *"...hēo ne dorhste for Gode him swā lēanian swā hē hire tō geearnud hæfde"*.

[33] Presumably he was said to have stolen the sword that was found on him when he was drowned {cf. S 1457 (in Robertson 1956: no.59); S 877 (in Robertson 1956: no.63); S 886 = *EHD:* i, no.119}.

[34] E.g. the Will of the Ætheling Æthelstan {S 1503 (in Whitelock 1930: no.20, p. 56. 11)}. A particular estate is regularly land, but the totality which sustains the person's rank is his or her *ār*; e.g. S 1211 (King Edward deprives Goda of his lands and gives them to Eadgifu): *"and se cynincg hine þa 7 ealle his āre, mid bōcum 7 landum, forgeaf Ēadgife..."* (Harmer 1914:37, l. 25); then, Eadgifu is deprived of her lands: *"man Ēadgife berypte ǣlcere āre"* (Harmer 1914:38, l. 11); but later, they are replaced: *"hī hire āre gerehton 7 āgēfon"* (Harmer 1914:38, l. 17). In that context, however, it means 'benefit', 'honour': *"þan hyrede on ēcnesse tō āre 7 hire sāwle tō reste"* (Harmer 1914:38, l. 20).

[35] Queen Eadgifu lost her lands as soon as the second of her sons, King Eadred, died, even though the successor was her grandson, Eadwig: S 1211 (in Harmer 1914:no. 23; cf. Stafford 1981:24-6).

know that it did not prohibit alienation outside the kindred. Nonetheless, Ceolfrith thought it wise to include a special clause in the anathema warning against anyone 'of my kindred or any outsider', *ex parentela mea vel externorum*, who might seek to undo the gift. On the other hand, even though the original charter witnessing to Æthelbald's grant did not prohibit alienation outside the kindred, its purpose was, in fact, to create a family monastery for one son. There may have been other sons, who, because they were not intended to be heads of monasteries, inherited a share in the normal way, without benefit of any royal grant.

Surviving wills show that, once laymen came to possess bookland for themselves, the benefit of doing so was not normally to alienate the land outside the kindred, but to give the testator freedom to apportion his estate as he wished within the kindred {e.g. S 1508 (Harmer 1914: no.10=*EHD* i, no. 97)}. This allowed him to give one son much greater resources than others;[36] or grant land to a kinswoman for life;[37] or lease land to a man and one set of heirs after him {S 1412=*CS* 271 (786 x 796)}. This flexibility allowed a nobleman to plan the succession to his estate so as to ensure, given the king's good will, that at least one of his sons retained wealth and power. In that sense, it had the advantages of primogeniture, but it still allowed provision to be made for other kinsmen and allies (Holt 1982:195-7).

For persons of lower rank, such as the reeve Abba, bookland did not perhaps make so much difference and was probably also less common. According to his will, Abba's kinsmen, apart from his wife Heregyþ, included: Alchhere (Ealhere), who is described as *mīn brōþar*, and Æthelwold (he and Ealhere are called *twaegen mine megas*) {S 1482 (ed. Harmer 1914:no. 2)}. Probably Æthelwold was also a brother. Freothomund's relationship is unspecified, but he is to receive Abba's sword and is to inherit the land if neither of the brothers has an heir. A possibility is that Freothomund is Abba's father's brother's son. This is supported by the fact that in the order of succession he comes after Abba's brothers (and their children, if any are born) and before his sister's sons (*mīnra swestarsuna*). Abba's will is that

(1) if God should grant him a child, that child 'should inherit the land and enjoy it with [Abba's] wife'.

(2) If God does not grant him a child,

   (a) his wife is to enjoy it as long as she remains single (but as a laywoman); she is to be aided by Ealhere his brother; and in return for this help Ealhere is to be given half a sulung at Chillenden.

   (b) If she prefers to marry again, Abba's *megas* are to inherit the land, and the widow is to be given her own possessions.

   (c) If she prefers to enter a monastery or 'to journey south' (as a pilgrim), Abba's two megas, Ealhere and Æthelwold, are to give her 2,000 pennies and they are then to take the land. They are also to give 50 ewes and 5 cows to Lyminge on her behalf.

---

[36] Notoriously, King Alfred's Will advantaged his eldest son Edward (S 1507 = *EHD:* i, no.96).

[37] E.g. a grant by Aldred, sub-king of the Hwicce, of a monastery to his kinswoman, Æthelburg, the monastery to go to Worcester after her death {S 62=*CS* 238 (778 x 781)}.

The sequence of heirs, therefore, seems to have been something like this:

F   = father, B = brother, FB = father's brother etc.
(1)   = order of succession of existing relatives.
((1))   = place in the order of succession of those not yet born, such that ((1)) comes after (1) and excludes (2).

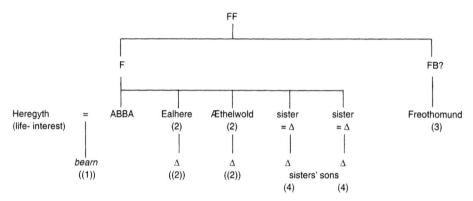

The pattern is clear enough: preference given to lineal descendants as against collaterals; among the latter, preference given even to more distant patrilineal kin over nearer matrilineal kin. These relatives may be all that Abba considered to be kinsmen. After detailing the order of succession, he declares that "if it comes to pass that my *cynn* dies out so utterly that there be none of them able to hold land, then let the community at Christ Church and their lord take it". This then shows exactly what benefit his testamentary capacity confers on Abba: he makes Christ Church his residuary heir on condition that the archbishop acts as advocate and patron of his heirs. The document also includes provisions made by Abba's wife, Heregyth, about an estate at Challock which may have been her *morgengifu*; this would probably also have been bookland, but she does not prescribe an order of succession, but rather imposes on any heir a food-rent to be paid to Christ Church. Since, therefore, it was characteristic of the nobility to enjoy book-right, it follows that they were also the characteristic benefactors of churches.

Abba appears to have been of commoner status (Harmer 1914:78 note). His possession of book-right marks him out as a very thriving *ceorl*. Most men of his rank, however, will have possessed folkland, which I take to be land subject to the full range of public burdens, but which also was land handed on by partible inheritance. Partible inheritance appears to have been taken for granted in the early period.[38] The main problem at this level of Anglo-Saxon society is the relationship between partible inheritance and the standard units of land, such as the hide and

---

[38] Æthelberht 80, implies partible inheritance; Bede, *Historia abbatum*, c. 11, shows that the eldest son had some preference (probably by being entitled to the *frumstōl* of Ine 38): *"Inter spiritales suos liberos eum maiorem qui ampliori spiritus gratia sit praeditus aestiment, quomodo terreni parentes, quem primum partu fuderint, eum principium liberorum suorum cognoscere, et caeteris in partienda sua hereditate praeferendum ducere solent"*.

the yardland. By the twelfth and thirteenth centuries there is a fairly sharp divide between the free peasants, who had much greater power to hand on their land to their heirs, and the unfree yardlanders or half-yardlanders who had impartible inheritance imposed on them by their lords. Lords wished to retain standard holdings from which they could demand standard services. They therefore took care to exercise control over the transmission of villein holdings by making all land transfer subject to the manorial court. At the end of the Anglo-Saxon period, it is evident from Domesday Book as well as from such texts as the *Rectitudines singularum personarum* or the Tidenham survey that the yardland was already a standard feature of the landscape {*Rectitudines singularum personarum*, 4. 3 (Liebermann 1903-16, i.447) provides two oxen for the *gebur*; cf. Lennard 1959:349-58, esp. 351; Robertson 1956: no. 109}. In the survey of Hurstbourne Priors, however, which Finberg dates to the tenth century, the hide is the standard unit from which dues are demanded (Finberg 1964; Robertson 1956: no. 110). In Ine's laws, the yardland is already mentioned, but the reference to a Welshman who may rise as far as possessing a full hide of land, also suggests that very many of Ine's Welsh subjects were not so well off (Ine 23.3). My suspicion is that the Anglo-Saxon settlers attempted to impose a pattern by which even their rank and file received a hide of land; the settlers were then marked off from the native Britons because they included a large proportion of very prosperous peasants. This division between English and Briton could not survive large-scale anglicization of subject Britons. With the demise of a polity of two nations came the end of any assumption that all native freemen should have a hide of land.[39] One hide or five hides could function as standards to which those with less wealth must aspire if they were to rise in the social hierarchy; but they were no longer standards of landed wealth which one had to satisfy in order to remain in the rank into which one had been born. They were the targets of the thriving, not the stumbling block of the declining peasant.

The kinship of the slave was overshadowed by his low status: at least in publicly recognized circumstances, such as the payment of wergild, the lord replaced an unfree kindred:

> If a Welsh slave kills an Englishman, then he who owns him shall surrender him to the lord and kinsmen [of the slain man], or pay 60 shillings for his life. If, however, he will not pay the price for him, the master must then set him free; his kinsmen are then to pay the wergild if he has a free kindred; if he has not, the avengers are to deal with him (Ine 74-74.1; transl. Whitelock 1979; *EHD:* i. 372).

Yet, among freedmen, kinship varied according to status, just as it did for kings, nobles and freemen. This is neatly demonstrated by comparing the above passage from Ine's laws with a contemporary Kentish rule, given in Wihtred 8. Both concern themselves with manumission, but with different effects on the kinship of those freed. Wihtred's freedman remains under the protection of his lord: even though he is personally free and can go where he wants, nevertheless he still looks

---

[39] What follows is derived from Charles-Edwards 1972 with an extra dose of speculation.

to his lord rather than to his kindred for protection, even beyond the bounds of Kent. Ine's freedman, however, is in a very special situation, having been manumitted as a consequence of killing a freeman. His lord could have paid compensation on his behalf or he could have handed him over to the kindred of the dead man, but he can also free him so completely that his former slave has no claim on him for protection or support. Now that he has been freed to this extent, the former slave can seek the support of his own kinsmen in the feud, if any are free. The kinship of the unfree is thus ineffective in the feud; the kinship of the freedman may be ineffective, in that the lord continues to act as if he were the freedman's kin, but this depends on the extent of the manumission and upon whether the freedman has any free kinsmen.

The language of status is applied directly to kindreds, not just to individuals. Kindreds are free or unfree, as in the passage from Ine; they may be of a two-hundred or a twelve-hundred wergild, as in the Ordinance of the Bishops and Reeves of the London District (VI Athelstan 8.2; *EHD:* i. 389). Such language reflects reality: the kinship of king, of noble, of free and unfree were not the same. Yet, there was not a gulf between them: many nobles were the descendants of kings; the economically independent free, who might have bookland, like the reeve Abba, were in a different position from the dependent, who, in turn, resembled the unfree in some respects. As kinship was only one source of friendship, so different kinships offered different kinds of friendship: the brother of a king might be his rival, while the brother of a free peasant was much more likely to be his daily collaborator, in ploughing, in harvesting and in the sharing of scarce tools.

References

Textual sources:
[Abbreviations: *ASC=Anglo-Saxon Chronicle*; CCCC 183=Corpus Christi College, Cambridge, MS 183; *CS=Cartularium saxonicum*; *EHD= English Historical Documents*; *Hist.=Libri historiarum decem*; S=Document number in Sawyer 1968]

Æthelberht: see Liebermann 1903-16 (ed.)
Alfred's laws: see Attenborough 1922 (trans.); Liebermann 1903-16 (ed.); Whitelock 1979.
Anglian Collection: see Dumville 1976.
Anglo-Saxon Chronicle A: see Plummer 1892-99; Dumville & Keynes 1983-.
Asser
          Vita Ælfredi: see Stevenson 1904.
The Astronomer
          Vita Hludovici: see Rau 1968:255-381.
Athelstan
          VI, 7, *Ordinance of the Bishops and Reeves of the London District*: see Liebermann 1903-16, i: 173-183; Withelock 1979: no. 37.
Bede
          Baedae continuatio: see Plummer 1896, i: 361-363.

Baedae vita S. Cuthberti prosaica: see Colgrave 1940.
Epistola ad Ecgberhtum: see Plummer 1896, i:405-423, Withelock 1979: n. 170.
Historia Abbatum: see Plummer 1896, i:364-387
Historia ecclesiastica gentis Anglorum: see Colgrave & Mynors 1969.
Beowulf: see Klaeber 1950.
Be Wifmannes Beweddunge: see Liebermann 1903-16: i. 442.
Cartularium Saxonicum: see Birch (ed.) 1885-93.
Cassiodorus
      Variae: see Mommsen 1894.
Collectio canonum hibernensis: see Wasserschleben.
Corpus Christi College, Cambridge, MS 183: see Dumville 1976.
CS: see Birch 1885-1893.
EHD: see Withelock 1979.
Felix
      Vita S. Guthlaci: see Colgrave 1956.
Gregory of Tours
      Libri historiarum decem: see Krusch & Levison 1951.
Historia Brittonum: see Mommsen 1898.
Ine's laws : see *EHD:* no.32; Liebermann 1903-16.
Leges Henrici primi: see Downer 1972.
Norðleoda Laga: see Liebermann 1903-16, i: 458-461.
Pactus legis salicae: see Eckhardt 1962.
Paul the Deacon
      Historia Langobardorum: see Waitz 1878.
Rectitudines singularum personarum: see Liebermann 1903-16.
Stephen
      Vita S. Wilfridi: see Colgrave 1927.
Vita S. Cuthberti anonyma: see Colgrave 1940.
Wer: see Liebermann 1903-16: i. 392-3.

Bibliography:

Alcock, L.
    1987   *Economy, Society and Warfare among the Britons and Saxons*. Cardiff: University of Wales Press.
Angenendt, A.
    1984   *Kaiserherrschaft und Königstaufe*. Berlin: de Gruyter.
Attenborough, F. L. (trans.)
    1922   *The laws of the earliest English kings*. Cambridge: Cambridge Univ. Press.
Birch, W. de Gray
    1885-93   *Cartularium Saxonicum*, 3 vols. London: Whiting & Co.(Ltd.). [Rep 1964 by Johnson reprint Co., New York & London].
Brooks, N.
    1971   The development of military obligations in eighth- and ninth-century England. In *England before the Conquest: Studies in Primary Sources presented to Dorothy Whitelock*. P. Clemoes & K. Hughes (eds.), pp. 69-84. Cambridge: Cambridge University Press.

Campbell, J.
1989   The sale of land and the economics of power in Early England: Problems and
            possibilities. *The Haskins Society Journal: Studies in Medieval History* 1: 23-37.
Chadwick, H. M.
1905   *Studies on Anglo-Saxon Institutions.* Cambridge: Cambridge Univ. Press.
Charles-Edwards, T. M.
1972   Kinship, status and the origins of the hide. *Past and Present* 56: 3-33.
1976   The distinction between land and moveable wealth in Anglo-Saxon England.
            In *Medieval Settlement Continuity and Change.* P. H. Sawyer (ed.), pp. 180-
            187. London: Edward Arnold.
1993   *Early Irish and Welsh Kinship.* Oxford: Clarendon Press.
Colgrave, B.
1927   *The Life of Bishop Wilfrid by Eddius Stephanus.* Cambridge: Cambridge
            University Press.
1940   *Two Lives of Saint Cuthbert.* Cambridge: Cambridge University Press.
1956   *Felix's Life of Saint Guthlac.* Cambridge: Cambridge University Press.
1968   *The Earliest Life of Gregory the Great.* Kansas: University of Kansas Press.
            [Reprinted Cambridge: Cambridge University Press (1985)].
Colgrave, B., & R. Mynors
1969   *Bede's Ecclesiastical History of the English People.* Oxford: Oxford
            University Press.
Dinneen, P. S., & T. O'Donoghue
1911   *Dánta Aodagáin Uí Rathaille.* London: Irish Texts Society.
Downer, L. J.
1972   *Leges Henrici primi.* Oxford: Oxford University Press.
Dumville, D. N.
1976   The Anglian Collection of royal genealogies and regnal lists. *Anglo-Saxon
            England* 5: 23-50.
1979   The Ætheling: A study in Anglo-Saxon constitutional history. *Anglo-Saxon
            England* 8: 1-33.
1985   The West Saxon Genealogical Regnal List and the Chronology of Early
            Wessex. *Peritia* 4: 21-66.
Dumville, D. N., & S. Keynes
1983-   *The Anglo-Saxon Chronicle: A Collaborative Edition.* (23 vols.).
            Cambridge: D. S. Brewer.
Eckhardt, K. A. (ed.)
1962   *Pactus legis salicae. Monumenta Germaniae historica. Legum sectio* I, iv. 1.
            Hannover: Hahn.
Finberg, H. P. R.
1964   *Lucerna: Studies of Some Problems in the Early History of England.*
            London: Macmillan.
Fleming, R.
1991   *Kings and Lords in the Conquest of England.* Cambridge: Cambridge
            University Press.
Franz, A.
1909   *Die kirchlichen Benedictionen in Mittelalter.* Freiburg-im-Breisgau: Herder.
Godman, P (ed.)
1982   Alcuin. In *The Bishops, Kings, and Saints of York.* Oxford Medieval Texts 11.
            P. Godman (ed.), pp. 786-835. Oxford: Clarendon Press.

Goody, J.
1983   *The Development of the Family and Marriage in Europe*. Cambridge: Cambridge University Press.

Harmer, F. E.
1914   *Select English Historical Documents of the Ninth and Tenth Centuries*. Cambridge: Cambridge University Press.

Hart, C.
1966   *The Early Charters of Eastern England*. Leicester: Leicester University Press.

Holt, J. C.
1982   Feudal Society and the Family in Early Medieval England: I. The Revolution of 1066. *Transactions of the Royal Historical Society*, 5th ser. 32: 193-212.

Hunter Blair, P.
1948   The Northumbrians and their southern frontier. *Archaeologia Aeliana*, 4th ser. 26: 98-196 [Reprinted as no. IV in *Anglo-Saxon Northumbria*. M. Lapidge & P. Hunter Blair. London: Variorum 1984].

John, E.
1960   *Land Tenure in Early England*. Leicester: Leicester University Press.
1966   Folkland reconsidered. In *Orbis Britanniae and Other Studies*. E. John (ed.), pp. 64-127. Leicester: Leicester University Press.

Jolliffe, J. E. A.
1935   English book-right. *English Historical Review* 50: 1-21.

Kelly, S.
1992   Trading Privileges from Eighth-Century England. *Early Medieval Europe* 1: 3-28.

Kirby, D. P.
1974   Northumbria in the time of Wilfrid. In *Saint Wilfrid at Hexham*. D. P. Kirby (ed.), pp. 1-34. Newcastle upon Tyne: Oriel Press.
1991   *The Earliest English Kings*. London: Unwin Hyman.

Klaeber, F. (ed.)
1950   *Beowulf and the Fight of Finnsburg*. Lexington, MA: Heath & Co.

Krusch, B., & W. Levison
1951   *Libri historiarum decem. Monumenta Germaniae historica. Scriptores rerum merovingicarum*, I. 1. Hannover: Hahn.

Liebermann, F.
1903-16 *Die Gesetze der Angelsachsen*. Halle: Niemeyer.

Loyn, H. R.
1974   Kinship in Anglo-Saxon England. *Anglo-Saxon England* 3: 197-209.

Lynch, J. H.
1986   *Godparents and Kinship in Early Medieval Europe*. Princeton, NJ: Princeton University Press.

Moisl, B.
1983   The Bernician royal dynasty and the Irish in the seventh century. *Peritia* 2: 103-126.

Mommsen, T. (ed.)
1894   *Cassiodori senatoris Variae. Monumenta Germaniae historica. Auctores antiquissimi*, 12. Berlin: Weidmann.
1898   *Chronica minora. Monumenta Germaniae historica. Auctores antiquissimi*, 13. Berlin: Weidmann.

Ó. Corráin, D.
    1971   Irish regnal succession: A reappraisal. *Studia hibernica* 11: pp. 7-39.
Plummer, C. (ed.)
    1892-1899   *Two of the Saxon Chronicles Parallel*, 2 vols. Oxford: Clarendon Press.
    1896   *Venerabilis Baedae opera historica*, 2 vols. Oxford: Clarendon Press.
Rau, R. (ed.)
    1968   *Quellen zur Karolingischen Reichsgeschichte*, 3 vols. Ausgewählte Quellen
                zur deutschen Geschichte des Mittelalters. R. Buchner (ed.). Darmstadt:
                Wissenschaftliche Buchgesellschaft.
Robertson, A. J.
    1956   *Anglo-Saxon Charters*. Cambridge: Cambridge University Press.
Sawyer, P. H.
    1968   *Anglo-Saxon Charters: An Annotated List and Bibliography*. (Royal Historical
                Society Guides and Handbooks, no. 8). London: Royal Historical Society.
Stafford, P.
    1981   The King's wife in Wessex, 800-1066. *Past and Present* 91: 3-27.
    1989   *Unification and Conquest: A Political History of England in the Tenth and
                Eleventh Centuries*. London: Edwin Arnold.
Stenton, F. M.
    1971   *Anglo-Saxon England*, 3rd edn. Oxford: Clarendon Press.
Stevenson, W. H.
    1904   *Asser's Life of King Alfred*. Oxford University Press.
Vinogradoff, P.
    1893   Folkland. *English Historical Review* 8: 1-17.
Waitz, G.
    1878   *Historia Langobardorum. Monumenta Germaniae historica. Scriptores
                rerum langobardicarum et italicarum, saec. VI-IX*. Hannover: Hahn.
Wallace-Hadrill, J. M.
    1988   *Bede's Ecclesiastical History of the English People: A Historical
                Commentary*. (Oxford Medieval Texts). Oxford: Clarendon Press.
Wasserschleben, F. W. H.
    1885   *Die irischen Kanonensammlung*, 2nd edn. Leipzig: Bernhard Tauchnitz.
Whitelock, D. (ed. & trans.)
    1930   *Anglo-Saxon Wills*. Cambridge: Cambridge University Press.
    1955   *English Historical Documents* c. 500-1042. London: Eyre & Spottiswoode.
    1968   *The Will of Æthelgifu*. (Roxburghe Club). Oxford: Oxford University Press.
Wormald, P.
    1984   Bede and the conversion of England: The charter evidence. Jarrow Lecture
                1984 (Jarrow, n.d.), pp.19-23.
Yorke, B.
    1989   The Jutes of Hampshire and Wight and the origins of Wessex. In *The
                Origins of Anglo-Saxon Kingdoms*. S. Bassett (ed.), pp. 84-96. London:
                Leicester University Press.

Discussion

AUSENDA: Did constructed kinship reflect a social group's need to increase its kinship network by non-biological means? Is there a nexus between this and territorial or population increase?

CHARLES-EDWARDS: When the influence is coming from the top of society, this is a level of society where it is absolutely necessary to create as many alliances as you possibly can. Particularly, as I think I argued, because your pragmatic tool is very often your enemies. I am sure this can be paralleled elsewhere.

AUSENDA: If a feud was extinguished by compensation, I understand this to mean that there were no socio-economic reasons for it to continue. In other words, is it possible that the people south of the Humber were willing to be annexed by Mercia?

CHARLES-EDWARDS: I think this is one stage in a long-running population feud where you have interesting characteristics. One of the things, in fact, is that the Northumbrian and the Mercian royal lineages both inter-marry like anything at this stage, and also fight each other. So there is lots of peace weaving. In this sort of situation, slightly later than this, Osthryth, a Northumbrian princess who had been married off like several others in that generation to a Mercian, Æthelred, was killed by the Mercians. There was strong political competition between these two royal dynasties and given the basis of that competition, there is no reason why it shouldn't have continued after 679. In fact what happened is that the Northumbrians were defeated by quite another bunch of people in 685 and their power declined. So they never recovered the territory they lost south of the Humber in 679. But that couldn't have been foreseen at this stage.

AUSENDA: You made an interesting point concerning the "...liability of two wergilds, one to the kindred as normal, the other to the king". Is this an example of the increasing interference of the administration, represented by the person of the king, in 'private' feuds?

CHARLES-EDWARDS: It may be. But as far as I can see kings were always concerned with feuds, particularly of course feuds of the nobility. They did not always succeed—certainly on the Frankish evidence—in appeasing the feuding parties. Nonetheless, obviously, for political reasons, it may be disastrous to have a major feud within your nobility. But I think there are other pressures too, to do with notions of honour, why the intervention of kings was important not merely from the king's point of view, to get his paw in, but also for the feuding parties; in the sense that, if you make peace, in part by accepting that you are both parties that have been feuding and are now within the king's peace, and if you accept what the king's notion of appropriate compensation is, and build that into the ceremony of making peace, it helps to get over the problem about whether it is honourable to accept cash. The king is a source of honour.

AUSENDA: Your observation that there were different kinships among the Anglo-Saxons is quite correct. In my opinion even feuds varied according to status. In my experience, feuds within the close kinship group are virtually unknown in pre-industrial society. If murders occur within close kin at the normal level they are ascribed to madness or justified in some way. When murders occur between members of a ruling family they acquire considerable significance because members represent different popular factions. So the ensuing feuds develop along non-customary lines and respond to the prevalence of the factions represented.

CHARLES-EDWARDS: So you would see feuding as characteristic of the higher levels?

AUSENDA: No, I see feuding varying from the higher levels to the lower ones.

CHARLES-EDWARDS: But if it was the lower ones who said, "He must have been mad, or he must have been drunk", you wouldn't get feuding at the lower levels. But as soon as political factions are involved then feud develops.

AUSENDA: This corresponds to what you were saying about kinship.

CHARLES-EDWARDS: Yes.

HINES: What you said on the question of feud provokes me to think in terms of feud being not so much a particular institution as a way of looking at the world, with God himself and his faithful followers in a state of feud against a group led by the pre-eminent *feond*, Satan. This touches on a potentially important point, which is that in the course of the Anglo-Saxon period you apparently get a sense of right and wrong introduced into the concept of feud. There is then more involved than which side you happen to be on to. It's quite different from the idea that one tried to maximize one's own good fortune and well-being, and your reward came in this world. That was entirely a matter of self interest. In England one can trace an increasing sense that you fight on the right side, and that the moral rectitude of your case gives you a reason for fighting and dying, and this is better than the simple fact that you owe loyalty to a certain group or person. I wonder if the involvement of Christianity in this way takes place as the scope for the pursuit of self-interest decreases. If you are a chief's retainer, you are increasingly less likely to get very much materially out of the relationship, and you have to be persuaded to fight by other arguments. In *Beowulf*, Grendel's kin are God's enemies, and there is glory in attempting to oppose Grendel which is quite different from butchering (or being butchered by) some chap who is exactly the same as you, but on the other side.

CHARLES-EDWARDS: Well, I certainly think that it may be important. It is a long story and I think, perhaps, one critical element in it might be when you decide, that Christ is the *dryhten*. This is someone to whom you owe your loyalty in war, and by doing that, you're introducing this kind of military perception into a moral economy.

HINES: The great difficulty is to know precisely when that particular concept is introduced, because you have the problem not only of the representativity of the written sources but also that the manuscript of a particular source in which a concept is used may be two-hundred years later than the composition of the text.

FOWLER: Does the idea of moral rectitude arise to provide motivation within a warring society, which is geared up to feuding and fighting, or is it actually the other way around. Is it because they are a fighting society that the idea of battle fighting evil gets embedded into Christianity?

CHARLES-EDWARDS: I would say that one of the things that is done is to relate Christ as lord, or God as lord, to king as lord. And thus you vote the king of the world qualities of your loyalty to your worldly lord.

HINES: I wouldn't disagree with that but I do not think it is entirely a one-way process: at the same time as there are changing circumstances, both social and religious, there are changing attitudes towards the military life.

CHARLES-EDWARDS: I have a question to archaeologists on the cessation of having weapon burials. You talk so much about gender differences in terms of burials, and implicit in frequent weapon burial may be the attitude to war. Yet this warlike conception of the Anglo-Saxon male carries right on in spite of the change in burial practice.

HÄRKE: Yes, but you have this warlike conception in post-Roman Celtic society, too, and they don't have weapon burials. On the Continent, the Christian Franks practise weapon burial, in some parts of the country until the early eighth century. I don't necessarily see it as a kind of male symbol. To me it is more a symbol of the power of one section of society.

CHARLES-EDWARDS: You mean in ranking terms.

HÄRKE: Well, in the sixth century I would say it is ethnic, and then it becomes transformed in the seventh century into a purely social symbol, when the ethnic differentiation does not matter any more. So, initially, I would actually see it as a kind of material-culture version of the conquest myth.

AUSENDA: I wanted to add that the presence of weapons does not necessarily mean that people are warlike. The Hadendowa go around with long swords hanging from their left shoulder and I have never seen meeker people in my life. [Laughter]

HINES: Surely the real point is that you can have a weapon cult, and a material weapon cult, without having weapon graves. A medieval knight is not necessarily buried with his sword but nonetheless can be portrayed in full armour in sculpture over his tomb.

HÄRKE: But, again, it is a mark of social rank, rather than manly values.

HINES: And there is the apparently ritual deposition of weapons in rivers. It seems to become rather more common as weapons disappear from the graves and may be an alternative to that practice (see Hines, this volume).

SCULL: Interpreting weapon burial as symbolic of the right to use violence is a very valuable analytical distinction which may have both ethnic and social dimensions. It seems clear that this ideology survives into the Late Anglo-Saxon period and beyond, and we need consider why it is expressed in burial in the fifth, sixth and seventh centuries, and whether this status may be expressed in different ways in life, or in death, from the late seventh century onwards.

LENDINARA: The *Miles Christi* topos is found quite early in Anglo-Latin literature. At the same time I think that St Guthlac's story is one of the earliest sources where the problem is raised in a rather complex way. You remember Guthlac developing a disgust for the actions of his forefathers and deciding not to be a warrior anymore. Guthlac's story is a good example as it states that Guthlac had been a warrior for a certain period of time (Felix, *Life of St Guthlac* XVIII). I wonder how the new religion would affect the Anglo-Saxon's view of a *feond*. We should always bear in mind the role of literate men in the transmission of this and similar stories. I think it is important to stress the way Christian religion affected the world view of the Anglo-Saxons, e.g. with regards to war, the role of a warrior and the nature of the enemy, but also to realize the contrasting opinions which existed side-by-side and were expressed in the literature of the time. A new awareness superseded the old one which was conditioned by the old religion, but the pattern is quite complex and, at least in the seventh century, one had to cope both with the old and the new religion, facing a further dichotomy.

WOOD: That point raises the question about chronology. The chronology of feuding seems to me to be even more complicated than you're implying. One of the problems is that not everything that historians have identified as feuds are described as feuds in the early sources; they are only re-described as feuds in the seventh- and eighth-century sources. They are not feuds in sixth-century sources. I just wondered to what extent a feud is actually something that develops later as a concept rather than being indigenous already in the fifth and sixth centuries.

CHARLES-EDWARDS: There is a difficulty about what passes as feud. What I take to be important in the state of feud is the possibility of there being accepted forms of reconciliation which may not work or you may not accept.

WOOD. Yes, but that does not have to imply feud. Wergild can simply imply a settlement.

CHARLES-EDWARDS: That is feud. I don't think you will ever find it later on, anything like that. There may be terminological differences but the central question is whether you continue the feud or whether you make peace along the simple pattern which includes paying compensation. That's it. So, when Gregory of Tours hands cash to make peace that is, to my mind, cast iron evidence of the presence of feud.

WOOD: I don't agree at all. [Laughter]

DUMVILLE: Can I take up the relationship between kindred, kingship and religion as seen in terms of established ecclesiastical houses. You have an interesting passage where you were talking about Guthlac's entry to Repton and you said that this was a house probably associated with the Mercian royalty, and had Guthlac not made it clear that he was renouncing all political ambitions he would not have been welcome. If you put that point alongside your genealogy of the Mercians which you drew out, it seems to me that one could in fact argue that it's not quite as simple as that; that the relationship is not so much with the Mercian royal house as with a segment, a lineage within it. This is made particularly manifest in the case of Æthelbald later. But Æthelbald, as you say, is not of the same lineage as the people of Guthlac and therefore his turning to Guthlac could itself be a political statement and could have further political implications. He may be renouncing the world but he was not necessarily going so far as to renounce the world and put himself in the hands of the people he had been fighting against.

I wonder if too you could elaborate a bit on the etymological connection of *cynn* and *cyning*. I pick this up particularly because of what you have to say about the possible relationship with *æþeling* but also I'm reminded that people studying ninth-century Denmark often argue that the word 'king' was used there for any member of the royal lineage. I have never seen any evidence produced for that. I suspect it is a means for covering up difficulties. But anyway the point has been prominent in discussion on ninth-century Denmark. You suspected that this might be the case in Wessex in particular because of the opposition you set up between the idea of the king of West Saxons, as perhaps artificial historiography, and the evidence for the local, possibly competing, kingships. That's not the way I would read the Wessex evidence and would be dubious about that particular kind of construction. But it seems to me a part of this turns on how one handles this question of *cynn* and *cyning*.

CHARLES-EDWARDS: One might perhaps explain *cyning* much better in the Frankish situation than you can in some of the other cases. It may be that the term comes straight from *Francia* and that would then mean that it spreads, probably in the sixth-century. You don't get a cognate word, of course, in Gothic. You don't get it in the Ostrogothic kingdom, but you get it in Scandinavia, you get it in the West and North-West. What is the explanation apart from the fact that it looks simply like a member of a *cynn*? Which *cynn*? You don't even have the royal *cynn* yet. So how on earth do you explain this extraordinary word?

DUMVILLE: I was trying to provoke you into an explanation.

CHARLES-EDWARDS: I had abandoned the Frankish interpretation and gone in for some kind of explanation along the lines of a change in the meaning of the word.

WOOD: I wouldn't have thought that the Frankish model could apply and I must say I have increasing doubts about whether you can take the Merovingians as a model, because I think they are a 'constructed' family. The fact that people do not actually know who is related to whom in the Merovingian family suggests that royal blood didn't really matter very much. The family seems to have been a political construct—blood connections could be dubious.

It is very interesting that, in the middle of the seventh century when the king was very powerful, there were kings whose descent nobody knew. And historians forget this, because nineteenth-century historians created nice genealogical trees. In fact when you look at the contemporary sources, you don't always know who is whose father.

I think the Merovingians are not a very good norm to look at for the Franks. One of the things about the Merovingians is that they have sex with everybody just to prove how splendid they are and they don't follow any social norms. And there was trouble in the sixth century when people started throwing the law book at them. There is one king who has two sons by a slave. By law the child of the slave girl would be enslaved. In Merovingian society the king is completely exonerated from this social standard. The kings deliberately break all the legal norms just to show us what they are.

HINES: This sounds interestingly reminiscent of what happened in the late Viking period in Norway.

HÄRKE: I was wondering about your memorable phrase, 'a polity of two nations'. Do we know anything about differences or similarities between Anglo-Saxon/Germanic and British/Celtic kinship systems to speculate whether they had anything to do with a maintenance of this polity for a while, or were there enough similarities to enable assimilation, particularly from the seventh century onwards?

CHARLES-EDWARDS: What I was thinking of particularly actually was Ine's laws, which I regard as seventh-century essentially, and the presence there of provisions for the Welsh. In other words you've got there a parallel hierarchy. In the sixth century you've got people who are Roman and noble within the Frankish realm. But it is usually argued that in the seventh century you have increasing diffusion and therefore you are moving away from a polity of two nations towards assimilation. And I would see this as happening in England earlier in a case like Kent, and later in places like Wessex or Northumbria.

HÄRKE: To come back to the actual kinship system, do you see differences there or do you think that the Welsh very quickly adapted their kinship system to the Anglo-Saxon one, if there was a difference at all initially?

CHARLES-EDWARDS: In a lot of ways I would caution against using the term 'Celtic' in respect of social systems, I think there are differences between Welsh and Irish, in terms of status. It is simply that in a patterning of status the Welsh evidence is much later, when Wales was much more like early Anglo-Saxon England than other parts. In terms of kinship it may be a very important question why it is the case that an awful lot of Anglo-Saxon men are marrying British women because then, of course, ethnicity is presumably descending patrilineally. It must have been. Otherwise they wouldn't.

AUSENDA: I just want to make a comment on the status of slaves. In my experience slaves have no genealogical status. This differentiates them completely from both free and half-free. When asked about their clan they mention the clan of their owners or patrons. I had a personal experience with one man who told me he was a member of the dominant clan when actually he was a descendant of a slave of the dominant clan.

References in the discussion

Textual sources:

Felix

        Life of St Guthlac: see References at end of paper.

THE KENTISH LAWS

PATRIZIA LENDINARA

Università degli Studi di Palermo, Facoltà di scienze della formazione, Istituto di Lingue e Letterature straniere, Piazza I. Florio 24, I-90139 Palermo

Introduction

The 'Kentish laws' have come down to us in one sole manuscript, Rochester, Cathedral Library, MS. A.3.5, a twelfth-century collection of Anglo-Saxon laws and charters known as *Textus Roffensis* (Ker 1957:443-7).[1] We have four English law-codes which all originated in the seventh century; the first three sets of laws were issued by the kings of Kent Æthelberht I, Hlothhere and Eadric, and Wihtred. The fourth compilation issued in the seventh century is that of Ine of Wessex. His legal code met a different fate from the *dōmas* (laws) of the Kentish kings and survives only because it was preserved in Alfred's law-code. With Offa of Mercia's laws it is different. These laws are considered lost, although we have no sure proof that they ever existed in written form (Wormald 1991). It is interesting that all evidence of law-making then stops—or is lost—until Alfred's time.

It is remarkable that the Kentish laws (with the exception of the laws of Eorcenberht, whose decrees are mentioned by Bede, *HE* III. 8, but have not come down to us) experienced a fate different from Ine's laws, as they were not (at least not evidently) reworked by Alfred. In my opinion, this means that a peculiar significance was attributed to these law-codes. Bede wrote of the laws issued by Æthelberht, as if they were still in use in the eighth century, remarking that "*decreta illi iudiciorum iuxta exempla Romanorum cum consilio sapientium constituit; quae conscripta Anglorum sermone hactenus habentur et obseruantur ab ea*" (*HE* II.5) {He established with the advice of his counsellors a code of laws after the Roman manner. These are written in English and are still kept and observed by the people. (Trans: Colgrave & Mynors 1969)}.

In fact these laws are an extraordinary source, both as legal documents and as Old English texts, and the question as to why they were written in the vernacular is still an open one—if they were really written in the vernacular at first— when all the other laws of the Continental *Germani* were written in Latin.[2] This first set of laws is the only documented instance of vernacular writing *ca* 600 in England, as no other Old English text (with the sole exception of a few runic inscriptions) can

---

[1] This was copied from a Canterbury manuscript of the early eleventh century. For a facsimile of the manuscripts see Sawyer 1957-1962.

[2] The origin and function of the so-called Malberg glosses (written in the Old High German vernacular) to the *Lex salica* is still an open question.

211

be dated so early; the same can be said of the other Kentish laws. But, as far as I
know, no scholar has put forward the hypothesis that these seventh-century codes
might have been written in Latin and afterwards translated into English.
Æthelberht issued the first series of laws following the example of his
contemporaries on the Continent,[3] and law-writing can be regarded as another
proof of Frankish influence in England (Wallace-Hadrill 1971:21-6; Wood 1991;
1992), although this does not explain the reason why the Kentish laws were
written in the vernacular. The influence of the Church was also important, as it is
likely that it immediately undertook the function of recording written legislation, a
task which its members would continue to perform in the following centuries: all
the major collections of the laws which survive from Anglo-Saxon England were
copied at ecclesiastical centres, such as Canterbury where the exemplar of *Textus
Roffensis* was written (Sawyer 1957:20).

The Laws of Kent

The laws issued by the Kentish kings constitute a continuum, none wholly
superseding the preceding code. At the same time, the aspects covered by each law-
code seem to keep up with the evolution of Kentish society. In the second and third
law-codes trade is a more developed theme and the machinery of justice more
complicated (see, for example, the provisions in Hl. 15). The last chapters of the laws
of Hlothhere and Eadric (Hl. 15 and 16) lay out provisions for foreigners (possibly
traders) and transactions taking place in London. The same code attributes great
importance to the role of the compurgators (Hl. 5, 6 and 16), not mentioned in the first
set of laws. In the laws of Hlothhere we read how the king's revenues are
supplemented by the profits of justice (Hl. 12, 13 and 14); we also read of judges or
arbitrators (Hl. 8). The laws of Wihtred register the growing influence of the Christian
Church upon society and cover new matters such as Sunday observance (Wi. 9-11).

The three codes are different in the lay-out and number of their sections; Æthelberht's chapters are generally one sentence long, while the other laws have longer
chapters as the matter involved is more complex or, rather, cannot undergo the
same process of synthetic formulation as the subjects expounded in the laws of
Æthelberht. Contrast, for example:

> *Gif þēo steleþ, II gelde gebēte* (Æbt. 90).
> (If a slave steals, he shall pay twice the value [of the stolen goods,] as compensation).

with:

> *Gif þēuw stēle 7 hine man ālēse, LXX scll', swā hweder swā cyning wille; gif hine
> man ācwelle, þām āgende hine man healfne āgelde* (Wi. 27).

---

[3] Compared with that of the Visigoths and the Burgundians, Frankish legal activity was limited
in character.

(If a slave steals, and is released, 70 shillings [shall be paid]—whichever the king wishes. If he is put to death, half his value shall be paid to the man who has him in his power).

At the same time, the clauses maintain the same style, as is evident from a comparison of:

Gif esne ōþerne ofslēa unsynnigne, ealne weorðe forgelde (Æbt. 86).

(If one servant slays another, who has committed no offence, he shall pay his full value).

with:

Gif man leud ofslēa an þeofðe, licge būton wyrgelde (Wi. 25).

(If anyone slays a man in the act of thieving, no wergild shall be paid for him).

Although each code has its individuality and its primary concerns (for example, the king in the laws of Æthelberht), each shares features with the others; for example the avoidance of the first person, the use of the same formulas and a similar word-choice.

The three prefaces to the laws, two of which are, in my opinion, a later addition, are also quite similar in lay-out and style and might stem from the hand of the same reworker. Both the prologues to the laws of Æthelberht and to the laws of Hlothhere and Eadric say: "*þis syndon þā dōmas...þe āsette....*" (Æbt.) (These are the decrees which...established); "*þis syndon þā dōmas þe āsetton....*" (Hl.) (These are the decrees which...established), with the subordinate clause in the preterite. In the prologue to the laws of Wihtred only the present tense is used in the much simpler formula: "*þis synd Wihtrædes dōmas....*" (Wi.) (These are the decrees of Wihtred), a choice which shows that the first reworking of the Kentish laws must date from no later than Wihtred's time.[4] Both the mention of Augustine in the prologue to the laws of Æthelberht and the description of the (lay and) religious assembly where the laws of Wihtred were issued, which is recalled in the prologue with a pomp reminiscent of the poem on "The Coronation of Edgar" (Krapp 1942:21-2), show how closely the history of English legislation is tied to that of Christianity.

The Kentish laws, as well as the other Anglo-Saxon laws, are concerned with practice and codify established customs. Such compilations could not address all the relevant points of concern, and the three Kentish law-texts are far from being comprehensive codes. Alfred's law-code will cover a greater variety of subjects. Of the Kentish law-codes, that of Æthelberht is the compilation which attempts to be most comprehensive, but it addresses relatively few legal matters and deals almost exclusively with 'criminal law', that is 'feud' in its different aspects, including a detailed list of possible acts of violence (33-72). Eleven clauses (2-12) involve the king himself; two concern the noblemen (13-14) and several more the commoners; the first chapter (which contains

---

4 The first clause of Æbt. has also been considered an interpolation (see Richardson & Sayles 1966:2-4).

seven decrees) concerns the Church and churchmen. The last clauses address women (73-84) and the family retainers, servants and slaves (85-90).

At the same time there were probably unwritten customary laws in use, now lost. We cannot be sure of the extent to which a given code was operative. *Textus Roffensis* is a late compilation, dating from the time of Bishop Ernulf (1115-24) (Ker 1957:443), and we can do little more than guess at the amount of reworking which was done, both on the Kentish laws and on the other laws contained in the manuscript. This is especially true for the Kentish laws, none of which survives in any other manuscript. When Alfred drew up his legal code, he incorporated the legislation of the kings of the past, as he explained in the prologue to his law; he also explained how past laws were modified and revised.

When all these limits and caveats are borne in mind, those laws can be used as a source of information about several aspects of Anglo-Saxon society. Those early laws were well known to scholars; since the beginnings of Old English studies they have been frequently mentioned and often quoted for their contents, which have been used to re-create a picture of Kentish society in the seventh century (or, what is worse, a generalized picture of Anglo-Saxon society). Such representations are often unrealistic because they are based on the assumption that laws provide an accurate image of the social situation. As with other literary and historical documents, laws reflect only a partial view of society. Circular arguments should also be avoided, such as "if the *laadrincman* (Æbt. 7) is a king's escort, then the kings of Kent used to travel with guides". Moreover several chapters of the laws are difficult to interpret. An instance is provided by the contrasting suggestions put forward for the meaning of *frīwīf locbore* (Æbt. 73), literally "a freeborn woman, with long hair", with reference to a free, unmarried woman, but a "woman in charge of the keys", according to a recent suggestion (Fell 1983). Also, apparently simple and plain sentences are problematic and open to different interpretations, as, for example, the meaning of *medume* in the sentence *medumam lēodgelde forgelde* (Æbt. 7) (he shall pay an ordinary wergild).

All these problems bear on the sort of picture of society which can be drawn by using these sources, and especially on the 'jural relations' which are the main subject of the Kentish laws. It has been remarked that "The laws are practical documents.... Function predominates, and four practical matters receive, as might be expected, special attention: the feud, wergild payments, marriage arrangements and succession to land" (Loyn 1974:202).[5]

Jural relations

Large sections of the Kentish laws (as, in particular, the largest part of the law-code of Æthelberht) are devoted to the condition of feud which came to exist

---

[5] A different opinion on the nature and purpose of Germanic law-codes is held by Wormald (1977).

between the kindred of a man (killed, wounded, wronged, or robbed) and that of
the man responsible (for the killing, wounding, wrongdoing, or stealing). Kindreds
were to take charge of reparation and they could (with a few exceptions, for
example, when the conflict was too close in blood-line) arrange either for
vengeance or for the payment of compensation to the kin of the killed. Material
compensation requited woundings and offences. The reparation (expressed by the
Old English verbs *forgildan,* 'to pay for' and *gebētan,* 'to amend'), is meant to
recover the lost equilibrium and to maintain the *friđ,* 'peace'.

The complex system of wergild, with its different levels, which were fixed in
relation to the status of the offended person, is strictly connected with feud.
Payment could be made in one or more installments: the *healsfang,* which was the
first payment of the wergild (that is, the first twenty shillings of the hundred-
shilling wergild of a freeman), must be paid *æt openum græfe* (Æbt. 22), "when
the grave is still open". All the details of the feud were regulated by law, which
fixed the amount of composition and the time-schedule for payment.

Two different opinions have been put forwards as regards Anglo-Saxon
legislation concerning feud. According to some scholars the kinship system
appears to have been made the subject of such a large amount of legislation
because it did not work: the chapters of the laws concerned with feud, in all its
aspects and details, testify to an increasing failure of family concern (cf. Bridbury
1992). Other scholars have expressed the opinion that feud maintained its
importance and vitality well beyond the seventh century. The bond of kinship was
undeniably very important in Anglo-Saxon society and the support of the kindred
was needed in all aspects of a man's life: "kinship remained immensely strong in
ordinary social life" (Loyn 1974:199); at the same time, however, a strong state-
authority soon developed. Kinship appears to be still powerful in the laws of
Æthelberht and in those of Hlothhere. If a homicide departed from the country, his
kindred were responsible for paying half the wergild (Æbt. 23). The consequence
of the growing power of the king resulted in the well known duality of kingship vs.
kinship, which is evident in some chapters of the laws of Wihtred:

> *Gif man frīgne man æt hæbbendre handa gefō, þanne wealde sē cyning đrēora ānes;*
> *ođđe hine man cwelle oþþe ofer sǣ selle oþþe hine his wergelde ālēse* (Wi. 26).

> (If anyone catches a freeman in the act of stealing, the king shall decide which of the
> following three courses shall be adopted whether he shall be put to death, or sold
> beyond the sea, or held to ransom for his wergild).

And further:

> *Gif þēuw stēle 7 hine man ālēse, LXX scll', swā hweder swā cyning wille; gif hine*
> *man ācwelle, þām āgende hine man healfne āgelde* (Wi. 27).

> (If a slave steals, and is released, 70 shillings [shall be paid], whichever the king wishes.
> If he is put to death, half his value shall be paid to the man who has him in his power).

In the later legal codes it becomes evident that the law attempted to control feud,
as the higher authority of the king attempted to exercise some of the power that the

kin used to enjoy. As for the Church, it encouraged settlements by composition rather than 'vendetta'. Bede tells of the role of Theodore of Canterbury in the settlement of the feud between Mercians and Northumbrians after the killing of King Ecgfrith's brother, Ælfwine (*HE* IV.21). At the same time, the penitentials stressed the negative side of killing, including that perpetrated by a kinsman carrying out a vendetta. In the Penitential of Theodore we read: "*Si quis pro ultione propinqui hominem occiderit peniteat sicut homicida VII vel X annos*" (*Canones Theodori cantuariensis* IIII, 1; see Finsterwalder 1929:294) (If a man slays another one to avenge a relative, he shall do penance as a murderer for seven or ten years).

The three laws contain a series of decrees about matrimony and have been made the object of considerable research into the (legal) position of women and its evolution (*cf.* Hill 1979; Richards & Stanfield 1990). Laws address only a few aspects of the relations between man and woman, such as sexual crime and marriage: their provisions have been considered cynical but, of necessity, the lawyers were concerned with the practical (that is the financial) aspects of marriage and divorce. One of the most controversial chapters is Æbt. 31, which deals with a betrayed man and his (eventual) re-marriage, for the provisions of which several interpretations have been put forward (Rivers 1976; 1991). The terms of marriage-agreements are clearly stated in the laws (Æbt. 76-84; Hl. 6): different provisions are set for widows (Æbt. 76) and maidens (Æbt. 77-84). This is one of the fields where the control of the kindred remained stable: the kinsmen arranged marriage and, after the wedding, continued to watch over the woman. On the other hand a woman was an independent legal subject and if she refused to participate in the illegal activities of her husband (Wi. 12) she would not be fined. Marriage was redefined, as a consequence of the influence of the Church, in the laws of Wihtred:[6] four chapters (Wi. 3-6) condemn illicit unions—namely unconsecrated unions, bigamous unions or unions within the forbidden degrees.[7]

The Kentish laws also provide an overall survey of the social structure of seventh-century Kent, as compensation varied with social standing, which is minutely described. The highest rank was that of a nobleman (Æbt. 13, 14 and 75; Hl. 1 and Wi. 5); in Kent he was called *eorl* and described as *eorlcund* 'earl kind, of an earl's degree', a word which provides evidence for the existence of a hereditary aristocracy. In the laws of Æthelberht there occurs also a specialized use of the term *lēod* (Æbt. 2) to refer to the king's lieges (a possible influence of the Frankish *leudes* ?). The intermediate class was that of freeman (*frīgman*), who is also called *ceorl* (see Charles Edwards 1972:10-3). The clause listing the penalties

---

[6] See Imbert 1967; the evidence of Anglo-Saxon law-codes needs to be examined anew, without forcing their meaning.

[7] See the fifth question of Augustine to Pope Gregory: "*Vsque ad quotam generationem fideles debeant cum propinquis sibi coniugio copulari: et nouercis et cognatis si liceat copulari coniugio*" (*HE* I.27) {Within what degree may the faithful marry their kindred; and is it lawful to marry a stepmother or a sister-in-law? (Trans. Colgrave & Mynors 1969)}; the Church regarded as legitimate only those marriages contracted within the recognized degree of consanguinity. Bede condemned illicit unions in the *Historia ecclesiastica* (e.g., *HE* III.22).

for violating the *mund* of widows (Æbt. 75) mentions the widows of nobles (the highest class) and of men of the second, third and fourth class, without any further specification. The code of Æthelberht is the only one to mention an intermediate class between freemen and slaves, that of the *læt*, 'semi-free', divided in turn into three classes (Æbt. 26). The dependent class of slaves also had several divisions and the law makers devoted several chapters to their specialized roles, such as that of the *hlāfǣta*, 'loafeater' (Æbt. 25), or the *grindend þēow*, 'grinding slave' (Æbt. 11).

The accepted view of a marked difference in Kentish society, as far as the wergild of the ordinary freeman was concerned, has been shown to be untrue by Bullough (1965:650) on the monetary evidence put forward by Grierson (Grierson & Blackburn 1986:165).

The Kentish laws portray a society where the change from movable to landed wealth was under way so much so that even the oldest laws contemplate fines for the breach of enclosures (Æbt. 27-9). It is clear here that land is no longer handled in tribal terms but as belonging to individuals (Charles-Edwards 1972; 1976). The word *feoh* meant not only 'cattle' but also 'money' and 'property', and it is hard to believe that the amount of coins which made up the different levels of wergild did not circulate and were only a unit of account.[8]

The language

The laws issued by the three Kentish kings are a very peculiar source: they are both the earliest witness to a legal system in England and the first Germanic laws written in vernacular. The Kentish laws are also regarded as the first works written in Old English and are frequently labelled as documents of the Kentish dialect.[9] The 'Kentish laws', as well as the other laws which are contained in *Textus Roffensis*, are, in fact, written in Late West Saxon. Their language, as often happens with Old English texts, is not homogeneous and shows mixed features.

The study of 'word-geography' applied to the Old English corpus (focusing on the occurrence and distribution of certain words, the so-called 'dialectal synonyms') has yielded important results in recent years and several words can now be safely labelled as 'Anglian', 'West Saxon' or common Old English.[10] On this and other evidence the dialectal origin of a share of Old English texts has been established and now for many works it is also possible to follow the steps of the re-writing in West Saxon.

With the sole exception of those which had been written or reworked by Wulfstan and, in their language, show clear signs of his hand, the Anglo-Saxon laws have not

---

[8] On the limited circulation of money in the first half of the seventh century see Grierson & Blackburn (1986:161): "It would appear that coinage before *ca* 650 was indeed very small and used by a limited group of people for special purposes and transactions".

[9] For the 'truly' Kentish texts, see Hogg 1992:7 and references.

[10] The state of research has been conveniently presented by Wenisch 1979 and Hofstetter 1987.

yet been studied from this point of view. The fact that the Kentish laws have only survived in one manuscript inhibits linguistic analysis. Moreover the peculiarity of their lexicon hinders lexical comparison with other works; however, this does not explain or justify their neglect by lexicographers until recently.

If we analyse the lexicon of the Kentish laws, looking for its dialectal components, we obtain some striking results which suggests a re-writing (of originally Kentish laws) in an Anglian dialect, followed by a further re-writing in West Saxon. There is no proof for the existence of a 'Kentish version' and we might even surmise that it was in Anglian that the three law-codes were written for the first time (or translated from the Latin, see above); a supposition confirmed by the large role played by Anglian, presumably Mercian, in Kent (Seebold 1992).

The Anglian component of the three Kentish laws is evident, as far as their lexicon is concerned (Hofstetter 1987:364; Wenisch 1979:19). Among the (lexical) Anglian features we find *lēafness,* 'permission'; *hrēow,* 'sorrow' (a rare word in West Saxon, which prefers *dǣdbōt* and *(be)hrēowsung), gestliþness,* 'hospitality' (vs. West Saxon *cumliðness); ambihtsmið,* 'court-smith' (an Anglian word, as well as *ambeht* and the other compounds); *ǣlcor,* 'elsewhere' (vs. West Saxon *elles).*

The use of the preposition *in,* 'in' or 'on', is a commonly accepted dialectal test. The Kentish laws yield the following picture: *in* (Anglian) x17 vs. *on* (West Saxon) x5. This means that the texts, if originally written in Kentish, underwent a total anglianization, followed by a partial de-anglianization at the hands of West Saxon scribes. In the Kentish laws there occur both *nǣnig* 'no one' x1 (Anglian) and *nān* x1 (common Old English): it is interesting to compare Æbt. 18: "*Gif man mannan wēpnum bebyred, ðǣr cēas weorð, 7 man nǣnig yfel ne gedēþ....*" (If one man supplies another with weapons when a quarrel is taking place, no injury however being inflicted...) with Hl. 13: "*Gif man wǣpn ābregdeð þǣr men drincen 7 ðǣr man nān yfel ne dēþ....*" (If, where men are drinking, a man draws his weapon, but no harm is done there...).

The chapter of the oldest law maintains the Anglian *nǣnig,* replaced, in the laws of Hlothhere, by *nān.* Elsewhere *nān* has been introduced in works which were originally written in Anglian (and survive in more than one manuscript), such as the Old English Martyrology, or the translation of the *Dialogues* of Gregory the Great.

On the other hand the Kentish laws are marked by several West Saxon features, such as the use of *būtan,* 'without' (West Saxon) and not of *nemne, nymðe* (Anglian); of *mete,* 'food' (West Saxon) and not of *symbel* (Anglian) and of *hraþe,* 'quick' (West Saxon), which replaced *recen* in the more West-Saxonized manuscripts of the translation of the *Dialogues* of Gregory the Great (MS. C). The word *wīsdōm* is used with the meaning *sapientia* (and not *scientia,* as in Anglian) (Seebold 1974); also the choice of *tīma,* 'time' is typical of (Late) West Saxon, as well as the ample use of *ætforan,* 'before'.

The language of the Kentish laws also shows a mixture of early and late word-choices, as well as of early and late variants: for example, the pronominal forms (gen. pl. f.) *hīora* (Early West Saxon) and *hēora* (Late West Saxon). There occurs *scyld,* 'sin' (x1), which is dominant in Early West Saxon and Anglian, and not *gylt*

(Büchner 1968); the Early West Saxon form of the suffix -*ness* is met throughout (*gestliþness* 'hospitality' Wi. 7, *gewitness*, 'witness' Hl. 16; *lēafness,* 'permission' Wi. 7). Archaic also is the frequent occurrence of *esne,* 'slave' (x13), which, at the end of the Anglo-Saxon period, is entirely superseded by *þēow* (x4). The Late West Saxon Word word *lagu,* 'law', which is a borrowing from Old Norse, was not introduced in the process of linguistic up-dating of the Kentish laws, and in the text we meet *dōm* (x7), *riht* (x5), and once (in the prologue to the laws of Hlothhere) *æ*.

All these features show that the laws were used somehow, or at least circulated, for more than four centuries, being copied repeatedly and probably undergoing several changes, perhaps not only as far as their content was concerned, but also as regards their language.

The lexicon

If we look at the Kentish laws as literary texts and study their language we can collect a series of data which help to shed light on their composition, the aims of their authors, and the problems which they had to face when they undertook the task of writing the customs of the people of Kent in the vernacular. According to Dorothy Bethurum (1932:271), notwithstanding the ecclesiastical flavour, the laws maintain several features of the Germanic tradition and "in style...go back to a pre-Christian tradition". In my opinion, their model was Latin (the legal compilations known to or brought along by Augustine and his companions) and the Kentish laws follow closely the Latin codes of the Continental *Germani* in style and layout: for example the usual beginning of the chapters of the Latin compilations: "*Si quis...*" is reproduced by "*Gif man...*" (If one man...). Word-pairs and parallelisms are also met with in the Latin law-codes, as well as assonance and other adornments.

As far as the lexicon is concerned, Æbt. contains 996 words, Hl. 608 and Wi. 665 (the numbers refer to the total amount of words occurring in each law); in the total of 2,269 words there are several words with high-frequencies, such as the conjunctions *and,* 'and' (x69), *gyf,* 'if' (x144), *oþþe,* 'or' (x28); the prepositions *æt,* 'at' (x21), *an,* 'on' (x21), *in,* 'in' (x17), *mid,* 'with' (x18), *tō,* 'to' (x20); and the pronouns *hē, hīo, hit,* 'he, she, it' (x88) and *sē, sēo, þæt,* 'he, she, it, that, this' (x133). The substantives with the highest occurrences are *cyning,* 'king' (x35), *mann,* 'man' (x95) and *manna,* 'man' (x13), which is often used indefinitely, like Modern English 'one'; *scilling,* 'shilling' (x108) and *sceatt,* 'silver penny' (Grierson & Blackburn 1986:164-5) (x13). As far as the verbs are concerned we notice the high frequency of *forgeldan,* 'to pay for' (x20) and *gebētan,* 'to amend, to pay compensation' (x63).

As the codes had to deal with manifold aspects of Anglo-Saxon society, besides the frequently used words, there is a large number of words occurring only occasionally. The Kentish laws are characterized by an amazing number of *hapax legomena.*[11]

---

[11] I shall reckon as *hapax legomena* the words which occur only in the three Kentish laws, even when a word is met more than once in the same law-code or when it occurs in more than one law-code.

Several of the rare terms are difficult to translate as, in the instance of these law-codes, we do not have the help of the *Quadripartitus*, a Latin translation of several Anglo-Saxon laws (see Wormald 1994). The *hapax legomena* are, in large part, compound words, coined to express a complex technical meaning in a synthetic way. The possibility should also be considered that simple words and compounds which do not occur elsewhere may have been loan-translations of Latin terms. The limited occurrence of several words, found only in these three law-codes, yields proof, in my opinion, for a partial reworking of the two foregoing sets of laws, at the time when the third one was written, which produced a certain amount of lexical homogeneity. On the other hand also the lexicon confirms the evolution which marked Kentish society and law in the seventh century, as is evident from the presence of words, for example *eorlcund* 'of an earl's degree' (Æbt. 75 and Hl. 1), whose occurrence is limited to one or two of the law-codes.

In the Kentish laws we also meet *hapax legomena* which do not properly belong to the lexical field of law, such as *blice*, 'exposure' (Æbt. 34). Such a term, as well as other *hapax legomena* which occur in the list of penalties for injuries, might, on that account, be brought back to the legal lexicon too; and the first set of laws, which is particularly rich in rare words for the parts of the body or the different kinds of injuries, has a parallel in the Old Frisian legal compilations.

An alphabetical list of the *hapax legomena* which occur in the Kentish laws is given in Appendix A.[12]

Several words are of limited occurence in the Old English corpus (further occurrences of this group of terms are—with one exception—found only in legal compilations, both civil and ecclesiastical). These words are listed in Appendix B.

Also limited to legal texts, but with a larger number of occurrences, are technical terms such as:

> *halsfang/healsfang*, 'fine prescribed in substitution for capital and other punishment,
>   preferential share of the wergild' (Wi. 11, 12 x 2 and 14);
> *gesīþcund*, 'of the rank of thane' (Wi. 5);
> *tihtan*, 'to accuse' (Hl. 8 and 10, Wi. 22; 23; 24 x 2);
> *twībōte*, 'with double compensation' (Æbt. 2 and 3);
> *twīgylde*, 'liable to a double fine' (Æbt. 1);
> *þrīgelde/þrīgylde*, 'liable to a three-fold fine' (Æbt. 1 and 28).

In the Kentish laws there occur several key-words for features which are typical of the Anglo-Saxon legal system, but whose occurrence is not limited to the laws. This is the case of technical terms such as *morgengyfe*, 'gift of a husband to the wife the morning after the wedding' (Æbt. 81), which also occurs in several charters (Sawyer 1968: S 939, S 1445, S 1458, S 1487, S 1539), in the Antwerp glossary { 'Dos: *morgengifu*' (Kindschi 1955:66)} and in the translation of Apollonius of Tyre (!); *mund*, 'protection, guardianship', here 'the value of guardianship, the compensation to be paid for violation of the *mund*' (Æbt. 75, 76)

---

[12] I have created a complete glossary of the three law-codes and hence checked the occurrences of each lemma in the entire Anglo-Saxon corpus with the help of *A Microfiche Concordance to Old English*.

and 'the guardianship of the freedman's family' (Wi. 8), which occurs, in the sense of 'protection', for example in one of the Old English poetic traslations of the *Pater Noster,* line 48, in the doublet *miht ond mund*; *mundbyrd* 'protection, patronage', here 'the amount to be paid for breach of the peace of the king' (Æbt. 8), 'of a churl' (Æbt. 15), 'of a (free)man' (Hl. 14) and 'of the Church' (Wi. 2), which, in the sense of 'protection', occurs both in poems and in several glosses; *wergeld,* 'value of a man' (Æbt. 31, etc.), whose further occurrences are limited to prose: the laws, some charters, two lists, one of the *Prognostics,* and—as well as other legal terms—in the *Life of St Mildred* in London, BL, MS. Cotton Caligula A.XIV.

Other words of limited occurrences are listed in Appendix C.

Among the rare words which occur in the Kentish laws there are the names of peculiar occupations, such as *birel,* 'cup-bearer' (here 'serving maid'); *grindend,* a present participle, which refers to a particular category of (women) servants, possibly those who were in charge of grinding the corn (cf. *grindere,* 'corn-grinder' in one of the Prognostics) or worked as assistant of the smith as 'knife or sword grinder'. Among words of limited occurrence in the Old English corpus are further terms for injuries and wounds such as *bite,* 'sword-cut' (Æbt. 35), *dynt,* 'blow, stroke' (Æbt. 58; etc.), and *sceard,* 'cleft, gap' (Æbt. 42 and 49).

Several words occur in a meaning which is not witnessed elsewhere, such as *āsettan,* 'to take away' (Hl. 12 x 2) or *gepeahtendlīc,* 'deliberative' (Wi. prol.). Some words share their technical meaning with the other Anglo-Saxon legal compilations, for example, *āweorðan,* which here means 'to become worthless' (Æbt. 52 and 64); *clǣnsian* which has the meaning 'to justify oneself' (Wi. 18 x2; 19; 20 and 22); *forsittan,* in the meaning 'to delay' (Wi. 6); *geblōdgian,* in the meaning 'to make bloody' (with reference to bloodshed resulting from a quarrel); *geclǣnsian,* in the meaning 'to clear oneself' (Wi. 23 and 24); *gecȳðan,* in the meaning 'to prove' (Hl. 16. 3); *gesellan,* in the meaning 'to offer (a security)' (Hl. 6); *gescrīfan,* in the meaning 'to prescribe' (Hl. 8); *rihtan,* 'to amend' (Wi. 4); *tēam,* 'vouching to warranty' (Hl. 16. 1); *tīeman* (Hl. 16. 1) and *getīeman* (Hl. 7), 'to vouch to warranty'; *unāgen,* 'not one's own or under one's control' (Æbt. 76).

The need for a complete study of Anglo-Saxon legal terminology is evident, and it would be interesting to discover if the legal meaning of a word is the primary one or the result of (secondary) semantic evolution. The occurrence of legal terms in other kinds of texts would also help to shed light on the background or inclinations of their authors. Ælfric rarely used legal terms in his sermons, whereas Wulfstan as well as some anonymous homilist, seem to have a penchant for legal terminology. It is interesting to remark how a series of words which occur in the Kentish laws are not found elsewhere in Old English prose texts, for example homilies or translations, but are, rather, found in Old English poetry. This is also true of words with a very low frequence in the entire Old English corpus (such as *lysu,* 'what is depraved'). The lexicon of the Kentish laws has several parallels in *Beowulf* and in *Andreas,* the Riddles of the Exeter Book, *Solomon and Saturn* I, *The Fates of Men,* and *Maxims* I and II. This is the case with words such as *ābregdan,* in the meaning 'to draw' (said of a sword) (Hl. 13); *āgend,* 'owner'

(Hl. 1; etc.); *berigea*, 'a surety' (Hl. 6; etc.) (cf. *leodgebyrga*, 'the protector of a people' of *Beowulf* line 269, etc.); *fācne*, 'fraudulent' (Æbt. 77. 1); *flet/flett* in the meaning 'hall'(Hl. 11; etc.); *gesēman*, 'to reconcile' (Hl. 10); *mæðel*, in the meaning 'council' (Hl. 8); *sēman*, 'to pacify' (Æbt. 65. 1); *undeornunga*, 'openly' (Hl. 16. 2); *unfācne*, 'without malice' (Æbt. 30; etc.). In this instance the similarities might be due to several factors: the 'legal terminology' of the Riddles is due, in my opinion, to their tendency to anthropomorphization of the objects/subjects of the riddles and the stress on 'function', which characterizes this genre. On the other hand, social description is the object of 'catalogue-poems' such as the *Gifts of Men* and the *Maxims*, which aim to show how society works or ought to work and such a feature produces the overlaps with the laws.

Conclusion

The information which can be drawn from the laws is seldom matched by other Old English or Anglo-Latin literature, for the content of the law-codes is eminently technical. In some instances the evidence of the earliest laws finds a counterpart in the works of the historians and the authors of the first prose hagiographies. Bede's *Historia ecclesiastica* (whose limitations are now too often stressed) provides us with a great deal of information about some of the matters treated by the laws and it is, for example, interesting to compare the provisions about theft of the Church's property set forth in Æbt. 1 "*Godes feoh 7 ciricean XII gilde*" {(Theft) of God's property and the Church's shall be compensated twelve fold} with *HE* I.27 "*Addes etiam quomodo eas, quae furtu de ecclesiis abstulerint, reddere debeant. Sed absit ut ecclesia cum augmento recipiat quod de terrenis rebus uideatur amittere, et lucra de uanis quaerere*" ("You should also add that they ought to restore whatever they have stolen from a church. But God forbid that the church should make a profit out of the earthly things it seems to lose and so seek to gain from such vanities") (Trans. Colgrave & Mynors 1969).

The archaeology of the seventh century has a particular importance; the great increase in excavation research and the studies of material culture yield impressive information on the gradation of rank (which is chiefly reflected in cemeteries) and other relevant features of early English society. Anthropologists and their knowledge of other societies whose development was at the same stage as Anglo-Saxon England of the seventh century can provide data concerning similar systems which occurred in different places at different times (for example, about the general principles governing the feud) and discover apparent differences and essential similarities with other 'primitive' peoples which have been studied by the ethnologists. A joint work might yield a new picture of seventh-century England, clear and accurate.

Acknowledgement—I wish to thank David Dumville for reading the first draft of this paper. I also thank Helmut Gneuss for his help with questions relating to Old English dialects and my daughter Camilla Piedimonte for her advice on jural aspects.

Appendix A: list of *hapax legomena* which occur in the Kentish laws

ætgebrengan, 'to buy for himself' (Æbt. 82);

ætgebrengan, 'to bring to' (Hl. 7);

æwda, 'witness, one who affirms the truth by oath' (Hl. 2 and 4; Wi. 23);

æwdamann, 'witness' (Hl. 5): the compound-word has the same meaning as *æwda*; its
second member, *mann* 'man', re-determines the difficult *æwda*;

ambihtsmið 'official carpenter' (Æbt. 7);

bismærword, 'insult' (= Latin *contumeliosum uerbum*) (Hl. 11);

blice, 'exposure' (Æbt. 34);

cearwund, 'badly wounded' (Æbt. 63): the emendation *scearwund,* 'wounded in the share'
has been put forward (Toller 1921:695);

ciricanmann, 'churchman' (Wi. 24 x 2): if not two words *cirican mann*;

drihtinbeag, 'money for slaying a freeman, payment (to the lord) for killing a freeman'
(Æbt. 6), a word which will be superseded by *manbot* in the Laws of Ine and other
law-codes;

edorbrec, 'breach of an enclosure' (Æbt. 27 and 77. 1): a similar compound-word,
edorbrice, occurs in the Laws of Alfred (40);

eorlcund, 'of an earl's degree' (Æbt. 75 and Hl. 1), which is superseded by *gesi cund* in the
Laws of Wihtred (Wi. 5);

feaxfang, 'seizing or dragging by the hair' (Æbt. 33);

folcesmann, 'layman' (Wi. 24 x 2);

forewyrcan, 'to amend on someone else's behalf' (?) (Hl. 15), literally 'to work for': cf. the
hapax, forwyrcend, 'servant', which occurs in The Life of Eugenia by Ælfric, where
it is said that a woman was left with "*unlytle æhta on lande and on feo and on
forewyrcendum*" (very large possessions in land and money and servants);

freolsgefa, 'emancipator' (Wi. 8);

friwif, 'free woman' (Æbt. 73);

gecænnan, 'to clear oneself' (Hl. 2; 4 and 5);

gelæmed, 'lame' (Æbt. 38): an original past participle of *gelæmian* 'to cripple'; cf. *lemian*
in *Beowulf* line 905; the simple verb also occurs, in the meaning 'to subdue', in the
translation of Gregory's *Cura Pastoralis*;

gesam, 'reconciliation' (Hl. 10);

hlafæta, 'loafeater', that is 'a dependent servant' (Æbt. 25);

hion, 'membrane of the brain' (Æbt. 36) (see Liebermann 1905:177);

hrifwund 'wounded in the belly' (Æbt. 61): for a different formulation see the Laws of
Alfred (61) *Gif mon bið on hrif wund* (If one man is wounded in the belly), but the
compound word is documented in the Alamannic Laws, "*si in interiora membra
transpunctus fuerit, quod hrefwunt dicunt...*";

inbestingan, 'to penetrate, to pierce' (Æbt. 64. 2);

laadrincmann, 'conductor, escort, guide' (Æbt. 7): cf. *ladmann* 'leader, guide';

læt, 'man of the class between the slave and the *ceorl*' (Æbt. 26);

leodgeld/leudgeld, 'wergild for manslaughter' (Æbt. 7, 21 and 64); in the same law also the
simple *leod* is used with this meaning (Æbt. 22 and 23);

locbore, literally 'with long hair' (Æbt. 73), otherwise 'who is in charge of the keys' (Fell 1983);

mægþ bot, 'fine for assault on an unmarried woman' (Æbt. 74);

mægþ mon, 'maiden' (Æbt. 82);

mæthlfriþ, 'peace secured by law at a public assembly'[13] (Æbt. 1);

---

[13] Liebermann restored the word also on the authority of a sixteenth-century transcript.

manwyrþ, 'value or price of a man' (Hl. 1; 2; 3 and 4);

mōnanǣfen, 'Monday-eve' (= 'Sunday') (Wi. 9);

nēadhǣs, 'order which one must obey' (Wi. 1. 1);

rihthāmscyld, 'legal means of protection to a homestead' (Æbt. 32) (see Liebermann 1905: 389);
   Toller (1921:688), basing his suggestion on similar chapters of the Continental laws,
   proposed to amend to: *gif man on unriht ham oððe scyld þurhstinð* (If a man pierces
   a dress or a shield unrighteously ?);

siexgylde, 'requiring a six-fold payment or fine' (Æbt. 1);

stermelda, (possibly to be emended to *stelmelda*) 'one who gives information of the theft' (Hl. 5);

tōfōn, 'to take possession ' (Hl. 16. 3 and Wi. 3);

þrīgebētan, 'to pay a triple compensation' (Æbt. 9);

twelfgylde, 'to be restored twelve-fold' (Æbt. 1);

ungestrodyn, 'not subject to confiscation' (Wi. 4. 1);

unlǣgne, 'not to be questioned' (Wi. 16 and 21), cf. the other *hapax, unlygen* 'truthful',
   which occurs in the Laws of Æthelstan (II) (12);

wǣlt, 'sinew of the thigh' (Æbt. 68);

wegrēaf, 'highway-robbery' (Æbt. 19 and 89);

ymcyme, 'assembly' (Wi. prol.).

Appendix B: list of words with limited occurrences in the Old English corpus, found almost only in legal compilations.

ætfōn, 'to lay claim to' (Hl. 7 and 16. 1) which occurs only here and in the Laws of Edward
   the Elder (1. 5) and Æthelstan II (9);

cænn/cann, 'clearance, expurgation, positive assertion' (Hl. 16. 3; Wi. 17 x2; 21. 1 and 22)
   is met here and in the translation of extracts from the Penitential of Theodore (Mone
   1830:525);

cēas, 'quarrelling' (Æbt. 25) is found only here, in the Laws of Alfred-Ine (Introduction to
   Alfred 18. 1) and in a gloss of the third Cleopatra glossary (ed. Quinn 1956:141),
   where it renders Latin *lis,* 'quarrel';

ceorlǣs, 'unmarried woman' (Æbt. 25) here and in the Laws of Cnut (II) (73);

ciricfrið, 'right of sanctuary, penalty for breach of the right of sanctuary' (= Latin *ecclesiae
   pax*) (Æbt. 1) here and in the Laws of Alfred (2. 1);

endlyfgylde, 'entitled to eleven-fold compensation' (Æbt. 1) here and in *Be griðe 7 be munde* (7);

folcfrȳ, 'having full right of citizenship' (?) (Wi. 8) here and in the Laws of Cnut (II) (45. 3);

frēolsdōm, 'emancipation' (Wi. 1) here and in a charter (Sawyer 1968: S 488);

hūslgenga, 'communicant' (Wi. 23 x2) here and in the Laws of Ine (15. 1 and 19);

nigongylde, 'entitled to nine-fold compensation' (Æbt. 1 and 4) here and in *Be griðe 7 be munde* (7);

prōfian, 'to assume to be, to take for' (Wi. 28) here and in one chapter of the Laws of Ine
   (20), which is a verbatim repetition of clause 28 of the Laws of Wihtred;

sǣmend, 'conciliator, arbitrator' (Hl. 10) here and in *Wer* (4);

tohȳran, 'to belong to' (Hl. 5) here and in the Laws of Edgar (II) (1. 1);

þurhþirel, 'pierced through' (Æbt. 61. 1) here and in the Laws of Alfred (67. 2).

Appendix C: other words of limited occurrence.

beberan 'to supply with' (Æbt.18), which is met only here and, with a different meaning, in
   a gloss of the first Cleopatra glossary "Municipales: *innihte* [read *in rihte*]
   beborene" (Stryker 1951:314 M 359, who suggests that "the gloss...is an attempt to
   translate *in loco officium gerentes*");

fēdesl, 'fattened animal' (Æbt. 12) which is found here, in two glosses of the Antwerp
glossary "Altile: *fedels*", "Altilis: *fedels*" (Kindschi 1955:77, 249) and in one gloss
of the Corpus glossary "Altilia: *foedils*" (Lindsay 1921:A 467), where it renders
Latin *altilis* in the meaning 'fattened bird' (cf., for its meaning, *fēdelsswīn*, 'fattened
pig', which occurs in a charter (Sawyer 1968: S 1448));

fæderingmǣg, '(paternal) kinsman' (Æbt. 81 and Hl. 6), which occurs in the laws and
Beowulf line 1263;

gǣngang, 'return' (Æbt. 84) which occurs here and in the Durham Ritual (Lindelöf
1927:195) (= *gēangang*, cf. *gēanfær*, 'return' in the *Anglo-Saxon Chronicle* (MS. E)
s. a. 1119, and *gǣnhwyrft* which glosses Latin *conuersio* in the Lambeth Psalter,
Ps. 107, 12);

hēafodgemaca, 'companion' (Wi. 21), which also occurs in the translations of Bede's
Historia ecclesiastica and Gregory's *Cura pastoralis,* and in the Life of St Margaret
in London, BL, MS. Cotton Tiberius A.III;

lysu (gen. *leswæs*/*lyswæs*), 'what is depraved' (Æbt. 3 and 73) which occurs here and in
Maxims I line 189 (the adjective *lysu,* 'base, false, evil' occurs in *Andreas* line
1222);

mægdenman, 'maiden' (Æbt. 10) is used only here and in the translation of the *Historiae
aduersus paganos* of Orosius;

opberstan, 'to break away, to escape' (Hl. 2 and 4) is found also in the *Anglo-Saxon
Chronicle* (MS. E) *s. a.* 1101 and in a charter (Sawyer 1968: S 886);

tōgecwædan, 'to utter, to address' (Hl. 11) here and in the first Blickling Homily;

tōgedōn, 'to add thereto' (Hl. 2) here and in the West Saxon Gospels (*Luke* 10, 34);

þēowweorc, 'servile work' (Wi. 9) here, in the Laws of Edward the Elder (II) and in
Ælfric's Letter to Wulfsige;

wlitewamm, 'disfigurement of the face' (Æbt. 56) occurs here and in two glosses in the first
and third Cleopatra glossary "*Neuorum wlitewomma*" (Stryker 1951:322 N 84;
Quinn 1956:101).

References

Textual Sources:

[Abbreviations: Æbt. = Law of Æthelberht; Hl. = Law of Hlothere and Eadric; Wi. = Law of Wihtred;
S=Document number in Sawyer 1968].

Aldhelm
    Carmina ecclesiastica: see Ehwald 1919.
    Carmen de virginitate: see Ehwald 1919.
    De virginitate: see Ehwald 1919.
    Enigmata: see Ehwald 1919.

Ælfric
    Life of Eugenia: see Skeat 1881-1887.
    Letter to Wulfsige: see Fehr 1914.

Andreas: see Krapp 1932.
Anglo-Saxon Chronicle: see Plummer 1892-1899.
Antwerp glossary: see Kindschi 1955.
Apollonius of Tyre: see Goolden 1958.

Bede

        De temporum ratione: see Jones 1977.

        Historia ecclesiastica gentis Anglorum: see Colgrave & Mynors 1969.

        Life of St Cuthbert: see Colgrave 1940.

Be griðe 7 be munde: see Liebermann 1903-16.

Beowulf: see Dobbie 1953.

Blickling Homilies: see Morris 1874-1880.

Corpus glossary: see Lindsay 1921.

The Coronation of Edgar: see Krapp 1942.

Durham Ritual: see Lindelöf 1927.

The Fates of Men: see Krapp & Dobbie 1936.

Felix

        Life of St Guthlac: see Colgrave 1956.

The Gifts of men: see Krapp & Dobbie 1936.

Gregory the Great

        Cura pastoralis: see Sweet 1871.

        Dialogi: see Hecht 1900-1907.

Isidore

        Etymologiae: see Lindsay 1911.

Lācnunga and *Leechbook*: see Cockayne 1864-1866.

Lambeth Psalter: see Lindelöf 1909-1914.

Laws of Alfred, Athelstan, Æthelberht, Cnut, Edgar, Edward the Elder, Hlothere and
        Eadric, Ine, Wihtred: see Liebermann 1903-16 (ed.).

Laws of Æthelberht, Hlothere and Eadric, Ine, Wihtred: see Attenborough 1922 (trans.).

Life of St Margaret in London BL Cotton Tiberius A. III: see Clayton & Magennis 1994.

Life of St Mildred in London BL Cotton Caligula A. XIV: see Cockayne 1864-1866.

Maxims I and *Maxims II*: see Krapp & Dobbie 1936; Dobbie 1942.

Menologium: see Dobbie 1942.

Old English Martyrology: see Kotzor 1981.

Orosius

        Historiae adversus paganos: see Sweet 1883.

Prognostics: see Förster 1912.

Quadripartitus: see Liebermann 1903-16.

Riddles of the Exeter Book: see Krapp & Dobbie 1936.

Solomon and Saturn I: see Dobbie 1942.

Symphosius

        Enigmata: see Shackleton Bailey 1982.

Theodore of Canterbury

        Canones Theodori cantuariensis: see Finsterwalder 1929.

Venantius Fortunatus

        Carmina: see Leo 1881.

Wer: see Liebermann 1903-16.

West Saxon Gospels: see Skeat 1871-1887.

Bibliography:

Attenborough, F. L.
    1922   *The Laws of the Earliest English Kings*. Cambridge: Cambridge University
           Press.

Bethurum, D.
1932   Stylistic features of the Old English Laws. *The Modern Language Review* 27: 263-279.

Büchner, G.
1968   Vier altenglische Bezeichnungen für Vergehen und Verbrechen *(firen, gylt, man, scyld)*. Dissertation. Berlin: Freie Universität.

Bridbury, A. R.
1992   Seventh-century England in Bede and the Early Laws. In *The English Economy from Bede to the Reformation.* A. R. Bridbury (ed.), pp. 56-85. Woodbridge: The Boydell Press.

Bullough, D. A.
1965   Anglo-Saxon Institutions and Early English Society. *Annali della fondazione italiana per la storia amministrativa* 2: 647-659.

Charles-Edwards, T. M.
1972   Kinship, status and the origins of the hide. *Past and Present* 56: 3-33.
1976   The distinction between land and moveable wealth in Anglo-Saxon England. In *Medieval Settlement. Continuity and Change.* P. H. Sawyer (ed.), pp. 180-187. London: Arnold.

Clayton, M., & H. Magennis (eds.)
1994   *The Old English Lives of St Margaret.* Cambridge: Cambridge University Press.

Cockayne, T. O. (ed.)
1965   *Leechdoms, Wortcunning and Starcraft of Early England.* 3 vols. (Roll Series 35). London: Longman.

Colgrave, B. (ed.)
1940   *Two Lives of Saint Cuthbert.* Cambridge: Cambridge University Press.
1956   *Felix's Life of Saint Guthlac.* Cambridge: Cambridge University Press.

Colgrave, B, & R. A. B. Mynors
1969   *Bede's Ecclesiastical History of the English People.* Oxford: Clarendon Press. [Repr. with corr., 1991].

Di Paolo Healey, A., & R. L. Venezky
1980   *A Microfiche Concordance to Old English. The List of Texts and Index of Editions.* (Publications of the Dictionary of Old English, 1). Toronto: Pontifical Institute of Mediaeval Studies. [Repr. with rev., 1985].

Dobbie, E. van K. (ed.)
1942   *The Anglo-Saxon Minor Poems.* (The Anglo-Saxon Poetic Records, 6). New York/London: Columbia University Press/Routledge & Kegan Paul.
1953   *Beowulf and Judith.* (The Anglo-Saxon Poetic Records, 4). New York: Columbia University Press.

Ehwald, R. (ed.)
1919   *Monumenta Germaniae historica, Auctores antiquissimi,* 15. *Aldhelmi opera.* Berlin: Weidmann.

Fehr, B. (ed.)
1914   *Die Hirtenbriefe Ælfrics.* Hamburg: Henri Grand. [Repr. Darmstadt: Wissenschaftliche Buchgesellschaft 1966].

Fell, C.
1983   A *friwif locbore* revisited. *Anglo-Saxon England* 13: 157-165.

Finsterwalder, P. W. (ed.)
1929   *Die Canones Theodori Cantuariensis und ihre Überlieferungsformen.* Weimar: Böhlau.

Förster, M. (ed.)
1912   Beiträge zur mittelalterlichen Volkskunde VIII. *Archiv für das Studium der neueren Sprachen und Literaturen* 129: 16-49.

Goolden, P. (ed.)
1958   *The Old English 'Apollonius of Tyre'*. Oxford: Clarendon Press.

Grierson, P., & M. Blackburn
1986   *European Medieval Coinage. I: The Early Middle Ages (5th-10th centuries)*. Cambridge: Cambridge University Press.

Hecht, H. (ed.)
1900-1907 *Bischof Waerferths von Worcester Uebersetzung der Dialoge Gregors des Grossen*. Leipzig/Hamburg: Henri Grand. [Repr. Darmstadt: Wissenschaftliche Buchgesellschaft 1965].

Hill, R.
1979   Marriage in seventh-century England. In *Saints, Scholars and Heroes: Studies in Medieval Culture in Honour of Charles W. Jones*, 2 vols. M. H. King & W. M. Stevens (eds.), vol. I, pp. 67-75. Collegeville, MN: Hill Monastic Manuscript Library-Saint John's Abbey and University.

Hofstetter, W.
1987   *Winchester und der spätaltenglische Sprachgebrauch*. München: Fink.

Hogg, R. M.
1992   *A Grammar of Old English*. Vol. I *Phonology*. Oxford: Blackwell.

Imbert, J.
1967   L'influence du christianisme sur la législation des peuples francs et germains. In *Conversione al cristianesimo nell'Europa dell'alto medioevo*, pp. 365-396. Atti delle Settimane di Studio, XIV. Spoleto: C.I.S.A.M.

Ker, N. R.
1957   *Catalogue of Manuscripts Containing Anglo-Saxon*. Oxford: Clarendon Press.

Kindschi, L.
1955   The Latin-Old English Glossaries in Plantin-Moretus Manuscripts 32 and British Museum Manuscript Additional 32, 246. Dissertation. Stanford University, Dept. of English.

Kotzor, G.
1981   *Das altenglische Martyrologium*. München: Beck.

Jones, C. W. (ed.)
1977   *Bedae venerabilis opera, Pars VI. Opera didascalica 2*. (Corpus Christianorum, Series Latina, 123B). Turnhout: Brepols.

Krapp, G. P. (ed.)
1932   *The Vercelli Book*. (The Anglo-Saxon Poetic Records, 2). New York: Columbia University Press.

Krapp, G. P., & E. van K. Dobbie (eds.)
1936   *The Exeter Book*. (The Anglo-Saxon Poetic Record, 3). New York/London: Columbia University Press/Routledge & Kegan Paul.

Leo, F. (ed.)
1881   *Monumenta Germaniae historica. Auctores antiquissimi*, 4.1. *Venanti Honori Clementiani Fortunati presbyteri italici opera poetica*. Berlin: Weidmann.

Liebermann, F. (ed.)
1903-16   *Die Gesetze der Angelsachsen*, 3 vols. Halle: Niemeyer. [Repr. 1960, Aalen: Scientia].

1905a   Kentisch *hionne*: Hirnhaut. *Archiv für das Studium der neueren Sprachen und Literaturen* 115: 177-178.

1905b   Ags. *rihthamscyld*: echtes Hoftor. *Archiv für das Studium der neueren Sprachen und Literaturen* 115: 389-391.

Lindelöf, U. (ed.)
1927   *Rituale ecclesiae dunelmensis. The Durham Collectar.* Durham: Surtees Society.

Lindsay, W. M. (ed.)
1911   *Isidori hispaniensis episcopi etymologiarum sive originum libri XX.* Oxford: Clarendon Press.

Lindsay, W. M. (ed.)
1921   *The Corpus Glossary.* Cambridge: Cambridge University Press.

Loyn, H. R.
1974   Kinship in Anglo-Saxon England. *Anglo-Saxon England* 3: 197-209.

Mone, F. J. (ed.)
1830   *Quellen und Forschungen zur Geschichte der teutschen Literatur und Sprache.* Aachen-Leipzig: Mayer.

Morris, R. (ed.)
1874-1880 *The Blickling Homilies.* London: Oxford University Press. [Repr. 1967].

Plummer, C. (ed.)
1892-1899 *Two of the Saxon Chronicles Parallel.* Oxford: Clarendon Press. [Reissued by D. Whitelock 1952].

Quinn, J. J. (ed.)
1956   The Minor Latin-Old English Glossaries in MS Cotton Cleopatra A. iii. Dissertation, Stanford University, Dept. of English.

Richards, M. P., & J. Stanfield
1990   Concepts of Anglo-Saxon Women in Law. In *New Readings on Women in Old English Literature.* H. Damico & A. Hennessey Olsen (eds.), pp. 89-99. Bloomington, IN: Indiana University Press.

Richardson, H. G., & G. O. Sayles
1966   *Law and Legislation from Æthelberht to Magna Carta.* Edinburgh: University Press.

Rivers, T. J.
1976   A Reevaluation of Æthelberht 31. *Zeitschrift der Savigny-Stiftung für Rechtsgeschichte, Germanistische Abteilung* 93: 315-318.

1991   Adultery in Early Anglo-Saxon society: Æthelberht 31 in comparison with Continental Germanic Law. *Anglo-Saxon England* 20: 19-25.

Sawyer, P. H.
1957-1962 *Textus Roffensis: Rochester Cathedral Library MS. A.3.5.* (Early English Manuscripts in Facsimile, 7 and 11). Copenhagen: Rosekilde & Bagger.

1968   *Anglo-Saxon Charters. An annotated List and Bibliography.* London: Offices of the Royal Historical Society.

Seebold, E.
1974   Die ae. Entsprechungen von lat. *sapiens* und *prudens*. Eine Untersuchung über die mundartliche Gliederung der ae. Literatur. *Anglia* 92: 291-333.

1992   Kentish - and Old English Texts from Kent. In *Words, Texts and Manuscripts. Studies in Anglo-Saxon Culture Presented to Helmut Gneuss on the Occasion of his Sixty-Fifth Birthday.* M. Korhammer (ed.) with the asst. of K. Reichl & H. Sauer, pp. 409-434. Cambridge: Brewer.

Shackleton Bailey, D. R. (ed.)
   1982   *Anthologia latina*, I. Stuttgart: Teubner.
Skeat, W. W. (ed.)
   1871-1887   *The Four Gospels in Anglo-Saxon, Northumbrian, and Old Mercian
               Versions*. Cambridge: Cambridge University Press. [Repr. Darmstadt:
               Wissenschaftliche Buchgesellschaft 1970].
   1881-1887   *Ælfric's Lives of Saints*. London: Oxford University Press. [Repr. 1966].
Storms, G.
   1948   *Anglo-Saxon Magic*. The Hague: Nijhoff.
Stryker, W. G.
   1951   The Latin-Old English Glossary in Ms Cotton Cleopatra A III. Dissertation.
               Stanford University, Dept. of English.
Sweet, H. (ed.)
   1871   *King Alfred's West-Saxon Version of Gregory's Pastoral Care*. London:
               Trübner. [repr. 1958].
   1883   *King Alfred's Orosius*. London: Trübner. [Repr. 1959].
Toller, T. N.
   1921   *An Anglo-Saxon Dictionary, Supplement*. Oxford: Clarendon Press.
Wallace-Hadrill, J. M.
   1971   *Early Germanic Kingship in England and on the Continent*. Oxford:
               Clarendon Press.
Wenisch, F.
   1979   *Spezifisch   anglisches   Wortgut   in   den   nordhumbrischen
               Interlinearglossierung des Lukasevangeliums*. (Anglistische Forschungen,
               132). Heidelberg: Carl Winter.
Wood, I.
   1991   The Franks and Sutton Hoo. In *People and Places in Northern Europe 500-
               1600. Essays in Honour of Peter Hayes Sawyer*. I. Wood & N. Lund (eds.),
               pp. 1-14. Woodbridge: The Boydell Press.
   1992   Frankish hegemony in England. In *The Age of Sutton Hoo, The Seventh
               Century in North-Western Europe*. M. O. H. Carver (ed.), pp. 235-241.
               Woodbridge: The Boydell Press.
Wormald, P.
   1977   *Lex scripta* and *Verbum regis*: Legislation and Germanic Kingship, from
               Euric to Cnut. In *Early Medieval Kingship*. P. H. Sawyer & I. N. Wood
               (eds.), pp. 105-138. Leeds: The School of History, University of Leeds.
   1991   In Search of King Offa's 'Code'. In *People and Places in Northern Europe
               500-1600. Essays in Honour of Peter Hayes Sawyer*. I. Wood & N. Lund
               (eds.). Woodbridge: The Boydell Press.
   1994   Quadripartitus. In *Law and Government in England and Normandy. Essays
               in Honour of Sir Jones Holt*. G. Garnett & J. Hudson (eds.), pp. 111-147.
               Cambridge: Cambridge University Press.

Discussion

DUMVILLE: I found the paper extremely exciting and offering some interesting possibilities to follow up. I wish to explore one, which is your textual history, because it seems to me that how we take that determines in some measure how we take the information which the text provides. Now, our first fixed point, as you say, is Bede's mention in 731 that Æthelberht's code exists even in Old English.

LENDINARA: That is what Bede says in the *Historia ecclesiastica* (II.5).

DUMVILLE: OK, that's our fixed point and I take it that there are three possible histories before this point: one is that it's written, as you first mentioned, in Old Kentish, and that we have as yet no demonstrated traces of this; the second possibility, as you say, is that it was originally written in Latin and that at some point an Old English translation was made and Bede was not in a position to say how it was originally. He could only speak of how it was in his own time and what his informants told him. The third possibility is that it was an oral text which only came into writing significantly later than Æthelberht's own time. I find that possibility increasingly attractive because of the very interesting evidence you're providing about the Anglian dimension. What we've had held up to us for a long time—which I think now is quite untenable—is this basically inserted gloss as a product of Kent, but written in the Mercian dialect; which is then cited as an example of what could happen with dialects being used outside their natural areas in circumstances of overkingship, *imperium*. Before 731 there is a good bit of history in which the Mercians have been active in Kent politically, and before then in which the Northumbrians dominated Kent.

Now, what I wonder is whether the following possibility exists. Formally, I think, it must. The text first came into writing in Anglian in Kent, because Anglian conquerors of Kent wanted to know about Kentish law. That seems to me to be one development of the third possibility, in that you said you have an oral cultivation of the law until you have some necessity to bring it in to writing, which may not be at that initial point. One can put that together (though this is not the way that they intended it) with the point that was made by Richardson and Sayles in their book on law and legislation in medieval England (1966:1-12) where they argued that Æthelberht's laws were originally a pre-Christian text—and they stressed text— and this has been treated with contempt by other scholars. But if you think in terms of an oral set of laws it perhaps is not so outrageous.

LENDINARA: Yes, this is what has been put forward also for the laws of Offa. The hypothesis of a former oral transmission of the Kentish laws is very interesting. We have a few texts which represent a strict form of Kentish (see Hogg 1992:7) and others (e.g. those in MS London, BL Cotton Vespasian D, vi) with remarkable West-Saxon influence. So we should also decide which layer of Kentish the laws belonged to, if/when they were written in Kentish. Of course, Anglian is the best candidate for their first rewriting or for their first writing down.

DUMVILLE: Now the physical point, your point about money. If one feels some reserve about having money mentioned in the late sixth or the beginning of the seventh century, and the text is in fact a text of the seventh or eighth century, this may not seem such a problem. There may be other ways to come out of that.

LENDINARA: Richard Hodges thinks that money had a 'real' circulation in Kent as early as the time of Æthelberht (1989:92). He puts forward the suggestion that 'the plentiful access to imported goods' (1989:39) explains the different ranking of social classes in Kent, which differs from that of other kingdoms. According to him, the greater circulation of wealth in Kent (owing to trade, etc.) was responsible for the narrower distinction existing there between the *ceorl* and the *eorl*, which was clearly represented in the Kentish Laws.

AUSENDA: I wrote down some observations on the Kentish laws because Professor Lendinara kindly told me that she was going to discuss especially the linguistic aspects of the laws, so I thought I would add some 'socio-economic' comments. But let's start with the linguistic ones. I am going to add a fourth possibility to your three: the idea that indeed originally they were oral texts, as is the case of customary law among pre-literate societies, and that they were committed to writing with the help of the Christian missionaries who arrived in Kent around the beginning of the seventh century—this, by the way would help explain the seniority of the Kentish laws. It is true that the language may have been changed and 'modernized' in subsequent centuries, but it looks to me as if we have some valid clues for this hypothesis.

The 'introductory' clue is the privileged position given to the Church by Æthelberht's laws, in as much as theft of Church property required elevenfold compensation as against ninefold for theft of the king's property. There must have been the hand of missionaries or the Church in this transcription.

As well known, contemporary missionaries normally translate religious literature and even subjects of 'social' import. It would not be outlandish to think that a Christian mission arriving in England, realizing that the population was in a pre-literate state in which customary law was entrusted to the memory of elders, thought they could make themselves useful to the population, and at the same time strengthen the position of the king who protected them, by writing them down in the vernacular.

The phonetic transcription of an unwritten language by means of an alphabet is a very sophisticated operation which requires not only literary but also linguistic expertise including knowledge of grammar and syntax. As proven by Ulfila's translation of the Scriptures into Gothic, Christian missionaries had that expertise as early as the fourth century, whilst it is reasonable to believe that no one in Britain could have possessed this knowledge until at least a generation after the beginning of the mission to the *Angli*, which gave religious instruction to the 'natives' in the vernacular and presumably taught them to read and write.

My second observation is of a socio-economic nature. It concerns Æthelberht's controversial 31 (604) which states that, 'If a freeman lies with the wife of another freeman, he must bring him a second wife...'. This is not surprising if one bears in mind the meaning of compensation. Even when someone was killed, in many cases the murderer's group could offer a girl in lieu of compensation and extinguish the feud (Lewis 1962:24; Munzinger 1890:255). In fact the purpose of compensation was that of re-establishing the balance of prestige of a clan or smaller group wronged by the murder of one of its members or, in this case, by adultery. Giving a girl in marriage meant that, despite the affront, members of the offending group did not consider themselves on a higher status level than those of the offended group. In fact marriage only obtained between social groups of equal status and indeed was often hypergamic in the sense that women were readily given to men belonging to higher status groups. Further redress to the wronged group was consequent on the fact that the offended group did not have to effect any marriage payment, viz. 'buy' the girl (cf. Æthelberht 77) and pay *morgengifu* for the girl received in compensation.

My third comment concerns blood-money compensation in general, noting that this was originally a 'private' affair between two social groups, whether clans or fractions thereof. Only in later times is an overarching authority, i.e. the king, established which enforces payment and eventually levies fines.

The fourth comment follows on the previous point to show that even in Æthelberht's laws there is a trace of the fact that feuds were originally 'private' affairs where blood-money compensation was discussed between elders of the two groups with some 'neutral' person of authority acting as an arbiter between the feuding parties. This surfaces in Æthelberht's 65.1, "If he becomes lame, the settlement of the matter may be left to friends"—it would be impossible in fact to foresee all degrees of lameness in a law, so that was left to the traditional mechanism. One may add that the 'posted' wergild is not a fixed tariff (cf. Cerulli 1964:93; Lewis 1955), it serves as a level of departure for discussion. The actual amount, rarely paid in coinage but more often in livestock, varies according to socioeconomic conditions and a fraction of the 'posted' amount may be eventually agreed upon.

My next remark concerns the expression *locbore*, 'long-haired' found in Æthelberht law 73, which, according to Attenborough (1922:178), means "the freeborn woman as opposed to the slave". In my opinion, instead, this expression refers without a doubt to an unmarried woman, presumably a virgin. A similar expression exists in Langobardic law (*Edictus Langobardorum*), namely Li. 2, 3, 4 & 145. This is the Latin expression *in capillo* or *in capillis*, which is in complementary distribution with 'married woman', e.g. Li. 2, "*Si quis Langobardus se vivente filias suas nupto tradiderit, et alias filias in capillo in casa reliquerit...*". The sense of the expression *in capillo* is 'maiden'. In fact a maiden's misconduct was economically more damaging than that of a married woman, because the unmarried girl, as long as she was a real or presumed virgin, could be 'bought' and given a considerable *morgengifu* which could potentially benefit her agnatic relatives in case of inheritance.

The simultaneous presence of veiled and unveiled women is attested in the church of Santa Maria della Valle at Cividale del Friuli in a sculpture of the eighth or ninth century where both veiled women and unveiled maidens, *in capillo*, may be seen—those veiled, i.e. married, in a more prominent position, i.e. closer to the central icon. This interpretation of *locbore* is strengthened by ethnographic

Fig. 7-1: Ninth-century relief in the church of S. Maria della Valle in Cividale, showing women, some wearing a veil, others *in capillis*.

experience. Hadendowa unmarried girls do not cover their hair/head, while they do immediately upon marriage.[14]

My next comment concerns the position of the *læt*. Æthelberht's 21 established that the 'ordinary' wergild for a free man was 100 shillings. Æthelberht's 26 establishing a wergild of 80, 60, 40 shillings for *læt* according to their class seems quite generous. One should recall that the *Pactus legis salicae* 42.4 established a much lower wergild, one half of that of a free man, for Romans and *leti*.

One may observe that the Saxon and Frankish *læt* or *leti* were probably equivalent to the Langobardic *haldii*. Individuals belonging to this group were semi-free in that they were not slaves, but had to perform certain services for their patrons from whom they obtained property in a form similar to present-day sharecroppers. This property reverted to their patrons' heirs in case the *haldii* died without heirs. A similar situation obtained until recently (1948) among Beni Amer in eastern Sudan and northern Eritrea and among Libyan Bedouin and other Saharan pastoralists. While some pre-Second World War ethnographers called them 'serfs', recent scholars, e.g. Barth, Peters, etc., preferred the term 'clients' in that their position was similar to that of clients in ancient polities, i.e. foreigners who had no rights in a given territory and depended entirely on the protection of local 'patrons' (Ausenda 1995:25).

I finally would like to point out the similarity, both in value and description, between injury compensations in Æthelberht's laws and Rothari's laws issued a few years later (see Table 7-1). One could interpret this as showing that injury compensations were roughly similar among some Germanic groups or that Æthelberht's laws were taken as a partial model in the preparation of Rothari's

---

[14] The habit of Germanic married women of wearing a veil over the head may have been taken from Roman customs. There is a parallel among Beja in Sudan where reports of nineteenth-century travellers describe women without veils over the head whereas nowadays all married women wear one, having taken the custom from the Arabic-speaking Sudanese populations living along the Nile.

Table 7-1
Comparison of injury compensations between Æthelberht's & Rothari's laws

Aethelbert (601-4)	Shillings	Rothari (643)	Solidi
34. Bone laid bare			3
35. Bone damaged			4
36. Outer covering of scull	10	46. *Plaga in caput (cutica)*	6
37. Both broken	20	47. *Plaga in caput (ossa)*	12
38. Shoulder disabled	30	384. *Brachium super gubitum ruptum*	20
39. Hearing of one ear	25		
40. Ear struck off	12	53. *Aure abscisa 1/4 (80:-100)*	20
41. Ear pierced	3		
42. Ear lacerated	6	54.. *Plaga in aurem si resolidaverit*	16
43. Eye knocked out	50	48. *Oculo evulso 1/2 (80—100)*	50
44. Mouth or eye disfigured	12	54. *Plaga in facie*	16
45. Nose pierced	9	55. *Plaga in naso si resolidaverit*	16
46. One cheek pierced	3		
47. Both pierced	6		
48. Nose lacerated	6		
49. Nose [throat] pierced	6		
50. Smashed chin bone	20		
51. Front tooth (incisor)	6	51. *Unum dentem priorem*	16
(canine)	3		
(molar)	1	52. *Unum dentem maxillarem*	8
53. Arm pierced	6	57. *Brachio transforato*	16
1. Arm broken	6	384. *Subter gubitum ruptum*	16
54. Thumb struck off	20	63. *Policem 1/6 (100)*	16
2. Forefinger	9	64. *Secundum digitum*	16
3. Middle finger	4	65. *Tertium digitum*	5
4. Ring finger	6	66. *Quartum digitum*	8
5. Little finger	11	67. *Quintum digitum*	16
57. Strike nose with fist	3	44. *Pugno*	3
64. Destroy gen. organ 3 X wergild			
1. Pierce through or partially	6	59. *Capsum plagaverit*	20
65. Broken thigh	12	384. *Coxa rupta super geniculum*	20
1. If lame settle through 'friends'.			
67. Thigh pierced	6	60. *Coxa transforata*	16
69. Foot struck off	50	68. *Pedem excussum 1/2 (100)*	50
70. Big toe	10	69. *Policem pedis*	16
71. Second toe (1/2 equiv.finger)	4.5	70. *Secundum digitum pedis*	6
Third	2	71. *Tertium digitum pedis*	3
Fourth	3	72. *Quartum digitum pedis*	3
Fifth	5.5	73. *Quintum digitum pedis*	2

slightly later and more complex collection. On the other hand, it may point to the previous 'orality' of customary laws and their inherent similarity among early Germanic populations, in that a 'head-to-toe' model may have been used prior to committing customary law to writing.

LENDINARA: Just a remark. J. M. Wallace-Hadryll (1971:38) suggests that nineteen chapters of the Laws of Æthelberht might be borrowed from the *Lex salica*. There is a lot of overlapping in the corpus of Germanic laws (Visigothic, Burgundian, etc.) and also in that of the Roman laws, which weakens the value of such estimates and prevents from arguing that there is an undoubtable borrowing from one law code to another. There are apparent similarities between laws, as they are often written in the same style and use the same technical vocabulary. Another thing I want to say concerns the first chapter of the laws of Æthelberht where it is said that a breach against the Church will get a compensation greater than that due to the king. After this chapter follows a series of provisions about the king and it is possible to highlight a precise pattern underlying the laws of Æthelberht, which are far from being an inorganic text. The first chapter might be spurious and a later addition, interpolated in the text to please the Church and dating to the time when the prologues to the first two Kentish laws were written, that is at least at the time when the prologue to the third Kentish law (and its text?) were composed.

DUMVILLE: That's what Richardson and Sayles say.

LENDINARA: What is said in this chapter contrasts with what Bede says in the *Historia ecclesiastica* (II.27), where he asserts that the Church should not get rich with the money paid to atone detriments and injuries committed against it. This is one of the few places where the Kentish laws show a complete disagreement with Bede. The first chapter of the law of Æthelberht looks quite an embarassing subject to deal with.

CHARLES-EDWARDS: I might add that one of the assumptions behind Richardson and Sayles's theory that the laws of Æthelberht were pre-Christian was that Liebermann's chapter 1 is a single entity—but it isn't in the manuscript. The numbering provided by Liebermann is completely misleading. If you look at the manuscript (although it is much later than the supposed date of the text it is the only evidence we have) there is a system of rubrication of the initial letter of each item, each decree. Chapter 1, by this criterion, is a series of distinct *dōmas*. So, one shouldn't base anything on the notion that as a piece of text it is a single entity. One can argue from syntactical parallels, but this criterion doesn't correspond to the ecclesiatical contents. Part of this syntactical group of decrees (which is Liebermann's number 1) is the clause about the *mǣthlfrið*, which is not ecclesiastical.

LENDINARA: This chapter seems to draw some sort of a genealogy or rather a hierarchy of the Church. This list of religious offices—bishop, priest, deacon, etc.—looks like an effort to produce a hierarchy of the Church matching the hierarchy of lay society, which will be portrayed in the following chapters. This is something else which makes me suspicious about this chapter. There is also the occurrence of XII-*gilde* and XI-*gilde*, without a verb, which are hard to define from a grammatical point of view, as it can be taken both as an adjective or an adverb. The first chapter raises more problems than all the following sections of the of Æthelberht.

POWLESLAND: I am totally unconvinced by the idea that this was written down by Augustine's little group. In fact, there is probably much more evidence of missionaries destroying everything they find than actually writing it down. I am thinking of Central and South America, where they were pretty good at wiping out every piece of native law they came across.

CHARLES-EDWARDS: But that is in a context of a political takeover by conquistadores. Whereas in this case you've got a native king on whom the missionaries are dependent for protection.

POWLESLAND: Still, I am very sceptical.

HINES: On the question of the origin of the laws, I supervised the work of a student, Lorraine Miller, writing a doctoral dissertation on Anglo-Saxon orality, literacy and mentality, working particularly with the Old English prose records, which is unusual. Sadly, she died before she could successfully complete her thesis. She did, however, identify possible evidence for claiming that the symptoms of oral tradition in the laws gradually decrease as one comes through from Æthelberht, right the way down to Alfred. In the earlier codes she noted in particular the prevalence of syntax that was formulaic, but also truncated, creating a high level of semantic and syntactic interdependency between separate *dōmas*. Put simply, you had to remember what had been said several clauses further back to understand the reference to, for instance, a certain part of the body and a particular fine in a clause of this kind. In respect of this she proposed that a law speaker would be more likely to conceive of the law code as a whole while the literate lawyer would be more likely to conceive of its clauses as a series of discrete utterances.

Oral formulae will survive in succeeding literate contexts, and the notion of an oral tradition at the beginning gradually becoming more and more literate seemed to be supported by the close analysis she made of the Old English law codes down to Alfred's. That in itself, of course, wouldn't tell us exactly when they got written down and by whom. On the other hand, to allow for the question of a possible tradition of literacy in both England and vernacular literacy in *Francia* preceding these laws isn't quite as preposterous as people have been suggesting. The runic tradition in England is represented by only about a dozen inscriptions datable before about 600 and they are all very short. But one curious feature of the early inscriptions which shows a degree of linguistic sophistication is the fact that they frequently have the words divided in them—something which in other contexts has been picked up as evidence of sophistication (Parkes 1987). There is no detectable influence from the runic writing tradition on the Roman script tradition in England, but these people were not virgins as far as literacy went. There is also the story in Gregory's Histories of the Franks about new letters being introduced for the writing of Frankish—which otherwise simply do not survive. We have only that one anecdote as evidence for such a thing.

WOOD: The letters are written down in manuscripts of Gregory of Tours.

HINES: And Augustine brought Frankish interpreters with him in order to be able to speak to the Kentishmen. We've got various bits of evidence that enable us to put quite a plausible picture together.

WOOD: I have one or two points about Frankish law and in a sense it is more addressed to Giorgio's comments than to Patricia's original comment. There has been a suggestion, I suppose it is unprovable, that there was a recension of Frankish law made around the year 600 which underlies both Æthelberht's code and the original Langobardic codes. That's reasonably likely and you don't need to consider this in terms of *Francia* being an economic centre. At precisely that time the Franks were bullying a lot of people. They were intervening in the Langobardic royal succession, they were intervening in the Visigothic royal succession, they were involved with the English mission to Kent. It does seem that that is more likely to explain the parallels between all the laws than that a copy of Æthelberht's code was taken back to Italy.

There are a couple of points at which I think that current work on *Francia* and on England is going in different directions and soon someone will have to pull the two together. One of these relates to the word *laeti* who, in the area of modern Belgium, appear to have been Frankish troops settled by and working for the Romans. The only reason why I was shaking my head about your point about different wergilds, Giorgio, was not that I think you're wrong, but I think you cannot actually argue that particular case even in *Francia* simply because there are different law codes enforced in different parts of *Francia*. In Aquitaine the *Codex theodosianus* is enforced, and in the Church, and therefore you can't actually use your model of different wergilds, simply because the same law code is not being enforced in the whole kingdom.

LENDINARA: As far as England is concerned, J. N. L. Myres (1989:142) put forward the suggestion that the *lætas* derive their name from that of the *laeti*. But he is alone in maintaining such a point.

WOOD: Yes. But people have been discussing *laeti* on the Continent since Myres. There seems to be a discrepancy now between the meaning of the word on the Continent and in England. Either they are two separate words or people have to re-think the English word in the light of what has been on the Continent.

LENDINARA: Has anyone put forward a suggestion about the Old English word?

WOOD: I don't know.

CHARLES-EDWARDS: Let's suppose you compare some later Frankish forms *lidi*: it looks as if you've got a change from [t] to [d] which you might have in late Latin; but also there appears to be a long vowel. Now, in *læt* you've got a short vowel and the [t] preserved. So, this surely looks rather too different.

LENDINARA: If Old English *læt* is a loan-word with a long *æ* its evolution is similar to that of *strǣt* ('street'), which was borrowed from Lat. *strata* with a long *ā*, which underwent the (first) fronting of long *ā*, a phonetic evolution which affects all the early borrowings from Latin.

If, meanwhile, you look at the Old English word from an etymological point of view (excluding the hypothesis of a borrowing) you can connect *læt* with the verb *lætan*, 'to let, let go', hence a *læt* was a person who was 'let free'. The Continental laws have the words *litus*, *latus* and *lazzus*. Does a Frankish *litus* have the same social position as the Anglo-Saxon *læt*?

WOOD: Well, no. It is a Latin word rather than Frankish.

LENDINARA: What was the condition of the Frankish *litus*?

WOOD: Presumably these are warriors who have been, or are descendants of, groups of warriors who have been settled in Batavia.

SCULL: I understood *laeti* in the Late Roman world to be semi-servile settlers, rather than autonomous military groups such as the Frankish *foederati*.

WOOD: They are now seen as military.

SCULL: Are they seen as military in the sense they were a manpower reserve or somehow semi-autonomous in their own right? I thought that they were not autonomous, but a servile manpower reserve settled under Roman prefects.

WOOD: But they seem to have had a military role. And this fits with what the *Pactus legis salicae* says.

SCULL: Do you reckon this from Frankish rather than late Roman sources? There is no evidence for *laeti* or indeed for *foederati* (in the sense of the Frankish *foederati*) settled in England.

CHARLES-EDWARDS: But if one examines the implication of connecting *læt* with *laeti*, is the idea that the late Roman state in Britain gets hold of a bunch of mercenaries, is sufficiently firmly in control of them that it can settle them in what appears to be low-status condition? They are not the mercenaries who are flexing their muscles. Alternatively, the *læt* come from earlier Germanic incomers who have been defeated by the Romans and settled by them as low-status *laeti*. Then, curiously, when Kent is taken over by a later-group of Germanic incomers, the latter do not say of their *laeti* neighbours, "They are our kith and kin; let us free them".

WOOD: Well, that could be the implication of the Frankish evidence. These people are likely to have been defeated Franks resettled in the fourth century as troops to be used by the Romans. The Franks in the late fifth century do not recognize them as kith and kin, but recognize them as being Romans, not Franks. So you could argue a parallel case for England if you wanted to see them as the same institution in England as on the Continent.

CHARLES-EDWARDS: So, having been defeated, having been controlled by the Romans, you perhaps so lost honour that you were not worth freeing.

LENDINARA: There are three classes of *læt* (Æthelberht 26), but they do not seem to be so low in the social pyramid, as there are other people who occupy a class which is inferior to that of the *læt*.

WOOD: Well, in a sense they are not so low in *Francia*: they are still equivalent to Romans.

HINES: We should not confuse the history of the word with the history of the group. But it seems that both are very uncertain.

POWLESLAND: Archaeologically, they were largely used to explain Late Roman military belt assemblages, and particular types of military equipment. And small groups of them are based in the smaller Roman military installations like, for instance, Malton which has a scruffy little fort and a scruffy little town and about fifty of these people buried in a small enclosed cemetery, but is very much within the area of Roman control.

SCULL: There is no secure archaeological evidence for the settlement of *laeti* or *foederati* in England.

CHARLES-EDWARDS: I would like to go back to an earlier issue: the possible rewriting of the laws in Anglian and then West Saxon. I wonder whether we know enough about Kentish in the seventh century to identify words that were not Kentish at that period. Suppose the usual story, namely that these are written texts from the beginning, and suppose that they were written in Kentish. Do we know enough of the differences between Anglian and Kentish in the seventh century to be able to say that a given word is one rather than the other?

LENDINARA: Of course we do not know anything of the seventh century [laughter]. There is a German scholar, Elmar Seebold, who has recently put forward the hypothesis of a dialectical stratification in Kent. According to Seebold there were three types of Old English spoken (and written) in Kent: Jutish-Kentish, Kentish-Mercian and Kentish-West Saxon (which also contained Anglian elements) (Seebold 1990:409-34). Seebold has also analysed the relationship between the inhabitants of Kent and their language and the Jutish invaders and their language (1992:335-52). This is something about which I would like to hear the opinion of the historians and know more about the recent evaluations of the role and number of the Jutish 'invaders'. In the future we will possibly get some further clues from the research carried out by Seebold and other German scholars working on the dialects of Anglo-Saxon England. We know much more about the Kentish dialect and the Canterbury scribes for the later centuries. There are documents which are written in Kentish (charters, a translation of a hymn and a psalm, glosses to the *Book of Proverbs*) and there are several phonetic features which can be considered Kentish. But there is no lexical item which can be labelled as a Kentish word. There are a number of Old English words which might be considered dialect words, in so far as they only occur in works which were written in Mercia or Northumbria: e.g. *ambeht*, 'office', or *medmicel*, 'small'. For a series of words which have been made the object of detailed analysis it is possible to say not only that they are Anglian, but also that they are either Mercian or Northumbrian, e.g. *hoga*, 'Lat. *prudens*', (North.) and *glēaw*, 'Lat. *prudens*', (Merc.)

DUMVILLE: If one does not know what is Kentish, how can one conclude this?

LENDINARA: There are also suffixes which have a different form in early and late West Saxon, in Anglian and in West Saxon, e.g. verbal nouns in *-ness* are formed with the stem of the verb in Anglian, but in late West Saxon are formed with the past participle of the verb (e.g. *forgyfnys/forgifennis*). But nothing like that can be said of Kentish, possibly owing to the nature of its corpus.

The Kentish dialect is quite a mystery. There are other Old English works which have been reckoned among the Kentish documents, e.g. some charters (Sawyer 1968: nos. 1067 and 1500) but these might not be Kentish. Also the glosses to the *Book of Proverbs* show a mixed language. Glosses are the hardest texts to deal with to ascertain a possible dialectal origin, as they are made up of batches of words drawn from different sources and which might have different origin, also as far as their original dialect is concerned.

HINES: It's interesting to note that early eighth-century Englishmen could be just as confused over the Kentish language as we are now. This is clear when Bede refers to vernacular place-names in what he knows to be Anglian or Saxon areas. There he is quite precise and consistent in referring to forms as *in lingua Anglorum* or *in lingua saxonica* respectively. When he comes to a vernacular place-name in Kent he goes into circumlocutions to try to avoid saying *in lingua jutica* or *in lingua Cantuuariorum* or anything like that. He says 'in the place which the *gens Anglorum* call so and so' (e.g. *HE* II.3). It is perhaps interesting if he does much the same thing with the laws of Æthelberht, which he says were *conscripta Anglorum sermone*. He doesn't normally use the word *sermo* in such contexts.

CHARLES-EDWARDS: Doesn't *Anglorum sermo* mean 'speech of the English'?

HINES: Usually the context leaves one in no doubt as to when *Angli* means 'Angles' or 'Englishmen'. When it comes to Kent suddenly it becomes difficult.

CHARLES-EDWARDS: One thing which might be important about Bede's statements on Kent, is that he himself was getting information through Nothelm, who appears to have been a Mercian.

LENDINARA: I tried to compare Bede's words about the Kentish laws (*HE* II.5) with the story he tells about Cædmon (*HE* IV.24) as in both instances Bede is reporting a story—that some witness told him—about a literary composition of some sort: a legal code in the case of Æthelberht and a series of songs on the Old Testament in the case of Cædmon. In the first instance Bede stresses the fact that the laws of Æthelberht were written down and were written in the vernacular. Telling the story of Cædmon he does not specify whether the poems were composed in Latin or in vernacular (though, of course, Cædmon knew no Latin); Bede is also silent about the possibility that the stories, sung by the 'brother' living in the monastery of Hild, were eventually committed to writing. I am amazed by the importance which has been attached to the story of Cædmon, which has found a place in every book dealing with the Anglo-Saxons, especially so if one compares it with Bede's remark about the laws of Æthelberht. In fact Bede himself does not accord to the writing down of the first Anglo-Saxon vernacular law code the importance that it was due. He speaks of King Æthelberht several times, but mentions his legal activity only in connection with his death, adding this detail in a careless way, as if he attached a limited importance to this accomplishment of the king. Hence it was Cædmon's poem which came to be considered the first document of the Old English literature.

DUMVILLE: But the Cædmon story is not a literary story, it's a divine revelation isn't it?

LENDINARA: This is probably the reason why Bede gave so much space to Cædmon. I looked at his story as it was a story about a vernacular composition, as well as that of the laws of Æthelberht.

SCULL: I should like to come back to an earlier point, that the suggestion of money in early English society may be suspect. There is in fact archaeological evidence for some circulation of continental coinage in sixth-century England. There are finds of coins and of balances, found most commonly in Kentish graves, which may have been used to weigh gold and/or coins.

DUMVILLE: I'm sorry, that wasn't my suggestion. I was simply responding to Patrizia's point that if there was some unhappiness about the existence of money, one of those textual histories might sort that out.

CHARLES-EDWARDS: The Welsh and the Irish used the Latin *scrupulus* in the sense of one twenty-fourth of an ounce and it seems to be a standard measure of silver. In other words what they are weighing is silver, and the weight of silver is the standard measure of value.

SCULL: I don't believe that this was a monetary economy or society in any modern sense, but there is evidence for special-purpose currency use in the sixth century, especially in Kent.

HINES: Especially in the second half of the century.

SCULL: The coinage seems to be circulating from the second quarter or the middle of the sixth century.

HINES: Yes, I would put it's inception before the middle of the sixth century. It seems to be reasonably continuous from then onwards.

CHARLES-EDWARDS: Is it Kentish use of Frankish coins?

HINES: Primarily, yes.

AUSENDA: I would like to say something about coinage and wergild. I do not know anything about whether there were coins or not in the seventh century, but in non-literate societies with the feud system, wergilds are fixed in some kind of unit of account, whether it is camels or cows or cattle or whatever. When people get down to discussing these things, they don't take the law and say you owe me twenty-five cows or twenty-five *solidi*. They start discussing and at a certain point they agree on a given number of different kinds of livestock, whatever is offered by the culprit's side. If everybody agrees the feud is finished. The interesting point about that is that this is true also of Sudan's present law. Sudan has re-introduced the *shariah*, the Islamic law. According to the *shariah,* people arrange their differences as to feuds on the basis of *diya*, blood money or compensation. *Diya* is fixed by law and when I was there last it was fixed at 20,000 Sudanese pounds. Of course there is now a galloping inflation, and 20,000 pounds are worth about ten dollars. So, theoretically you could kill a person for ten dollars [laughter]. It goes up all the time; I believe it has gone way up above that figure. This is all to say that if the two parties meet at this juncture—the man who committed murder is put in jail in the meantime—and say that they have reconciled their differences, the murderer is let out of jail without direct concern about the blood compensation agreed upon. In conclusion, wergild figures should be taken as indicative of the level at which you start discussing. I calculated that a cow was worth about 3 *solidi* (see Ro.332, Ro.333 and Ro.334) so that a 'normal' wergild of 80 *solidi* for a free man was worth approximately 27 cows. This is quite a large number for a society like that and would involve many more owners than the extended family. It is probable that settlement was reached on a lower figure.

References in the discussion

Textual sources:

Æthelberht's Laws: see Liebermann (ed.) 1903-16; Attenborough (trans.) 1922.
Bede
   Historia ecclesiastica gentis Anglorum: see Colgrave & Mynors 1969.
Edictus Langobardorum: see Bluhme 1868 (ed.).

Bibliography:

Attenborough, F. L.
    1922   See References at end of paper.
Ausenda, G.
    1995   The segmentary lineage in anthropology and among the Langobards. In
                Atfer Empire: Towards an Ethnology of Europe's Barbarians. G. Ausenda
                (ed.), pp. 15-50. Woodbridge: The Boydell Press.
Bluhme, F. (ed.)
    1868   *Edictus Langobardorum*. In *Monumenta Germaniae historica. Legum
                tomus IIII*. G. H. Pertz (ed.), pp. 1-234. Hannover: Hahn.
Cerulli, E.
    1964   La tribù somala. In *Somalia. Scritti vari editi ed inediti*. Vol. 3. Roma:
                Ministero degli Affari Esteri 1964.
Colgrave, B., & R. N. L. Mynors
    1969   See References at end of paper.
Hodges, R.
    1989   *The Anglo-Saxon Achievement*. London: Duckworth.
Hogg, R. M.
    1992   See References at end of paper.
Lewis, I. N.
    1955   *Peoples of the Horn of Africa*. London: International African Institute.
    1962   *Marriage and the family in Northern Somaliland*. (East African Studies 15).
                Kampala: East African Institute of Research.
Liebermann, F. (ed.)
    1903-16   See References at end of paper.
Munzinger, W.
    1890   *Studi sull'Africa Orientale*. Rome: Tipografia Voghera, Carlo.
Myres, J. N. L.
    1989   *The English Settlements*. Oxford: University Press.
Parkes, M. B.
    1987   The contribution of Insular scribes of the seventh and eighth centuries to the
                "grammar of legibility". In *Grafia e Interpunzione del Latino ned Medioevo*.
                Ed. A. Maieru. Roma: Lessico Intelletuale Europeo XLI. pp 15-30.
Richardson, H. G., & G. O. Sayles
    1966   See References at end of paper.
Sawyer, P. H.
    1968   See References at end of paper.
Seebold, E.
    1990   Was ist jütisch? Was ist kentish?. In *Britain 400-600: Language and
                History*. A. Bammesberger & A. Wollmann (eds.), pp. 335-352. Heidelberg:
                Carl Winter.
    1992   See References at end of paper.
Wallace-Hadrill, J. M.
    1971   See References at end of paper.

FARMING IN EARLY MEDIEVAL ENGLAND: SOME FIELDS FOR THOUGHT

PETER J. FOWLER

Dept. of Agricultural and Environmental Science, University of Newcastle, Newcatle upon Tyne, GB-NE1 7RU

Introduction

"Should anyone be more interested in learning about the countryside than about the religion professed by its inhabitants, he will find the answer to his every question obstructed by lack of evidence...." (Blair 1976:228). Twenty years later, the auguries are still not good; but at least "learning about the countryside" of Anglo-Saxon England has become, through the assiduous scholarship of such as Della Hooke and David Hall, a legitimate field of study rather than merely a peripheral facet on which incredibly, as Blair implies, a few off-beat persons may wish to waste their time.

We can begin, though not entirely propitiously, with England's first historian. "Britain is rich in grain and timber; it has a good pasturage for cattle and draught animals...": thus Bede writing about AD 700. "Most of the work of settlement was done, and the problems of the future were of a different shape from the struggles of the past": thus Hallam (1988:44) writing of "the land the Conqueror won from Harold [which] was one of the richest in western Europe".

Two scholars nearly thirteen centuries apart seem to be speaking as one of a land where good husbandry combined with rich natural resources to effect a considerable agrarian achievement by 1066. The model Bede and Hallam propose is in general credible and acceptable, though—perhaps 'because'—much is currently unknown. It is extremely likely, however, that further research will tend not to reinforce the apparent smoothness of the model with, for example, evidence for continuous linear development. Rather will more evidence distort it with contours of regional diversity in space and of non-synchronous changes in time. Time in particular is a most important dimension in seeking a useful generalization for, easy though it is to conceptualize 'Anglo-Saxon farming' as of a single period, the period from the sixth to the eleventh century is sufficiently long for its interpreter to expect waxings and wanings and for the topic itself to demand subdivisions. Here we are concerned primarily with the sixth to the mid-eighth century, thinking of the time of Bede in particular, spanning parts of archaeologists' Early and Middle Anglo-Saxon periods but definitely confining our field to pre-Viking times.

The Venerable Bede, one of that outstanding first generation of genuinely Anglo-Europeans in seventh-century England, is both my starting point and, with patience, my end. Yet in truth, despite a previous use in this sort of context by

THE ANGLO-SAXONS FROM THE MIGRATION PERIOD TO THE EIGHTH CENTURY:
AN ETHNOGRAPHIC PERSPECTIVE

Della Hooke (1988:1) of the quotation from him above, Bede had little to say about contemporary or earlier farming. We have no evidence that he himself farmed or was much interested in the activity; indeed, his writings are high-mindedly almost barren of *agraria*. This is slightly odd as well as disappointing, for other practical matters caught his attention and were described with good detail. He was, for example, apparently intrigued by building work, glass-making, cement-mixing and wood-working, particularly lathe-turning (Blair 1976:205-7).

Probably his most detailed passage about farming is in his *Life of Cuthbert*. Chapter 19 there relates how the hermit induced a crop of barley to grow on (Inner) Farne when he decided to pursue a policy of self-sufficiency. "He asked for implements to work the land with and wheat to sow, but though he planted in spring there was nothing ready by mid-summer. 'It's either the nature of the ground', he said to the brethren, 'or the will of God, but the wheat certainly is not growing. So bring barley and we shall see whether that will produce anything....' The barley was brought long past the proper time for planting, when there was no hope of it growing, but it soon sprang up and brought forth a very good crop" (Farmer 1988:68). This is a reasonably well-informed account from a farming point of view, though no spring-sown crop of wheat on Farne would be 'ready' by mid-summer anyway; but how one wishes that Bede's interest had been sufficient to have led him to tell *what* and *what sort of* implements were used on what sorts of fields, and *why* and *how* Cuthbert knew that the right thing was to change to barley from wheat. If only we knew too what counted as 'a very good crop', on a seed/yield ratio for example, in seventh-century Northumbria.

Yet it is unreasonable to expect that sort of information, for the point of this story for Bede appears not to have been the barley's late but successful germination and fruiting. Rather it was that the birds which devoured the grain as soon as it ripened flew off at Cuthbert's first word of admonition and "did no further damage". The story reminded him of St Anthony "who, by words alone, restrained wild asses from trampling his little garden" (Farmer 1988:69), and obviously its metaphorical value far exceeded its agrarian interest. Better, seems the implication, for a man to wield a word-power over fauna than make much of a fairly routine miracle with a cereal crop. Indeed, Bede's few references to food production suggest an adherence to the 'it's a miracle' school of explanation. At the personal level, when St Cuthbert was hungry in a sheiling near Chester-le-Street, his horse conveniently dislodged from the inner thatch "a warm loaf and meat carefully wrapped up in a linen cloth". At the other end of the country, South Sussex was suffering famine as a result of a three-year drought when Wilfrid arrived to convert them: "on the selfsame day on which that people received the baptism of faith, there fell a gentle but abundant rain. The earth blossomed once more and as the fields turned green a joyous and a fruitful season followed" (Blair 1976:200, 202).[1]

A realistic counterpart to Bede's arguably wishful-thinking, almost Old Testament approach to farming is hinted at by human bones, not documents: "...the

---

[1] For a well-documented view of food processing and consumption in the period, see Hagen 1992.

average life-expectancy up to the seventh century is only about thirty years.... A high degree of osteoarthritis of the spine suggests back-breaking field work in a damp climate...." (Longworth & Cherry 1986:130). While Bede's mind was doubtless justifiably on higher things, one of the beauties of farming history is that understanding it can allow room for both theory and pragmatism.

Nevertheless, Bede and his brethren had to eat, and his monastery at Jarrow— *Gyrwe*—was both dependent on and manager of an agricultural estate. That in itself—the existence of an institutionally-centralized, legally-recognized landed estate—is a fact illustrative of a significant development in English agrarian history within the seventh century. The formation of the monastic estate at St Paul's, probably under royal aegis, actually happened quite late in a process which, as much as any other, transformed sub-Roman Britain into Anglo-Saxon England. By AD 700, clearly and in a way which we cannot similarly say with confidence was the case in AD 600, land was owned in a recognizably modern sense. Much of England had come to belong to people, families, organizations, and it could therefore be shaped and parcelled, inherited and bought, sold off and amalgamated, and, critically in this case, given for the glory of God and the good of a man or woman's soul—especially the latter. Land therefore acquired a 'worth', an iconographic value, over and above its financial value quantifiable as annual rent, as a source of materials, or in producing daily bread. Both values were of basic importance within a pre-industrial society where, in a sense, land was currency as well as capital, within agrarian communities which did not have the facility to generate wealth by enhancing value through, for example, large scale production or major landscape works.

This is all academically common ground; yet the image of simple, even barbaric, Anglo-Saxons flourishes still, their farming at best 'primitive'. Bede may well not have involved himself in the running of the estate from which his community drew its daily bread, though he might have been a little surprised had he known what we now know about contemporary bread-production, or had he had to learn about such agricultural basics as stock-raising, curing and supply-lines if, for example, the delivery of parchments for his scriptorium failed. Such basics are, 1300 years later, once again being learnt the hard way, and demonstrated to a late twentieth-century society which has largely lost touch with them. For, within the obviously late twentieth-century concept of 'Bede's World', land near the late seventh-century monastic site and its surviving church where Bede worked and worshipped is once more being farmed in an Anglo-Saxon sort of way. Some elements of a new landscape are beginning, it is intended, to make the area look a little like that which Bede might have seen had he looked up from a Latin text and glanced out of his cell window in AD 700.

Landscape

Both England and the Anglo-Saxons, the farmed and the farmers, look rather different to students in the late twentieth-century compared to those of even a generation earlier. England was being farmed, even by the eighth-century, much more extensively, in a more organized way and probably more successfully, than was conceivable to, for example, historians a century ago trying to understand what happened from premises such as that of primitive Teutonic pioneers hacking their way through virgin forest. This new image has been increasingly apparent over the last generation as part of a conceptual 'revolution' largely triggered by air photography and 'rescue archaeology' and developed under the banner of 'landscape archaeology'. This last is not of course period-specific—indeed, that is largely its point and its strength; but the early medieval period has shared with other times a quantitative increase in data and a consequential change in perception of Finberg's (1972) scholarly but rather static countryside to what seemed to be an increasingly 'busy' landscape. This began to be realized 20-25 years ago (e.g. Fowler 1976) and ten years later it was possible to synthesize this new view of the early medieval landscape (Hurst 1986:202-6).

This has corresponded with results from documentary and topographic research to reinforce an impression of 'busyness': that is of a landscape not only fuller with things—settlements, cemeteries—and activities—farming, silviculture—but witnessing changes resulting from the working out of processes. Among the last were not only human impacts on the countryside—forest clearance, drainage—but new situations and other, new processes created by the interaction of people and environment. Among the many factors contributing to the development of the particular form of urbanism in late Anglo-Saxon England, for example, was, it could be argued, a special dynamic of town and countryside which no one planned and which no one could have foreseen. Many aspects of these three topics, people/environment interactions, the dynamics of processes, and urbanism, are illuminated in a seminal volume which came out after the initial preparation of this essay (Rackham 1994). It is flagged here as a significant contribution to Anglo-Saxon studies, but it has not been possible to digest all its data or think through its implications for our fields here.

It nevertheless seems implausible to think of adventurous bands of Continental incomers exploring a wild and woolly landscape in the lowland southern Britain of the sixth century; and by the seventh century, behind the recorded 'history' of regal and religious development, that landscape is by implication increasingly witnessing the development of an *organized* agriculture. A guess would see the framework as new but the actual farming as fundamentally unchanged: a new legal framework increasingly reflecting the *mores* of Teutonic rather than British society, within which operated a basically British way of farming using indigenous technology, botany, stock and methodology. It is very difficult to see the incomers adding anything to the operative side of farming before the eighth century; but, by channelling its products to certain ends through the mechanisms of ownership, tenure and estate, circumstances were created in which change was encouraged, indeed had to occur. Archaeologically, and to a certain extent documentarily, agrarian change can be detected from Bede's time onwards.

Yet, even with the recent accession of a great deal more evidence, in truth the Anglo-Saxons do not 'show' as dynamic farmers in contemporary material culture.

Archaeologically, in particular, farming of the eighth century is not well attested in terms of structures, e.g. field systems, or implements, e.g. cultivating tools. Yet complexity, even chaos, has grown interpretatively from the simplicity of earlier ideas like "The Anglo-Saxons brought open fields to England". It is difficult at the moment to see where the complexity is leading. Certainly it is not heading towards a model of an homogeneous and uniform farming regime by, say, AD 1000. The diversity of agrarian landscapes which Kerridge (1973: fig. 1) illustrated for the sixteenth and seventeenth centuries, Thirsk (1967, 1984b) espied regionally at the end of the Middle Ages and later, which Domesday Book attempted to disguise beneath bureaucratic uniformity, and which Hooke demonstrated within southern and central Anglo-Saxon England (Hooke 1988:123-51)—it is a fair guess that such diversity was there long before King Ine's laws provide such a tantalizing glimpse of some well-established agrarian practices in a Wessex contemporary with Bede. Much of the 'Anglo-Saxon landscape' then was neither Anglian nor Saxon; indeed, it was not racially-specific at all but, in various parts of the country differentially, the product of various processes, dead, dynamic and embryonic.

Though such a view is closed to those whose perspective of agrarian history begins with "early and remote times" indeed but *sensu stricto* either side of AD 700 (Kerridge 1992:17), the fact is that similar variety and diversity existed in farming matters in Britain during the first seven centuries of our era and at least for a millennium before Christ.[2]

Fields

Let us not forget that present-day scholarship has already enjoyed a generation of liberation from the Teutonic 'ancestor model' of how medieval fields began in England. It was as long ago as 1964 that Thirsk published her seminal paper on 'The Common Fields' in which she summarized her, and others', argument with the statement that "...it is no longer possible for English scholars to argue that the Anglo-Saxons brought from Germany in the sixth century a fully-fledged common-field system" (Thirsk 1964, reprinted in Thirsk 1984a:43). The current complexity has flowed in part from the release from that historical parameter (Dodgson 1980; Rowley 1981). Subsequently, it has also flowed from a physical and tenurial 'reality' which archaeology has discerned in the landscape in terms of boundaries, field systems and settlements (Hurst 1986:196-236; Taylor 1983). That actuality, though not necessarily on the same sites or even in the same areas, both reflects and is echoed by detailed tenurial and regional studies (e.g. Gelling 1992, Hooke 1985). Furthermore, attempts have increasingly been made to create an environmental dimension for early medieval

---

2   This is not the place to pursue British agrarian prehistory any further but see Bowen & Fowler 1978, Cunliffe 1991, Fleming 1987, Fowler 1983, Mercer 1981, Piggott 1981; for Europe, Barker 1985, Randsborg 1991; for Roman Britain, Salway 1981: ch. 17-19; and for agricultural regions in general Coppock 1964.

farming, particularly for its arable fields and pastures, and their products (Fowler 1981; superseded by Rackham 1994: *passim*).

Now, complexity is confounded or, as the author would doubtless argue, reduced to simplicity once more by the arresting proposition that, as in days of yore, common fields originated "in one particular heartland". That place was Anglo-Saxon England of *ca* AD 700 or earlier. The idea thereafter diffused thence, "west to east, from England right across to Russia" (Kerridge 1992:4, ch. 1-2). We merely flag that an issue many thought long-deceased, i.e. that Anglo-Saxon immigrants brought the common field to Britain, has struggled back to life. There is not, in this writer's view, a shred of evidence that such was the case nor that they then exported the idea—with woollen cloaks and Christianity, presumably?—back to Europe.

A prehistoric, Roman or sub-Roman background may or may not be germane to field systems and indeed the whole agrarian process in the sixth to eighth centuries. The chances are that, both in general and in many details, it is, but the difficulty is to understand the starting points of developments which give us the sort of landscapes which we can dimly perceive by the days of Bede and the reign of King Ine. Even the word 'developments' begs a question, for it assumes a 'before' and a 'later' and an explanatory, a processual, connection between them; but perhaps it did not happen that way at all. Maybe we have been and still are asking the wrong questions, or at least making the wrong assumptions in respect of agrarian history: e.g. that before *ca* AD 700 farming was distinctively Anglo-Saxon at all—rather may it have been technologically, even culturally, British. If, indeed, we have to envisage the common field operating in seventh-century England, perhaps it was Britons, not Saxons, who developed it? Though this is not the place to enlarge on the idea, it can be envisaged as a development which might have occurred in some places from late-Roman times onwards (cf. Loyn 1991:152-205). This would allow some three centuries during which sharing out lands and resources through a system of allotments and 'rights' with corresponding responsibilities could become what appears to be a traditional practice when it at length appears in written form in Ine's laws.

Perhaps, nevertheless, we have been misled for these early post-Roman centuries by concepts of order implicit in regal laws and estate charters which survive generally from later times. Maybe too, we should not be looking for patterns of linearity, yet we assume such at the most elementary level when we talk of "from Roman Britain to Anglo-Saxon England". Why should there be any straight-line, progressive explanation taking us from landscapes in the fourth century to those in the seventh century? Or of cultivating implements between these same centuries? Same sort of question, different framework: why should there *not* be a continuum of cultivated crops from first to second half of the first millennium? Crop management may vary but cereals, for example, do not change their characteristics every time the land changes hands.

Nevertheless, taking fields specifically, it is reasonable to look at late-Roman Britain for prototypes of what we see in the Early if not the Middle Anglo-Saxon period (Taylor & Fowler 1978:159-60). It is equally reasonable to look archaeologically for origins of seventh-century fields in England in fifth- to sixth-century north-west Europe, though the search is unlikely to bear fruit (van Bath 1963; Randsborg 1991; Unwin 1988:85-91). A different approach may be as valid, albeit non-historical, that is to proceed on an anthropological or even merely theoretical basis. England, after all, is characterized by a remarkable natural variety in its landscape, a fact which, as noted above, had through interaction with people already produced by the sixth century an equal variety of *cultural* landscapes. In economically agrarian societies, unlike the English today, it is the farmer's job to exploit that variety, releasing its potential for food production while maintaining the potential of the basic resources of the landscape through good husbandry. In general terms, there are many anthropological models, even ethnographic analogues, and plenty of theory for such situations and what could happen in them; though an understandable reluctance to pursue such an approach is apparent in agrarian studies of what always has been regarded as an historical period primarily to be elucidated by written evidence (e.g. Finberg 1972). Who, after all, needs theory when we have King Ine's laws?

Theory or not, a useful working premise from which to proceed envisages that basically, despite some prehistoric and Roman agrarian accidents which had scarred the landscape with barren zones like Dartmoor and Salisbury Plain, the potential of England's farmland was in good heart as European *emigrés* moved into a much-used and much acculturated countryside. In no farming sense were the Anglo-Saxons pioneers. They did not push forward into virgin wilderness, for these *nouveau arrivé(e)s* were latecomers, harbingers of England may be, but along the east coast and up the river-soft countryside of southern Britain, unlikely to farm where no farmer had previously worked (Hallam 1988). Indeed, for some, arrival might have been not much different from getting off a tourist boat at a York riverside landstage today, or rowing through the summer waterways of the Broads bravely, but with lots of people watching. Perhaps an exaggeration, but throughout the area of primary colonization (accepting the concept for present purposes) many of the Teutonic folk would have had a long search, probing up a river in what was to become Norfolk, for example, before finding a bank where they could pull in without someone telling them to "push off". Perhaps it was only the lucky would-be farmer's group which found an area long-abandoned where ruins lay overgrown with elder and bramble surrounded by former pasture and arable now scruffily almost unrecognizable beneath thistles, embryonic blackthorn and Yorkshire fog.

Archaeology in the Oxford region now tends to support such scenarios, of incomers probably having to look hard across the fertile properties—that is, tenured farms with land attached—of the Middle Thames before finding a patch where they might settle and earn their daily bread. They could of course just kill the natives, but that sort of behaviour tends to make the new neighbours suspicious and to make restive subjects. The history of colonization, the Spaniards in North America, for example, and the English in Australia, provides a multitude of analogues for possible agrarian situations that might have arisen in sixth- to eighth-century England. Among a range of possibly relevant points are, short-term, that food acqusition could become a real problem for incomers in hostile country from the second year onwards, and, longer-term, that a sort of unintentional synergy created by the dynamics of the new situation could have quite unexpected results (Cronon 1983).

Various theories about field creation exist, some based on assumptions about the dynamics of socio-economics in agrarian societies. To enter this field may seem unnecessary, even distasteful, when we have lots of archaeology and good documentary evidence (Whitelock 1979). But in matters agrarian, especially fields, we do not have a good archaeology, and we cannot even reach agreement about the simplest of references to fields in Ine's law. A little theory seems justifiable, if only as an alternative. One theory of field creation sees two fundamental processes as having taken place (Houston 1953:49-50). There is the process of 'evolution' which leads to the development of traditional field systems; and the other process is 'creation', a deliberate act leading to enclosure (though deliberate enclosure may not in fact demand physical enclosure—delineation of areas for various purposes may suffice). Either process could have taken place anywhere at any time; both processes were almost certainly at work in what was undoubtedly an evolving cultural landscape in first millennium England. Such had been the case for millennia beforehand: the evidence of both 'organic' and 'organized' field systems in prehistoric and Roman Britain is plentiful and their development was characteristically synchronous (Fleming 1987; Fowler 1983). Indeed, an interesting hypothesis to explore elsewhere is that the period AD 400-700 is unusual in that both processes were not going on, that is that no 'organized' landscapes were being created then. They certainly were in late Saxon times—on the improving monastic estates, for example, as at Glastonbury and Wells—and probably were in similar estate contexts, secular as well as ecclesiastical, from the eighth century onwards (Hall 1988:99-122; Hallam 1988; Loyn 1991:194-205; Williams 1970:19-23).

Field systems, and especially arable field systems, are a particular problem in early medieval England, extending far beyond the small 'blindspot' of the 'Dark Ages' in the sense of the fifth and sixth centuries. If we ask "What sort of fields did the Anglo-Saxons cultivate?", the only sensible answer now would seem to be "Lots of different sorts", depending on where you are in the British Isles and where you are in the Anglo-Saxon period. Overall, the impression from numerous detailed local studies is that everywhere a general trend towards localized piecemeal assarting and enclosure was in progress throughout the post-Roman centuries. Further, this was not so much a racially-specific (Anglo-Saxon, British etc.) activity, as an adaptation by particular agrarian communities to local circumstances of environment, tenure and need. My model would be of a pattern of arable continuing broadly within existing landscape arrangements (from prehistoric and/or Roman and/or sub-Roman times) in southern and Midland England until the late seventh/early eighth century. Thereafter, we can discern a response to increasing demands from an increasingly large élite and infer improved management of often newly-integrated estates embracing a range of resources for successful farming. Such estates were also increasingly expected to meet newly-desirable activities such as building in stone and hunting for pleasure. From this gradually emerged a more idiosyncratically Anglo-Saxon landscape, with new emphases in cereal production and animal husbandry. This mid/late farmed Anglo-Saxon landscape included large arable fields, increasingly cultivated and grazed in common. As the charters in general illustrate, however, its characteristic features became the extensive and productive exploitation through detailed management of a range of familiar resources in a mixed economy.

In contrast was the infield/outfield system, making the point, it has been argued, about local adaptation to circumstances (Dodgson 1980: ch. 4). The essence of this system has been taken to be expressed physically by a cluster of small, continuously-cultivated fields set in an extensive area of rough-grazing, some of it enclosed but mostly open moorland and fell-side; with temporarily cultivated areas coming and going in this 'outfield'. This method of using land agriculturally was not of course specific to Anglo-Saxons, or any other racial group, nor need it have been confined, as it is in our perception now, to highly marginal and culturally archaic upland landscapes. Perhaps within, as well as that away from, the light soils of eastern and southern England it could well have been a widely-practised system. It hardly leaves a distinctive archaeological imprint, however, though it has been claimed to have existed, largely on documentary and inferential grounds, in areas as widely separated as, for example, East Anglia and south-western England. Nevertheless, its outlying, temporary arable, even if leaving its mark for the percipient fieldworker, was and is not labelled 'outfield', could of itself result from any act of cultivation, and can only be interpreted knowingly within its context (see Foster & Smout 1994: ch. 2, 3, 11).

Nor can we turn for illumination to regnal dooms like Ine's in Wessex, for no-one at the time sat down and wrote the rules for using an infield/outfield system (or 'runrig'). Dodgson argues (1980:99-100), however, that we miss the point by thinking of it in terms of a 'system': "Far from being a farming system and no more, infield-outfield farming formed only one aspect of a diverse range of patterns moulded around the distinction between assessed and non-assessed land...fully-matured systems of infield-outfield farming could only have taken shape with the overflow of townships into non-assessed land; this began to occur in England at least over the twelfth and thirteenth centuries". This judgement reminds us of familiar arguments about when and why 'common field' farming developed in England (p. 249 above) and places us in the well-known territory of colonizing movements on to marginal land in post-(Norman) Conquest times. A point not to be missed, however, whichever landscape and whatever century we are considering, is surely that an infield-outfield arrangement could have been very effective in certain circumstances. This is not because it is 'primitive' but because the characteristic spatial variability of its inputs—intensive and extensive—could have been appropriate. It could well have represented a sensible modulation not just of tenurial and financial factors but of environmental and resource ones too; and it is not difficult to imagine circumstances in which such would have been the appropriate response in the sixth to eighth centuries. An Anglian trying to establish a homestead on the flanks of a Cheviot valley or a Briton high up on his ancestral lands in Wharfedale now paying something called a rent to an absent, ecclesiastical landlord may not have thought of it quite in those terms, but it can help the modern, non-agrarian English mind to grasp the elements of a way of farming which disappeared long ago from England (but continues to be practised elsewhere).

Because it has disappeared, 'runrig' can easily be historically underestimated. Infield/outfield need not necessarily be thought of only in topographical terms on the edges of those higher and poorer lands where, long after our period here, it is both documented and recorded. We see it then associated especially with a particular type of settlement, the hamlet or farm-hamlet, and with a dispersed settlement pattern. Though not necessarily taking the implication, a dispersed pattern of small settlements is now accepted as the general picture in Early/Mid-Anglo-Saxon England, in a landscape relatively under-populated compared to third- and fourth-century Roman Britain. It is therefore conceivable that, from the fourth century into the seventh century—up to the variable local time when estate-creation altered the tenurial landscape—among a probable range of local adjustments to the challenge of producing a living, a dispersed pattern of small settlements developed their livelihoods on an intensive/extensive basis. This would certainly have included periodic stock-treks to outlying pasture quite as much as ploughing up some distant lands. It seems probable that such a system was in operation in early Northumbria, for example, and such may also have been the case further south at about the same time where people were thin on the ground. Would abandoned Roman villa estates on the Cotswolds, for example, or upland British farms on the Chilterns and the Peak have been in such areas in, say, the hundred years either side of AD 500? And if there really had been a population collapse followed by a long, slow recovery, then areas with few people might well have continued to be common through the seventh century too. Bede's monastery illustrates the point: was St Paul's founded at Jarrow as an extension of St Peter's at Monkwearmouth to meet the needs of an existing, pagan (and non-Anglian?) local population, or was the attraction the emptiness of the muddy landscape where the River Don met the Tyne?

Cereal crops

Knowledge of the botany, and in particular of the crops, of Anglo-Saxon England, has been transformed in the last twenty years. While we are still a long way from resolving all our interpretive problems, we know much about the range of what was being grown and can see something of regional variations. The following summary draws heavily on published work by Murphy, Monk, Green and Greig but is unable to explore the implications of the mass of new data throughout Rackham (1994). We note, however, the judgement of one of the contributors, himself a pioneer in Anglo-Saxon cereal research: "The evidence suggests that it is

[now] no longer possible or wise to make any generalizations about which crops may have been most important" (Green 1994:84). We shall be knowingly unwise, briefly, for what can new research test without interpretation?

The late prehistoric species pattern of crop production in the British Isles essentially continued into the first millennium AD. Relevant evidence from the fifth and sixth centuries is very scarce, even in intensively focussed projects (Campbell 1994:67). In general it seems, however, that when evidence becomes available again in the seventh and eighth centuries, the pattern of what can perhaps be seen as a distinctively Anglo-Saxon cropping régime is different from late-Roman times in certain respects. *T. aestivum* (einkorn), *Secale cereale* (rye), *Hordeum vulgare* (barley) and *Avena sativa* (oats) are the main cereals in England, supplemented by peas and beans.

An example of the type of evidence in use here, and of its interpretation, is also relevant to 'Bede's World'. It is a sample of a large deposit of charred grain from an early/mid-third-century military granary at *Arbeia*, South Shields, at the mouth of the Tyne, 3 km. downstream from *Gyrwe* (van der Veen 1988). It consisted almost equally of two wheats, spelt and bread wheat (*T. aestivum/compactum*), with a little barley. Whereas the spelt could well have been a local product, the bread wheat was probably imported. The latter was very rare in late-Roman Britain; whereas spelt was virtually ubiquitous as a major component, often the predominant species, across the range of military, urban and rural sites in the first half of the millennium.

A second example illustrates the change in the principal crop. At West Stow, Suffolk (Murphy 1985), spelt occurred in contexts (?pre-Anglo-Saxon) up to the mid-fifth century, but not thereafter. Rye in sufficient quantities to indicate its presence as a crop occurred in Anglo-Saxon pits from the seventh century. This new prevalence of rye apparently continued: among large amounts of charred cereals from ninth-century pits and ovens at Stafford, for example, were considerable quantities of rye rachis (Moffett 1988). In contrast, wheat and barley were most common in late-Saxon urban contexts in central southern England, with rye rare.

Such palaeobotanical studies are probably picking up not so much general change within the Anglo-Saxon period as indicators of those regional trends first hinted at in the pioneer analyses of this sort of material (summarized in Fowler 1981). While the entire range of cereals seems to have been grown in most regions suitable to arable farming, more rye occurs where sandy soils best accommodate it and barley and oats were cropped more widely in less favourable regions. In sum, the cereal cultivars of embryonic Anglo-Saxon England are quite different, in some species and in their pattern of incidence, from those of late-Roman southern Britain. The main components of the crop from the seventh century onwards were einkorn and rye; conversely, their equivalents of the earlier centuries AD and later prehistory, spelt and emmer wheats, became rare. Barley remained common and oats continued to be cultivated.

Nevertheless, these changing emphases were occurring within a range of cereal production suggesting that, in all significant respects, crop husbandry in the first millennium AD was similar to that of the last prehistoric centuries. Nothing in the palaeobotanical evidence of the cereals suggests any major, long-term improvement. Indeed, in reverting to a more primitive favoured cereal, rye, and all but abandoning the well-tried insular staples of spelt and emmer, the crop husbandry of southern England in the eleventh century was perhaps less advanced than it had been a thousand years earlier. In considering these matters, however, it is crucial to appreciate that, at the moment of any one attempted generalization, its validity can only at best reflect the author's information about current work in a dynamic field where knowledge is changing all the time. As one of the researchers himself remarks at the end of his recent attempt to synthesize, "...it is difficult to establish overall trends or a general pattern through time. The surviving plant remains appear to reflect a complex pattern of agricultural production and utilization" (Green 1994:88). And he was writing particularly of Hampshire: if a multiplier effect is applied for other regions and a wider range of site-types, then we are indeed looking at complexity. Such complexity may actually be our most significant discovery. Certainly it needs to be set beside well-founded generalizations such as Loyn's (1991:346) that "...over a great swathe of country from the Tees to the Tamar a general picture of uniformity in agrarian techniques is not too distorted and misleading".

'Bede's World', Jarrow

The essence of experiment in field archaeology is simplicity. Straight away, therefore, a question must arise about a proposal to 'experiment' in early medieval farming: how valid can it be if, to proceed, complexity has to be reduced to simplicity? Butser Ancient Farm, Hampshire (Reynolds 1979) has provided some answers, theoretically and empirically. The farming aspects of the Bede's World project are well aware of the 25-year experience of 'Iron-age' farming on Wessex chalk, scientifically and also of farming in the public gaze for educational and income purposes. Compared to the Arcadia of the Hampshire/Sussex border, Jarrow on Tyne is a different country, and we have to do things differently there; but the practice of presenting a worthwhile experience for visitors based on principles of scholarship, authenticity, discovery and involvement is similar.

Butser began as a seriously experimental 'ancient farm' and then had to accommodate the public's interest. Bede's World is immediately different. The project's prime motivation is veneration for a great (local) man. It is also very much inspired by the thought of achieving that aim by creating an educational centre and international visitor attraction, including a beautifully conceived large, new museum building, in an environmentally upgraded setting in the post-industrial landscape of South Tyneside.

The 'early medieval farm' is but an element within that conceptual framework but it is an important one. At the moment, certainly, its immediate prime function is as a visitor attraction, for the finances of the project demand that visitor numbers rise now while the project develops, funds are assembled and buildings are constructed. Serious experiment is therefore as yet minimal and not a major priority; but since we have to plough the fields, sow and harvest, and keep animals which visitors love to see, a tentative beginning has been made. We have in any case learnt a lot merely by starting and having to face such basic questions as "What sort of arable field would Bede have looked out on?" and "How and with what did his brethren cultivate it?" It is amazingly disconcerting to be looking at an empty chunk of landscape, cleared of its industrial débris, and have to answer such questions knowing that, with the power of modern machinery and an obliging civil engineer, you can have whatever sort of 'Anglo-Saxon landscape' you care to define.

Gyrwe, the OE original of Jarrow, was first resuscitated and then applied to the new 'old landscape' physically created in 1992-3 on some 12 acres of former petrol storage 'tank farm'. Then, obviously, the landscape had to be provided with various features to meet statutory requirements, access for a fire-engine and ambulance, for example, and to enable it to meet its intended function of receiving visitors. The principal archaeological/historical elements defined for inclusion were timber buildings, fields, trackways, a ford, a stream and a pond, set in a 'valley landscape' with wooded slopes. They presented some probems individually, but the real issues arose over their spatial relationships and their dynamics, for basic to the whole concept was the intention to make this landscape 'work'. We knew we did not have enough land to replicate a complete early medieval agrarian system, but we wanted to demonstrate the workings of elements within such, not merely exhibit a static display.

To that end, the 'valley slopes' were planted with some 10,000 trees and shrubs, all of species known to have been growing in Northumbria around AD 700 and none of them later introductions. Millions of appropriate flower seeds were also sown. A combination of very poor soil, severe drainage problems and extremes of weather in 1993-5, notably very cold Mays and long, very dry periods, have severely inhibited growth, however, and it has not yet been possible to see the development of either the botanical aspects of the farm or to begin a serious experimental programme. Beginning with tiny amounts of 'ancient' cereal seed bought from Butser, however, we have moved through two successful harvests (1993, 1994) to a position of self-sufficiency in our seed corn, namely in einkorn, spelt, emmer, barley, rye and oats. In 1995, therefore, while our first aim is to demonstrate to visitors the range of cereal crops available to be grown on St Paul's monastic estate, the first serious experiment is planned. It is of the simplest, counting grains sown, in drills and 'broadcast', and then counting the grain produced: of no great moment, but the beginning of a long haul to build up a databank of what can happen in these environmental circumstances using different methods. We have also begun trials with different types of ard, plough and traction, but we still have some way to go before we can begin to emulate the splendid work now laid before us from Denmark (Lerche 1994).

As much as anything, Bede's World is a medium of communication about the early medieval world to the present day. The workings of farming in an agrarian society—indeed the very nature of an agrarian society, so alien in the post-industrial context of South Tyneside—are an integral part of that message. We have not added anything yet to scientific knowledge of early medieval farming, but we have already learnt a lot ourselves and can increasingly share the learning and the experience with others. In an age when, sadly, many find themselves with too much time on their hands, there may be merit in extending some people's time horizon from merely the immediate present to thirteen centuries. The land may have been "rich in grain and timber" but, unlike the Arcadia of our dreams, people died at 30 then, crippled from working in the fields.

References

Bibliography:

Barker, G.
  1985   *Prehistoric Farming in Europe*. Cambridge: Cambridge University Press.
van Bath, B. H. Slicher
  1963   *The Agrarian History of Western Europe A.D. 500-1850*. London: Arnold.
Blair, P. H.
  1976   *Northumbria in the days of Bede*. London: Gollancz.
Bowen H. C., & P. J. Fowler (eds.)
  1978   *Early Land Allotment in the British Isles*. (British Archaeological Report 48). Oxford: BAR.
Campbell, G.
  1994   The preliminary archaeobotanical results from Anglo-Saxon West Cotton and Raunds. In *Environment and economy in Anglo-Saxon England: A review of recent work on the environmental archaeology of rural and urban Anglo-Saxon settlements in England*. Proceedings of a conference held at the Museum of London, 9 - 10 April, 1990. J. Rackham (ed.), pp. 65-82. York: CBA.
Coppock, J. T.
  1964   *An Agricultural Atlas of England and Wales*. London: Faber & Faber.
Cronon, W.
  1983   *Changes in the Land. Indians, Colonists and the Ecology of New England*. New York: Hill & Wang.
Cunliffe, B.
  1991   *Iron Age Communities in Britain*. London: Routledge.
Dodgson, R. A.
  1980   *The Origin of British Field Systems: An Interpretation*. London: Academic Press.
Farmer, D. H.
  1988   *The Age of Bede*. Harmondsworth: Penguin.
Finberg, H. P. R. (ed.)
  1972   *The Agrarian History of England and Wales* I.2, *A.D. 43-1042*. Cambridge: Cambridge University Press.
Fleming A.
  1987   *The Dartmoor Reaves*. London: Batsford.

Foster, S., & T. C.
1994   *The History of Soils and Field Systems.* Aberdeen: Scottish Cultural Press.
Fowler, P. J.
1976   Agriculture and rural settlement. In *The Archaeology of Anglo-Saxon England.* D. M. Wilson (ed.), pp. 23-48. London: Methuen.
1981   Farming in the Anglo-Saxon landscape: an archaeologist's review. *Anglo-Saxon England* 9: 263-280.
1983   *The Farming of Prehistoric Britain.* Cambridge: Cambridge University Press.
Gelling, M.
1992   *The West Midlands in the Early Middle Ages.* Manchester: Manchester University Press.
Green, F. J.
1994   Cereals and plant foods: a re-assessment of the Saxon economic evidence from Wessex. In *Environment and economy in Anglo-Saxon England: A review of recent work on the environmental archaeology of rural and urban Anglo-Saxon settlements in England.* Proceedings of a conference held at the Museum of London, 9 - 10 April, 1990. J. Rackham (ed.), pp. 83-88. York: CBA.
Hagen, A.
1992   *A Handbook of Anglo-Saxon Food. Processing and Consumption,* Pinner, Middlesex: Anglo-Saxon Books.
Hall, D.
1988   The Late Saxon countryside: Villages and their fields. In *Anglo-Saxon Settlements.* D. Hooke (ed.), pp. 77-98. Oxford: Blackwell.
Hallam, H. E.
1988   England before the Norman Conquest. In *The Agrarian History of England and Wales II, 1042-1350.* H. E. Hallam (ed.), pp. 1-44. Cambridge: Cambridge University Press.
Hooke, D.
1985   *The Anglo-Saxon Landscape. The Kingdom of the Hwicce.* Manchester: Manchester University Press.
1988   *Anglo-Saxon Settlements.* Oxford: Blackwell.
Houston, J. M.
1953   *A Social Geography of England.* London: Duckworth.
Hurst, J.
1986   The medieval countryside. In *Archaeology in Britain since 1945: New Directions.* I. Longworth & J. Cherry (eds.), pp. 197-236. London: British Museum.
Kerridge, E.
1973   *The Farmers of Old England.* London: Allen & Unwin.
1992   *The Common Fields of England.* Manchester: Manchester University Press.
Lerche, G.
1994   *Ploughing Implements and Tillage Practices in Denmark from the Viking Period to about 1800 Experimentally Substantiated.* Herning: Poul Kristensen.
Longworth, I., & J. Cherry (eds.)
1986   *Archaeology in Britain since 1945. New Directions.* London: British Museum.
Loyn, H. R.
1991   *Anglo-Saxon England and the Norman Conquest.* London: Longman.
Mercer, R. (ed.)
1981   *Farming Practice in British Prehistory.* Edinburgh: Edinburgh Univ. Press.

Moffett, L.
1988   The Archaeobotanical Evidence for Saxon and Medieval Agriculture in
            Central England *circa* 500 AD to 1500 AD. M. Phil. thesis, University of
            Birmingham (unpublished).
Murphy, P.
1985   The cereals and crop weeds. In *West Stow: The Anglo-Saxon Village*. S. E.
            West (ed.), pp. 100-108. (East Anglian Archaeology 24). Ipswich: Suffolk
            County Planning Department.
Piggott, S. (ed.)
1981   *The Agrarian History of England and Wales I.1, Prehistory*. Cambridge:
            Cambridge University Press.
Rackham, J. (ed.)
1994   *Environment and Economy in Anglo-Saxon England: A review of recent work
            on the environmental archaeology of rural and urban Anglo-Saxon
            settlements in England*. Proceedings of a conference held at the Museum of
            London, 9 - 10 April, 1990. York: CBA.
Randsborg, K.
1991   *The First Millennium A.D. in Europe and the Mediterranean*. Cambridge:
            Cambridge University Press.
Reynolds, P. J.
1979   *Iron Age Farm: The Butser Experiment*. London: British Museum.
Rowley, T. (ed.)
1981   *The Origins of Open Field Agriculture*. London: Croom Helm.
Salway, P.
1981   *Roman Britain*. Oxford: Clarendon Press.
Taylor, C.
1983   *Village and Farmstead. A History of Rural Settlement in England*. London:
            George Philip.
Taylor, C., & P. J. Fowler
1978   Roman fields into medieval furlongs? In *Early Land Allotment in the British
            Isles*. H. C. Bowen & P. J. Fowler (eds.), pp. 159-162. (British Archaeological
            Report 48). Oxford: BAR.
Thirsk, J.
1964   The Common Fields. *Past and Present* 29: 3-29.
1967   The farming regions of England. In *The Agrarian History of England and
            Wales IV, 1500-1640*. J. Thirsk (ed.), pp. 1-112. Cambridge: Cambridge
            University Press.
1984a   *The Rural Economy of England*. London: Hambledon Press.
1984b   *The Agrarian History of England and Wales V, 1640-1750*. 1. Regional
            Farming Systems. Cambridge: Cambridge University Press.
Unwin, T.
1988   Towards a model of Anglo-Scandinavian rural settlement in England. In
            Anglo-Saxon Settlements. D. Hooke (ed.), pp. 77-98. Oxford: Blackwell.
van der Veen, M.
1992   *Crop Husbandry Regimes. An Archaeobotanical Study of Farming in northern
            England 1000 BC-AD 500*. (Sheffield Archaeological Monographs 3).
            Sheffield: J. R. Collis Publications, University of Sheffield.
Whitelock, D. (ed.)
1979   *English Historical Documents I, ca AD 500-1042*. Oxford: Oxford
            University Press.

Williams, M.
   1970   *The Draining of the Somerset Levels.* Cambridge: Cambridge Univ. Press.

Discussion

AUSENDA: Is it possible that Saxon peasants used digging sticks?

FOWLER: No evidence has been found for the use of digging sticks. They are known from Scandinavian sites. But there is both documentary and archaeological evidence for the use of spades in Anglo-Saxon times. We've been concentrating on finding out about, and how to use, different sorts of ards at Bede's World this first year, but I guess some of the things we've done, especially with modern spades, would have been done 1,300 years ago with iron-edged wooden spades. There's quite a lot of evidence for them—from the Roman period right through to medieval illustrations. And they don't seem to change much—once you've acquired the idea of a spade, there's not much fundamental that you can or need to do with it, though there's a myriad of detailed modifications of course. On the other hand, though ards may seem equally simple, archaeologically there is a typology and a progression. And ploughing implements had undoubtedly become much more efficient by the end of the Anglo-Saxon period—the questions are when and where the technological changes developed and by when they came into common usage. I don't see answers in stories about what Anglo-Saxon may have brought with them.

HÄRKE: You mentioned that there is no convincing evidence that Anglo-Saxon influence brought any new type of ard or plough. But under the lowest settlement level of Feddersen Wierde there are plough marks that appear to come from a mouldboard plough because the furrows have quite clearly been turned over. Their stratigraphic position would date them to the first century BC. The question is, how did that knowledge get lost, because there is, as far as I know, no further mouldboard plough evidence until the seventh century at least.

FOWLER: I think this is one area where you've got to use experiments. It's a great pity that serious experiments begun in the '60s at Lejre in Denmark have not been continued there—or if they have, have not been published, although Lerche's great work is soon to be published and of course we have accumulated a lot of experimental data about prehistoric cultivation and farming at Butser Iron Age Farm in England. I don't see myself how, for our period, we are going to be able to get direct evidence for whether or not they used a mouldboard and proper share on their ploughs in order to produce an inverted turf—we're going to have to experiment and extrapolate. It's theoretically possible that a proper plough was around before the Anglo-Saxon period and not forgotten—apart from the evidence Heinrich quotes, I saw deep furrows and cultivation ridges under Hadrian's Wall at Denton in the western suburbs of Newcastle a few years ago which could be interpreted as suggesting such a plough was around before 122 AD in what six-hundred years later became Anglian Northumbria. Because I had the opportunity to examine the evidence in detail in the ground, I came away convinced that it was an ard which had turned the soil over, probably an ard with a wing on it being held at a very acute angle, which is not the same as a plough with a coulter. We need to do a lot of experiments, on clay for example, to try to replicate this sort of archaeological evidence, using a range of different cultivating implements. One clue is Gwithian in Cornwall, but the disappointing fact is that, as far as I know, the type of evidence there has simply not been followed up by similar evidence of comparable date from western Britain. Occurring in a well-dated context there, about 900 AD, the evidence of cultivation in wind-blown sand showed clearly that the turf had been turned over. I always took this to indicate that a mouldboard plough had been in use, though I would argue that this was a technological survival from Roman Britain rather than a new tool introduced by the Saxons. It's still an issue, but it remains the one good example of that sort of date—though the furrow-marks from Hen Domen, apparently of the mid-eleventh century, might of course represent earlier activity. Perhaps experiment will show whether this sort of evidence can be produced without using a mouldboard plough.

HOOKE: In commenting upon the rotation of crops it is interesting to look at the evidence of charters, which make reference to such things as 'the bean land', 'the oat land', 'the flax land', 'the wheat land', 'the barley acres', almost suggesting, unless they are being treated as some very ephemeral land mark, that there was some sort of monoculture.

FOWLER: Well, first of all we know already that we haven't got enough room on our 'Anglian farm' at Bede's World to farm properly. We certainly need more room to introduce some serious experiments with different variables. But I think the key to this historical question—and I would be very grateful for any guidance on this—is, given 700 as our central date and Northumbria, what sort of field should we have? Never mind about the rotation. I've avoided this question about field-types so far. What people see is a small field with a bank round it. Not everyone needs to be told that it is modelled on a 'Celtic' field, or a Roman field or whatever, any more than we always need to explain the genetic background to our animals or the details of our implanted botany. We must never forget that we made this landscape in 1992: it's not a real historical one. But it has now produced enough seed for us to think bigger next year. We have to take a view on whether we go on growing our cereals in plots or strips within these little enclosed fields or whether we start having longer strips in the open area we have so far just used for grazing. I might add that our land is awful from a farmer's viewpoint.

HOOKE: There were all sorts of fields by the late Roman period weren't there?

FOWLER: My gut feeling is that whenever we get our dexters to work efficiently with an ard we'll keep them going in the same direction as long as we reasonably can, perhaps stopping at some arbitrary 25-metre mark or something like that. Maybe the question will settle itself purely pragmatically. Maybe that's how they did it. Could you give me any guidance as to what sort of field we should have, about its shape?

AUSENDA: My hundred-year-old informant told me they had two ploughs amongst 52 families because this was considered very expensive equipment. So they only ploughed fields more than ten metres long. For less than ten metres, and five metres wide, they would work them with the spade.

FOWLER: Well, perhaps oddly, that is about what our 1994 strips look like: about 25 yards long and 5 yards wide, which is quite a convenient unit. Mind you, we didn't have our 'oxen' in the Spring, so we pulled our various ards ourselves, and our seed-corn was so scarce that we planted every grain carefully by hand. A 25-yard length has to be seen in relation to that one-off and very un-Anglo-Saxon method!

POWLESLAND: We've only got one early Saxon field down and beyond the settlement. It would be about a kilometre away. It is not really a great help, but does give you something very low, long and thin rather than big and square.

FOWLER: That's interesting; but maybe we shouldn't try to replicate exactly what may have been—when we don't actually know. Anyway, it sort of freezes history. Perhaps our problem here is merely a presentational one: to have a plausible story to tell people like you and visitors and so on. But, on the other hand, presentation does concentrate the mind wonderfully and raise fairly basic questions. I take the view that it matters profoundly now, and it mattered profoundly in Anglo-Saxon times—if you were living on a monastic estate or in a kinship group, perhaps as a labouring man with rights over a little bit of land—it mattered tremendously, what range you had and what you had to do on what shape of land. It is not a big historical question in one sense but it actually mattered day to day. It seems to me that we don't know the answer, do we?

CHARLES-EDWARDS: You said you have a bit of bad land, yet there is good germination on the rest of it. Can you explain how well you've done on that bad land?

FOWLER: I think you can say that ours is bad land. Basically we are on Boulder Clay which is good land in Northumbria for mixed farming, indeed arable farming, in the area of its lowlands. But ours is bad because we are creating this Anglian farm on what was an industrial site: it had had huge petrol tanks on it. It was completely cleared, thousands of tons of soil and rubbish taken off it, and dug out to get rid of chemical pollution. Then it was reshaped into our design for an early medieval farmed landscape, but unfortunately it was covered with the wrong sort of topsoil from the site of a new car factory down the road. No Anglian in his right mind would have attempted to cultivate it!

CHARLES-EDWARDS: But at least it hasn't come from very far away.

FOWLER: No, it hasn't come from very far away, but that soil is bad in two senses: it has got no structure and has got no organic life in it. We are offering a prize for the first person who sees a worm on the site, and that is literally true. So, the reason why we've got a good crop this year is simply because it happens there was a high phosphate content in the soil that was dumped on the site. I suspect we burnt it off and we'll have a real problem next year in getting anything like that sort of fertility. We've got to manure like mad.

HOOKE: Will you be able to judge the effects of the folding of sheep across the land?

FOWLER: Absolutely. In a sense the big experiment has started because we are using our sheep systematically, to manure the soil where we are going to cultivate but not on some other areas—just as Reynolds has done at Butser where he was, until recently, getting high productivity on land, fertilized and unfertilized, used over twenty years.

SCULL: You were discussing comparanda for the fields. There are late Roman Iron-age field systems on the Continent, at Flögeln, for instance. So there are Continental examples which are not too far from Anglo-Saxon England in date and cultural context.

FOWLER: I have looked very hard on the Continent for Anglo-Saxon fields and I can't see any. Of course there are ancient fields across Continental north-western Europe but, although I would not claim to have made a comprehensive search, I find it difficult to pin any down to the time at which Saxons and so on would have been leaving for Britain. I can't see what the about-to-be English were using as old-time *Germani*, and therefore it's difficult to see what idea of field layout they may have brought with them. Of course there are a number of field systems in Holland and north-western Germany where you have long 'Celtic'-type fields which on their radiocarbon dates come through to about 500 AD. I don't know to what extent that date is just a convention—a lot seems to come to an end in north-western Europe about then!

HÄRKE: And do you expect proto-historic fields to look profoundly different?

FOWLER: No.

SCULL: Another point which interests me is your harvesting technique (cutting the stalk near to the ears). The absence of cultivar weeds in environmental asssemblages is often cited as evidence for off-site processing, and so for the local importing of cereals. But if the techniques you describe were used, weeds would rarely if ever have got mixed with cereals at harvest. A common axiom of environmental analysis would fall!

FOWLER: Nothing I've said must be taken as gospel—we've only just taken in our first harvest, a few days ago, and all we've been doing in 1994 is experimenting in experimenting, just getting a feel for the site and its possibilities. I'm certainly not saying what we did is the only way, what I am saying is that it was imperative to build up our seed bank. That's why we hand-plucked the ears, just like we'd hand-planted the seed. We decided to take every ear off and we took it in various ways. We just found that one particular way worked well: putting the fingers of your left hand round the stem and then running them up towards the tip of the ear, pulling the plant taut while simultaneously cutting the stem just below the ear with one of those familiar little knives that you find on many post-Roman sites. They're not 'Saxon'—they are just ubiquitous in these centuries, and maybe we've stumbled on one of the reason why. Of course one result of harvesting that way is that all plants shorter than the cereal ear are excluded from the 'take'. But I'm not suggesting that a whole field could have been harvested in this way—it would take for ever. And, that clearly was not done for there is quite a lot of evidence now for all sorts of mixes of grains and seeds and ears and weeds and so on—there's a lot of detail in the recently published CBA book edited by James Rackham (1994). And don't forget hay in all this, with all its floral richness. We keep on about cereals but hay is just as important a crop.

HOOKE: Did you look at the Tiberius calendar? The reapers depicted there have a short sickle.

POWLESLAND: Those people are hussing and trying to extract straw for special purposes. They cut the ears off first and then they cut the straw at the base; they do exactly what you've done.

FOWLER: Yes. I was just going to say that maybe accidentally we've illustrated one of the reasons for doing what Dominic has just said—and maybe this was done in the eighth century for these reasons. You want to get as many uses out of your crop, any crop, as you can. The big advantages of just taking the ears off are 100 per cent recovery and no weeds, as already said, and while you also leave a lovely stalk which can then be cut separately *en masse*, perhaps using a scythe, to give you your thatch, your bedding material and so on.

HAWKES: I have an idea that this is based on the Harley psalter. My understanding of the Harley psalter is that most of the illustrations are based on the Utrecht psalter which in turn is based on a late antique prototype, and certainly in terms of details of dress there is nothing there that indicates it would be of interest in an Anglo-Saxon context. So I'm not sure to what extent that is a piece of evidence for Anglo-Saxon practice.

WOOD: The armour is not late antique in style but later.

LENDINARA: There are four descriptions of sowing in the works of Aldhelm (*Carmina ecclesiastica* IV, ii, line 4; *Carmina de virginitate* line 225 and *De virginitate* p. 264, line 16 and p. 270, line 15) where he uses the unusual word *occa* (a homonym of *occa* 'harrow') which means 'ploughed field'. All the passages are steeped in 'Scriptural' images, such as the description of the careless driver of a plough (Luke IX, 62), but there is also some reworking by Aldhelm when he describes the furrowed earth and the broken sods. I'm not a very good observer of fields, but these Aldhelmian passages might give some clue. I have spotted the word *occa*, which seems exclusive to Anglo-Latin authors, also in a small poem which follows St Boniface's riddles in MS Cambridge, UL Gg. 5 .35 and in a Vatican MS (Pal. 591), where the plural *occis* occurs, once again with the meaning 'clods'.

FOWLER: Well that would be interesting because I'm trying to play to the documentary evidence in our farming at Bede's World quite as much as the archaeology and botany. Any hints of farming practices or technology are welcome and sometimes they turn up in unexpected places. Whenever a student asks me for some ideas for a dissertation, I give him or her a Saint's Life and say "Right, go through that and take out all the references you can find to anything agrarian". Incidentally, there's a reference to a mill, it may be a water mill, in Adomnán's *Life of St Columba*.

LENDINARA: Both in MS London, BL, Cotton Tiberius B.v, f.3 and in the Bayeux tapestry there are amazing drawings of ploughs in all their detail.

POHL: I would like to make two points: one about field sizes. We have tried to extract information about sizes and values of agricultural units from Langobardic charters of the eighth century. Of course what you don't get are exact measures of actual sizes of fields. What you could get are values of agricultural property that is being sold or bought or given away. These values range from one and a half *solidi* to 900 *solidi*; sometimes, not with fields, but with other forms of agriculture, you get sizes like the smallest olive grove that is being talked about which consists of six olive trees. That doesn't seem to give you any clue about typical field sizes or typical sizes of agricultural units. It probably goes right through the range depending on the quality of the soil and the type of crop.

The second point concerns agricultural technology. I don't know if you ever came across a huge book by an eastern German called Joachim Henning. He made an amazing collection of all agricultural tools, scythes, sickles, ploughs, etc. from the first millennium AD, all along the Danube, from Noricum down to Moesia. It has been published in German a few years ago with a lot of illustrations (Henning 1987). He planned to do the same for the Rhineland but I do not think this has appeared yet. I recently heard a paper given by him which came to some surprising conclusions: for instance that throughout the Roman period along the Danube, the technology involved in farming and growing of crops was not as highly developed as the one for raising cattle, whereas it was the other way round along the Rhine. Then around 500 the situation changed: along the Rhine they reached the highest standards of growing crops, although along the Danube they didn't reach the highest standards in cattle raising. Henning built far-reaching conclusions on that to explain why there was more prosperity and progress from that period onwards along the Rhine than in the region of the Danube. I cannot really judge whether that can be maintained. But my question is: have you ever made a comparison of respective standards of agricultural technologies in England and on the Continent? Was there a marked difference in the Anglo-Saxon period?

FOWLER: In terms of productivity?

POHL: Well, in terms of technology, the standard of tools and equipment found. His evidence was largely from excavations, of course.

FOWLER: Well, all I have done is look at the obvious major excavations of *terpen* and so on. In general, setting aside specifically Roman material which turns up on some sites, the technological position seems to be pretty much the same; that is that there does not seem to be a great deal of change from late pre-historic times right through the period that we are talking about, at least as far as the basic agrarian technology is concerned. Once you've developed a particular tool which does the job you want done—a rake which rakes, a spade with which you can dig your ditches in your particular subsoil, an ard which churns effectively through your soil—there's not much change you can make, or incentive to do so, until you have machinery or until you change the traction power.

POHL: What surprised me about Henning's method was that he developed a very sophisticated terminology and argued that a number of little changes added up to a major technological change in a period that we rather associate with decadence.

FOWLER: Well, let us go back to the very first question asked, about digging sticks which I changed into spades. At the end of the spade development, by the middle of the nineteenth century in Ireland, there are 170 or so different types of spades all of which are morphologically recognizable and were known to exist to people at the time. This was more and more a matter of specialization in the function rather than a purely cultural thing.

I came across this because there is a spade mill, Patterson's, just outside Belfast, which was working until a few years ago. It went out of business and was eventually taken over and restored to working order by the National Trust. I had the chance to see it during that change, and was both surprised and delighted to see hundreds of spade moulds—all slightly different and forming a real typology, not just an academic's one. You know, you could say 'I'll have a Connemara type 3B' [laughter] or whatever—a specialist implement for a specific task, to fit local soil conditions and functions and, doubtless, ways of working. So, although there have been so many types of one particular implement up to our own day in Ireland, the example actually illustrates my point: if it works, don't change it. It should be no surprise if in general terms the agrarian tool kit is pretty much the same throughout much of Europe, especially outside the Empire, during the first millennium AD.

AUSENDA: You were talking about manuring. It seemed to me that you intimated that manuring was always obtained from sheep.

FOWLER: The principle of farming practice which is attested archaeologically was to have domestic middens, farmyard middens. This is a circular argument because when we find potsherds, prehistoric, Roman, Anglo-Saxon, scattered over areas of ancient fields, we identify the fields as arable because of the sherds and say the sherds got there accidentally in manure; and we then infer that there were domestic middens to explain the sherds on the 'arable'. Actually, I think it's quite a good circular argument—just look at the modern potsherds on eighteenth- to twentieth-century fields. But the problem is that, once you are into the post-Roman period, especially in north and west Britain, pottery tends to become a little scarce, to put it mildly. It is, therefore, difficult to recognize the manuring, and particularly that of the sixth-seventh centuries and, therefore, the fields of that period. Farming common sense tells us, however, that you've got to manure on certain soils to maintain at least certain crops, even if 'runrig' farming was attractive precisely because you did not have to do that. Manuring would, I am sure, have been carried out by sheep too: that's one main reason for keeping them, even if to say so may be to be looking backwards a bit from later documentary evidence. People feuded over grazing rights.

I also think that cattle should not be underestimated as a manure machine, one which you occasionally take out to pull an ard. And you keep your precious ox, or pair of oxen if you're well-off, in a building like that we're putting up at Jarrow. That's based on the ground plan of one excavated at Thirlings in Northumberland. But again, although we're in the very early stages of construction, a most interesting inference has already been suggested empirically, that the very large amount of timber required for this modest building by Anglo-Saxon standards would have had to come from carefully managed woodland, probably some way away elsewhere on the estate, where, before transport, it would probably have been prefabricated. The prefabrication takes place on the estate, not down in Jarrow because there is no point in carrying down tons of bark and wood which you don't want, so you adze it off site. So, Dominic, you've got to find where they got the timber.

POWLESLAND: I most wholeheartedly agree. That's another thing to support the issue of prefabricated construction. It's the perfect way of building them.

SCULL: There is evidence for manuring at Witton (Norfolk), where fieldwalking detected a very thin scatter of pottery around the Anglo-Saxon settlement which does seem to represent manuring from domestic middens.

FOWLER: Has anybody done some serious work on Middle-Saxon settlement complexes using phosphate analysis as has been done on prehistoric sites and some Irish setlements? You might be able to show up an infield area if it had been heavily manured.

SCULL: Not in England, but there has been good work using phosphate analysis to define infields in Scandinavia.

References in the discussion

Textual sources:

Aldhelm

> *Carmina ecclesiastica, Carmina de Virginitate, De virginitate*: see Lapidge & Herren 1979; Lapidge & Rosier 1985.

Bibliography:

Henning, J.
  1987   *Südosteuropa zwischen Antike und Mittelalter: archäologische Beiträge zur Landwirtschaft des 1. Jahrtausends u.Z.* Berlin: Akademie-Verlag.
Lapidge, M., & M. W. Herren (trans.)
  1979   *Aldhelm: The Prose Works.* Cambridge: D. S. Brewer.
Lapidge, M., & J. L. Rosier (trans.)
  1985   *Aldhelm: The Poetic Works.* Woodbridge: D. S. Brewer.
Rackham, J. (ed.)
  1994   See References at end of paper.

CHRISTOPHER SCULL

English Heritage, 23 Savile Row, London, GB-W1X 1AB

Introduction

Ethnography and urbanism raise general issues of approach, definition and interpretation. Because, however, the societies of pre-Viking England were not urban, more detailed discussion narrows to an evaluation of the character and context of a few settlements, and of how they may be located within general models of urbanism and urban development. This paper focuses on these questions. Other related issues, in particular the economic structures of seventh- and eighth-century England, the broader patterns of settlement structure, function and hierarchy, and their social contexts, are considered in so far as they are relevant to this central discussion, but are not otherwise pursued: more detailed treatments may be found in other contributions to this volume and in the discussions.

Ethnography and Anglo-Saxon archaeology

The seminar title, "The Anglo-Saxons: towards an ethnography", invites an approach which views the Anglo-Saxons as a definable social or ethnic group, with characteristic identities, institutions and circumstances which are accessible, and which can be described and characterized, if not fully understood, without undue difficulty. There may be areas of Anglo-Saxon studies for which this is indeed the case, and for which the nature of the source material is suited to the construction of an ethnography, and I anticipate learning here from colleagues in other disciplines. However, the archaeological record is the primary source for urban life and urban economy in Anglo-Saxon England, and while there are good reasons why the archaeologist should attempt to characterize aspects of society and economy at a particular place and time, the nature of the source material presents problems, and the intellectual climate in which debate has developed is not necessarily sympathetic to an ethnographic approach to Anglo-Saxon England.

Ethnographies such as Evans-Pritchard's study of the Nuer (Evans-Pritchard 1940) or Chagnon's study of the Yanomamö (Chagnon 1968) are very largely concerned with the contemporary and are based on direct testimony and observation. Archaeology, by contrast, is an historical and forensic discipline. Its primary source is material evidence which, however actively constituted in the systemic context (Schiffer 1976), is in the archaeological context most commonly the detritus of human activity. This limits the extent to which the dynamics of past

269

© C.I.R.O.S.S.
San Marino (R.S.M.)

societies can be approached directly through the archaeological record, and since the 1960s an explicit thrust of mainstream archaeological theory has been to overcome these constraints through the use of generalizing models derived from cultural anthropology in archaeological explanation. An important aspect of this processual or social archaeology, in which archaeology is seen as the historical dimension of cultural anthropology, has been the rejection of culture history in favour of culture process, and an emphasis on the explanation of culture change rather than the description of 'cultures' (Renfrew & Bahn 1991; Trigger 1989). The tenets of processual archaeology have been subject to re-evaluation over the last decade (cf. Hodder 1986; Shanks & Tilley 1987; Yoffee & Sherrat 1993), but even though more recent trends have to some extent rehabilitated the concerns of traditional culture history, the certainties of a monolithic 'Anglo-Saxon archaeology' are being replaced by an appreciation of both the complexity of the material record of the early medieval period in the British Isles, and the range of perspectives on this material offered by the so-called 'post-processual' archaeologies (Scull 1993:65-6).

The study of post-Roman urban development in north-west Europe has been a major beneficiary of cross-cultural and inter-disciplinary comparative study (e.g. Clarke & Ambrosiani 1991; Clarke & Simms 1985; Hodges & Hobley 1988), and Hodges' benchmark *Dark Age Economics* (Hodges 1982a) is a paradigmatic processual study. The emphasis of these approaches has been on investigating the underlying causes of urban development as a widespread socio-economic phenomenon. David Hill (1988) has argued the need for a theoretical framework which encompasses common inter-regional trends and the regionally or culturally specific, but this has not been forthcoming. While there is no question that the nature and trajectory of urban development in Anglo-Saxon England differed significantly in some respects from other areas of Europe, it is debatable to what extent we should see these as 'Anglo-Saxon towns' rather than towns shaped by the specific and historically contingent circumstances of place and time. Thus, whereas it may be legitimate to treat Anglo-Saxon symbolism, ideology, or kinship structures as characteristic social constructs it is more difficult to argue persuasively that this must also be true of towns. This is not to say that they had no social or ideological dimension, or to deny that England differed from the Continent, but to emphasize that the fundamental factors which governed their existence and success or failure were not culturally specific.

Another point to emphasize, especially in view of the immediate, synchronic nature of twentieth-century ethnographies, is that the society and economy of Anglo-Saxon England were not static. The circumstances of the seventh century were very different from those of the fifth, and those of the tenth century to those of the eighth (cf. Hinton 1990:1-105). Limiting the scope of this seminar to the seventh and eighth centuries has gone some way towards minimizing the problems this poses for constructing an ethnography, but there is evidence for considerable change over these two centuries, and even allowing for the relatively poor chronological precision afforded by archaeology (Chagnon's initial study of the

Yanomamö was completed within fifteen months, whereas we are lucky if we can date a recognizable archaeological event to within a generation) there is a danger that evidence might be conflated, masking important dynamics. There is also a danger of ethnocentricity, to which any researcher is prone who comments on a culture not their own. A vivid illustration of this is given by Martin Biddle's famous analysis of the contemporary terms applied to Winchester and Southampton from the late seventh to the ninth century (Biddle 1973:246-7; 1976:114). By most modern analytical criteria (below) Southampton has a claim to be urban and Winchester does not, but it is Winchester which is referred to as *civitas* or *urbs*. We need not discard our own criteria, but we must accept that our understandings of the signifier and the signified do not coincide with that of the Anglo-Saxon scribes. A final danger is that of anachronism, which may be generated by the different perspectives of ethnography on the one hand and a processual archaeology on the other. The concept of 'proto-urbanism', which has assumed an important place in debate on urban origins in early medieval Europe (Clarke & Simms 1985:673; Hodges 1982a:23), is the product of an historical perspective. A particular settlement may appear proto-urban when viewed against its precursors and successors in a developmental sequence, but whether it is valid or useful to use the term in a pre-urban context is debatable—a point discussed in more detail below.

What is a town?

The definition of urban character is a long-standing and complex issue which transcends disciplinary boundaries, but which has been constrained by them. Clarke and Simms (1985) have broadly characterized the debate as one between legalistic and functional definitions, the former rooted in historical scholarship, the latter deriving ultimately from Weberian sociology. It has been recognized for over twenty years that legalistic definitions are not appropriate to the settlements of the early medieval period which are known largely from archaeological evidence, and an influential response to this has been the definition of a body of urban criteria, possession of a number of which would make a *prima facie* case for urban status. Biddle (1976:100) has made a list of twelve criteria relevant to early medieval towns which remains influential,[1] but which still leans heavily towards institutional and morphological criteria, and which if applied uncritically to the spectrum of settlement in the seventh and eighth centuries would identify clearly non-urban settlements as towns. Archaeological opinion in north-west Europe and

---

1 These criteria are 1) defences, 2) a planned street system, 3) a market(s), 4) a mint, 5) legal autonomy, 6) a role as a central place, 7) a relatively large and dense population, 8) a diversified economic base, 9) plots and houses of 'urban' type, 10) social differentiation, 11) complex religious organization, 12) a judicial centre. Possession of more than one of these characteristics is held to establish a prior case for urban status. This follows the approach adopted in *The Erosion of History* (Heighway 1972).

Scandinavia has moved towards broader functionalist definitions which emphasize the economic character and roles of urban settlements, aspects which can be addressed more readily through archaeological evidence than can institutional criteria, and which are sufficiently broad to accommodate the range of complexity and regional variation apparent in early medieval Europe but which do not rule out more refined characterization. Thus Ambrosiani (1988:63) takes as his definition of urban "any settlement with a densely populated and permanently occupied site and a specialized non-agrarian economy.... It should also have the functions of a central place". This definition is widely echoed in recent archaeological studies. In emphasizing thresholds of population size and economic complexity this embodies the valid notion of an urban settlement as other than rural, and the economic assumptions which lie behind a modern definition—not wholly facetious—of a town as a settlement with a Woolworth's store. This might be taken further, and an analytical distinction drawn between towns as institutions and urban settlements as economic and social phenomena.

A feature of functionalist approaches to the study of towns and urban origins in post-Roman north-west Europe has been the development of the concept of the *Frühform*; the proto-urban state. This depends largely upon the retrospective identification in non-urban settlements, some of which later became towns and some of which did not, of elements which are typical of, or which foreshadow those typical of, later towns. Thus ecclesiastical centres and magnate residences have been identified as proto-urban because they sustained a resident non-agrarian population, albeit below the threshold of size and complexity which would be considered urban (Clarke & Simms 1985:672-4). As noted above, this perspective is conditioned by the context of historical enquiry, and may be considered anachronistic if applied uncritically in a synchronic analysis. In any case, as is argued below, the term may be better applied to a society as a whole or to a range of social and economic conditions rather than to specific sites in particular. Although they meet the analytical criteria, post-Conquest monastic complexes in England, in contrast to their pre-Viking counterparts, are not considered candidates for proto-urban status, presumably because they were components of a society which sustained and recognized towns. Implicit in the use of the term proto-urban in the context of early medieval Europe is the recognition that urban settlements manifest a threshold of economic sophistication within the societies which sustain them. At any one time particular settlements may be more likely than others to develop urban characteristics, but these circumstances are not necessarily immutable, as the eventual failure of the major trading settlements of seventh- to ninth-century England shows.

Urban development in Anglo-Saxon England

Pre-Viking England was not urban even by the standards of pre-industrial societies. It has been estimated that between seven and ten per cent of the population of England lived in a town by the time of the Norman conquest (Biddle

1976:141; Dyer 1985:92; Hinton 1990:115), but this can be attributed almost entirely to developments during the two centuries from the later ninth century. Before this time, the number of settlements in Anglo-Saxon England which have a genuine claim to be considered urban can be counted on the fingers of one hand.

Whether or not genuinely urban communities were a major feature of later Roman Britain, or whether the character of towns had changed to what Reece (1980) has described as administrative villages, town life did not long survive the end of Roman rule in Britain (Esmonde-Cleary 1989; Millett 1990). The economic and political trauma of rupture from the Roman state deprived the towns of late Roman Britain of their administrative and economic functions, of the economic structures which supported them, and of the ideological system of which they were a manifestation. The fifth and sixth centuries, by contrast, were a period of relative political fragmentation and more localized and subsistence-orientated economic structures. The archaeological evidence indicates small-scale agrarian societies without the degree of political integration required for rulers to wield powers of extraction and coercion comparable to those available to the Roman state, and, as Carver (1993:56) has pointed out, strategies of surplus extraction and re-distribution in the immediate post-Roman period were quite different—and very probably consciously different—from those which had sustained towns, being geared instead towards providing the portable wealth which buttressed the élites around whom the Anglo-Saxon kingdoms eventually crystallized. There is evidence for craft specialization and both regional and long-distance exchange, but not on any large or commercial scale. There is no evidence for a market economy, commercial transactions appear to have been socially embedded, no coinage was minted and currency-use appears to have been restricted to élites.

There is evidence for early (that is fifth- or sixth-century) post-Roman activity within the walls of a number of late Roman towns, and a strong case can be made that some—notably London, Canterbury and York—were the sites of high-status secular settlements before important ecclesiastical sites were established there in the immediate aftermath of the Augustinian mission (Clarke & Ambrosiani 1991:10-5). It is also true that most major Roman walled towns re-emerged as major towns in the Late Saxon period. This appears to argue for some continuity, but there is as yet no evidence that any Roman town in Britain retained its urban character through the fifth century, nor is there any direct evidence that any Roman town retained the importance of its counterparts in North Gaul such as Reims or Soissons, let alone of those in the Mediterranean provinces. It might be argued instead that secular settlements within the walls of Romano-British towns were no more urban—in the sense defined above—than their counterparts in the open countryside, and that the establishment of sees at these sites in the seventh century reflected what the metropolitan Church of Rome saw as appropriate rather than the true status of the existing settlements. If so, the eminence of Winchester, for instance, from the seventh century might be attributed to a post-conversion re-invention rather than the survival of some special status from the fifth century.

It is not until the seventh century that there is widespread evidence for the development of a settlement hierarchy, implying the formal administration of territory and the systematic extraction of an agrarian surplus, for political hegemony on a regional scale, for large-scale regional or inter-regional exchange, and for any but the most restricted use of coinage. It is also during the seventh century that the first post-Roman sites for which a case for urban status can be made emerge. These are the extensive coastal or riverine settlements, now usually referred to as 'wics' or 'emporia', which have been physically identified at Ipswich, Southampton, London, and possibly York. The English sites had their counterparts on the Continent at Dorestad, Domburg, and Quentovic, and were linked to a long-distance trading system which flourished from the seventh to the ninth centuries. They were, however, a relatively short-lived phenomenon. Of the four known sites in England, only that at Ipswich survived the ninth century with no marked hiatus in activity or relocation of the main focus of settlement; they cannot, therefore, be represented as part of an unbroken trajectory of urban development. Instead, as already noted, the level of urbanization apparent in eleventh-century England can be attributed to developments from the late ninth century. The initial momentum is conventionally attributed to the establishment of the *burhs* by Alfred of Wessex and his successors, and to the Scandinavian armies, but alongside the conscious re-foundation of Roman cities and the establishment of new towns on the same model it is possible to discern other factors at work. In particular, it has been argued that high-status secular settlements, and ecclesiastical centres, sites which might be identified as proto-urban, acted as the *foci* for more organic urban development, functioning as they did as both administrative and economic central places, and so exercising a pull on craftsmen and traders. Both the emergence of major medieval towns such as Northampton (Williams 1984; Williams *et al.* 1985) and smaller centres (Blair 1988) have been explained in this way. That such developments might occur in the tenth and eleventh centuries, but not in the seventh or eighth, must be due in a large part to differences in the economic infrastructure, and it appears that whereas the economy of seventh- and eighth-century England was largely redistributive, the towns of later Saxon England had truly commercial market functions. Biddle (1976) has drawn attention to the fact that the administrative, jurisdictional and economic functions which would be integrated within a classical or later medieval town are split between a range of sites in the seventh and eighth centuries, and are not re-aggregated in an urban form until the second half of the ninth century or later. The eighth- and ninth-century settlement at Southampton probably had an administrative role in addition to its economic functions (below), but both the scale of urbanization by the time of the Norman conquest and the character of towns such as Winchester and London by the late tenth century support the general distinction which has been voiced by O'Connor (1994:142): we may define a handful of seventh- to ninth-century sites as urban, but unlike their later counterparts it may be difficult to see them as towns in the complex way that we understand the word.

The material evidence

There is written evidence for trading sites in England, some of which bear the suffix *-wic*, from the seventh century, and there is a presumption that a number of such sites in Kent may have been operating from the sixth century (Hawkes 1982:76; Vince 1994:110). However, neither involvement in exchange nor the place-name element *-wic* need imply that a settlement was in any way urban. The Old English term *wic* has been appropriated to describe an archaeological phenomenon, but it was a common settlement term, applied to a range of sites, most of which did not share the economic and physical characteristics which underpin the current archaeological usage (for this reason the term 'emporium' is used in this paper). While acknowledging their close relationship, it is also important to differentiate between trade and urbanism. Archaeological evidence shows clearly that non-urban communities in England exploited inter-regional or long-distance exchange systems from the fifth century (below; Huggett 1988; Scull 1990). Type B emporia in Hodges' developmental typology are large permanent settlements, but Type A are periodic trading places which need have no permanent inhabitants (Hodges 1982:50-2). These might be linked to existing settlements, but there is evidence that this was not always the case. A number of so-called 'productive sites', where coins and metalwork of the period have been found in profusion but where archaeological intervention has revealed no sign of a settlement, have been interpreted as the sites of fairs or periodic markets: Barham (Suffolk) is an example (Hinton 1986:12; Newman 1992:35; Webster & Backhouse 1991:56).Thus, however likely it may be that there were large permanent settlements at Sandwich or Fordwich in Kent, and whatever the possibility that further coastal trading centres may have existed at sites such as Pagham, Sussex (Munby 1984:322), we remain dependent on the excavated data from three or four sites for direct evidence for urban settlements in pre-Viking England. It is essential, therefore, to review the salient features of this evidence before going on to consider the character, function and context of these settlements in greater detail.

Southampton

The settlement at Southampton was situated on the west bank of the River Itchen *ca* 3 km north of its confluence with the River Test and Southampton Water. It can be identified convincingly with the place-names *Hamwic* and *Hamtun* recorded in eighth- and ninth-century sources, and referred to as *mercimonium* and *villa*; the site is now conventionally referred to as *Hamwic*, emphasizing its status as a trading site (Morton 1992a:1, 26-8; Rumble 1980). Excavations since 1946 have identified and defined the settlement area and approximately three per cent of the total area has been excavated. It is the most extensively investigated of the four English sites, and although analysis is by no means complete the scale of publication of finds and structural evidence from recent excavations also makes it the best documented (e.g. Andrews 1988; Hinton 1996; Hodges 1981; Holdsworth 1980; Morton 1992a). As a result, it has assumed the status of a type-site and a lynch-pin of generalizing interpretation of emporia and their socio-economic role and significance (Hodges 1982a,b; 1988:5). However, it should be borne in mind that this pre-eminence may reflect the current state of knowledge as much as the actuality of the seventh and eighth centuries; the identification of similar sites at London and York in the 1980s tripled the number of archaeologically-known comparanda for Southampton in this country.

At its greatest extent the eighth- and ninth-century settlement covered an area between 42 and 45 ha (Brisbane 1988; Morton 1992a:29-30). The settlement had an orthogonal street configuration, the earliest elements of which are broadly contemporary with a ditch which is assumed to bound the settlement area. The archaeological dating evidence is consistent, and points to the establishment of the earliest elements of the settlement in the years immediately around AD 700. The extent of the settlement area and the degree of control apparent in the street layout and boundary ditch suggest a planned settlement, established by royal initiative. This is attributed to Ine of Wessex, and the political context proposed is the conquest by Cædwalla, his predecessor, of the Isle of Wight and subsequent control over the Solent (Welch 1991:268). Around the middle of the eighth century there appears to have been both an intensification of development within the original settlement area and an expansion of the settlement area, which took in land which had previously been cemeteries (Morton 1992a:53-4); a very similar development has been documented at Ipswich (below). There is strong evidence that the settlement had administrative functions (Rumble 1980), and there was a mint from the 720s if not a little earlier (Metcalf 1988). It has been argued that the settlement may have been established at the site of a royal vill in existence by the middle of the seventh century (Yorke 1982:80), and it is not impossible that some of the earlier burials may be associated with settlement in the immediate vicinity before the end of the seventh century, but otherwise evidence for antecedent settlement on the site is sparse and fragmentary (Morton 1992a:28; Scull n.d.a). The archaeological evidence suggests that the settlement flourished for about 150 years, and was largely abandoned during the middle and later ninth century. It is suggested that it was superseded as a regional administrative centre by Winchester, and that within the immediate environs the focus of population had shifted south-west to the site of the later Saxon and medieval town by the beginning of the tenth century (Morton 1992a:70-6).

Much of the excavated evidence for buildings and associated features is fragmentary (cf. Holdsworth 1980:31-2), but there is good evidence from the Six Dials site which accords with that from elsewhere (Brisbane 1988). Here, rectangular earth-fast timber structures, interpreted as dwelling houses, were identified. They were aligned along the street frontages, and in some cases were associated with smaller structures interpreted as workshops or ancilliary buildings. There is evidence for property boundaries both here and at other sites (Morton 1992a:46). Seven cemeteries have been identified, at least one apparently associated with a church; these do not all appear to be contemporary, and have been assigned to two groups, earlier or later within the lifetime of the settlement (Morton 1992a:41; 1992b; Scull n.d.a). No waterfront structures have been identified.

A wide range of artefacts provides evidence for long-distance exchange contacts: principally pottery and coins, but also vessel glass, millstones and hones. The ceramic evidence indicates links with the Rhineland and the Low Countries, but the bulk of the imported pottery has been provenanced to northern France (Hodges 1981). There is evidence for a wide range of craft production: smithing, glass-working, bone and antler working, copper-alloy working, textile manufacture and pottery production. However, whether the scale and organization of these activities can be considered industrial is open to question. Concentrations of waste may indicate bone and antler-working areas (Riddler n.d.), but otherwise there is little evidence for zoning of craft activity across the settlement area, and at Six Dials the evidence suggests that production was organized by household unit (Hinton 1996:98; Morton 1992a:57). Imported pottery, however, is found in the greatest quantities towards the waterfront (Timby 1988:117-8). There may be a number of reasons for this, but whether it represents mercantile activity, a foreign enclave within the settlement, or chronological factors remains unclear (Hodges 1982:57-8; Morton 1992a:68; Timby 1988:117-8). There is little or no evidence for direct involvement in agriculture or animal husbandry. On the contrary, the faunal evidence suggests controlled provisioning of the settlement from a well-organized rural hinterland (Bourdillon 1988; 1994).

Ipswich

The Saxon settlement, like the medieval and modern town, is situated at the head of the Orwell estuary in south-east Suffolk. It appears to have been a new settlement of the seventh century, but the evidence of cemeteries and fieldwalking indicates fifth- and sixth-century settlements in the immediate area in the Deben and Gipping valleys (Newman 1992), and there are two sixth-century cemeteries within 3 km of the settlement, at Boss Hall and Hadleigh Road (Layard 1907; Newman 1993). As a result of systematic rescue excavation since 1974 approximately two per cent of the Anglo-Saxon settlement area has been excavated and the outlines of its development are fairly well understood (Wade 1988; 1993).

The earliest phase of settlement appears to date from the first half of the seventh century and to have covered an area of *ca* 6 ha. Immediately to the north of this an extensive cemetery is known, which remained in use until the end of the eighth century; other graves elsewhere suggest that this may have been part of a larger zone of burials around the settlement. From the middle of the seventh century Ipswich ware was produced on a large scale in an area *ca* 300 m north-east of the settlement focus. A revetted waterfront has been identified.

The major expansion of the settlement, to cover an area of *ca* 50 ha, occurred in the ninth century. Streets were laid out to an orthogonal pattern to the north of the original settlement, the best evidence for this coming from the Butter Market excavation where the cemetery, abandoned by the end of the eighth century, was superseded at the beginning of the ninth by metalled streets whose frontages were developed with buildings. Associated with this phase is evidence for metalworking and antlerworking, and a pottery kiln which produced Ipswich-ware bottles. Ipswich is unique among the known Anglo-Saxon emporia in that settlement survives on the same site through the Viking period, representing a continuous sequence of occupation and activity from the seventh century to the present day. However, the evidence from the extensive excavations at the Butter Market and Foundation Street indicates that from the late ninth or early tenth century occupation became less dense and the urban landscape changed. At this later period there were fewer buildings, and they were set back from the street frontages (Wade 1993).

Imported pottery, the so-called 'Merovingian blackware', is known from the earliest phases of the settlement, indicating cross-Channel exchange contacts from the first. Imported pottery, hones, quernstones and vessel glass indicate long-distance exchange throughout the eighth and ninth centuries. The main mint for the East Anglian Series R sceattas has been identified as being at or near Ipswich (Metcalf 1984:58; 1994:504, 523), and the apparent paucity of sceattas from Ipswich (Hinton 1986:12; Wade 1988:96) has been redressed by finds from the Butter Market excavation. Rhenish pottery dominates the imported assemblage, but the ceramics also indicate links with Belgium and northern France. Ipswich wares were produced on a large scale from the middle of the seventh century. There is evidence for leatherworking, bone and hornworking, metalworking and textile production across the settlement area, although only at the Butter Market is the evidence sufficiently intense to suggest that it may represent something more than production on a domestic scale. There is also some evidence for functional zoning or differentiation within the settlement. The concentration of pottery production in the Cox Lane area to the north-east of the original settlement nucleus from the middle of the seventh century has already been noted. The number of sceattas recovered from the Butter Market might suggest that the cemetery associated with the original settlement also served as a trading place (Scull n.d.a). A distinction has also been drawn between ninth-century activity at Foundation Street on the east side of the settlement and at the Butter Market in its centre. At the former, buildings are not as dense, evidence for craft activity is not as intense, and environmental evidence suggests cereal cleaning and the keeping of livestock (Wade 1993:148). Contemporary ditches, interpreted as field ditches, have been excavated elsewhere immediately adjacent to the settlement area. The evidence of faunal remains indicates that Ipswich was a consumer rather than a producing or self-sufficient community (Crabtree 1994). However, taken with the differential evidence from the Butter Market and Foundation Street, the evidence for fields might suggest that households on the margin of the settlement were agricultural or semi-agricultural. Something similar has been suggested for the contemporary site at Dorestad, on the Rhine (van Es 1969:194-7; 1973:212-6), which has been identified as Ipswich's primary trading partner. There is also evidence from London which would be consistent with a similar model.

London

London was the site of a mint from the middle of the seventh century, and Bede records the foundation of St Paul's as the seat of Mellitus' Bishopric of the East

Saxons from AD 604 (*HE* II.3). The *Lundenburh* of ninth- and tenth-century written sources has been identified with the area of the Roman walled city, and, despite the lack of archaeological evidence for contemporary occupation, it has been presumed that there was a high-status site within the walls, perhaps within the area of the Roman fort at Cripplegate. However, Bede refers to London as an *emporium* (*HE* II.3), other seventh- and eighth-century sources refer to *Lundenwic*, and there is secure written evidence for the existence there of a trading site by the 670s. In 1984 it was suggested on the basis of finds distributions that this was located not within the Roman walls, but around Aldwych and the Strand (Biddle 1984; Vince 1984; 1990:13-25). Since then a series of excavations and watching briefs has confirmed the hypothesis (Cowie 1988; Cowie & Whytehead 1988; 1989; Rackham 1994:126-7).

The site of the emporium at London has not seen structured long-term campaigns of excavation comparable with those at Southampton and Ipswich, and our understanding of the settlement is correspondingly less precise. The maximum area of seventh- to ninth-century occupation has been estimated at between 55 and 60 ha. There is some evidence to suggest an initial settlement nucleus in the area of the Strand before the middle of the seventh century, with an expansion of the settlement area from the later seventh century, when a waterfront embankment was constructed (Cowie 1992). A few contemporary burials are known, including a late sixth- or seventh-century grave with palm cups from St Martin-in-the-Fields and inhumations which suggest a cemetery in the area of Covent Garden. The evidence appears to suggest a zone of burials skirting the original core of the settlement, similar to the configuration known at Ipswich; there is also evidence from Covent Garden to suggest an expansion of the settlement in the late seventh or eighth centuries over areas previously used for burial (Scull n.d.a). Very little can be inferred about the morphology of the settlement, but it has been assumed that its principal axis ran west-east along the line of what is now the Strand (Cowie & Whytehead 1989:710). It appears to have been abandoned during the second half of the ninth century, and by the early tenth century occupation had shifted to the walled area of the Roman city (Cowie & Whytehead 1989; Vince 1990).

Evidence has been recovered for iron smelting, smithing, copper-alloy working, bone, horn and antler working, and textile production. As elsewhere imported material, in particular pottery and quernstones, provides direct evidence of overseas exchange. The imported pottery is mainly from northern France, but ceramics from the Low Countries and the Rhineland are also represented. Regional contact with other areas of England is suggested by pottery sourced to Surrey, the Chilterns or North Downs, and the East Midlands (Cowie & Whytehead 1988:81). The environmental and faunal evidence from excavations at Jubilee Hall and Maiden Lane indicates that both cereals and meat were being supplied from elsewhere. (Cowie & Whitehead 1988:80; Rackham 1994:128-31). By contrast, assemblages from sites on the margins of the settlement (the Treasury and National Gallery Basement sites) are more characteristic of production than consumption, and may be interpreted as supplying livestock to the Strand settlement (Rackham

1994:131-2). There is also evidence that the settlement was being supplied with sea fish and with foodstuffs such as figs and grapes which may have been shipped from the Continent.

York

Excavation of 0.25 ha east of the confluence of the rivers Ouse and Foss at Fishergate has revealed three structures, boundary ditches and pits dated to between the late seventh or early eighth century and the mid-ninth century (Kemp 1996). The interpretation of this as a small area of a larger settlement comparable to Southampton, Ipswich or London is based on the location of the site and material evidence for long-distance exchange contacts, in particular coins and lava querns which suggest contacts with the Rhineland and pottery which indicates contacts with northern France (Mainman 1993; Rogers 1993). The excavation also yielded evidence for a range of craft activities: antler and bone working; textile production; iron and other metal working (Rogers 1993). The narrow range of species and kill pattern apparent in the faunal material suggests controlled provisioning (O'Connor 1991; 1994). Like the Strand settlement at London, the Fishergate site is close to a major walled Roman city which was a major ecclesiastical centre and which is assumed to have housed a high-status secular establishment. A contemporary cemetery is known *ca* 800 m east of the Fishergate site at Lamel Hill and Belle Vue House, but whether or not the two are directly associated is unclear (Briden 1984a; 1984b; Scull n.d.a; Thurnham 1849).

Comparative discussion

York is the least well understood of the four settlements and, without greater and more detailed data, interpretation of the Fishergate site as part of an extensive settlement on the same scale and with the same functions as those known at London, Southampton and Ipswich—however likely in view of circumstantial evidence—remains hypothetical. The other three settlements clearly exhibit common features. Most strikingly, in their developed phases they are very much larger—in some cases an order of magnitude larger—than contemporary rural settlements. There is no evidence to suggest periodic occupation, and even allowing for a seasonally transient element it is a sound inference that they housed substantial permanent populations; certainly larger than those which can be inferred from contemporary rural settlement evidence. There is consistent and abundant evidence for direct and large-scale exchange contacts with the Continental mainland, and for a range of craft practices. The faunal and environmental evidence indicates that these settlements, or at least constituent elements of them, were net consumers of agricultural produce rather than producers or self-sufficient communities. However, despite these general similarities there are variations in the patterns of evidence which suggest that it would be erroneous to accept too simple or general a characterization of the sites as a group. What follows, therefore, is a brief comparative discussion of morphology and development, economic and administrative function and status, hinterland, and community and demography. It is important when considering these dimensions of the evidence to bear in mind not only the extent to which the characteristics of these sites conform to models of urbanism, but also the extent to which they are shared by other, non-urban, settlements.

Morphology and development

Major episodes of settlement expansion or intensification have been identified at Southampton in the middle of the eighth century and at Ipswich at the turn of the ninth century. At London, the evidence from Covent Garden may suggest a similar expansion of settlement in the later seventh or eighth centuries. At all three sites these appear to represent significant thresholds of urban development.

Further comparative discussion is hampered by the fact that only at Ipswich and Southampton has archaeological investigation been sufficiently extensive to allow secure and detailed inferences. The similarities between Hamwic and ninth-century Ipswich are striking. Both appear to have been laid out over a very short period of time, with metalled streets in an orthogonal pattern, and buildings fronting on to the streets. There is direct evidence for bounded plots at Southampton, and the configuration of structures at the Butter Market and Foundation Street suggests something similar at Ipswich. These are not the classic urban properties of later Saxon and medieval towns, but the suggestion that the expansion of Southampton around the middle of the eighth century saw intensification of occupation within the settlement area as well as an expansion of the settlement area argues that land within the settlement bounds was at a premium, and can be interpreted as a first step towards the subdivisions which produced the characteristic urban strip properties of later towns.

Where Southampton and Ipswich differ is in the date at which the extensive settlement was established, and in what preceded it. Ipswich has been represented as an example of a type A emporium which develops into a type B site (Hodges 1982a:50-65; 1988:3-4), but in fact there appears to have been a permanent settlement for the best part of two centuries before its dramatic expansion early in the ninth century. Although no larger than some contemporary rural settlements at *ca* 6 ha, the density of occupation may have been greater, and the settlement was involved directly in long-distance exchange and—from the middle of the seventh century—was the centre of the major pottery industry of seventh- to ninth-century England. Three components of this settlement have been identified: an occupation area, a pottery manufacturing area, and a cemetery (or cemeteries) which may also have been used as a trading-place. The sixth-century cemeteries at Boss Hall and Hadleigh Road indicate antecedent settlement in the immediate area, and so it is not inconceivable that the seventh-century settlement succeeded a periodic trading place or beach-market here or in the immediate vicinity. The initial settlement at Ipswich is clearly different from other elements of the contemporary settlement pattern in East Anglia, and from Southampton and ninth-century Ipswich, although it is worth noting that the fragmentary evidence for seventh-century activity at Southampton *could* be consistent with a beach-market or type A emporium adjacent to a high-status settlement (Hodges 1982, 1988; Scull n. d. a). However, the configuration of the earlier phases of the Strand settlement at London—an occupation focus with a cemetery or cemeteries on the margins—is very similar to that known at Ipswich. Here, too, the evidence is consistent with a permanent settlement in the seventh century rather than simply a periodically-occupied trading place.

There is a further similarity between Ipswich and London in that, unlike Southampton, households on the periphery of these settlements appear to have been engaged in agricultural activity or animal husbandry. Apart from the identification of the kiln area at Ipswich, and the possibility that the Butter Market cemetery may have been the site of monetary transactions, the bone and antler waste from Southampton provides the only evidence for zoning by economic activity. None of the other evidence for craft production suggests that specific areas of the settlements were given over to specific crafts in the way reflected in documentary sources for eleventh-century Winchester, for instance, but it should be noted that even in Winchester the spatial distribution of finds does not appear to reflect the craft quarters known from documentary evidence (Biddle 1990:42-73). There is little or no evidence from any of the sites for variations in the scale and plan of buildings which might indicate social differentiation, and no evidence for the scale of construction or structural features which might be considered characteristic of high-status buildings (Marshall *et al.* 1984; Williams *et al.* 1985). At Six Dials, Southampton, where the best sample has been excavated, the main structures conform to the criteria of the early medieval building tradition defined by Marshall, Millett and James (1984) and would not look out of place on contemporary rural settlements. None of the sites has evidence for defences, and there is evidence for a physical boundary only at Southampton.

Demography and community

There can be little doubt that, in their prime, Ipswich, Southampton and London had permanent populations which were very significantly larger than any other contemporary settlements, probably in the thousands rather than the hundreds. Estimates of the maximum population at Southampton have ranged between 2,000 and 10,000, with the most recent estimate between 2,000 and 3,000 (Morton 1992a:55); some indication of the order of population size may also be gleaned from the fact that at Domesday Ipswich had a population of more than 2,000 (Darby 1952), but any figure remains guesswork. The possibility that the permanent population of these settlements may have been augmented seasonally or periodically must also be borne in mind. Trade usually requires the presence of both parties to an exchange, and long-distance exchange dependent on crossings of the Channel or the North Sea is more likely to have been a summer than a winter activity. However, there is no reason to assume that a seasonal population need have been entirely foreign. The principals in any large-scale dealing—foreign traders and the representatives of Anglo-Saxon élites—would have been accompanied by their crews, handlers and other assistants. It is argued below that the emporia were integrally linked, economically and socially, to the contemporary rural estate system. During the trading season one might therefore expect an influx from the regional hinterland alone of individuals involved in handling and transportation, for example, or of drovers involved in provisioning the increased population. Whatever the structure of the permanent population, the overall demographic profile may have been abnormal at such times.

The size of these populations is not yet reflected in the number of excavated burials (Scull n.d.a). The largest excavated samples are eighty-one graves at SOU 13, Southampton, dated to the eighth century (Morton 1992a:121-41), and seventy-seven at the Butter Market, Ipswich (Scull n.d.a; n.d.b) and the demographic conclusions to be drawn from the mortuary data are correspondingly limited. Men, women and children were buried at both Ipswich and Southampton. Twice as many men as women have been identified at SOU 13 (Morton 1992a:MF1,C1-7), an imbalance which may perhaps suggest a predominantly male population of craftsmen and traders (Brisbane 1988:104). There is a similar ratio at the Butter Market, but here bone survival was so poor that only twelve individuals could be sexed osteologically and so this evidence—although tantalizing—cannot be used safely to argue for any wider pattern (Cox n.d.; Scull n.d.a).

Evidence from the Butter Market cemetery suggests ranking—or at least higher-status elements—within the seventh- and early eighth-century population at Ipswich. At London there was a higher-status burial at St Martin-in-the-Fields and, although the evidence from Southampton is less easy to interpret, the clearest indications of social differentiation come from burials associated with the earlier rather than later phases of the settlement (Morton 1992a; 1992b; Scull n.d.a). There is little overt evidence for social differentiation among the later graves at the Butter Market, or at the later Southampton cemeteries, and, as noted above, there is nothing about the excavated buildings or settlement layout from Southampton or ninth-century Ipswich to suggest marked social differentiation. This apparent contrast may simply be a function of changes in burial practice during the seventh and early eighth centuries, but it is worth bearing in mind the possibility that it genuinely reflects differences in the social character of these settlements in their initial and developed phases.

Historically, the experience of urbanization has generated changes in demography, community structure, and social relations. One of the most extreme examples is the deracination and the breakdown of traditional social networks experienced by the new urban populations of late eighteenth- and nineteenth-century England. On a different scale, changes in burial practice during the first century AD apparent in the King Harry Lane cemetery at St Albans have been interpreted in terms of social realignment related to the beginnings of town life (Millett 1993). As discussed above, episodes of settlement expansion or intensification which may represent significant thresholds of urban development can be identified at Southampton, Ipswich and London, and there is evidence for contemporary changes in cemetery location and character (Morton 1992b; Scull n.d.a). In theory, this coincidence should allow investigation of whether or not an expansion of settlement, and any associated social change, was accompanied by, or precipitated, changes in demographic structures and patterns of disease, and if so whether these might be considered distinctively urban. The osteological data from Southampton, if presented uncritically, could be used to suggest a change in the sex-structure of the population which coincided with just such a threshold of development; however, the sample is too small to validate this argument (Scull n.d.a).

Economic functions and status

Hodges (1982b; 1988:5) has characterized Southampton as a monopolistic trading and production centre controlled by the kings of Wessex. The evidence for direct involvement in overseas trade at all four sites is overwhelming, but it has been questioned whether a settlement the size of Southampton (or rather a population the supposed size of that at Southampton) could be sustained by its direct involvement in overseas trade alone (Vince 1994:117). This presupposes that the population was economically independent, and can be answered by adopting a redistributive rather than a true market model to explain the settlement's economic function (below); however, it is equally legitimate to query whether craft production, on the scale for which there is evidence, could have directly sustained any significant element of the population. The exclusively riverine and estuarine locations of the emporia strongly suggest that their existence was dependent upon overseas contacts, and it follows from this that the primary importance of the sites to those who administered and maintained them was as long-distance trading centres. The inference from this must be that their manufacturing functions were secondary to their trading functions; if not, we might legitimately expect to find evidence for inland settlements of comparable size with evidence for intensive craft production but not for long-distance exchange on the same scale. Such centres are not known until the later ninth century at the earliest. In any case, it is difficult to argue convincingly that the emporia could deliver craft skills or manufactured products which were not available through contemporary rural economic structures, or indeed through those which had existed in the fifth and sixth centuries. Evidence for the range of craft manufacture apparent at the emporia is known from contemporary higher-status settlements, variously interpreted as estate centres, magnate residences or monastic establishments, such as Brandon (Suffolk) (Carr *et al.* 1988), Flixborough (Humberside) (Webster & Backhouse 1991:94-101), Jarrow (County Durham) (Cramp 1969) and Barking (Webster & Backhouse 1991:88-94). There is also evidence that the rural estate structure accommodated non-agricultural sites with specialist production or extractive functions (Kelly 1992:15-7); the iron-smelting evidence excavated at Ramsbury (Wiltshire) may be part of such a site (Haslam 1980). The one exception to this generalization is the production of Ipswich ware, for which there is nothing comparable in contemporary England. The organization of craft production, and the distribution of its products, is discussed further below.

Hodges (1982b) has stressed the role of such settlements as 'gateway communities', regulated by royal officials to control access to overseas trading partners and to control the profits—both economic and ideological—accruing from long-distance exchange. Although there has sometimes been a tendency to assume that centres such as Southampton were maintained by élites for the purposes of gift exchange (Bourdillon 1994; O'Connor 1994) this is not consistent with the material assemblages (cf. Hinton 1996:93-104), nor with the absence of such centres from fifth- and sixth-century England, when there is clear evidence for the long-distance movement of prestige items and luxuries, almost certainly through the medium of élite gift exchange and redistribution (Huggett 1988; Scull 1990:199-209). A more plausible explanation is that the development or establishment of emporia reflects exchange on a significantly larger scale than in the period before the seventh century, and with a commercial element. These were coin-using sites, and the weight of evidence suggests that the sceatt coinages were genuinely a medium of exchange rather than primarily a display or special-purpose currency (Metcalf 1984). It is recognized that most of the imported items found at emporia are not the main traded goods, but merely the surviving fossils of a bulk movement of perishable organic commodities (Hodges 1982a:104-29; Kelly 1992:14), a definition which should include slaves (Hinton 1996:101; Pelteret 1981). The products of an agrarian surplus must have formed a significant component, and must have been moved in quantities which could be deployed only by the king, the Church and other land-controlling groups. If this was so, the emergence of emporia as an economic phenomenon can be linked to the social and economic dynamics which underpinned the emergence of the Anglo-Saxon kingdom structure in the sixth and seventh centuries (Scull 1993). Trends towards socio-political stratification and the territorialization of authority would have presented the regional élites of the seventh century with the ability to extract, process and dispose of agricultural surplus on a scale which would simply not have been possible under the more fragmented political circumstances and less formal extractive mechanisms of the fifth and sixth centuries, and it is realistic to envisage the resulting larger-scale trade developing along the earlier axes of élite exchange.

There remain, however, the problems of defining the hinterlands served by these settlements, and the mechanisms of exchange. At the highest level their hinterlands can be defined by their direct trading contacts, and this places them firmly in an international context. Hodges's suggestion that each of the major kingdoms of seventh- to ninth-century England was served by one or more such sites has been widely accepted (Hodges 1981:93-4; Welch 1991:268). On the basis of the ceramic assemblages he proposed that Ipswich and East Anglia traded preferentially with the Low Countries and the Rhineland, whereas Wessex, through Southampton, looked primarily towards northern France, but the recognition of new sites at London and York, as well as a more sophisticated understanding of Continental ceramics (cf. Piton 1993), requires that this simple monopolistic model of Continental hinterlands be refined. The written evidence for the involvement of Frisians in cross-Channel exchange has allowed the hypothesis that contact between the major trading centres of England and their counterparts on the Continent was articulated by middlemen, and this might explain the discrepancy between the coin evidence from Southampton, which suggests contacts with the Rhine mouth, and the evidence of the imported pottery, which points to links with northern France (Metcalf 1988:19-20). In this context of broader hinterlands and political geography it is also worth considering the extent to which the locations of the emporia conform to the theoretical prediction that periodic markets or ports-of-trade are likely to be situated on boundaries, or otherwise be territorially marginal. Neither Southampton nor York were on political boundaries, and although Ipswich is within 10 km of the River Stour, conventionally the border between the *prouinciae* of the East Angles and the East Saxons, this area of south-east Suffolk has been identified as a core territory of East Anglian royal power in the seventh century, and so any marginality may be more apparent than real. The model may be more applicable to London, but it would appear that in so far as any of the emporia are territorially marginal this is because they are sited at the junction of land and navigable water, communications being a primary locational factor.

Defining the local and regional hinterlands of the emporia has proved more difficult. In the case of Southampton there is little archaeological evidence for the redistribution of artefacts and commodities known or expected from the trading settlement (Hinton 1996:98-101). The series H sceattas of types 39 and 49, minted at Southampton, may represent a currency produced specifically for use in the trading settlement, and largely restricted to it: finds outside of Southampton are rare, and are mostly within Wessex (Metcalf 1988:18-9; 1994:321-33). There is some ceramic evidence from London for regional contacts inland, and the distribution of series L sceattas minted at London suggests contacts up the Thames valley and into the West Midlands in the eighth century (Metcalf 1994:368-83, 406-15; Vince 1988: fig. 45). The respective distributions of finds of sceattas minted at Southampton and at London appear to be largely complementary (Metcalf 1994:323, 412), which may suggest some genuine economic or political demarcation between the regional hinterlands of the two settlements, and may in turn support the model that each of the emporia served one of the major kingdoms. However, perhaps the most immediate evidence is for the hinterland of Ipswich. Ipswich wares are found on virtually every known settlement site of the seventh to ninth centuries in East Anglia, and there is evidence that imported wares reached some of the same sites, although in much smaller quantities (Rogerson 1988; Wade 1980). Ipswich ware is also distributed more widely through eastern England and is found at London and York, raising the possibility of direct contacts between the major regional trading centres, and redistribution through regional networks. This contrast with Southampton must primarily reflect the simple fact that Ipswich ware is a highly-visible marker which can be sourced to the settlement. However, it also emphasizes that imported perishable commodities such as wine would be no more archaeologically visible in the hinterland than at the port, that most items manufactured at the emporium would be archaeologically indistinguishable from those manufactured at rural settlements, and that, even if commodities were traded for currency, coin-loss is a function of coin-use. Thus, although the scarcity of series H sceattas outside Southampton may reflect a low level of monetary exchange in the hinterland of the emporium, it does not rule out other mechanisms such as barter or controlled redistribution (Hinton 1996:99). The incidence of sceatt finds from rural sites in East Anglia may be consistent with a greater degree of monetary exchange in the immediate hinterland of Ipswich than Southampton, and the possibility that more local periodic trading sites existed alongside the major emporia is raised by evidence from sites such as Barham. As well as the possibility that there may have been regional variations in the articulation of economic relationships between emporia and their hinterlands, it is important to bear in mind that different activities may have generated contacts of varying range and intensity. The known distribution of East Anglian series R sceattas, whose principal mint is thought to have been at or near Ipswich (Metcalf 1994:504), is rather more restricted than that of Ipswich ware (cf. Metcalf 1994: 503, 505; Wade 1988: fig. 54), which may suggest that the factors conditioning circulation of the coinage on the one hand and acquisition and re-distribution of the pottery on the other were not identical. None the less, if it is accepted that exchange through the emporia was both controlled and socially constrained then the range of hinterland contacts would have been very much more restricted than those of later towns.

The faunal assemblages from all four settlements are characterized by relatively little diversity of taxa, which O'Connor (1991:276-82) considers may indicate a command economy. The species range and kill-patterns are not consistent with self-sufficient communities, nor with patterns of market supply as these are understood from later urban assemblages, and, although there is evidence for agriculture or animal husbandry on the margins of the settlements at Ipswich and London, the evidence suggests that all four settlements were provisioned wholly or substantially from an administered hinterland. The inference must be that they were supplied from rural estates, and it is logical to conclude that the élites with an interest in long-distance exchange were those who organized the supply. In the case of Southampton it has sometimes been assumed that this was a royal undertaking, and that the settlement was supplied through royal food rents or similar exactions (Bourdillon 1994:124), but there is no reason to assume this. Hodges's model identifies royal interest in the emporia as in control of trade rather than monopolistic involvement in trade. Documentary evidence from the eighth century demonstrates that other élite groups such as monastic houses were involved in long-distance exchange (Kelly 1992), and so settlements such as Southampton may best be seen as royally-controlled areas where any party with sufficient mobility and resources could trade, subject to tolls and royal control. If trade was founded on the ability to dispose of an agricultural or extractive surplus, this would have been collected and processed through the same estate system as provided the livestock for provisioning, and this raises the possibility that provisioning was undertaken by the parties actually involved in trade.

This has several important implications. It raises the possibility that these were largely if not entirely consumer settlements maintained by the élites with an interest in long-distance exchange, rather than integrated into a local hinterland on a market basis. It also raises the possibility that these were not free or autonomous communities but that a high proportion of the permanent inhabitants held the same status as the majority of the rural population, tied to an estate or estate centre. It has been suggested that the initial sub-division of Alfredian Winchester was into large properties which were in effect urban estates (Biddle 1976:133). It is possible to envisage something similar at Southampton, with a variety of magnates having property interests under overall royal authority. The settlement could therefore be viewed institutionally as a conglomerate of independent elements, each part of a discrete network of estates and estate centres through which the surplus of extensive or multiple holdings could be redistributed or re-deployed.

Under such a system one might expect permanent structures and a permanent population, but—as argued above—there might be considerable seasonal fluctuations in the population level. The primary function of the settlements would be long-distance exchange. The range of craft practices is similar to that known from contemporary rural settlements, and in most cases there is no reason to assume a greater degree of full-time specialization; even at Ipswich, it may be argued that pottery production was likely to be a seasonal rather than a year-round activity. It should also be remembered that the cattle and sheep with which the settlements were provisioned provided hides, horn and bone as well as beef and mutton. It is therefore possible that, in addition to commodities processed inland, some of the raw materials for craft production came in on the hoof and were eaten by the population which then processed their skin and skeletal remains. The evidence from Six Dials, Southampton, has been interpreted to mean that craft production was household-based from the eighth century (Hinton 1996:98). Where not for domestic consumption, both the permanent and transient population of the port might provide a market for craft products, but at present it is difficult to gauge the extent to which there existed any wider sphere of circulation for low-value manufactured items. Wider distribution may to some extent have been linked 'piggy-back' to the redistribution of higher-value or bulk trade goods, but it may be more satisfactory to envisage different spheres of circulation for different categories of imports and local craft products (cf. Hodges 1982a:105, 126-8). There need be no contradiction in the co-existence of different modes of production and exchange related to different levels of activity and different social spheres (cf. Carver 1993:16-7).

Administration

The evidence strongly suggests that these were controlled settlements, presumably administered by officials such as the port-reeve mentioned in the laws of Hlothhere and Eadric (Attenborough 1922:22-3). Both the Strand settlement at London and the Fishergate site at York can be linked plausibly with nearby high-status establishments. There is a temptation to link Ipswich with the seventh-century princely cemetery at Sutton Hoo and the *vicus regius* recorded by Bede at Rendlesham in a context of the 650s or 660s (*HE* III.22), especially now that field survey has identified extensive seventh- to ninth-century settlements at both Sutton and Rendlesham (Carver 1986:33, Figs. 4 and 22; Newman 1992:36-8). However, Ipswich is on a different tidal estuary, 26 km from Sutton Hoo and 38 km from Rendlesham, and any direct administrative relationship is likely to have been with a much closer establishment. Biddle (1976) has linked Southampton with

Winchester, but Southampton had a mint, and there is good evidence that as *Hamtun* it was the administrative focus of *Hamtūnscīr* (Rumble 1980); Winchester's importance may therefore post-date Southampton's decline. This may call into question any automatic distinction between emporia as administered sites and higher-status settlements with administrative functions. At both Ipswich and London there is burial evidence which might be interpreted as indicating a high-status presence in the seventh century, and the fragmentary evidence for high-status seventh-century graves at Southampton may be consistent with an élite presence before the foundation of the eighth-century trading settlement (Morton 1992:28; Scull n.d.a; Yorke 1982:80). However, it is important to emphasize that any administrative status would be vested in the royal vill—or more properly the royal representative—rather than the settlement as a whole. This duality is preserved in the two recorded names for the settlement at Southampton: *Hamwīc* and *Hamtūn* (Rumble 1980).

Conclusions

The settlements at Ipswich, London and Southampton exhibit a range of characteristics which set them apart from contemporary rural settlements. The evidence from Fishergate at York may suggest a similar site.

These settlements may be linked to the development of regional economies and the desire of kings to regulate trade. Generally speaking they may be seen as the legitimate points of access to regional networks of extraction and redistribution, which were themselves controlled by élites. However, it is important not to over-simplify their role and status. They may have existed alongside more local periodic markets, and there are a few instances, notably Barking Abbey, where the range of material suggests that individual high-status sites enjoyed direct access to long-distance exchange. With the exception of Ipswich there is no evidence for production which cannot be found on other settlement sites of the period, and although the numbers of individuals involved may have been greater it is not clear that production was necessarily any more intense or its organization any more industrialized. Functionally, it is their role as ports for long-distance trade which sets these sites apart. Institutionally and socially they may be best seen as integral parts of a primarily redistributive economy and its associated settlement hierarchy, and in this sense they are special-purpose settlements rather than towns offering a diversity of economic services and locked into a system of local and regional markets. This calls into question the extent to which they may be considered central places in the strict sense of Christaller's terminology (Wagstaff 1986); a dendritic model is more appropriate (Astill 1985:227-29; Collis 1986; Hodges 1982a:16-7, 47-50; Smith 1976). Although there may be an unusual demographic structure at Southampton, there is no evidence to consider these autonomous communities, or to presume that their indigenous inhabitants were in any way outside the normal constraints of kinship, custom, rank and law. Institutionally, these settlements can be viewed as agglomerations of discrete social constituents with specific economic and administrative functions which coincide within the same settlement area, but which individually remain more closely linked to their parent systems than integrated with each other.

Both the typology and the sequence of development proposed by Hodges for emporia may now require re-assessment. Periodic fairs on boundaries, Kentish ports of the sixth and seventh centuries, which it has been argued were linked to royal vills, and trading sites like those now being identified in association with central places or chieftain farms in Scandinavia where trade appears to have been directed to or linked with an existing settlement or community (Carver 1993:53-6; Ulriksen 1994), might all be characterized by default as type A emporia. Some further refinement might therefore be useful; a distinction might be drawn, for instance, between genuinely periodic activity at a single-function site and seasonal activity at or near a permanent settlement. Sites such as Barham provide evidence for periodic trading places operating in the hinterlands of larger permanent trading settlements, but which did not themselves develop into such sites; any developmental model should therefore take account of diversity of site character and trajectory of development.

The earliest emporia for which there is good archaeological evidence in England are Ipswich and London, both of which appear to have been established well before Southampton. In some ways, particularly in the evidence from the Butter Market cemetery (Scull n.d.a), there appears to be little archaeological distinction to be drawn on the grounds of size or structure between the Ipswich community and that of a contemporary rural settlement, but the settlement was none the less involved in exchange with the Continental mainland and in large-scale pottery production. Although the evidence from London is fragmentary and does not include any indication of large-scale production, a case can be made that it was initially a settlement similar to that at Ipswich. Both have been characterized as type A emporia (Cowie & Whytehead 1989:709; Hodges 1988:3), but neither conforms particularly well to this model, although it is entirely possible that both may have developed from impermanent periodic sites or been established deliberately to funnel contacts which had previously been targeted directly at élites. Hodges (1988:3-4) has identified Southampton as the first type B emporium. It has been accepted more widely that the eighth-century settlement was a radically new phenomenon, and it has been identified as the first Anglo-Saxon urban settlement (Hodges 1988:5), but this assertion minimizes the special nature of the settlement at Ipswich, and ignores the possibility that something similar may have been associated with the expansion of the Strand settlement in the later seventh century. The evidence also allows the possibility that all three sites originated as small communities with an élite element which were subsequently transformed, a reading which would emphasize a common trajectory of development rather than Southampton's singularity. However, the evidence of coinage, faunal remains and settlement morphology combine to suggest that Southampton may have been more tightly regulated than eighth-century Ipswich or

London. One explanation for this may be sought in the preferential locations for cross-Channel exchange enjoyed by Ipswich and London. Southampton is the furthest from the Continental mainland as well as the last of the three settlements to be established. It is possible, therefore, that the early development of Ipswich and London was linked organically to the growth of existing exchange contacts whereas at Southampton a greater degree of élite intervention was required to establish the trading settlement. The possibility that there was a greater degree of monetary exchange in the hinterland of Ipswich, which might suggest a more developed regional economy, may be consistent with this suggestion.

A strong case for urban status can be made for Southampton and ninth-century Ipswich both by the criteria detailed by Biddle and by more fundamental functionalist criteria. The Strand settlement at London may be considered urban on the grounds of size and economic diversity, but as yet there is insufficient evidence to make any such judgement about the Fishergate site at York. Ipswich in the seventh century is a classic candidate for proto-urban status in that although very similar in many respects to contemporary rural communities it is a manufacturing and exchange centre. However, this illustrates the problem of applying the concept of proto-urbanism to individual sites: although Ipswich expands massively in the ninth century, there is little evidence that its economic base changes, and in its pottery industry Ipswich in the eighth century has a manufacturing element greater and more sophisticated than anything known in contemporary Southampton. Despite the hostile reaction which it has provoked (cf. Clarke & Simms 1985:673; Hines 1994:17) it is therefore difficult to disagree with Richard Hodges's assessment that "a site is either urban or it is not" (Hodges 1982a:23). As argued above, it is unrealistic in a synchronic study to characterize a settlement as proto-urban on the basis of what it later became or because it had individual functions or characteristics which are also found in earlier or later urban settlements. Even where the case for an urban character is strong, it is worth re-emphasizing O'Connor's warning that we should not expect emporia to conform to our modern understanding of a town. Indeed, this reservation should be extended to all classes of settlement site. Like the anachronistic use of the term proto-urban, the spurious certainties embodied in the uncritical application of categories such as 'town', 'village' and 'monastery' to archaeological sites is more likely to obfuscate than enhance our understanding of settlement character and diversity in seventh- to ninth-century England. A more critical approach is needed to characterization and study of both individual settlements and settlement systems, seeking as far as possible to describe and explain them in their own terms, and addressing such issues as function, character, status, differentiation and hierarchy through the material signature of individual sites and their comparative study.

Having said this, it is valid to speak of a proto-urban sequence when seeking from an historical perspective to identify the development of the social and economic conditions which eventually sustained urban settlements. There is clear evidence for social differentiation and economic diversity in seventh- to ninth-century England, but the social organization of production and exchange, like that of lordship and jurisdiction, was articulated through a rural structure of multiple or complex estates and its associated settlement hierarchy (cf. Austin 1986; Blair 1989; Hooke 1986). This sustained a handful of settlements which may be claimed as having an urban character, but these are best seen as integral special-purpose components of the system, rather than as towns in any modern sense. Thus, while it is misleading to apply the term to individual settlements, it may in this context of enquiry be appropriate to consider the economy and society of seventh- to ninth-century England as proto-urban.

Acknowledgements—I should like to thank Giorgio Ausenda and John Hines for their invitation to contribute to the seminar and this volume, and the other seminar participants for their rigorous discussion of the first draft of this paper and the issues it raised. David Hinton, Ailsa Mainman, John Newman, Bob Cowie and Alan Vince also commented on an earlier draft, and I am very grateful for their comments and advice. Responsibility for the opinions expressed, however, remains mine alone.

References

Textual sources:

[Abbreviation: HE = Bede, *Historia ecclesiastica gentis Anglorum*]

Bede
        Historia ecclesiastica gentis Anglorum: see Colgrave & Mynors 1969.

Bibliography:

Ambrosiani, B.
    1988   The prehistory of towns in Sweden. In *The Rebirth of Towns in the West AD 700-1050.* R. Hodges & B. Hobley (eds.), pp. 63-68. (CBA Research Report 68). London: CBA.
Andrews, P. (ed.)
    1988   *The Coins and Pottery from Hamwic.* Southampton: Southampton City Museums.
Astill, G.
    1985   Archaeology, economics and early medieval Europe. *Oxford Journal of Archaeology* 4 (ii): 215-231.
Attenborough, F.
    1922   *The laws of the earliest English kings.* Cambridge: Cambridge Univ. Press.
Austin, D.
    1986   Central Place Theory and the Middle Ages. In *Central Places, Archaeology and History.* E. Grant (ed.), pp. 95-103. Sheffield: Sheffield University.
Biddle, M.
    1973   Winchester: the development of an early capital. In *Vor- und Frühformen der europäischen Stadt im Mittelalter.* H. Jankuhn, W. Schlesinger & H. Steuer (eds.), pp. 229-261. (Abhandlungen der Akademie der Wissenchaften, Philologische-historische Klasse Serie 3, 83). Göttingen: Akademie der Wissenchaften

1976   Towns. In *The Archaeology of Anglo-Saxon England*. D. Wilson (ed.), pp. 99-150. Cambridge: Cambridge University Press.

1984   London on the Strand. *Popular Archaeology* 6 (i): 23-27.

1990   *Object and Economy in Medieval Winchester*. Oxford: Oxford Univ. Press.

Blair, J.
1988   Minster churches in the landscape. In *Anglo-Saxon Settlements*. D. Hooke (ed.), pp. 35-58. Oxford: Basil Blackwell.

1989   Frithuwold's kingdom and the origins of Surrey. In *The Origins of Anglo-Saxon Kingdoms*. S. Bassett (ed.), pp. 97-107. London: Leicester Univ. Press.

Bourdillon, J.
1988   Countryside and town: the animal resources of Saxon Southampton. In *Anglo-Saxon Settlements*. D. Hooke (ed.), pp. 177-195. Oxford: Basil Blackwell.

1994   The animal provisioning of Saxon Southampton. In *Environment and Economy in Anglo-Saxon England*. J. Rackham (ed.), pp. 120-125. (CBA Research Report 89). York: CBA.

Briden, C.
1984a   Belle Vue House. *Interim* 9/3: 11-13.

1984b   Belle Vue House. *Interim* 9/4: 5-8.

Brisbane, M.
1988   Hamwic (Saxon Southampton): an 8th-century port and production centre. In *The Rebirth of Towns in the West AD 700-1050*. R. Hodges & B. Hobley (eds.), pp. 101-108. (CBA Research Report 68). London: CBA.

Carr, R., A. Tester & P. Murphy
1988   The Middle Saxon settlement at Staunch Meadow, Brandon. *Antiquity* 235: 371-377.

Carver, M.
1986   Project Design. *Bulletin of the Sutton Hoo Research Committee* 4.

1993   *Arguments in Stone: Archaeological Research and the European Town in the first Millennium*. Oxford: Oxbow.

Chagnon, N.
1968   *Yanomamö: The Fierce People*. Orlando, FL: Holt, Rinehart and Winston.

Clarke, H., & B. Ambrosiani
1991   *Towns in the Viking Age*. London: Leicester University Press.

Clarke, H., & A. Simms
1985   Towards a comparative history of urban origins. In *The Comparative History of Urban Origins in non-Roman Europe*. H. Clarke & A. Simms (eds.), pp. 671-714. (British Archaeological Report, S 255). Oxford: BAR..

Colgrave, B., & R. Mynors
1969   *Bede's Ecclesiastical History of the English People*. Oxford: Oxford University Press.

Collis, J.
1986   Central Place Theory is dead: long live the Central Place. In *Central Places, Archaeology and History*. E. Grant (ed.), pp. 37-39. Sheffield: Sheffield University.

Cowie, R.
1988   A gazetteer of Middle Saxon sites and finds in the Strand/Westminster area. *Transactions of the London and Middlesex Archaeological Society* 39: 37-46.

1992   Archaeological evidence for the waterfront of Middle Saxon London. *Medieval Archaeology* 36: 164-168.

Cowie, R., & R. Whytehead
  1988   Two Middle Saxon occupation sites: excavations at Jubilee Hall and 21-22
          Maiden Lane. *Transactions of the London and Middlesex Archaeological
          Society* 39: 47-163.
  1989   Lundenwic: the archaeological evidence for Middle Saxon London. *Antiquity*
          241: 706-718.
Cox, M.
  n.d.   The human bones from St. Stephen's Lane/Butter Market. In *Anglo-Saxon
          Cemeteries at Boss Hall and St. Stephen's Lane/Butter Market, Ipswich.* C. J. Scull
          (ed.), n.d.b.
Crabtree, P.
  1994   Animal exploitation in East Anglian villages. In *Environment and Economy
          in Anglo-Saxon England.* J. Rackham (ed.), pp. 40-54. (CBA Research
          Report 89). York: CBA.
Cramp, R.
  1969   Excavations at the Saxon monastic sites of Wearmouth and Jarrow: an
          interim report. *Medieval Archaeology* 13: 24-66.
Darby, H.
  1952   *The Domesday Geography of Eastern England.* Cambridge: Cambridge U. P.
Dyer, C.
  1985   Towns and cottages in eleventh-century England. In *Studies in Medieval
          History presented to R. H. C. Davis.* H. Mayr-Harting & R. I. Moore (eds.),
          pp. 91-106. London: Hambledon Press.
van Es, W.
  1969   Excavations at Dorestad, a pre-preliminary report. *Berichten van de
          Rijksdienst voor het Oudheidkundig Bodermonderzoek* 19: 183-207.
  1973   Die neuen Dorestad-Grabungen, 1967-72. In *Vor- un Frühformen der
          europäischen Stadt im Mittelalter.* H. Jankuhn, W. Schlesinger & H. Steuer
          (eds.), pp. 202-217. (Abhandlungen der Akademie der Wissenchaften,
          Philologische-historische Klasse Serie 3, 83). Göttingen: Akademie der
          Wissenchaften.
Esmonde-Cleary, S.
  1989   *The Ending of Roman Britain.* London: Batsford.
Evans-Pritchard, E. E.
  1940   *The Nuer: A description of the modes of livelihood and political institutions
          of a Nilotic people.* Oxford: Clarendon Press.
Haslam, J.
  1980   A Middle Saxon iron smelting site at Ramsbury, Wiltshire. *Medieval
          Archaeology* 24: 1-68.
Hawkes, S.
  1982   Anglo-Saxon Kent c. 425-725. In *Archaeology in Kent to AD 1500.*
          P. Leach (ed.), pp. 64-78. (CBA Research Report 48). London: CBA.
Heighway, C. (ed.)
  1972   *The Erosion of History. Archaeology and Planning in Towns.* London: CBA.
Hill, D.
  1988   Unity and diversity: a framework for the study of European towns. In *The
          Rebirth of Towns in the West AD 700-1050.* R. Hodges & B. Hobley (eds.),
          pp. 8-15. (CBA Research Report 68). London: CBA.
Hines, J.
  1994   North-Sea trade and the proto-urban sequence. *Archaeologia Polona* 32: 7-26.

Hinton, D.
1986   Coins and commercial centres in Anglo-Saxon England. In *Anglo-Saxon Monetary History: Essays in Memory of Michael Dolley.* M. Blackburn (ed.), pp. 11-26. Leicester: Leicester University Press.
1990   *Archaeology, Economy and Society: England from the Fifth to the Fifteenth Century.* London: Seaby.
1996   *The Gold, Silver and Other Non-ferrous Objects from Hamwic.* Stroud: Alan Sutton.

Hodder, I.
1986   *Reading the Past: Current Approaches to Interpretation in Archaeology.* Cambridge: Cambridge University Press.
1981   *The Hamwic Pottery: The Local and Imported Wares from 30 Years Excavations at Middle Saxon Southampton and their European Context.* (CBA Research Report 37). London: CBA.

Hodges, R.
1982a   *Dark Age Economics: The Origins of Towns and Trade AD 600-1000.* London: Duckworth.
1982b   The evolution of gateway communities: their socio-economic implications. In *Ranking, Resource and Exchange. Aspects of the Archaeology of Early European Society.* C. Renfrew & S. Shennan (eds.), pp. 117-123. Cambridge: Cambridge University Press.
1988   The rebirth of towns in the early Middle Ages. In *The Rebirth of Towns in the West AD 700-1050.* R. Hodges & B. Hobley (eds.), pp. 1-7. (CBA Research Report 68). London: CBA.

Hodges, R., & B. Hobley (eds.)
1988   *The Rebirth of Towns in the West AD 700-1050.* (CBA Research Report 68). London: CBA.

Holdsworth, P.
1980   *Excavations at Melbourne Street, Southampton, 1971-76.* (CBA Research Report 33). London: CBA.

Hooke, D.
1986   Territorial organisation in the Anglo-Saxon West Midlands: Central Places, Central Areas. In *Central Places, Archaeology and History.* E. Grant (ed.), pp. 79-93. Sheffield: Sheffield University.

Huggett, J.
1988   Imported grave goods and the early Anglo-Saxon economy. *Medieval Archaeology* 32: 63-96.

Kelly, S.
1992   Trading privileges from eighth-century England. *Early Medieval Europe* 1: 3-28.

Kemp, R.
1996   *Anglian settlement at 46-54 Fishergate.* (The Archaeology of York 7/1). York: York Archaeological Trust.

Layard, N. F.
1907   An Anglo-Saxon cemetery in Ipswich. *Archaeologia* 60: 325-352.

Mainman, A.
1993   *The Pottery from 46-54 Fishergate.* (The Archaeology of York 16/6). York: York Archaeological Trust.

Marshall, A., M. Millett & S. James
1984   An early medieval building tradition. *Archaeological Journal* 141: 182-215.

Metcalf, M.
  1984   Monetary circulation in southern England in the first half of the eighth
            century. In *Sceattas in England and on the Continent*. D. Hill & D. Metcalf
            (eds.), pp. 27-69. (British Archaeological Report 128). Oxford: BAR.
  1988   The coins. In *The Coins and Pottery from Hamwic*. P. Andrews (ed.),
            pp. 17-59. Southampton: Southampton City Museums.
  1994   *Thrymsas and Sceattas in the Ashmolean Museum Oxford*, Vol. 3. London:
            Royal Numismatic Society Special Publication 27c.

Millett, M.
  1990   *The Romanization of Britain*. Cambridge: Cambridge University Press.
  1993   A cemetery in an age of transition: King Harry Lane reconsidered. In
            *Römerzeitliche Gräber als Quellen zu Religion, Bevölkerungsstruktur und
            Sozialgeschichte*. M. Struck (ed.), pp. 255-282. Mainz: Gutenberg
            Universität.

Morton, A.
  1992a   *Excavations at Hamwic: Volume 1*. (CBA Research Report 84). London: CBA.
  1992b   Burial in Middle Saxon Southampton. In *Death in Towns: Urban Responses
            to Dying and the Dead, 100-1600*. S. Basset (ed.), pp. 68-77. London:
            Leicester University Press.

Munby, J.
  1984   Saxon Chichester and its predecessors. In *Anglo-Saxon Towns in Southern
            England*. J. Haslam (ed.), pp. 315-330. Chichester: Phillimore.

Newman, J.
  1992   The late Roman and Anglo-Saxon settlement pattern in the Sandlings of
            Suffolk. In *The Age of Sutton Hoo: The Seventh Century in North-Western
            Europe*. M. Carver (ed.), pp. 25-38. Woodbridge: The Boydell Press.
  1993   The Anglo-Saxon cemetery at Boss Hall, Ipswich. *Bulletin of the Sutton
            Hoo Research Committee* 8: 32-35.

O'Connor, T.
  1991   *Bones from 46-54 Fishergate*. (The Archaeology of York 15/3). London:
            CBA for York Archaeological Trust.
  1994   8th-11th century economy and environment in York. In *Environment and
            Economy in Anglo-Saxon England*. J. Rackham (ed.), pp. 136-147. (CBA
            Research Report 89). York: CBA.

Pelteret, D.
  1981   Slave raiding and slave trading in early England. *Anglo-Saxon England*
            9: 99-114.

Piton, D. (ed.)
  1993   *Travaux du Groupe de Recherches et d'Études sur la Céramique dans le
            Nord - Pas-de-Calais*. Numéro hors-série de Nord-Ouest Archéologie.

Rackham, J.
  1994   Economy and environment in Saxon London. In *Environment and Economy
            in Anglo-Saxon England*. J. Rackham (ed.), 126-135. (CBA Research Report
            89). York: CBA.

Reece, R.
  1980   Town and country: the end of Roman Britain. *World Archaeology* 12 (i): 77-92.

Renfrew, C., & P. Bahn
  1991   *Archaeology: Theories, Methods and Practice*. London: Thames & Hudson.

Riddler, I.
    n.d.   The spatial organisation of boneworking. In *Wics and Emporia: the pre-Viking Trading Centres of Europe*. D. Hill, R. Cowie & I. Riddler (eds.). Sheffield: Sheffield University (forthcoming).

Rogers, N. S. H.
    1993   *Anglian and Other Finds from 46-54 Fishergate*. (The Archaeology of York 17/9). London: CBA for York Archaeological Trust.

Rogerson, A.
    1988   Appendix 1: The medieval pottery. In *The Fenland Project 3: Marshland and the Nar Valley, Norfolk*. R. J. Silvester (ed.), pp.174-175. (East Anglian Archaeological Report 45). Gressenhall: Norfolk Archaeological Unit.

Rumble, A.
    1980   HAMTUN alias HAMWIC (Saxon Southampton): the place-name traditions and their significance. In *Excavations at Melbourne Street, Southampton, 1971-76*. P. Holdsworth (ed.), pp. 7-20. (CBA Res. Rep. 33). London: CBA.

Schiffer, M. B.
    1976   *Behavioural Archaeology*. New York: Academic Press.

Scull, C.
    1990   Scales and weights in early Anglo-Saxon England. *Archaeological Journal* 147: 183-215.
    1993   Archaeology, early Anglo-Saxon society and the origins of Anglo-Saxon Kingdoms. *Anglo-Saxon Studies in Archaeology and History* 6: 65-82.
    n.d.a   Burials at *emporia* in England. In *Wics and Emporia: the pre-Viking Trading Centres of Europe*. D. Hill, R. Cowie & I. Riddler (eds.). Sheffield: University Press (forthcoming).
    n.d.b   *Anglo-Saxon Cemeteries at Boss Hall and St Stephen's Lane/Butter Market, Ipswich* (in prep.).

Shanks, M., & C. Tilley
    1987   *Re-constructing Archaeology: Theory and Practice*. Cambridge: Cambridge University Press.

Smith, C.
    1976   Exchange systems and the spatial distribution of elites: the organisation of stratification in agrarian societies. In *Regional Analysis*. C. Smith (ed.), pp. 309-374. London: Academic Press.

Timby, J.
    1988   The Middle Saxon pottery. In *The Coins and Pottery from Hamwic*. P. Andrews (ed.), pp. 73-122. Southampton: Southampton City Museums.

Thurnham, J.
    1849   Description of an ancient tumular cemetery, probably of the Anglo-Saxon period, at Lamel-Hill, near York. *Archaeological Journal* 6: 27-39, 123-136.

Trigger, B.
    1989   *A History of Archaeological Thought*. Cambridge: Cambridge Univ. Press.

Ulriksen, J.
    1994   Danish sites and settlements with a maritime context, AD 200-1200. *Antiquity* 261: 797-811.

Vince, A.
    1984   The Aldwych: mid-Saxon London discovered? *Current Archaeology* 8 (iv): 310-312.

Vince, A. *(cont.)*

1988   The economic basis of Anglo-Saxon London. In *The Rebirth of Towns in the West AD 700-1050*. R. Hodges & B. Hobley (eds.), pp. 83-92. (CBA Research Report 68). London: CBA.

1990   *Saxon London: an Archaeological Investigation.* London: Seaby.

1994   Saxon urban economies: an archaeological perspective. In *Environment and Economy in Anglo-Saxon England.* J. Rackham (ed.), pp. 108-119. (CBA Research Report 89). York: CBA.

Wade, K.

1980   The pottery. In *Excavations in North Elmham Park 1967-72.* P. Wade-Martins (ed.), pp. 413-478. (East Anglian Archaeological Report 9). Gressenhall: Norfolk Archaeological Unit.

1988   Ipswich. In *The Rebirth of Towns in the West AD 700-1050*. R. Hodges & B. Hobley (eds.), pp. 93-100. (CBA Research Report 68). London: CBA.

1993   The urbanisation of East Anglia: the Ipswich perspective. In *Flatlands and Wetlands: Current Themes in East Anglian Archaeology.* J. Gardiner (ed.), pp. 142-151. (East Anglian Archaeology 50). Norwich: Scole Archaeological Comittee.

Wagstaffe, M.

1986   What Christaller really said about Central Places. In *Central Places, Archaeology and History.* E. Grant (ed.), pp. 119-122. Sheffield: Sheffield University.

Webster, L., & J. Backhouse

1991   *The Making of England: Anglo-Saxon Art and Culture AD 600-900.* London: British Museum.

Welch, M.

1991   Contacts across the Channel between the fifth and seventh centuries: a review of the archaeological evidence. *Studien zur Sachsenforschung* 7: 261-269.

Williams, J.

1984   A review of some aspects of Late Saxon urban origins and development. In *Studies in Late Anglo-Saxon Settlement.* M. Faull (ed), pp. 25-34. Oxford: Oxford University Department for External Studies.

Williams, J., M. Shaw & V. Denham

1985   *Middle Saxon Palaces at Northampton.* Northampton: Northampton Development Corporation.

Yoffee, N., & A. Sherratt

1993   *Archaeological Theory: Who Sets the Agenda?* Cambridge: Cambridge University Press.

Yorke, B.

1982   The foundation of the Old Minster and the status of Winchester in the seventh and eighth centuries. *Proceedings of the Hampshire Field Club and Archaeological Society* 38: 75-83.

Discussion

DUMVILLE: Would you explain, in as few words as seems decent, the difference between a redistributive and a market economy.

SCULL: Karl Polanyi (1957) defined redistribution as the aggregation of resources to the centre and out again, and drew a clear distinction between this and market economics. Since then the idea has been greatly developed and refined. I use the term to describe the exaction and re-deployment of resources by élites through non-market mechanisms. One theoretical example would be the 'cross-subsidizing' of specialist constituents (such as sheep farms or iron-smelting sites) of multiple estates. Another would be the re-deployment of a surplus from point A to point B through a network of estate holdings and their tied labour: which is how I imagine goods for trade reaching sites such as Southampton.

HOOKE: Droitwich almost certainly did not disappear from the record between the late Roman and the Middle to Late Anglo-Saxon period. So *wics* could remain functioning throughout this period. We have the documentary evidence and we are just beginning to get the archaeological evidence. Some *wics* may, moreover, have been places of marketing and exchange. Goods were probably coming in to London in exchange for salt.

SCULL: The question is whether you see the functioning of Droitwich as exchange or whether you see it as something controlled—with a controlling interest which didn't need to exchange wood for salt. It could bring wood in, and it could have salt, and it could then dispose of the salt as it liked.

HOOKE: It depends how you envisage the organization behind it, which I think is open to question.

SCULL: When considering Droitwich in the same breath as Southampton, we also have to remember that we are not comparing like with like. The term *wīc* has been appropriated by archaeologists to mean large, permanent, trading settlements, and it is those settlements I am discussing. It does not follow that all Anglo-Saxon -*wīc* names have this meaning: clearly they do not. There is a danger of confusion because archaeologists are using an Anglo-Saxon term in a loose and simplistic way.

DUMVILLE: There is a serious point here, isn't there? Terms travel across disciplinary boundaries all too easily and can cause a good deal of confusion.

SCULL: Where Della and I seem to disagree is over the extent to which extractive production such as of iron and salt fits the sort of model I'm advocating.

HOOKE: It may be more than pure extraction. There is trading going on there.

SCULL: I'm talking about fundamental production. The land produces more than crops and cattle: iron smelting and salt boiling can be accommodated within a 'controlled' estate model as easily as farming.

HOOKE: I nevertheless think you don't get salt from Droitwich unless you give something in return.

SCULL: If salt production were controlled by a magnate he could appropriate the salt and dispose of it as he wished, or control access to the resource as he wanted.

FOWLER: There is another dimension here which is very much concerned with exchange. I think the whole idea of not just a settlement site, *a* Droitwich, having a specialist function, but also the idea of people having specialist functions is actually a very modern idea bound up with specialist production. The traditional way of producing salt or mining iron ore is that the people who do it are actually farmers who make salt or mine when they are not farming. Smallholders working the coal mines in the Forest of Dean would be a living example—there were very few of those who were full-time miners. It's the same with lead mines in Derbyshire. It seems to me that this sort of fuzziness about what people do actually fits the redistributive model you're talking about very well.

SCULL: I agree. There is no reason why we should consider all specialist production as full-time. For instance, pottery production at Ipswich may well have been seasonal. We also have to think about different models of control in the Saxon countryside. There are two ways that control may have operated: one is strict lordly control from the top down; the other is lordly control exercised through the extraction of rents—and that beyond a certain level of extraction people are left to get on with whatever they want to do. This second situation would allow one to argue that there is a level of activity which allows élites to dispose of very large surpluses through places like Ipswich and Southampton; but that underneath this there is a level of economic activity—production and exchange—which the more humble people are involved in.

FOWLER: Sorry if I just come back to this. We are dealing with an agrarian society and I should have stressed this yesterday, it was so important, but I got involved in the details. It's so easy to make an assumption that because we are dealing with farmers, peasants to use a slightly derogatory term, that farming is a non-specialist activity. If everybody farms but some people mine iron ore and coal or whatever, it is only they who are specialized. But in fact, of course, farming actually encompasses activities which are just as specialist as getting iron ore out, like being a specialist cattle farmer or being the one who looks after the swine or whatever it is in your particular area. And from that sort of activity could come some of your supplies, for your *wics* or whatever you want to call them, which are then redistributed.

SCULL: That's exactly what I mean.

HAWKES: How do you see the monastic centres in relation to 'centres of production' and even 'farms'?

SCULL: Exactly the same way. I would take the view that there is no fundamental difference between an ecclesiastical lord and a secular lord: I don't see that one would need to make any economic distinction. Some sites which have been identified as monastic at this time are clearly very rich. Barking has a lot of evidence for overseas trade. Unfortunately little has been published on the recent Barking excavations.

DUMVILLE: I don't see much of importance there; not very much in literary terms.

SCULL: But I wouldn't see the need to draw an economic distinction between an ecclesiastical and a secular landlord. Is there anything in the documents which says that ecclesiastical landholding is economically different from landholding by a secular lord?

CHARLES-EDWARDS: Two points, one more precise, one much more general. The more precise one is that there is evidence for administrative and seigneurial interventions in trading networks in terms of the capacity to make the people who transport the stuff go long distances. And if they transport commodities like wine, it gives them a major advantage in terms of trade networks. Now is that an interaction of political or of seigneurial power with trade networks?

CHARLES-EDWARDS: I was wondering about the example you gave (Southampton) with a hinterland which was very narrow. It's precisely the function of seigneurial intervention to overcome the problems of transportation.

SCULL: That is more or less how I would see these sites operating in seventh- to ninth-century England. I do not see the *wics* having a hinterland in the conventional, market model, sense of the word. I would see as their hinterlands just those estate networks through which lords could move goods. What I'm trying to say in this paper is that the *wics* are aggregates of the end points of a whole series of such chains. They are not integrated settlements. They are the individual end points of interlinked elements of seigneurial power.

CHARLES-EDWARDS: There is a classic point made by A. H. M. Jones (1974:37) about ancient city trade, which is that, apart from high-cost, low-weight goods, every other commodity that was moved any distance was traded by sea or river. It was only the state that had the power to transport bulky goods over land. All you're saying is that lords had taken over the power of the Roman Empire.

That in fact relates to my second point which is on your characterization of Middle-Saxon England. Again it comes from A. H. M. Jones, namely that the economy of the Roman Empire was essentially rural and that most towns were political entities first and economic entities only second. Approaching Middle-Saxon towns from the Roman Empire going forwards in time, rather than from the later medieval or modern periods going back, one would not set up criteria of urban status that privileged the economic sphere as against the political.

SCULL: I explain in my paper my reasons for privileging economic criteria. There is no reason to apply classical models to this period.

CHARLES-EDWARDS: But seigneurial power is even more important.

SCULL: The towns, if we can possibly call them towns, in this period are primarily economic phenomena. Control of economic activity that takes place in them may be 'important' but political power is vested in other communities and other settlements.

CHARLES-EDWARDS: I think, in fact, that consumption was more important than economic production, and that towns were primarily units of consumption.

SCULL: As I have argued in my paper, there are very few settlements known from seventh- and eighth-century England which can be considered urban in any way and I do not think that they really are such units of consumption. The élites consume, the élites redistribute, but they mostly do this on other sites: consumption and investment are targeted elsewhere.

HINES: It seems to me that it's precisely into this gap that the concept of proto-urbanism can usefully be dropped. Could I first just clarify one point that seemed to be an important element in your slight embarrassment over dealing with this topic. You emphasize that the fundamental factors which governed the existence and success or failure of Anglo Saxon towns were not culturally specific. Does this mean that the lack of distinctively Anglo-Saxon towns, as opposed to towns in the Anglo-Saxon period, leaves them with little or nothing to contribute to an ethnographic study?

SCULL: Ethnography may help us understand those sites—or the broader phenomena of urbanism—but it is very difficult to contribute to an ethnography from such fragmentary material evidence. Also, I have difficulty in putting Anglo-Saxon towns, urban settlements, on the same level of cultural specificity as Anglo-Saxon kinship systems.

HINES: I wouldn't disagree with that. Although I also think one might want to take in the idea of proto-, quasi-, or pseudo-urban states [laughter].

SCULL: I deny proto-, quasi-, or pseudo-urban *sites*, not states.

HINES: Which indeed you deny, and I would like to talk about that a bit more. When you discuss the definition of a town is, or of 'urban character', you seem to come down on the side of the 'bundle of criteria' as the best answer.

SCULL: My instinct has always been not to use the word 'town' in this period, but to talk more generally of urban settlements. The problem with the bundle of criteria, as adopted by Biddle (1976) is that possession of more than one of these allows a claim to urban status. However, there are sites in seventh- to ninth-century England with two or more of these characteristics which are clearly not towns, nor are they urban. For this reason I think that this approach must be refined, and I prefer broader functionalist criteria.

HINES: One of the recurrent words in your characterization of what you think is really urban is 'complexity', and I made a connection between complexity and the presence of more than one definitive characteristic.

SCULL: Yes. I would see thresholds of population size and economic complexity as the fundamental criteria for urban status. These would imply something beyond a direct agricultural economy.

HINES: That's an interesting point if such thresholds vary from culture to culture rather than a threshold being something which is uniform world-wide. Looking at the bundle of criteria, which you are not relying on but which is very important to the general concept of 'the town' in studies of this period, those criteria seem to me to have a clear common factor which effectively defines a town as what I would call a site of specialized exchange. This is not just material exchange, not just the exchange of goods, but also the social exchange involved in organizing people, judging people, participating in all sorts of interpersonal transactions. I'm not suggesting that every site of specialized exchange is a town. But this function seems to me to be central to the concept of a town. Beyond that I would agree that a town must be a built site and, if it cannot be permanent, it must at least be durable. And rather than talking about thresholds of size, I would like to build in to the notion of size some more fluid concept of growth; a 'town' must somehow have the capacity to grow beyond a certain culturally specific threshold.

SCULL: According to this model a wide range of non-urban sites have to be considered as possible towns?

HINES: Yes. I think what I'm doing is allowing all of these sites to fit into a system which has a substantial proto-urban zone within it; an urban margin at one end and a purely rural margin at the other. There are then these intermediate phenomena.

SCULL: You're thinking of a series of interactions and functions which are characteristic of towns. I would argue that a great many sites which are not and cannot be considered urban have a range of such functions, hence the example of later Medieval monastic houses in my paper. It is a feature of this period that many functions integrated in towns in the Roman period or the later Middle Ages are disaggregated and performed at rural sites. This does not make them towns, or urban—any more than the large villas of fourth-century Britain or the manors of fifteenth-century England were urban. For those reasons I am very unhappy with viewing Barking Abbey or Flixborough as proto-urban.

HINES: I agree with you fully that one's talking about a proto-urban atmosphere, as it were, rather than a series of proto-urban sites. But in the archaeological record I would suggest that we can observe the emergence of a markedly increasing level of specialized exchange at sites like Flixborough, Brandon and so on, and that perhaps we should consider this as experimentation in the establishment of built sites for that specialized exchange. I would take consumption as an important symptom of this specialized exchange. The sites are not there purely to consume: the sites are there for social functions and along with that you have high consumers at those particular sites.

SCULL: Those sites can be viewed as magnate residences drawing on and processing the resources of rural estates. Nothing about the range of intensity of activities is inconsistent with this, or requires us to consider them as proto-urban.

POWLESLAND: I have a number of questions about the *wīc* sites. I'm very worried about the suggestion that there are just a few of them—I think there were lots of them—and I see absolutely no reason why many have not been lost, because as beach markets are affected by changes in the coastline, we would have lost a lot of these sites. One of the things that worries me about seeing these as sort of embryonic urban centres is that the mechanics of their working is that, as far as we can see on the Continent, they are not places that are thriving every day of the year. So people leap into their long boats and cruise up and down the coast stopping off at a particular location for what is, in effect, a large fair. And the population there during the rest of the year is not necessarily huge. But there will be a time of the year when each one of these sites is at its most active and supports a very large population. And the question then is to what degree is that population controlled? I would argue that it is very, very tightly controlled. One of the mechanisms of control is that if you're a Frankish trader and you go to Hamwic you have to transfer your Frankish currency to English sceattas before you can use them and you are not allowed to trade before you've done that: through that mechanism the king exerts absolute control over these sites. Thus they are very much not urban, because they have a very particular function, and that function is directly controlled. Hamwic is the most important simply because we have the best evidence in this country from there. I don't know what anybody else thinks about the position of the Roman site of *Clausentum* there, because it seems to me critical that we have failed miserably to look at this site, which has a gas works sitting on top of it, and a large part of it is Roman. It is one place in which there is good reason to believe we may have a rural *villa* contained within a Roman fortification.

SCULL: In general we appear to agree.

WOOD: I was delighted with your comments about Franks in the pre-circulated paper. It seems to me that the Frankish evidence does not point the way that Richard Hodges argues it does, although most people follow Richard Hodges's model. Indeed, I did originally. One of the problems with the Frankish evidence is that it does not suggest royal control at all. Part of the problem here is the absence of excavation on French emporium sites. But it is very peculiar that Quentovic is close to the royal villa at Crécy. The best evidence comes from Dorestad where the dendrochronology gives very precise dates. And Dorestad was being laid out in precisely the years when the Franks had no power whatsoever. In fact it is emerging that Dorestad was being laid out in the decade after a major royal defeat. The dates for Dorestad are almost impossible to fit into Frankish politics. One may actually have to come up with a much more complicated view of the relationship between merchants and kings, which I thought you were actually suggesting.

SCULL: I'm trying to do two things: I'm trying to say what conventional wisdom is, and I'm trying to offer some sort of critique. One point is that this simple typology of type A and type B *emporia* does not really work, but this is not surprising given the amount of new data since Hodges published it in 1982. It does not look as though Ipswich is precisely the same as early London. Neither of them appears to be the same as Southampton. There are indications that there may have been a precursor settlement to *Hamwĩc*. If Southampton was genuinely a new planned settlement, then it is plausible that it was established as a controlled area where dues were exacted on trade, and the coin evidence may support this. Contemporary Ipswich and London were different. At Ipswich the formal laying out occurred during the ninth century, by which time there had been a permanent settlement with a manufacturing element and trade with the Continent for two-hundred years. It is difficult to accept the primacy given to Southampton by Hodges given that London and Ipswich developed as trading centres long before Wessex appears to have got in on the act. Hamwic may look most impressive in the eighth century, but you can't really argue that East Anglia or Mercia are economically retarded. The situation is more complex than has been represented. I'm not really sure yet how we can go about explaining it or modelling it. I like the idea of these sites as places of free enterprise under control—the places where people who have control over the networks of redistribution can take their surplus to get rid of it for profit and pay their dues to the king at the same time. I want to see no more royal control than that; though we must consider royal protection.

POWLESLAND: It is not royal imposition on the landscape, but the king's shopping centre here. Yet whatever goes on is under control.

WOOD: Control will vary according to how successful an individual king is and so on...which raises questions about lordship.

HÄRKE: I find the beach-market model very attractive. On the other hand I wonder whether it does not simply shift the question of where full-time specialist population was to somewhere else. Jankuhn (1984) has pointed to the existence of *Langwurten* along the North German and, I believe, the Dutch coast, where a specialist craft production is supposed to have been going on without much if any agricultural elements. Unfortunately I have not seen any of these sites published. He considered them as transitional between the conventional, agriculturally orientated *Wurten* with some craft activities, like Feddersen Wierde, and the full blown Hedeby-type emporia. If you think about emporia or their predecessors as essentially seasonal beach markets, then you might still wonder whether such full-time craft production existed, and how the interaction between all these elements should be conceived.

SCULL: I don't deny beach markets, but I'm very uneasy at the thought that in Anglo-Saxon England we might postulate hundreds of them without any direct material evidence whatsoever.

DUMVILLE: But we have a good deal of numismatic evidence for other kinds of markets.

SCULL: Not a good deal. There are a few sites such as Barham, which I mention, with coins but nothing to suggest a settlement. In my paper I mention these and the possibility of other, periodic markets operating alongside the *emporia*. I'm not totally unhappy about a beach market every two miles, but I'm not very happy with the idea either. There are certainly sites in western Britain where material found at beaches suggests trading sites.

HINES: There is a substantial project going on around Wijnaldum in Frisia which suggests that that was a centre of production and exchange (Gerrets 1995). I believe this site shows a sequence of increasing specialization of precisely the kind that Heinrich has described.

HÄRKE: Jankuhn called it the emancipation of crafts from the rural background.

HINES: Besides that, there is a clustering of *terpen* there, one of which as I understand it specialized in both craft production and indeed consumption. As far as I know what was produced is nothing extraordinary in relation to other production sites of the same period.

Turning from this to the question of the diversity of different early urban settlements, I'm sure that here the notion of geographically discrete trading networks is a significant one: the idea that sites differ because they were associated with their own trading areas and so the circumstances for their development were different. I think this is borne out by the study of numismatic distribution (cf. Hines 1996).

WOOD: I think Quentovic poses problems. It is an absolutely standard Merovingian royal mint. And it was a place where such travellers as Theodore and Hadrian could be controlled.

HINES: Quentovic is not an ideal type-site in this respect. I'm much happier coping with apparent inconsistencies and incongruencies at Dorestad than in relation to Quentovic.

FOWLER: The impression I get is that all down the coast of eastern England there were a series of car boot sales in fields which were scattered with coins, but which don't have any physical installations.

SCULL: There are so-called 'productive sites', known from surface finds of coins and metalwork, but in most cases it is unclear whether these represent settlements or some other activity.

FOWLER: I would like to return to the question of the definition of a 'town'. 'Urban' clearly does not exist in the period that we are talking about in western Britain. But if you're looking at this sort of definition on a functional basis, it seems to me that there are one or two places, especially in Somerset, where a number of those functions which are urban criteria occurred not on a single site but dispersed in different but linked places, in particular at Glastonbury, but also at the two Cadburys. At the one I excavated, we had a hill fort which you can take as an archaeological site and say, "That is not urban; there is nothing urban about the hilltop there". People were struggling to maintain a sort of way of life up there which looked backwards to later Roman Britain rather than forwards. The one thing it is not is 'proto-', as in 'proto-urban'. But people were living there. There were big buildings there, there are important functions being carried out on the hill top behind *de novo* defences, and a kilometre below it you've got the quay at the tidal end of the river there.

SCULL: What you have there is probably similar to Biddle's model of the disaggregation of urban functions and their later re-integration.

FOWLER: And the next stage goes back to your other point about control—royal control, seigneurial control—is that once you've got these different functions coming together spatially, then it seems to me that your local lords will say, "this is a good idea; there are things going on here; I really ought to bring this together in political terms"—so that a number of elements which perhaps sprang up in different ways formed an entity. I don't know whether that's how it happened. It could be what happened: that you got the imposition of political control on to something which had developed over a century or so, say during the fifth or sixth century.

DUMVILLE: In relation to Glastonbury, could you specify which period you are talking about?

FOWLER: I was thinking of the fifth and sixth centuries. In that sense you can say it's not relevant because the whole point about this is not that it's urban but that the culture is pre-Saxon. That's the interesting thing about Somerset at this stage. In that sense it is representative of quite a large area of western Britain, it is pre-cultural-Saxon and pre-political-Saxon.

DUMVILLE: I'm not sure we're engaging in directly with Chris's point about the prejudicial nature of using terms like 'proto-'. You can speak of people on the hilltop who maintained a series of functions which at other times could be described as partly urban, but dismiss 'proto-urban' because the situation and the suffix look in different directions. You're within the same framework as Chris, looking at things in diachronic terms in order to judge definitions. Is that way of looking at things not itself prejudicial?

SCULL: In this context I'd say it's prejudicial. If we want to understand the place of such settlement in seventh- to ninth-century England rather than to explain the development of towns, then it may be inappropriate to adopt a diachronic rather than a synchronic perspective.

CHARLES-EDWARDS: There are serious dangers in trying to use a single category of 'town' defined by a single set of criteria. That's just exactly what historians have been trying to get away from by using *burh* as against *wīc*.

SCULL: Indeed as I emphasize in my paper, I think it is important to realize that the *wics* do not represent a continuing tradition of urban development.

LENDINARA: I'm becoming confused [laughter]. The criteria you list in your paper, are they the criteria for being a town?

SCULL: They are the criteria which people have suggested. If these can be identified there is a case that a settlement may be a town.

LENDINARA: Then what would be the most important difference between a *burh* and a *wīc*? What's going to be our model for a *burh* and what for a *wīc*?

CHARLES-EDWARDS: Well a *burh* is fortified. That's one criterion.

DUMVILLE: It can be a matter of how you deploy the judiciary; or mean a fortification against Vikings.

POWLESLAND: There are 690 places that claim this status in England and if you analyse them all you will find that while at one end you have your Winchesters, and at the other end there are a very large number of much smaller sites that can never be considered in any way as being substantially urban in the way that somewhere like Winchester was. But they have a gateway through which you can administer control; an enclosed area which only needs a fence around it with a gateway to which you can actually apply a door.

LENDINARA: Does the *burh* need specific legislation?

POWLESLAND: The *burh* had a legal status in the Late Anglo-Saxon period.

LENDINARA: Yes, but what about seigneurial power? I have been hearing about seigneurial authority and seigneurial control. Would that be an important matter for a *burh* and a *wīc*? Can there be a *burh* without seigneurial authority?

DUMVILLE: There is again a problem of definition of terms to start off with.

SCULL: It is a question of terminology. Archaeologists have appropriated the term *wīc* to denote a particular site type of the seventh to ninth centuries. There are three or four such sites: large settlements which appear to be primarily involved in long-distance trade. There are then at a later period of enclosed or fortified settlements to which the term *burh* has been applied, which in their date, layout and size, and apparently in their legal status and their organizational context, are quite different from the earlier sites which we call, for want of a better term, *wics*. We need to adopt a more neutral, less loaded terminology.

DUMVILLE: We need a new terminology, and then we could discuss the Old English terminology in relation to a modern terminology. At the moment we are confusing the two all the time.

CHARLES-EDWARDS: But we must pay attention to the words that they used.

HINES: I think there is another important point here. Chris's approach is thoroughly archaeological and therefore tends to define these things in terms of material characteristics. A significant point here is the question of how far a town or an urban settlement or even urbanism is essentially a cognitive concept. Towns in a given culture may be what people *see* as being distinctive. I can fit Winchester as a sort of *urbs* as easily into my understanding of the range of urbanism and its related phenomena in the Middle Anglo-Saxon period in this light as well as by what was actually happening there and what is left behind in the ground.

SCULL: I still think the danger there is not a cognitive problem but rather a terminological one. The danger is that we are using heavily loaded vocabulary which is inappropriate to the period. I have no problems with most of your individual points, but I am troubled by the use of the term 'town' in that sort of sense when we discuss seventh- to ninth-century England. In using loaded terminology we are erecting a barrier to real understanding of settlement character and function.

AUSENDA: I would like to comment on the 2:1 ratio of men to women found in your urban cemeteries. In contemporary pre-industrial society this occurs in cases where male children are the main source of manual labour for the extended family. Thus among Beni Amer in the mountains the ratio of men to women is 55:45, in the shanties on the edge of town it is the same, whereas in the town itself it goes down to 50:50. In your case, however, such a lopsided 2:1 ratio may be due to the presence of seasonal craftsmen in the town, as used to be the case until not so long ago, whereby at certain times of the year there were many more men than women.

SCULL: That did indeed occur to me. I would agree that there could be a seasonal element to activity at those sites, and that population size may fluctuate seasonally. The men who cart the fleeces, the wool, and other products into the *wics* may also have swollen the population temporarily. The other point to make is that the excavation in Southampton which gives us that 2:1 ratio is a relatively small area and the number of bodies is only about 80. It may very well be that this genuinely reflects the wider population structure, but it's equally possible that it is a function of a small sample, a product of a sample bias.

HÄRKE: There are several Anglo-Saxon cemeteries which have a similarly strange ratio between the sexes without being unusual otherwise.

FOWLER: We were talking earlier on about a frontier society (pp. 135-6, 163, this vol.), and I wonder whether, paradoxically, the *wics* and all your other 'towns' in the way they actually operated might have been more frontier in the eighth century than in the fifth century. If, for instance, you take Jennifer Bourdillon's evidence about the cattle from Hamwic, where they were evidently slaughtered, you've got to think of cowboys coming down from Basingstoke driving their cattle herds (Bourdillon 1994). Taking Giorgio's point, that is likely to have been in September, at the end of the feeding time. So that for a brief few days Hamwic would not have looked like a car boot sale on a Sunday, but like a frontier town. Extra people would come in along with the cattle, whereas the products of sheep were coming on wagons. It would have been a sort of Wild West.

DUMVILLE: We now have to look for the saloons.

AUSENDA: Your remark about saloons is interesting. One would think that in such pre-industrial societies these institutions did not exist. Not so. In 1842 two

German explorers, Ferdinand Werne and his brother, followed the Egyptian governor of the Sudan on his expedition to conquer the Hadendowa, a semi-nomadic pastoralist population in eastern Sudan. When they got to the area where the Hadendowa roamed, they found villages surrounded by Hadendowa encampments where there were several beer joints where they could drink "refreshing" sorghum beer (Werne 1852:95)!

POHL: All I can do is to jump in with Continental parallels again. One is about terminology. Certainly in central Europe whatever is called *urbs* in the early Middle Ages has nothing to do with a town whatsoever. The same applies to *burg*: you can even see this in the semantic development of the word. In German, a *burg* is nothing like a town but a fortified settlement on top of a hill. And in Italian *borgo* is not a town but a kind of shanty town, a settlement outside the walls. As the use of the term spread, it took on different characteristics, so we cannot argue on the basis of the terminology of the early Middle Ages.

The second point is about royal or state control. What seems to me to be a feature that occurs in many countries in the early Middle Ages is that most trading settlements which became important were not established near political centres but rather somewhere else, for instance in Italy in places like Venice or Comacchio in the north, or Amalfi in the south: places which were not political centres to begin with. And the attempt of the Langobardic or later kings of Italy to establish control over trade was not really an attempt to control the traders, but rather to control distribution. We have Langobardic legislation from the eighth century involving very detailed regulation of trade routes and trading activities along the River Po and its tributaries, where two things seem to be important: one is that supply must be guaranteed in a general way, and the second that money has to go from the traders to the king—and it is specified how much and at which point. There is no attempt to tell the traders, who clearly came from Comacchio or Venice, how they were to organize themselves in the towns where they stayed even though at that point these places were more or less under Langobardic royal control.

AUSENDA: It would be like attempting to choke the hen laying the golden eggs to establish too rigid a control over traders. The rulers' interest would be to favour trade while imposing reasonable taxes on the incoming or outgoing goods.

POHL: There is something else about specialized activities in the Langobardic laws, in the regulations for the *magistri commacini*, which regulated timber work, and especially cases like timber buildings being erected and breaking down or falling on somebody's head or injuries during work and things like that. This gives the impression that there must have been a very specialized group of people, not necessarily staying in one place, but employed in timber work, which links up quite well with examples that Peter Fowler gave that such work is a very specialized activity which could not easily be done by just anybody.

References in the discussion

Bibliography:

Biddle, M.
  1976   See References at end of paper.
Bourdillon, J.
  1994   See References at end of paper.
Gerrets, D.
  1995   The Anglo-Frisian relationship seen from an archaeological point of view. In
              Friesische Studien II. V. F. Faltings, A. G. H. Walker & O. Wilts (eds.),
              pp.119-128. Odense: Odense University Press.
Hines, J.
  1996   Coins and runes in England and Frisia in the seventh century. In
              Amsterdamer Beiträge zur älteren Germanistik 45: 47-62.
Hodges, R.
  1982   See entry 1982a in References at end of paper.
Jankuhn, H.
  1984   Die historische und sozialgeschichtliche Bedeutung der Handelsplätze. In
              *Archäologische und naturwissenschaftliche Untersuchungen im deutschen
              Küstengebiet. Vol. 2: Handelsplätze des frühen und hohen Mittelalters.*
              Deutsche Forschungsgemeinschaft (ed.), pp.441-449. Weinheim: Chemie.
Jones, A. H. M.
  1974   *The Roman Economy: Studies in Ancient Economic and Administrative
              History.* Oxford: Blackwell.
Polanyi, K.
  1957   The economy as instituted process. In *Trade and Market in the Early
              Empires.* K. Polanyi, C. Arensberg & H. Pearson (eds.), pp. 243-270.
              Glencoe, IL: The Free Press.
Werne, F.
  1852   *African wanderings or, an expedition from Sennar to Taka, Basa and Beni-
              Amer, with a particular glance at the races of Billad Sudan.* London:
              Longman, Brown, Green & Longman.

JANE HAWKES

Dept. of English Literary and Linguistic Studies, University of Newcastle, Newcastle upon Tyne, GB-NE1 7RU

Introduction

The topic of this paper will be the 'symbolic life' of the Anglo-Saxons in England between the sixth and eighth centuries, as represented in the extant visual arts of that period. In this instance, 'symbolic life' is understood to refer to those views of life and death apparently current among the Anglo-Saxons in England which are revealed symbolically in their visual arts (i.e. by the symbols used in the decoration of their artefacts).

The vagaries of time have ensured that these artefacts are, to all intents and purposes, limited to metalwork, manuscripts and stone sculpture, the more perishable media of leather, textiles and wood having, with one or two remarkable exceptions, been lost to us. The parameters of this discussion will further be limited to those motifs (or symbols) most commonly employed in the decoration of these artefacts during the centuries in question, namely animals and interlace.

Given that this period, historically, is that which marks the transition from 'pagan' to 'Christian' in Anglo-Saxon England, it is to be expected that the visual arts produced in this 'transitional culture' (Geertz 1973) will reflect changing outlooks, as well as some sense of continuity; in some cases these attitudes will be clearly expressed, in others they will be less apparent.

The limits of debate

Discussion (or indeed, definition) of the 'pagan' and 'Christian' aspects of Anglo-Saxon culture is not the concern of this paper, but it is necessary to identify some basic preconceptions regarding these communities as a background against which to view the art (Cohen 1985; Geertz 1973). In doing this, however, we come to the first of a number of problems inherent in discussing the subject of 'symbolic life' represented in the visual arts, namely the relationship between art and the culture which produced it.

Within an early Christian community, art can generally be regarded as produced by a people (whatever their particular status or role in that community), whose production, use and knowledge of art is explicitly recorded for observation and analysis. This is largely because early Christian cultures were literate, and have left written commentaries on their art and its perceived role in their society which, with some application, can be interpreted by later scholars.

311

For early pagan (pre-Christian) communities, however, who are largely illiterate, such insights are not as readily available, and *our* perception of the relationship between the art and the people who produced it depends on a process of 'disciplined' reconstruction; in this it is often the case that art is as helpful in interpreting ethnography, as ethnography is in interpreting the art (Morphy 1989:10-2). Much therefore, depends on the insights of the interpreter.

As regards Anglo-Saxon England, the Christian culture introduced to the Germanic peoples of Britain in the late sixth and early seventh centuries, whether (immediately) originating in the Mediterranean world or the Irish world, was not only highly literate, but imbued with symbolic meanings and significances, particularly in its perceptions of life and death. This is apparent in a number of cultural phenomena, not least of which is the literature.

It was generally believed that mankind's understanding of life was viewed "through a glass, darkly" (I Cor. 13, 12), and a full(er) understanding was thus necessary for the attainment of everlasting life; this could be achieved through knowledge of the sacred texts. However, it was never sufficient to understand the mere narrative of the text; rather, it was vital to appreciate what it revealed of God's scheme of salvation for mankind. Thus, an interpretative approach to the sacred texts was established early, being found within the Bible itself (e.g. I Cor. 10, 1-11), and even more so in the great body of exegesis which soon proliferated, deliberately cultivating the notion of symbolic meaning, of ways of reaching a fuller understanding of 'God's Truth'. For example, Augustine (*De civitate Dei*, XV.27, (*C.C.S.L.* 48, 497), declared:

> *Nec inaniter ista esse conscripta putare quisquam vel durus audebit, nec nihil significare cum gesta sint, nec sola dicta esse significativa non facta, nec aliena esse ab ecclesia significanda probabiliter dici potest; sed magis credendum est et sapienter esse memoriae litterisque mandata, et gesta esse, et significare aliquid, et ipsum aliquid ad praefigurandam ecclesiam pertinere.*

> (No one, however stubborn, will venture to imagine that this narrative [the Bible] was written without an ulterior purpose; and it could not plausibly be said that the events, though historical, have no symbolic meaning, or that the account is not factual, but merely symbolical, or that the symbolism has nothing to do with the Church. No; it is rather to be believed that the writing of this historical record had a wise purpose, that the events are historical, that they have symbolic meaning, and that this meaning gives a prophetic picture of the church....) (Trans. H. Moisl, pers. comm.).

A symbolic approach to life is thus clear in the literary arts of early Christian communities in western Europe.

Not surprisingly, the visual arts played a very similar, indeed complementary role, reflecting the symbolic meanings and reinforcing them. Moreover, this not only provided the *raison d'être* for early Christian art, but also one of its principal justifications in a world cautious of raising up "graven images" (Exodus 20, 4). In the often-cited words of Gregory the Great at the end of the sixth century, art could be used to instruct, and in that, was justified (Epist. 13 to Serenus, Bishop of Marseilles, Letters XI.xiii, *P.L.* 77:1128):

Aliud est enim picturam adorare, aliud per picturae historiam quid sit adorandum addiscere. Nam quod legentibus scriptura, hoc idiotis praestat pictura cernentibus, quia in ipsa etiam ignorantes vident quid sequi debeant, in ipsa legunt qui litteras nesciunt. Unde et praecipue gentibus pro lectione pictura est.

(A picture is to be revered in so far as that which is to be revered through the story which the picture tells, is to be learned. As scripture is to those who can read, so a picture stands before unlearned viewers, for in it the ignorant see what they ought to follow, and in it, those who do not know letters, can read. A picture is, first and foremost, that which serves in the place of reading for the heathen) (Trans. H. Moisl, pers. comm.).

In the early eighth century, John of Damascus restated the case, somewhat more emotively (*Adversus Constantium*. Trans. Didron 1886:3):

Etiam loquuntur [imagines] nec mutae prorsus sunt omnisque sensus expertes...imagine loquente, enarrat; sensumque ac mentem aperit, ut miris eos infandisque modis aemulemur.

(Images speak. They are neither mute nor lifeless blocks.... Images open the heart and awake the intellect, and in a marvellous and indescribable manner, engage us to imitate the persons they represent).

It is clear that the views represented by writers such as Gregory and John of Damascus, which were current in the Christian communities of the Mediterranean world between the sixth and eighth centuries, were known in Anglo-Saxon England. They are evident, for example, in Bede's work (*ca* 672-735 AD), particularly his allegorical interpretation of Solomon's Temple {*De Templo, II* (*C.C.S.L.* 119A:212-3)}, and his account of the artefacts imported to Northumbria from Italy at the end of the seventh century {*Historia Abbatum* 6. See Plummer 1896:369-70, cf. Homily on Benedict Biscop, *Homilies* I.13 (*C.C.S.L.* 122:93)}.

Furthermore, it is clear that the visual arts were not only written about, but also played a physical role in the Christian communities of Anglo-Saxon England. Apart from material evidence (for summary see, e.g. Dodwell 1982:1-24), we have written accounts, such as that of the painted boards diligently accumulated to adorn the church at Monkwearmouth. These depicted the Virgin, the twelve apostles, the Apocalypse, and events from the Old Testament and the Life of Christ, while their arrangement within the church deliberately drew out meaningful juxtapositions (*Historia Abbatum* 9):

...de concordia veteris et novi Testamenti summa ratione compositas exibuit; verbi gratia, Isaac ligna, quibus inmolaretur portantem, et dominum crucem in qua pateretur aeque portantem.... Item serpenti in heremo a Moyse exaltato, Filium hominis in cruce exaltatum conparavit.

(...ably describing the connection between the Old and New Testament, as, for instance, Isaac bearing the wood for his own sacrifice, and Christ carrying the cross on which he was about to suffer...again the serpent raised by Moses in the desert was illustrated by the Son of Man exalted on the cross) (Trans. Plummer 1896:373).

Thus, within a clearly Christian context in Anglo-Saxon England, we might expect the visual arts to have a double, but complementary function: to elucidate the subtleties of the Christian views of life, and to propagate those views.

Against this, however, the particular 'meaning' of any given piece of art may not always be clear. For instance, an iconic (figural) image, one based on look-alike criteria, such as an image of Christ and his apostles, can be interpreted by someone who has never seen such an image before; it can be recognized, at the very least, as an illustration of thirteen people. In such images there is a recognizable relation between form and content which can be expanded upon as needed.

Where animal and interlace patterns are concerned, however, there may be a relatively arbitrary relation between the signifier (the form of the pattern) and the signified (the content, or what is referred to). Such art requires an interpreter who is familiar with the 'code' for the meaning, if any, to be grasped. Not only is the purpose of such art often hidden from a late twentieth-century audience, it may be that even within their own context, the 'transitional' culture of sixth- to eighth-century Anglo-Saxon England, non-iconic patterns were deliberately employed for their very ambiguity. It is possible that they were not easy to decode even for a contemporary audience, and were not meant to be.

Symbols, particularly non-iconic symbols, are by their very nature ambiguous, and so are malleable; they can express things in ways which allow for their common form to be retained and shared among members of more than one community, whilst not imposing upon them the constraints of uniform meaning. While this permits a potential diversity of meanings for a contemporary audience, it also raises the possibility that "everything may be grist to the mill of symbolism" (Cohen 1989:18) for late twentieth-century audiences, particularly those who try to reconstruct the context for looking at, and the knowledge required to interpret, any meaning(s) in the art.

This is certainly the case with the visual arts of 'pagan' Anglo-Saxon England, as this culture was virtually illiterate. Contemporary written accounts of the (pre-Christian) religious beliefs and rituals of the early Anglo-Saxons are non-existent, and the only records we have of its perceptions of life and death are either comments by (often hostile) 'outsiders', or descriptions far removed from the culture concerned, in both time and place.

There are, for instance, accounts by Roman commentators, discussing the Germanic tribes making inroads to the Empire (e.g. Tacitus, *Germania*, first century AD, or Procopius, *De bello gothico*, sixth century). There are also early Christian accounts, which include 'histories' (e.g. Gregory of Tours, *Libri historiarum decem*, sixth century. Trans. Thorpe 1974:153-4), and ecclesiastical decrees and denouncements of 'pagan' rites {e.g. Councils of Auxerre 573-603 AD; Cæsarius of Arles, d. 542 AD; Martin of Braga, d. 560 AD; Isidore of Seville, d. 636 AD (See Klingender 1971:117)}. Descriptions such as these are marked by attitudes, generally unfavourable, towards peoples regarded as either 'barbarians' or 'heathens', and fall far short of the standards of objective and/or empathetic observation expected (if not always attained) in modern anthropological studies. Furthermore, they concern the Germanic tribes of mainland Europe, and not those who had been settled in the British Isles for some generations by the sixth century.

Commentaries originating in Anglo-Saxon England are few and far between, and, emerging from Christian contexts, use the material in a generally uncomplimentary manner for didactic purposes. Bede's discussion (in *De temporum ratione, P.L.* 90:293-578) in the eighth century, for instance, (re-used in the tenth century by Ælfric in his homily *De falsis deis.* Trans. Pope 1968:676-712), is an explanation of Germanic paganism in terms of classical (Greek and Roman) paganism, both being largely misunderstood and viewed as morally reprehensible {cf. Aldhelm's letters, d. 685 AD (see Klingender 1971:117; Lapidge & Herren 1979:155-70)}.

Later references are perhaps less pejorative, but they are nevertheless of doubtful relevance to sixth-century Anglo-Saxon England. These sources, usually accepted as the most untainted, are the twelfth- and thirteenth-century literary versions of Scandinavian mythology. Most, however (like the earlier Old English poetry written down in the late tenth and eleventh centuries), were shaped within Christian communities and cannot really be taken as direct evidence of the beliefs of the earlier pagan peoples of Scandinavia (Bailey 1980:101-3), let alone those of fifth- and sixth-century Anglo-Saxon England.

One solution to the problem of reconstructing an understanding of the 'symbolic life' of the pagan Anglo-Saxons from their visual arts has been to extract references to any given symbol from the entire corpus of 'relevant' literature. The assumption is that if a number of sources, widely separated in time and place from the object of reference, seem to agree in interpretation, it is likely that such an explanation comes close to providing an insight as to the 'meaning' of that symbol current among those by whom, and for whom, it was originally produced. For example, if Tacitus describes attitudes towards 'boars' current among early Germanic tribes, and a similar attitude is reflected both in Old English literature and the later Scandinavian material, this is regarded as a valid basis for interpreting images of boars decorating sixth-century Anglo-Saxon artefacts. This, in fact, has been the methodology commonly adopted by those discussing the Germanic animal art of Anglo-Saxon England (e.g. Åberg 1926, 1943; Klingender 1971; Speake 1980).

Inferring the significance of a symbolic motif (such as boars) in Anglo-Saxon art according to this procedure can, however, be problematic. The written sources *do* relate to such different aspects of various cultures and are of such different dates from the archaeological sources which they are invoked to elucidate that their use of similar elements cannot mean those elements are necessarily invested with the same meaning.

Tacitus (*Germania* VL), for instance, mentions the boar in the context of the ritual worship of a goddess (by the *Aestii* in the first century AD); her emblem was "the device of a wild boar", which, when worn by her acolytes, "instead of armour or human protection...ensures the safety of the worshipper even among his enemies" (*insigne superstitionis formas aprorum gestant: id pro armis omnique tutela securum deae cultorem etiam inter hostis praestat.* Trans. Stephenson 1894:54-5). In Saxo Grammaticus' late twelfth- or early thirteenth-century *Gesta Danorum* (Trans. Elton 1894:49) the boar's head is also mentioned as an emblem, among the Danes, but of Odin/Woden, who, in later Scandinavian literature, is described as the god of death and battle, while in the (ninth-century) *Anglo-Saxon Chronicle* he is credited with being the ancestor of almost all the Anglo-Saxon royal dynasties (Garmonsway 1972:13, 16, 18, 20, 24, 50, 66). The boar also features in the Old English poem *Beowulf*, written down in the late tenth or early eleventh century; here a boar-banner is given to Beowulf by Hrothgar (l. 2152) and boars decorate the warriors' helmets (e.g. ll. 1286, 1453). Later (Scandinavian) references to Freyr and Freyja seem to attest to a continuing function of boars as symbols of fertility (Davidson 1964:98-9).

Having accumulated these references to boars and their association with religious ritual, fertility, tribal identity, and the male concerns of battle and dynastic power, there is then the problem of interpretation. Because symbolism is a particularly imprecise language which has to be deciphered, much depends on this process. In this particular analogy, any image of a boar could be interpreted as having a multivalent significance, referring simultaneously to fertility, protection, victory and kingship; indeed, some scholars have put forward such inclusive interpretations of animal symbolism in attempts to create single 'Grand Narratives' (e.g. Salin 1959; Speake 1980; see Poulsen 1986 for further comments). Other scholars, however (e.g. Hicks 1986; 1993; Stevenson 1974; 1983; Wickham-Crowley 1992), have mediated this tendency, attempting to assess the material evidence in light of both the literary references and its archæological context. Images of boars decorating protective armour, such as helmets and shields (e.g. the Sutton Hoo helmet (Evans 1986: pl. III)) may thus be interpreted as having a primarily apotropaic significance, but this reference is slightly different from the use of such images to decorate weapons {e.g. a sword from the River Lark, Cambs. (Speake 1980:78)}, where the boar-motif may also have had a more 'magico-religious' significance, the weapon being regarded as imbued with the aggressive and, one might have hoped, victorious nature of the beast decorating it. In turn, such symbolism is distinct from that associated with images of boars decorating women's bracelets, brooches and pendants {e.g. Faversham and Kingston Down, Kent; Womersley, Yorks. (Speake 1970: pl. 1d; 1980: figs. 11k-l, 11p)}, where they may have been associated with fertility. This interpretation is given credence by the high percentage of boar-tusk amulets discovered in women's (but not men's) graves in Anglo-Saxon England in the fifth and sixth centuries (Meaney 1981:131-47). Again, a different symbolism may attach to the use of images of boars to decorate men's jewellery, such as buckles and shoulder-clasps {e.g. the Faversham buckles (Speake 1980: pls. 6c, 8a-c); or the Sutton Hoo shoulder-clasps (Evans 1986: pl. VI)}; in contexts such as these, the image of the boar seems to have signified (high) social rank or status. Used to decorate harness mounts {e.g. Faversham (Speake 1980: fig. 11i)}, it is unclear whether the boar-symbol had a primarily protective function, or signified the social rank of the rider; it may be that in this context both were equally present.

Of necessity, therefore, the relation between art and its culture, and our understanding of the symbolic motifs decorating the artefacts produced in the context of 'pagan' Anglo-Saxon England, have to be consciously, and carefully reconstructed. It is likely that no single explanation can be provided; the likelihood that we are dealing with a diversity of meanings, each of which may be both specific and multivalent, must be accepted.

Animal symbolism

Due to the problems inherent in de-coding the animal symbolism of Anglo-Saxon art, it is perhaps understandable that most discussion of the subject has, until recently, favoured examination of the stylistic development of the various motifs. This has charted the evolution of two distinct methods of representing animals in the visual arts: Salin's so-called 'Style I' and 'Style II'.

Put briefly (as it is not my intention to contribute to this aspect of animal art studies), Salin's Style I animals, which embrace, as a sub-group, the so-called Helmet-style animals current in Anglo-Saxon art in the fifth and sixth centuries, can be defined as creatures whose bodies have been exploded into a number of component parts (the head, trunk and limbs) which are arranged on the field of decoration, sometimes with no apparent 'physiological' relationship to each other (e.g. Haseloff 1974; Kendrick 1938: figs. 15-16).

It is no longer accepted that this type of animal motif "was frankly and fundamentally ornamental, merely a device for filling spaces on the flat" (Smith 1923:10), but such is the nature of these creatures, that any symbolism once associated with them is, in most cases, considered to be irretrievable.

It has alternatively, been argued (Klingender 1971:103-6) that the essentially undecipherable form is the (symbolic) point: the animals were deliberately broken up to render them, and their potential powers, innocuous. Whether this was the case, there is one apparent exception to the general obscurity of the symbolism of these animals, and that is their use on gold bracteates, objects which form part of the grave-goods of high-status burials in England in the sixth century (Leeds 1946:22; Smith 1923:8-10; Speake 1980:66-76).

On the bracteates, Style I creatures are associated with images (often very stylized), originally derived from imperial portraits (the bracteates themselves having apparently evolved from imperial coinage). Moreover, the bracteates from Anglo-Saxon England are exclusively associated with female burials, strongly suggesting that they functioned as women's dress accessories (Speake 1980:66). In these instances, Style I animals may well have played an integral part in the symbolic manifestation, not only of (high) social status, but of female identity (although see Speake 1980:66-76 for possible amuletic significance). However, while this may be true of Style I animals on the bracteates, it does not follow that they would necessarily have had the same symbolic function on other artefacts, where the relationship between artefact, gender, social status, signifier and signified is more ambiguous.

Salin's Style II creatures, sometimes referred to as Ribbon-style animals, or zoomorphic interlace, and current in Anglo-Saxon art by the late sixth century, are, compared with the Style I beasts, easier to identify as animals, the body being contiguous with the head and limbs (if there are any). These creatures are characterized by elongated bodies which inter-twine both with themselves, and with those of other animals; tails, limbs, tongues and lappets (projections growing from the back of the head) contribute to a general interlacing effect (Kendrick 1938: fig. 17).

Although most attention has concentrated on these two types of animal motif, there was another, co-existent with them, which featured in Anglo-Saxon art from its earliest (fifth-century) stages: namely, 'recognizable' animals (Hicks 1993), which in their earliest stages of development, have most commonly been referred to as 'Quoit Brooch'-style animals. Viewed in profile, these creatures are shown (sometimes confronted and in friezes) running or crouching, with their hind-quarters raised and their head (sometimes) back-turned. Often heavily stylized, they are discrete individuals, readily identifiable as such (Kendrick 1938: fig. 17).

These beasts, along with the Style II animals, are evidently more open to symbolic interpretation than the Style I creatures, and indeed there is a small, but growing trend away from stylistic analyses towards iconographic studies (of individual artefacts), although, in reaction, the tendency is perhaps to read 'meanings' into everything. When dealing with such a subject we should not overlook the possibility that any given 'symbol' may also have functioned as a purely decorative motif with, in some contexts, the shape of the object determining the 'species' of animal used (Speake 1980:77). In light of these more recent (iconographic) studies, however, we can look at some of the animal symbols in more detail, bearing in mind that any depiction of an animal can be regarded in a number of ways. An image can be simply a depiction of an animal, but it can also be regarded as making a statement about the selection of that particular animal, as referring to the underlying qualities of the animal, and as illustrating a specific iconography (Hicks 1993:6-9).

From the surviving material it is clear that set types of animal motifs do recur in apparently 'pagan' contexts, and some of these continue to be used in early Christian (or late pagan) contexts, as well as in the clearly Christian. It is possible that the continued use of some of these, and the rejection of others, in the more overtly Christian visual arts, will provide information about attitudes towards 'symbolic life' in Anglo-Saxon England.

In order to assess the information I shall limit the discussion to the more reliably 'identifiable' creatures which feature regularly in the art, as the process of reconstructing the symbolism of quadrupeds of indeterminate species is riddled with pitfalls. For instance Klingender (1971:108) interpreted the horizontal panels of Style II quadrupeds with elongated jaws which frame the central cross and interlace medallion on a carpet page in the seventh-century Book of Durrow {Dublin, Trinity College Library MS A. 4. 5 (57), f. 192^V (Alexander 1978: pl. 22)} as "a swarm of evil demons, an impression strengthened by the non-zoomorphic interlace thicket that seems to protect the cross against them"; an Irish literary reference to magic hedges is invoked to support this interpretation. Set against this explanation, however, are a number of others. Speake (1980:87), for instance, disregards the interlacing limbs of the animals, and interprets them as pagan Germanic world-serpents biting their own tails, which, in the context of a Christian manuscript have been transformed into symbols of eternity. Alternatively, Hicks (1993:87-91), who also views them as Christian symbols, sees their numbers as significant. Based on the writings of Augustine, Isidore of Seville and the liturgy of the eighth-century Stow Missal, the side panels, each containing three linked beasts, are understood to refer to the Trinity. The inner horizontal panels, each containing eight intertwined beasts, are thought to refer to Creation, the Crucifixion and the Resurrection (the world 'beginning' on the eighth day of creation, the resurrection occurring on the eighth day of Holy Week, during which the Passion was celebrated, and eight being a combination of the five wounds of Christ and the three persons of the Trinity). The outer horizontal panels, each containing ten interlaced animals, refer to the unity of the Christian community. While the decoration of this page may well involve some symbolism (see Stevenson 1981/2:15, and further below), consideration of quadrupeds of no specific species seems to be an infinitely extendable exercise of limited value.

The identifiable animals occurring most frequently in the 'pagan' period include predatory birds, 'serpents', boars, and stags (Hicks 1993:19-31; Speake 1980:77-92). The bird, generally seen in profile and characterized by a prominent curved beak, is used to decorate a wide range of artefacts from weaponry to jewellery, hanging bowls, drinking horns and musical instruments.

Its use to decorate military equipment seems to be limited to protective armour {e.g. the helmet and shield at Sutton Hoo (Evans 1986: pl. III, fig. 35); cf. shield fragments from Gilton and Hackington, Kent (Speake 1980: figs. 17a and 17c)}. It does not feature on any of the extant swords, although its aggressive appearance might be deemed to make it appropriate to such a weapon. Its apparent restriction to protective equipment would seem, therefore, to indicate that the symbol had, at the very least, an apotropaic function {but the bird is also interpreted as a depiction of the literary 'beast of battle'; as symbolic of the life after death; and as a bringer of victory (see Klingender 1971:103-12; Speake 1980:81-5; Wickham-Crowley 1992:45-53)}.

The iconography of the bird on the Sutton Hoo shield, however, may have had an additional, more specific, symbolism. It has been argued (Wickham-Crowley 1992:45-50) that the tear-shaped heads which are set in the leg and tail of the bird may represent images of Odin (Fig. 10-1), the whole creature being thus transformed from a general image of the predatory bird of battle, to a more specific image of Odin metamorphosed into the eagle (according to the later Scandinavian mythological account of Odin stealing poetry from the giants by changing first into a serpent, and then into an eagle). In this particular instance the symbol would seem to be, potentially, extraordinarily potent.

The same (Odin-eagle) symbolism is also associated by Wickham-Crowley (1992:50-3) with the bird-heads decorating the neck of the Sutton Hoo lyre (Evans 1986: fig. 54), although in this context it is the poetic connotations of the Odin-eagle motif which have precedence, given the assumed use of the lyre for poetry

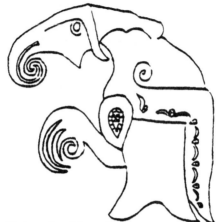

Fig. 10-1: Bird appliqué from Sutton Hoo shield (App. scale 1:3).

recitals. There is a certain attractiveness to this interpretation, in light of the metamorphic qualities associated both with Odin and the act of poetic recitation in early Anglo-Saxon culture (e.g. Shippey 1972:53-79), but the (stylistic) differences between the symbols on the shield and the musical instrument, and the application of a single explanation (based on later literary references) to fit such diverse contexts, makes it less convincing.

The significance of the bird-motif set in confronting pairs decorating the hanging bowls {Lullingstone (Hicks 1993: fig. 1.7); patch on the large hanging bowl, Sutton Hoo (Evans 1986: fig. 60)}, is not clear, largely because the function of these bowls, both in their original Celtic, and later Anglo-Saxon, contexts, is unknown. It is generally assumed that they had a 'ritual function', although the possibility that they were 'simple' wash-basins has also been proposed. On the Lullingstone bowl (which is of Anglo-Saxon manufacture), pairs of confronting birds are set above another predatory bird grasping a fish in its talons. The arrangement is repeated round the bowl, interspersed with the escutcheons and depictions of stags. In such company the birds would seem to refer to the activities of hunting and hawking, well-established pastimes among the Germanic Anglo-Saxon warrior-class, and could therefore be regarded as symbols of social status (Hicks 1986:162-5; 1993:26-9, 69-70; Klingender 1971:112; Wickham-Crowley 1992:53).

The use of these birds in the decoration of drinking horns {e.g. Sutton Hoo (Evans 1986: fig 50); Taplow, Bucks (Smith 1923: fig. 5)} and buckles {e.g. Sutton Hoo (Evans 1986: pl. VII)} would seem to confirm this symbolism, and it certainly appears to be the reference on the purse lid from Sutton Hoo, where the bird with its prey is part of a complex symbolism referring to the rank and status of the owner (Evans 1986: pl. VIII; Hicks 1986:164-5; 1993:69-70). It has also been suggested, however, that the three creatures (birds, fish and stags) on the

Lullingstone bowl may, in a non-Christian setting, be symbolic of the three elements of air, water and earth, although no explanation is given for this attribution (Hicks 1993:28-9).

Being well-established with a number of symbolic references in the visual arts of pagan Anglo-Saxon communities, the bird-motif continued to be used on late pagan/early Christian artefacts, but in slightly different settings. On the early seventh-century composite disc brooch from Sarre, Kent (Webster & Backhouse 1991: no. 31a), for instance, two conjoined, opposed birds' heads form a collar round the catch-plate on the back, the side not intended to be seen; on the front, gold-filigree and gilt-silver metalwork are arranged with shell- and garnet-inlay to form a series of cross shapes. This is done in such a way that the whole can be viewed either as a series of 'hidden' crosses, or as variations on a deliberate theme. Here, the association of 'hidden' crosses and bird's heads may have had a complementary symbolic function, both acting to protect the wearer.

On the mid seventh-century Hunterston brooch (Stevenson 1974; 1983:464-72; Youngs 1989: no. 69) we find the same set of symbols, this time arranged together on the front but positioned so that both are hidden under the pin (Fig. 10-2). Here the minute cross-motif is designed so that it resembles the cover of a manuscript, and, arranged in confronting pairs above and below it, are the birds' heads. It may well be that the birds are arranged (in time-honoured fashion) to 'protect' the cross; their apotropaic function, established in pagan contexts, has been co-opted into a Christian setting, perhaps helping to establish the new symbolism of the cross. However, set above and below the cross, between each pair of beaks, is a small gold boss which the birds could be seen as pecking. They may, therefore,

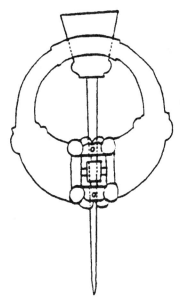

Fig. 10-2: Hunterston Brooch, showing cross - and bird-motifs 'hidden' (App. scale 1:3).

also be regarded within a completely Christian context, in which they symbolically (by eating the fruit of life) receive sustenance from the Book of Life.

The apparent flexibility of the predatory bird-motif, which enabled it to be incorporated into the decoration of artefacts emerging from a transitional late pagan/early Christian culture, seems to have ensured its survival in the decoration of more overtly Christian artefacts. The stone sculpture at Monkwearmouth, for instance (an art-form introduced to the Anglo-Saxons with Christianity), includes a grave-cover dated to the early eighth century (Bailey 1992:35-6; Cramp 1984: no.5). On it, a pair of confronting predatory birds (with ribbon-like bodies) flank and enclose the central cross and epitaph of the stone (Fig. 10-3). Here, the symbolism used (potentially ambiguously) on the Hunterston brooch, has been invoked in an unequivocally Christian setting—with (presumably) similar references to protection (in the overall arrangement of the birds) and spiritual life—in their close association with the cross, and the fact that they decorate a funerary monument.

Thus the predatory bird, with its social, protective and iconographic significances in pagan contexts, continued to be used apotropaically in Christian

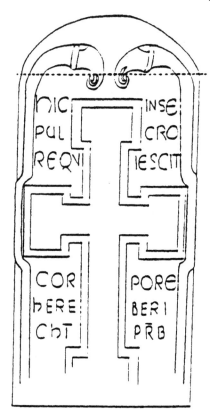

Fig. 10-3: Herebrecht Stone, Monkwearmouth, showing restoration (App. scale 1:13).

contexts, while its specific iconographic meanings changed from ones apparently associated with the old world view to refer to the ever-lasting life available through the new.

A similar process of adoption and adaptation seems to have occurred with the serpent-motif, characterized by bodies lacking limbs or wings, which (sometimes) taper to a pointed tail, and heads which are either rounded, or have open, extended jaws. In a sense, this symbol was even more common in pagan Anglo-Saxon art than the bird, as its form lends itself to the interlacing patterns definitive of Style II creatures; the decorative potential of the motif is thus probably primary in most instances, but there are suggestions that in some cases the serpent could have a symbolic function (cf. Speake 1980:85-92, for a range of possibilities).

On the Sutton Hoo helmet (Evans 1986: pl. III), for instance, the crest running from the eyebrows to the neck terminates at both ends in a serpent's head with teeth and garnet eyes, strongly suggestive of apotropaic qualities, and a similar function may have been intended for the interlacing serpents featured on some buckles. Kitzinger (1993:3) has recently cited an eighth-century Irish tale in which a snake slithers into the belt of the hero, Conall Cenach, enabling him to overcome his enemies and conquer a fortress (cf. Ross 1967:151; Speake 1980:90), and while no zoomorphic (serpentine) interlacing decorates extant Irish belt buckles (which are, in any case, extremely rare artefacts), the motif is certainly present on Anglo-Saxon versions {e.g. Sutton Hoo (Evans 1986: pl. VII); Taplow, Bucks (Campbell 1986: pl. 39)}. There is no apparent (direct) relationship between an Old Irish tale and an Anglo-Saxon buckle, but it is hard to imagine what symbolic function other than apotropaism the serpent-motif could have had in these contexts. It might be argued that it is merely decorative, but motifs other than serpents are found on the buckles, suggesting the snake, when it does appear on such items, was deliberately chosen, and therefore had a specific symbolic purpose {cf. the shoulder clasps from Taplow (Webster & Backhouse 1991: no.38)}.

Certainly, the serpent continued to be used on later (seventh-century) buckles, in potentially Christian contexts. On a buckle from Eccles, Kent, for instance, two interlacing snakes flank a double-headed serpent; one head grasps a cross-bar in its jaws (Webster & Backhouse 1991: no. 7). Apart from the potential cross-shape in the division of the field of decoration, the front of this buckle seems to repeat a long-established tradition of (talismanic) symbolism associated with the serpent-motif. On the back of the buckle, however, hidden from sight, is a sheet-metal fish appliqué (Fig. 10-4).

The depiction of this fish on its own, placed centrally in the field of ornament (and directly under the double-headed serpent on the front), might seem to indicate a Christian symbolism, in which the fish denotes Christ. Before him, the wearer displayed the traditional symbols of protection; hidden next to his body, he bore the new. Against this explanation, however, is the existence of a number of sixth-century brooches and shields which carry fish appliqués on the back, always hidden from view (e.g. Dickinson & Härke 1992:27-30, fig. 18c). The use of the fish motif on the back of the Eccles buckle may, therefore, simply represent the

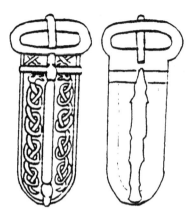

Fig. 10-4: Eccles Brooch, front and back (App. scale 1:1).

continuation of a long-established tradition, in which the fish had a specific symbolism, now lost to us.

On the near-contemporary Crundale buckle (Webster & Backhouse: no. 6), however, a Christian symbolism may be more likely; the fish has been moved into sight, on to the front of the plate, where it is set between interlacing serpents (Fig. 10-5). Here, the dominant position and form of the fish (it is in high relief, its features outlined in beaded wire, and the eyes picked out as small cabochon settings), suggests it is of primary (and probably Christian) significance. It may well illustrate the transference of pagan images to a new Christian iconography, possibly that of Christ recognized between the beasts, a scheme symbolic of Christ's life-giving victory over death, celebrated daily in the Eucharist.

Also incorporated into an overall Christian iconography, is the use of the

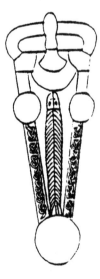

Fig. 10-5: Crundale Buckle, front (App. scale 1:3).

(double-headed) serpent-motif on the helmet from Coppergate, York, dated to the second half of the eighth century (Webster & Backhouse 1991: no. 47). One of these apparently apotropaic creatures decorates the crest of the helmet, while another, grasped in the mouth of the serpent-head set over the nasal, acts as the 'eyebrow guards': together they function as appropriate protectors. This significance is intensified, however, by the inscription in the 'body' of the serpent lying over the crest of the helmet, which invokes the Trinity. Set cross-wise to it, over the crown of the head, is an abbreviated version of the same inscription. The inscription thus functions as a cross set over the head of the wearer which incorporates a triple invocation to the (trinitarian) deity. Protection is complete.

More overtly Christian is the setting of the interlaced snake motif on the late seventh-century portal stones of the church at Monkwearmouth (Bailey 1992:33; Cramp 1984: no.8; Kitzinger 1993:4-6). These two snakes (Fig. 10-6), are related stylistically to other Style II serpents, but the exact form of their interlacing (they are twisted together so that their tails form a Tau-cross), and their position (at the entrance to the church), is very suggestive of a specifically Christian apotropaism, whose effect is hidden by the way the cross is disguised in the interlace, and the way the snakes are very lightly engraved on the *inner* sides of the portal stones; they would not be seen until the threshold was actually being crossed. Thus situated, these serpents have proved a fount of inspiration to those interpreting the motif (cf. Hicks 1993:82-5; Speake 1980:89, on the chthonic association of snake, its relevance to notions of death and rebirth, and rites of passage), and clearly it has a potentially rich significance; many of the diverse readings available to modern scholars may well have been understood by contemporary viewers.

Fig. 10-6: Portal Stones, Monkwearmouth (App. scale 1:7).

In the eighth-century Durham Cassiodorus {Cathedral Library MS B. II. 30, f. 172^V (Alexander 1978: pl. 75)} the (double-headed) serpent has been incorporated into a recognizable Christian iconography: the Old Testament figure David stands on the serpent holding a spear. The text of the manuscript is a commentary on the Psalms, and the image of David has been used (as in the Psalters) to highlight those psalms especially attributed to David and held to be prophetic of Christ the Saviour. In this particular instance, however, the picture has a double reference: the prophetic nature of the psalms and the typological, foreshadowing role of David explained in the text are expressed in visual terms (Bailey 1978:11). Not only is David the psalmist, he is also a type of the Saviour. Thus the image depicts, not only David, but also Christ trampling the beasts (overcoming evil and death); the latent apotropaic qualities of the (ancient) double-headed serpent motif are here vanquished once and for all.

Again, like the predatory bird, the potential significances of the serpent appear to have ensured its continued use, with changing symbolic values, in the transitional culture of sixth- to eighth-century Anglo-Saxon England. In each case recognized animal symbols were re-used, along with their associated symbolism, although the specific iconography attached to the motifs could alter quite dramatically to reflect the changing concerns of the culture. In this way the familiar connotations of recognized motifs were 'made anew', and the newer associations were initially rendered acceptable by their incorporation with the old and familiar, eventually emerging as 'new' symbols in their own right.

This perhaps is not such a startling observation. We should expect continuity and change to be reflected in the visual arts of a transitional culture. But what is then surprising, is that the other animal motifs (the boar and the stag) commonly featured in pagan Anglo-Saxon art, do not appear in overtly Christian contexts.

As we have seen, the boar motif, identified by the tusk rising from the lower jaw to cross the upper, could be used (potentially) for a number of purposes in the sixth-century pagan period, and it continued to feature in the art of the late pagan/early Christian period. On the mid seventh-century helmet from Benty Grange, Derbyshire (Webster & Backhouse 1991: no. 46), for instance, the boar is a striking three-dimensional figure riveted on to the crest of the helmet, its tusks picked out in gilt copper-alloy. Below it, on the nasal of the helmet, is a silver cross. It has been thought that the use of the cross here reflects the Christian faith of the wearer (Bruce-Mitford 1974:223-52). However, the helmet-setting of the cross, and the date of the piece, might equally suggest that the boar is the primary symbol, and the cross another talismanic symbol functioning in the same way, as another symbol of strength, rather than as a deliberate statement of Christianity. Certainly the two symbols work together as protective agents; the new sign of Christ is employed alongside the age-old sign of the boar.

The striking use of the two symbols in this way might be thought to augur well for the continued use of the image of the boar in the decoration of later, more clearly Christian, artefacts. This, however, is not the case; it seems, almost without exception, that the boar was excluded from the menagerie of creatures featured in the extant Christian artefacts of early Anglo-Saxon England. The exception is a boar featured on part of a seventh-century architectural frieze from Hexham, Northumberland (Cramp 1984, no. 34, pl. 185:1012). Here, however, the context indicates that the depiction of the boar was inspired, not by local decorative traditions, but by imported models. It is one of a number of motifs which includes 'putti', cows, lions, cockerels, as well as the vine-scroll and four-lobed marigold designs, all of which were common to the Christian art of the Mediterranean world, but were not part of the pre-Christian Anglo-Saxon artistic repertoire. In this case, the boar was part of Wilfrid's deliberate attempt to recreate Rome in the north of England, and so represents a 'foreign implant', which happens to coincide with the motifs available in the established (pre-Christian) decorative repertoire, rather than a (unique) reproduction of the pagan boar in clear Christian context.

The stag is also absent from the early Christian art of Anglo-Saxons. In pagan contexts, this animal features in hunting-scene friezes on cremation urns, testifying to its early use as a symbol of social status (Hicks 1993:23-4), but apart from these instances, it is not depicted in Anglo-Saxon contexts until the tenth century, when it reappears in Viking-age art associated with the hound. Here it functions as a Christian motif denoting the Christian harried by the devil, the hound (Bailey 1977:68-9).

What is surprising about this is the fact that in the visual arts of other early Christian cultures of the British Isles (particularly those of the Irish and Pictish), the stag (and boar) feature, on stone carvings, as part of full hunting scenes. In most instances these scenes are associated with a large cross-motif (on one side of the Pictish cross-slabs, or on the base of the Irish High Crosses), and seem to refer to the close relationship between the ruling secular warrior-classes and the ecclesiastical communities in each culture. Although a similar relationship is believed to have existed in Anglo-Saxon England (e.g. Wormald 1978), it is (apparently) not reflected in the same way in the visual arts.

This discrepancy between the Anglo-Saxon and Irish and Pictish material is probably a result of differing perceptions of the role of the stone carvings in the various cultures. In Ireland and Pictland the art of stone sculpture was already practised when the Christian monument form (the cross-slabs and the high crosses) on which the hunt scenes feature were developed, and in Pictland particularly, the (possibly pre-Christian) Symbol Stones are sometimes associated with centres of royal power. In Anglo-Saxon England there was no tradition of stone-carving prior to the introduction of Christianity; thus Anglo-Saxon sculpture seems in its earliest phases, to be associated with ecclesiastical attempts to create monuments (church buildings and cross-shafts) which were deliberately impressive and, in a real sense, propagandist. It may well be that the more common depiction of secular scenes on Pictish and Irish monuments would have been less controversial than in early Christian Anglo-Saxon England.

The absence of the two motifs in early Christian Anglo-Saxon art might, therefore, suggest a conscious rejection in the early Anglo-Saxon ecclesiastical communities of activities popular in secular life (for references to denunciations see Hicks 1986:162-3; Klingender 1971:117), or, more specifically, of the symbols obviously associated with these activities: the boar with war (and possibly fertility rites), the stag with hunting. The retention of the predatory bird motif in Christian Anglo-Saxon art, however, implies this was probably not the case or at least that such censorship was not universally applied.

As we have seen, although the bird-motif was associated throughout the period with the aristocratic pastimes of falconry and hawking (Hicks 1986:162-5; 1993:69-70; Kitzinger 1993:10-2), it featured widely in the Christian arts. It appears in illuminated manuscripts, for instance, often as the symbol for John the Evangelist {e.g. Book of Durrow, f. 84^V; *C.C.C.C.* MS. 197B, f. 1; Echternach Gospels, f. 176^V; cf. Lindisfarne Gospels, f. 139; Vespasian Psalter, f. 93^V (Alexander 1978: pls. 17, 58, 59, 33, 145)}. Even more relevant is the image of the bird of prey preserved in a secular portrait, in the carving of the mid eighth-century cross-shaft at Bewcastle in Cumbria.

At the base of the west face of this monument (Bailey & Cramp 1988: ills. 90, 96; Karkov 1997; Kitzinger 1993:10-2), below nimbed images of John the Baptist with the Agnus Dei, and Christ recognized between the beasts, and separated from them by a lengthy runic inscription, is the full-length figure of a man (without a halo) in secular dress with the gauntlet, short staff and bird-perch often used by those involved in falconry; standing on his wrist is a large bird of prey. The runic inscription is damaged so that specific names cannot be deciphered, but it still records that the cross was raised as a commemorative monument. It would seem the figure, portrayed with his 'hawk', the symbol of his social status, represents either the person commemorated by the cross, or the patron responsible for its production. Clearly, secular activities (and their associated symbols in the visual arts) were not rejected outright by the early ecclesiastical communities in Anglo-Saxon England.

It has nevertheless to be admitted that images such as that at Bewcastle are very rare in early Christian Anglo-Saxon art {cf. the Repton stone (Biddle & Kjølbye-Biddle 1985:238-73)}, and it is probable that what determined the retention of symbols, such as the bird and the serpent, was their (formal) malleability; they could be 'disguised' in the Style II animal-form, and generalized into bird- and serpent-shapes, whose symbolism could be adjusted according to need. The boar, with its distinctive tusks, and the stag, generally a discrete animal, were perhaps considered less flexible symbols. If this was the case it would seem that the process of continuity and change evident in the visual arts of Anglo-Saxon England was a subtle and conscious process. Decisions were made about the use of various symbols which depended not only on their symbolic content, but also their form, and cultural associations.

Interlace symbols

Plain interlace (as distinct from the interlac*ing* patterns of the Style II animals) is another very common motif in Anglo-Saxon art, but only from the mid seventh century onwards. Before that it is rare, as most of the interlacing patterns decorating the metalwork of the sixth and earlier seventh centuries are zoomorphic; they have, at the very least, heads with eyes and jaws. For this reason Anglo-Saxon interlace has been described as a development of Style II art (e.g. Haseloff 1958:80-2), itself thought to have derived (ultimately) from interlace patterns featured in the visual arts of the Mediterranean world (Åberg 1926; 1947; Haseloff 1958). More recently however, it has been argued that the derivation (of Anglo-Saxon interlace from Style II art) is probably incorrect (Adcock 1974:7-50; Stevenson 1981/2:15-8); the forms of zoomorphic interlacing featured in early Style II art are not usually repeated in the plain interlace patterns decorating the (later) Christian artefacts.

Nor does it seem that Anglo-Saxon interlace was introduced from the Mediterranean. The few examples of plain interlace which occur in the decoration of non-Christian artefacts, and which are thought to represent the influence of new (Christian Mediterranean) cultural contacts (e.g. Lullingstone bowl) are not repeated in the decoration of the Anglo-Saxon Christian artefacts {except for derivative patterns in the mid seventh-century Durham Gospel fragment, MS A. II. 10, f. 3^V (Alexander 1978: pl.10)}. This (early) type of plain interlace is characterized by thick ribbons arranged on the field in a tight, and often incoherent, mesh; it is a type of interlace which had a very short life-span in Anglo-Saxon art of the first half of the seventh century (Åberg 1926, 1943; Adcock 1974:35-42; Haseloff 1958:80-2). Other interlace patterns available to Mediterranean artists are also absent from the repertoire of such designs current in Anglo-Saxon England.

In other words, the types of interlace apparently derived from Mediterranean art circulating in England, did not have a lasting impact on the types of interlace which became synonymous with Anglo-Saxon art. Thus although it is clear that during the seventh century the Anglo-Saxons, in ecclesiastical communities, began to use interlace widely in their visual arts, it was not copied from Germanic or Mediterranean patterns. Certainly, these sources may have inspired the *idea* for the design, but they did not provide the actual *types* which became dominant. These are characterized by the use of (generally) fine lines arranged in precise designs (based on a square grid) in which complex patterns could be constructed (Adcock 1974:7-15; 1978:33-5; Cramp 1984: xxviii-xlv). In fact, these distinctive patterns seem to have originated in ecclesiastical centres in Anglo-Saxon England (cf. Åberg 1943; Adcock 1974:7-42; Stevenson 1981/2:11-8).

If this is the case, it follows that in these communities it was felt appropriate to 'invent' a specific type of interlace; this raises the question of why. One answer may lie in the *form* of the interlace adopted. This is distinguished by the heavy use of 'breaks', the technique by which the flow of the ribbons is broken, and their direction changed, resulting in a pattern which can be divided into a series of discrete sections. Stevenson (1981/2:5-18) has demonstrated that in many of the designs a variety of repeated cross-shapes are 'hidden' (or reserved) in the spaces between these sections.

Fig. 10-7: Book of Durrow, f. 85^V (App. scale 1:2).

In manuscript art the phenomenon is relatively easy to decipher, as colour separates interlace and background. On f. 125^V of the Book of Durrow (Alexander 1978: pl. 21), for instance, three crosses with diamond (or lozenge-shaped) ends and centres are visible in the black background between the back-to-back curves of the brightly coloured interlace. Furthermore, the eight interlace knots each contain, diagonally, a cross formed by their strands; in the upper and lower borders further, smaller, crosses of varying design are both reserved in the background, and in the way blocks of colour are used to break up the geometric patterns (Stevenson 1981/2:12-5, fig. 6.4).

Again, on f. 85^V (Alexander 1978: pl. 20), the central roundel of the page contains a small gold-coloured cross set between a four-lobed marigold design, itself often used to form a repeated-cross pattern in Anglo-Saxon art {e.g. a sculptural frieze at Ledsham, Yorks (Bailey 1992: fig. 1c)}. In the spaces between this marigold design is another cross with splayed arms containing small knots of interlace. On the page as a whole, this central roundel works with the three above and below which are similarly coloured to form a double cross-motif (like that illustrated in geometric form on f. 1^V; Alexander 1978: pl. 11); between the roundels a series of eight crosses with lozenge terminals overlapping each other are visible in the background {Fig. 10-7; cf. ff. 3^V, 192^V (Alexander 1978: pls. 12, 22; Stevenson 1981/2:15)}.

The same principle is also found operating on the early stone carvings of Anglo-Saxon England. It should be remembered that originally these monuments (like the manuscripts) were probably highly coloured (e.g. Bailey 1980:25-7; Lang 1990), and although they are now monotone, cross-shapes are still clearly visible in the spaces between the knots carved on the sides of some of the cross-shafts. At the base of the south face of the Bewcastle Cross, for instance (Bailey & Cramp 1988: ills. 92, 101), a panel of interlace contains a small diamond-armed cross at the top, whose centre is traversed by a double, interlocking diagonal cross. At the centre of the panel is a larger cross, carved so that its central point rises to a plane level with that of the carved interlace (Fig. 10-8); if an onlooker were to kneel before the monument, this central cross would lie at eye-level.

Stevenson (1981/2:11-20) has demonstrated that this method of 'reading' the interlace can be applied to many of the manuscripts and carved stone monuments of seventh- and eighth-century Anglo-Saxon England (cf. Coatsworth 1989:291-6), and while it might be argued that once looked for, any shape could be picked out in such contexts, it has to be admitted that crosses cannot be deciphered in *all* examples of Anglo-Saxon interlace. On the other hand, where they are most visible in the early Christian art, the context is not inappropriate.

Fig. 10-8: Panel of Interlace, south face, Bewcastle Cross (App. scale 1:10).

For instance, in manuscripts, the cross-shapes proliferate on the so-called 'carpet pages'. These are the pages which mark the beginning of each gospel; they function both as a cover, and as a way into the sacred text (much as a door which can be closed and opened). In such a context, it is highly apt to have pages decorated in such a way that they have to be meditated upon before the 'hidden' symbol can be picked out. Interlace, of its very nature is a positive pattern, and the negative patterns of its background are not easy to see. Both interlace and cross . therefore, cannot be seen simultaneously; a sudden 'jump' from one form to the other has to take place. In the setting of the carpet-page, the cross protecting the text is hidden in the interlace, while the life-giving symbol(ism) of the cross has to be discovered. In this respect it functions both as a metaphor, and as a preparatory mental exercise for the reading of the text which follows: the symbolic (life-saving) meaning held within the narrative of each gospel has to be meditated upon and deciphered. Thus, on the carpet-pages, the cross (of salvation) literally forms the 'way in'; it is the symbol to be held in the mind during the subsequent reading of the text. In fact, it almost seems that the hidden pattern understood by the early Christians to exist in God's created world was being re-created in the visual arts of the Anglo-Saxons.

If, as seems likely, the desire to present 'hidden' symbols is one explanation for the adoption and ensuing popularity of interlace in the visual arts of Christian Anglo-Saxon England, it presents us, not so much with the continuing use of a particular symbol, as with an apparent continuation of attitude: an attitude towards the visual arts, and also perhaps, towards the 'symbolic life'.

In the early Christian (late pagan) visual arts of the mid-seventh century, we have already seen a predilection for 'things hidden' in the decoration of artefacts as diverse as the portal stones of the church at Monkwearmouth, the Eccles buckle, and the Sarre and Hunterston brooches. To this set of metalwork artefacts can be added the decoration of the Kingston Down and Boss Hall brooches, as well as that of pendants from Ash, Old Westgate Farm, Ixworth and Epsom (Webster & Backhouse 1991: nos. 32, 33, 8, 10, 11, 35). In these, a series of cross-shapes is disguised in the relationship between the metalwork and inlays of which they are constructed. As all of these artefacts emerge from seventh-century contexts when ambiguous Christian references seem to be deliberate, such reserved symbols might be expected.

However, the same tendency is also prominent in the decoration of 'pagan' artefacts. A number of sixth-century saucer brooches, such as those from Fairford, Gloucs., and Kempston, Beds. (Smith 1923: figs. 27, 31), are decorated with a repeated motif composed of stylized human faces; repetition and stylization ensures that the form of the face is not clearly visible. In the early seventh century the boar-motif is similarly hidden in the decoration of a bracteate-pendant from Womersley (Yorks.), while a serpent with elongated jaws is hidden in the border decoration of similar pendants from Forsbrook and Bacton, Norfolk (Speake 1980: figs. 11a).

Again, in pre-Christian contexts, cross-shapes are disguised in the zoomorphic interlace patterns decorating the shoulder-clasps from Taplow (Webster &

Backhouse 1991: no. 38), and the 'millefiori' decoration of the Sutton Hoo shoulder-clasps and a small harness mount (Webster & Backhouse 1991: nos. 14 & 41); in these (pagan) contexts it is unlikely that a specific symbolism was attached to the crosses, but the shapes are an integral part of the decorative patterns. And the potential of these designs for containing hidden cross-motifs was clearly recognized by later (Christian) artists, in their use of the same patterns. One example of this phenomenon is the chequer-board decoration carved onto the north face of the Bewcastle Cross (Bailey & Cramp 1988: illus. 93, 105), where, originally picked out in colour, it would have presented the onlooker with a large panel encrusted with crosses {cf. 'millefiori' and zoomorphic interlace decoration on the carpet-pages of the Book of Durrow, ff. 1^V, and 21^V, the Lindisfarne Gospels, ff. 2^V, 26^V, 94^V, 138^V, and the Lichfield Gospels, p. 220 (Alexander 1978: pls. 11, 14, 34 -36, 38, 77)}.

In other words, the adoption of the interlace motif by the early Christian Anglo-Saxons seems to represent a variation on a theme current in the visual arts of the culture since its earliest stages: namely, the ambiguous presentation of shapes and symbols. In fact, it would seem to be yet another instance of the ambiguity which seems to have delighted the Anglo-Saxon 'sensibility', being characteristic not only of their visual arts, but also their poetry.

It is probably not co-incidental, for instance, that riddles form a significant part of the surviving corpus of Old English poetry, while riddling plays a structural and thematic role in a number of other poems, such as the Vercelli Manuscript version of *The Dream of the Rood* and *The Seafarer* (Gordon 1979; Swanton 1987). While this literature survives in much later (tenth- and eleventh-century) manuscripts, the Franks Casket, dated to *ca* 700 AD, demonstrates that the apparent predilection for ambiguous presentation was also present at a much earlier date, not only in its iconography, but also in the inscriptions which frame the pictures on all sides (Elliott 1959:96-109; Wilson 1984: pls. 34-7). That which accompanies the illustrations of Weland the Smith and the Adoration of the Magi on the front of the box is particularly illustrative of the riddling aspect of so much of the later literature. It does not refer to the illustrations, as do the inscriptions elsewhere on the casket; rather, it refers to the material from which the box is fashioned, whale-bone:

Fisc flōdu āhōf on fergenberig
warþ gasrīc grorn, þær hē on grēut giswom
Hronæs bān.

(The flood lifted up the fish on to the cliff-bank/The fish lifted up the flood onto the cliff-bank, the savage animal became sad, where he swam up on the shingle, the bone of the whale) (Trans. Elliott 1959:99).

The subject of the first 'sentence' is deliberately (gramatically) ambiguous, and thus the role of the beast as hapless victim or willing sacrifice is left open. It is not a serious, or extended verse, but (or indeed, because of this) it does give a glimpse of the extent to which it was 'normal' to define, or explain something by means of apparent paradox. It would seem, therefore, that ambiguity of presentation was quite widespread in both the pagan and Christian communities of Anglo-Saxon England, and is perhaps a reflection of a fairly deeply-seated attitude prevalent among them: a symbolic way of viewing the world. Thus, in the adoption and use of interlace in the visual arts of the Anglo-Saxons we can perhaps see, in a very real way, the meeting of the two cultures which transformed Anglo-Saxon culture during the sixth to eighth century: on the one hand, the Christian culture, with its symbolic world view, and on the other, the 'pagan' Anglo-Saxon, with its own predilection for symbolic ambiguity realized in their visual arts. The cross-fertilization of these approaches ensured the continued use of recognized motifs, whose associated iconographies transcended the restrictions of each community, to embrace them both, and also allowed for the creation of new motifs. A continuing richness of design and significance in the visual arts, reflecting their 'symbolic life', was thus ensured in Anglo-Saxon England.

References

Textual sources:

[Abbreviations: C.C.S.L. = *Corpus Christianorum Series Latina;* P.L. = *Patrologia Latina*]

Ælfric
        Homilies: see Pope 1968.
Aldhelm
        Letters: see Lapidge & Herren 1979.
Anglo-Saxon Chronicle: see Garmonsway 1972.
Augustine
        De Civitate Dei adversus paganos: see Dombaut & Kald (eds.) 1955.
Bede
        Historia Abbatum: see Plummer 1896.
        Homilies: see Hurst 1955.
        De templo II: see Hurst 1969.
        De temporum ratione: see Jones (ed.) 1943.
Beowulf: see Klæber 1950.
The Dream of the Rood: see Swanton 1987.
Gregory the Great
        Epistolae: see Migne 1849.
Gregory of Tours
        Libri historiarum decem: see Thorpe 1974.
John of Damascus
        Adversus Constantium: see Didron (trans.) 1886.
Procopius
        De bello gothico: see Havry 1963.
Saxo Grammaticus
        Gesta Danorum: see Elton 1894.
The Seafarer: see Gordon 1979.
Tacitus
        Germania: see Stephenson 1894.

Bibliography:

Åberg, N.
   1926   *The Anglo-Saxons in England During the Early Centuries After the Invasion.*
          Uppsala: Almqvist & Wiksell.
   1943   *The Occident and the Orient in the Art of the Seventh Century 1: The British
          Isles.* Stockholm: Wahlström & Widstrand.
   1947   *The Occident and the Orient in the Art of the Seventh Century 3: The
          Merovingian Empire.* Stockholm: Wahlström & Widstrand.
Adcock, G.
   1974   A Study of the Types of Interlace on Northumbrian Sculpture (unpublished
          M. Phil. Thesis, 2 vols, University of Durham).
   1978   The theory of interlace and interlace patterns in Anglian sculpture. In *Anglo-
          Saxon and Viking Age Sculpture and its Context.* J. Lang (ed.), pp. 333-346.
          (BAR, British Series 49). Oxford: BAR.
Alexander, J. J. G.
   1978   *Insular Manuscripts: 6th to the 9th Century.* London: Harvey Miller.
Bailey, R. N.
   1977   The meaning of the Viking-age shaft at Dacre. *Transactions of the
          Cumberland and Westmorland Antiquarian and Archaeological Society,*
          ser. 2, 77: 61-74.
   1978   *The Durham Cassiodorus.* Jarrow: Jarrow Lecture.
   1980   *Viking Age Sculpture.* London: Collins.
   1992   Sutton Hoo and seventh-sentury art. In *Sutton Hoo: Fifty Years After.*
          R. Farrell & C. Neuman de Vegvar (eds.), pp. 31-41. (American Early Med.
          Studies 2). Oxford, OH: Am. Early Med. Studies, Dept. of Art, Miami Univ.
Bailey, R. N., & R. Cramp
   1988   *Corpus of Anglo-Saxon Stone Sculpture 2: Cumberland, Westmorland and
          Lancashire North-of-the-Sands.* Oxford: Oxford University Press.
Biddle, M., & B. Kølbye-Biddle
   1985   The Repton Stone. *Anglo-Saxon England* 14: 233-292.
Bruce-Mitford, R. L. S. (ed.)
   1974   *Aspects of Anglo-Saxon Archæology.* London: Gollancz.
Campbell, J. (ed.)
   1986   *The Anglo-Saxons.* London: Phaidon.
Coatsworth, E.
   1989   The pectoral cross and portable altar from the tomb of St Cuthbert. In
          St Cuthbert, His Cult and His Community to AD 1200. G. Bonner, D. Rollason
          & C. Stancliffe (eds.), pp. 287-302. Woodbridge: The Boydell Press.
Cohen, A. P.
   1985   *The Symbolic Construction of Community.* London: Ellis Horwood.
Cramp, R.
   1984   *Corpus of Anglo-Saxon Sculpture 1: County Durham and Northumberland.*
          Oxford: Oxford University Press.
Davidson, H. R. E.
   1964   *Gods and Myths of Northern Europe.* Harmondsworth: Penguin.
Dickinson, T., & H. Härke
   1992   Early Anglo-Saxon shields. *Archaeologia* 110.
Didron, A. N.
   1886   *Christian Iconography.* London: G. Bell.

Dodwell, C. R.
  1982   *Anglo-Saxon Art: A New Perspective.* Manchester: Manchester Univ. Press.
Dombaut, B., & A. Kalb (eds.)
  1955   *Sancti Aurelii Augustini De Civitate Dei, Libri I-X* (C.C.S.L. XLVII), *Libri XI-XXII* (C.C.S.L. XLVIII). Turnhout: Brepols.
Elton, O. (ed. & trans.)
  1894   *Saxo Grammaticus: The First Nine Books of the Danish History.* London: David Nutt.
Evans, A. C.
  1986   *The Sutton Hoo Ship Burial.* London: British Museum
Garmonsway, G. N. (ed.)
  1972   *The Anglo-Saxon Chronicle.* London: Dent.
Geertz, C.
  1973   *The Interpretation of Cultures.* London: Basic Books.
Gordon, I. (ed.)
  1979   *The Seafarer.* Manchester: Manchester University Press.
Haseloff, G.
  1958   Fragments of a hanging-bowl from Bekesbourne, Kent, and some ornamental problems. *Medieval Archaeology* 2: 72-103.
  1974   Salin's Style I. *Medieval Archaeology* 18: 1-15.
Havry, J. (ed.)
  1963   *Procopii caesariensis opera omnia 2: De bellis.* Berlin: B. G. Teubner.
Hicks, C.
  1986   The birds on the Sutton Hoo purse. *Anglo-Saxon England* 15: 153-165.
  1993   *Animals in Early Medieval Art.* Edinburgh: Edinburgh University Press.
Hurst, D. (ed.)
  1955   *Bedae Venerabilis homeliarum evangelii, Libri II* (C.C.S.L. XXII). Turnhout: Brepols.
  1969   *De Templo. Bedae Venerabilis opera. Pars II, opera exegetica* (C.C.S.L. CXIX A, pp. 141-234). Turnhout: Brepols.
Jones, C. W. (ed.)
  1943   *Bedae opera de temporibus.* Cambridge, MA: Medieval Academy of America.
Karkov, C.
  1995   The Bewcastle Cross. In *The Insular Tradition.* R. Farrell, C. Karkov & M. Ryan (eds.). (American Early Medieval Studies 3). Oxford, OH: American Early Medieval Studies, Dept. of Art, Miami University, Oxford, OH 45056.
Kendrick, T. D.
  1938   *Anglo-Saxon Art to A.D. 900.* London: Methuen.
Kitzinger, E.
  1993   Interlace and icons: Form and function in early insular art. In *The Age of Migrating Ideas.* R. M. Spearman & J. Higgitt (eds.), pp. 3-15. Edinburgh: National Museums of Scotland.
Klæber, F. (ed.)
  1950   *Beowulf and The Fight at Finnsburgh* (3rd edition). Lexington, MA: Heath & Co.
Klingender, F.
  1971   *Animals in Art and Thought to the End of the Middle Ages.* E. Antal & J. Harthan (eds.). London: Routledge.

Lang, J.
   1990   The painting of pre-Conquest sculpture in Northumbria. In *Early Medieval Wall Painting and Painted Sculpture in England*. S. Cather, D. Park & P. Williamson (eds.), pp. 135-146. (BAR, British Series 216). Oxford: BAR.
Lapidge, M, & M. Herren (eds.)
   1979   *Aldhelm: The Prose Works*. Cambridge: Cambridge University Press.
Leeds, E. T.
   1946   Denmark and Early England. *Antiquaries Journal* 26: 22-37.
Meaney, A. L.
   1981   *Anglo-Saxon Amulets and Curing Stones*. (BAR, British Series 96). Oxford: BAR.
Migne, J. P.
   1849   *Sancti Gregorii Papae I, cognomento magni, opera omnia. Tomus III. (*P.L. LXXVII, col. 431-1352). Paris: rue d'Amboise. [Repr. Turnhout: Brepols].
Morphy, H. (ed.)
   1989   *Animals into Art*. London: Unwin Hyman.
Plummer, C.
   1896   *Venerabilis Baedae opera historica*. Oxford: Clarendon Press.
Pope, J. C. (ed.)
   1968   *Homilies of Ælfric: A Supplementary Collection 2*. (Early English Text Society, OS 260). Oxford: Oxford University Press.
Poulsen, G. S.
   1986   The complementarity of magic in nordic mythology and in archæological sources. In *Words and Objects: Towards a Dialogue between Archaeology and History of Religion*. G. Steinsland (ed.), pp. 168-179. Oslo/Oxford: Norwegian University Press/Oxford University Press.
Ross, A.
   1967   *Pagan Celtic Britain: Studies in Iconography and Tradition*. London: Routledge.
Salin, E.
   1959   *La Civilisation Mérovingienne* 4. Paris: A. & J. Picard.
Shippey, T. A.
   1972   *Old English Verse*. London: Hutchinson.
Smith, R. A.
   1923   *Guide to Anglo-Saxon Antiquities*. London: British Museum.
Speake, G.
   1970   A seventh-century coin-pendant from Bacton, Norfolk, and its ornament. *Medieval Archaeology* 14: 1-16.
   1980   *Anglo-Saxon Animal Art and its Germanic Background*. Oxford: Clarendon Press.
Stephenson, H. M. (ed.)
   1894   *Tacitus: Agricola and Germania*. Cambridge: Cambridge University Press.
Stevenson, R. B. K.
   1974   The Hunterston brooch and its significance. *Medieval Archaeology* 18: 16-42.
   1981/2   Aspects of ambiguity in crosses and interlace. *Ulster Journal of Archaeology* 44-45: 1-27.
   1983   Further notes on the Hunterston and 'Tara' brooches, Monymusk reliquary and Blackness bracelet. *Proceedings of the Society of Antiquaries of Scotland* 113: 469-477.
Swanton, M. (ed.)
   1987   *The Dream of the Rood*. Exeter: University of Exeter Press.

Thorpe, L. (ed. & trans.)
  1974   *Gregory of Tours: The History of the Franks*. Harmondsworth: Penguin.
Webster, L., & J. Backhouse (eds.)
  1991   *The Making of England: Anglo-Saxon Art and Culture A.D. 600-900.*
            London: British Museum.
Wickman-Crowley, K.
  1992   The birds on the Sutton Hoo instrument. In *Sutton Hoo: Fifty Years After.*
            R. Farrell & C. Newman de Vegvar (eds.), pp. 43-62. (Am. Early Med.
            Studies 2). Oxford, OH: Am. Early Med. Studies, Dept. of Art, Miami Univ.
Wormald, P.
  1978   Bede, Beowulf and the Conversion of the Anglo-Saxon Aristocracy. In
            Bede and Anglo-Saxon England. R. Farrell (ed.), pp. 32-95. (BAR, British
            Series 46). Oxford: BAR. .
Youngs, S. (ed.)
  1989   *The Work of Angels, Masterpieces of Celtic Metalwork, 6th-9th Centuries A.D.*
            London: British Museum.

Discussion

HOOKE: You've given us some new ideas to consider, the linking of the riddles with what's hidden within interlace. I personally was intrigued by whether a hidden sense might lie in the beaching of the whale providing the material for the casket.

HAWKES: I had always understood that the whale was thrown up on the Northumbrian coast somehow.

HOOKE: They sometimes beach themselves, don't they?

POWLESLAND: It's interesting if there is a suggestion that the material has come from a beached whale rather than a hunted whale because of whales represented in the Early Anglo-Saxon period. We have some remains on site. The question is whether they are hunting the whales or just collecting material from beaches.

HAWKES: There was a porpoise jaw included with the St Ninian's Isle hoard.

HOOKE: The Franks Casket text does not necessarily refer to a hunted whale.

POWLESLAND: No. That's very interesting. I would rather have them using the beached whales than rushing off whaling in their coracles.

CHARLES-EDWARDS: The Franks Casket is actually very useful. The narrative is extremely eclectic. Really it demonstrates how difficult your task was, in a single artefact.

HAWKES: Iconographically it is extremely eclectic as well.

DUMVILLE: Can I take up the riddling matter to hang a couple of other points on? You started off what you were saying just now by discounting quite explicitly what you described as the imported Latin literature of Aldhelm and Bede; I'd urge that you reinstate that.

HAWKES: In terms of Bede's and Aldhelm's riddles?

DUMVILLE: I think one would be unwise to assume that because Aldhelm and Bede wrote in Latin, and because they wrote early in Anglo-Saxon history, they weren't doing something new in Latin literature. There is a good deal of evidence that they were. And obviously, one of the aspects of this is Aldhelm's riddles.

HAWKES: I'd understood that as regards Aldhelm's riddles there was some question as to whether they have a Germanic background, translated into Latin, or he was using a Latin riddling tradition, and translating that into an Anglo-Saxon context.

DUMVILLE: There certainly is a late Latin riddling background.

LENDINARA: The collection of riddles which exerted the largest influence on Latin medieval riddling practice was that by Symphosius (an African writer of the fourth/fifth century), who was the author of one hundred *enigmata*, each one consisting of three hexametres. Aldhelm, Eusebius, Tatwine and the authors of the Old English riddles of the Exeter Book all drew from Symphosius. The Anglo-Latin riddles are 'literary' riddles and are quite different from the 'popular' ones; they are provided with a title which gives the solution of the riddle, hence spoiling the ludic side of riddling and highlighting the erudite aspect of the compositions. There is some originality in Aldhelm's riddles, especially in the longer ones, such as no. 100 (*De creatura*), where the poet offers a moving description of the different elements of creation. A few features of Germanic riddle literature can be found in his *enigmata*.

DUMVILLE: Although he gives these titles, there are plenty of these riddles to which the solution is by no means necessarily the title advertised. So there is a further element of ambiguity built in, which is perhaps carried over into the vernacular riddles that we have later on, which are in part sub-Aldhelmian anyway. It has also been argued with increasing force that Aldhelm's poetic, his versificatory techniques, are heavily influenced by Germanic poetry. I'm sure this is controversial in a variety of ways, but the material is being produced more and more. There is work on this by my colleague Andrew Orchard, which lays this out with, for someone who is not a metrist, stupefying detail (e.g. Orchard 1994).

HAWKES: I left that whole argument out because I was very unsure about what the state of the current debate was between the Germanic and Latin inheritance of Latin Anglo-Saxon riddles.

DUMVILLE: Well, I think that what's happened is simply that Anglo-Latin literature has started to be studied in a more intensive way and all manner of things have now started to appear.

HOOKE: Am I right in thinking that riddles were quite common in many early societies?

DUMVILLE: Well, there is another stupefying piece of work (again it sounds rude; it's not at all intended to be, but it's simply the weight of documentation involved) by Patrick Sims-Williams (1978). The reason I mention him in particular is because he did a vast comparative trawl for material. He has a vast bibliography, from everywhere, and that's what is stupefying about it. There is a huge literature.

LENDINARA: The Finnish school (Aarne 1918-20) focussed its attention on the form (the pattern) of riddles. There is a likeness of motives of riddles of different times or locations (e.g. the 'year riddle' or the riddle about 'writing') which might be due to common origin, transmission and identity of processes of the human mind.

HOOKE: This goes right back to prehistoric art. We have little knowledge of what that conveys, and different ideas have been put forward.

HINES: Yes, but one surely shouldn't postulate a riddling tradition on the grounds that we have no idea of what the art actually means. Is there any argument except this totally circular one for a Germanic riddling tradition? The claims for the antiquity of this tradition in Anglo-Saxon culture are based on the fact that we have this art for which we cannot put forward interpretations in the sense of translations into another language. The Old English riddles often end up by saying, "Now discover what I am; discover the hidden message of the words". And there is a tendency to try and take that over to Style I art and to imagine that it says to you, "Now discover what I am". This could very well be anachronistic.

CHARLES-EDWARDS: But if Patrick and David are right, you have to argue that there wasn't. Since riddling is so widespread, right across Eurasia, the burden of proof should be on the person who tries to argue that there wasn't any such tradition.

HINES: There are two issues. One is the question: was there an ancient riddling tradition? And if there was one, there is the question of whether the art actually had anything to do with it. You talked about things like the 'meaning' of this, use the word 'decoded'. In one sense the art ought to have some meaning. But that meaning is also surely something that we can decode in the sense of identifying what it is that is speaking to us and going on to try to identify its meaning in much more functional terms. Why should one decorate one's artefactual environment in so many different ways? It's not necessarily the case that you hide little coded messages there. I would look for some consistent meaning in some consistent purpose which we can call a symbolic meaning. The terms in which one could analyse and articulate this meaning are a very difficult issue for us. One way of doing it, of course, which has been explored, is in terms of ethnic information, marking the identity of the people. One certainly ought not to assume that is the only or the major function. But it is at least an example of how this material can be interpreted.

CHARLES-EDWARDS: But if you think of the similarity between the Pictish stuff that was mentioned and some of the earliest Gospel books, it looks as though they were extremely ready to take material from other people.

DUMVILLE: Except there is an argument for one of those Gospel books being Pictish, if not two.

HOOKE: I strongly disagree that just because it's difficult to decode, we shouldn't analyse it. We analyse everything else in literature down to the last dot over the 'i', so why shouldn't we try in this case?

HINES: I'm not for a moment suggesting that it shouldn't be analysed. But we need to think about the terms in which we analyse it and we probably need to think carefully about what sort of information we might get out of it.

SCULL: I should like to draw attention to the cemetery evidence, which has a rich symbolic dimension. Provision of grave goods varies with sex and age at death, and there are other patterns which suggest that the social identity of the deceased was in some way symbolized in burial practice. Perhaps this points us towards another way of investigating symbolism: a comparative approach to the contexts in which symbols occur. This leads me to a second point, relevant to our discussion of Style I. Because so little organic material has survived, we have no idea whether Style I, for instance, was ubiquitous—on wood, textiles, or even tattoos—or whether it was one of a range of treatments which may have had only a very restricted niche on fine metalwork. We think of Style I as the characteristic decorative style of the Migration period, but in fact the great majority of known examples is on high-quality metalwork produced for women. Might this contextual evidence tell us something about its symbolic sphere and symbolic functions?

HAWKES: We can say that a significant number of the bracteates with Style I decoration on them are associated with female burials.

HINES: It's only in Norway and in England that they turn up in grave finds; elsewhere they are hoarded. But in Denmark they are regularly hoarded with women's jewellery, so there is no serious doubt that these pendants are women's dress accessories. You noted that one apparent exception to the general lack of comprehension surrounding Style I animals, is their use on gold bracteates, objects which occur in high-status burials in the sixth century. This exception is a pretty serious exception, because Style I originates in the late fifth century in southern Scandinavia and in its earliest occurrences it's limited to just two types of artefact. The one is the gold bracteate and the other is the relief brooch, a very expensive and splendid type of brooch that is worn by the richest women. So, if Style I actually emerged on the bracteates, and genuinely is interpretable in that context, it's not by any means a marginal area. I, however, do not believe one can make a very good case for actually reading Style I art on the bracteates. You certainly cannot make any case for reading the art on the equally early square-headed brooches in the same way.

HAWKES: I'm extremely unhappy with Style I. I felt very much as if I was pushing it to try to get something out of nothing.

SCULL: It's worth noting that contemporary with the very stylized zoomorphic ornamentation of Style I in England, animals are depicted very differently on pottery, this can be seen at Spong Hill. Might a structuralist approach to the different traditions as fine metalwork and cremation pottery be useful? Does the context affect or dictate the symbolism here? Is Style I appropriate only to fine metalwork?

HÄRKE: This continuity of animal symbolism from pagan to Christian I found intriguing. Do we also have any overlap or continuity of symbolism from Roman to post-Roman? I'm not talking about art styles; what I mean is symbolism itself, the use of certain symbols.

POWLESLAND: Well, it is simple really. There are swastikas, both ways round, right through. They occur in the metalwork throughout, they are there in the Roman period, and you get them both in wall plaster and in mosaics.

HAWKES: You also get in the mosaics—I'm not sure if this is strictly relevant to your question—but those mosaic floors that you have in the villas in the south of England, include the use of characters like Poseidon turning up in demonstrably Christian contexts; they are associated with pictures of Christ. So, you get a continuation of pagan, or secular imperial art, carrying through, or being picked up again—I think it's more a case of being picked up again—in early Anglo-Saxon

Christian art. For instance, just within the end of this period, possibly, if you date the Rothbury Cross to the late eighth century, which I think is more likely than the early ninth century, on the back of the cross-head, on the reverse side of the crucifixion, you have three figures surviving, holding what I think are two crowns of victory, the *mappa circensis* (the napkin depicted on the consular diptychs, which was dropped to start the circus games celebrating the inauguration of the consul), and the short small sceptre that the consul holds on the consular diptychs. So you have three symbols that are very specifically associated with consular diptychs in a non-Christian context. They are part of imperial art of the fifth and sixth centuries, and presumably go back earlier that that as well. And you get that turning up, being re-used and re-defined, in the Christian context.

AUSENDA: Concerning Salin's Style I animals defined "as creatures whose bodies have been exploded into a number of component parts" I would like to refer you to Franz Boas' *Kwakiutl Ethnography* where he expressed the idea that they cut them up in order to fit them in the surfaces they had (Boas 1966:329).

My second point is on the possibility that bracteates evolved from imperial coinage. Tacitus relates that the *Germani* preferred *serratos bigatosque* coins confirming that they were used for their 'religious' connection since the chariot and horses were sacred, connected with the cult of Woden, I believe. I do not understand the religious connection of the *serratos* coins.

There is a parallel with the Sudan and northern Ethiopia concerning what you said about bracteates being women's ornaments and that the remains were found of a man wearing one. In eastern Sudan and northern Ethiopia, Maria Theresa thalers are indeed worn always by women as amulets on necklaces except during a wedding ceremony. On this occasion the mother or a female relative gives her Maria Theresa thaler as a fertility talisman to the bridegroom who wears it throughout the ceremony.

My final remark on this very interesting paper concerns the use of animals in iconography. I thought that if animals were that important in iconography they would be just as important in peoples names. So I took a look at the *Deutsche Namenkunde* (Bach 1978) which discusses Germanic names. It appears that the boar, the eagle and the snake were quite popular. The boar, Old High German *ebur*, was the animal which 'accompanied' Freyr, the god of fertility (Page 1990:9). However its use in male accoutrements and names was surely connected with the fighting qualities of the animal. Most names made up with *ebur* and *aro* as the first part of the compound were also names of males. The eagle, OHG *aro* or *arn*, was an animal connected with Odin (Bach 1978:212). Odin was capable of assuming the forms of a serpent (Mundkur 1983:170). Snake in OHG is *lint* and there were names of males with that term as the first part of the compound. The word for 'stag', OHG *hiruz*, was very seldom used in Germanic names.

What surprised me was the absence in the iconography of the images of a 'wolf', which was quite commonly used in names, and 'hraban', the crow which perched on Woden's shoulder. In fact there were several Anglo-Saxon names with 'wolf' as the first part of the compound.

HOOKE: There were many wolves in Anglo-Saxon England.

CHARLES-EDWARDS: There is an early enough story about an ancestor of the Uí Neill being reared, very interestingly, by wolves. As with those riddling things, there are possibilities of polygenesis.

AUSENDA: It's strange that the wolf does not appear in iconography despite its being so popular in names.

HAWKES: I have a list of the compounds of animals in Anglo-Saxon names. As far as I can remember there are 'eagle and bear', 'eagle and boar', I think. You don't get as many pictures of wolves. The wolf seems to be a very common name, and compound element of a name.

SCULL: It is very difficult to identify most Style I or Style II animals as specific species; indeed, it has been argued by David Leigh (1984) that the images are deliberately ambiguous.

HINES; I think, in fact, that in all of this one's got to remember that in both Style I and Style II it can be quite a matter of guesswork to identify a given animal: to say that 'this is a wolf; this is a serpent'. It could be a crocodile or a worm or all sorts of things. I have often thought that the models for the so-called dog's heads in the Book of Lindisfarne could just as well be seals. Quite seriously, there are lots of seals around the island. These pictures are just as seal-like as dog-like.

DUMVILLE: Let's keep off the Lindisfarne origin of the thing!

HINES: The point is that even the current identification of the depicted animal is highly conventionalized.

Every so often we have introduced the British population into discussions. In early Welsh literature and poetry there's a lot of imagery using crows and so on. Is there anything that seems usefully comparable, in terms of the use of animals there? It might in fact provide us with an important context. These animals' function within the British symbolic world could in fact affect their presence in the Anglo-Saxon context.

DUMVILLE: It is an extremely interesting question, but should prove a bit of a challenge to answer.

POWLESLAND: I remember we have a serpent in a pattern-welded sword. And there is actually a literary description of such a sword which remarkably resembles the one that we've excavated. That led me on to wondering how many bits of decoration there were on iron objects that don't survive because, of course, we tend just to get these nasty piles of rust. And if they are not very serious like pattern welding, they are not even going to appear in x-rays. It's something that I as an archaeologist have to remind myself of constantly that what we see as, in a sense, an art or decorative material is a tiny percentage of what we have to assume existed. Not just even in the metalwork; we get large quantities of ironwork which is very likely to have been decorated, given that decorated metalwork was the ultimate form of decoration. I can see them very probably decorating other stuff, much as some people did in the nineteenth century, by using a different handwriting when finishing things off.

SCULL: The Alamannic cemetery at Oberflacht is interesting. This was waterlogged, and so a wide range of wooden objects survives, including coffins made from hollowed tree trunks. Some of these have easily identifiable serpents—albeit with two heads—carved on the lid (Paulsen 1992; Schiek 1992).

HAWKES: No legs?

SCULL: No legs, no.

References in the discussion

Textual sources:

Aldhelm

    Riddles *(Enigmata)*: see Ehwald 1919; Lapidge & Rosier 1985.

Symphosius

    Enigmata: see Shackleton Bailey 1982.

Bibliography:

Aarne, A.
    1918-20   *Vergleichende Rätselforschung.* Helsinki: Suomalaisen tiedeakatemian kustantama.

Bach, A.
    1978   *Deutsche Namenkunde. Band I, 1: Die deutschen Personennamen.* Heidelberg: Carl Winter.

Boas, F.
    1966   *Kwakiutl Ethnography.* Chicago: University of Chicago Press.

Ehwald, R. (ed.)
    1919   *Aldhelmi opera. Monumenta Germaniae historica, Auctores Antiquissimi* 15. Berlin: Weidmann.

Lapidge, M., & J. L. Rosier (trans.)
    1985   *Aldhelm: The Poetic Works.* Woodbridge: D. S. Brewer.

Leigh, D.
    1984   Ambiguity in Anglo-Saxon Style I art. *The Antiquaries Journal* 64: 34-42.

Mundkur, B.
    1983   *The Cult of the Serpent: An Interdisciplinary Survey of its Manifestations and Origins.* Albany: State University of New York Press.

Orchard, A.
    1994   *The Poetic Art of Aldhelm.* Cambridge: Cambridge University Press.

Page, R. I.
    1990   *Norse Myths.* London: British Museum Press.

Paulsen, S.
    1992   *Die Holzfunde aus dem Gräberfeld bei Oberflacht und ihre kulturhistorische Bedeutung.* (Forschungen und Berichte zur Vor- und Frühgeschichte in Baden-Württemberg 41/2). Stuttgart: Konrad Theiss Verlag.

Schiek, S.
    1992   *Das Gräberfeld der Merowingerzeit bei Oberflacht.* (Forschungen und Berichte zur Vor- und Frühgeschichte in Baden-Württemberg 41/1). Stuttgart: Konrad Theiss Verlag.

Shackleton Bailey, D. R.
    1982   *Anthologia latina, I.* Stuttgart: Teubner.

Sims-Williams, P.
    1978   Riddling treatment of the "watchman device" in *Branwen and Togail Bruidne Da Derga. Studia celtica* 12/13: 83-117.

THE TERMINOLOGY OF OVERKINGSHIP IN EARLY ANGLO-SAXON ENGLAND

DAVID N. DUMVILLE

Girton College, Cambridge, GB-CB3 9DP

Since Eric John published his celebrated essay, *'Orbis Britanniae'* (John 1966:1-66), the problems of early Anglo-Saxon kingship and overkingship have been among the principal issues discussed by historians of the period (e.g. Keynes 1992; Scharer 1988; Vollrath-Reichelt 1971; Wormald 1974/5; 1983; 1986; 1992; Yorke 1981). But it has not always been so. For a half-century before 1966 there had been almost no discussion of this large series of interlocking problems. Before John's work appeared, the subject had been dominated by the views of Sir Frank Stenton, whose formidable learning and authority in matters touching early English history seem, in hindsight, to have left little room for scholarly debate (cf. Drögereit 1952 and Stengel 1960 from outside the English tradition of historiography). Stenton's first, and seminal, contribution to our immediate subject was his paper on 'The supremacy of the Mercian kings', issued in 1918 (Stenton 1970:48-66). Striking out in a new direction by basing his arguments on a critical attitude to the evidence of royal diplomas, Stenton evidently felt little in need to refer back to the work of other scholars who had studied Anglo-Saxon kingship and overlordship. In one particular respect, his omission created an unhappy tradition, one which controlled Anglo-Saxon historiography until very recently and whose effects are still with us.

For in 1905 had been published one of the most important modern works on the political and social structure of the Anglo-Saxon kingdoms. Hector Munro Chadwick's *Studies on Anglo-Saxons Institutions*, a book which has not since received the credit which it properly deserves (beginning with the review by Stenton 1905; cf. Bullough 1965; Loyn 1962:390), investigated the nature—*inter alia permulta*—of early Anglo-Saxon kingship (Chadwick 1905:249-307). Students of English history have long been consumed with a fascination of the so-called *'Bretwalda'* and his authority in the 'heptarchich' period of Anglo-Saxon England. Stenton directed this interest into the study of specific phases of Anglo-Saxon royal overlordship. In so-doing, he reinforced that general tendency of English scholars to concentrate on the importance of overkingship as a theme in the constitutional history of the Anglo-Saxon peoples. But royal overlordship necessarily implies dependent royalty, and here is where Chadwick's book comes into its own (for comparative purposes, the contemporary work of Eiten 1907 remains useful). Early Anglo-Saxon kingship is a very complex subject; yet, from 1905 until the 1970s, little scholarly attention was devoted to it.

The dependants, or potential dependants, of an Anglo-Saxon overlord have never been the subject of a special study. Until recently, the petty kings of Anglo-Saxon England have been fodder only for local antiquaries (Bonser 1957 provided

345

THE ANGLO-SAXONS FROM THE MIGRATION PERIOD TO THE EIGHTH CENTURY:
AN ETHNOGRAPHIC PERSPECTIVE

© C.I.R.O.S.S.
San Marino (R.S.M.)

most of the relevant bibliography). The results of an investigation of the more local rulers of Anglo-Saxon England necessarily have an immediate bearing on our ideas of overlordship in that period (for recent large-scale treatments, see Bassett 1989, Kirby 1991, and Yorke 1990; for summary, tabular treatment see Dumville 1986). Our conclusions as to the quality of English royal authority when it emerges into history will inevitably tend to determine our responses to subsequent indications of its changing nature.

The general tendency has indeed been to look at relationships between kings through the overlord's eyes. Along with this has gone the assumption that the overlord is a 'proper' king—one, that is to say, who conforms to some modern expectation of royal power—and that the other, dependent, ruler is scarcely worthy of the title. Consider, for example, the following typical passage, which I take from Stenton's *Anglo-Saxon England*, where I have emboldened the relevant passages (1943:45-6=1971:46):

> A little before the year 700 a certain Oshere...had styled himself 'king of the Hwicce' without any qualification [Sawyer 1968: S 53]. Some forty years after his death **his real position** was defined by an archbishop of Canterbury, who described him as *comes*, or retainer, of Æthelred, king of the Mercians, and *subregulus*, or under-king, of the Hwicce [S 1429]. Oshere was succeeded in his kingdom by four of his sons, and in 736 one of them attests the oldest original Mercian charter as 'under-king and retainer of Æthelbald king of the Mercians' [S 89]. But in 736 the archaic conception of a king or under-king who was also a member of a lord's household was itself becoming obsolete, and the last of these early rulers of the Hwicce—three brothers who held the throne jointly under Offa of Mercia—ignore the association with an overlord's court *which their ancestors had regarded as an especial honour*. They assert, and even emphasize, the *shadow of kingship* that belonged to them. In 777 one of them styles himself 'under-king' of the Hwicce by the dispensation of the Lord' [S 113]. But in the same charter King Offa, his overlord, expressed the **realities of his position** by calling him 'my under-king, ealdorman, that is, of his own people of the Hwicce'.

Leaving aside the distinct possibility that Stenton mistranslated two key terms—*regulus* ('petty king', not 'under-king' which would be *subregulus*) and *dux* ('leader', not 'ealdorman')—we may note that he rejected the Hwiccian kings' own statements of their position, and relied on those of their overlords as exclusive statements of fact when in reality they describe only the relative standing of the two parties. Stenton indicated his deductions quite plainly when he wrote of two Hwiccian kings of the time of Æthelred of Mercia (AD 675-704): "whatever rank may have been theirs by birth, they owed their authority to his gift" (1971:45). It seems to me that this approach is highly prejudicial, and distorts our perception of early Anglo-Saxon kingship. We can learn much from Midland charters of the eighth century about the workings of the Mercian overlordship, and on this question Stenton (1970:48-66) is our mentor. But he largely ignored the dependent rulers, their origins, their claims, their power. We shall discover a great deal about these questions if we learn to look up and (especially) to look around, rather than simply continue to look down from the overking's lofty heights.

Comprehension of the royal terminology used by our Anglo-Saxon sources becomes difficult in situations where royal power is diminished. If we are to understand the nature of early Anglo-Saxon kingship, we must study these circumstances. A king's authority within his kingdom may be circumscribed by the need either to co-exist with co-rulers or to make allowance for the interests of a powerful overlord. Of these pressures the former is fragmentarily—though convincingly—illustrated by the sources for the period. Such a situation naturally has implications for terminology employed to describe the kings, their authority, and their territorial holdings. Comprehension of this terminology—and of that used in other, less complex, situations in the early kingdoms—is essential for an approach to the difficult problems presented by the sources which illustrate the workings of early Anglo-Saxon overkingship.

From the late sixth century to the early tenth a variety of terms was employed to describe Anglo-Saxon kings. In Old English, *cyning* and *hlāford* are the normal words, with *undercyning* making an occasional appearance. But most of our evidence is not couched in the vernacular. In Latin, *rex* is of course the most common, but *regulus* and *subregulus* are also important. The nature of a king's power is expressed in terms of *regnum* and *imperium*. His people may be described as a *gens* or *populus* (very occasionally as *genus* or *natio*), and the territorial unit as *prouincia, regio,* or *regnum*.[1] An accurate correlation of these various terms should tell us much about the structure of early Anglo-Saxon kingship. We must, of course, be on our guard against both inconsistent usage (particularly as between different Latin writers, and especially the writers of charters) and the greatly varying viewpoints and political circumstances reflected by different sources. For example, use of *subregulus* or *undercyning* (Sawyer 1968: S 126) necessarily implies subordination and overkingship (as perhaps *regulus* does too); such usage represents a vertical view of political relationships, expressed in terms likely to have been employed by someone looking down from above. This is even more pronounced where a person seen to be exercising royal power is nonetheless described as *dux, comes,* or *miles*.

In our sources for the period beginning at the close of the sixth century, we see royal authority being divided in a number of different ways in the various Anglo-Saxon kingdoms. Committee-rule seems to be attested among the Hwicce, East Saxons, and perhaps South Saxons; there is some implication in such circumstances of the operation of a seniority-system. The people, but not their territory, might be divided into their separate units (without concern to achieve territorially compact or exclusive units); this is uncertainly attested for the East Saxons, and there are other Germanic parallels for such arrangements (Wood 1977:18-22, on the Burgundians; cf. Wood 1990a), while the practice was known also in early medieval Ireland. The territory might be divided, as is variously seen in Kent, Essex, and (less clearly) Sussex; plainly this might be achieved in a

---

[1] For discussion of these Latin terms in an Irish context, see Charles-Edwards (1993:154-65, 469-72); his treatment of their English use (1983:49-50) is troublesome, however.

number of different ways, with different types of relationships between the co-rulers. Division of royal authority would perhaps tend naturally to provoke a redistribution of power within the kingdom to the extent of the development of an internal overlordship. We seem to see this at its fullest, most institutionalized extent in seventh-century Wessex (discussed by Dumville 1985). In a number of the kingdoms, it would seem, the internal administrative divisions either did habitually support or could support, in the case of occasional joint government, rulers of royal status. Inevitably, the following question is whether these administrative sub-units were original kingdoms or merely the creations of seventh- or eighth-century kings.

As some kings became overlords outside their own kingdoms, so others fell prey to such expanding authority. Already in the second half of the seventh century in Northumbria, the Bernician kings were appointing their close relatives to be dependent rulers of the subject kingdom of Deira (discussion by Miller 1979 and Abels 1983). Such a procedure is found again in the treatment of Kent by King Cenwulf of Mercia from 798 when he appointed his brother as its king (Brooks 1984:129-32). And the West Saxon kings, overlords of south-eastern England from 825 x 828, continued this practice by appointing their sons to rule in the east of Greater Wessex (namely, Essex, Kent, Surrey, and Sussex) (Brooks 1984:136-7, 197-206; Dumville 1979; 1992: ch. I).

One of the few Anglo-Saxon kingdoms which we know to have lost territory to a neighbour by annexation in these circumstances is Essex. The detachment in the early eighth century of London and its hinterland—of Middlesex, in other words—from Essex and its fairly rapid absorption into Mercia has long been known, if perhaps insufficiently stressed in modern literature (Dumville 1992:3-6). This inevitably raises questions about the structure of early Essex, especially in view of its known history of multiple kingship. Could Middlesex have been, under some other name, a self-contained province of the East Saxon kingdom? Given the appearance of a sub-king in late seventh-century Surrey, the southern district of the East Saxons, and of kings of the East Saxon line in Saxon West Kent whenever the vagaries of seventh- and eighth-century south-eastern politics permitted, we might think this a reasonable speculation: but it can be no more than that (Dumville 1993: ch. IX).

In general, it is perhaps surprising that the incidence of joint rule did not encourage or allow more such annexations. The potential for external intervention created by joint rule is well illustrated by the case of Hlothere and Eadric, co-rulers of Kent in the 680s (Kirby 1991:44, 113-9). But such situations seem usually to have led to changing patterns of overkingship rather than to annexations. It is, in fact, striking in general how multiple kingship does not seem to have led to permanent fragmentation of kingdoms. (The trend seems in fact to have been in the opposite direction). This implies that the mesne kingdoms—in spite of evidence for their origins as agglomerations of much smaller kingdoms—were generally recognized as constituting political units, *gentes*, enjoying a strong degree of cohesion.

A factor tending to reinforce the cohesion of the whole unit was the rule, which seems to have operated in kingdoms enjoying multiple kingships, that a grant of land in hereditary tenure by one king required a co-ruler's assent. We see this in Kent, in Sussex, and among the Hwicce. It was perhaps no more than an extension of this rule which caused an external overlord to expect to exercise a comparable right of veto over a dependent ruler's grants (cf. Sawyer 1978:101-2). But eventually this led, via joint grants by overlord and local king, to the making of direct grants of land by an overking within a subject kingdom without (at least explicit) reference to the local ruler; we find this last prerogative exercised by Mercian overlords, from the beginning of our records among the Hwicce, and from the later eighth century in Kent.

Perhaps it was precisely because there was so much overlapping of royal functions that royal titles were often so unspecific. From the early 760s we have two grants made by Sigered, East-Saxon king of West Kent: in one he is styled *rex dimidiae partis prouinciae Cantuariorum* (Sawyer 1968: S 33), in the other merely *rex Cantie* (S 32). If, in the more general case, we were to translate with the definite article, the title would be patently untrue; the indefinite article ('a king of Kent') might seem to us demeaning but would have the merit of being accurate; perhaps a compromise such as 'a king [exercising power] within Kent' should be adopted.

We may have here the makings of one disctintion between kingship and overkingship. Kingship of a country may divisible, but the nation itself remains a unity. An overlordship, on the other hand, may be created and held by an individual ruler, but it is difficult to transmit to a successor since it has no natural unity; only a long, continuous period of enforcement, and the vigurous reduction of factors tending to emphasize the separate identities of the constituent parts, could hope to create a kingdom from an overlordship (Dumville 1993:28).

How was the distinction between early Anglo-Saxon kingship and overkingship expressed by contemporary witnesses? The title of an overlord was no different from that of an ordinary king: he was still *rex*, and his overlordship was simply an extension of this prerequisite kingship. Bede's invariable usage (in his *Historia ecclesiastica gentis Anglorum*) for an English king, however powerful, is *rex*. Only in the charters of the eighth-century Mercian supremacy can we see moves being made to express the powers of overlordship in an appropriate formula: however, the word *rex* remains central to any such formula.

As far as we can see, overkingship consisted of a king's power being formally recognized by another kingdom, normally by the ruler of that second kingdom. This would usually be established by a military campaign, but the reputation of an overking might be such that other, less powerful kings would wish to seek him as their lord. A marriage-alliance and perhaps a relationship of spiritual kinship might be the chosen means (Angenendt 1984; Campbell 1985:73-6). *Gecēosan tō hlāforde* is an expression studied by Chadwick who indicated that it would apply to recognition as well of overkingship as of lordship within a kingdom (Chadwick 1905:360-6); he made the further useful point that although *gecēosan tō hlāforde* was "the act of an individual and involved the relationship of 'lord' and 'man'", that individual's dependants and lands would nonetheless pass with him to his lord (Chadwick 1905:352; cf. Stenton 1971:35). Under these circumstances an overkingship would be unlikely to be transmitted from one king to his successor (Stenton 1971:36), who would not necessarily be a close relative at all. Under conditions of overlordship, we find the overking's writ running from one end of his territories to another and we see the overking beginning to dispose directly of lands in the subordinate kingdoms.

Hlāford (or *dryhten*: for discussion see Green 1965) was represented in Latin by *dominus*. The power of overkingship itself was represented in Bede's *Historia ecclesiastica* by the word *imperium*. *Imperator*, however, was invariably reserved for the Roman (or Byzantine) emperor; as I have just mentioned, Bede gave no English king a more imposing title than *rex*. However, his use of verbs tells us more. *Imperare* he twice used of Æthelberht I of Kent (*HE* II.3; II.5), and on the second occasion it applies also to the other kings having power over all Southumbrians (also in a document, quoted by Bede in *HE* IV.17 [15], in reference to Ecgfrith of Northumbria and Æthelred of Mercia); and verbs compounded with *prae-* and *super-* are employed to express, *inter alia*, the power of overlordship.

The sources of early Anglo-Latin political terminology, as well as the associated ideologies, still require sustained investigation. The role of the Bible (McClure 1983) and of Christian authors of late antiquity (Fanning 1991a; 1991b) will of course need close and particular consideration. More tantalizing because as yet less tangible are the direct contributions of those who were the evangelists and neighbours of the Anglo-Saxons: sixth- and seventh-century Romans (Evans 1986 and references), Britons and Irish (Charles-Edwards 1983, Dumville 1994), and Franks. The still somewhat indefinable but, thanks to Ian Wood's dogged and imaginative campaign (Wood 1983; 1990b; 1991; 1992; 1994a; 1994b:176-80), increasingly certain overkingly roles of Frakish rulers in south-eastern England in the sixth and earlier seventh centuries may have left as yet unrecovered traces in vernacular and Latinate locutions.

Charles Plummer (1896: II.43 and 86) notes the opposition of *regnum* ('royal power or authority'; 'reign'; 'kingdom') and *imperium* ('overkingship'). This observation has since been attacked (cf. Campbell 1985:85-6; McClure 1983:96-8; Wormald 1983:107-9) but it seems to me that it stands yet. Detailed study of Bede's use of this terminology reveals some interesting evidence. *Imperium* he used sparingly; it states the nature of the power of the seven overkings of the southern English, whom he named in the *Historia ecclesiastica* II.5, and is employed also to refer to the power of some of them individually (Æthelberht, *HE* I.25 [twice] and II.5; Edwin, *HE* II.9 [twice] and II.16; Oswald, *HE* II.14; Oswiu, *HE* IV.3). He used it, furthermore, of English power over Celtic neighbours (*HE* II.5; II.9), on Edwin's authority over the Mevanian Islands (*HE* IV.12), and on the subjection of the Picts, or some of them, to Ecgfrith of Nurthumbria. Additionally, however, we find the word used of the power of a series of Northumbrian rulers who do not seem to have exercised overkingship of all the Southumbrians: Ecgfrith, 670-85 (*HE* IV.12), Aldfrith, 686-705, and his son and eventual successor

Osred, 705-16 (*HE* V.18 and 19; Stephanus, *Vita S. Wilfridi*, par. 60, called Osred *Aquilonalium regem*). This usage is not to be taken as an expression of Bede's Northumbrian patriotism, however, for more credible explanations are available. Ecgfrith was for some years (674-9) overlord of Lindsey and Mercia, and in his later years was recognized as overking by British Dál Riata and by Strathclyde; he seems also to have annexed some Pictish territory (Stenton 1971:85, 87-8; Thomas 1984). He was, then, a powerful ruler whose authority extended well beyond his own boundaries. However appropriate may seem the use of *imperium* to describe his power, the reason for Bede's use of this word cannot in fact lie here. For Aldfrith and Osred cannot be shown to have possessed authority outside Northumbria; Osred's power seems never to have been fully assured even there. We must conclude, and the evidence from Wessex will tend to support this, that the *imperium* of Northumbrian rulers derived from their control of two kingdoms (*prouinciae, regna*), Bernicia and Deira; Northumbria in the seventh century at least should, therefore, be seen as an overkingship, not as a single kingdom (Myres 1935/6; cf. Charles-Edwards in Wallace-Hadrill 1988:226-8). Only after a substantial space of time during which the two units had been continuously united would this sense of an *imperium*, consisting of two potentially independent *regna*, cease to be operative. It is interesting that Bede did not use the word *imperium* to define the rule of Ceolfwulf, his own king (on their relationship, cf. Kirby 1979/80).

When writing of Northumbria (or Wessex), Bede often alternated in his usage—within the same sentence or paragraph—between *imperium* and *regnum*. The consequent apparent risk that the alleged distinction may generally in fact be no more than the result of elegant variation of vocabulary is, however, to be discounted. *Imperium* was used sparingly and, it seems, carefully by Bede; while *regnum* might be alternated with it for elegant variation, the reverse is certainly not the case.

We may now address the final examples, those relating to Mercia. Bede referred to two Mercian kings as possessing *imperium* (*HE* V.24, *recapitulatio, s.aa.* 675 and 731): Wulfhere (658-674) and Æthelbald 716-757). This corresponds exactly to the picture derived by Stenton in 1918 from an examination principally of documentary evidence (Stenton 1970:48-66; crucial evidence is also provided by Stephanus, *Vita S. Wilfridi*, par. 20); the overkingship of the southern English (which Bede described in *HE* II.5) fell, after Oswiu, to Wulfhere and then, after about half a century in which no ruler achieved such power, to Æthelbald. The only problem which emerges in this connection is Bede's statement in his summary chronicle, *sub anno* 675, that Wulfhere left his *imperium* to his successor Æthelred; it is noteworthy that, in the annal (704) recording the next Mercian successor, Bede wrote "Aedilred...Coenredo regnum dedit". Bede had already noted, in an aside from another subject (*HE* IV.12), that Ecgfrith of Northumbria defeated an invasion by Wulfhere and seized Lindsey from Mercia (an event usually attributed to 673 x 675, following Colgrave 1927:166): and Stephanus, in the *Life of Wilfrid* (written in 709 x 731), remarked that Mercia was itself for a while reduced under tribute ("*regnumque eius sub tributo distribuit*", par. 20). If

Wilfrid's biographer, whom Bede read (Goffart 1988:235-328), was correct, then Wulfhere can hardly have been in a position to transmit his *imperium* of the southern English to his successor in Mercia. In that case we should have to understand *imperium* in this context as the Midland overlordship which constituted the basis of Mercian power in the period.

Bede's famous list of the seven kings who had held the *imperium* of the Southumbrian English (*HE* II.5) has given rise to much speculation. His clear recognition of Æthelbald's power in 731 (*HE* V.23) suggests that his motive in terminating the list of overkings with Oswiu of Northumbria was not racial or nationalistic unwillingness to recognize the extent of Mercian power.[2] What does not seem to have been remarked in this connection is that Bede nowhere in his account of the seven overkings hints that there were *only* seven such rulers. The passage occurs as a tangential development of a remark about Æthelberht I of Kent, with a notice of whose death the chapter begins. Æthelberht, wrote Bede, was the third such overking but—and here is the point of specifying that he was the third overking—he was the *first* English king to enter the kingdom of heaven. Bede then named the first two overkings, mentioned Æthelberht in the sequence, and continued with notices of four more. After devoting some lines to Oswiu, Bede realized—or so it seems to me—that he was straying badly from his main point; with an abrupt '*Sed haec postmodum*' (and *haec* may refer either to Oswiu's activities or to the whole of the preceding excursus) he returned to his principal subject-matter, Æthelberht's death and its effects on the progress of the Christian mission in the south-east.

We have no reason to assume, therefore, that Bede could not have extended the list towards his own day. Indeed, there is every reason to suppose that Bede knew perfectly well of Wulfhere's ascendancy, and he is certainly quite explicit about Æthelbald's Southumbrian overlordship (*HE* V.23). As always, arguments from Bede's silence about secular matters are weak, and apt to be misleading; they provide instead an index of his reticence and his severe criteria of relevance in respect of non-ecclesiastical affairs.

If Bede's invariable term for a king was *rex*—however imposing that king's *imperium*—we must ask further questions about the famous passage of the *Anglo-Saxon Chronicle, sub anno* 827, where Bede's list of overkings is rendered into the vernacular and with the additional name of Ecgberht of Wessex. This is the sentence which has given rise to so much talk of 'Bretwaldas' and 'Bretwaldaships'. In the words of the early tenth-century A-text, "*geēode Ecgbryht cyning Miercna rīce 7 al thæt be sūthan Humbre wæs, 7 hē wæs se eahtetha cyning sē the bretwal'd'a wæs*"; "King Ecgberht conquered the kingdom of the Mercians and everything which lay to the south of the Humber, and he was the eighth king who was *Bretwalda*". Eric John discussed this passage, to radical effect (John 1966:6-8). It is as clear as anything can be that *Bretwalda* cannot be the original

---

[2] Such a motive, or an equally great ignorance, may rather be attributed to the ninth-century West-Saxon chronicler (*Anglo-Saxon Chronicle* s.a. 827=829) who copied out Bede's list, adding Ecgberht of Wessex (802-839; overking 829/30) as the eighth.

reading of the sentence of the *Chronicle* (Whitelock 1979:186 n.2, 493). The testimony of the other manuscripts (which do not share a single immediate common ancestor independent of A) assures us that the primary wording employed the noun *b/Brytenw(e)alda*, whose meaning still requires discussion.[3] As evidence of the poor quality of the A-text, initially given by Plummer (1892/9: xciv, cii-civ) who first clearly established the distance between A and the archetype, has accumulated, that conclusion has become progressively more secure. The title *Bretwalda*—if that indeed is what any Anglo-Saxon ever perceived it to be—thus becomes a scribal curiosity, no longer a peg on which to hang large hypotheses of English constitutional history or a secure foundation on which the archaeologists can build a circumstantial superstructure of court-furnishings, regalian ritual, and imperially wealthy funeral-practices (as, for example, by Bruce-Mitford 1975-83). If the scribe of MS A, or a proximate ancestor, thought about the consequences of or even noticed his omission of a single syllable (*b/Bre/yt[en]walda*), he may have believed the first element to have been *Bret-*, or *Bryt-*, as in *Bre/ytwalas*, 'Britons', indeed, *Bretwala* is what the scribe of MS A first wrote (ed. J. M. Bately in Dumville & Keynes 1983- : III.42; facsimile eds. Flower & Smith 1941: fo. 12r; cf. Yorke 1981:173-4). But even if the creation of this form—at some date between 891 and the 920s (Dumville 1992: ch. III)—was the result of thought, it remains far from clear that its creator thought it a formal institutional title. Attempts to turn this broad conclusion aside, by insisting that the form *b/Brytenw(e)alda* replaced an earlier *Bretwalda* in a common ancestor of Chronicle MSS B, C, D, E and F, must be rejected. The A-text is the corrupt deviant, not the others. We have no reason to allow that *Bretwalda*, in effect a ghost-word, was an ancient title.

That conclusion throws into prominent relief the Ismere charter issued by Æthelbald, king of Mercia, in 736 and surviving as an original single-sheet document, in which he was styled "*rex Britanniae*", "*gloriosissimus princeps*", "*rex Suutanglorum*" and "*rex non solum Marcersium sed et omnium prouinciarum quae generale nomine Sutangli dicuntur*" (Sawyer 1968: S 89). Taken together with the A-Chronicle's rendering of Bede's list of overkings, the styles of this document seemed to offer the clearest indication of a formalized notion of a British overkingship based on Southumbrian England (Stenton 1971:34-5). We need to take stock of how our perceptions of this question must now change.

In fact, very little difference is made to what the principal sources have to say. What we have lost is the word '*Bretwalda*' and, with it, we may cast Modern English 'Bretwaldaship' into the flames. And good riddance!—for it takes with it all the institutional structure which the ingenuity of nineteenth- and twentieth-century constitutional historians has been able to erect (cf. Graus 1986 for useful relevant discussion which may be taken as commentary on Wenskus 1961). We can now consider the sources afresh.

---

[3] On the problems see Yorke (1981:172), and J. M. Bately in Dumville & Keynes (1983: cxvii n.332); John's attempt (1966:7-8) to build on a locution from the Old Saxon *Heliand* introduced into this discussion by Carl Erdmann (1951:4) fails on comparative philological grounds, as has been pointed out by Charles-Edwards (1991:24-5, 31 n.32) and by D. H. Green in Keynes (1992:120 n.52).

Bede still tells us of a discontinuous series of overkings of the Southumbrian English, and the Ismere charter still reeks, even more strongly than Bede's paragraph, of ideology. The *Anglo-Saxon Chronicle* offers us, in late ninth-century form, an interesting vernacular noun; but beyond that its annal has no immediate value for our purpose, save in as much as it implies that the idea of Southumbrian overkingship no longer had much meaning by AD 892 (on this date of the original common stock of the *Chronicle* see Dumville 1992:89-90, and references given there). If the *Su(u)tangli* of the charter are "the southern English" rather than "the South Angles", then we may legitimately bring this document into association with Bede's list of Southumbrian overkings. And when we do so, we are still confronted with familiar questions. What is significant of the Humber as a frontier and why do Southumbrian overlords merit separate and special attention? How did these kings exercise their overlordly powers, and did extra power or authority accrue to a king by virtue of achieving this status?

If scholars have been correct in viewing Bede's list as something special in his eyes, but also as something inherited from a written source (cf. Wormald 1974/5, and Yorke 1981:195-6 n.19; but I am not convinced), then there is an institution to be explained. And if such an institution was visible by and in AD 731, the evidence of the charter cannot very well be brushed aside. After all, for Bede, "*Et hae omnes prouinciae, [Cantuariorum, Orientalium Saxonum, Orientalium Anglorum, Occidentalium Saxonum, Merciorum, popul(orum) qui ultra amnem Sabrinam ad occidentem habitant, Huicciorum, Lindisfarorum, Uectae insulae, Australium Saxonum] ceteraeque australes ad confinium usque Humbrae fluminis cum suis quaeque regibus Merciorum, regi Aedilbaldo subiectae sunt*" (*HE* V.23).

Bede had already stated the qualifications of the overkings whom he listed (*HE* II.5). Each "*in regibus gentis Anglorum cunctis australibus eorum prouinciis, quae Humbrae fluuio et contiguis ei terminis sequestrantur a borealibus, imperauit*", "ruled over the kings of the English race with all their southern kingdoms (which are separated from the northern [kingdoms] by the River Humber and the territories adjoining it)". The resulting power was immediately described by Bede as *imperium*. The four non-Northumbrian kings receive no further description of their power, but their three Northumbrian successors are accorded treatment of how they dominated various of their Celtic neighbours.

If we are looking for a veritable kingship or overkingship of Britain, we could therefore hardly do better than to study Northumbria between 616 and 670. But there is little reason to suppose that that is what we must seek. For we have to hand a parallel which might be thought to provide an explanation, if not an origin, for the idea of a special Southern overlordship. I shall not treat this fully here, for I shall discuss it elsewhere; in any case, the beginnings of the argument have been made by Eric John (1966:9-11) and by Professor Francis John Byrne (1969:5-7; cf. 1995), so that they will not be wholly unfamiliar.

Adomnán, abbot of Iona, in his Life of the founder, St Columba, written between 688 and 704 (for discussion see Herbert 1988), referred to King Oswald of Northumbria, victorious against Cadwallon, king of Gwynedd, thus: "*Totius*

Britanniae imperator a Deo ordinatus est" (I.1). Very similar thinking informed his notices of two Irish kings: Diarmait mac Cerbaill (544-65) he described as *"totius Scotiae regnatorem Deo auctore ordinatum"* and *"totius regem...Scotiae"* (I.26, slightly misquoted by Byrne 1969:6-7); and Diarmait's son, Aed Sláine, was warned by the saint against action which would cause him to forfeit the "prerogative, fore-ordained to you by God, of the monarchy of the kingdom of all Ireland", *"tibi a Deo totius Euerniae regni praerogatiuam monarchiae praedestinatam"* (I.14). Two essential elements are to be identified in his accounts: the debt to God and the kingship of the whole island (whether Ireland or Britain). It is clear in all these cases that the stated dominion over the whole island is an indication of desire, not of fact. It must be taken as an ideological statement, and certainly one representing Adomnán's views. What is less clear is the extent to which these views are original. Is he, for example, simply recording what was claimed by Oswald, or is he instead defining an historical role for a king of whom the Church of Iona must have strongly approved?

Adomnán's most likely contribution is the religious element, especially in view of his account of royal succession in Dál Riata (for recent discussion, cf. Enright 1989). There is sufficient evidence to suggest that he could not have been an originator of the claims of the Uí Néill dynasty (to which the abbots of Iona hereditarily belonged) to be supplying 'kings of Ireland'. The Uí Néill kings increasingly dominated the north of Ireland, but had no standing in the south. Their claim seems bound up with the idea of a 'kingship of Tara' which probably had ancient roots. What Adomnán might have done was to transfer that idea to an English, or British, context and to have done so in the reign of an approved Northumbrian king, Aldfrith (686-705), a man of Gaelic education and perhaps, but much more doubtfully, blood (Dumville 1990:149-52), with reference to a greater and more approved ancestor.

A conclusion on this point will turn on what evidence can be adduced to suggest the antiquity of the Southumbrian overkingship. This is very problematic before the time of Æthelberht I of Kent (the third king in Bede's list), and is still somewhat uncertain thereafter. An eighth-century source is necessarily poor evidence for fifth- or sixth-century events. What we must ask is when the idea of a Southumbrian overkingship emerged. But since that is likely, of necessity, to remain uncertain, we must ask another question, a poor substitute. What evidence is there which would justify the description of Ælle and Ceawlin in such terms? Ælle's career is wholly unrecorded. However, Ceawlin could be placed at the time when the events represented *sub anno* 571 in the *Anglo-Saxon Chronicle* were taking place (but for discussion of the chronography of Ceawlin, see Dumville 1985), when the *ciuitas Catuuellaunorum* based on Verulamium was, on one theory (Rutherford Davis 1982), finally being reduced by the Anglo-Saxons. Such a move would have linked southern, East Anglian, and East Midland English territory, and could perhaps have justified such a title being accorded him. But is such calculation misguided? Should we see the list as a later construct based ultimately on national recollections of the heroic age? If so, precise motive is for the moment lacking.

If we were to take the idea of describing Edwin and previous kings in such terms as having originated at a later but perhaps still seventh-century date, we could attribute its development to Irish influence mediated by ecclesiastics including Adomnán. If, on the other hand, we were to allow it more ancient roots, we should have to regard the kingship of Tara and the Southumbrian overlordship as being parallel developments, possibly from a common ultimate Celtic origin (on early British kingship and overkingship see Charles-Edwards 1970-2 and 1974). But, whatever the case, by 736 an idea of a kingship of Britain was being expressed in a Mercian charter, yet couched also in terms which equate it with Bede's Southumbrian overkingship. To the extent that statement and fact do not coincide, we must suspect that we are in the presence of an ideology to the door of which we have not yet found the key.

The terminology used by other contemporary writers to describe the rulers of the Southumbrian overlordship and their powers was thoroughly discussed by Stenton (1970:48-66), and that study will not be repeated here. But the use of formulae like *rex Britanniae* and *Su(u)tangli* raises questions about the relationship between Anglo-Saxon rulers and the racial or tribal groupings which comprised the early Old English polity. Even at the beginning of the historical period we see Anglo-Saxon kingdoms in very different states of organization and development. In Northumbria, Mercia, and Wessex, for example, we see, through often differing sources, three overkingships in varying degrees of advance.

The creation of Northumbria as a permanent unit took almost a century of recorded history. Its immediate constituents were the Anglian kingdoms of Deira and Bernicia, each with its own royal line. As far as we know, these kingdoms were first brought together during the reign of Æthelfrith of Bernicia (592/3-616). During the following century, one Deiran and four Bernician kings each ruled the whole, three of these five achieving this by conquering their fellow-ruler; Deira and Bernicia enjoyed two periods of separation (633-4, 642-51), and Deira was ruled by two or three sub-kings (or co-rulers) of the Bernician dynasty (Miller 1979). From 685, at the latest, the old division between Deira and Bernicia is not among the factors presented by our sources as overly important in the continuing political life of Northumbria (for Ecgfrith as *rex Derorum et Bernicorum*, see Stephanus, *Vita S. Wilfridi*, par. 20).

The kingdom of Lindsey, situated to the south of the Humber, but whose inhabitants may have been tribally related to those of the Lindisfarne area in Bernicia (Myres 1935/6), was for much of the seventh century a source of contention between Northumbria and Mercia. We know only from the Anglian collection of genealogies (Dumville 1976) that it had its own native royal line, although we might have deduced that fact from Bede's use of *prouincia* to describe Lindsey. No king of Lindsey is known for his deeds, and we have no sense whatever of when any of these Lindsey rulers lived (Stenton 1970:127-35).[4] We

---

[4] Stenton's interpretation offered inspirational use of Sawyer (1968: S 1183), but this must now be discounted.

have one piece of evidence for national feeling within Lindsey which expressed itself strongly against Oswald of Northumbria, reckoned as a foreign conqueror (Bede, *HE* III.11; cf. Stenton 1971:83); we do not know if the men of Lindsey felt the same about the Mercian rulers who incorporated that border-kingdom within their overlordship. In any event, there is every reason to regard Lindsey as an old-established kingdom (against Davies & Vierck 1974:237) which by the bad fortune of its geographical location came to be a disputed area between the Mercian and Northumbrian overkingships; only after the battle of the Trent (679) does it seem to have gravitated permanently into the Mercian sphere of influence (for most recent review see Foot 1993).

The earliest history of the Mercian overkingship of midland England is utterly obscure. By the time when Mercia appears clearly in our sources, it was already an overkingship extending over most of midland England between the Thames-Severn and the Humber-Mersey (or even Humber-Ribble) lines.[5] The Mercians had disputed successfully with Wessex for the Hwicce, in Penda's reign, probably with East Anglia for supremacy over Essex, which was achieved most likely in Penda's and certainly in Wulfhere's reign, and with Northumbria for Lindsey; Oxfordshire continued to be debated between Mercia and Wessex until the ninth century. These conquests gave a certain geographical conpactness to Greater Mercia (for discussion of the process, see Dumville 1993: ch. IX). The stages by which the Mercian rulers extended their overkingship to comprehend the whole of southern England, and the styles used in official documents to reflect their growing strength and prestige, were studied by Stenton (1970:48-66). On a much less sure footing, however, is our understanding of the process by which Mercia came to be, by the mid-seventh century, one of the contenders for supreme power in southern England.

The document known as the 'Tribal Hidage' (Dumville 1989, cf. Kirby 1991:9-12) gives ample evidence of the racial or tribal variety of early central England. Whether each of the almost thirty named population-groups originally constituted a kingdom, we do not know. Certainly a few did, and there seems to be little reason to doubt that this was the general rule. We may perhaps associate the thirty *duces regii*, 'royal leaders', in Penda's army at the battle of Winwed in 655, with these units (*HE* III.24). At least two centuries of settlement had passed in some areas before we begin to obtain a glimpse of midland England from historical sources; even the late seventh and eighth centuries are far from well documented at a local level. We should, therefore, be most unwise to argue from the absence of direct evidence about numerous local royal dynasties; the comparative evidence from the south-eastern kingdoms and from Wessex should also caution against such negative reasoning (Chadwick 1905:269-90).

In recent years there has been an increasingly pronounced tendency to argue that some of the midland kingdoms seen in our sources were administrative creations

---

[5] The appearance of the Elmetsǣte of south-west Yorkshire in the 'Tribal Hidage' presumably indicates that they too were drawn into the Mercian overkingship; this would perhaps make a Humber-Ribble boundary more likely; but cf. Davies & Vierck 1974:226-7.

of the Mercian overkingship.[6] This case was originally made for Hwicce by Sir Frank Stenton (1971:44-6) who urged the proposition that Penda "first brought the Angles and Saxons of the middle and lower Severn under a single lordship, and that the under-kingdom of the Hwicce which is known to have existed within a generation of his death was in fact his creation" (1971:45; cf. Hooke 1985; Sims-Williams 1990). This proposition has been extended by Professor Wendy Davies to the Middle Angles and to Lindsey and the Magonsæte (Davies 1973), and the further argument has been advanced "that such kingdoms as there are in the early Saxon period [viz, those which are identifiable in our imperfect sources] do not embrace the whole population"; therefore, "groups of people exist alongside but outside the kingdom structure"; accordingly, we are told, a theory of the development of overlordship which requires one "to suppose a straighforward replacement of some 'tribal' system by a political one will not do" (Davies & Vierck 1974:237-8). Davies has set up the Middle Angles and Middle Anglia as constituting a model for the development of English administrative units, especially in the seventh century. She has demonstrated that Middle Anglia seems best explained as a royal administrative unit created by Penda (with his son Peada as king) following the Mercian domination of this area—I should prefer to describe Peada's kingdom as an intermediate overkingship or mesne kingdom—, which event happened to coincide with the introduction of Christianity to the area and the establishment of a diocese bearing the name of the 'kingdom' and thus perpetuating its currency. From this demonstration Davies has proceeded to the assertion that other major units, Hwicce, Lindsey, etc., bordering the 'original' Mercia were similarly administrative creations. This seems singularly unjustified: the criteria employed to establish the point are different in each case. And there is no demonstrable example of Mercian, or other, creation of royal lines: in Anglo-Saxon England such lines do not seem to have been made thus. The only units which Davies has admitted as kingdoms are the 'Heptarchic' ones; but the 'Heptarchy' is not an original feature of the Anglo-Saxon polity, as Northumbria, for example, shows, and the 'Heptarchic' kingdoms are hardly to be taken as 'tribal'.[7]

We are fortunate to have as much evidence as we possess concerning local population-groups and administrative units in the seventh century. Not the least among our sources is that laconic, but nonetheless eloquent, document known as the 'Tribal Hidage'. We encounter in these sources an extreme variety, when measured against what we see in the eighth century, which should be a sufficient warning to us against assuming that the sixth century would be no more complex and varied; for there is every possibility that the larger of the units, seen through the Tribal Hidage, other seventh-century sources and Bede, would then have appeared instead as a plurality of minor peoples.

The standing of Middle Anglia, however temporary, as a mesne kingdom or intermediate overlordship reminds one of another comparable case in the history of

---

[6] Davies 1973 and Davies & Vierck 1974, developing to a fundamental degree suggestions of Stenton 1971:38-48; see also Arnold 1984:139-40.

[7] On problems of the term 'Heptarchy', see Dumville 1993: ch. IX.

Mercia's seventh-century expansion. Bede referred to the baptism in Mercia of King Æthelwalh of Sussex at the instance of the Mercian King Wulfhere (658-674) who became his godfather and in token of this relationship gave him two *proiuinciae*, Wight and the Meonware (*HE* IV.13). Mercian control of Sussex may not have survived Wulfhere's death in 674. Before 685, Cædwalla of Wessex, then an exile from his native land, attacked and killed King Æthelwalh; shortly thereafter, during the kingship of Wessex (685-8) Cædwalla was overlord of Sussex (*HE* IV.15). King Cædwalla also seized Wight (which Wulfhere had given to Æthelwalh of Sussex, perhaps having detached it from Wessex for the purpose), where he ruthlessly exterminated both its royal line and its population. The Meonware, it would seem on the evidence of the same Bedan passage (*HE* IV.16[14]), were already back under West Saxon control (Yorke 1989). It is tempting to account for Cædwalla's savage behaviour towards Sussex and Wight by reference to the events of Wulfhere's overlordship; Sussex had then suddenly expanded, thanks to Mercia, at the expense of Wessex, and this vigorous West Saxon king was presumably determined to ensure that that would never again be possible. We may tentatively conclude from Bede's account that, while Æthelwalh of Sussex ruled Wight, that island-kingdom's native dynasty nonetheless remained in power; for a King Arwald reigned there at the time of Cædwalla's onslaught. In other words, while Wulfhere was Æthelwalh's overlord, Æthelwalh was in his turn overlord of the kings of Wight and the Meonware (Campbell 1985:91-2).

In its turn, then, Mercia was a developing overkingship. Within the Midlands and without, its power developed by the extension and manipulation of overkingly authority. At a certain point, that overkingly authority seems to have started to bear severely on the subject kings. We begin to sense, via the terminology used in royal diplomas, that the Mercian overkings' view of their dependent kings had taken a downward turn. Kings of Sussex and the Hwicce gain more lowly titles, for example, *dux*, the East Saxon kings disappear from the record under Offa (only to return in Cenwulf's reign). Grants by Ecgberht II, king of Kent, were revoked by Offa, with the Kentish king being described by the Mercian ruler as his thane (Brooks 1984:114-5, 321-2, 350 n.23). Whether these verbal assaults were followed up with decisive political action is less easy to say. After Offa's reign, we know of no more kings of Sussex, Lindsey, or the Hwicce (Kirby 1991:163-84). After 798, no more native kings of Kent are found, although a Mercian kingship of Kent was preserved until the end of Mercian rule in 825 x 828. Offa's apparently treacherous killing of King Æthelberht of East Anglia should, therefore, be remembered here. There is perhaps, then, some evidence that Offa was acting vigorously to reduce local independence. His successes were restricted, however—the last generation of scholars has surely grievously overestimated Offa's importance in his own day— and the nature of his repression may have created rather than suppressed dissidence in some areas. There are also some grounds for the suspicion that Offa was afraid of Frankish overlordship being asserted in England.[8]

---

8   On early Carolingian behaviour in this regard, cf. Wallace-Hadrill 1971:115-7.

Cenwulf, who followed the ill-fated Ecgfrith, son of Offa, as king of Mercia in 796, seems to have been a ruler of more temperate and measured frame of mind, with a better grasp than Offa's of some political realities. A new arrangement was worked out for Kent. The, apparently loyal, kings of Essex emerge into the light once again. But evidently in some areas the depression of dependent royalty had been terminal. Among the Hwicce, for example, from *ca* 800, the old royal family was replaced by or turned into an ealdormanly line; one harbours the suspicion that this is what Offa desired to achieve, by forcing the pace, throughout his *imperium*.

Such depression in status is probably not, then, merely a matter of Latin terminology. But the last quarter of the eighth century represents the end of the process in some areas. From the nature of earlier evidence it is possible to say that the apparent right of the overking to interfere in the internal affairs of the dependent kingdom paved the way for this further assault. That is no doubt true in part. But, as we see the dependent kings almost exclusively through documents promoted by the overking, it is difficult to be clear as to exactly what was happening.[9] What is certain is that, to the end, at least some local rulers went on exercising local kingly functions, especially including the granting of land by charter and in hereditary tenure.

Nevertheless, in the ninth century the number of royal lines in a position to exercise the function of granting land reached an all-time low. Only in Northumbria and East Anglia—for both of which in fact we have no evidence on this point—, in Mercia and Wessex were there lines of sufficient standing. The last known grants by other local kings occur in the 770s (Hwicce and Sussex) or 780s (Kent). Native kings of Essex continue to be met in Mercian charters until 823, but we know nothing of their ability to make such grants by virtue of their royal standing.

We should not imagine, however, that the story of Anglo-Saxon overkingship ends at this point. The relationship between Alfred and Edward of Wessex, on the one hand, and Æthelred II of Mercia on the other has, it seems to me, been widely misunderstood, and elaborate theories have ben generated to explain Æthelred's position. He seems to have come to the throne of Mercia in 879, and only to have accepted King Alfred as his overlord in the 880s, perhaps by 883, certainly in 886 at the latest. In 887, a royal marriage between Æthelred and Alfred's daughter Æthelflæd confirmed the relationship (Dumville 1992:1, 7, 17-8). Throughout his long reign (879-911) Æthelred II continued in his own right to exercise royal prerogatives in Mercia; these powers were assumed by his queen after his death, and exercised further until 918. Their daughter succeeded briefly to the kingdom, but she was deprived of her position by Edward, king of Wessex, who then became direct ruler of all Southumbrian England until his death in 924 (Dumville n.d.). Only in the next reign does the practice of Anglo-Saxon overlordship of other Anglo-Saxon kings cease and the story of the English monarchy begin (Dumville 1992: ch. IV).

What are we taught by our sources for the whole period down to the 920s is, I think, that Anglo-Saxon overkingship is a more complex and diverse phenomenon

---

[9]   For a comprehensive study of the charters of the period see Scharer 1982.

than has often been admitted. To my mind, the best available points of comparison are to be found in early medieval Ireland where similar complexities are frequently attested, but that is another subject. To understand overkingship one must also understand kingship, its essential prerequisite, and to comprehend the practice of kingship one must look beyond the surface-meanings of texts issued by overkings themselves. We need to be able to view relationships of royal authority from every possible angle. Precise perceptions of terminology are essential for such purpose. This is perhaps an elementary series of points, but in Anglo-Saxon scholarship they do not seem to have received their due of serious attention.

References

Textual sources:

[Abbreviations: *HE* = *Historia ecclesiastica gentis Anglorum*; S = Document number in Sawyer 1968]

Adomnán
          Life of Columba: see Anderson & Anderson 1991.
Anglo-Saxon Chronicle: see Earle & Plummer (eds.) 1892: Dumville & Keynes (eds.) 1983-
Bede
          Historia ecclesiastia gentis Anglorum: see Colgrave & Mynors 1969.
Ismere charter: see Birch 1885:222-3, no. 154.
Stephanus (Eddius)
          Vita S. Wilfridi: see Colgrave 1927.
Tribal Hidage: see Dumville 1989.

Bibliography:

Abels, R.
    1983   The Council of Whitby: a study in Anglo-Saxon politics. *Journal of British Studies* 23: 1-25.
Anderson, A. O., & M. O. Anderson
    1991   *Adomnán's Life of Columba*. Oxford: Clarendon Press.
Angenendt, A.
    1984   *Kaiserherrschaft und Königstaufe*. Berlin: de Gruyter Verlag.
Arnold, C. J.
    1984   *Roman Britain to Saxon England: An Archaeological Study*. London: Croom Helm.
Bassett, S. (ed.)
    1989   *The Origins of Anglo-Saxon Kingdoms*. London: Leicester University Press.
Birch, W. de G.
    1885   *Cartularium saxonicum*. Vol. I. London, Whiting & Co. [2 further volumes were published in 1888 and 1895 by Whiting and Co. and Clark, London respectively].
Bonser, W.
    1957   *An Anglo-Saxon and Celtic Bibliography* (450-1087), 2 vols. Oxford: Blackwell.

Brooks, N.
1984   *The Early History of the Church of Canterbury: Christ Church from 597 to 1066.* Leicester: Leicester University Press.
Bruce-Mitford, R. L. S.
1975-83 *The Sutton-Hoo Ship-Burial*, 3 vols. London, British Museum.
Bullough, D. A.
1965   Anglo-Saxon institutions and early English society. *Annali della Fondazione italiana per la storia amministrativa* 2: 647-659.
Byrne, F. J.
1969   *The Rise of the Uí Néill and the High Kingship of Ireland.* Dublin: National University of Ireland. [Revised in Byrne 1995].
1995   *Irish Kingship and Historiography in the Early Middle Ages.* Woodbridge: The Boydell Press.
Campbell, J.
1985   *Essays in Anglo-Saxon History.* London: Hambledon.
Chadwick, H. M.
1905   *Studies on Anglo-Saxon Institutions.* Cambridge: Cambridge University Press.
Charles-Edwards, T. M.
1970-2 The Seven Bishop-houses of Dyfed. *Bulletin of the Board of Celtic Studies* 24: 247-262.
1974   Native political organisation in Roman Britain and the origin of MW *brenhin.* In *Antiquitates indogermanicae.* M. Mayrhofer *et al.* (eds.), pp.35-45. Innsbruck: Institut der Sprachwissenschaft der Universität Innsbruck.
1983   Bede, the Irish and the Britons. *Celtica* 15: 42-52.
1991   The Arthur of history. In *The Arthur of the Welsh.* R. Bromwich *et al.* (eds.), pp.15-32. Cardiff: University of Wales Press.
1993   *Early Irish and Welsh Kinship.* Oxford: Clarendon Press.
Colgrave, B. (ed. & trans.)
1927   *The Life of Bishop Wilfrid by Eddius Stephanus.* Cambridge: Cambridge University Press.
Colgrave, B., & R. A. B. Mynors (eds. & trans.)
1969   *Bede's Ecclesiastical History of the English People.* Oxford: Clarendon Press.
Davies, W.
1973   Middle Anglia and the Middle Angles. *Midland History* 2: 18-20.
Davies, W., & H. Vierck
1974   The context of Tribal Hidage: social aggregates and settlement patterns. *Frühmittelalterliche Studien* 8: 223-293.
Drögereit, R.
1952   Kaiseridee und Kaisertitel bei den Angelsachsen. *Zeitschrift der Savigny-Stiftung für Rechtsgeschichte* (germanistische Abteilung) 69: 24-73.
Dumville, D. N.
1976   The Anglian collection of royal genealogies and regnal lists. D. N. Dumville (ed.) *Anglo-Saxon England* 5: 23-50. [Revised in his *Histories and Pseudo-histories of the Insular Middle Ages.* Aldershot: Variorum 1990].
1979   The ætheling. A study in Anglo-Saxon constitutional history. *Anglo-Saxon England* 8: 1-33.
1985   The West Saxon genealogical regnal list and the chronology of early Wessex. *Peritia* 4: 21-66. [Reprinted Dumville 1993].

1986   The local rulers of Anglo-Saxon England to A.D. 927. In *Handbook of British Chronology*. E. B. Fryde *et al.* (eds.), pp. 1-25. London: Royal Historical Society.

1989   The Tribal Hidage: an introduction to its texts and their history. In *The Origins of Anglo-Saxon Kingdoms*. S. Bassett (ed.), pp. 225-230, 286-287. London: Leicester University Press.

1990   Two troublesome abbots. *Celtica* 21: 146-152.

1992   *Wessex and England from Alfred to Edgar.* Woodbridge: The Boydell Press.

1993   *Britons and Anglo-Saxons in the Early Middle Ages.* Aldershot: Variorum.

1994   The idea of government in sub-Roman Britain. In *After Empire: Towards an Ethnology of Europe's Barbarians*. G. Ausenda (ed.), pp. 177-216. Woodbridge: The Boydell Press.

n.d.   The Mercian Monarchy, A.D. 874-959. In *Kings, Currency, and Alliances*. M. A. S. Blackburn & D. N. Dumville (eds.).

Dumville, D. N., & S. Keynes (ser. eds.)

1983-   *The Anglo-Saxon Chronicle. A Collaborative Edition.*, 23 vols. Cambridge: Brewer.

Earle, J., & C. Plummer

1892   *Two of the Saxon Chronicles Parallel.* 2 vols. Oxford: Clarendon Press.

Eiten, G.

1907   *Das Unterkönigtum in Reiche der Merovinger und Karolinger.* Heidelberg: Carl Winter Verlag.

Enright, M. J.

1989   *Iona, Tara and Soissons.* Berlin: de Gruyter Verlag.

Erdmann, C.

1951   *Forschungen zur politischen Ideenwelt des Frühmittelalters.* Berlin: Akademie-Verlag.

Evans, G. R.

1986   *The Thought of Gregory the Great.* Cambridge: Cambridge University Press.

Fanning, S.

1991a   Jerome's concepts of empire. In *Images of Empire*. L. Alexander (ed.), pp. 239-250. Sheffield: Sheffield University Press.

1991b   Bede, *imperium*, and the Bretwaldas. *Speculum* 66: 1-26.

Flower, R., & H. Smith (eds.)

1941   *The Parker Chronicle and Laws (Corpus Christi College, Cambridge, MS 173). A Facsimile.* London: Early English Text Society.

Foot, S.

1993   The kingdom of Lindsey. In *Pre-Viking Lindsey*. A. Vince (ed.), pp. 128-140. Lincoln: City of Lincoln Archaeological Unit.

Goffart, W.

1988   *The Narrators of Barbarian History (A.D. 550-800).* Princeton, NJ: Princeton University Press.

Graus, F.

1986   Verfassungsgeschichte des Mittelalters. *Historische Zeitschrift* 243: 529-589.

Green, D. H.

1965   *The Carolingian Lord.* Cambridge: Cambridge University Press.

Herbert, M.

1988   *Iona, Kells and Derry.* Oxford: Clarendon Press.

Hooke, D.
  1985   *The Anglo-Saxon Landscape. The Kingdom of the Hwicce.* Manchester: Manchester University Press.
John, E.
  1966   *Orbis Britanniae and Other Studies.* Leicester: Leicester University Press.
Jones, P. F.
  1929   *A Concordance to the* Historia ecclesiastica *of Bede.* Cambridge, MA: Medieval Academy of America.
Keynes, S.
  1992   Ræwald and Bretwalda. In *Voyage to the Other World. The Legacy of Sutton Hoo.* C. B. Kendall & P. S. Wells (eds.), pp. 103-123. Minneapolis: University of Minneapolis Press.
Kirby, D. P.
  1979/80   King Cedwulf of Northumbria and the *Historia Ecclesiastica. Studia Celtica* 14-15: 168-173.
  1991   *The Earliest English Kings.* London: Unwin Hyman.
Loyn, H. R.
  1962   *Anglo-Saxon England and the Norman Conquest.* London: Longman Green.
McClure, J.
  1983   Bede's Old Testament kings. In *Ideal and Reality in Frankish and Anglo-Saxon Society.* P. Wormald *et al.* (eds.), pp. 76-98. Oxford: Blackwell.
Miller, M.
  1979   The dates of Deira. *Anglo-Saxon England* 8: 35-61.
Myres, J. N. L.
  1935/6   The Teutonic settlement of northern England. *History,* N. S. 20: 250-262.
Plummer, C. (ed.)
  1892-9   *Two of the Saxon Chronicles Parallel,* 2 vols. Oxford: Clarendon Press.
  1896   *Venerabilis Bedae opera historica,* 2 vols. Oxford: Clarendon Press.
Rutherford Davis, K.
  1982   *Britons and Saxons: The Chiltern Region, 400-700.* Chichester: Phillimore.
Sawyer, P. H.
  1968   *Anglo-Saxon Charters: An Annotated List and Bibliography.* London: Royal Historical Society.
  1978   *From Roman Britain to Norman England.* London: Methuen.
Scharer, A.
  1982   *Die angelsächsischen Königsurkunde im 7. und 8. Jahrhundert.* Wien: Böhlau Verlag.
  1988   Die Intitulationes der angelsächsischen Könige im 7. und 8. Jahrhundert. In *Intitulatio,* III. H. Wolfram & A. Scharer (eds.), pp. 9-74. Wien: Böhlau Verlag.
Sims-Williams, P.
  1990   *Religion and Literature in Western England 600-800.* Cambridge: Cambridge University Press.
Stengel, E. E.
  1960   *Imperator* und *Imperium* bei den Angelsachsen. Eine Wort- und begriffgeschichtliche Untersuchung. *Deutsches Archiv für Erforschung des Mittelalters* 16: 1-72.
Stenton, F. M.
  1905   Review of Chadwick 1905. *Folklore* 16: 122-126.
  1943/71   *Anglo-Saxon England.* Oxford: Clarendon Press.
  1970   *Preparatory to 'Anglo-Saxon England'.* Oxford: Clarendon Press.

Thomas, C.
1984   Abercorn and the *provincia Pictorum*. In *Between and Beyond the Walls*.
         R. Mike & C. Burgess (eds.), pp. 324-337. Edinburgh: John Donald.
Vollrath-Reichelt, H.
1971   *Königsgedanke und Königtum bei den Angelsachsen bis zur Mitte der
         9. Jahrhunderts*. Wien: Böhlau Verlag.
Wallace-Hadrill, J. M.
1971   *Early Germanic Kingship in England and on the Continent*. Oxford:
         Clarendon Press.
1988   Bede's *Ecclesiastical History of the English People. A Historical
         Commentary*. Oxford: Clarendon Press.
Wenskus, R.
1961   *Stammesbildung und Verfassung: Das Werden der frühmittelalterlichen
         gentes*. Köln: Böhlau Verlag.
Whitelock, D. (trans.)
1979   *English Historical Documents c. 500-1042*. London: Eyre Methuen.
Wood, I. N.
1977   Kings, kingdoms and consent. In *Early Medieval Kingship*. P. H. Sawyer &
         I. N. Wood (eds.), pp. 6-29. Leeds: University of Leeds.
1983   *The Merovingian North Sea*. Alingsås: Viktoria.
1990a   Ethnicity and ethnogenesis of the Burgundians. In *Typen der Ethnogenese
         unter besonderer Berücksichtigung der Bayern*, I. H. Wolfram & W. Pohl
         (eds.), pp. 53-69. Wien: Österreichische Akademie der Wissenschaften.
1990b   The Channel from the fourth to the seventh centuries A. D. In *Maritime
         Celts, Frisians and Saxons*. S. McGrail (ed.), pp. 93-97. London: CBA.
1991   The Franks and Sutton Hoo. In *People and Places in Northern Europe 500-
         1600*. I. Wood & N. Lund (eds.), pp. 1-14. Woodbridge: The Boydell Press.
1992   Frankish hegemony in England. In *The Age of Sutton Hoo*. M. O. H.
         Carver (ed.), pp. 235-241. Woodbridge: The Boydell Press.
1994a   The mission of Augustine of Canterbury to the English. *Speculum* 69: 1-17.
1994b   *The Merovingian Kingdoms 450-751*. London: Longman.
Wormald, P.
1974/5   Review of Giovanni Mosca. *Il Venerabile Beda* (Bari: Dedalo). *Durham
         University Journal* 67 (N.S., 36): 231-233.
1983   Bede, the *Bretwaldas* and the origins of the *gens Anglorum*. In *Ideal and
         Reality in Frankish and Anglo-Saxon Society*. P. Wormald *et al.* (eds.),
         pp. 99-129. Oxford: Blackwell.
1986   Celtic and Anglo-Saxon kingship, some further thoughts. In *Sources of
         Anglo-Saxon Culture*. P. E. Szarmach & V. D. Oggins (eds.), pp. 151-183.
         Kalamazoo, MI: Medieval Institute.
1992   The Venerable Bede and the 'Church of the English'. In *The English
         Religious Tradition and the Genius of Anglicanism*. G. Rowell (ed.), pp. 13-32.
         Wantage: Ikon.
Yorke, B. A. E.
1981   The vocabulary of Anglo-Saxon overlordship. *Anglo-Saxon Studies in
         Archaeology and History* 2: 171-200.
1989   The Jutes of Hampshire and Wight and the origins of Wessex. In *The
         Origins of Anglo-Saxon Kingdoms*. S. Bassett (ed.), pp. 84-96, 256-263.
         London: Leicester University Press.
1990   *Kings and Kingdoms of Early Anglo-Saxon England*. London: Seaby.

Discussion

AUSENDA: I would like to make some comments on the pre-literate situation. I take it that the consensus of opinion is that during the early phase of Anglo-Saxon settlement in Britain, kinship was the most important network on which relationships were based.

DUMVILLE: Over the last century that has been argued about a great deal.

AUSENDA: Let us say that this is an assumption. Taking it as such, I would like to observe that in many contemporary non-literate societies kinship groups at the local level are linked by 'demonstrated descent', while at clan level and beyond they are linked by 'stipulated descent'. Genealogical maps are made up with remarkable consensus between groups to 'explain' through a kinship terminology, the relationship between the various components of the system. This was described in its earliest formulation during the 1940s as 'tribal genealogical' (Evans-Pritchard 1940:192; Bacon 1958:viii). Generally, the component units of such systems are not 'ruled', in the modern sense of the word, but 'headed' by an elder, e.g. in Arabic *sheikh*, in Tigré *diglel*, in To Bedawie *surkenab*, all terms meaning elder—the same seems to have been true of some early Anglo-Saxon groups. This elder acts primarily as an arbiter in council with elders from the various units in resolving controversies between kin groups from feuds to less serious questions.

Among Beni Amer, for example, such component units are territorial and consider themselves as genealogically related sections of a dominant clan (Nadel 1945:93). They act as 'patrons' to members of client clans which have their own genealogical network but are not related to the dominant clan; they live in the dominant clan's territory. They also owned slaves, who were characterized by lack of genealogy.

It was recognized later that 'tribes' "may be viewed as a reaction to the formation of complex political structures" (Fried 1967:170 ff.). This seems to have been true also among the Anglo-Saxons, as intimated by your remark that Offa was afraid of Frankish overlordship being asserted in England, and it would also explain the success of Roman missionizing as against a possible Frankish effort. The reaction described above formed 'tribes' and by extension 'overlordships'. It may also have been produced by long-distance trade and/or religious and cultural penetration. My question is: has there been any research trying to 'reconstruct' those early kinship networks and the outside influences which turned them into tribes and later into kingdoms and overlordships?

DUMVILLE: I think the simple answer to the question itself is 'Not in recent times' though I stand to be corrected on that. Going back into the body of your remarks, the role of genealogical relationships is at present much less easily demonstrable in the early Anglo-Saxon material that we've got than it would be, say, in Irish material. It is much easier to translate classical anthropological work dealing with genealogy and social organization into the early Irish and possibly the early Welsh situation. I tried suggesting a good number of years ago now that there was an ultimate defining genealogy, an ultimate defining characteristic of Anglianism, in the position of Woden in the genealogies. There has been a lot of debate about this, and I am not sure that the suggestion has been terribly well received. It does seem difficult to demonstrate this kind of thing very clearly from the surviving genealogical record, in spite of the evidence for construction of the kind of internal layering of genealogical schemes in precisely the form you described. Where we have the most difficulty with what you described is simply relating this question of 'elders' to the material I know.

CHARLES-EDWARDS: To me 'elder' suggests a way that people gather around and decide the difficult questions.

DUMVILLE: And that raises the whole horrible semantic question about the origins of the word *ealdorman* and what that means. One way of explaining that, I take it, would be to invoke the kind of model which Giorgio has described.

CHARLES-EDWARDS: There is a sufficiently clear element of 'age' in the semantic background to the term to suggest that there is something to this. In the case of Bede, it seems to me that his use of the word *gens* is highly contentious and most obviously so in Northumbria. He is so careful on the whole to say that the Northumbrians are a *gens* and the Deirans and Bernicians are two *prouinciae*, suggesting a deliberate downgrading of political entities which would have regarded themselves as *gentes*. And this may be because of the connection between *gens* and *rex gentis*: *þeod* and *þeoden*. A people deprived of their own king, a *þeod* deprived of their *þeoden*, may cease to be regarded as a *gens*, a *þeod*. Bede's use of *gens* and *prouincia* is probably not just a scholarly construction: people would have known what he meant.

DUMVILLE: His scholarly interests are only part of the story, and to that extent I agree with you. He had to produce, by a scholarly process, something appropriate to the circumstances. If what he said was obviously inapplicable then his work would be useless in terms of at least one of its functions. But I'm not sure to what extent Bede's usage is so loaded with a heavily ideological element in his use of the term *gens*. Although we have a concordance to the *Ecclesiastical History*, the material has not been pulled out and discussed thoroughly in each of its instances. I'm not clear that Bede's use of *gens*, unlike his use of some other terms for power and rule, has the kind of consistency which ought to have made it contentious in his own time. It ought to be contentious for us, insofar as at least some of us don't yet understand what's going on here. But I don't know to what extent that particular element would have produced contention in his own time. I would entirely agree that the ruling class in Deira took as dim a view as possible of Bernicians and their activities. But where the difficulty lies for me is in your interpretation of the Latin terminology, because it seems to me that Bede uses the word *prouincia* of Deira and uses it quite consistently until his account of the very late seventh century. It means that he is recognizing its people, therefore, in your terms, as a *gens*.

CHARLES-EDWARDS: I was thinking of the Meonware. There is no question at all about this territory being detached by Wulfhere from the West Saxons and given to someone else, the South Saxon kingdom. They wouldn't have been and they were not a *prouincia* in the way that the Deirans might have been.

DUMVILLE: Why not?

CHARLES-EDWARDS: Well, simple geographical extent for one thing.

DUMVILLE: Yes, but you're leaving out the historical development. I wouldn't accept geographical extent as a factor in this discussion. You leave out of account what, in the particular case of Meonware, Bede states as clearly as he possibly can, that they were earlier a separate people.

CHARLES-EDWARDS: In what sense?

DUMVILLE: In his discussion of the question of Jutishness.

CHARLES-EDWARDS: Right, but there too there are no *reges Iutarum*.

DUMVILLE: I think I'm being consistent here—you may very well argue I'm being too consistent and too schematic—but I would argue that in principle the territory and the people of, let us say the Meonware, have in Bede's descriptive process, and for good historical reasons and good political reasons, the same status as Bernicians or Deirans. And therefore they were people who were subjected, as the Deirans came to be, through a long-term process, to an overlordship which might in one case or the other have been more or less contentious over the long term. And I take it that the Meonware would have had their *rex*—we are coming back to the Latin terminology of *cyning*—just as the Deirans did.

HÄRKE: I would like to try to link one point that you are making here to the wider question of ethnic groups and ethnogenesis that we talked about a bit earlier. You make the point here that kingship of a country may be divisible, but the nation itself remains a unity. What does that mean to our perception, and perhaps the perception at the time, of regional and political units? It appears to imply that there was a primary perception of ethnic or political unity, and the limit imposed by kingship comes later. Does this have implications for our notion of ethnogenesis and of how ethnic groups are composed?

DUMVILLE: What it implies for the prehistoric period, in Anglo-Saxon terms, is inevitably highly speculative. The way I was coming at it there, I think, was to imply that people such as the Cantware do have an identity of their own which the kingship arrangements, the overkingship arrangements reflect, but within which the kingship arrangements point to more local divisions. Then there comes the question of whether these more local divisions have their own separate earlier origins which we then need to go on to try to quantify and talk about, or whether these are in some senses essentially administrative divisions—but they are divisions, for political or governmental purposes, of this larger whole. I'm on the horns of a dilemma here undoubtedly, but what has struck me for a number years is how whenever you have this divided rule within certain regions, you seem to have it over the long term. And yet in spite of the political ups and downs the region holds together. The explanation I was tending to give, was that there was a unity of sorts to these Saxons, or the people in Kent, etc.

HÄRKE: Your answer brings us back to the original point Walter made about ethnogenesis very often being the outcome of a political process. And here it actually would then have been a political process that was lost in what you call prehistory, while later political processes impinged only marginally on its outcome.

DUMVILLE: We have odd places where we can see that kind of model being disrupted. The obvious one I cited already is Middlesex, which we can see being shorn off from Essex and incorporated within Bernicia. We don't know what the detailed arrangements for that were.

LENDINARA: May I ask a question? I was intrigued by the idea that Bede used Isidore's *Etymologiae* as a storehouse for technical vocabulary of some sort. I wonder if there is any difference between the prose *Life of St Cuthbert* and the *Historia ecclesiastica* as far as this kind of terminology is concerned. There are instances when both works tell similar stories, e.g. the relapse into pagan practices (*HE* IV.27 and *Life of St Cuthbert*, ch. IX), with a different emphasis and in a different style.

DUMVILLE: This still needs to be looked into.

LENDINARA: The feeling I have is that Bede changed his style when he came to write the *Historia ecclesiastica*.

DUMVILLE: I have been collating some of the early manuscripts of Bede's history. It's been taken as read that our standard editions are based on manuscripts which are so close in date and arguably in origin to the time of writing of the *Ecclesiastical History* that that is the end of the story. But the early manuscripts have clearly not been collated together in spite of what has been said by the editors. What happened was that the previous edition had been taken as a base and random editorial activity proceeded from that. Close collation of the manuscripts is not too difficult because we got facsimiles of the two earlier manuscripts. What it produces is a range of interesting variants which enable us to deduce something about the relationship of the early manuscripts to one another and to the origin of work. That doesn't produce a great wealth of new historical information, which is a great pity. But it is possible to show various lines of the early transmission of the work. We have the descendants of a number of eighth-century Northumbrian copies which are linguistically quite different in respect of OE name-forms. In the end, these other lines of transmission, which we now have to get at through ninth-century and later manuscripts, may possibly produce some variant readings which are of greater substance to the historian than those which are in OE from earlier manuscripts. The other thing which has to be said about this is that I think there is a good case to be made that the earliest manuscripts of Bede's history aren't as early as they are usually said to be and they should be re-dated to the second half of the eighth century. This doesn't affect yet the quality of the text and the context of the received text, nor this discussion, bearing on the question of terminology.

FOWLER: I hesitate to join in: it's wonderful to hear Northumbria discussed in the European context when Northumbria is my personal local history. We've discussed when, and to a certain extent why, Bede was writing. I want to raise the point about where he was writing. I'm very conscious that every time I go to Jarrow I have to cross the river Tyne, crossing into old County Durham. There is an argument that the river Tyne was the division between Bernicia and Deira. Perhaps Bede was right at the interface between these two kingdoms. My second point is that before this—again it's obviously a very difficult area—you could argue that behind the documentary evidence, the river Tyne could have been the division between the northern edge of the *Brigantes* and the southern edge of the *Uotadini*.

DUMVILLE: I regard the latter as a more dangerous and more important possibility than the former. You know probably better than most of us that the frontier line between Deira and Bernicia has been much debated in our time and as far as I can see the question hasn't been settled satisfactorily. I always come down on the side of the Tees rather than the Tyne, and therefore I would see Bede firmly within the physical Bernician context.

FOWLER: Bede, of course, had a vested interest in the concept of Northumbria, not Bernicia or Deira, whether or not he was actually sitting on the frontier between them.

HINES: Could I raise a couple of questions? The first one is that you assert that Surrey was the southern district of the East Saxons. I know that the etymology of 'Surrey' defines it as a region that is south of somewhere; what exactly it is defined in relation to is a very interesting question. One can, provocatively, consider various alternatives.

DUMVILLE: I hope I do give there reference to a fuller discussion on it. It would be useful if you would elaborate on that point. What else could it be south of?

HINES: The Thames, Middlesex, and London are the obvious alternatives.

CHARLES-EDWARDS: There is only Middlesex.

HINES: I think Middlesex is the least likely. But it is certainly the option most widely favoured in place-name studies. I personally would look to London. But this may be a minor point.

DUMVILLE: I'm not sure that it is, because it has a lot of larger implications. I would have great difficulty accepting that it is the southern district of Middlesex, and I have argued against that, for reasons to do with the history of Middlesex. But, I entirely agree that somebody concentrating on political history can perhaps have a blind spot: one can see it as the southern district of what is above, and for me what is above in this period is Essex, whereas Middlesex was a division of Essex. But what about this question of the word *gē*. It's always been described as an archaic word which is not productive in the historical period in Anglo-Saxon England. It has also become of the very greatest importance in how we see the growth of English administrative territories and, of course, in nineteenth-century discussions because of its etymological relationship with *gau*. So, what about this word, philologists?

HINES: The basic point is that from the very limited distribution of the place-name element in England, *gē* does indeed seem to be a word that went out of productive use very early as far as linguistic chronology goes, probably by around the middle of the seventh century. Beyond that we can't tell what the antiquity of a name like 'Surrey' is. It seems to me equally possible as a late fifth-century formation as an early to mid-seventh-century one. It's not, as far as I'm aware, an element that can be usefully dated in a way that is going to clarify this particular problem.

DUMVILLE: Except that if it goes out of use after the first half of the seventh century that is a very interesting fact in itself: it belongs to early Anglo-Saxon political history.

CHARLES-EDWARDS: Bede was well aware of what it meant.

HINES: Maybe so. But it appears not to have been producing new names. You may have had a certain phase in which this was a term which was used to label, say, a *regio*: it would then be used in new place-names in political circumstances in which you're producing new *regiones*. That there's a later lack of productivity doesn't mean that the political sense of the word was forgotten.

CHARLES-EDWARDS: But when you're moving westward territorially there is no reason why you shouldn't create and name new *regiones* in the same way as you've done things in the past.

DUMVILLE: We need to break out of what is a circular argument, which is allowed to be circular by the use of two languages. If every time you said *regio* you'd use the vernacular term or vice versa, the argument would have been visibly circular.

HINES: What may be one of the most interesting things is that *gē* is a term to describe an area of land whereas a lot of the other names like *-sǣte*, *-ware*, and *-ingas* are clearly terms that are specific to groups of people. This is the point that Walter touched upon by noting that it is very rare to find, in Latin sources, terms like *Anglia* and *Saxonia* being used. There is a peculiarity in the use of this term to mark out the landscape.

Can I pursue another question? You say that the first fact of English royal history is the overlordship of Æthelberht I of Kent. What do you mean by the first fact of English royal history?

DUMVILLE: It's self-explanatory. It's the first specific piece of information we have relating to matters of high politics.

HINES: You mean the first dependable piece of information? After all, there is a claim that Ceawlin was an overking before Æthelberht.

WOOD: If you accept Æthelberht's overlordship of southern Britain as a fact, and add what Bede says, and what Gregory the Great says, you have a picture of overkingship as far as the Severn and quite far north. To what extent is it possible that Southumbria is actually something created by Æthelberht?

DUMVILLE: It's highly possible.

WOOD: So that in a sense one might be looking at something very substantial taking place in Æthelberht's reign which then, for all sorts of possible ecclesiastical reasons, becomes a model which sticks.

DUMVILLE: Yes, and the overkingship created by Æthelfrith in Northumbria might be the exact and almost immediately successive parallel to this.

HINES: When you look at the Southumbrian boundary from the perspective of the Anglo-Saxon archaeology of the fifth and sixth centuries, it looks very odd. In terms of material culture, North and South Humberside have a lot in common. In fact, unusually late, right up to the late sixth century, they seem to form a very cohesive unit. In terms of ethnic affiliation, as far as one can reconstruct that, you have the Angles both to the north and to the south.

DUMVILLE: It may be so, but while the concepts are stable, the boundary between them may not be equally so. There is no problem in terms of intra-kingdom and overkingly politics here, in that it's quite clear that down to the battle of the Trent in 679 Lindsey on the one side and Deira on the other side were territories which were disputed over by the two brutes next door, the Bernicians and the Mercians. It was only with the stabilization of the Mercians in 679 that this area had a more stable frontier rather than that being just the frontier which was aspired to on the Mercian side. What was aspired to on the Northumbrian side has got to be Lindsey as an absolute minimum. And this may be why feelings were so bad in both Lindsey and Deira.

SCULL: To what extent might our perceptions of Æthelberht's power be fiction? Is it possible that any power wielded by Æthelberht outside Kent was limited, and dependent upon consent? That other kings may have found it expedient or advantageous to play along with the idea of an overking, but that in reality Æthelberht's independent coercive power may have been very limited?

DUMVILLE: Well, I can show off my flexibility or my sheer lack of principle by agreeing with that as wholeheartedly as I agreed with Ian [laughter]. Yes, other evidence could mean that overkingship is essentially Bedan: you are quite right. And, if we were to wash away all that we take from Bede about the sixth and early seventh centuries, and put ourselves back into the situation when Bede was in when he wrote *De temporum ratione* in 725, this would be an entirely possible way of looking at things. One of the most fundamental problems which Early Anglo-Saxon period historians have is that much of what we write and like to think about seventh-century England is dependent upon our accepting Bede's views and Bede's sources. There is an extreme argument nobody would really care to make, because it would put him out of business, that things have been so contaminated by whatever Bede's agenda was that we have nothing left.

SCULL: How frequently could a seventh-century overking flex his muscles? How often would Æthelberht be in a position to say, "OK, East Anglians and people of the West Saxons we're going to fight Northumbria", without them responding, "Well, you know, it's come to the point where it's not really in our interests". Is overkingship on this scale nominal?

DUMVILLE: I think nominal would be the wrong word. It wouldn't be difficult to cite other cases where dependent people or political leaders said to their overkings, "Well, sorry, we won't do that", or indeed leave overkingship altogether and say to their king, "I'm terribly sorry, you're asking too much from us".

CHARLES-EDWARDS: Most of the evidence would suggest it was possible to say "Well, we're only going to fight for you once every three years": that kind of thing. You try to limit your obligations.

DUMVILLE: The question is at what point—if you are deeply distrustful of Bede's formulation—at what point does other evidence come in to support him? You do get to a point, I think, in the second half of the seventh century where you've got to accept this situation.

SCULL: The archaeological evidence is consistent with a model which would see the seventh-century kingdoms developing from smaller local groupings as a result of conflict and competition in the fifth and sixth centuries. Excluding this model would explain the higher level of political integration embodied in overkingship as a function of regional dynastic conflict between these kingdoms. For this reason I would be happier with the concept of a powerful overkingship later rather than earlier in the seventh century. Again, I wonder if we are losing sight of the limits of the written evidence. Is it possible that there may have been quite a rapid development in the integration of regional political power in the seventh century, and that this is what we see in Bede's formulation? Perhaps we are in danger of anachronism: projecting the political geography of the early eighth century back into a period when political structures were more fragmented, simply because our written sources reflect this later situation.

DUMVILLE: That's a very clever point.

References in the discussion

Textual sources:

Bede

> *De temporum ratione*: see Jones 1977.
> *Historia ecclesiastica gentis Anglorum*: see Colgrave & Mynors 1969.
> *Life of St Cuthbert*: see Colgrave 1940.

Isidore

> *Etymologiae*: see Lindsay 1911.

Bibliography:

Bacon, E.
    1958   *Obok: A Study of Social Structure in Eurasia.* Chicago: University of Chicago Press.
Colgrave, B. (ed.)
    1940   *Two Lives of Saint Cuthbert.* Cambridge: Cambridge University Press.
Colgrave, B., & R. A. B. Mynors (ed. & trans.)
    1969   See References at end of paper.
Evans-Pritchard, E. E.
    1940   *The Nuer: A description of the modes of livelihood and political institutions of a Nilotic people.* Oxford: Clarendon Press.
Fried, M. H.
    1975   *The Notion of Tribe.* Menlo Park, CA: Cummings.
Jones, C. W. (ed.)
    1977   *Bedae Venerabilis opera pars. VI, Opera didascalica* 2. (*Corpus Christianorum, Series latina*, 123B). Turnhout: Brepols.
Lindsay, W. M. (ed.)
    1911   *Isidori hispaniensis episcopi etymologiarum sive originum libri XX.* Oxford: Clarendon Press.
Nadel, S. F.
    1945   Notes on Beni Amer Society. *Sudan Notes and Records* 25 (1): 1-94.

RELIGION: THE LIMITS OF KNOWLEDGE

JOHN HINES

School of English Studies, Communication and Philosophy, University of Wales, Cardiff,
P. O. Box 94, Cardiff, GB-CF1 3XB

> The theologian may indulge the pleasing task of describing Religion as she descended from Heaven, arrayed in her native purity. A more melancholy duty is imposed on the historian. He must discover the inevitable mixture of error and corruption which she contracted in a long residence upon earth, among a weak and degenerate race of beings (Gibbon, *The Decline and Fall of the Roman Empire*, Ch. XV).

The possibility that religious beliefs and practices might be explicable in human rather than supernatural terms has been recognized in Western thought throughout the Christian era. The division between the theological and the historical, which Gibbon wittily but cynically magnified, was, however, effectively bridged in a medieval view that saw the history of religion in transcendental and providential terms. Scriptural revelation and ecclesiastical authority were the touchstones that made sense of everything in medieval Christendom. Truth, God, and God's purpose were identical; the muddled events and haphazard eddies of worldly history, and human error in understanding the divine, were emblematic of the inferior state of mankind in this cosmos. As far as I am aware, it was with the Enlightenment, after the 'general crisis' of the seventeenth century and the consolidation of the division of Christian Europe and her colonies into Catholic and Protestant, that a crucial shift in Western thought took place which made every aspect of religion an object of humanist investigation and explanation. Inevitably this approach was sacrilegious in some quarters, while itself it has more often than not displayed a hostile attitude behind its 'deconstruction' of religious beliefs. But there are also those who employ this kind of analytical approach to validate religious beliefs (e.g. Mitchell 1973).

It is, of course, important for the ethnographer to be aware of the constructed nature and lack of perfect critical objectivity in his or her own position in relation to any topic of study; this may, however, be especially the case in respect of the sensitive and often mystical topic of religion. In work that has been published over the last thirty years or so, we have at our disposal a thorough examination and discussion of the evidence for the nature of Anglo-Saxon 'paganism'[1] and early Anglo-Saxon Christianity (Mayr-Harting 1972; Owen 1981; Stanley 1975; Wilson

---

1 The previous year's symposium (see Foreword) enjoyed an unexpectedly heated discussion of the appropriateness of the term 'paganism' as a label for the non- and pre-Christian religion(s) of Germanic Europe. Experimentally, I have sought to use this term with particular care in this discussion. *Post factum*, my view is that this does add a welcome refinement to the terms in which early Germanic religion is discussed. See the section `Conclusion', below.

THE ANGLO-SAXONS FROM THE MIGRATION PERIOD TO THE EIGHTH CENTURY:
AN ETHNOGRAPHIC PERSPECTIVE

1992). In an attempt to add something worthwhile to this material and not merely to summarize it, I have sought, in this paper, to emphasize the procedural decisions that have to be taken in studying early Anglo-Saxon religion, and the range of interpretations of the evidence which can be made.

What is religion?

Any attempt to discuss religion in the pre-Christian period in Anglo-Saxon England faces us squarely with the fearsome problem of how religious activity is to be identified in the surviving record, a question which in turn poses the question of how religion itself is to be defined. If we look at the term lexicologically, we find that it has been a very elastic term, which can for instance be used seriously to describe creeds such as Marxism or humanism. At the 1993 symposium in this series, David Turton interpreted the characterization of religion produced by Émile Durkheim as a definition of religion as "characteristically social", with God and the Church being effectively metaphors for society: "the diagnostic feature of religion is a community activity" (see Wood 1995, although these particular words are omitted from the edited transcripts). In fact, Durkheim's final position seems to have been to postulate a universal cognitive pattern that divides all things into classes of *sacred* and *profane*, and then to define religion as the communal beliefs of what was sacred and rites that embody how one should behave in respect of the sacred (Durkheim 1915:23-47). From here on, his application of this definition (in relation to Australian Aboriginal religion in his classic study, first published in 1912) was thoroughly sociological (Durkheim 1915:141-239, 431-47).

While one can readily accept, as a valid proposition, the notion that the social-ideological role represents an important and consistent *function* of religion, it seems to be quite unhelpfully free, even misleadingly so, to allow all ideological commitments and practices that ritually enhance social cohesion to be included in the category of religion. At the very least I should prefer a definition of religion that would exclude trivia such as intense loyalty to sports teams—"He supports Manchester United religiously"—from the study of religion, however important such phenomena may be sociologically. More positively this is a matter of looking for some more essential and substantial characterization of Durkheim's *sacré*, so that the sacred/profane relationship does not remain a purely configural universal. Much of what follows also argues the importance, in historical study, of being able to distinguish between social and religious rituals.

What, then, is this 'religion'? If we look through discussions of religion in dictionaries, encyclopedias, books on theology and religious studies etc., we can quite easily identify recurrent characteristics of what is commonly recognized as being religion. It was of course precisely the intuitive sense of religion as a naturally distinct category that Durkheim sought to counter with his analyses. With him, we cannot but recognize the frequently ceremonial and ritual character of religious activity, but this cannot serve as a definition. There are many conventions of behaviour, more and less elaborate, in societies both large and small, which would swamp any attempt to discuss religion so identified. To recognize that religion regularly imposes ethical demands and taboos on its adherents gets us closer to what I regard as essential to religion in that it involves a recognition that religion is to be defined in ideological rather than in formal terms—but would we want, pragmatically, to regard any and everybody who has some sort of ethical code as a religious person? And is there indeed anybody who is totally devoid of such a code?

One phenomenon that seems *only* to exist within what everyone would accept to be religion is a belief in a divine power or powers: God, gods or goddesses. In itself, this cannot be regarded as the essence of religion for at least one major world religion, Buddhism, is non-theistic. If, however, we expand the concept of divinity beyond the personalized god into a general recognition of spirituality, I believe we will have got as close as we can get to a workable and appropriate definition of religion. *Religion*, for this study, *is defined as a human response to a perceived but intangible spirit world that coexists with the real and concrete human world.* It is tempting, but really oversimple, to justify this approach in the present context on the grounds that what we know of Christianity and of Germanic religion before Christianity shows we are dealing with theistic religions. We may only be able to recognize as religion what is substantially similar to religion as we know it. Conversely, of course, we have to discuss religion in terms that make sense to us. To approach early Anglo-Saxon religion on the basis of this definition is at least both practical and theoretically sound—in my view more so than any other approach.

The next question is how we can identify religious elements in the remains of the past. Religion as defined here resides in the mind of the doer of an act rather than in the act itself—or at very least in the communal explanation of an act—and I would presume that to a mind not formed by Western scientific traditions, distinctions between practical, ritual and religious behaviour could be impossible to make: for instance a distinction between manuring a field, feeding the earth, and making a sacrificial offering for fertility. For us it is especially important to try to distinguish the 'merely' ritual—the equivalent, for instance, of a society's Annual Dinner—from the religious; consequently while the strangeness, or apparently impractical, symbolic or pseudo-magical nature of actions represented in our sources may rightly encourage speculation as to their religious character, such leads should only ever be followed up with rigorous objectivity. It is much better, certainly in the present context, to seek to work strictly from the known—and this means working totally under the direction of written sources which can explicitly identify religious implications. This may leave us with a seriously limited and thus distorted view of early Anglo-Saxon religion. Conversely it definitely provides us with a consistent image of the nature of early Anglo-Saxon religion—one in fact that is very much in accord with Gibbon's and Durkheim's characterizations of religion as an instrument with which Man controls his social circumstances.

Of course, that consistency may in turn simply be a reflex of the social and political circumstances in which historical sources from this period could be generated and preserved. As I hope the following will show, however, I doubt that this is entirely the case. In this essay I have consciously sought to resist the relatively easy option of pouring the raw evidence into the Enlightenment mould and so emphasizing virtually exclusively the social and political aspects of the picture. I have found that the categories under which I have sought to order the evidence have repeatedly led to explorations of the intellectual and emotional role of religion in individual life in this period alongside its communal, cultural role.

A historical framework

It would probably be helpful to summarize the outline of early Anglo-Saxon religious history as we know it. It is the story of a large community that adopted Christianity. The Anglo-Saxon peoples were established in Britain by non-Christian settlers from northern Germany and Scandinavia in the fifth century AD. Although both Christian and non-Christian cults seem to have been flourishing in late-Roman Britain (cf. Henig 1984:217-28), Christianity is the only religion that can be seen to have been handed down from this period to the early medieval period in Britain. Whatever else the relations between the descendants of the native British population and those of the Germanic settlers may have been, the Britons are clearly condemned in Bede's *History* for making no effort to impart Christianity to the Anglo-Saxons (*HE* II.2, II.4 and V.23). Parts of Anglo-Saxon England, however, were in contact with converted Germanic communities on the Continent, and around 570 Æthelberht, King of Kent, took a Frankish princess as wife who was accompanied to Kent by a bishop and priests, who, however, it seems had no missionary role. In 597 a mission sent by Pope Gregory led by Augustine arrived in Kent (see Wood 1994). The subsequent progress of the conversion of the Anglo-Saxons was initially slow, apparently haphazard, and subject to vicissitudes, but it was formally complete around the early 680s with the conversion of Sussex and the Isle of Wight. Of especial importance is the fact that a distinctly Gaelic Christianity was introduced into Northumbria under King Oswald (634-642) who had been converted, while in exile, at Iona. The Mercian Church was at first Gaelic too. A decision to conform to Roman practices in these English Churches was taken at the Synod of Whitby in 664. It seems to be broadly true that this decision cleared the way for consolidatory reorganization in the English Church in the late seventh century, which in turn allowed concentrated efforts to be applied in missionary work, art and scholarship in the eighth century.

Religious practices and behaviour

It is practically impossible to identify both convincingly and substantially traces of religious practices in the silence of true prehistory, and the Anglo-Saxons effectively became a people with a comprehensive history only when they became Christian. At least we know very well what behaviour and practices Christianity enjoins upon the people and can identify, sometimes with absolute certainty, at other times with reasonable probability, instances of these requirements being put into practice. An intriguingly problematic area is that of how far the existence of Christian behaviour may itself create pagan practices. The fallacy of assuming that a rite is religious in one context—e.g. burial in sixth-century England—because it is so in a Christian context need not detain us. But in what ways would the religious character of a traditional Anglo-Saxon burial rite have been changed by the contextual presence, contemporary and in the immediate vicinity, of Christianity and Christian burial? We shall repeatedly see that our picture of religion in early Anglo-Saxon England provides instances of apparent responses in traditional practices to Christian norms even when those responses hardly seem to reflect the adoption of Christianity.

Historical evidence for the customary practices of the non-Christian English comes primarily from the writings of the Northumbrian monk, Bede (*ca* 672-735). In Ch. XV of his work *De temporum ratione* (On the Reckoning of Time), entitled *De mensibus Anglorum* (On the Months of the English), he explains a calendar in terms of such religion. The survey reveals a pattern of regular sacrificial feasting and rites closely connected to the cycle of fertility and the agricultural year. The year begins in the middle of a double month *Giuli* (Yule) with a midwinter festival of *modranect* (Mothers' Night) on which unspecified ceremonies are hesitantly alluded to. The second month, *Solmonath*, is a month in which cakes were sacrificed to gods. The third and fourth months, *Hredmonath* and *Eosturmonath*, were named after goddesses Hreda and Eostre, for whom sacrifices and a feast were held. The ninth month is *Halegmonath* (Holy Month), which Bede also calls the "*mensis sacrorum*"—probably to be translated 'month of offerings' but possibly 'month of festivals'. It cannot be a matter of chance that this coincides with the time of the traditional Christian Harvest Festival in this area. The eleventh month is *Blodmonath* (Blood Month), a month in which the livestock that has to be slaughtered for the winter is 'devoted' to the gods. Sacrificial slaughtering of cattle is also referred to in a letter from Pope Gregory to Abbot Mellitus in Kent dated to the year 601 (*HE* I.30). Such notices have been called upon in suggesting interpretations of archaeological deposits such as a pit full of ox-skulls in a postulated temple-building at the seventh-century royal vill of Yeavering, Northumberland (on which more below), a very large deposit of ox-skulls at a possible temple site on Harrow Hill, Sussex, and various finds of animals' skulls in Anglo-Saxon graves (Owen 1981:45-9).

The second important passage in Bede's writings is the story of Edwin of Northumbria's conversion and the council at which Coifi, "*primus pontificum*" (the chief of the priests), renounces his old religion (*HE* II.13). This purportedly provides evidence of certain taboos that Coifi deliberately violates to profane the sacred customs and sites of the old religion. He carries weapons, which was forbidden a priest, and rides upon a stallion when only a mare was allowed him; he profanes the shrine (*fanum*) itself by casting a spear into it. Although negative, the two constraints upon the priest can be seen as active, creative factors in that they impose an emblematic feminization upon him, something which rings true in terms both of its coherency and of certain further historical echoes. In his *Germania* of the end of the first century AD, Tacitus refers to a priesthood within the old Germanic religion (*Germania* X; see also Wood 1995:257-9). The importance of feminine deities is reflected by evidence for the cults of Nerthus, Hreda, Eostre, Frige *et al.* (Tacitus, *Germania* XL; Bede, *De temporum ratione* XV), and the importance of their femininity may be reflected by the rules designed to keep representatives of normal masculinity at a distance from them. Nerthus' cart, according to Tacitus, is drawn by cows; no one but the priest can approach her; the slaves who wash her chariot and vestments in a secluded lake are then drowned.

There are two major categories of site in the archaeological record in which religious ritual is widely argued to be represented, human graves and ritual hoards. In both cases the basis for imputing a religious character is solid, though of varying significance; in both cases too we can argue that even if a religious element was prominent in some earlier stage, the history of the development of these practices seems to show a growing subordination to purely secular, social needs.

In the late Roman period, the ritual hoards of the Continental groups from which Anglo-Saxon culture was derived are dominated by a series of sometimes huge weapon hoards (Geißlinger 1967; Hines 1989). These are quite reliably interpreted as sacrificial deposits of the equipment of defeated enemy armies at established votive sites as a form of propitiatory and contractual gift to the gods. Such rites are rather vaguely, but, in light of the archaeological finds, still adequately attested to in Classical historical sources from Caesar to Orosius. The weapon hoards are characteristic of southern Scandinavia. In the fifth century the range of such hoarding becomes more complex, apparently under the pressure of a need to increase the scope for such ritual consumption, and showing a presumably socially-governed shift from group to individual offerings. We may thus argue that ritual hoarding was losing its religious character. In the later fifth and sixth centuries ritual hoards of jewellery and amulets are recurrent finds in the Continental Saxon areas too (Hauck 1970).

It is usually held that this form of ritual is simply absent from the Anglo-Saxon archaeological record. A more accurate view of the situation would be to note that the need for ritual consumption that the hoards apparently represent is satisfied in England by the provision of grave goods (hence in England, as in Norway, the majority of bracteates found in context have been found as grave goods rather than as hoarded items: on bracteates see further below). This fact can in turn be used to bolster the argument that funerary deposition in Anglo-Saxon England is to be interpreted in social terms rather than in religious ones. From Anglo-Saxon England we do, however, have several brief but largely neglected reports of considerable quantities of weaponry recovered from rivers, above all from the Thames. Such river-finds form part of an extensive series of material from the Neolithic to the late Middle Ages, and the persistence of the phenomenon and the large number of objects involved renders a simple explanation in terms of casual loss highly implausible (cf. Bradley & Gordon 1985). The condition of the majority of these weapons also indicates that loss in battle is practically out of the question, and deliberate deposition has to be regarded as highly probable.

There is a crying need for further research on this phenomenon, to quantify its frequency and range, not only in England but also elsewhere in Europe, and to evaluate the biases inherent in the normal circumstances in which such material is recovered (by dredging). With even late-medieval swords frequently recovered from rivers, it appears that the presumed rite of deliberate deposition occurs in too many different historical contexts for any single religious explanation to be plausible, and socially-directed destructive rites are a possibility (cf. the fate of Excalibur at the end of the Arthurian cycle). It also appears that the evidence for genuinely early Anglo-Saxon riverine deposition may be less strong than has been thought. Michael Swanton's catalogue (1974) of early Anglo-Saxon spearheads lists more than 120 examples from the Lower Thames and its tributaries. If, however, we compare the range of types from this area of river with that from fifth- to seventh-century grave finds in the adjacent counties of south-eastern England (Berkshire, Middlesex and Surrey) we find large discrepancies: for instance ten examples of Series D from rivers against one from a grave; sixteen examples of Series I from rivers against three from graves; thirty-five examples of Series H from graves against fifteen from rivers. (This is in the context of an overall ratio of river to grave finds in this area very close to 1:1.) These figures seem to imply that most of the river-deposited spearheads are not drawn from the same collection of weapons that can be dated to the Early Anglo-Saxon period by the grave finds. It is perhaps also appropriate at this point to note that one essential sacrament of the Christian Church, baptism, could take place in rivers, as in the case of Paulinus baptizing in the River Glen at Yeavering.

Burial rites figure very prominently in the standard accounts of pre-Christian Anglo-Saxon religious practices. One cannot deny the common association of funerary ritual and religion. The weakness in admitting the archaeological evidence for burial into a discussion of early Anglo-Saxon religion can be exemplified by posing two questions: what, in this case, does the archaeological record definitely tell us about the supposedly implicit religion; and what features of the archaeological record does the imputation of religion specially and successfully explain? The answers are nothing and none respectively. Although it is impossible to quote chapter and verse to demonstrate the Church's insistence on specifically Christian burial practice, we know that the Church preferred and in effect eventually enforced certain funerary norms (Thomas 1981:228-39; Watts 1991:38-98; Young 1977; discussion, this vol., pp.407-8). In consequence, a trend towards the orientation of graves and the abandonment of grave goods must, in the historical context of the advance of Christianity, be seen as a form of Christian influence. Even in these circumstances, however, it is perfectly conceivable for the burial practices to be adopted without the religion being so, and indeed there are many fluctuations in the provision of grave goods in Germanic funerary ritual that cannot have anything significant to do with Christianity—or, in all probability, with any other religion.

It is the phenomena of the transitional phase, of the period of conversion in seventh-century England, that are of most interest in this regard, especially where we see either the adaptation of Christian practices in what nevertheless appears to be a non-Christian context or the maintenance of what might otherwise be classified as pagan practices in an ostensibly Christian context. An example of the latter is the persistence of the provision of grave goods, and even the provision of explicitly Christian grave goods—above all gold or jewelled pendant crosses, even in the second grave of St Cuthbert of Northumbria. The provision of grave goods becomes genuinely exceptional in Anglo-Saxon England only in the late seventh century, and effectively disappears early in the eighth. The shift to burial in consecrated ground, eventually in churchyards, is difficult to trace archaeologically but seems likely to have been a similarly gradual process. A number of new, seventh-century, 'Final-phase' cemeteries with oriented graves could qualify as distinctly Christian cemeteries, but the continuity of seventh-century burials with Christian insignia in cemeteries founded before the conversion is broadly as well attested, especially in Kent (Hyslop 1963).

Most interesting are a few special instances of burials that seem quite deliberately to select the opposite of all the most distinctive features of Christian burial: for instance a small group of richly furnished barrow burials of the seventh century with cremated bodies and unburnt grave goods (Davidson & Webster 1967). The famous Sutton Hoo boat grave may indeed be one such example. Precisely the same range of features seems to have been deliberately selected for the emphatically pagan funeral of the hero in the Old English heroic epic *Beowulf* (esp. lines 3136-68). It would be relatively easy to attribute these phenomena to a self-consciously pagan reaction in the face of Christianity. But again one should be cautious in making such religious interpretations. Just as in the case of Cuthbert's burial noted above, it might be possible for such contraversions of Christian rule to be allowable, for some special emphasis, safely within the framework of the Christian religion. Thus we have a few instances of distinctively furnished barrow graves in the latest phases of what should have long been Christian Merovingian-period row-grave cemeteries in Frankish and Alamannic Germany (Ament 1975:80-93; Christlein 1978:56-62). Eventually, however, the social and ecclesiastical élite had its special position marked by reserved burial within churches or mortuary chapels and the use of special memorial monuments rather than burial in the common graveyard.

A further field of human behaviour in which religion is often represented as being typically influential is that of ethics. It is not unduly cynical to doubt that ethics—people's views on how they ought to behave—ever has more than a marginal influence on how people actually do behave. As far as I can see it is impossible to attribute any definitely religious character (as religion is defined here) to any of the traditional Germanic ethical codes, for instance those concerning sexual fidelity or military loyalty that we can read of in Tacitus and later sources, and pointless to speculate on this matter.

We are, however, presented by our early sources with a series of images of Christian behaviour in the first century or two after the conversion in England which seem to be consistent in one particular, and potentially very important, way. Hagiography, Bede's *History* and Aldhelm's treatises inevitably puff up exhortations to and stories of personal vocations to monastic service and lives of outstanding piety (e.g. *HE* III.6, 14, 27). But through all such stories, and minor ones of, for instance, royal pilgrimages to Rome late in life, bequests to the Church and so on (*HE* IV.11, V.7, 19), it is possible to see that a fear of damnation (and a hope of salvation) did become widely imbued in at least that stratum of Anglo-Saxon society that such sources take notice of. Such an understanding, according to Felix, was effectively what led Guthlac to abandon the life of a military adventurer for that of a monk, in his mid-twenties, in the year 699 or 700.

> *Nam cum antiquorum regum stirpis suae per transacta retro saecula miserabiles exitus flagitioso vitae termino contemplaretur, necnon et caducas mundi divitias contemptibilemque temporalis vitae gloriam pervigili mente consideraret, tunc sibi proprii obitus sui imaginata forma ostentatur, et finem inevitabilem brevis vitae curiosa mente horrescens, cursum cotidie ad finem cogitabat.... Haec et alia his similia eo cogitante ecce subito instigante divino numine se ipsum famulum Christi venturum fore, si in crastinum vitam servasset, devovit.*

> (For when he contemplated the pitiful deaths and shameful end of the ancient kings of his kindred, and likewise meditated with wakeful mind upon the transitory wealth of the world and the contemptible glory of this passing life, a vision of his own death came to him. And troubled in his mind, horrified by the inevitable end of this brief life, he considered that it was daily coming towards its close.... Thinking over these things and others like them, he suddenly vowed, with divine inspiration, that if he should live till the morrow, he himself should become one of Christ's servants) (*V.S.G.* XVIII).

The most general point I would make on this basis is that it is in this field of religion that we can best see a sense of individualism in early Anglo-Saxon England. Even though the evolving Church introduced various forms of collective intercession and expiation, Christianity made morality not only a highly individual responsibility but also a deeply internal matter. Attitudes and thoughts counted as much as actions. One of the great myths of modern History is the notion that a sense of personal individuality was somehow created in Europe only with (variously) the twelfth-century or the fifteenth-century Renaissance (e.g. Bloch 1962:106-8; Burckhardt 1960:121-44). It is certainly not claimed here that it was actually Christianity that introduced such a concept to early Anglo-Saxon England. Indeed there would appear, *prima facie*, to be a good deal of continuity between a heroic concern for immortality in the form of a heroic reputation and a Christian concern with salvation:

> *Ūre ǣghwylce sceal ende gebīdan*
> *worolde līfes; wyrce sēþe mōte*
> *dōmes ǣr dēaþe; þæt bi∂ drihtguman*
> *unlifgendum æfter sēlest.*

> (All of us must come to the end
> of this worldly life; let him who can create

> a reputation before death; that is the best thing
> a noble man no longer living can leave behind him).
>   (*Beowulf*, ll. 1386-9) (Trans. Klaeber 1950).

Hence the parade of heroic saints and saintly heroes in Anglo-Saxon literature. We, however, can only observe this as an aspect of the Christian community and culture, and can see here a subtle and substantial feature of general cognition that clearly influenced some important people's behaviour.

Religious sites in the natural and social environments

Looking at evidence for religious sites in the Early Anglo-Saxon period, we find some considerably more concrete elements to put into our overall picture. We have already seen an example of how elements of the natural environment can be endowed with religious significance, in the case of rivers and other watercourses and lakes that could be used for baptism or for sacrificial offerings. Perhaps drawing substantially on traditions of the British and Gaelic Churches, early Anglo-Saxon Christianity was also much given to distinguish islands, either in the sea or in wasteland such as the Fens, as secluded sites that were appropriate to a sanctified life, though they were not holy in themselves. Hence the monastery at Lindisfarne on Holy Island off the Northumberland coast, Cuthbert's cell on the nearby Farne Islands, and Guthlac's cell at Crowland. Christianity took such suitable locations and built religious sites upon them.

Religious sites can leave their mark on the place-names of an area; representing English Christianity, for instance, we find numerous forms in *minster* and *church* (not necessarily early place-names), and the small number of *eccles* place-names in England notoriously represents some form of presumably late- or sub-Roman Christian centre (*ecclesia*) recognized as such in the English place-name set (Thomas 1981:262-4). Place-names are in a certain sense a historical source. English non-Christian religious-site names are a particularly important source of evidence for this early phase of religious history, which apparently ended in the seventh century (Brooks *et al.* 1984:150-1; Gelling 1962; Stenton 1941). There are two basic categories of diagnostic elements that identify such names: the name or designation of a god, and an element meaning temple (*hearh*) or shrine (*weoh*). The range of specific terms found in either category is small, and the two are never found in combination. The deities thus represented are Woden (Weden in its developed Old English form), Thunor, Tiw and Frige (see Table 12-1). These are precisely the four pre-Christian deities used in the probably third-century West Germanic translations of the Latin names of the days of the week, rendering the Roman days of Mars, Mercury, Jove and Venus as Tuesday, Wednesday, Thursday and Friday respectively. It is curious that no Germanic equivalent of Saturn was put forward. Mythology indicates that this small pantheon included both war and fertility deities.

Table 12-1

English 'pagan' place-names included in the maps, Figs. 12-1a/b*

	Woden	Thunor	Tiw	Frige	weoh	hearh
simplex					Wye, Kent	Harrough, Suffolk Harrow Hill, Sussex
lēah	Wensley, Derbys.	Thunreslea, Hants. (x2) Thursley, Surrey Thunderley, Essex Thundersley Essex Thurs lege broc, Rutland	Tuesley, Surrey Tislea, Hants.		Whillig, Sussex Willey, Surrey Wheely Down, Hants. Weoley, Worcs.	
feld	Wodnesfeld, Essex Wedynsfeld, Essex Wednesfield Staffs.	Thunresfelda, Wilts. Thunderfield, Surrey				
land					Weoland, Wilts.	
ford					Weeford, Staffs. Wyfordby, Lincs.	
wiella					Wyville, Lincs.	
mere			Tyesmere, Worcs.			
dūn					Weedon Beck/ Weedon Lois, Northants. Weedon, Bucks.	Harrowden Beds. Harrowden, Northants. Harrowdown, Essex
beorg	Wodnes beorg, Wilts.					
hōh			Tysoe Wariwcks.		Wysall, Notts.	
denu	Wodnes denu Wilts.			Friden, Derbys.		
ham(m)					Wyham, Lincs.	
-inga						Gumeninga hearh, Middlesex Besinga hearh, Hants.
Personal name					Patchway, Sussex Cusan weoh, Surrey	Peper Harow, Surrey

* Names in italics are recorded only in historical sources.

The published discussions of this quite well-known place-name set seem to be rather too trusting in accepting as authentic evidence a small number of names that link one of the gods with a human artefact such as a barrow (*hlæw*) or an earthwork—e.g. Wenslow, Beds., *Thunreslau*, Essex, and Wansdyke, Wilts. These seem to me to be too readily attributable to later, imaginative formation, like Weyland's Smithy in Berkshire, the Devil's Punch Bowl in Surrey or several Drakelows (= dragon's barrow). Much more convincingly authentic are a range of topographical features that seem to have been regularly used as cult sites. Two in particular, *lēah* (grove) and *feld* (field), recur several times with the names of gods. Hills, valleys and watercourses seem also to be reliably attested to as religious sites. Tacitus testifies to the use of sacred groves in his *Germania* (X, XXXIX), and the Norse word for a grove, *lundr*, is frequent in Scandinavian pre-Christian religious place-names. We have four examples of the combination of *wēoh* with *lēah*.

Of particular interest is a small but coherent group of proprietorial names with the specifics *wēoh* and *hearh*. Three of these have a personal name with one of

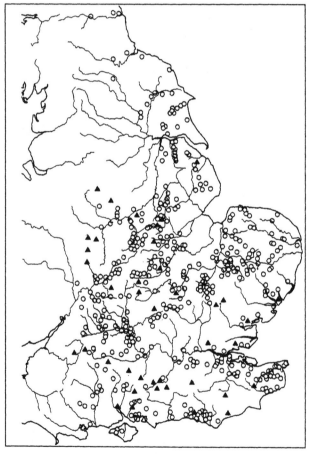

Fig. 12-1a: Migration-period Anglo-Saxon burial sites (open circles) and the pre-Christian religious place-names listed in Table 12-1 (filled triangles).

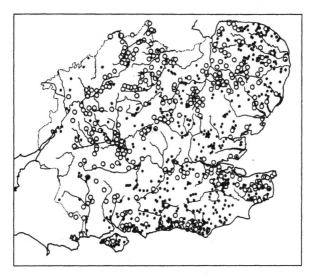

Fig. 12-1b: Migration-period Anglo-Saxon burial sites (open circles) and place-names in *-inga-* or *-ingas* (filled dots) in the southern counties of England, adapted from Dodgson 1966.

these words, twice certainly in the genitive case with *wēoh*; two have the genitive plural *-inga* with *hearh*. The English non-Christian religious place-names as a whole have a geographical distribution which is similar to that of the famous stratum of *-ingas*, *-inga-* place-names in that a number are found beyond the western limits of early Anglo-Saxon material culture as represented by furnished burial sites, and they are especially frequent within void areas inside those limits on the distribution map (Dodgson 1966; Fig. 12-1a, 12-1b).

Contributory factors explaining this distribution might be that these religious sites were typically located in remote and secluded areas, and that in such areas such names had a better chance of surviving a Christian purging of the place-name set.

Neither of these explanations, however, fits the evidence with ideal consistency. It is at least equally likely that the formation of these religious place-names should be linked to the later sixth- and seventh-century processes of social organization reflected in the multiplication of *-ingas* and *-inga-* names. It may be appropriate to note here that in a paper read by the late John Dodgson to the Viking Society of London in November 1986—never published, as far as I know—he revived the argument that various names in *Wing*, such as Wing, Bucks., and Wingham, Kent, contained Old English *wēoh* and the suffix *-ing*, giving a name interpretable as 'the people of the shrine'. Altogether this view of the place-name evidence implies, quite simply, that we can correlate the emergence of this layer of evidence for religion with the consolidation of an aristocratic social and political order in England. Consequently we may see here a trace of a late, politicized re-organization of traditional religious cult at a time when the conversion to Christianity had already begun.

To translate *hearh* as 'temple' and *wēoh* as 'shrine' is potentially misleading in that in neither case does the word itself imply the existence of any particular structures at those sites. Presumably the best-informed reference to a non-Christian religious building in Anglo-Saxon England is Bede's reference to the *fanum* at Goodmanham desecrated by Coifi (this vol., p. 379) as an enclosed and flammable structure containing idols. Bede also records Pope Gregory's various instructions to Augustine on what to do with pagan *fana idolorum* and *fanorum aedificia* (*HE*, I.30, 32). One archaeological site has a claim to identification as such a temple that has to be taken seriously—Building D2 at Yeavering, Northumberland (Fig. 12-2;

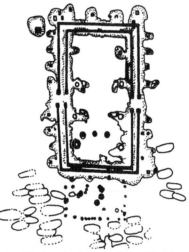

Fig. 12-2: Yeavering, Northumberland, building D2. After Hope-Taylor 1977.

Hope-Taylor 1977:154-69). This was a rectangular timber building, rather small in comparison with the other halls on the site, aligned north-south on its long axis. It had an external fenced enclosure with post-settings beyond the southern end, an interior row of three post-settings also towards the southern end, and a pit filled with the remains of butchered oxen, predominantly their skulls, by the eastern door. The building was a focus for human graves. It eventually burnt down with the rest of the site but was not rebuilt in the following phase; in that phase another building (Building B), interpreted as a church, appeared at the other end of the site, located upon a burial area already used and itself a focus for later graves. It is enlightening here that the presence of the putative church is an important factor in the identification of the possible temple. There is good reason to suppose that temple buildings were not typical of traditional Germanic religion. Tacitus, for what his testimony is worth, categorically stated that the Germanic peoples did not enclose their gods within walls (*Germania* IX). In the later, reasonably well-evidenced phase of traditional Germanic religion of Viking-period Scandinavia special temple sites seem to have been extremely rare (Turville-Petre 1964:236-50). There are two plausible sources of influence that may have modified Germanic practice. One was Roman religion, with which many Germanic soldiers and officers would have been familiar in the days of the Empire. There is even a third-century door-pillar with an inscription recording a fulfilled vow to a romanized Germanic deity, *Mars Thincsus*, and an altar apparently to the same god, from the fort at Housesteads, Northumberland (Collingwood & Wright 1965: no. 1593). The other source, of course, is Christianity—itself an heir to the habits of Roman religion.

Even without attributing the appearance of temples in late sixth/seventh-century Anglo-Saxon traditional religion to an appropriation of a Christian feature, we simply cannot disassociate the establishment of built religious centres that was so important to the earliest Christians in Anglo-Saxon England from the apparently contemporary establishment—or even just redefinition—of non-Christian religious sites. Christianity preferred consecrated ground for burial and for worship; it preferred consecrated buildings for the latter and, eventually, as houses for God's most devoted servants, the monastic orders. According to Bede's account, establishing churches was clearly a high priority for Augustine, firstly seeking out and restoring an old Roman church of St Martin at Canterbury, and later restoring a second church, which he dedicated to the Holy Saviour and which apparently was the site of the present cathedral (*HE* I.26, 33). Two known early (i.e. pre-650) Anglo-Saxon churches at Canterbury and two further ones at Stone-by-Faversham and Lydd, Kent, appear, accordingly, to incorporate Roman material or buildings (Cherry 1976; Fletcher & Meates 1969; Taylor & Taylor 1965:134-48, 405-8, 575-7). By 601, Gregory was sending Augustine books, vestments and relics to be housed in Canterbury (*HE* I.29).

The earliest Anglo-Saxon churches known to archaeology have an uncomplicated and quite consistent plan. Further early examples from Kent are SS. Peter and Paul, Canterbury, thought to be Augustine's monastery, and churches at Lyminge and Rochester (*HE* I.33; Taylor & Taylor 1965:134-48, 408-10, 518-9). The Kentish churches all have a nave measuring thirteen to fifteen metres long by eight to nine wide with a chancel or apse five to eight metres long. They are masonry-built. Bede, however, tells us that churches built "*more Scottorum*" (in the Gaelic tradition) in England were typically wooden. He tells the tale of Bishop Aidan dying leant against such a church at a *villa regalis* in Northumberland (*HE* III.17)—usually identified as *Maelmin*, though it could have been Yeavering. The postulated wooden church at Yeavering, Building B, measured about twelve metres by six. It is interesting that the naves of these churches are typically a little smaller than the contemporary buildings that have the best claim to be identified as aristocratic halls. The smallest of these is apparently that at Dinas Powys, South Glamorgan—a British site—which seems to have measured about fifteen metres by six (Alcock 1963). The seventh-century halls at Yeavering measured from eighteen to thirty metres long and six to ten metres wide, and those at Cowdery's Down, Hants., from seventeen to twenty-two metres by nine (James *et al.* 1985; Millett & James 1984). The churches either could not rival the halls, or perhaps were careful not to.

For the Church as much as for the traditional religion, the location of religious sites was of great importance. Even more than the islands referred to above, this involved man-made sites, such as the abandoned church of an old Roman city that Augustine first latched upon (*HE* I.26). This pattern of re-use is widely repeated.

The site of St Paul-in-the-Bail, Lincoln, has proved a difficult one archaeologically, and has been interpreted in many different ways; the now established view seems to be that this was the site of a Roman wooden church and Christian graveyard that may have seen continuous, Christian use through the early Middle Ages (Eagles 1989:207-8). The sequence of churches of St Paul began there at some uncertain date from the seventh century to the ninth. At Exeter, the Saxon minster overlies a late- or sub-Roman cemetery (Bidwell 1979:104-14). Both these sites are in the *forum* of the Roman city. An odd though nevertheless comparable situation is the gift of the old Saxon Shore fort at Burgh Castle by King Sigiberht of East Anglia to Fursa as the site for a monastery (*HE* III.19). The common interest of Crown and Church in the designation and use of such sites seems to have been of great importance in the history of urbanization in England, as it is this which is probably the single most important factor in the revival, as administrative cities, of a series of old Roman towns which otherwise had no clear, special economic function: most notably Canterbury, Winchester, Leicester and Lincoln.

In the whole view, this consistent relationship between religion and landscape deserves to be taken very seriously. At a relatively superficial level, the phenomenon can on the one hand be interpreted as a product of a sort of religious personification of the landscape. The hidden depths of waters and forests, and the tops of hills, could be imaginatively populated with spirits—as Guthlac's fens could be imaginatively populated with demons. Similarly the landscape can be imbued with value as emblematic of religious beliefs, as islands and the sea became linked with ascetic isolation and sanctity, and Roman sites became emblematic of Christian civilization. But the religions concerned are emphatically not merely topographically governed, nor is religion the only phenomenon that culturally governs human use of the landscape. Both the spiritual world and the landscape are huge, permanent environments in which Man lives; across the whole range of early Anglo-Saxon religion we can see these environments being imaginatively compounded.

A further special type of Christian site is the monastery—the home of a dedicated religious community. Within the wider community it appears that these communities were designed to be materially self-sufficient, a series of surviving charters giving us moderately good evidence as to the nature of monastic endowments and estates (Stenton 1943:303-6). Our best view of an earlier Anglo-Saxon monastic centre comes from the excavations of the monastery at Whitby, North Yorks., which have revealed residential cells and chapels, and, of economic importance, workshop areas too (Cramp 1976a; Cramp 1976b; Rahtz 1976; Webster & Backhouse 1991:138-47; cf. Sawyer 1986:67). This separation of the monasteries from the remainder of the community was clearly an important element in their perceived and attributed status. Legally it is clear, from a letter of Bede to Ecgberht, then bishop of York, of 734, that the monasteries enjoyed privileges, for instance of tenure, and exemptions, for instance from military service, which according to Bede gave rise to an abuse with noblemen having their homes designated as monasteries to obtain these advantages (Whitelock 1979:799-810; cf. Charles-Edwards, this volume). In this context it is clear that the lay and religious character of relatively high-status settlement sites could be thoroughly confused—something which leaves one wondering whether there is any point in archaeological speculations on the possible monastic character of certain fairly rich eighth-century sites that have been excavated, for instance at Flixborough, South Humbs., and Brandon, Suffolk (Webster & Backhouse 1991:81-101).

Here too we would appear to have a very clear example of a communal religion being perceived and used as an instrument to serve the interests of a powerful group within society. It is not, however, the whole picture in respect of the aristocratic-monastic relationship. It does also appear that by the late seventh/eighth century, monastic devotion could be quite in vogue for some of the aristocracy, such as the royal ladies of Whitby, Barking and many other nunneries, the abdicating kings, and Guthlac in his hermitage. Of course there are pragmatic considerations here—the scope afforded for independence and power, perhaps especially for the royal women; the desire for security from the risks of political life—from which it is not a great step to a desire for eternal salvation. But in all respects we can see how close to the heart of English cultural life the Church was by about the beginning of the eighth century.

Art, literature and the imagination

Such are the monuments of this period that have been passed down to us that early Anglo-Saxon Christianity and art are seen as quite inseparable. It was in the workshops and scriptoria of the early Church that the so-called 'golden age of Northumbria' was produced; the British Museum can put on a special exhibitions of art from this period adopting Giraldus Cambrensis' phrase 'The Work of Angels' as its title (Youngs 1989). This Christian art is best known to us in the form of illuminated manuscripts, metalwork and sculpture; less evidence of other media such as textiles, woodwork and painted glass now survives. A point of particular interest in respect of early Anglo-Saxon Christian art is the existence of two quite distinct traditions within the whole range—a Roman, relatively Classical one, and a Hiberno-Saxon one that drew massively on the Germanic zoomorphic and the Celtic La Tène traditions. Many illuminated manuscripts show that the Roman and Hiberno-Saxon styles can be combined, but it is invariably possible in these cases to identify one tradition as the dominant mode. As Jane Hawkes's discussion of Anglo-Saxon art and symbolism (this volume) indicates, ecclesiastical art was more than the mere ornamentation of venerated objects and places, casually using whatever artistic traditions happened to be at hand. The distinctive distributions and detailed style-histories of the Roman and in particular the Hiberno-Saxon tradition lend themselves to interpretation in political terms (Hines 1992; Høilund Nielsen n.d.). On top of its religious functions, such art symbolized identity and allegiance.

The most robust attempts that have been made to identify non-Christian Germanic religious art have been based explicitly on similarities with and possible derivations from Roman religious—often Christian—art. These are to be found in Karl Hauck's compendious series of studies *Zur Ikonographie der Goldbrakteaten* (published principally in the periodical *Frühmittelalterliche Studien*). This series has as its domain a special set of finds from the fifth and sixth centuries, a large series of pendants which are quite unusually made of the most precious metal available, gold; which are predominantly deposited in ritual hoards in southern Scandinavia; which use a range of artistic motifs that are substantially different from those on other contemporary objects; and some of which carry runic inscriptions that can be interpreted amuletically, for instance as invocations of good fortune: *alu!*; *auja!*. The whole topic is far too large a one to summarize adequately here; I would simply say that I would judge the case for regarding motifs like the cross, the swastika and the triskele on the earlier bracteates (up to Type C) as symbols, and recurrent figural scenes like the three figures on B-bracteates or the head and quadruped of C-bracteates as originally iconographic, to be a strong one. That the iconography can be translated into terms suggested by later Germanic mythological records, however, and specific gods identified, seems a far more speculative issue.

I would regard one of the more useful and positive points that can be made concerning the religious and amuletic significance of bracteates to be to note their testimony as to the persistent association of medicinal effects and healing with divine power—again an association apparently shared quite equally by both traditional Germanic and Christian religion. The later books of Bede's History are stuffed with healing miracles (e.g. *HE* III.9-13, V.2-6). The medicinal role of the bracteates in particular offers an explanation of the otherwise strange appearance of the word *lauk-* (onion or leek) in a number of bracteate inscriptions, a plant whose powerful invigorating properties are widely recognized and exaggerated in folklore (e.g. Pliny, *Natural History* XX.20-23). In England, it is the much trumpeted reference to a pre-Christian deity, Woden, in the Old English metrical *Nine Herbs Charm* (known in an eleventh-century text) that first appears to represent this aspect of traditional religion (Owen 1981:12). A pair of comparable Old High German charms imply a deeper historical background (Bostock *et al.* 1976:26-42). We can also recall Bede's condemnation of how countrymen in Tweedsdale lapsed into "*erratica idolatriae medicamina per incantationes vel fylacteria vel alia quaelibet daemonicae artis arcana*" {false remedies of idolatry, by means of incantations or amulets or diverse other mysteries of devilish art (*HE* IV.27)}, when suffering afflictions such as a plague. Such accusations are echoed in the early Anglo-Saxon Penitentials associated with Theodore of Canterbury and Ecgberht of York (Wilson 1992:37-8, 97-102, 115). We ought not, however, to jump to conclusions about how much real religious belief may have been involved in such superstitious rituals—it is at least as difficult a matter as to know how much such belief to attribute to charm-bracelets now worn in the West, or lorry drivers' evil-eye beads in the Near East. There is every reason to suppose that

Woden could only appear in the late text of the *Nine Herbs Charm* because he had become a harmlessly fictional supernatural figure or a mere sprite—and in these circumstances he could perfectly well be a late introduction to the charm. A charm against a 'stitch' in the same eleventh-century manuscript uses the old gods, the **ēs*, merely as an imagined possible source of the 'shot' that the sudden pain of the stitch represents, on an equal basis with elves and witches.

The number of bracteates known in England is small. They are persistently of a character that suggests they are losing any religious significance their prototypes may have had. In Anglian England they often appear in silver and once in bronze as well as in gold, and their 'iconographic' designs degenerate substantially. Two runic inscriptions are known on bracteates found in England, an early one (possibly imported) which reads quite clearly and unmystically "...reward to a kinsman/-woman", and a late one which may be a degenerate version of the word *laþu* (invitation). Most of the Kentish finds, which are of gold, are D-bracteates, a later type which carries fairly simple Style-I zoomorphic ornament that lends itself very poorly to iconographic interpretation. In several respects these Style-I motifs look like precursors of the stately, rather heraldic, Style-II animals of the late sixth century onwards. It seems quite possible, then, that D-bracteates functioned more as badges of wealth and social status than as religious tokens. D-bracteates never carry runic inscriptions.

A more common pendant amulet which practically supersedes the bracteate in Anglian England—and eventually in Kent—is the scutiform pendant: a little model shield with a perfectly obvious and simple emblematic protective character (Hines 1984:221-43). Interestingly, cross designs on such pendants become quite frequent as we move into the seventh century; Christian influence seems undeniable, although cross-motifs are used in pre-Christian contexts. We also have examples from the seventh century of the pendant gold and/or jewelled cross used as personal jewellery, both for women {an outstanding case is the woman's necklace buried in a grave at Desborough, Northants. (Smith 1923:75-6 and Pl. IV)} and men, most notably in St Cuthbert's second grave (Bonner *et al.* 1989:231-366).

From the period of settlement itself, the Anglo-Saxon culture was a literate one, albeit to a highly restricted degree. Writing, in such contexts, always has an element of secrecy about it and is thus inevitably mysterious, but good evidence for the religious use of the earliest, runic writing is extremely limited. Miscellaneous statements by Tacitus and Venantius Fortunatus have been cited as evidence for the use of runes in divination by Germanic peoples into the Anglo-Saxon period (cf. Owen 1981:51-60; Lendinara 1994). Later Old English sources might imply that the myth of Woden's role in the introduction of runic writing to the world was known in England (Owen 1981:11-2), although the attribution of the introduction of letters to the Roman god Mercury, represented as a giant in the Old English prose *Solomon and Saturn* (cf. *dies Mercurii* = *Wednesday*, above) may have its roots in purely Classical myth (cf. the links between the Roman Mercurius and the Greek Hermēs, the communicator) and need not depend on an Anglo-Saxon identification of Mercury with Woden, while in the line:

ᚠ *byþ ordfruma...ælcre spræce*
(*ōs* is the originator of all speech)

in the tenth-century Old English *Rune Poem*, the word *ōs* clearly lends itself to interpretation as the Latin word for 'mouth' rather than in its English sense, a pre-Christian god, the singular of **ēs* (cf. *The Nine Herbs Charm*, above). At most these references could illustrate the controlled use of some elements drawn from pre-Christian religious traditions in the imaginative mythography of Christian England.

Tacitus records that Germanic peoples cultivated mythological poetry, and our richest source for traditional Germanic mythology is the Scandinavian Eddic mythological poetry collected in the thirteenth-century *Codex Regius* and studied and re-presented by the medieval Icelandic man of letters Snorri Sturluson (1179-1241) {Faulkes (ed.) 1982; (trans.) 1987}. Myth and religion are not the same thing, though they are usually closely related. There is actually no direct evidence that the Anglo-Saxons ever had any substantial, pre-Christian mythological poetic tradition, and only slender echoes of traditional mythology can tentatively be identified in the literary sources we do have. There is, for instance, the teasingly evocative reference to all creation weeping between Christ's passion and resurrection in *The Dream of the Rood*, recalling the death of Baldr in Norse mythology, the slain god who could not be brought back from Hel because not quite all creation would weep for him (*The Dream of the Rood*, lines 55-6; *Gylfaginning* XLIX). There seems no good reason to doubt that the unintentional slaying of Baldr by Hǫð has been transformed into the historical legend of the killing of Herebeald by Hæðcyn in *Beowulf* (Dronke 1969).

The same adaptation of the pre-Christian pantheon to secular pseudo-history is more widely seen in the royal genealogies, where, for instance, we find Woden, Bældæg and Seaxneat, together with other figures with clear links to fertility myth but whose original divinity is rather more obscure, such as Bedwig and Sceaf (Owen 1981:27-33). In a very real sense, these gods and mythical characters are still being used mythically in the Christian context. Their function there, however, is different, and they have clearly been removed from a suppressed non-Christian context in which their names and characters were of greater, and at least partly religious, significance.

Christianity introduced to England a much enhanced role for literacy and a new form of literacy in the Latin language and letters. Parchment books became necessary for the written texts. In due course this gave rise to the production of original Christian literature in England, in both Latin and the vernacular English language. The outstanding Latin authors of the early Church in England are the presumably West Saxon Aldhelm, Abbot of Malmesbury and later Bishop of Sherborne, Dorset, and his younger contemporary Bede. Their writings are characterized by a deep and thorough intellectual Christianity. Bede, for instance, in his writing on literary analysis, e.g. *De arte metrica* and *De schematibus et tropis,* distinguishes himself amongst contemporary and Classical works in this critical tradition by using examples predominantly from Christian Latin literature (Irvine 1994:272-98). Both Bede and Aldhelm were deeply imbued with the allegorical method of Christian interpretation of the Bible, as appears especially clearly in Bede's studies *De templo* and *De tabernaculo*, for instance, and in the opening section of Aldhelm's *Epistola ad Acircium*. This Acircius can be identified as Aldfrith, king of Northumbria (685-705). Bede and Aldhelm were writing to—if not for—a readership which evidently could include clerically educated laymen, not in a vacuum. They can hardly be considered as figures representative of Anglo-Saxon Christian culture around the late seventh/early eighth centuries in simple sense of being typical. But they can well be regarded as archetypes, representing the culmination of the direction and dynamism of that culture.

A comparison of this Latin writing with the earliest Christian literature in English makes one more important and interesting point. As that literature I would count three poems: *Cædmon's Hymn*, purportedly of the late seventh century; *Bede's Death Song*, of 735, and the Ruthwell Cross inscription, certainly no later than the eighth century. Cædmon is represented by Bede as the first Christian English vernacular poet, and the Hymn is allegedly his first, miraculously inspired composition (*HE* IV.24[22]). Bede's further development of this story in his *History*, referring to Cædmon's versification of Biblical material, shows little or no expectation that this vernacular verse would become written. He gives Cædmon's Hymn only in a Latin version, and one of the famous discrepancies between Bede's Latin and the tenth-century English translation of his History is that the original "*doctores suos vicissim auditores sui faciebat*" (he made his teachers in their turn become his listeners) is changed to "*seolfon þā his lāreowas æt his mūðe wreoton and leornodon*" (his teachers themselves *wrote* and learnt from his mouth). The earliest written texts of *Cædmon's Hymn* in English appear in mid-eighth-century manuscripts of Bede's *History*. *Bede's Death Song* appears earliest in what can be accepted as eighth-century language in a ninth-century manuscript; the verses on the Ruthwell Cross are inscribed in runes.

All of these early English Christian poems are embedded in a significant context. *Cædmon's Hymn*, as a hymn of praise to God as Creator, can make perfectly good sense on its own, and indeed critical ingenuity can discover or attribute various subtleties and ambiguities of meaning and structure to it (e.g. Conway 1995). *Bede's Death Song* is a five-line, rather laconic statement that Judgement is inevitable and to be approached apprehensively. Both poems, however, have clearly been passed down as details—important details, certainly—of larger stories which have their own rather different, effectively hagiographic significance. The Ruthwell Cross verses are beyond significant doubt all components of a monologue spoken by the Cross itself describing the Crucifixion and Passion. A longer version of this monologue appears in the manuscript poem *The Dream of the Rood*, not attested to before the late tenth century. It is impossible to determine whether or not the Ruthwell Cross inscription is an extract from such a larger poem extant as early as the eighth century; it does not need to be for the lines to function and to be understood as part of what the cross as a monument says and stands for. The point is that writing can make discourse context-free: *precisely* the same text can be transmitted and read in virtually infinitely different circumstances. We can perhaps see here that these implications of literacy were only slowly learnt in respect of Christian English poetry; they had been learnt by whenever the speech of the Cross was enclosed within the dreamer's vision in *The Dream of the Rood*, and by the time the poet Cynewulf was inscribing such details of himself as he wanted to and his signature into his Christian poetry, probably sometime in the ninth century (see, for instance, Gradon 1977:22-3).

Conclusion

> In one view...the history of scholarship is a history of error, and looked at that way the search for paganism comes near the centre of any historical account of Anglo-Saxon scholarship of the last hundred and fifty years. In that period the unknown (as I think, the unknowable unknown) was so firmly used to explain the known that scholars felt no doubt in their methods or results (Stanley 1975:122).

This study too has been very much on the theme of the nature and limits of the known and the knowable in early Anglo-Saxon history. Like Stanley, but not entirely with him, I conclude that the essential *known* is the historical and that the historical, in terms of Anglo-Saxon religion, means Christian culture. To me it appears, however, that Christianity makes the final phases of the traditional Germanic religion in England knowable in a reasonably substantial way since here, as apparently in late-Roman Britain, the introduction of Christianity was accompanied by a late 'pagan' florescence—the use of the term *pagan*, I think, becoming absolutely unobjectionable when applied to an actively non-Christian religious movement in the presence of Christianity which thus becomes effectively anti-Christian. We see most of the traditional Germanic religion as it overlaps, formally and chronologically, with Christianity. We also see a functional continuity between the different religions—not just in their social roles (cf. the introductory references to the Durkheimian view) but in the cultural use, control and development of the landscape, or in the (limited) continued use of mythological material in a new range of myths. Across the whole range of Anglo-Saxon culture, technical, social and intellectual, we can nevertheless see that the conversion to Christianity brought about profound changes. In all of this, religion appears as considerably more than the ideological drudge of social and economic interests, a repressive opium of the people. It must correlate with its cultural circumstances but can modify those circumstances to suit itself; in early Anglo-Saxon England, religion had a substantial degree of institutional and intellectual autonomy and power.

References

Textual sources:

[Abbreviations: *HE* = Bede, *Historia ecclesiastica*; *V.S.G.* = Felix, *Vita Sancti Guthlaci*]

Aldhelm
      Epistola ad Acircium: see Lapidge & Herren.
Bede
      Bede's Death Song: see Dobbie 1942; Smith 1978.
      De arte metrica: see Kendall 1975.
      De tabernaculo: see Hurst 1969.
      De templo: see Hurst 1969.
      De temporum ratione: see Jones 1943; 1977.
      De schematibus et tropis: see Kendall 1975.
      Historia ecclesiastia gentis Anglorum: see Colgrave & Mynors 1969; Miller 1890/98.
Beowulf: see Klaeber 1950.
Caedmon
      Hymn: see Dobbie 1942; A. H. Smith 1978.
The Dream of the Rood: see Krapp 1932; Swanton 1970.
Felix
      Vita Sancti Guthlaci: see Colgrave 1956.
The Nine Herbs Charm: see Dobbie 1942.
The Old English Rune Poem: see Dobbie 1942.
Pliny
      Natural History. Books XX-XXIII: see Jones 1951.
Snorri Sturluson
      Gylfaginning: see Faulkes 1982 (ed.); Faulkes 1987 (trans.).
Tacitus
      Germania: see Winterbottom & Ogilvie 1975.
Theodore
      Poenitentiale: see Migne 1851.

Bibliography:

Alcock, L.
    1963   *Dinas Powys*. Cardiff: University of Wales Press.
Ament, H.
    1975   Merowingische Grabhügel. In *Althessen im Frankenreich*. H. Beumann & W. Schröder (eds.), pp. 63-93. Sigmaringen: Thorbecke.
Bidwell, P. T.
    1979.   *The Legionary Bath House and Basilica and Forum at Exeter*. Exeter Archaeological Reports I. Exeter: Exeter City Council & the University of Exeter.
Bloch, M.
    1962   *Feudal Society*. [Trans. L. A. Manyon]. 2 vols. London: Routledge & Kegan Paul.
Bonner, G., C. Stancliffe & D. Rollason
    1989   *St Cuthbert: His Cult and Community to AD 1200*. Woodbridge: The Boydell Press.

Bostock, J. K., K. C. Kay & D. R. McLintock
    1976   *A Handbook on Old High German Literature.* Oxford: Clarendon Press.
Bradley, R., & K. Gordon
    1985   Human skulls from the River Thames. *Antiquity* 62: 503-59.
Brooks, N., M. Gelling & D. Johnson
    1984   A new charter of King Edgar. *Anglo-Saxon England* 13: 137-155.
Burckhardt, J.
    1960   *The Civilisation of the Renaissance in Italy.* [Trans. S. G. C. Middlemore,
              rev. I. Gordon]. New York: New American Library.
Cherry, B.
    1976   Ecclesiastical architecture. In *The Archaeology of Anglo-Saxon England.*
              D. M. Wilson (ed.), pp. 151-200. Cambridge: Cambridge University Press.
Christlein, R.
    1978   *Die Alamannen.* Stuttgart: Theiss.
Colgrave, B. (ed. & trans.)
    1956   *Felix's Life of Saint Guthlac.* Cambridge: Cambridge University Press.
Colgrave, B., & R. A. M. Mynors (eds. & trans.)
    1969   *Bede's Ecclesiastical History of the English People.* Oxford: Clarendon Press.
Collingwood, R. G., & R. P. Wright
    1965   *The Roman Inscriptions of Britain.* Vol. 1. Oxford: Clarendon Press.
Conway, C. A.
    1995   Structure and idea in 'Cædmon's Hymn'. *Neuphilologische Mitteilungen*
              96: 39-50.
Cramp, R. J.
    1976a   Monastic sites. In *The Archaeology of Anglo-Saxon England.* D. M. Wilson
              (ed.), pp. 201-252. Cambridge: Cambridge University Press.
    1976b   Analysis of the finds register and location plan of Whitby Abbey. In *The
              Archaeology of Anglo-Saxon England.* D. M. Wilson (ed.), pp. 453-457.
              Cambridge: Cambridge University Press.
Davidson, H. R. E., & L. Webster
    1967   The Anglo-Saxon burial at Coombe (Woodnesborough), Kent. *Medieval
              Archaeology* 11:1-41.
Dobbie, E. van K.
    1942   *The Anglo-Saxon Minor Poems.* (The Anglo-Saxon Poetic Records VI).
              New York: Columbia University Press.
Dodgson, J. McN.
    1966   The significance of the distribution of the English place-name in *-ingas-,* -
              inga- in south-east England. *Medieval Archaeology* 10: 1-29.
Dronke, U.
    1969   Beowulf and Ragnarǫk. *Saga-Book* 17: 302-326.
Durkheim, E.
    1915   *The Elementary Forms of the Religious Life.* [Trans. J. W. Swain]. London:
              George Allen & Unwin.
Eagles, B. N.
    1989   Lindsey. In *The Origins of Anglo-Saxon Kingdoms.* S. Bassett (ed.),
              pp. 202-212. London: Leicester University Press.
Faulkes, A. (ed.)
    1982   *Snorri Sturluson: Edda. Prologue and Gylfaginning.* Oxford: Oxford
              University Press.
    1987   *Snorri Sturluson: Edda.* London: Dent.

Fletcher, E., & G. W. Meates
  1969   The ruined church of Stone-by-Faversham. *Antiquaries Journal* 49: 273-294.
Geißlinger, H.
  1967   *Horte als Geschichtsquelle*. (Offa-Bücher NF 19). Neumünster: Karl Wachholtz.
Gelling, M.
  1962   Place-names and Anglo-Saxon paganism. *University of Birmingham Historical Journal* 8: 7-25.
Gradon, P. O. E.
  1977   *Cynewulf's 'Elene'*. [Revised ed.]. Exeter: University of Exeter Press.
Hauck, K.
  1970   *Goldbrakteaten aus Sievern*. München: Fink.
Henig, M.
  1984   *Religion in Roman Britain*. London: Batsford.
Hines, J.
  1984   *The Scandinavian Character of Anglian England in the pre-Viking Period*. (BAR British Series 124). Oxford: BAR.
  1989   Ritual hoarding in Migration-period Scandinavia: a review of recent interpretations. *Proceedings of the Prehistoric Society* 55: 193-205.
  1992   The Scandinavian character of Anglian England: an update. In *The Age of Sutton Hoo*. M. O. H. Carver (ed.), pp. 315-329. Woodbridge: The Boydell Press.
Høilund Nielsen, K.
  n.d.   Animal art and the weapon-burial rite: a political badge? In *Burial and Society*. C. K. Jensen & K. Høilund Nielsen (eds.). Århus: Århus University Press.
Hope-Taylor, B.
  1977   *Yeavering: An Anglo-British Centre of Early Northumbria*. (D.o.E. Archaeological Reports No. 7). London: Her Majesty's Stationery Office.
Hurst, D.
  1969   *Baedae Venerabilis opera. Pars IIA: Opera exegetica. De tabernaculo, de templo etc.*. (Corpus Christianorum Series Latina CXIX A). Turnhout: Brepols.
Hyslop, M.
  1963   Two Anglo-Saxon cemeteries at Chamberlain's Barn, Leighton Buzzard, Beds. *Archaeological Journal* 120: 161-200.
Irvine, M.
  1994   *The Making of Textual Culture: 'Grammatica' and Literary Theory 350-1100*. Cambridge: Cambridge University Press.
James, S., A. Marshall & M. Millett
  1985   An early medieval building tradition. *Archaeological Journal* 141: 182-215.
Jones, C. W. (ed.)
  1943   *Bedae opera de temporibus*. Cambridge, MA: Medieval Academy of America.
  1977   *Bedae Venerabilis opera. Pars VI: Opera didascalica* 2. (Corpus Christianorum Series Latina CXXIII B). Turnhout: Brepols.
Jones, W. H. S. (ed. & trans.)
  1951   *Pliny: Natural History Books XX-XXIII*. (Loeb Classical Library). London: Heinemann.

Kendall, C. B. (*et al.* eds.)
    1975   *Bedae Venerabilis opera. Pars VI: Opera didascalica 1.* (Corpus
            Christianorum Series Latina CXXIII A). Turnhout: Brepols.
Klæber, F. (ed.)
    1950   *Beowulf and the Fight at Finnsburg.* [3rd. ed]. Lexington: Heath & Co.
Krapp, G. P.
    1932   *The Vercelli Book.* (The Anglo-Saxon Poetic Records II). New York:
            Columbia University Press.
Lapidge, M., & M. Herren (trans.)
    1979   *Aldhelm: The Prose Works.* Cambridge: Brewer.
Lendinara, P.
    1992   Considerazioni sulla scrittura dei Germani in Venanzio Fortunato. *Annali*
            dell'Istituto Orientale di Napoli, sez. germ. (n.s.) II: 25-49.
Mayr-Harting, H.
    1972   *The Coming of Christianity to Anglo-Saxon England.* London: Batsford.
Migne, J.-P. (ed.)
    1851   *Patrologiae cursus completus, et coetera.... Patrologiae Tomus XCIX.*
            Paulinus aquileiensis - Angilbertus centulensis - Leidradus lugdunensis.
            Accurante J.-P. Migne. Series prima. Paris: Publisher in rue d'Amboise.
            [Repr. Turnhout: Brepols].
Miller, T. (ed.)
    1890/98 *The Old English Version of Bede's Ecclesiastical History of the English*
            People. (Original Series 95-6, 110-11). London: Early English Text Society.
Millett, M., & S. James
    1984   Excavations at Cowdery's Down, Basingstoke, Hampshire 1978-81.
            Archaeological Journal 140: 151-279.
Mitchell, B.
    1973   *The Justification of Religious Belief.* London: MacMillan.
Owen, G. R.
    1981   *Rites and Religions of the Anglo-Saxons.* Newton Abbot: David & Charles.
Rahtz, P.
    1976   The building plan of the Anglo-Saxon monastery of Whitby Abbey. *The*
            Archaeology of Anglo-Saxon England. D. M. Wilson (ed.), pp. 459-462.
            Cambridge: Cambridge University Press.
Sawyer, P.
    1986   Early fairs and markets in England and Scandinavia. *The Market in History.*
            B. L. Anderson & A. J. H. Latham (eds.), pp. 59-77. London: Croom Helm.
Smith, A. H. (ed.)
    1978   *Three Northumbrian Poems.* (Exeter Medieval Texts). Exeter: Exeter
            University Press. [Rev. edition].
Smith, R. A.
    1923   *A Guide to Anglo-Saxon and Foreign Teutonic Antiquities.* London: British
            Museum.
Stanley, E. G.
    1975   *The Search for Anglo-Saxon Paganism.* Cambridge: D. S. Brewer.
Stenton, F. M.
    1941   The historical bearing of place-name studies: Anglo-Saxon heathenism.
            Transactions of the Royal Historical Society. (4th ser.) 23: 1-24.
    1943   *Anglo-Saxon England.* (The Oxford History of England II). Oxford:
            Clarendon Press.

Swanton, M. (ed.)
    1970   *The Dream of the Rood.* Manchester: Manchester University Press.
    1974   *A Corpus of Pagan Anglo-Saxon Spear-Types.* (British Archaeological Report 7). Oxford: BAR.
Taylor, H. M., & J. Taylor
    1965/78 *Anglo-Saxon Architecture.* 3 vols. Cambridge: Cambridge University Press.
Thomas, A. C.
    1981   *Christianity in Roman Britain to AD 500.* London: Batsford.
Turville-Petre, E. O. G.
    1964   *Myth and Religion of the North.* London: Weidenfeld & Nicolson.
Watts, D.
    1991   *Christians and Pagans in Roman Britain.* London: Routledge.
Webster, L., & J. Backhouse (eds.)
    1991   *The Making of England: Anglo-Saxon Art and Culture AD 600-900.* London: British Museum.
Whitelock, D.
    1979   *English Historical Documents I: c.500-1042.* [2nd ed.] London: Eyre Methuen.
Wilson, D.
    1992   *Anglo-Saxon Paganism.* London: Routledge.
Winterbottom, M., & R. N. I. Ogilvie (eds.)
    1975   *Cornelii Taciti opera minora.* Oxford: Clarendon Press.
Wood, I. N.
    1994   The mission of Augustine of Canterbury to the English. *Speculum* 69: 1-17.
    1995   Pagan religion and superstitions east of the Rhine from the fifth to the ninth century. *After Empire: Towards an Ethnology of Europe's Barbarians.* G. Ausenda (ed.), pp. 253-280. Woodbridge: The Boydell Press.
Young, B.
    1977   Paganisme, christianisation et rites funéraires mérovingiens. *Archéologie Médiévale* 7: 5-81.
Youngs, S. (ed.)
    1989   *'The Work of Angels': Masterpieces of Celtic Metalwork, 6th-9th centuries A D.* London: British Museum Publications.

Discussion

DUMVILLE: For Bede there were aspects of religious history, as it affected Britain, which were deeply controversial. Given that he took that attitude and given that there was presumably a serious attitude about not rushing to damnation, it's likely that his attitude to paganism will in fact have been quite vehement. One can pick up points from around the *Ecclesiastical History* which would make this clear. We might ask ourselves whether we should not, in spite of what people have stressed about what Gregory had to say, start with the presupposition that, for the missionaries too, it was a deeply controversial matter. But also that whatever hostility they may have arrived with to Anglo-Saxon religion or religions may have been tempered by experience in some ways, while in other ways contact may indeed have made them more hostile.

There are different ways of coming to this. Partly there is how Anglo-Latin writers tackled this sort of thing, partly there is the comparative question, partly there is the question of how vocabulary was handled in the transition from pagan to pre-Christian and Christian use. And I wonder in particular whether the last of those couldn't have helped you in this discussion.

Two other points relate to this. There is the question which doesn't get discussed much, as to whether there was a reason why the Anglo-Saxons in the end responded favourably to Christianity. The place where I've seen this sort of thing most prominently discussed is in Edward Thompson's book on the Visigoths and the time of Ulfila where he devoted a considerable amount of time trying to find socio-economic reasons for why the conversion took place. And the answer was essentially simple and Marxist. But it seems to me that there is a controversial context there within scholarly writing which could be pursued a bit more.

Lastly, on the comparative point there has been some interesting recent work done in the Irish context, to do with pagan reaction to the process of conversion. There are two papers of some importance on this, one, by Richard Sharpe (1979) arguing that one of the Irish non-Christian reactions to the dissemination of Christianity throughout is a military militant pagan reaction, which persists in Ireland perhaps even into the eighth century. This has been followed up, perhaps more controversially, but with a wider range of references and in some ways more interestingly, by Kim McCone (1986) in a paper which pursues some of the broader issues. Thus we may already have that kind of problem and that kind of response within the Insular context, and given then that Irish missionaries acted in England, they may have anticipated this situation.

HINES: I'll take the points in turn. First of all the suggestion that this is a rather 'uncontroversial' topic: I was referring here quite specifically to there not having been as much critical controversy in modern scholarship as there ought to have been; I certainly didn't want to give the impression that religion was not a site of serious conflicts between different parties in the past. But I would again stress the point that these parties were apparently capable of influencing one another and then merging to some degree in fascinating ways that make their religions significantly interdependent when looked at in the whole—though they could still be very antagonistic to one another.

On the issue of why Christianity should have been accepted within Anglo-Saxon England at this time, in my anxiety not just to reproduce the familiar argument of political expediency I may have gone too far, and ought perhaps to have said a bit more about, for instance, the pressures that there would have been to conform with western Continental Europe in this respect, and the political interests that would thus have been involved. But once one has put that in, it may or may not seem naively Marxist, but it certainly seems insufficient to explain the range of different religious behaviour and religious monuments that we have from the period. I think it can only be seen as a contributory factor.

I'm grateful for the references to the analogous pagan—pagan in my sense—reaction in the process of conversion in Ireland. As I say, I think something markedly similar, though perhaps not militant, can be seen in later Roman Britain as well, where the introduction of the new cult (Christianity) coincides with a florescence of activity in the old cults. I'm inclined to believe that, if not a universal experience, this is certainly to be regarded as quite usual at the point of conversion.

FOWLER: I think one can also argue from the agrarian point of view that the study of religion has been too separatist. The positive point I want to make is that we may appear to be very unrealistic with you writing about religion and me talking about farming. Not least in the minds of the people at the time, the two were really the same thing. For early agrarian prehistoric north-western Europe, some of the best interpretation comes from a perspective of farming in a religious context. The Swedish talk about it on their petroglyphs; a very clear connection appears to exist between pre-Roman religion and its contemporary agriculture. What strikes me from the peasant's point of view is the way in which, once you get Christian religion coming in as the latest of religions, it very quickly colonizes the agrarian cycle, which is, if you like, God-given. The new Church says that of course you've got to plough at a certain time of the year 'So, let's invoke God's blessing', and then you harvest, exactly as I said in my paper, you harvest and thank God for a good harvest. And, you know, it doesn't take a great deal of energy to say a prayer: it's a good thing to do and it's not much effort. It seems to me that the Christian religion very quickly moved in and took over in the thought processes that go along with the physical activity of farming.

HINES: I quite agree. I would be grateful to hear if anyone knows how rapidly the Christian Church converted or appropriated the agricultural calendar.

WOOD: You could argue almost exactly the opposite, and emphasize the confrontational, with the Christian year having to accept local festivals which it didn't have before that.

FOWLER: Does that explain why you get slightly different dates between the Celtic year and the Christian dates?

CHARLES-EDWARDS: Yes, I think it is usually said that the first of November and the first of May are the dates when, in transhumance, people moved their animals, and there does seem to be tolerable evidence for that at a later period. Unfortunately the evidence is mostly Welsh.

FOWLER: These new saints coming in, do they accompany the days attached to them? Is that why there is diversification between the old days and the pagan days?

WOOD: If you want to fit a new religion into a previously existing agrarian year you have to have new feasts which are not in the pre-existing calendar.

HINES: It would be very nice to have an example of a specific saint.

LENDINARA: A very common example—I'm not able to remember any example about saints' festivals—is the Easter festival (Old English *eastre* < Germanic **austron*) which derives its name from that of a goddess whose feast was celebrated at the vernal equinox, as Bede says in Ch. XV of *De temporum ratione*. The pagan Spring festival was substituted by a festival of the Christian Church, but the old name was maintained.

AUSENDA: I would like to confirm what people have said about Christian festivities. In the foothills of the Alps throughout the yearly cycle, nearly all Church festivities signalled agricultural starts and stops, and they were fairly closely respected. I could give you a list of the coincidences between church feasts and agricultural activities. There is also an interesting point in connection with animal husbandry. Even though there is no transhumance there, because the place is located on top of a mountain, on the first of May a hired cowherd came from another hamlet and drove all the cows from the village out to the mountain pastures in the morning and back in the evening. The cowherd left during the month of October and the cattle were left to graze stubble in the fields and were stabled on the 25th of November, the day of St Catherine. These dates seems to be the same all over Europe.

HÄRKE: Your paper mentions the apparent need for ritual consumption. Whilst in principle I'm very much in sympathy with that line of argument, you say that the apparent need for ritual consumption in early Anglo-Saxon England may have been satisfied in England by the provision of grave goods. That would still leave you to explain the rather big difference in the nature of the Danish depositions of military goods, where brooches and beads, for example, are conspicuously missing.

HINES: Well, the Danish depositions of military goods and so on go through chronological stages, and the deposition of military equipment that seems almost certainly to be the equipment of some defeated army becomes very rare once you get into the fifth century. Instead you find what seems much more plausibly to be interpreted as those groups for whom that sacrificial site is their own site depositing expensive samples of their own gear there. This, I think, is easily interpreted in terms of there being a need for these displays. In the good old days you could be sure of a suitable enemy turning up and being defeated once every sixty or seventy years, which would satisfy the demands of ritual. When your enemies let you down, you have to produce your own expensive gear and sacrifice it within those sites. This is the start of a process which sees the range of hoarding diversifying considerably so that by the second half of the fifth century a considerably larger proportion of female-associated items are being hoarded and sacrificed in this way.

HÄRKE: Which hoards are you talking about?

HINES: Bracteates would be the best example. Very nearly all bracteate depositions in Denmark, when one has good evidence of the circumstances of retrieval, look like so-called votive or ritual hoards of this kind. At the same time one gets a gradual shift from the deposition of material that seems to belong to a group, material that represents more than one person, to deposition that seems to represent an individual.

HÄRKE: So that's where you see the connection with the burial ritual.

HINES: Richard Bradley in fact, in relation to the Bronze Age in Britain, talked about hoarding of this kind as a sort of surrogate burial, as if the pressure was such that you couldn't wait for a convenient person to die and had instead to dispose of personal gear in this ritualized way without the person dying (Bradley 1984:110-13).

HÄRKE: If you want to put ritual deposition in hoards and burials under this one heading of ritual consumption, where then do you put into this overall scheme of things these river depositions, where you emphasized that their spearheads are not drawn from the same collection of weapons as grave finds that can be dated to the Early Anglo-Saxon period? Are you saying that they are different chronological horizons?

HINES: I suspect it is largely a different chronological horizon. I certainly wouldn't assert that I know that river deposition of weapons began only as the weapon-grave rite died out. I will admit that I'm inclined to believe that the great difference could very well be due to a considerable intensification of ritual deposition of weapons in the eighth century, with weapon deposition in graves having effectively ceased.

HÄRKE: But there must have been a substantial overlap because some of the types you mentioned here from river deposits, H and I for example, are not late types.

HINES: I'm very interested to hear that. Nonetheless the discrepancies in figures between what you get in graves and rivers in the same area are clear enough.

POWLESLAND: But if the bulk of river finds are the possessions of the vanquished, that may explain why you have a different material in river finds. You are dealing with a beaten community.

HINES: No, this was a point I made early on. In fact there is practically no evidence that these are weapons which were used in battle. When you go back to the big third- or fourth-century bog finds, there are all sorts of battle-marks on the weapons.

HÄRKE: Moreover the earlier finds make up functional complexes of military equipment whereas the later river depositions appear to be consecutive deposits of single, or a few, items.

POWLESLAND: The graves at Wetwang included square barrows in a Middle-Saxon cemetery. I think one or two of the graves had a number of spears which they claim were all stuck in from the outside some twenty or thirty in a single grave.

You also talked about pagan religion and it seems that it has a number of different gods, and a number of place-names in which they may be represented. Do we see this as some sort of animism or is there any reason we should identify archaeologically ritual space? As an excavator, one of the things I'm concerned about is if such ritual space exists, do you believe we should be able to identify it? How can we see it if it consists of trees?

HINES: Personally I don't believe one should continually search for this; only in exceptional circumstances might you be able to identify a religious site of the pre-Christian period; and once you get into the Christian period you've got a good idea of what a church looks like. By chance we've got the site at Yeavering, and I'm interested in what the other archaeologists think of Yeavering building D2. It seems to me it merits serious consideration as a possible temple site, though it could be interpreted in other ways. All I could say prescriptively from that starting point is that if you find something that reproduces the features of Yeavering building D2 then perhaps you could carefully draw attention to those parallels and leave it to your readers to draw their own conclusions. Otherwise I couldn't tell you what to look for as a pre-Christian religious site.

LENDINARA: Before I get to my main question I would say that one needs to be extremely careful about the attributes of Woden, Thunor and Tiw as far as the

Anglo-Saxon religion is concerned. The only evidence we have comes from late homilies, such as *De falsis deis* by Ælfric and the sermon on the same subject written by Wulfstan, whose source is Martin of Braga, who is a Spanish bishop (sixth-century) and Pirmin, who probably came from the Visigothic kingdom (eighth-century). There is nothing Anglo-Saxon behind what is said in the homilies on the 'false gods', written in the late tenth century. We do not have any picture of Thunor throwing his hammer for Anglo-Saxon England and there is always the risk of forcing on it something which is Old Norse or is drawn from the *interpretatio romana* of the names of the week. E. A. Philippson (1929) has some good pages on this.

I wanted to point out to you an article of mine concerning the lines where Venantius Fortunatus mentions the runes (Lendinara 1992). The words of Fortunatus have often been misused and in my article I try to explode former arguments. In his poem (VIII, xviii) he addresses a friend who has not written him for a long time and, using the topos of the different kinds of writing, he asks him: "Why do you not write me using a papyrus scroll, why do you not engrave runes for my sake?" What I want to explain is that Venantius Fortunatus is a highly sophisticated poet who employs a topos (commenting on the difference between Romans and barbarians). In the same poem he mentions the Persian language, but we do not have any evidence that it was known in the Middle Ages. Venantius Fortunatus speaks of the runes as something typical of the barbarians and compares them to the other kinds of alphabets.

There are some new publications on the Alamannic runes. There is a book by an Italian scholar, Marcello Meli (1988), where he studies some seventy inscriptions which can be considered Alamannic and which are, in many instances, new finds. According to Max Martin (1977), in the sixth century, northern influence gave the old runic tradition new vitality in France and Germany.

HINES: On the question of the character of the gods and the particular gods of the Early Anglo-Saxon period, I take your point and think I tried to address that by saying that the mythology *indicates* that their character includes particular features. Nonetheless, there is some continuity and consistency between, say, the *interpretatio romana* and the characters as they later appear in the Scandinavian mythology.

LENDINARA: You know that, according to some scholar, what linked Mercury and Woden (and justified the *interpretatio romana* of his name) was that both gods dealt with trade and they were both cheaters and, on occasion, thieves. So they did not have in common a high status, but qualities such as being tricksters. If the link between Woden and Mercury was such, this produces a complicated assessment of the Anglo-Saxon pantheon: who is the most important god?

POHL: Can I say two more words about Woden. And again I have to come up with a Langobardic comparison. It is interesting how often Woden comes up in Anglo-Saxon material. You mention him throughout your paper and I think you quite rightly say he can only come up so often because he has evolved into a more generally supernatural figure for general mythic functions. It is interesting to see that in the Langobardic *Origo gentis* Woden has a very central function in giving the Langobards their name and victory in their primordial battle against the Vandals. So, in this case he is not just a god of merchants, but a god of war who can give victory. He's not the one who tricks everybody but he is being tricked by Freia, who is the one to whom the Langobards appeal for victory in the first place. Now this is in a mid-seventh-century written version of the *Origo gentis Langobardorum*, where the story is told quite straightforwardly without any comment. Obviously, when it was later copied, there was a sort of tension connected with this story and it's interesting to watch how different authors treat the story differently. Our main witness for Langobardic history is Paul the Deacon, who wrote at the end of the eighth century. He comes up pretty much with the same story, but then he goes on to say "Now this is obviously a *ridicula fabula*". *Fabula*, in this sense, is a term which can be traced back to Isidore as meaning something which cannot be true because it is against nature. So that's what the story means to Paul the Deacon even though he writes it down. Then he says, "It's a *ridicula fabula* which cannot be true because men cannot give victory to other men, that is what only God can do". So, quite clearly Woden is not regarded as a god here, but as a man. There is another version of the story which completely omits Woden so as to regain the concept of some divine intervention that brings victory. The earliest form is found in Fredegar, interestingly enough, where it is just a voice from heaven that gives victory and the name to the Langobards. But the Christian and providential elements are only fully developed in a short Langobardic history in the so-called *Codex gothanus*, which dates to the beginning of the ninth century, where all the pagan elements have disappeared. Whenever stories are treated in these different ways you can see that there is a fundamental tension, that comes as a challenge to authors to somehow resolve this tension by narrative means.

CHARLES-EDWARDS: It's a little bit similar to Daniel's letter to Boniface where he says there, "Don't argue about the genealogies of the gods, just point out that if they were conceived and were born, they must be simply men and women".

HÄRKE: I wonder if I may briefly turn back to burial evidence but in the context of Christianization now. Your opinion on the effect of Christianity on burial rites and grave goods appears a bit ambiguous or uncertain, and I just want to encourage you to pursue a bit further the line that the change in burial rites we see mostly in the seventh century has much to do with Christianity; you mention, for example, the orientation of graves and the abandonment of grave goods. Orientation of graves and also the standardization of the body position within the grave are part, as far as I can tell in my sample, of a gradual change from the late sixth century onwards. That makes it too early for Christianity to play a role in.

DUMVILLE: There is a circular reasoning archaeologically over the relationship between the abandonment of grave goods and the advent of Christianity.

HÄRKE: Certainly, there has been a lot of discussion about this question and whether it had to do with Christianity; periodically there is a swing of opinion. At the moment there is a firm swing towards clear ambiguity and uncertainty.

SCULL: Perhaps it's the post-modern paradigm.

HÄRKE: Thank you for that rider. A question to the historians: is it true that there is very little evidence for Christianity discouraging grave goods?

POHL: An important piece of evidence in this respect is a letter in the *Variae* of Cassiodorus, written in the name of Theoderic. It was intended to prohibit and discourage the use of precious grave goods. But, interestingly enough it doesn't lean so much on any Christian argument. Rather it argues about wise men in ancient times who had invented gold and silver. One of them, by the way, was a king of the Scythians and, therefore, in Cassiodorus's understanding, one of Theoderic's predecessors. They invented these beautiful things for the use of living men, not for stuffing them away in graves. But although there must be a Christian background, there is not any clear reference to the Christian religion.

SCULL: In *The Development of the Family and Marriage in Europe*, Goody (1983) argues that the Church discouraged grave goods not on religious grounds but because it preferred to see wealth that would otherwise be buried re-invested in the Church.

HINES: There is a range of indirect evidence that the Church did not favour furnished burial and so I think that that general point is a valid one. What I wanted to say, however, was that in the larger perspective in western Europe during the late Roman period and early Middle Ages we find a remarkable spread of a particular burial rite with orientation and the absence of grave goods. That Christian influence is in some way operative there in every area where that particular rite is imitated is the point that I wanted to make. It is, if you like, the presence and the expansion of Christianity in western Europe that sets this whole process off. It is then increasingly imitated in different places. Thus material culture can be influenced by Christianity, even if the group or culture hasn't adopted Christianity and may even be violently opposed to it.

POHL: I think it is very important to put it like you do in a positive way and not to say it's just the end of putting objects in graves. It is the diffusion of another burial rite.

AUSENDA: I think you shouldn't look for the Church to give orders on what should be deposited in graves. I don't think the Church cared, at least it doesn't in our time. I think you should look at the views of the pagans and Christians on what happens after death. According to the Church the soul goes to Paradise to contemplate God and it doesn't have to wear jewellery to be recognized. But as far as pagans are concerned, it is possible that they thought that they had to have a symbol of status to be recognized and that presumably was the difference.

HINES: I would, in fact, regard the proposition that there was any widespread concept of the afterlife in Anglo-Saxon 'paganism' as a highly contentious matter. We actually have no evidence for it.

AUSENDA: Usually when people get buried with something it's because they believe that it will be useful to them in their afterlife.

HINES: That's the usual interpetation, yes. There are several other possible explanations.

AUSENDA: That is what the ancient Egyptians used to do.

HINES: Indeed, in some cases it can mean that. I think one can't force that analogy on to the Anglo-Saxon furnished burial rite. This is essentially what the standard books on Anglo-Saxon pre-Christian religion do. They simply say "grave goods must be things that are going to be useful to these people in the afterlife". I think it is a highly uncritical statement.

POWLESLAND: Yes, there is a frequent inclusion of broken objects. Surely a very simple way of looking at the decline of grave goods is "Thou shalt not put goods in your graves because I shall want them as taxes".

HINES: Well, the Church's role is not necessarily to encourage wealth to circulate for the good of the community; it encourages wealth to circulate to itself. In the long term this may be a very important factor.

LENDINARA: This is the explanation which Richard Hodges (1989: ch. 3) gives for the impoverishment of grave goods in the late seventh century, after an 'inflation' period in which the Church had been involved in great funerary ceremonies.

HÄRKE: The tenth-century *Sachsenspiegel* refers to the *Gerade* and the *Hergewäte* that had to be given to the Church on an individual's death. Some scholars have extended that back to the pagan period to explain the grave-goods custom, which I would be rather wary of.

AUSENDA: You could say that the Church influences the disposal of these things because it gives its followers clear rules on how to go to heaven: you perform good deeds for the Church and for fellow Christians and are thus sure of being admitted to Paradise. So that, instead of taking your earthly goods into the grave, you will them to the Church and the Church uses its influence and prayers to get you into heaven.

References in the discussion

Textual sources:

Ælfric
> *De falsis deis*: see Pope 1967.

Cassiodorus
> *Variae*: see Mommsen (ed.) 1894.

Codex gothanus: see Waitz (ed.) 1878.

Daniel's letter to Boniface: see Tangl (ed.) 1916; Talbot (trans.) 1954, 75-78.

Origo gentis Langobardorum: see Waitz (ed.) 1878.

Paul the Deacon
> *Historia Langobardorum*: see Waitz (ed.) 1878.

Sachsenspiegel: see von Schwerin (ed.) 1953.

Wulfstan
> *De falsis deis*: see Bethurum 1957.

Bibliography:

Bethurum, D.
> 1957   *The Homilies of Wulfstan*. Oxford: Clarendon Press.

Bradley, R.
> 1984   *The Social Foundations of Prehistoric Britain*. London: Longman.

Goody, J.
> 1983   *The Development of the Family and Marriage in Europe*. Cambridge: Cambridge University Press.

Hodges, R.
> 1989   *The Anglo-Saxon Achievement*. London: Duckworth.

Lendinara, P.
1992   Considerazioni sulla scrittura dei Germani in Venanzio Fortunato. *Annali dell'Istituto Orientale di Napoli, sez. germ.*, n. s. II (1-3): 25-49.

McCone, K. R.
1986   Werewolves, cyclopes, *díberga*, and *fíanna*: juvenile delinquency in early Ireland. *Cambridge Medieval Celtic Studies* 12: 1-22.

Martin, M.
1977   Die Runenfibel aus Bülach Grab 249. Gedanken zur Verbreitung der Runendenkmäler bei den Westgermanen. In *Festschrift Walter Drack zu seinem 60. Geburtstag*. K. Stüber & A. Zürcher (eds.), pp. 120-128. Stäfa (ZH): Gut.

Meli, M.
1988   *Alamannia runica. Rune e cultura nell'alto medioevo*. Verona: Libreria Universitaria Editrice.

Mommsen, T. (ed.)
1894   *Cassiodori senatoris Variae. Monumenta Germaniae historica. Auctores antiquissimi*, 12. Berlin: Weidmann.

Philippson, E. A.
1929   *Germanisches Heidentum bei den Angelsachsen*. Leipzig: Tauchnitz.

Pope, J. C.
1967   *Homilies of Ælfric: A Supplementary Collection*. (O.S. 259). London: Early English Text Society.

von Schwerin, C. (ed.)
1953   *Sachsenspiegel*. Stuttgart: Reclam.

Sharpe, R.
1979   Hiberno-Latin laicus, Irish láech and the devil's men. *Ériu* 30: 75-92.

Talbot, C. H.
1954   *The Anglo-Saxon Missionaries in Germany*. London & New York: Sheed & Ward.

Tangl, M. (ed.)
1916   *Die Briefe des heiligen Bonifatius und Lullus. Monumenta Germaniae historica, Epistolae selectae*, I. Berlin: Weidmann.

Thompson, E. A.
1966   *The Visigoths in the Time of Ulfila*. Oxford: Clarendon Press.

Waitz, G.
1878   *Monumenta Germaniae historica, Scriptores rerum langobardicarum*. Hannover: Hahn.

CURRENT ISSUES AND FUTURE DIRECTIONS IN THE STUDY OF THE EARLY ANGLO-SAXON PERIOD

Summary of participants' concluding discussion, comments by

GIORGIO AUSENDA

CIROSS, 6 C.da S. Francesco, San Marino (R.S.M.)

Introduction

During the concluding discussion a participant proposed that it would be useful to take an overview and perhaps define more precisely targeted research aims. This seemed a good idea which prompted me to submit an overview from an anthropological perspective, checked by a cultural historian, to serve as a guideline for future research. The topics touched upon are those which were brought up under the heading 'Problems' and 'Untouched topics' during the concluding discussion.

Model of Roman decline

Discussion: world into which the Anglo-Saxons came

WOOD: One of the things that seems to me to arise out of discussions is that we need to think more about the world into which the Anglo-Saxons came. This point was already raised in Edward Thompson's final research on the idea of social stress in fourth-century Britain.

SCULL: The fundamental point to treat here is that of material changes which you see in the late Roman period before we have the evidence of an Anglo-Saxon cultural presence.

POWLESLAND: This is an absolutely key point: what was the scene into which the Anglo-Saxons emerged. We have tended in the past to see the Anglo-Saxon as a purely Continental culture that came in, and if we have a context that already exists upon which it was built, then things are quite different. We have a detailed understanding of the last fifty years of the Roman period, and reassessment of what goes on in the immediately post-Roman phase which tends to be conveniently forgotten.

SCULL: Actually, I am arguing against this. The thrust of scholarship in England over the last twenty years has been the *opposite* of what Dominic says: a tendency to emphasize long-term endogenous change, to minimize the impact of migrations, and to ignore the Germanic/Scandinavian Continental background.

DUMVILLE: What I should like to see are more regional studies of Roman Britain and in particular late Roman Britain. One of the things I would like to find much more useful than I have yet found it is that series on peoples in Roman Britain where the weakest section appears always to be the last century of Roman Britain for the particular area in question. That kind of approach could be very illuminating, and in principle should allow the author to demonstrate a lot about an area. And we could then go on to compare the conclusions. But that series on the whole hasn't done that. It may have done so for earlier parts of the Romano-British period but not for the late.

POWLESLAND: In reality we don't know much about the Roman countryside. We know a great deal about Roman towns, a great deal about Roman military sites, and a great deal about villas in parts of the country, but....

SCULL: This is one of the problems. The 'romanized' Britain of the fifth century is not the insular context of the Anglo-Saxon migrations: it is post-Roman, or sub-Roman Britain. What questions are we addressing here?

DUMVILLE: You have two enormous problems which Peter Fowler has been insisting on all through this meeting. One he has described—and I disagree with him—about the great density of settlement within late Roman Britain which is now inferred although we don't know anything about it. And secondly the importance of addressing the successor states and the successor society to Roman Britain.

FOWLER: We sense that more than just the late Roman period is important for our concern; but we are beginning to see the sorts of change that were happening in late Roman Britain, and Dominic has given us a lead on that. The point I would like to go back to is that if you'd accept that as a principle, the nature and, above all, the timing of that late Romanity in which change is taking place depends on where you are in the country. It does so now, in terms of the evidence we have and what you can do with it, and it certainly did so then, in terms of what was happening. It is quite different in Somerset from Hertfordshire when you tackle the problem in this period. There are a whole lot of changes in Somerset, but they have nothing to do with the Saxons. It is the society, the self-contained society with its own cross-currents, which was changing by itself.

SCULL: We need to be very careful about what questions we are asking and how we will answer them. The dying late Roman Britain will tell us very little about the economic structures of the sixth century. Are we dealing with Anglo-Saxons? Are we dealing with Britons? Are we dealing with Europe?

AUSENDA: I think it would be extremely important to find out what was going on in the late Roman period because there must be some reason for depopulation. Something must have changed considerably. Trade must have changed momentously. When taking into account the Early Anglo-Saxon period we seem to be starting with the beginning of the world. But there was a world there before and it changed and influenced what happened in the period we are focusing on.

SCULL: I'm not denying that, but I think that automatically to take the late Roman period in Britain as the starting point for the study of what occurs in the fifth and sixth centuries in eastern England is to deny the uniqueness or the cultural specificity of what happens in fifth- and sixth-century England. I'm coming to this from a very, very narrow Anglo-Saxonist point of view. But, too often in the last ten years I have heard the archaeology of Migration-period England dismissed out of hand by people who take the long-term view and argue—very simplistically in my view—that most change in post-Roman Britain should be explained by endogenous development. I'm not denying that we have to know the context of Anglo-Saxon settlement, but I'm wondering where we're coming from and what we are looking for and whether we are going to compare like with like. So I'm not reacting really against what Ian said or what Dominic said; I suppose I'm trying to sound a note of caution as to how and why we should go about it.

DUMVILLE: Could you put your first point again with positive rather than negative verbs? Where do we start?

SCULL: No, my reactions are negative ones.

DUMVILLE: I sympathize because this is the way I am usually perceived. But if somebody listens to you and wants to know where to go and how to proceed, he needs a positive agenda, agendum even. Is what you were saying, that the place to start is in the sub-Roman period, scrap late Roman Britain and start looking in the fifth century?

SCULL: To define the context of Anglo-Saxon migration, yes.

FOWLER: There are two things being argued here. One is the nature of the Anglo-Saxon conquest and migration—or whatever—from the Anglo-Saxon point of view. That is a rather different question from a history of Britain in which the Anglo-Saxon settlement is but one facet of a period of migration. They are two different things.

SCULL: I agree.

HÄRKE: I think Peter is reacting against the debate of the last ten, fifteen, twenty years.

SCULL: But is this going to be a seminar on the Anglo-Saxons, or is it going to be a seminar on early medieval Britain?

POWLESLAND: One little point to add really, I suppose, is an unstated question: but do we know when the end of the Roman period is? I don't as far as the countryside is concerned. And I don't know when, archaeologically, the Roman period ceases to exist in terms of material culture. If identifying the sub-Roman is possible in the West, it is not necessarily so easy or possible in the East. I just throw this in because it goes within the context of my desire to understand the late Roman period, the ending of Roman civilization and the mechanics of it in terms of what really happened to allow this fundamental change in the landscape and population structures.

Comment

During the concluding discussion a participant suggested that models for the end of the Roman government in Britain should be proposed and tested against the available historical and archaeological evidence.

With the recall of the two remaining legions in Britain and the retreat of Honorius to Ravenna, to all intents and purposes the Western Empire ceased to exercise its defensive and administrative functions and became an appendix of its Eastern counterpart, while Constantinople took over as the hub of creativity and trade. Italy thus became peripheral and Britain, until then peripheral to Italy, faded back into the fog of barbarism.

The socio-economic consequence of this may have been a gradual 'drainage' of 'Romans' from the lowlands of Britain where it was becoming increasingly hard to make a living according to the lifestyle to which they were accustomed—it would be surprising it they would have hung on—to the Continent where regional trade was sufficient to keep Gallo-Roman and Italo-Roman societies alive and where some trade to and from Britain was still possible with the recently established Anglo-Saxon populations, through 'agents' who may have stayed on in southern ports.

With few exceptions the Roman *villae*, which had thrived in provisioning the Roman army and the neighbouring towns, were abandoned. They were quickly followed by the towns—thriving cities became ghost towns for lesser reasons, such as famine, plagues or high taxes, as Gregory of Tours makes abundantly clear (*H.F. passim*)—whilst trade with the formerly Roman Continent continued from the southern towns of Britain, as seems to be ascertained by archaeology (Scull, this vol., pp. 277, 285). At the same time regional trade picked up and we are told of Frisians and Saxons trading in London.

It appears as if Bede's use of the term 'Britons' varies according to the period. Until the battle of Mount Badon, Bede's Britons are what we would call Romano-Britons. After the hiatus between that date and the reign of Ida in Northumbria, by Britons Bede meant those who lived in the West and in the North.

One of the problems of this pattern lies in explaining the constant enmity between Romano-Britons and Gaels or Picts and the early apparent, if testy, collaboration between the former and the Saxons. The solution probably lies in the competitiveness between the Romano-Britons and the Britons because they exploited the same eco-niches, while the recently immigrated Saxons may have exploited different ones.

Another problem lies in extending the above pattern to the countryside since what has been described only explains the situation of towns and *villae*. It may be that, ever since early urban civilizations, in lands without a strong overarching authority there was a dichotomy between towns or villages and the countryside. Agriculturalists lived in villages and towns whence they walked off in the morning to till their fields and came back in the evening. John Wacher writes:

> The interdependence between the towns and the countryside is often stressed, and we can see now the nature of the relationship, which was heavily weighted in favour of the towns; the pattern of agricultural settlement that emerged in Roman Britain could not have been produced without the towns and villages and could not have survived, indeed did not survive in isolation (Wacher 1974:72).

Those who roamed the countryside probably were nomadic or semi-nomadic herders who may have belonged to different ethnic groups from those living in towns and villages. In Britain they would have stayed on after the Romans left the lowlands but upon the arrival of the Saxons they may have gradually retracted to safer areas in the West and North. Their lowly status may have justified the contempt Saxons felt for them.

Migration

Discussion

Charles-Edwards noted the possibility of a difference between the patterns of migration in southern and northern Europe and wondered whether recent work on the Goths could be applied to northern Europe.

Pohl expressed his ideas concerning comparisons between the migration of Anglo-Saxons to Britain and long-distance migrations on the Continent. He averred that the idea of whole populations migrating in search of land had been abandoned in favour of "specialized warriors migrating in a precise context of *foedera* relationships with the Roman Empire and being accommodated under precise circumstances" and wondered whether this situation could be really compared with that in Britain.

Wood asserted that the Franks were high-status warriors.

Charles-Edwards dissented in that, while Vandals travelled "huge distances", the Franks did not.

Wood acknowledged that one "might better see Rhineland *Francia* in terms closer to the Middle Saxon 'shifts' rather than in terms of migration".

Härke said that different situations arose from the different influence of the Roman administration in different parts. He favoured a model which assumed that "Rome had a profound impact" in certain areas, e.g. Denmark, based on the relatively large quantity of prestige goods found there. Such links would have had a "profound influence on migration", but because of local circumstances they would have differed from place to place.

Charles-Edwards objected that if it was high-status people who had access to Roman wealth, "it's precisely high-status people who don't have the need to migrate". "Unless [their status] depends on Roman wealth" added *Wood*.

For *Härke* "high-status people never migrate on their own, otherwise they haven't got anybody to measure their own high status against", and *Pohl* suggested that they might "find somebody new".

Scull mentioned a model which "perfectly answers [Charles-Edwards's] objection". The explanation was that, since the political system in *Germania* was 'fissile', and so depended on 'organization', to avoid collapse, élite groups would have to "look outside *Germania* for status and glory" and hence needed to migrate.

Härke proposed a comparison with the Viking period in Scandinavia.

Charles-Edwards interpreted Scull's suggestion to mean the *wics* in that Danish kings in the ninth century trying to get hold of places like Dorestad implied that to achieve political pre-eminence they would have to control trade with the Franks.

According to *Pohl*, two economic factors sustained power in the early Middle Ages: one is that any high-status group must make a living by 'exploiting' peasants and obtaining their daily need of foodstuffs from the local population. The second is the demand for prestige luxury goods, to demonstrate high status with the *wics* being the ideal way to obtain prestige goods from "far away". In his opinion it was "not very difficult" to subdue a local population to obtain "any quantity" of produce; however, he admitted that there was a second school of thought which held that "this was not so easily achieved", so that it was necessary to rely on preceding Roman or sub-Roman ways of "taking revenue out of the local population".

Scull ventured that "clear evidence" showed that during the Anglo-Saxon Migration-period élites "were gathering prestige" before the establishment of *wics*. Hence his opinion that prestige goods were not necessarily linked to *wics*. *Härke* agreed. *Scull* said that good evidence proved that the exchange of prestige items was in process "before the *wics* were established" and that it was "difficult to see large settlements maintained purely by prestige goods exchange" which suggested to him that the linking of *wics* with prestige goods acquisition was fallacious.

Charles-Edwards asked archaeologists whether the exchange of prestige goods in the Migration period represented a "change from the late Roman pattern" and whether prestige goods came from *Romania* to *Germania* via the Roman authorities or via trade.

Scull underscored the complexity of the picture which excluded the possibility of pointing solely to one or the other of the proposed avenues.

Wood, going back to Charles-Edwards's question, proposed to compare migrations at their inception rather than, as usually happened, at their end. He gave the Goths as examples, whose first settlements were known, and the *Rugii* "because of the new evidence from Noricum"; "freezing the picture of migration [of the Goths and the Vandals] ten years from the start" was bound to produce a useful comparison for the Anglo-Saxon migration.

Hines partially dissented, noting immediate problems in comparing overseas migration with gradual overland migration.

Pohl's remark was to turn the question to Wood whose "favourite comparison is between the Anglo-Saxons in Britain and the Rugians in Noricum"—a sensible idea, according to Pohl, because they were areas where Roman authority had collapsed, but where there were local populations "organized according to the Roman model". He pointed out, nevertheless, that the *Vita Severini* described "an amazing variety of forms of cooperation/confrontation between the Rugians and the local population", "robbers crossing the Danube to rob the Roman population on a small scale,...large-scale military actions by Rugian kings to enlarge the area under their control,...all sorts of settlements, peace talks, negotiations,...overall transfer of commodities from the Romans to the Rugians". He concluded that there could not be "a monocausal explanation for what happened when the Anglo-Saxons came to Britain".

Ausenda observed that, firstly, there was "no opposition between peasants and warriors"; secondly, he pointed to the difference between the Rugians, separated from Roman territory by the Danube, as against the Anglo-Saxons who had to cross the sea. He also told of a recent migration across the Red Sea of members, about 30,000 all told, of a Bedouin population from Arabia which took place in the second half of the last century and is still remembered, during which groups "arrived in small numbers, never in an army: they started infiltrating all over eastern Sudan and then slowly coalesced" and that, in the beginning, the social structure was much less differentiated than later.

Härke concluded that "one of the key points that we are beginning to agree upon here is that there is an almost infinite variety of models for population movements" and "to realize that, in a situation like the Anglo-Saxon one, all these models might, with variations, apply at the same time or successively". He cautioned against adopting one model in preference to another, but suggested one should keep them all in mind and see how they "relate to the evidence". He suggested comparing "the Roman Iron-age social and economic structures on the Continent before migration and in England after migration".

The comparative method was discussed later in the concluding discussion when *Hines* referred to the "consistent avoidance of the nature of the Anglo-Saxon conquest", suggesting that the topic had been debated in the literature for decades and that it would be pointless to review it once again with no "new views" nor any "new evidence that would validate any given view, new or old, on the nature of the Anglo-Saxon conquest".

Dumville agreed in part but complained that "the fundamental aspects of this" had not been "discussed, they've been asserted over the last generation". He went on to stress that "even if analysis has been done, there has not been great competition of views". He confirmed his conviction that there "could have been a very significant comparative dimension to this", not in terms of a comparison between what happened in northern and southern Europe, "but in comparison with what we know about migration from the anthropological record on the evidence of what David Turton had to say the last time: that there is a fair amount of literature on this which can be brought to bear" (Turton 1995:47). He also expressed his opinion that despite the fact that "to try to get illumination from the Viking Age for the Migration period...was shot up very thoroughly...in the 20s and 30s", but that there was some scope for going back to that in that much had been learnt about the Viking Age in the meantime.

Charles-Edwards pointed out that in the late Roman period different groups had made successful inroads in different parts of the country, e.g. the Irish in Scotland and western Britain.

Härke, à propos of the Vikings, concluded that one could envisage a southern Scandinavian model whereby population movements by Goths, Danes, Jutes, Angles, Vikings, were triggered every "two hundred to five hundred years" and try to pinpoint the "factors, such as agriculture, or population growth" which were behind them.

Comment

Looking at a map of Britain and of the north-west Continental coastline one realizes that the latter slants south-westwards towards southern Britain where the closest point to the Continent is Kent. It stands to reason that, while a few hardy mariners may have crossed the North Sea making directly for the north-eastern shores of Britain, the great majority would have followed the Continental coastline until they reached the *fretum gallicum*, the present-day Pas de Calais, where the crossing narrows to as little as 35 km, or about five hours for loaded ships. The

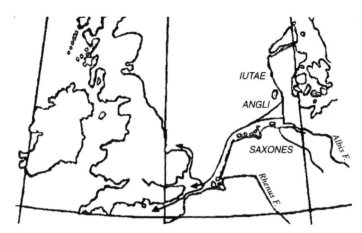

Fig. 13-1: Most probable invasion route of north-eastern barbarians.

length of the direct passage from Frisia to the Yarmouth coast is about 200 km; this entails a crossing of at least 30 hours during which the weather can easily change making the crossing quite dangerous. Feats like the colonization of Iceland, when ships sailed from Denmark or Norway to the Shetlands and the Faroes, were to follow some three or four hundred years later.

Another important variable concerns the season preferred for crossing and migration. The choice of dates had to accommodate both the risks of navigation and those inherent in sowing and harvesting. It would seem that winter travel must have been very rare, as Bede makes quite clear when describing Bishop Theodore's companion Hadrian's trip to Britain:

> Hadrian went first to Emme, bishop of Sens, and then to Faro, bishop of Meaux, and lived comfortably with them for a long time, *for the approach of winter compelled them to stay quietly where they could* (*HE* IV.1. Trans. McClure & Collins. My emphasis).

The best time for crossing was between late spring and early fall. If Theodore, as averred by Bede, "came to his church on Sunday 27 May" (*HE* IV.2), one can probably conclude that travel started in earnest about the beginning of May. It would seem expedient for those migrants to carry out the July or August cereal harvest before negotiating the trip. History tells us that land migration of whole tribes also started in the spring, but they were wholesale expeditions where cereals could be plundered, whereas the Anglo-Saxon migration is believed to have been mostly based on small contingents.

According to Bede, the migratory movement started in 449, a reasonable date if one considers that in other peripheral places in the Roman Empire, e.g. the *agri decumates*, the 'invasion' started about fifty years after Roman garrisons had moved out of the area. However, the date given by Bede may only be indicative of an increase in the momentum of migration since the establishment of Germanic *foederati* in Britain had apparently preceded it, perhaps for as long as a couple of centuries. The Britons did nothing but conform to a well-established tradition in allowing Germanic *foederati* into Britain giving them land "and for this the soldiers were also to receive pay" *HE* I.15): this was the cheapest solution to obtain protection from their enemies. Little did these impoverished heirs to the Roman Empire know that they would be hard put to pay those soldiers in the long run, causing their *foederati* to do what all those troops had done in similar circumstances, seize the land and ultimately the administration and governing power as security for their pay.

As for the "three ships" in which the "race of the Angles or Saxons" came to Britain called by the Britons, this figure may be not so far off the mark: Bede specifies that they were "warships" (*HE* 1.15). Each warship may have transported as many as thirty soldiers for a total of about one hundred, not a mean force for those days. It is probable that this contingent was also used, as in the case of Carausius, for 'coastguard' operations, for which they would have been sufficient (cf. Higham 1994:39-40). The fewer women and children may have come later on transport ships.

The likelihood that the contingents of migrants were small is supported by the fact that, well into the eighth century, Continental Saxons, and most probably also Angles and Jutes, had a clan structure (*HE* V.10). Within a clan, except in case of immediate danger from enemy raids or when a raid would be considered attractive because of the possibility of easy plunder, it would have been quite difficult to raise a contingent of more than a hundred individuals. In fact Bede adds that when members of the ethnic group were told about "the fertility of the island and the slackness of the Britons...at once a much larger fleet was sent over with a stronger band of warriors".

The impression is that the 'invasion' of Britain was based mainly on the arrival of small contingents or family groups. In fact it took these groups of immigrants at least a hundred years to coalesce into larger territorial units with explicit governing functions.

There is no reason to doubt Bede's clear assessment about where the three nations were settled in Britain: in his day, knowledge of the 'ethnic' demarcations of the colonizing groups must have been fairly precise. According to Bede the Saxons were grouped in the South, the Angles in all the lowlands to the north, while the Jutes were predominant along the southern coasts of Britain, on the Isle of Wight and in neighbouring territories on the mainland. This does not mean that there weren't other groups in those territories. Field experience has shown how frequently small groups from different tribes live in another tribe's territory without causing any disturbance. Among the Tigré-speaking Beni Amer, the To Bedawie-speaking Labad or Hedareb are considered Beni Amer to all intents and purposes. Ethnic dominance does not necessarily entail ethnic uniformity, a fact which does not seem to bother populations at that level of socio-cultural integration.

One aspect of the settlement of the three major nations, Saxons, Angles and Jutes, concerns the chronological sequence of their arrival and their settlement pattern. If the 'castle of cards' model of 'collapse' into Roman territory applies to those northern populations as it did to other border populations, e.g. Odoacer, followed by Ostrogoths and Langobards into northern Italy, it would seem possible for the same model to apply to the populations along the north-western coast of

Germany. Since the closest landfall in Britain was the coast of the Pas de Calais it would be reasonable to expect the closer Saxons to be the first to arrive and to settle in the areas of southern Britain, followed by the neighbouring Angles, who had to seek locations further to the north. According to that pattern, the Jutes would have been the last to move; why were they allowed to choose their abodes in strategically important Kent and along the southern shores of Britain?

Finally there is the question of the name of the new ethnic entity. Despite the fact that the Saxons were in the majority, as also indicated by the ethnic terminology at the time of the Norman invasion, the country took its name from the Angles. Could this have been due to the fact that there was a semantic space available for the Angles as a territorial unit because they no longer had one on the Continent, whilst both Saxons and Jutes still had territories in their name on the Continent which would have made it necessary to use additional specifiers such a 'new' or 'great', that the new territorial unit in Britain was given their name? Or perhaps it was a political choice so as not to create embarassing allegiances based on terminology?

Total population displacement/replacement

Discussion

It was suggested that genocide and total population displacement/replacement should be taken into consideration as they would represent the logical extremes of the problem.

Fowler picked up an idea raised in another context by Dumville, expressing the opinion that the model of "total population displacement" could provide a fairly clear testing ground for "other things which [could] happen" and could be detected in the documentation or the archaeology.

Dumville declared he was struck by the fact that archaeologists active in the study of the Early Anglo-Saxon period in the last twenty years do not believe in the genocide of the Britons by Anglo-Saxons "in the most literal sense". The level of hysteria raised in some such discussions led him to believe that "somebody had something to hide". He continued asserting that he would be "a lot more impressed" if scholars who seriously wanted to tackle the problem would set up a model, e.g. of total replacement, and follow through the implications that the model would involve, such as for language, material culture and so on.

Fowler expressed his agreement asserting that the opposite extreme would be that of the "three boats" and what that would imply after fifty or one hundred years.

Charles-Edwards remarked that the problem went hand in hand with that of ethnogenesis, in that "the English did not simply replace the Britons because those who migrated were not yet English".

According to *Dumville*, the UN charter's definition of genocide would certainly apply to the change which took place after the arrival of Germanic populations "because Englishness was something thrust down a lot of peoples' throats. Hence the question is fraught with problems of definition, terminology and so on".

Wood interjected that in the *Lex ribuaria*, one's law is associated with where one is born. As soon as there is an English government, one becomes an Englishman.

Powlesland pointed out that if there was indeed genocide he would like to "have at least one piece of evidence for it" because "there is no way [one] can identify it".

Comment

When two ethnic groups are thrust together and, after a while, the language, customs and traditions of one of them prevail as happened some time after the Anglo-Saxons 'invaded' Britain, two possible social mechanisms may be at work: (a) gradual acculturation by assimilation of one ethnic group to the other or (b) the disappearance of one group leaving the field to the other. In turn, disappearance may be due either to the physical elimination of one group by genocide and 'ethnic cleansing', or to the voluntary abandonment of the area by one of the populations, in this case the Romano-Britons, due to unfavourable socio-economic conditions.

It seems strange that, in the face of a numerous Romano-British population, as it surely was at the beginning of the fifth century, the Anglo-Saxon language and customs should have prevailed as they did at the beginning of the seventh century. Indeed the acculturation would have had to take place in about 150 years, generally a short time for such a wholesale change; furthermore, with equal population numbers interacting, acculturation generally goes in the direction of the higher, the Roman, not of the lower level of socio-cultural integration, the Anglo-Saxon.

This leaves only two possible models, either physical elimination, i.e. genocide, or voluntary abandonment, called 'total displacement/replacement' in the preceding discussion. Genocide seems improbable on account of the relatively small numbers of 'invaders' and the erstwhile large numbers of Romano-Britons. Genocide could have occurred only if the original large number of Romano-Britons had waned, for whatever reasons, to the point where genocide could have been possible. However, in this case genocide could not be assumed to have been the primary cause but only the final consequence of an overwhelming population displacement/replacement mechanism.

That genocide was unlikely is borne out by archaeology:

> Contrary to some still current views, it is now known that few towns suffered violent destruction, some villas went up in flames with their inhabitants massacred, but the majority slid into slow decay.... There is virtually no evidence of battle cemeteries such as were connected with native British sites during the Roman invasion period of AD 43 (Wacher 1974:414).

We thus come to consider a model of total displacement/replacement. Once more Bede gives us a clue:

> To begin with, the inhabitants of the island were Britons...from the land of Armorica, and appropriated to themselves the southern part of it (*HE* I.1. Trans. McClure & Collins 1994:9).

Armorica ranges from the Seine estuary to Cape Finisterre and from the Loire to the Channel. Bede could not have known the 'origin' of the populations of southern Britain—who in fact, in Roman times, were highly fractionated along the southern coast, comprising *Dumnonii*, *Durotriges*, *Regnenses*, *Atrebates*, *Dobunni*, *Catuuellauni* and *Trinouantes*, none of whom seem to have been directly connected to the Armoricans—whereas he certainly had information about the situation which obtained shortly before his times, in the twilight of Romano-British dominance. The most convincing interpretation of his statement is that the Romano-Britons living in the southern part of Britain shortly before his time were closely related to the Armoricans living across the Channel.

It would make sense to surmise that trade to and from Britain was controlled by related groups on both sides of the Channel and that there was a continuity of interests, hence kinship, between the 'Romans' on the Continent and those on the facing British coast across the Channel, so much so that they even gave the same names to territories on both sides of the sea (cf. Hooke, this volume, p. 68).

It might be worth analysing the possibility that the Romano-British population thrived until Roman garrisons were provisioned, 'strategic' goods were shipped to the central administration in the Western Roman Empire and prestige goods were shipped back to be sold to the local populations which earned money by providing food and services to the Roman garrisons.

As previously suggested, both the 'genocide' and the 'total population displacement/replacement' models should be tested against the available evidence, both documentary and archaeological. For instance, in favour of the 'total population displacement/replacement' model we have Gildas's testimony that many Romano-Britons were migrating to the Continent, *"...alii transmarinas petebant regiones..."* (Gildas I.xxv)—although he ascribed their migration to fear of unrest in Britain—and the permanence of autochtonous populations in non-romanized areas which, in many cases, even kept their names, e.g. the Picts and the Gododdin. In favour of the 'genocide' model we have some traces of violence in the archaeological record. The truth may lie in between, as both models could have co-existed. Research should clarify which model was prevalent and possibly give an idea of the relative importance of each one.

Population numbers

Comment

Population numbers are a basic concern for students of ancient societies because they condition all other aspects whether they refer to social relations, politics, religion, etc. During the conference it became apparent that ideas about the population of Britain at the time of migration were rather vague and discordant, that figures suggested were guesstimates and that no models were followed.

I shall try here to discuss some points of attack as first approximations to the problem by proposing a few population hypotheses to be tested by various methods to try to bring the problem closer to a solution.

The first model proposed is based on the consideration that, when migration took place, Britain's socio-economic situation may have been comparable to that

Table 13-1

Populations with less than 10 inhabitants per sq.km.

Country	Pop. density km.sq.	Urban pop. %	G.N.P. US $/per capita
Angola	8	28.3	1,555
Saudi Arabia	8	77.3	7,940
Australia	2	85.5	17,070
Belize	8.7	46.0	?
Bolivia	6	51.4	0,680
Botswana	2	45.7	2,590
Canada	2.7	76.4	20,320
Central Af.Rep.	5	46.6	0,390
Chad	5	33.3	0,220
Congo	7	40.5	1,030
Gabon	4	45.7	17,360
Guyana	3	34.6	0,330
Iceland	2	90.5	23,670
Kazakhstan	6	57.6	1,680
Libya	2	70.2	5,410
Mali	7	19.2	0,300
Mauritania	2	42.1	0,510
Mongolia	1	51.2	0,716
Namibia	2	32.8	?
Niger	7	19.5	?
Oman	8	10.6	6,490
Papua New Guinea	10	47.5	1,340
Russian Fed.	8.7	52.6	2,680
Somaliland	11	36.4	0,150
Sudan	10	22.0	0,400
Suriname	2	65.2	3,700
Turkmenistan	6	45.4	1,270
Zambia	11	55.6	0,290

of the poorest countries of the so called Fourth World. In fact in contemporary Fourth World countries modern medicine is available at least to the urban élites whereas in the Migration period it was available to no one.

The preceding table lists the countries, most of them in the Fourth World, with population densities at or below 10 inhabitants per square kilometre.

Leaving out countries, such as Australia and Canada, with high per capita GNPs, whose low population density is due to great expanses of barren land, one can see how even nowadays there are in the world several Fourth World countries with densities of 10 or fewer inhabitants per square kilometre. The size of Great Britain is 244,100 sq.km. which, on the basis of a density of 10 inhabitants/sq. km, would add up to a total population of about 2,400,000.

A second way to arrive at an approximate population figure is to reckon the number of tribes in Britain during the Migration period. By optimistically assuming that in the lowlands only the towns were abandoned while the tribal groups, the *Parisi, Coritani, Iceni, Catuellauni, Atrebates, Dobunni, Belgae, Trinobantes, Cantiaci, Regnenses* had remained intact, adding those of the western and northern highlands, *Dumnonii, Silures, Ordovices, Cornovii, Brigantes, Novantes, Demetae, Selgovae, Uotadini, Picti*, plus the three invading tribes, one reaches a total of twenty-three. By calculating the strength of each tribe at the optimistically high figure of 60,000, the average for modern tribal groups at similar levels of sociocultural integration, one obtains an approximate total of 1,400,000.

A third approach is to take the figures given by Bede. We are told (*HE* IV.3) that Wilfrid was given by the king 87 hides of land [1 hide = 24 to 49 ha][1] on which "250 male and female slaves" lived. Multiplying this figure by two to obtain the total population including children one obtains a density of 11.1 inhabitants/sq.km. This is certainly a high figure because it refers to a cultivated area, whereas, for the whole of Britain, one should take into account the great extensions of forested and barren areas.

Some have posited a greater density because of the apparent extension of cultivated land; it is quite possible that there was a system of rotation, as in fact described by Caesar for some Germanic tribes. A considerable extension of cultivated land has little bearing on the population size without the assessment of the intensity of cultivation of that land.

One should also bear in mind that, if a figure could be arrived at for the carrying capacity of the land, having deducted the extension of forests and barren areas, one still would have to reduce the carrying capacity to take into account plagues and famines and the slow recovery rate of the population due to the high infant mortality rate. Plague is mentioned about ten times by Bede in the *Historia ecclesiastica* (I.14; III.23; III.27; IV.1; IV.3; IV.7; IV.14; IV.19) and it looks as if one happened about every ten years in one part or another of the country. Famine may have been a fairly frequent occurrence. Bede mentions a drought which had continued during the three years prior to Bishop Wilfrid's "coming into the kingdom" (*HE* IV.13) and the 'Continuations' to the *HE* mention two droughts, one in 737 followed by another in 741.

On account of the high mortality rate, for populations at that level of subsistence it is difficult to recover losses caused by those occurrences. For populations at that level of nutrition and medical knowledge it would be unrealistic to estimate the prevailing mortality rate at a level lower than 40 per cent of live-born babies. In fact accurate statistics carried out in the crown lands of the Austro-Hungarian Empire show infant mortality rates including five-year-olds varying between a low of 26.4 per cent for Dalmatia to a high of 47.8 per cent in Silesia in 1872 (see page 161, this volume). Better nutrition and especially better medical care gradually reduced mortality rates to lower levels in 1913 between a minimum of 22.7 per cent for Carniola and a maximum of 34.7 per cent for Bukovina. The greatest reduction in Western Europe was achieved after World War I when improved medical practice and capillary medical care contained infant mortality rates within less than one per cent.

High infant mortality rates transpire even from Bede's account of events among royal families. In the case of five children of King Edwin, "...two were snatched from this life while still wearing the chrisom..." (*HE* II. 14), which amounts to a 40 per cent mortality rate within the first year of life even among the élite. A high rate applies to Edwin's children and grandchildren who had been rescued by Archbishop Paulinus after Edwin's death (*HE* II.20).

---

[1] The extension of a hide was obtained from Webster's New World College Dictionary. A figure closer to what a hide meant to Bede may be arrived at by recalling that he reckoned the extension of the Isle of Wight at 1,200 hides (*HE* IV.10), dividing this figure into its actual area would give Bede's value.

Nor can one invoke high fertility rates for the people of this epoch because these apply only to populations at a healthy nutritional level. Surveys carried out among Hadendowa in 1985 and Beni Amer in 1987 showed that among the former the average household consisted of 5.11 individuals, i.e. about three children (Ausenda 1987:342) and among the latter the average number of children varied from 2.65 per household in the mountains, to 3.2 within walking distance of routes of communication and about 3.6 in villages where fairly adequate medical care is available (Ausenda n.d.).

The low population level is also shown by the abundance of land available for grants to monasteries. Bede mentions eight land grants to monasteries (*HE* III.19, III.23, IV.3, IV.6, IV.13, IV.16, V.19). They amounted to a total of approximately 677 hides or about 300 sq.km. This is about 0.3 per cent of all available land in the Anglo-Saxon kingdoms. If one should further subtract the areas of barren lands and account for other probable grants of land, the figure would probably reach a level of the order of a few percentages of the available agricultural land. It is interesting to note that the extent of land required to feed the Roman army in Britain during the first century was calculated to have been 429 sq.km. (Wacher 1974:69-70), a figure comparable to that granted to monasteries. If colonization was as dense as some people maintain, Anglo-Saxon rulers would have been hard put to carry through such considerable giveaways.

The conclusion is that a figure of two million inhabitants in Britain during the Migration period should be considered an upper limit; the actual figure was probably closer to one million. Even the presence of the "twenty-eight noble cities" mentioned by Bede (*HE* I.1) would have made little difference as the population of towns calculated from the capacities of theatres was on average less than ten thousand (Wacher 1974:36). The difference would have been less than 250,000 at the height of the Roman presence.

Research on the population density from the height of Roman presence to the depth of Roman withdrawal, might be conducted by subsequent approximations along the lines suggested above.

Dwellings and settlements

Discussion

The only mention of dwellings during the concluding discussion came up during a debate on whether "daring reconstructions" were admissible in the trade, which is perhaps worth summarizing.

Hooke brought up the problem, saying that she was worried about the suggestion that "archaeologists need to be more daring in attempting to reconstruct", as it was distressing to see how many "elaborate reconstructions were completely misconstrued and misled the people".

Scull countered that one should not limit interpretation simply to make it more accessible to a non-specialist audience; and *Pohl* added that if one knows that the reconstruction is "daring" one is automatically put on guard.

Hooke added that if such a method were employed in the "field of historical documentation, it would be severely criticized".

Härke took up Pohl's argument that since the basic hypothesis was of complete ignorance the reader could not be told anything misleading.

Scull compared the situation to that of saying that medical research should stay away from certain areas simply because it was too difficult to explain to laymen, but one could "not constrain [one's] intellectual enquiry according to whether or not somebody who is not a specialist could understand it".

Hooke conceded that one might be justified in being daring as long as one used the facts at hand, but she was worried about stretching them and, for instance, suggesting "a structure that can't have been there"; one had to be "true to [one's] evidence".

Scull agreed, but he pointed out that the evidence would sustain a great range of interpretations; and *Powlesland* added that "it would be frightening if we were not to be daring", because it took imagination "to try to see a link between this feature and that one".

Pohl repeated that if he was told that a reconstruction was daring he would have no problem: he would "just want to know exactly what the evidence was to support it".

Härke brought in an international perspective pointing out that the argument that "one would have to be very careful that one did not do any reconstructions or suggest any interpretations which were not supported by the evidence" was very widespread in Germany; he concluded that "the danger of that argument was illustrated by the present state of German archaeology", which virtually confines itself, with few exceptions, to technology.

Hooke gave an example relating to buildings telling how she had been rebuked by a researcher when she had asked her for a "simple reconstruction of what [she] could expect of an Anglo-Saxon house".

Fowler concluded that at 'Bede's World', the project he is chairing at Jarrow, his team had just built "one quarter of one building", but that in any case they were not aiming at reconstructing an Anglo-Saxon village, they were putting together a "series of full-scale models". He pointed out that reconstruction is made much easier nowadays by computers and hyper-reality. He said that the aim was to get people to think, it was not to be "dogmatic".

Comment

The previous exchange gives an idea of the state of uncertainty concerning the real aspect of early Anglo-Saxon buildings, their functions and service.

On this topic one can get few pointers from Bede. While Romano-Britons had built extensively in stone or brick used especially in buildings for the administration, trade and public entertainment, the incoming barbarians used a less sophisticated architecture as also recognized by Bede (*HE* II.14).

The barbarians, and probably the Britons before them, built timber-framed houses with adobe walling and thatched roofs. They were suited to the climate and easier to heat because of their smaller size, but quite perishable.

For less permanent buildings used only during summer and early fall huts made "from the branches of trees" (*HE* I.30) were used by people engaged in activities away from their permanent winter quarters.

Among the merits of the mission to the Angles is that of having reintroduced the 'Roman manner' in the building of churches and monasteries. This paved the way for the resurgence of towns during the seventh and eighth centuries.

One needs to know the spatial relation between different kinds of livestock shelters or cattle byres, barns and houses better to understand the agrarian economy of the population. Models for comparison may be obtained from the local patterns during the years preceding industrialization.

Place-names

Discussion

The topic was brought up by *Härke* who interjected that if one was looking for "gaps" would it not be expedient to "re-write all the grand narratives based on place-names", such as the "assumed link between complete language replacement and population replacement by mass immigration". According to *Härke* the state of uncertainty causing repeated discussions "at every single conference" probably called for looking again at the "underlying models used as assumptions...at a fundamental level".

Hooke countered that place-name specialists were waiting for "a number of more detailed regional studies rather than for someone looking at the whole picture", or more information before "generalizations start again".

According to *Dumville* more articles were needed showing how far place-name specialists were prepared to "step back to re-survey the assumptions about the role which personal names played in place-names", in other words "something which tackles the present reference body of material and points out what some of the assumptions are in it".

Hines concluded the debate by pointing to the fact that the question brought up by Härke concerned "what [one needed] in terms of population to effect a linguistic change", a question which seemed a "matter of opinion all the way through". He asserted that he would prefer to "see more effort going into exploring the linguistic record rather than having another look at the old question concerning place-names".

Kinship and marriage

Discussion

Kinship was brought up during the concluding discussion by *Dumville* who suggested that Charles-Edwards might write a book on early English kinship. *Charles-Edwards*'s answer was that a study would have to focus on late rather than early Anglo-Saxons, "since the evidence is mostly late".

Comment

Small communities in simple societies generally have preferential marriage partners. Where movable property consisting of livestock is important for both subsistence and social relations, preferential marriage tends to be among close kin. This kind of alliance engenders a beneficial continuity in the management of livestock and other property belonging to the group (cf. Goody 1983:59).[2] One should mention that the most common form of 'endogamic' marriage, short of incest, is that obtaining between parallel first cousins, i.e. the son and daughter of siblings. In societies with patrilineal descent, preferential marriage usually concerns the offspring of brothers. That this may have been the model among tribes that settled in Britain may be inferred by the following excerpts from Bede:

> A certain secular law in the Roman State allows that the son and daughter of a brother and sister or of two brothers, or two sisters may be married (*HE* I.27);

and further:

> Now because there are many of the English race who, while they were unbelievers, are said to have contracted these unlawful marriages...they should be warned.... Nevertheless they are not to be deprived of the communion.... (*HE* I.27).

The Church went on to impose that "the faithful should only marry relations three or four times removed, while those twice removed must not marry in any case...." (*HE* I.27). The rationale behind the Church's stand was that "the offspring of such marriages cannot thrive" and in case of marriage with one's stepmother "because it is written in the law: 'Thou shalt not uncover thy father's nakedness'" (*HE* I.27). The real and more or less 'subconscious' motive probably was the need to break up the authority of the elders in the closely knit kinship network allowing their position to be taken over by religious 'elders', and also to prevent the automatism of inheritance within the close kinship network which was a consequence of such marriages since property was vested in the kin group rather than in individuals (cf. Goody 1983:45, 59, 134).

We also know that residence was virilocal, as Bede attests when he mentions that Bishop Paulinus came to his see in York in the train of the princess who had been given in marriage to Edwin (*HE* II.9). This was the practice among most Germanic people.

One may note the Church's prohibition upon married women of having intercourse until their newborns were weaned (*HE* I.27). In simple societies usually there is no alternative to maternal breastfeeding and suckling lasts about two years or longer. In later Anglo-Saxon times women who could afford to have their babies suckled by a wet nurse undoubtedly belonged to the highest levels of society. Engaging a wet nurse meant keeping her with board and lodging and in good circumstances so as not to impair the health of the newborn. For the élite this may have been a way of increasing the fertility of its women since having many children increased the possibility of surviving legitimate heirs and of contracting marriage alliances with other élite lineages.

One would like to know more about the wedding ceremony but Bede gives us no clues. Some may be obtained from descriptions of wedding ceremonies in later centuries.

---

[2] The pattern of close kin marriage was illustrated in some detail in a preceding volume of the series (Ausenda 1995:23).

A further problem concerns the terminology of kinship among the Anglo-Saxons during the early period as a key to understanding social relations. No information of this kind can be found in the *Historia ecclesiastica* and the solution to the problem lies in a careful reading of the Anglo-Saxon laws and comparison with similar laws among related Germanic populations.

Social relations

Discussion

Härke remarked how written sources present a different picture from that inferred from archaeological evidence. He recognized the "chronological discrepancy between the two types of evidence" but suggested looking at their overlap in the seventh century.

Charles-Edwards pointed to the disparities between "inherited status and wealth" whereby an impoverished person with "high inherited status may have had greater need to display grave goods".

Härke noted that Childe had postulated that the presence of grave goods implied "competitive display".

Dumville was not sure that Charles-Edwards assumed it was competitive.

Charles-Edwards countered that he would at least see that as proof that people were "sensible to...contrasts between their status and their wealth".

Dumville noted that what could be termed "pre-prosperity" in the seventh century reached a stable level in the eleventh and that "considerable social divergence" had taken place "in both directions" in the meantime, and that this trend was "already visible by implication in the seventh century".

Härke thought that several clauses in the laws could be found which implied that, and pointed out that the competition and display related to "aspired rather than real status".

Hines wondered whether, in contrast with the tendency in the early days of Anglo-Saxon archaeology to "think in terms of historical sources", and when looking at social differences in seventh-century Anglo-Saxon cemeteries to try to see whether the social strata uncovered correspond with those of the law codes, it would not be better to apply Fowler's chaos model, in that there will be discrepancies between what the law implies and what one might see. He went on to mention the untouched topic of craftsmen whose status appears to undergo interesting changes in the material record which do not appear in the written sources.

Hawkes noted the similarity with the fact that sculptors are absent from documentary records in England, whereas they appear in Ireland.

Hines adduced the "signed work of art" as a proof of the increasing status of craftsmen and noted that there was evidence from Northumbria of "ecclesiastical sculptors brought in from the Continent". He added that while it was relatively easy to identify a problem, it became very difficult to sort it out because of the lack of evidence. He then asked whether someone could suggest "a very obvious body of evidence waiting to be analysed" which could give a push forward on questions of social structure.

Dumville thought that "the obvious area" was "in the Anglo-Saxon law codes" and he cited Charles-Edwards's recent book on Irish and Welsh kinship which relied "very substantially on legal evidence but slotting it in to a vast range of other things".

Hines brought up the problem of slavery and asked whether anyone could define the role of slaves in that society accounting for the fact that there were various layers.

Hooke mentioned the importance of the role of the peasantry.

Comment

Understanding the social structure of the early Anglo-Saxon immigrants can help one explain many aspects of the early period and subsequent political developments. There is little information on social relations in the *Historia ecclesiastica*. However, the little there is is quite interesting.

We learn that Angles and Jutes had lineages and that these lineages were designated with patronymics ending in -*ingas*. The relevant citations are:

> Now Æthelberht was the son of Eormenric, the son of Oita, the son of Oeric whose surname was Oisc, whence the kings of Kent were known as *Oiscingas* (*HE* II.5);

and:

> Rædwald, who was noble by birth though ignoble in his deeds, was the son of Tytil, whose father was Wuffa, from whom the kings of the East Angles are called *Wuffingas* (*HE* II.15).

In Æthelberht's case the lineage was only three generations deep, four in the case of Rædwald. This means that lineages either started or were imagined to have started after settling in Britain. This is in harmony with lineage genesis: groups leaving an existing lineage usually give birth to a new one which takes the name of the individual who led the migration. In the Anglo-Saxon case too, no lineages appear to have carried over the name of their original lineage from the Continent.

Since lineages were designated by -*ingas* names, it follows that at least some -*ingas* place-names pertained to settlements of close kin with additions of affines and lower ranked followers. The fact that those place-names became permanent only in the late sixth- and seventh-century does not detract from their genesis; it only means that by that time those settlements had become fixed and large enough for their names to be adopted as those of permanent villages.

Contemporary examples may be found among the Hadendowa populations of the Gash Delta in eastern Sudan. Individual clans occupy different areas whence small groups consisting of lineages or parts thereof migrate during the wet season and where they return to weather through the peak of the dry season. As long as they are mobile their settlements remain nameless as it is preferable to indicate them by the name of the geographical location or canal or forest where they are temporarily settled. Once the settlement becomes permanent it soon receives a name of its own.

The -*ing* suffix expresses belonging, not necessarily to a lineage; it can express the relation of a person to a person, or of a person to a place, or of a place to a person, or of a place to another place or thing (Bach 1981:162 ff.). Belonging to a lineage would be a case of the relation of a person to a person. In the case of place-names in *-ingas* all those relations are possible and they should be carefully explored before deciding the category they belong to.

In connection with the conversion of Peada, king of the Middle Angles and Mercians, Bede mentions two main social classes of freemen:

> So Peada was baptised by Bishop Finian together with all his *gesiths* and thegns who had come with him...many, both nobles and commons, renounced the filth of idolatry (*HE* III.21).

There were two main classes of freemen, nobles and commoners. No reference is made to lower classes of partially free and slaves, probably on the assumption that these followed the pattern set by their patrons.

That conquering armies were made up exclusively of élite warriors is untenable from a practical viewpoint. An élite needs to be set against a background of common people in order to be one. An élite without commoners would no longer be an élite. There are also practical reasons for which barbarian élites were accompanied by commoners or clients, one of them the fact that they relied on livestock for their military requirements and for their nutrition. This service could in no way be performed by sedentary serfs in former *villae*. These relations between élites and clients existed until recently among contemporary populations which can be compared with those which settled in Europe at the end of the Western Roman Empire. The existence of commoners alongside the élite would prove the point. Further clarifications as to the composition of invading armies are required in order to answer the question exhaustively.

Another point to be clarified is why there were several classes of *læt* implied in the earliest Anglo-Saxon laws. One possibility is that they were classed according to their historical origins; in other words the clients of the Romano-Britons would be considered at a lower level than those of the Anglo-Saxon settlers. This point perhaps will bear on the question of the status of craftsmen which was aired during a concluding discussion. The answer may be related to which craft is involved. Goldsmiths generally have high status; less wealthy crafts may have entailed lower statuses. In general craftsmen may have had patrons, but quite seldom were they unfree.

As far as slaves are concerned one should try to understand how they would fit into such a social structure. In general slaves are usefully employed in urbanized societies or in agricultural establishments supplying them. They are rare in simple societies since their usefulness is limited by the traditional division of labour between genders and generations. In fact among simple societies slaves are treated mainly as valuable chattel to be traded, all the more so because they are usually sold to distant lands to ensure that they will not escape back to their kin.

These inferences are borne out in the *Historia ecclesiastica* both by the episode of Gregory the Great seeing "some boys put up for sale, with fair complexions, handsome faces and lovely hair" and learning that they came from "the island of Britain" (*HE* II.1), and by the story of Imma, a retainer of King Ælfwine, struck down in battle, imprisoned and later sent to London to be sold to a Frisian merchant and disposed of abroad (*HE* IV.22).

Bede also mentions that missions, in this case Aidan, the Irish bishop who had been sent to Oswald, king of the Northumbrians to convert his people, "...distributed gifts of money...for the use of the poor or for the redemption of those who had been unjustly sold into slavery..." (*HE* III.5). Those he redeemed were trained, instructed and later ordained as priests. This procedure was adopted also by the early Christian missions to Africa in the nineteenth century. Three years ago the Vatican canonized the first African saint, the Holy Bachita, a Sudanese slave who had become a nun.

Jural relations and conflict

Discussion

[The discussion centered on 'Relations between the Anglo-Saxons and their neighbours' and 'Warfare', here considered part of the topic 'Jural relations and conflict'].

Härke introduced the discussion asserting that he wanted to obtain more information on the Anglo-Saxons relations with their neighbours and how these related to "trade, economy, social development and so on", something akin to what Wood did for the relations between the Anglo-Saxons and *Francia*, but looking "in the other directions" as well.

Hines acknowledged that some 'directions', e.g. Scandinavia, had received due attention during the past ten years. Frisia should be "the boom area" in the immediate future on account of the archaeological work done there. Concerning British, Gaelic and Pictish populations in the West and North, Hines agreed that there was "a lot that could be done".

Dumville asserted that there were two aspects to the problem. The first consisted in reconsidering and reinterpreting existing evidence; on the other hand, he noted, there was no "book" which contained "readily accessible single items" on "the relationship between the Anglo-Saxons and their neighbours". He conceded that it would be a provisional effort, but "an enormously useful book for a lot of people".There was also scope for looking "eastwards and southwards", which would be "useful in focusing minds and drawing the attention of a larger academic public" so that "a CBA conference could be organized on the results".

Härke continued with a comment on the 'Warfare' topic, explaining that he meant to look at it "along the lines of what Chadwick characterized as a 'heroic society'", in the sense that warfare "must have played a huge role in the ideology of the ruling élite" and that that should be studied.

Wood observed that heroics were remembered as such by the following generations and that Chadwick's judgement was not enough to proclaim that one a heroic society; one should prove "internally" that it was a heroic society.

In *Hines*'s opinion whatever the genesis of the heroic image of a society one should take into consideration the fact that the myth existed. Mis-remembering might be a way for the myth to be built up.

Wood pointed out "how alarming the mis-remembering" was since the issue had got out of hand.

Härke asked whether the re-interpretation of that heroic society would swing the pendulum to the extreme that "Anglo-Saxon society was a haven of peace".

Wood ventured that he meant heroic in a different sense than warrior society and that a definition was required there. He guessed that one would get a different picture from "contemporary evidence" from that which one would get "using the whole batch of early medieval evidence as applying to the supposed heroic age which Chadwick brought up".

Härke conceded that "given the date of Chadwick's work, some reinterpretation was to be expected". He proposed to continue the discussion on the topic of 'warfare'.

Powlesland inquired whether one could get any evidence from the use of weapons.

Härke answered that very little evidence could be obtained from iron weapons. He was not looking for clues from "a dent here or a bent sword there" but "aiming at a much more general level".

Charles-Edwards noted that graves with weapons were not necessarily significant in that "so-called Frankish graves were not necessarily Frankish" but perhaps belonged to Gallo-Romans, who had acquired a "much more military character".

Wood acknowledged that warfare was not the only factor. Militarization of society began in the late Roman world with aristocrats creating their own war bands, the starting point probably being when weapons could be found only with soldiers. In his opinion the dividing line between antiquity and the early Middle Ages "had precisely to do with taxation".

Comment

No question was raised concerning jural relations, except concerning warfare, perhaps because of the exhaustive treatment dedicated to them. Little is said about them in the *Historia ecclesiastica* apart from the basic principles which seemed all important in Bede's times.

The first one concerned the "protection to those whose coming and trading he [King Æthelberht] had welcomed" (*HE* II.5), which was made part of the early Kentish laws although it did not reflect a customary procedure.

The second was the principle of agnatic succession, in one case applied to the succession of Edwin whereby the kingdom of Deira "passed to a son of his uncle Ælfric" (*HE* III.1), and in another transpiring from the fact that Oswiu, king of the Northumbrians, was attacked by the Mercians and "by his own son Alhfrith and his nephew Oethelwald, the son of his brother and predecessor" (*HE* III.14).

The third principle mentioned consists of the widespread practice of feud, i.e. private law enforcement, even when someone was killed in battle. In one case Archbishop Theodore succeeded in bringing the feuding parties to a compromise whereby "only the usual money compensation" was paid (*HE* II.21); the other case concerns Imma (see above) who should have been slain by his captor because he was a thegn of the enemy king and "...because all my brothers and kinsmen were killed in the battle". Selling him into slavery may have been akin to obtaining blood money compensation (*HE* IV.22).

There is still a lot to be learned about jural relations amongst the early Anglo-Saxons, especially about the division of personal property by gender, about the various exchanges of wealth at marriage and their traditional value, and about the relations and obligations between serfs or clients and their patrons.

Concerning conflict, a common misconception due to the weapons found in their graves and the epic poems sung by their minstrels is that the Anglo-Saxons were a heroic people. Concerning both these kinds of evidence one might mention recent ethnographic experience among Hadendowa and Beni Amer pastoralists in eastern Sudan and northern Eritrea. Most Hadendowa living in the bush carry swords having about a metre long blades, hung on their left shoulder by a *cingulum,* almost the same as those of the early Anglo-Saxons except that nowadays they are made from reclaimed automobile springs. Swords are carried mostly for prestige reasons and only occasionally for defence against hyenas. Wars, such as the recent one (1941-1945) between Hadendowa and Beni Amer, are fought by raids and counterraids and only seldom are there any direct engagements (Ausenda 1987:300).

The Habàb, a population living on the seaward side of the Eritrean mountains, in the face of an organized invading enemy, despite their war dances and boasts, fled with their livestock and families to desert or inaccessible areas so as to make it difficult for their raiders to follow them (Baratieri 1896; Munzinger 1890).

This is not to say that those populations were more or less heroic than others in complex societies. Heroism is a symbolic act conditioned by social relations and circumstances. It is less likely to occur in simple societies amongst which raids and ambush are more effective ways of conducting warfare than face-to-face combat.

Rural economics

Discussion

The discussion concerning this subject turned mostly on the topic of 'Impact on the environment' introduced by Fowler's mention of "environmentally-led field research".

Fowler aired the opinion that any human settlement made an impact on the environment. While the results should be widespread, the evidence "appeared incidentally in the course of holes in the ground made for another purpose". Environmentally-led field research implies asking "questions from the environmental standpoint", such as the impact that certain types of settlement may have in given areas. He asserted that the places where such questions could be asked were identifiable and that the techniques to answer them were available.

Hooke agreed with the change from 'random-sampling' techniques to making plans and "looking at things and making informed judgements".

Powlesland observed how "the whole question of the environmental framework in archaeology changed dramatically in the last twenty years". He recalled how "one of the nation's main environmental units" invited to express its opinion on the possible results of excavations at the site of West Heslerton, had recommended to abandon it because "it was a waste of time". He kept at it and came up with "absolutely enormous returns" which he was now trying to "set against a wider background", a difficult task because there was very little environmental evidence "for what was going on in Roman Britain in the countryside". He summarized the situation by saying that research on early Anglo-Saxon evidence invariably reached a point where it was necessary to "go back and look at more Roman evidence". He complained that archaeological knowledge on the topic was still "in a very primitive state" and that "an enormous amount" needed to be done archaeologically to move forward. He added that maybe a hundred years of research were needed to "radically change the picture".

Hines asked other historians whether they thought that their understanding of "aspects of Anglo-Saxon history that have to do with the exploitation of the landscape" would improve if they had "more concrete ideas of what was in the landscape in terms of crops and livestock, where they were being grown, how they were being grown". Having received a positive answer he ventured whether it was possible to put forward a set of proposals, for instance to focus on a specific problem with a set of charters.

Charles-Edwards said: "But it seems better to think not so much in terms of a particular document rather than our whole perception of the shape of the world. The danger with us historians is to argue back from the thirteenth century. For example, my temptation would be to take Titow's gloomy assessment of thirteenth-century crop yields (Titow 1972) and assume that things must have been as bad in the fifth and sixth centuries, namely that the amount of grain you got out at the end of the yearly cycle was not much more than what you put in. Peter's evidence for crop ratios therefore changes my estimate of what the early Anglo-Saxons world was like. The huge contrast in terms of crop yields which is suggested between the thirteenth century and this period also raises questions about the trustworthiness of the thirteenth-century evidence. It may well be that estate management was making relatively little out of arable farming, and that the texts make a failure of management look like a very poor crop yield".

Fowler admitted that one needed a lot of resources for environmental research but he thought that the exercise was worth putting "at the bow-wave of research". He suggested "modelling what a landscape could be like in the seventh century" and then doing environmental research on what "actually turned up in the right place". For the Migration period the question could be, "What should there be showing...if [one was] getting five thousand new souls moving into a certain landscape?". One should be asking that sort of question, but he was not sure that "we are even asking it".

Scull remarked that the 'impact' might be modelled in different ways, for instance the "end of intensive farming for profit" might bring "less intensive agricultural practice" resulting in changes in the "social and cultural economy in the equations".

Hines acknowledged the importance of the issue, which should be put on the agenda for the future. However, it was important not to kill artefact and cemetery research because it was 'out of date', a point to be underscored to avoid repeating the mistakes of the past.

Fowler observed that research in other directions should not be abandoned, but because of the potential of this new avenue of research and the fact that the know-how had been perfected one would wish that approaches could be adjusted. He related that it did seem that there was "a cereal difference", but "the question [was] whether this [was] a cultural difference between...the early Anglo-Saxon settlement area and the West".

To the same subject belonged a short discussion on the problem of *land tenure*, in particular that of folkland-bookland, brought up by *Hines* who asked whether it could be reassessed in a modern perspective.

Charles-Edwards suggested that bookland was easier to focus on than folkland because it could be followed through the charters which made the problem more manageable.

Dumville recalled that not only folkland but "other possible kinds of tenure" depended mostly on assumptions. Research had not yielded results on account of the scarcity of references to early tenure, whereas in later periods and with "another variety of tenures" one was considerably "impeded by the different terminology of the different Domesday commissioners". He was sure that there was "scope for another study and another good look at questions about tenure" provided the traditional problems were clearly stated and avoided.

Comment

There are few remarks made by Bede about the ecology of Britain in his days but nevertheless they are enlightening. In the story of St Cuthbert he relates the difficulty of growing wheat on certain soils where, however, barley thrived (*HE* IV.28). This condition must have been fairly widespread since wheat was extensively grown in Roman times.

Concerning animal husbandry Bede notes that in Ireland "Hay is never cut for winter use nor are stables built for their beasts" (*HE* I.1). This implies that in the area where he lived hay was cut for winter use, which would have meant the use of barns since haystacks rot easily in damp weather. One should also note that if hay is cut for winter, animals must be moved by transhumance to highland pastures in summer. This probably started at the beginning of May, as it does to this day in many parts of Europe. Yearly transhumance may have entailed the temporary abandonment of some settlements and might be one of the causes of the slow 'shuffles' of some others, in that temporarily abandoned houses could be destroyed by storms or rains and had to be rebuilt on different locations. The pattern of transhumance from Anglian regions may have been a factor in the relations between the Anglian and neighbouring Celtic population.

The practice of separate herding often causes tensions between herders and agriculturalists in that, especially when pastures are scarce, herders sometimes allow their animals to graze in cultivated fields. To protect these, cultivators surround them with enclosures made of thorny brush and, having built makeshift shelters, may also guard them day and night until harvest time. At harvest, cereals are sometimes threshed in a clearing in the middle of the field while dried stalks are tied in sheaves and stored for the winter. Once this operation is completed animals are allowed to graze the stubble.

The presence of stables means litter and hence forests in the vicinity where leaves can be easily gathered. Forests are also important for cutting wood as winter fuel. One can see how early agricultural settlements had to keep a balance between field and forest.

In simple herding societies calves are killed soon after birth so as to save milk for human consumption. Only about 3 per cent of male animals are allowed to grow to adulthood for breeding purposes. It is only with the growth of towns and villages that the supply of meat to the settled population becomes a profitable activity. In this case male calves are fattened until they are about two years old before selling them for slaughter. Some male calves may have been castrated to become oxen. In the early period castration may have not been practised by Anglo-Saxons as it is a delicate operation requiring considerable skill. Furthermore, oxen are powerful draft animals but, because of that, they also consume large quantities of fodder. As recently as the early 1900s in an alpine village probably somewhat more wealthy than early Anglo-Saxon settlers only six families out of 52 could afford to keep oxen and only two owned ploughs. These were considered expensive tools and men used spades to turn the sods before sowing. Only when fields were fairly long were ploughs used, and they were rented from their owners for a fee and drawn by two cows rather than oxen. In this same village cows were also used as draught animals for pulling carts to transport timber from the forest and manure to the fields, while wheat, hay, potatoes, pumpkins, turnips, leaves etc. were carried by women in large baskets strapped onto their shoulders or, when the load was too heavy for the women, by men.

Drought and famine were frequent and should be taken into account when calculating the carrying capacity of those lands.

Bede also supplies information about fishing. He writes that St Wilfrid taught the inhabitants of Northumbria stricken by famine "how to get food by fishing, for both the sea and the rivers abounded with fish but the people had no knowledge of fishing except for eels alone" (*HE* IV.13). The mention that "seals as well as dolphins are frequently captured and even whales" suggests that this was a haphazard operation mostly when these animals were beached. Both citations lead one to believe that some of the colonizers were not seafaring people and this leaves us with the problem of how, after the end of the Roman presence, they reached Britain: presumably by buying passage from coastal populations and paying with produce or livestock.[3]

Urban economics

Discussion

The one problem which came up during the discussion in the domain of urban economics concerned *taxation*.

---

[3] The cost of passage is an important variable: in the early nineteenth century Haussa pilgrims wishing to cross the Red Sea to reach Jidda and Mecca would walk some 500 km from Sawakin, where passage cost two Thalers (about $ 50), to Massawa where it cost only one Thaler (Burkhardt 1822:371).

Charles-Edwards noted: "An important general topic is suggested by Chris Wickham's argument in his article in *Past and Present* where he thought that the main divide between the Roman world and post-Roman was between a state which could tax and a state which could not (Wickham 1984). This addresses a big question which one might wish to take on board".

According to *Wood* the question could be made more specific with regards to the Anglo-Saxons in that, amongst all the barbarians settled in the Roman Empire, they were the only ones "incompetent enough to let all the tax systems collapse".

Scull ventured that it may have been an ideological stance, in that they considered "taxation as anathema".

Having remarked that the problem of taxation had cropped up with regards to 'seigneurial power' *Hines* asked whether everyone agreed that the term 'seigneurial' constituted a "possible anachronism" in relation to the Early and Middle Anglo-Saxon period.

According to *Dumville* opinion was divided.

Comment

In the introductory geographical précis to the *Historia ecclesiastica* Bede recalls that the "...country was once famous for its twenty-eight noble cities as well as innumerable fortified places..." (*HE* I.1). The number corresponds closely to the "twenty-three tribal areas for which there is evidence in Britain during the Roman period" (Wacher 1974:22). In fact the genesis of towns in Britain during the early stages of the occupation is explained by the presence of Roman garrisons in the central places of the tribal areas, due to the fact that the soldiers' salaries and the provisioning of the garrison were a considerable factor in the urbanization of these early centres. This was highlighted by archaeology:

> The importance of trade to a town is indicated by the speed with which shops appeared in the very earliest years after its foundation; Claudian shops have been excavated at Verulamium, London and Colchester, and Flavian shops at Cirencester and Leicester (Wacher 1974:59-60).

The removal of the Roman army and the cessation of 'strategic' trade in metals and slaves to the rest of the Empire sounded the death knell to the towns of Roman Britain.

An overview of the archaeological finds in those towns concludes:

> Evidence has yet to be produced that the towns were still properly functioning in the period of peace and British prosperity which came after the Anglo-Saxons suffered a major defeat at Mount Badon, towards the end of the fifth century.... The evidence may be there but, if it is, we cannot see it. But there is some reason to believe that by then many towns had already been deserted by the classes which had been foremost in their maintenance.
>
> Indeed, one of the most surprising aspects of the whole period is the almost total disappearance of what may be called the Romano-British culture (Wacher 1974:412).

Archaeology confirms that the end of Roman Britain was not due or accompanied by violence but rather to abandonment due to other causes (Wacher 1974:414), the almost total decline of trade being probably the foremost. In fact famines and plagues were just as frequent in Gaul, yet there was continuity because regional trade kept going on.

Three towns of the central lowlands, St Albans, Cirencester and Silchester, seem to have survived longest, perhaps into the sixth century. This may be due to their central position which allowed them to benefit from the little regional trade still going on.

Another interesting phenomenon consists in the continuity and, in some cases, the establishment of new port towns, especially in the south-eastern part of the country. These are London, Southhampton and Ipswich (see Scull, this volume). Southampton probably was the port of call of the remaining trade with central France and the Mediterranean, while trade through London and Ipswich was probably directed towards northern and eastern Europe, as also Bede implies when he relates how Imma was sold to a Frisian merchant in London (*HE* IV.22). Similar developments may have gone on at other southern ports.

The fact that Roman monumental town centres were little used if at all should be immediately apparent to anyone who is familiar with the difficulties of destroying or, worst still, renovating a pre-existing masonry or stone structure using hand tools. This is a very difficult and dangerous operation which requires considerable skill and luck since the structural integrity of an ancient building is usually impaired in places which are not immediately detectable, so that workers can be easily injured or killed by a suddenly falling wall or arch. It is not surprising that Anglo-Saxons who were completely unfamiliar with the intricacies of stone architecture would stay away from these structures, especially since land was easily available outside the Roman walls.

Primitive markets, especially when not permanent, like the preceding Roman ones, prefer open spaces where there is plenty of room for everyone arriving with his load of goods on a donkey or a mule to display them on a blanket laid down on the ground. The first buildings to go up are usually tea shops, or in the Anglo-Saxon case wine, beer or mead shops, where merchants could sit and discuss their business.

In Nacfa, the bastion of Eritrean resistance against the Ethiopians, a town destroyed by artillery and bombing, shortly after the war ended in 1991 a market took place every Friday with merchants coming all the way from Sudan and other parts of Eritrea. It was located on a wide plain immediately outside, but within easy walking distance from, the town. A few shops were beginning to open in makeshift huts among the destroyed buildings; there was a goldsmith, a vendor of seeds and herbs and about a dozen tea and coffee shops. In Kèren and Agordàt, which were still intact, the markets are located in permanent shops in the centre of town; the only market facility at the city limits was the enclosure for the sale or auction of livestock.

Archaeology should be able to give us some idea of the specialities of those early markets, and emporia, i.e. which kind of goods were sold and where they came from.

The collection of taxes is predicated on the creation of surplus. Very little surplus was produced in the Early Anglo-Saxon period. The explanation of why taxes were not collected probably lies in the fact that 'royal' administrations were of the scantiest type and that the king and his peripheral officers were supported by endowments of land sufficient to feed them and their retinues. Taxes may have not been levied because the administration did not need them badly and because trying to collect them would have cost more in good will and expense than it would have produced in resources. One should remember that the late Roman Empire was seen as oppressive on account of its fiscal pressure. The successor kings' main claim to fame was that they did not oppress the population with heavy taxes or easily remitted them (cf. *HF*. X.7).

Travel was either on foot or horse back. Bede gives an amusing example of the need to know how to 'drive' a horse for people in positions of responsibility where they had to cover distances relatively fast. He writes about Archbishop Theodore personally lifting Bishop Chad on to a horse to make sure that he would learn to ride it. This is the same as the case of modern priests who are expected to learn to drive an automobile.

Symbolic life

Discussion

Dumville pointed out that the advent of Christianity in Anglo-Saxon England was the "most obvious point of cultural change" during and immediately after the Migration period. He believed that Christianity was "where the literature [came] from which looks back on the period of migrations and transition from Roman to sub-Roman to Anglo-Saxons within what [became] England". Not only did Christianity preside over the "great series of changes... summarized in this changing conceptual base, but it had direct impact in creating the written evidence which we've been talking about nearly throughout the course of this conference". After this introduction the discussion focused on the spread of Christianity in the Early Anglo-Saxon period later to return to '*literacy and literature*'.

The suggested topic for discussion of '*the changing conceptual base of seventh-century English thought*' was introduced by *Hines* with the remark that he "found it difficult to interpret in terms other than Goody's and others' suggestions that the literate consciousness [was] fundamentally different from the oral consciousness" (Goody 1987). He went on to anticipate the objection that the upper chronological limit of the object of the conference was the eighth century, "but Old English literary manuscripts [were] mostly of the tenth century" and "very little material could be dated earlier". This justified the tendency to "deny the scope for any useful study of Old English literature in relation to this period". The tendency was also revealed by the attempt made around 1980 to establish that *Beowulf* had been composed in the tenth century, "still probably the majority view amongst Old English scholars".

Charles-Edwards asked his "view about the problem of the relationship of the runic material on the Ruthwell cross to the *Dream of the Rood*".

Hines passing the question on to Hawkes admitted that his views were "quite fluid". At first he had thought it was very difficult to understand the inscription unless "it was excerpted from some larger work". Later on he had changed his point of view to one which made it "easier to cope with the idea that the Ruthwell

Cross runic inscription [was] a single text", in that the verses may not be "complete in themselves, but they are completed by the stone monument".

Hawkes was unsure of that interpretation and recalled that Éamon ó Corragáin (1988) had argued that one should "think them in terms of the other inscriptions...on that monument" as being "the key phrases which bring the larger text to mind".

Wood related that it had been noticed "that there are very few hypermetric lines in the *Dream of the Rood*", which are also the lines of the Ruthwell Cross. This suggests the need to distinguish the Ruthwell poem from the *Dream of the Rood*.

Hines noted that this view had been expressed by Christopher Ball (1991) who pointed out that there was "a metrical coherence to the Ruthwell Cross inscriptions".

Comment

1) Language
In Bede's time there were:

> ...five languages in Britain.... These are the English, British, Irish, Pictish, as well as the Latin language; through the use of the scriptures Latin is in general use among them all (*HE* I.1).

The sequence in which they are listed suggests that little more than two centuries and a half after the beginning of the Saxon and Anglo-Jutish spread over lowland Britain, one could talk about a *koiné* called English, and that this had become the most widely spoken tongue in Britain, even if there were local dialects.

The status of Latin "in general use among them all" (*HE* I.1) must be interpreted. Was Latin the 'international' language of those times, as English is nowadays, or was Latin more akin to contemporary classical Arabic, the language of Muslim religion which is nowhere spoken in the Islamic world, but used all over for sermons, prayers and literature?

After the drafting of Kentish laws in Old English (see Lendinara, this volume, p. 257), most later documents are in Latin. This testifies to the spread of the legal and literary function of that language well into the eleventh century (Sawyer 1965:26 ff.).

Among clerics there were many learned men who not only read English and Latin, but Greek as well (*HE* V.8, .20).

2) Education
Even before the mission to the Angles there was a great desire, at least among the élite, to acquire a literate education:

> ...numbers of people from Britain used to enter the monasteries of the Franks or Gauls to practise the monastic life, they also sent their daughters to be taught in them and to be wedded to the heavenly bridegroom (*HE* III.8).

The most extraordinary fact of Anglo-Saxon settlement in Britain is that a population which had reached the threshold of the seventh century steeped in ignorance and superstition could transform itself in less than a century into one of the most advanced literate populations in Europe. This can only mean that during that century there was a strong resurgence of communication after the decline of the late Roman period. History and archaeology should be able to explain the new avenues and vehicles of communication.

The monasteries which the early Anglo-Saxons had seen in Gaul served as models for some of those established in Britain (*HE* III.18). Children were taught from as young as three (*HE* IV.8). Libraries were stocked with volumes from all over Europe.

Knowledge of sacred music, presumably what later came to be known as Gregorian chant, was considered a primary aspect of education. This is probably because, all liturgy being in Latin and not understood by most of the faithful, a musical accompaniment would be useful as mnemonic help. The Anglo-Saxon awakening also saw the beginning of religious vernacular poetry accompanied by music.

3) Medicine

Medical treatment mostly consisted in the use of the relics of official or reputed saints or even of the dust that could be gathered on their containers. Mentally affected people were considered bedeviled and exorcised.

The same kind of medicine is practised among Muslim populations in East Africa. The most effective preventive treatment consists of a small leather pocket in which a folded piece of paper with some verses of the Quran written on it is enclosed. Mentally affected people, called *majanìn* (Ar., sing. *majnùn*), literally 'bedeviled', are treated by an exorcist who repeats a prayer from the Quran a number of times proportional to the seriousness of the seizure.

When someone is sick he is made to drink water run over a paper inscribed with verses from the Quran, or made to inhale the smoke of the burning paper, depending on whether the sickness affects his entrails or his lungs. There is also traditional medicine, which is not practised by clerics but by lay people, based on cuts to let out blood, burns to treat jaundice and the symbolic sucking of poisonous fluids from the patient's body.

Reading the *Historia ecclesiastica* one gets the impression that part of the mission's success was due to the fame achieved by various holy men in effecting miraculous cures. Obviously the idea of punishment for sins in case of failure or reward for goodness in case of success placed the new religion head and shoulders above the traditional one which contented itself with outguessing the supranatural by various kinds of games of chance.

Politics

Discussion

No topics directly referring to the internal political structure during the Early Anglo-Saxon period were brought up during the concluding discussion. The following observations are taken from the *Historia ecclesiastica*.

Comments

Three important aspects of the political relations in early medieval Britain emerge from Bede's *Historia ecclesiastica*. The first one concerns the limited power of kings. This descends from the fact that the role of clan heads in simple societies is limited to arbitration. The same applies to 'tribal chiefs' whenever a measure of political unity is achieved, generally by the group of clans exposed to a 'polarized' antagonistic pressure which causes them to collaborate and choose a *primus inter pares* to act as their head in case of aggression. Absolute monarchy was a gradual side effect of feudalism which in the Anglo-Saxon period had not even begun.

The varying and limited power of kings is borne out by two passages in the *Historia ecclesiastica*: in the first, Æthelberht is called a "powerful monarch" whose suzerainty "stretched as far as the great river Humber" (*HE* I.25), in the second, concerning the refusal of the people of London to receive Mellitus "preferring idolatrous high priests", King Eadbald is said to have had "less royal power than his father and was unable to restore the bishop to his church against the will and consent of the heathen" (*HE* II.6). Such limited and varying power may help to explain aspects of early Anglo-Saxon history such as the waxing and waning and the splitting up of a kingdom into sub-kingdoms (*HE* IV.12).

The second aspect concerns the counselling role exerted by the local Church hierarchy on the various kings and the influence of the Papacy on politics (*HE* III.3, IV.1). This superiority of the religious hierarchy over the lay one was repeated in early colonial times wherever world religions had made any inroads. In Sudan and Eritrea in the 1880s and 1890s, colonial powers banked on the heads of Muslim religious sects to mediate with the local chiefs. The greater influence of religious hierarchies with local chiefs or even kings in pre-industrial societies does not need justification.

The third and very important aspect, perceptively higlighted by Bede, was the gradual decline of the first Anglo-Saxon 'resurgence' which, according to him, started around 685 when:

> ...the hope and strength of the English kingdom began to ebb and fall away. For the Picts recovered their own land which the English had formerly held, while the Irish who lived in Britain and some part of the British nation recovered their independence, which they have now enjoyed for about forty-six years (*HE* IV.26).

The ultimate consequence of that decline probably led to the Viking invasions in 793 and their intensification through the greater part of the ninth century until the rallying of King Alfred's troops at Edington in 878 inverted the motion of the pendulum of history bringing about a second Anglo-Saxon cycle, which in turn came to an end with the advent of the Danes undér Canute and eventually with the Norman conquest. Knowledge of the mechanics and background of those socio-economic cycles should be a primary target for an in-depth understanding of the period.

Religion

Discussion

Hines asked whether it was right to "make a conscious effort to problematize the issue of the conversion", insofar as present familiarity with Christianity blurs interest even in past "affairs of the Church". Because of the "substantial early sources giving us a story of what was supposed to have happened" it was necessary "to try to find problems".

Dumville concurred in saying that "we are going to have to explain [to students] a hell of a lot of things that we've been taking for granted". This would "need one great heave to start off with, but then others will find motives...."

The topic of '*ecclesiastical organization and the Church*' having been brought up, *Dumville* said that he had "always been struck" by the assumptions in the literature about "the nature of the ecclesiastical organization" which proved "intensely problematic". Despite the possibility that evidence is available for single religious institutions in the British Isles, the common assumption is that of an overarching similarity "which denies some of the variations which we do see in the written sources". He would like to see more discussion to help "better to understand the ways in which segments of the Church interacted with one another and with their society in the early English-Christian period".

Hines agreed that one could use "ecclesiastical organization as a key to fitting the Christianity of the late seventh- and eighth-century English with a lot of other topics...[amongst which were] relations with the rest of Europe". For instance, the idea of the Christianization of the Anglo-Saxons being a factor in the antagonism between Scandinavia and western Europe which "led to the Viking eruption" was being revived. *Jane Hawkes* had stressed the influence of monastic organization on crafts and art.

As an example of ongoing misconceptions *Dumville* cited the perception of the seventh-century "clash of Roman and Celtic Christianity" which is presented also "as a clash between the episcopal organization and the monastic organization". He continued pointing out the absurdity of that perception insofar as both Gaelic and Romano-Frankish 'dimensions' were "heavily monastic" hence the lack of any foundation to presenting the clash that way. Despite the importance of the question "there [was] not enough academic literature directed...at this kind of problem".

Wood observed that the interpretation of the Church of Anglo-Saxon England essentially comes through "the eyes of Bede". He suggested the need to "try to disentangle the differences" and, rather than seeing it as a monolith, one should see it as "Canterbury, as Barking, as Winchester".

Dumville expressed the opinion that before 669 there was a plurality of Churches and that the "starting point for the Anglo-Saxon Church was Theodore". However, it was improbable that Theodore succeeded in making it into a monolithic organization. He recognized that, although these were "purely organizational matters" they had "much greater implications".

Comment

Religion is the strong point of the *Historia ecclesiastica* and many points made by Bede on the subject are revealing. These will be discussed separately.

1) late Germanic aspects of religion

When the Augustinian mission reached Kent most Anglo-Saxons were still true to their native or traditional religion.[4] The first reaction of King Æthelberht to the arrival of Augustine's mission was that he:

> ...took care that they should not meet in any building, for they held the traditional superstition that, if they practised any magic art, they might deceive him and get the better of him as soon as he entered (*HE* I.25).

This attitude coincides perfectly well with the general tendency first highlighted by Tacitus of Germanic people not worshipping in closed spaces,[5] and the fact that archaeology has not found yet any trace of temples dedicated to native religion.

The anecdote concerning the spectacular abandonment of traditional religion by Coifi seems altogether specious, mainly because such a show would be counterproductive. However, the taboos enumerated in the anecdote ring true and may have been part of an oral tradition not yet forgotten in Bede's time about a century after the events, since the native religion endured until *ca* 650 in Kent (*HE* III.8) and even later in peripheral areas (*HE* IV.13).

2) Missions

A common misconception about missions to the Angles and Saxons is that fostered by Bede's interpretation of Gildas that "...to other unspeakable crimes [of the Britons]...was added this crime, that they never preached the faith to the Saxons or Angles who inhabited Britain with them" (*HE* I.22). This is a naive rationalization of a state of affairs which had little to do with the unwillingness of Britons or Romano-Britons.

Missions to populations practising a different religion require some basic urban or village life. Religion cannot be preached successfully to small settlements made up of kin-related individuals 'governed' by their own elders. In such settlements few or no men are available during the daytime, because they are all engaged in subsistence chores, and women are just as busy preparing food and tending small livestock, not to mention the embarassment caused by foreign men trying to talk to women while their men are absent.

In a town or even a village the situation is entirely different: there is production and consumption of surplus goods and the availability of 'surplus time'. In villages, missionaries have several possible lines of attack, whether concerning health matters or education, all important activities for members of a village or, better still, an urban population. A further advantage of towns for mission work lies in the presence of different classes of people whereby a given class, in general the 'have-nots', are motivated to'join the ranks of the new religion to improve their status vis-à-vis those who inherit it from tradition.

Even the establishment of central dispensaries, whose early medieval counterpart were monasteries, presupposes the existence of a central authority capable of guaranteeing the continuity of such important investments in labour and

---

[4]　This expression was preferred to the term 'paganism' since Germanic native religions were different from Roman or other urban 'paganisms'.

[5]　*Ceterum nec cohibere parietibus deos neque in ullam humani oris speciem adsimulare ex magnitudine celestium arbitrantur* (Germania IX).

time. Missionaries are not—and presumably were not—foolhardy adventurers to risk their lives and waste time and efforts without adequate protection.

Thus the beginnings of Christianity among the Anglo-Saxons, and for that matter among other Germanic populations, must be seen as a symptom of incipient urbanization of a particular group. The early Islamic missions to eastern Sudan at the end of the eighteenth century thrived in newly founded villages such as the Khatmia near present-day Kassala, where el Mirghani established his earliest inland mission having come to the port of Sawakin from the Arabian peninsula (Ausenda 1987:441). The same pattern was followed by Augustine and his party as they were given a dwelling "in Canterbury, ...[Æthelberht's] chief city" and "possessions of various kinds for their needs" (*HE* I.26).

Gregory's advice to the mission is quite instructive as to the methods followed:

> ...because they are in the habit of slaughtering much cattle as sacrifice to the devils,[6] some solemnity ought to be given them in exchange for this...let them make themselves huts from the branches of trees around the churches which have been converted out of shrines, and let them celebrate the solemnity with religious feasts. Do not let them sacrifice animals to the devils, but let them slaughter animals for their own food to the praise of God (*HE* I.30).

3) Deviance and reaction

While the Roman mission was making slow progress it was accompanied by deviances due to political differences covered by a religious varnish.

The long-lasting (until 707) (*HE* V.22) dispute over the date of Easter between the Roman catholic clergy and the Irish covered a deeper dissatisfaction which needs to be understood.

Bede himself extols "Theodoret, bishop of the city called Cyrus...[who] wrote about the true incarnation of the Saviour against Eutyches and Dioscorus, bishops of Alexandria, who denied the human in the flesh of Christ" (*Chronica magna*, §496), showing an undoubtedly diffuse leaning towards the Tricapitoline schism which had only recently been settled in Italy through the acceptance of Justinian's rescript by the schismatics.

When Pope Vitalian sent Theodore to be Archbishop of Canterbury he sent along Hadrian to make sure that he should not be tempted by monothelitic leanings in obeisance to the Byzantine political orthodoxy (*HE* IV.1). Did this mean that Britain was an, even if remote, bone of contention between the Eastern Empire and Western interests?

Then there was the expected but brief reaction to initial missionary penetration in that most traditionalist factions amongst the Anglo-Saxons came to the fore upon the death of those kings who had favoured and even aided the early missions, e.g. Eadbald at the death of Æthelberht, and his three sons at the death of Sæberht,

---

[6] Gregory the Great may have referred to the habits of urban 'pagans' because simple societies are not in the habit of slaughtering "much cattle", except on very special occasions. However, he was right in assuming that slaughtering "much cattle" would succeed in gathering large crowds.

king of the East Saxons (*HE* II.5). Did the traditionalist faction belong to the élite or did it thrive among the commoners, and did it manifest itself only on those first occasions, or did it maintain a critical attitude thereafter?

4) Monasticism

The quick spread of monasticism in Anglo-Saxon England was one of the factors aiding the spread of urban civilization. Indeed, there might be a relationship between the apparent lack of urbanization and the spread of monastic institutions during the Early Anglo-Saxons period in that the latter offered a vital 'international' communication network (see below) to a rapidly evolving social structure. Despite the frequent mention of monasteries, one knows relatively little of how they were organized, how they recruited their members, how they interacted with the surrounding populations, and on which model they were based. They must have owed something of their structural characteristics to preceding Roman *villae* which also were urban nuclei, albeit on a more modest level.

Undoubtedly the insecurity and poverty of the time made monasteries a haven of peace and well-being. In an economy which was slowly emerging from bare subsistence, monasteries produced surplus. Books copied and produced were precious intellectual surplus, but they may have produced surplus also on a more material level. Knowledge of architecture "in the Roman fashion" spread from monasteries or from the sites where they were being built or enlarged. It is quite probable that herbal medicaments were produced in monasteries and sold or given in exchange for alms. Monasteries served as hostels for travellers and among their early activities one can find a whole range of what later became widespread communicational initiatives in the modern world from schools to hospitals, etc.

It is understandable that, despite the rigid rule followed by most, the quality of life, both material and intellectual, was several steps above that of the commoners and even of some of the élite.

With characteristic critical perception, even though they may detract from the aura of holiness which surrounded the institutions, Bede brought out the less elating aspects of monastic life in his time. The suggestion that people might enter a monastery "for the sake of ease" was picked up by Bede (*HE* IV.3) when relating the story of Owine who, because he was less capable of study, applied himself more earnestly to manual labour.

There may have been extreme cases, as in that of Adomnán and the monastery of Coldingham, which echoes biblical prototypes and might be an exaggeration, in which:

> ...men and women alike, are sunk in slothful slumbers or else they remain awake for the purposes of sin. And the cells that were built for praying and for reading have become haunts of feasting, drinking, gossip, and other delights; even the virgins dedicated to God put aside all respect for their profession and whenever they have leisure, spend their time weaving elaborate garments with which to adorn themselves as if they were brides, so imperilling their virginity, or else to make friends with strange men (*HE* IV.25).

The conditions described here may have not been the rule, but they certainly were a possibility, especially in monastic institutions where for external reasons the motivation to achieve a 'holy' symbiosis with the surrounding lay reality had been thwarted and therefore substituted by more earthly attentions.

5) Pilgrimage to Rome
One of the characteristics of the early Anglo-Saxon Church was the apparently widespread desire on the part of its members, more than those of other Churches in Europe, to make a pilgrimage to Rome. According to Bede:

> [Oswiu] was so attached to the Roman and apostolic customs [*ca* 670] that he had intended, if he recovered from his illness, to go to Rome and end his life there among the holy places (*HE* IV.5).

After him Bede mentions Benedict who "visited Rome as he had often done before" (*HE* IV.18), Oftfor (*HE* IV.23), and Cædwalla, king of the West Saxons, who "...gave up his throne for the sake of the Lord to win an everlasting kingdom, and went to Rome [*ca* 679]" (*HE* V.7), and after him his successor Ine (*HE* V.7):

> At that time many Englishmen, nobles and commoners, layfolk and clergy, men and women, were eager to do the same thing (*HE* V.7).

Despite its long decline, Rome was still a monumental city and must have exerted a great fascination on the English who could rediscover there some of the models of the past greatness of the country in ruins their ancestors had settled in.

References

Textual sources:

[Abbreviations: *HE*=*Historia ecclesiastica gentis Anglorum*; *HF*=Gregory of Tour's, *Libri historiarum decem*]
Bede
        Chronica magna: see Jones 1977.
        Historia ecclesiastica gentis Anglorum: see McClure & Collins 1994.
Eugippius
        Vita Severini: see Régérat 1991.
Gregory of Tours
        Libri historiarum decem: see Thorpe 1974.
Tacitus
        Germania: see Page 1958.

Bibliography:

Ausenda, G.
  1987   Leisurely nomads: The Hadendowa (Beja) of the Gash Delta and Their Transition to Sedentary Village Life. Doctoral dissertation, Graduate School of Arts and Sciences, Columbia University, New York.
    1995   The segmentary lineage in contemporary anthropology and among the Langobards. In *After Empire: Towards and Ethnology of Europe's Barbarians*. G. Ausenda (ed.), pp. 15-50. Woodbridge: The Boydell Press.
    n.d.   Beni Amer and Habab: A Diachronic Ethnography (1890-1992).

Bach, A.
  1981   *Deutsche Namenkunde.* Band II, 1: Die deutschen Ortsnamen. Heidelberg:
          Carl Winter.
Ball, C.
  1991   Inconsistencies in the main runic inscriptions on the Ruthwell Cross. In *Old
          English Runes and their Continental Background.* A. Bammesberger (ed.),
          pp. 107-123. Heidelberg: Carl Winter.
Baratieri, O.
  1892   Negli Habab. *Nuova antologia: Rivista di Scienze Lettere ed Arti.* Anno
          XXVII, Serie III, Vol. XXXVIII, della Raccolta Vol. CXXII - Fascicolo 16
          marzo 1892, pp. 201-226.
Burckhardt, J. L.
  1822   *Travels in Nubia.* London: John Murray, Albemarle Street.
Cleary, S. E.
          The Ending of Roman Britain. London: Batsford.
Goody, J.
  1983   *The Development of the Family and Marriage in Europe.* Cambridge:
          Cambridge University Press.
  1987   *The Interface between the Written and the Oral.* Cambridge: Cambridge
          University Press.
Higham, N. J.
  1994   *The English conquest: Gildas and Britain in the fifth century.* Manchester:
          Manchester University Press.
Jones, C. W. (ed.)
  1977   *De temporum ratione liber, chronica maiora includens...(Corpus
          Christianorum, Series latina CXXIII B).* Turnhout: Brepols.
McClure, J., & R. Collins (eds. & trans.)
  1994   *Bede: The Ecclesiastical History of the English People, The Greater
          Chronicle; Bede's Letter to Egbert.* Oxford: Oxford University Press.
Munzinger, W.
  1890   *Studi sull'Africa Orientale.* Rome: Tipografia Voghera, Carlo.
O Carragáin, E.
  1988   The Ruthwell crucifixion poem in its iconographic and liturgical contexts.
          Peritia 6-7 (1987-88): 1-71.
Ong, W.
  1982   *Literacy and Orality: The Technologizing of the Word.* London: Methuen.
Page, T. E. (ed. & trans.)
  1958   *Tacitus: Dialogue, Agricola, Germania.* Cambridge, MA: Harvard
          University Press.
Régérat, P. (ed.)
  1991   Eugippius, *Vita Severini.* Sources Chrétiennes 374. Paris: Éditions du Cerf.
Sawyer, P. H.
  1968   *Anglo-Saxon Charters: An Annotated List and Bibliography.* London: Royal
          Historical Society.
Thorpe, L.(ed. & trans.)
  1974   *The History of the Franks.* Harmondsworth: Penguin Books.
Titow, J. Z.
  1972   *Winchester Yields: A Study in Medieval Agricultural Productivity.*
          Cambridge: Cambridge University Press.

Turton, D.
  1995   Discussion of 'The segmentary lineage in contemporary anthropology and
            among the Langobards'. In *After Empire: Towards an Ethnography of
            Europe's Barbarians*. G. Ausenda (ed.), pp. 45-50. Woodbridge: The
            Boydell Press.
Wacher, J.
  1974   *The Towns of Roman Britain*. Berkeley: University. of California Press.
Wickham. C.
  1984   The other transition: from the ancient world to feudalism. *Past and Present*
            103: 3-36.

INDEX

Abba 197, 198, 200
Aboriginal religion 376
Abortion 167
Acculturation 421
Adomnán of Coldingham 447
Adomnán of Iona 265, 354-356
Adoption 173, 178
Adovacrius; & Saxons on Loire 45
Adult(s) 128, 130, 133; burials 128, 132
Adultery 233
Ælffled 183
Ælfric 167, 221, 315, 406
Ælfwine 174-176, 181, 216
Ælle 355
Æscwine 189
Æthelbald of Mercia 21, 71, 75, 186, 188, 189, 194, 196, 208, 351-353; - 's letter to Wilfrid 193
Æthelberht I 19, 48, 49, 59, 130, 211, 212, 217, 231, 237, 350, 352, 355, 371, 372, 378, 430, 445, 443; - 's laws 141, 149, 162, 213, 215, 232-236, 240, 241
Æthelburh; wife of Ine 136, 186
Æthelflæd; daughter of Alfred 360
Æthelfrith of Bernicia 185, 186, 356, 371
Ætheling 189, 191, 192, 208
Æthelred of Mercia 174, 176, 181, 185, 192, 205, 346, 350, 351
Æthelred II of Mercia 360
Æthelric 71
Æthelwalh of Sussex 178, 184, 359

Æthelweard; Ealdorman - 192
Age(s) 125, 127, 128, 129, 140, 151, 340; Anglo-Saxon - structure 129; difference 163; for women's marriage 167; golden - of Northumbria 391; grades 126, 129, 166; groups 33, 127-129, 133, 152; of inheritance 126; related status 128; sets 126, 127; threshold(s) 126, 127, 129, 152, 163, 164; Viking - 327, 417
Agnatic; kin 179, 192; lineage 183, 185; succession 433
Agrarian(icultural) 114, 120, 282, 435; calendar 403; change 248; cycle 379, 403; economy(ies) 107, 109, 272, 302, 427; estate 247; hinterland 97; households 278; land 425; production 256; products 280; property 266; slaves 431; society(ies) 62, 162, 251, 258, 271, 300; starts & stops 404; surplus 274, 285, 287; techniques 256, 266; tools 266; units 265
Agriculturalists 414, 436
Agriculture 66, 88, 114, 248, 277, 287, 403, 417
Agropastoral; societies 162
Aidan; Bishop - 389, 432
Alamanni(c) 12; cemetery 343; runes 406
Alans 41
Alboin 9, 23, 24, 63
Alcester 76, 93
Alcuin 22, 176
Aldfrith of Northumbria 183, 195, 350, 351, 355, 395
Aldgisl; Frisian king 44

Aldhelm 265, 338, 339, 383, 394
Aldred; sub-king of the Hwicce 197 n37
Alfred of Wessex 22, 22 n 23, 130, 172, 186, 237, 274, 360, 443; - 's laws 149, 211, 214; - 's letter 20; - 's Will 134, 197 n36
Alhfrith 182
Alliance(s) 179, 180; into feud 173; marriage - 174, 349, 427, 428
Ambiguity(ous) 314, 333, 334; images - 343; relationship bw gender & status - 317
Amulet(s) 392, 393
Anachronism; danger of - 271; term seigneurial - 438
Ancestor(s); *duces* - of Kentish kings 59; Ida common - 183; of Anglo-Saxons 41, 316; Offa's - 188
Ancient; city trade 301; potsherds over - fields 267
Angles(i) 10, 12, 14, 18-21, 24, 33, 34, 41, 43, 48, 50, 51, 55, 57, 59, 63, 148, 419, 420, 430; mission to - 427, 441, 445; relations bw - & Franks 60; soldiers in *Brittia* 45
Anglia(n) 103, 121, 168, 218, 239, 240, 263, 371; bracteates in - England 393; cemeteries 168; Church 16; Collection 50, 182, 183, 186, 189, 356; élite 143; kingdoms 356; laws in - 218, 231, 239; model for - migration 58; Northumbria 261
Anglianization 218

Jacket motif by: *Severino Baraldi, Via F. Chopin 5, I - 20141 Milano*
Page setting: *Alta Qualità sas, I - 20144 Milano*
Printers: *Studiostampa S.A., Serravalle (RSM)*

CPSIA information can be obtained at www.ICGtesting.com
Printed in the USA
LVOW05s2005050915

452584LV00017B/69/P